Election Department Boston

Lists of streets, avenues, courts, places in Boston

Showing the numbers and divisions of those extending through more than one

ward or precinct

Election Department Boston

Lists of streets, avenues, courts, places in Boston
Showing the numbers and divisions of those extending through more than one ward or precinct

ISBN/EAN: 9783337210564

Printed in Europe, USA, Canada, Australia, Japan

Cover: Foto ©Andreas Hilbeck / pixelio.de

LIST OF STREETS, COURTS, PLACES, ETC., IN BOSTON.

EXPLANATION.

The date following the name is supposed to be the time at which the street or way first received that name.

Streets marked with a * are, in the opinion of the Street Commissioners, public highways.

Streets marked with a † are public in part.

B. . . . . Boston Proper, prior to annexation of Roxbury in 1868.
Rox. . . . Roxbury, as it existed at time of annexation in 1868.
Dor. . . . Dorchester, as it existed at time of annexation in 1870.
So. B. . . . South Boston, as it existed in 1870.
E. B. . . . East Boston, including Breeds Island.
Chsn. . . . Charlestown.
Bri. . . . Brighton, as it existed at time of annexation in 1874.
W. Rox. . . West Roxbury, as it existed at time of annexation in 1874.

The references to plans on file in the office of the Engineering Department and designated by the letter L, are given under the several streets where official action has been taken.

A street, B., 1828–30; from Mill-dam (now Beacon street) to Sumner (formerly Olive, now Mt. Vernon) street, established in 1828; includes part of unnamed passageway about twenty feet wide, established in 1804; name changed to River street, 1843.

A street, B., 1860; from Berkeley street, west, across Clarendon street, now part of St. James avenue.

†**A street**, So. B., 1804; from Dorchester avenue to Congress street, (formerly Eastern avenue); laid out from Turnpike street to Broadway, Feb. 27, 1805; ordered built from Broadway to the sea, Sept. 9, 1844; Midland street included in A street by change of name, April 20, 1868; A street relocated by Board of Aldermen from north-east line of Fifth (now W. Fifth) street across Eastern avenue (now Congress street) to "limit of solid structures," Nov. 17, 1868; part of same laid out again by Street Commissioners from "present northerly terminus" to Eastern avenue extended, March 14, 1879; authority to open from Congress street about 692 feet north-westwardly given by Street Commissioners, Aug. 12, 1896. L 27, L 58, L 254, L 1347.

A street, Rox., 1872; from Parker street to Halleck street; called New street, 1884; now Archibald street.

A street, Dor., 1892; from Pleasant street to Sumner street; authority to open given by Street Commissioners, May 4, 1892; now called Trescott street.

A street, W. Rox., 1868; from Boylston street to Spring Park avenue, laid out under name of Adelaide street, Nov. 17, 1893.

A street, W. Rox., 1877; from Forest Hills street, west, between Morton street and Keyes street; partly closed.

Abbotts block, } S. B.; from Ellery street, near angle, north-west;
Abbotts place, } called Ellery terrace in 1896.

***Abbot street,** Dor., 1872; from Blue Hill avenue to Harvard street; projected, 1872; laid out, Dec. 29, 1880. L 1509.

***Abbotsford street,** Rox., 1894; from Walnut avenue to Crawford street; authority to open given by Street Commissioners, May 31, 1894; laid out from Walnut avenue to Harold street, Sept. 19, 1895; extended to Crawford street, Dec. 29, 1896. L 2732.

Abbott street, So. B. 1859; from Dorchester avenue between Hyde street and Kemp street, to Richardson avenue.

Abbott street, W. Rox., 1890; east from Willow street near Weld street.

Aberdeen street, Rox., 1871; from Beacon street to Brookline Branch of B. & A. R.R.

Abney place, Rox., 1850; from Eustis street, north-east, crossing end of Mall street; part from Eustis street to Mall street, formerly part of lower road from Roxbury to Dorchester; part from Mall street, north, formerly part of ancient way called road to the town landing, which existed as early as 1796; now Dearborn street.

Abuttors' court, So. B., 1852; from Dorchester turnpike (now avenue), south-east next south from junction of Boston (now Dorchester) street; now part of Preble street.

Academy Hill street, or road, Bri., 1873; from Chestnut Hill avenue to High school; laid out, Dec. 17, 1873; and accepted conditionally, Dec. 30, 1873.

Acadia court, Dor., 1870; from Dorchester avenue east, between Ashmont street and Beale street.

Acadia street, Rox. and W. Rox., 1869; from School street to Atherton street; now Arcadia street.

Acorn street, B., 1823; from Willow street to West Cedar street.

***Acton street,** B., 1864; from Washington street to Bradford street; part from Washington street, west, called Washington court, in 1845; extended to present bounds and called Marlboro' street, in 1857; name changed to Acton street, Feb. 24, 1864.

Adams court, B., 1837; from Washington street, south-east to Waltham street; from Washington, east, called Adams place in 1837; part of included in extension of Waltham street in 1850.

Adams court, Dor., 1865; south of East street; Hall's court, so called; laid out as a part of Hecla street, Aug. 30, 1892.

Adams place, B., 1845; from North Anderson street to Blossom street; same from Bridge (now North Anderson) street to Blossom street called Bridge-street avenue, 1832; name changed to Adams place in 1845.

Adams place, B., 1837; from Washington street, east, nearly opposite Waltham street, which upon its extension east, in 1850, crossed and included part of Adams place; the remainder now called Adams court from Washington street to Waltham street.

Adams place, So. B.; from E street near West Third street, north-west.

Adams place, Rox., 1862; from Washington street north-west, then north-east to Williams street; shown as a "passway" in 1816.

Adams place, Chsn.; from Lincoln street, north-west.

Adams place, Bri., 1885; from Everett street, east, near Lincoln street; sometimes called Adams street.

***Adams square,** B., 1879; the area at the junction of Brattle street, Cornhill, Washington street and Devonshire street so named Nov. 17, 1879. L 65, L 124.

***Adams street,** B., 1788; from bottom of Water street to Milk street: called Cooper's alley in 1708; Kilby street in 1769; previous to 1784 called also Miller's lane; named Adams street, July 4, 1788; after naming of Liberty square considered to extend from Liberty square to Milk street; included in Kilby street, July 6, 1824.

***Adams street,** B., 1846–1850; from Sudbury street to Ivers (now Chardon) street; called Distill-House square in 1769; name changed to Adams street, Sept. 9, 1850; widened and name changed to Bowker street, April 20, 1868. L 351.

***Adams street,** Rox., 1836; from Hampden street to Dudley street; first mentioned, Oct. 22, 1836; laid out from Eustis (now Dudley) street to East (now Hampden) street, Sept. 8, 1856.

Adams street, Rox., 1849; from Warren street to Cliff street; name changed to Myrtle street, before March 19, 1860; now Glenwood street.

***Adams street,** Dor., 1840; from Eaton square (Meeting House Hill) to junction Washington street and Dorchester avenue at Lower Mills; formerly called Lower road from Roxbury to Milton, or Lower road to Milton, or Lower road to Boston, or the Lower road; named Adams street from Captain Eaton's to Lower Mills, March 11, 1840. L 1182, L 1256, L 1333, L 1334, L 1364, L 1365, L 1750, L 2712.

Adams street, W. Rox., 1871; from Gardner street, north-east, on Cow Island.

***Adams street,** Chsn., 1828; from Winthrop street to Chelsea street; staked out by selectmen from Mr Townsend's corner to Mr. Breed's dam pasture and approved by the Town in August, 1797; this was the old way from the training field (now Winthrop square) to the "dam pasture" before the laying out of the Salem turnpike; Common street and Adams street, laid out around Winthrop square and boundaries defined, Jan. 26, 1848. L 2492

Adams street, Bri.; 1895; from Franklin street opposite Alcott street; authority to open given by Street Commissioners, Nov. 4, 1895.

Adams street, Bri., 1846; from Everett street, east, near Lincoln street; sometimes called Adams place.

Adams terrace, Dor., 1895; authority to open between Adams street and Muzzy street, given by Street Commissioners, Oct. 8, 1895.

Addison avenue, W. Rox.; from Centre street to White avenue (now Custer street); laid out with the name of Ballard street, Oct. 3, 1891.

Addison street, E. B., 1838; from Saratoga street to Chelsea street at bridge.

***Adelaide street,** W. Rox., 1893; from Boylston street to Spring Park avenue; laid out, Nov. 17, 1893; formerly A street. L 2549.

Adelaide terrace, W. Rox., 1874; from La Grange street, north-east, across south end of Bellevue park; included in West Roxbury Parkway in 1894.

Adelaide terrace, W. Rox.; from Adelaide street, near cor. of Boylston street, north-west.

Ætna place, B., 1837; from Short (now Kingston) street, west, near Bedford street; now built over.

Agassiz avenue, W. Rox.; from Gould street, north-west, to Sunnyside avenue, near junction Weld street and Arnold street.

Agassiz park, W. Rox.; from Burroughs street, south-west.

Agawam street, Dor.; from Train street to Neponset avenue; authority to open given by Street Commissioners, Sept. 8, 1891.

Akron place, Rox.; from Akron street, north-east.

***Akron street**, Rox., 1845; from Alpine street to Regent street; laid out, Nov. 6, 1872. L 804.

Alaric street, W. Rox., 1870; from Spring street, near West Roxbury Branch R.R., south-east, then north-east to Centre street.

***Alaska street**, Rox., 1870; from Blue Hill avenue, north-west, to Perrin street; formerly Allston street; name of Allston street changed to Alaska street, April 21, 1868.

Alba court, B., 1844; from School street, north, near Washington street; closed.

***Alban street**, Dor., 1873; from Ashmont street to Welles avenue; laid out, Dec. 29, 1873. L 917.

†**Albano street**, W. Rox., 1852; from Kittredge street to Amherst street; south-east to Kittredge street (formerly Roslin avenue); laid out, Aug. 18, 1879. L 1372.

Albany avenue, Rox., 1874; from Dudley street between Greenville street and Mt. Pleasant avenue, south-west; now Oakland avenue.

Albany place, B., 1857; from Albany street, west, near Harvard street.

***Albany street**, B. and Rox., 1839; from Beach street in Boston to Eustis street in Roxbury; projected in 1839 by South Cove Corporation from Beach street southward; extended by said corporation to Troy street in 1845; extended by City to Roxbury creek (canal) April 21, 1855; extended across Roxbury canal and Roxbury Town wharf or landing-place to Northampton street, June 30, 1868; Davis street in Roxbury, from Northampton street to Eustis street named Albany street, April 21, 1868; this street in Boston was accepted in portions as follows:

Beach street to Harvard street, Aug. 10, 1847; Harvard street to Oak street, Oct. 10, 1853, "provided the South Cove Corporation convey the same to the City;" Oak street to East Orange (now Way) street, Dec. 17, 1855; part from East Orange street to Rochester street and part from Rochester street to Troy street seem never to have been expressly accepted; Troy street to Dover street, Dec. 22, 1865; Dover street to Malden street, Dec. 28, 1858, and May 28, 1859; Malden street to Springfield street (now discontinued), Sept. 4, 1866; part from Springfield street to Roxbury canal seems not to have been expressly accepted. L 59, L 104, L 150, L 212, L 260, L 261, L 303, L 308, L 349, L 377, L 498, L 941, L 1162, L 1331, L 1352, L 1512, L 1531, L 2299, L 2491, L 2708.

***Albemarle street**, B., 1879–80; from St. Botolph street to B. & P. (now N. Y., N. H. & H.) R.R.; laid out, Jan. 19, 1880. L 1426.

Albemarle terrace, B.; from Albemarle street, south-west.

Albert place, Dor.; from Adams street, between Park street and Gibson street, west.

Albert street, So. B.; from Abbott street to Kemp street.

†**Albert street**, Rox., 1872; from Heath street, south-west, across Bromley park and adjoining B. & P. (now N. Y., N. H. & H.) R.R.; laid out from Heath street to Bromley park, May 15, 1874. L 910.

***Albion court**, Chsn., 1857; see Albion place.

***Albion place**, Chsn., 1875; from Main street, north-east; laid out and accepted as Albion court, Sept. 7, 1857; name changed to Albion place, Dec. 31, 1875.

***Albion street**, B., 1849; from Dover street to Castle street; part from Dover street north called Tuckerman street in 1831; also called Parkman street, 1846–49; named Albion street, 1849; extended Nov. 20, 1855, from point about 42 feet south-west from Gardiner street, north-east, across Gardiner street to Castle street. L 54, L 230, L 544, L 546, L 837, L 838, L 1349.

***Albion street,** Dor., 1862; from Dudley street to Clifton street; laid out, Aug. 12, 1869.

Albion street, W. Rox., 1848; from Ashland street to Florence street; shown on plan from Poplar street, north-east; same part called Arnold place, 1843-49; part from Poplar street to Ashland street shown as part of Mt. Vernon street, 1874; same part laid out and name changed to Sycamore street, July 6, 1880. L 1468.

Albion street, W. Rox., 1870; from Shawmut avenue (now Washington street), south-east; probably same as Albano street.

Albright court, Dor., from Boston street, east, to Sumner street; shown as an unnamed court in 1846.

***Alcott street,** Bri., 1892; from Franklin street to Mansfield street; authority to open given by Street Commissioners, April 20, 1892; laid out, July 19, 1893. L 2521.

Alden court, B., 1824; from Alden street, north-west.

Alden lane, B., Alden street, formerly so called; earlier Alden's lane.

Alden place, W. Rox.; from Green street, north-east, near Washington street.

***Alden street,** B., 1846; from Court (formerly Cambridge) street to Sudbury street; called Alden's lane, 1732, and that name confirmed by selectmen, July 4, 1788; later sometimes called Alden lane; called Copeland's lane, 1820-29; Alden or Alden's lane again, 1829-46; named Alden street, July 20, 1846. L 1299.

Alden's lane, B., 1732; from Cambridge (now Court) street to Sudbury street; now Alden street.

Alder street, W. Rox., 1872; from Bellevue avenue, south-east, to Roslindale av.

Alder street, W. Rox.; from Mt. Vernon street to Keith street, between Libby street and Carroll street.

***Aldie street,** Bri., 1890; from Franklin street to Everett street; laid out from Franklin street to Athol street, Nov. 7, 1890; laid out from Athol street to Everett street, Dec. 28, 1892. L 2270, L 2477.

Aldine street, B.; from Atlantic avenue, south-east, to Gilbert place.

Aldrich street, W. Rox.; from Beech street to Brandon street; authority to open between Beech street and B. & P. (now N. Y., N. H. & H.) R.R. given by Street Commissioners, Dec. 1, 1891.

Aldworth street, W. Rox, 1896; from Centre street to Vane street; authority to open from Centre street, northwardly, given by Street Commissioners, Oct. 1, 1896.

Alexander avenue, Dor., 1873; from Dudley street, south-west, crossing Lebanon street and Oleander street; laid out as Alexander street, between Dudley street and Oleander street, July 14, 1890.

***Alexander street,** Dor., 1873; from Dudley street to Oleander street; formerly called Alexander avenue; laid out July 14, 1890. L 2248.

Alford avenue, Chsn., 1870; Alford street, from Main street, northward so called.

***Alford street,** Chsn., 1848; from Main street, northward to Malden bridge, and from north end of Malden bridge, northward to county line; formerly called Malden road, being County road through Malden; so called in records of 1803; named Alford street, from Main street to Malden bridge, March 24, 1848; altered, laid out 60 feet wide and accepted, Dec. 21, 1869; discontinued as a public street, Feb. 15, 1870; same altered, accepted and laid out 50 feet wide, Feb 15, 1870; same as laid out Dec. 21, 1869, again discontinued, June 28, 1870, same altered, accepted and laid out 50 feet wide, June 28, 1870; sometimes called Alford avenue. L 1100, L 1101.

Alford street, Chsn., 1858; a way leading from "Broadway" (now Main street) opposite the public street named Alford street, south to Sever street; discontinued and added to Sullivan square, Oct. 6, 1868.

Alford's corner, B., 1728; corner of Beacon street and Centrey or Century (now Mount Vernon) street, then so called.

***Alfred street**, W. Rox., 1881; from Green street, south-west, to Seaverns avenue; laid out, July 19, 1881. L 1540.

***Alfred street**, Chsn., 1810; from Summer street to Bartlett street; conveyed to Town for public highway by Oliver Holden, July 17, 1810; afterward made part of School street.

Alger street, So. B., 1856; part of street now Tudor street, on both sides of E street.

Alger street, So. B., 1857; from Dorchester avenue, south-east, nearly to Dorchester street.

***Algonquin street**, Dor., 1891; from Washington street to Harvard street: authority to open given by Street Commissioners, June 24, 1891; laid out, June 22, 1894. L 2602.

Allan or Allen place, Bri.; from Washington street, north, near Oakland street; called Allan place, 1875; Allen place, 1885.

***Allandale street**, W. Rox, 1863; from Centre street, north-west, opposite Arnold Arboretum; laid out as a public street from Centre street to Brookline line, April 7, 1885; at one time called "Franklin avenue or Allendale street." L 1854, 1855, 1856.

Allard court, Rox., 1876; from Pynchon street (now Columbus avenue) south-east; named, Dec. 5, 1876.

Allbright court, Dor.; from Boston street, east, to Sumner street; shown as an unnamed court in 1846.

Alleghany Lawn street, Rox., 1860; mentioned as a private street in Roxbury city records; not identified.

†**Alleghany street**, Rox., 1845; from Terrace street to Calumet street; portion between Parker street and Terrace street called Parker place: laid out between Terrace street and Parker street, Oct. 2, 1877; authority to open the portion from Delaware street to a point beyond Pontiac street, given by Street Commissioners, April 12, 1894. L 1268.

Allen court, B., from Allen street, north, between Allen court and Chambers street; also called Allen's court.

Allen place, B.; from Limestre et, south-east; now called Lime-street place.

Allen place, B., 1844; from Allen street, between Spring street and Chambers street; also called Allen's place.

Allen place, Rox.; from Roxbury street, north-east, between Shawmut avenue and Linden park.

Allen place, Bri; see Allan place.

***Allen street**, B., 1829: from Chambers street to Charles street; opened in 1729, by John Allen as a 40-foot highway from his 30-foot way (later Shute street, afterward Wiltshire street, now part of Chambers street) westward to another 30-foot way, near the position of the later Copper street, now Brighton street; named Allen's street, July 4, 1788 (Selectmen's list), and there described "From Shute street, westerly, by Capt. Job Prince's to Cambridge street," which indicates a way not shown on any map, turning southerly therefrom to Cambridge street, and called by the same name; called Allen's lane, 1800; shown on Carleton's map, 1800, from Wiltshire (formerly Shute) street, west to Charles river; called Green or Green's lane, 1803; called North Allen street, about 1807; name changed to Allen street, April 1, 1829; extended from Brighton street to Charles street, Oct. 29, 1870. L 409.

Allen street, W. Rox., 1872; from Anawan avenue, south-east, between Farrington avenue and Irving street.

Allen street, W. Rox., 1884; from Brown avenue to Rowe street, at Mt. Hope; shown as an unnamed street in 1874.

Allen street, Chsn., 1867; from Main street to Rutherford avenue.

Allen-street court, Chsn.; from Allen street to Thorndike street.

Allendale street, W. Rox., 1863; from Centre street, north-west; now part of Allandale street.

Allen's corner, B., 1732; cor. of Ann (now North) street and Wentworth's lane (now Barrett street), then so called.

Allen's court, B., 1836; from Allen street, north.

Allen's court, E. B.; from Paris street to Havre street, near Decatur street.

Allen's highway, B.; a way established by John Allen in 1717, probably from end of Green lane (now Green street) north, then curving westward and again running straight north-west toward, but not to, Charles river; shown as "Mr. John Allen's 30-foot highway" on plan made in 1725, and there extended to the river; see an obscure indenture made in 1728, by which probably the line of way at the northerly end was changed and extended to the river; called for many years "Allen's highway;" the southerly part "from Green street up the hill to Mr. Russell's rope-walk" (*i.e.*, as far as present position of Poplar street), named Shute street, July 4, 1788; substantially same part called in Edes list and marked on Carleton's map, both 1800, Wiltshire street; later included in Chambers street by change of name, 1812; from the Selectmen's list and Carleton's map it appears that the portion of this way north of the present Poplar street had been abandoned; the part of Gravel street, from Poplar street northward, seems to have been in the position of this northerly part of Allen's highway.

Allen's lane, B., 1800; the present Allen street, named Allen's street in 1788.

Allen's lane, B., 1733-89; from Orange (now Washington) street, east, opposite Nassau (now Common) street to the harbor; now closed.

Allen's plain, Dor., 1823; part of Pleasant street between Cottage street and Savin Hill avenue, then so called.

Allen's street, B., 1788; the present Allen street, so named July 4, 1788.

Allerton street, Rox., 1872; from Gerard street, south-east, near Farnham street.

Allston Heights, Bri.; from Cambridge street, south, opposite Gordon street; shown as an unnamed street on plan dated 1868.

Allston place, B., 1839; from Somerset pl. (now Allston street), south.

Allston place, Rox., 1858; from Warren street opposite Walnut avenue; name changed to Rockville place, April 21, 1868; named Rockville park, Feb. 9, 1885.

Allston square, Bri., 1872; from Allston street, south-east; shown as an unnamed street on plan dated 1857; called Allston-square street, 1875.

Allston-square street, Bri., 1875; Allston square, so called in 1875.

***Allston street,** B., 1842; from Bowdoin street to Somerset street; called Somerset place in 1807; named Allston street in 1842. L 249.

***Allston street,** Rox., 1856; from Blue Hill avenue to Perrin street; projected, Sept. 25, 1856; accepted, July 27, 1863; name changed to Alaska street, April 21, 1868.

***Allston street**, Dor., 1863; from Centre street to Melville avenue; laid out, Jan. 20, 1872. L 738.

***Allston street**, Chsn., 1854; from Bunker Hill street to Medford street; shown as an unnamed street on plan dated 1841; laid out, Oct 4, 1854.

***Allston street**, Bri., 1853; from Washington street to Brighton avenue; shown as an unnamed street on plan dated 1847; laid out by County Commissioners from Summit avenue (formerly Prospect street) to Washington street, Sept. 1, 1867; laid out by Selectmen from North Beacon street (now Brighton avenue) to way (now Summit avenue) formerly Prospect street, May 9, 1870, and same accepted by Town June 24, 1870.

Allston terrace, B., from Hobart street at angle, north-west.

Alma street, Dor.; from Morton street, near Norfolk street, to Hildreth street.

Almont place, B., 1846; from Blossom street, west.

Almont street, Dor., 1896; from Blue Hill avenue, north-west, near Mattapan station N. E. R.R.; formerly Mt. Hope avenue.

Almy street, Bri., 1892; from Seattle street to Windom street; laid out as Amboy street, July 18, 1892.

Alna place, E. B., 1853; from Webster street, south-west, toward Marginal street; originally branching on both sides, making a way T shaped.

Alphonsus avenue, Rox., from Whitney street, south-east.

Alpine avenue, Dor., 1845; from Grampian way to Indian way; closed in part and part included in Woodland avenue.

Alpine avenue, W. Rox., 1847; from Poplar street, north-east to B. & P. (now N. Y., N. H. & H.) R.R. called Belmont avenue, 1843–49; now Brown avenue.

Alpine place, Rox.; from Alpine street, north-east, then north-west, with two openings into Alpine street.

***Alpine street**, Rox., 1845; from St. James street, south-west, then south-east to Regent street; laid out, Nov. 6, 1872. L 802, L 803.

Alpine street, Dor.; from Arcadia street to Robinson street; shown on plan dated 1871, as "Draper street formerly Alpine street."

Alpine terrace, Rox.; from Circuit street, near Washington street to Alpine street.

Alpine way, Dor., 1883: from "Rockland" (formerly part of Alpine, now part of Woodland avenue), north-east, then east; probably part of former Alpine avenue.

Alston place, Rox., 1860; mentioned as a private street in Roxbury city records; same as Allston place.

Alton place, B., 1857; from Endicott street, east, near Cooper street; called Walters court in 1853; closed.

Alton place, Rox.; from Longwood avenue, between Parker street and Phillips street, south-west.

***Alveston street**, W. Rox., 1858; from Seaverns avenue to Greenough avenue; part shown as part of Roanoke avenue on plan dated 1847; laid out, Dec. 8, 1882. L 1668.

***Amboy street**, Bri., 1892; from Seattle street to Windom street; formerly called Almy street; laid out, July 18, 1892. L 2415.

***Ambrose street**, Rox., 1886; from Albany street to Chadwick street; Hartopp place laid out as a public street, Dec. 13, 1870; name changed to Ambrose street, March 1, 1886. L 535.

Amee place, B., 1855–82; from Shawmut avenue, south-east, near Arnold street; included in Woodbury street in 1882. L 1594.

Ames court, So. B., 1864; from Ames street, south-east.

Ames street, So. B., 1864; from Dorr street, north-east to O. C. (now N. Y., N. H. & H.) R.R.

Amesbury street, W. R., 1895; from Baker street to beyond Barnes street, authority to open, given by Street Commissioners, May 8, 1895.

Ames street, Bri.; from Dix street to Madison avenue, closed.

†**Amherst street**, W. Rox., 1881; from Brandon (formerly Williams) street to Dudley avenue; formerly called Cottage street between Brandon street and Prospect (now Penfield) street; laid out between Brandon street and Prospect street, Sept. 14, 1881. L 1556.

Amity street, E. B.; from Swift street to Harmony street.

Amory avenue, Rox.; from Amory street, west, between Centre street and Dimock street.

***Amory street**, Rox. and W. Rox., 1868; from Centre street near Hog bridge, Rox., to Boylston street, W. Rox.; name of part of School street, from Centre street to Boylston street, changed to Amory street, April 21, 1868; name of part of Boylston street from junction of Boylston avenue to junction of Amory street and School street changed to Amory street, Feb. 16, 1882. L 2010, L 2741.

Amory terrace, Rox., from Amory avenue, south-west.

Amory's corner, B., 1784; cor. of State street and Leverett's lane (now Congress street), then so called.

***Anawan avenue**, W. Rox., 1872; from Park street to Central station B & P. (now N. Y., N. H. & H.) R.R.; laid out, July 9, 1879. L 1366, L 1367.

Anchor street, So. B.; from B street to E street, north-east of and parallel with W. First street.

Anderson court, B., 1862; from Anderson street, east, between Cambridge street and Phillips street.

Anderson place, B., 1864; from Anderson street, east, between Cambridge street and Phillips street.

Anderson place, Dor.; from Washington street, west, between Algonquin street and School street.

***Anderson street**, B., 1861; from Cambridge street to Pinckney street; originally Centre street, established by Jeremiah Allen in 1729 from Cambridge street, south, to point 88 feet south from May (now Revere) street; appears as Centre street in 1800; and as Centre street (west), from Cambridge street to Myrtle street in 1817, later called W. Centre street; extended to Pinckney street, 1833; name of W. Centre street changed to Anderson street, May 21, 1861. L 2783.

Andover court, B., 1844; from Andover street, south; closed.

***Andover street**, B., 1837; from Causeway street to Minot street; accepted and laid out, July 19, 1852; taken, April 6, 1870, by B. & L. R.R. Corporation, by virtue of chap. 291, Acts of 1869; now built over. L 10.

Andrew place, B.; from Andrew street, east, to Thorn street.

***Andrew square**, So. B., 1891; square at the junction of Dorchester avenue and Dorchester, Swett, Boston and Preble streets named Andrew square, March 5, 1891.

Andrews road, Bri., 1892; from Coolidge street to Holland road (now Hooker street); laid out under the name of Arden street, Aug. 26, 1892.

Andrews street, B., 1874; from E. Canton street to E. Dedham street, between Albany street and Harrison avenue.

Angell street, W. Rox.; from Canterbury street, south-east, to Blue Hill avenue, near junction of those streets; formerly called Autumn street.

Angier street, E. B. (Breed's Island), 1876; from Ashley avenue, south-east, to Revere line.

***Ann** / **Anne** } **street**, B., 1708; from the conduit in Union street (now Dock square) over the drawbridge to Cross street, 1708–1823; extended through Fish street and Ship street by change of name to the foot of North (now Hanover) street, July 6, 1824; name of part from Hanover street to Commercial street changed to Commercial street, Feb. 17, 1834; from Dock square to North square changed to North street, Jan. 1, 1852; from North square to Commercial street changed to North street, April 10, 1854; called at different times Conduit street and Drawbridge street. Vol. 31, pp. 45, 51, 58.

Ann-street court, B., 1830; from Ann (now North) street, west, near Bartlett (now Harris) street; called Page's court, about 1837.

Ann-street passageway, B., 1831 and earlier; an ancient 4-foot passageway in which a city sewer was laid leading from that part of Ann street (formerly Fish street, now North street) near the bottom of North square to the sea. It was fenced up by some person unknown, and the City Solicitor was ordered to ascertain the rights of the City therein, July, 1831; no report has been found of record.

Anson street, W. Rox.; from South street, near Morton street, south-east to Percy street.

Anthony place, B., 1875; north-east from and then parallel with North Hanover court; named, Oct. 19, 1875.

Antram's corner, B., 1708; the end of the fish market, near the conduit, then so called; on North side of Dock square, now part of Faneuil Hall square.

Antrim street, E. B. (Breed's island); from junction of Ford street and Walley street to Bennington street; authority to open given by Street Commissioners, April 21, 1893.

Antwerp street, Bri., 1892; from Western avenue to Lincoln street; authority to open from Lincoln street, north-east, to unnamed street, given by Street Commissioners, Oct. 14, 1892; authority to open from Western avenue, south-eastwardly, given by Street Commissioners, Dec. 14, 1896.

Appian place, E. B., 1896; from Marion street, south-west, between London street and Havre street; formerly called Marion place.

Appian way, Bri., 1851; from Vernon (now Raymond) street to Franklin street; laid out, Dec. 16, 1873.

Appleton place, Rox., 1845; from unnamed street (Appleton place, now Short street), north-east and east to Brookline street (now avenue) accepted conditionally, June 29, 1863; later called Maple avenue.

Appleton place, Rox., 1845; from Brookline avenue to Maple avenue (now Bellevue street); shown as a "street" on plan dated 1845; now called Short street.

Appleton road, Bri.; from Lake street, south-west, near Commonwealth avenue.

***Appleton street**, B., 1862; from Tremont street to Columbus avenue; includes avenue J on plan dated 1855; from Avenue I (now Berkeley street) westward to point west of Avenue A (now Dartmouth street); laid out as a public street from Berkeley street to Clarendon street, May 21, 1867; from Clarendon street to Columbus avenue, Oct. 27, 1868; extended from Berkeley street to Tremont street, June 8, 1872, including part of Chapman street. L 354, L 764, L 770.

Arborway, W. Rox.; the name of the parkway between Prince street and Forest Hills street, connecting Jamaica Park, Arnold Arboretum and Franklin Park.

***Arcadia street,** Dor., 1871; from Adams street to Draper street; formerly Auburn street; laid out Nov. 10, 1871. L 712.

***Arcadia street,** W. Rox. and Rox., 1871; from School street to Atherton street; shown as Acadia street on plans dated 1869; part in W. Rox. accepted by Town, Sept. 27, 1871; whole laid out, Sept. 29, 1874. L 965.

Arcadia terrace, Dor.; from Arcadia street, south.

Arch place, B., 1846; from Hanover street, east, near Mechanic street.

***Arch street,** B., 1792; from Summer street to Milk street; from Summer street to Franklin place passing through archway under building on Franklin place, 1800; confirmed as a public street, Sept. 15, 1834; wholly opened to Franklin place, May 1, 1858; portion discontinued, Oct. 6, 1858; extended through Morton place to Milk street, April 18, 1873. L 131, L 139, L 840, L 841, L 869.

Archibald street, Rox.; from Parker street to Halleck street; called New street, 1844; A street, 1872.

Arcola street, Rox., 1896; from Day street, north-westwardly, opposite Creighton street; authority to open given by Street Commissioners, Sept. 16, 1896.

Ardee place, Rox., 1875; leads north-west from Ardee street, which leads from Rogers avenue; shown on plan dated 1875.

Ardee street, Rox., 1875; from Rogers avenue, west, north of Bayview place; shown on plan dated 1875.

Arden street, W. R.; from Colberg avenue to Belgrade avenue.

***Arden street,** Bri., 1892; from Coolidge street to Hooker street (formerly Holland road), formerly Andrews road; laid out, Aug. 26, 1892. L 2432.

Argyle road, Bri.; from Englewood avenue to Commonwealth avenue, now included in Strathmore road.

***Argyle street,** Dor., 1873; from Welles avenue to Talbot avenue; formerly from Welles avenue to Dorchester avenue; laid out, Dec. 29, 1873; part included in Talbot avenue, Oct. 10, 1892. L 916.

Argyle street, W. Rox.; from Cornwall street, north-east, between Washington street and Marmion street.

Arion street, Dor., 1884; from Davenport avenue, north-west.

***Arklow street,** Rox., 1881; from Posen street to Gay Head street; part of Heath place from Posen street to Ulmer street, laid out as Arklow street, Nov. 16, 1881; Heath place from Ulmer street to Walden street laid out, Dec. 15, 1875; name changed to Arklow street, March 1, 1882; Arklow street extended from Walden street to Gay Head street, Sept. 22, 1894. L 1118, L 1569, L 2661.

Arlington avenue, B., from Clinton street, northerly; at Mercantile market.

***Arlington avenue,** Chsn., 1870; from Alford street to Somerville line; laid out and named, Nov. 1, 1870; called also Arlington street; shown as Commercial avenue on plan dated 1870. L 1155.

Arlington place, Chsn.; from Tremont street near Chelsea street, south-west, south-east, north-east to Tremont street again; now Mansfield place.

Arlington place, Bri.; from Arlington street, north.

***Arlington street,** B. 1858; from Beacon street to Boylston street; shown as "street 80 feet wide" on plan dated 1854; established by the Commonwealth and the City by indenture dated Dec. 11, 1856, each contributing half of the street; westerly half, contributed by the Commonwealth, accepted, March 7, 1863. L 374.

Arlington street, Chsn., 1873; Arlington avenue, so called.

***Arlington street,** Bri., 1870; from Market street, opposite Sparhawk street, across Parsons street, westerly; shown as an unnamed street on plan dated 1851; accepted from Market street to Parsons street June 24, 1870; laid out west from Parsons street, Aug. 14. 1891. L 2321, L 2453.

***Armandine street,** Dor., 1871; from Washington street to Milton avenue; laid out Oct. 8, 1889. L 2180.

***Armstrong street,** Rox., 1887; from Chestnut avenue to Mozart street; laid out, May 19 1887. L 1990.

Arnold Arboretum, W. R.; park lying between Centre street and South street, from Arborway south-west, nearly to Mendum street.

Arnold place, W. Rox., 1849; from Poplar street, east: probably same as Albion street on plan dated 1848; now part of Sycamore street.

***Arnold street,** B., 1810; from Washington street to Shawmut avenue; laid out from Washington street west, 1810; accepted from Washington street to Suffolk street (now Shawmut avenue), Nov. 10, 1851. L 22, L 121.

***Arnold street,** W. Rox.; from Weld street to Newton line; lies in territory set off from Newton to Roxbury by chapter 167, Acts of 1838; relocated, July 24, 1884. L 1793, L 1794.

***Arrow street,** Chsn., 1819; from Bow street to Lynde street; formerly from Harvard street to Front street; mentioned April 12, 1819, as formerly Ropemaker's lane; portion from Harvard street to Bow street, made a part of Washington street, Sept. 17, 1866; portion from Lynde street to Front street taken June 5, 1874, by Eastern R.R. Co. by virtue of chapter 360, Acts of 1873.

Arrow-street court, Chsn.; from Arrow street; probably in territory taken by Eastern R.R., Co., June 5, 1874.

Arthur place, Chsn.; from Main street, south-west, between Lincoln street and So. Eden street.

Arthur street, W. Rox.; from Weld street to Joy street, between Willow street and Walker street.

***Arthur street,** Bri., 1884; from North Beacon street to Hichborn street; laid out, Dec. 26, 1884. L 1843.

Arundel park, Dor.; from Ashmont street, near corner of Carruth street to Elm road.

***Arundel street,** Rox., 1874; from Beacon street to Mountfort street; laid out, June 12, 1894. L 2601, L 2834.

Arundel street, Dor.; from Beaumont street to Elm road, between Carruth street and Fairfax street.

Arundel street, W. Rox.; from Walter street, near South street, to Centre street.

Asbury place, W. Rox.; from South street, south-west, near Jamaica street.

Ascension street, Rox., 1833; from Cedar street to Kenilworth street; now called Lambert avenue.

Ash place, B , 1859; from Myrtle street, south, nearly opposite Irving street.

***Ash street,** B., 1809; from Bennet street to Oak street; plan in 1816 shows it crossing Nassau street and Oak street; part south of Oak street called Oak place in 1834; extended conditionally from northerly end northward about 88 feet to Bennet street, July 28, 1834; order to open same, Sept. 22, 1834, shows conditions complied with.

Ash street, B., 1819; from Front street (now Harrison avenue), west, south from Bennet street, a little north of the present Nassau street; closed.

***Ashburton place**, B., 1845; from Somerset street to Bowdoin street; from Somerset street, west, called Somerset court, 1809; said court extended to Bowdoin street, 1843; named Ashburton place, Nov. 13, 1845; accepted as a street, Dec. 11, 1848.

Ashburton street, B., 1842; formerly Peck lane, now Oxford street.

***Ashfield street**, W. Rox., 1890; from Fairview street to Walter street; formerly Peters street; laid out, July 17, 1890. L 2251.

***Ashford street**, Bri., 1841; from Linden street to Malvern street; part shown in 1850 as a 40-foot street; shown extended from Malvern street east, to land of Francis on plan dated 1855; laid out by Selectmen, Dec. 17, 1873; accepted conditionally, Dec. 30, 1873, but no record of fulfilment of conditions; laid out as a public street, Sept. 16, 1876, from Linden street to Malvern street. L 1175, L 1176.

Ashland avenue, B., 1846; from Washington street to Harrison avenue, south of Dover street; part shown unnamed on plan 1844; called Ashland place, 1853.

Ashland avenue, W. Rox., 1849; from Norfolk and Bristol (or Dedham) turnpike (now Washington street) to Florence street; earlier called Ashland street; included in the County way laid out by Norfolk County Commissioners, Sept., 1856; afterward called Ashland street in W. Rox. and Oakland street in Dor.

Ashland avenue, W. Rox., 1854; a way 25 feet wide leading from land of B. & P. (now N. Y., N. H. & H) R.R. Co.; not identified; part of Granite street.

Ashland avenue, W. Rox., 1870; from Summer street, south-west, across Cass (formerly Granite) street to Ballinakill avenue (now Johnson street); sometimes called Ashland street.

Ashland place, B., 1853; from Washington street to Harrison avenue; called Ashland avenue, 1846; Ashland place, 1853; laid out under name of Laconia street, Feb. 15, 1896. L 2757. Volume 31, page 98.

***Ashland street**, B., 1845; from Leverett street, south-west, then south-east to junction of Chambers street and Poplar street, including part of street now appearing on maps as Chambers street; part from Poplar street, north-west, probably formerly part of Allen's highway; part from Leverett street, south-west, shown as Gravel street, 1769, 1800, and 1819; name of Gravel street changed to Chambers street, May 26, 1828; name of part of Chambers street, formerly Gravel street, changed to Ashland street, Feb. 24, 1845.

***Ashland street**, Rox., 1863; from Grove Hall (now Blue Hill) avenue to Maple street; accepted, Oct. 24, 1864: name changed to Sea View street, April 20, 1869, and to Schuyler street, May 24, 1870.

†**Ashland street**, Dor., 1851; from Park street to unnamed street near Barque Warwick cove, crossing Elm street and Mill street; accepted from Park street to Elm street, April 21, 1851.

***Ashland street**, W. Rox., 1848; from South street to Harvard street; part from Norfolk and Bristol (or Dedham) turnpike (now Washington street) to Florence street shown as Ashland avenue, 1843-49; is part in W. Roxbury, of the way from Dorchester Upper Mills, near corner of River street and Brush Hill turnpike (now Blue Hill avenue), to Norfolk and Bristol turnpike (now Washington street); laid out by Norfolk County Commissioners by way of Berry street and Ashland street (now avenue), Sept., 1856; extended from Washington street to South street, July 30, 1875. L 1066, L 1196, L 1197, L 1198.

Ashland street, W. Rox.; Ashland avenue, from Summer street to Ballinakill avenue, 1874.

Ashley avenue, E. B. (Breed's island), 1875; from Chelsea avenue to Revere line; the portion of Ashley avenue between B., R. B. & L. R R. and Bennington street was laid out as Walley street, July 3, 1888. L 2073.

*__Ashley street__, Rox., 1884; from Chestnut avenue to Armstrong street; laid out, May 19, 1887. L 1989.

__Ashmont avenue__, Dor.; see Ashmont street.

*__Ashmont street__, Dor., 1849; from Washington street to Neponset avenue (formerly turnpike); laid out by County Commissioners, Dec., 1849, for a part of the way through a private way called Ashmont avenue. L 881, L 976, L 1865, L 2189.

__Ashmont park__, Dor., from Ashmont street, near Peabody square, north-west.

__Ashton place__, B., 1868; from Charles street, east, north of Fruit street.

__Ashworth park__, Rox., 1882; from Columbus avenue, north-east, between Walnut avenue and Washington street.

*__Aspen street__, Rox., 1888; from Copeland street to Montrose street; laid out, Feb. 6, 1888. L 2048.

__Assabet street__, Dor.; from Train street to Neponset avenue; authority to open given by Street Commissioners, Sept. 8, 1891.

__Astor street__, Rox., 1883; from West Chester park (now Massachusetts avenue) to Parker street.

__Astoria street__, Dor.; from Flint street, south-west, between Norfolk street and N. E. R.R, and parallel with latter.

__Asylum street__, B., 1844; from Washington street to Harrison avenue. Volume 19, page 123; volume 31, page 56.

*__Athelwold street__, Dor.; from School street to Kilton street; laid out and extended over Jackson place from School street to Kilton street, May 6, 1896. L 2761.

__Athenæum court__, B., 1849–55; from Atkinson (now Congress) street, near High street, east; closed.

*__Athens street__, So. B., 1840; from W. Second street to Dorchester street; shown as an unnamed 20-foot passageway, 1809; some part of the present street accepted and laid out, Nov. 29, 1852; extended from a point west of C street about 209 feet to B street, March 14, 1861; laid out in parts as follows: from B street to D street and from Second street to A street, Sept. 1, 1871; from E street to F street, Feb. 29, 1872; from F street to Dorchester street, Feb. 2, 1874; from A street to B street, Aug. 3, 1874; from D street to E street, July 12, 1875. L 167, L 204, L 219, L 556, L 642, L 643, L 644, L 743, L 919, L 950, L 1055.

__Athens-street court__, So. B.; from Athens street, south-west, between B street and C street.

__Atherton avenue__, W. Rox., 1871; from Albano street to Washington street.

__Atherstone street__, Dor., 1896; from Bailey street to Fuller street; authority to open, given by Street Commissioners, Jan. 30, 1896.

__Atherton place__, Rox.; from Atherton street, north-east, opposite end of Arcadia street.

*__Atherton street__, Rox. and W. Rox., 1869; from Washington street to Amory street; laid out from Washington street to Arcadia street, Sept. 29, 1874; New Atherton street laid out from Copley street to Amory street, Aug. 27, 1886; Atherton street extended from Arcadia street to Copley street, April 16, 1888; name of New Atherton street, from Copley street to Amory street, changed to Atherton street, March 1, 1889. L 996, L 1942, L 2066, L 2807.

*__Athol street__, Bri., 1885; from Aldie street to Raymond street; formerly called Auburn street between Holton (now Pleasant) street and Vernon (now Raymond) street; laid out as Athol street, Sept. 3, 1885; laid out between Holton street and Aldie street, July 15, 1890. L 1883. L 2250.

Atkins street, Dor., 1872; north-east of and parallel with Hersey street, near Haven avenue.

Atkins street, Bri.; from Washington street to Stratton street.

Atkinson street, B., 1788; from Milk street to Broad street; shown unnamed from Milk street to Cow lane (now High street) 1722 and 1729; from Milk street to Cow lane called Atkinson street in list of 1732; had been extended to Purchase street through Green's lane and whole named Atkinson street, July 4, 1788; extended east to Broad street, May 12, 1851; name changed to Congress street, Aug. 4, 1854; at some time called Green lane or Green's lane. Volume 31, pages 5, 12, 13, 22, 26, 55, 88, 97; volume 19, pages 70, 129.

Atkinson's street, B., 1732; from Milk street to Cow lane (now High street); named Atkinson street, July 4, 1788.

***Atlantic avenue,** B., 1868; from junction of Commercial street and Eastern avenue to Federal street; laid out from junction of Commercial street and Eastern avenue to Broad street at Rowe's wharf, Dec. 18, 1868; name extended over part of Broad street, formerly Flounder lane, between Rowe's wharf and Federal street, March 17, 1874. L 339, L 425, L 426, L 427, L 487, L 488, L 608, L 609, L 610, L 611, L 622, L 674, L 874, L 875, L 876, L 1000, L 1001, L 1042.

Atlantic avenue, E. B. (Breed's Island); Beachmont avenue laid out from Saratoga street to Revere line, in part over a private way called Atlantic avenue, Aug. 12, 1887, but Railroad Commissioners refused confirmation of grade crossing; Atlantic avenue from Ashley avenue to Revere line, laid out and name changed to Beachmont avenue, July 25, 1888. L 2042, L 2043, L 2044, L 2081, L 2082.

Atlantic avenue, Dor., 1845; at Savin Hill, from south-east end Indian way in a circling course around the hill to junction of Savin Hill avenue and Indian way; laid out and included in Savin Hill avenue, Aug. 12, 1869.

Atlantic court, S. B., from Atlantic street; between Thomas park and East Ninth street, west.

†**Atlantic street,** So. B., 1867; from E. Fourth street to Thomas park, north side, and from Thomas park, south side, to E. Ninth street; between Fourth (now E. Fourth) street and Thomas park accepted conditionally, Nov. 25, 1867; laid out from Fourth (now E. Fourth) street to Thomas street (now Thomas park), Nov. 17, 1868; part from Thomas park to E. Ninth street, sometimes called New Atlantic street.

Atlantis street, W. Rox.; from Weld street to Lassell street; authority to open given by Street Commissioners, Oct. 12, 1893.

Atwood avenue, Rox., 1867; from Day street, west; laid out as Evergreen street, Aug. 10, 1894.

Atwood square, W. Rox.; from South street to Custer street, part of, from South street, formerly called Buchanan court.

Auburn avenue, B , 1859; from Poplar street to Auburn street; also called Poplar avenue; included in Auburns treet, Sept. 1, 1879. L 1375.

Auburn avenue, Chsn., from Auburn street, near corner of Main street, south-east.

Auburn court, B., 1846; from Cambridge street, south, between Joy street and So. Russell street.

Auburn place, Rox.; from Auburn street, north-west, between Ruggles street and Vernon street.

Auburn place, Chsn.; from Auburn street, south-east, between Main street and Russell street; shown as unnamed place, 1812.

Auburn square, Chsn.; from Auburn street, opposite Russell street, north-west.

***Auburn street**, B. 1838; from Poplar street to Leverett street; from Brighton-street avenue, north-east, across Livingston street, 1849; part from Livingston street, north-east, laid out and extended to Leverett street, Nov. 27, 1874; part from Livingston street, south-west, laid out and extended to Poplar street through and including Auburn avenue, Sept. 1, 1879. L 988, L 1375.

Auburn street, E. B.; from Swift street to Harmony street; shown as an unnamed street on plan dated 1838.

***Auburn street**, Rox., 1830; from Ruggles street to Vernon street; accepted conditionally, Jan. 14, 1850; accepted, Sept. 27, 1852. L 2175.

Auburn street, Dor., 1869; from Adams street to Draper street; laid out under name of Arcadia street, Nov. 10, 1871.

Auburn street, W. Rox., 1872; from Washington street to Bellevue avenue.

***Auburn street**, Chsn., 1863; from Bunker Hill street to Main street; shown as an unnamed street on plan dated 1812; laid out 30 feet wide, June 29, 1863, and subsequently widened.

Auburn street, Bri., 1847; from Pleasant (now Holton) street to Vernon (now Raymond) street, 234 feet south-east from and parallel with Everett street; now closed. L 1883.

Auburn street, Bri., 1851; from Pleasant (now Holton) street to Vernon (now Raymond) street; laid out by Selectmen, Dec. 17, 1873; part from Raymond street to Pleasant street laid out as a public street, with name of Athol street, Sept. 3, 1885.

Auchmuty street, B., 1777; part of Essex street was sometimes so called, from Short (now Kingston) street to South street.

***Auckland street**, Dor., 1875; from Belfort street to proposed street (part of Bay street); part from Belfort street, south, shown as an unnamed street on plan dated 1871; from Belfort street to Savin Hill avenue shown on plan dated 1875; south of Savin Hill avenue shown on plan dated 1885; Auckland street laid out from Bay street to Belfort street, Nov. 2, 1891; L 1760, L 2351, L 2352.

***Audubon circle**, Rox.; a circle 250 feet in diameter, having for its centre the intersection of the centre lines of Audubon road, and that part of Beacon street between Audubon road and Brookline line.

†**Audubon road**, Rox., 1884; from Ivy street to and across Beacon street at Audubon circle, south-east, to Back Bay Fens, named Jan. 28, 1884; portion from Beacon street across Ivy street, laid out Nov. 7, 1895; L 2745.

Augustus avenue, W. Rox., 1870; from Poplar street, south-west, and beyond Metropolitan avenue.

Austin avenue, E. B. (Breed's Island); from Ashley avenue to Bayswater street.

Austin avenue, Dor.; from Stoughton street, northward, between Sumner street and Bakersfield street.

Austin street, Rox.; from Brookline avenue, north, to Bellevue street.

Austin street, Dor., 1874; from Commercial street to Downer avenue; laid out with name of De Wolf street, June 21, 1880. L 1464.

Austin street, W. Rox., 1852; name of Centre street changed to Austin street, May 3, 1852; renamed Centre street, Dec. 2, 1861.

Austin street, W. Rox., 1884; from Canterbury street to Harvard street; opened by Arthur W. Austin over his land in 1868 with name of Austin terrace; called Austin street in 1884.

Austin street, W. Rox., from Canterbury street to Back (now Harvard) street; now a part of Morton street.

***Austin street**, Chsn., 1817; from Main street to Prison Point bridge; road made "from end Craigie's bridge" "through Austin street to Main street." Sept. 6, 1817.

Austin terrace, W. Rox., 1868; from Canterbury street to Back (now Harvard) street; now Austin street.

Austin's corner, B., 1800; cor. Marlboro' (now Washington) street and Bromfield's lane (now Bromfield street), then so called.

Austin's lane, Chsn., 1761; from Back street, west; not identified.

Austin's lane, Chsn., 1827; mentioned as "Austin's lane or Gill street" in Charlestown town records, May 21, 1827; Gill street discontinued, March 28, 1836.

***Autumn street**, Rox., 1871; from Longwood avenue to Park street: laid out, Sept. 1, 1871. L 658.

***Autumn street**, W. Rox., 1870; from Centre street to Summer street: laid out, April 29, 1878. L 1303.

Autumn street, W. Rox., 1872; from Blue Hill avenue to Canterbury street; now Angell street.

Avenue A, B., 1855; from a point south of Avenue K (now Montgomery street) to a point north of Avenue II (now Chandler street) part of Dartmouth street.

Avenue B, B., 1855; from Tremont street, northward, to point north of Avenue II (now Chandler street); part of Clarendon street.

Avenue H, B., 1855; from Tremont street, westward, to point west of Avenue A (now Dartmouth street) now Chandler street.

Avenue J, B., 1855; from Avenue I. (now Berkeley street), westward, to point west of Avenue A (now Dartmouth street): part of Appleton street.

Avenue K, B., 1855; from Tremont street, westward, to point west of Avenue A (now Dartmouth street); part of Montgomery street.

Avenue I., B. and Rox., 1853; projected from point west of Tremont street, opposite Lucas street, northward across Mill-dam (now Beacon street) to Charles river; abandoned.

Avenue I., B. and Rox., 1854; projected from west line of Tremont street, opposite Dover street, northward to Harbor Commissioners' line in Charles river, north from the Mill-dam (now Beacon street); now Berkeley street.

Avenue II., B. and Rox., 1853; projected from end of Boylston street at west side of Public Garden as then projected, westward to Cross-dam (now Parker street); same avenue projected to Brookline line; now part of Boylston street.

Avenue III., B. and Rox., 1853; projected from south end of Avenue I. (now abandoned), opposite Lucas street, westward to dike leading from Cross-dam (now Parker street) to B. and P. (now N. Y., N. H. & H.) R.R., opposite end of Camden street; abandoned.

Avenue III., B. and Rox., 1854; projected from Avenue I. (now Berkeley street), westward, being shown nearly to Cross-dam (now Parker street); shown to point west of Avenue A (now Dartmouth street); part of now part of Warren avenue, rest abandoned.

Avenue IV., B. and Rox., 1853; projected from Tremont street, nearly opposite Pembroke street, northward across Mill-dam (now Beacon street) to Charles river; abandoned.

Avenue IV., B. and Rox., 1854; projected from Tremont street, at a point opposite part from Brookline street to Pembroke street, northward across Mill-dam (now Beacon street) to Harbor Commissioners' line in Charles river; abandoned.

Avenue V., Rox., 1853; from Avenue I. (abandoned), westward, to Cross-dam (now Parker street); included in Commonwealth avenue.

Avenue V., Rox., 1854; projected from Avenue I. (now Berkeley street) westward to Brookline line; a part included in Commonwealth avenue.

Avenue VI., B. and Rox., 1853; projected from Tremont street, nearly opposite Chester square (now Massachusetts avenue) northward across Mill-dam (now Beacon street) to Charles river; abandoned.

Avenue VI., B. and Rox., 1854; projected from Tremont street, opposite Chester square (now Massachusetts avenue) northward across Mill-dam (now Beacon street) to Harbor Commissioners' line in Charles river; part of easterly side of said avenue made boundary line between Boston and Roxbury, by section 1 of chapter 210, Acts of 1859; abandoned.

Avenue place, Bri., 1884; from Western avenue, east of Waverly street, south.

Avenue street, Bri., 1840; the Mill-dam road from Brookline line to Watertown line so named June 15, 1840; name of Avenue street changed to Beacon street, Nov. 10, 1846; changed from Beacon street to North Beacon street, March 5, 1860; name of part of North Beacon street from former boundary line between Brighton and Brookline westward to Cambridge street at Union square changed to Brighton avenue, Jan. 28, 1884; name of part of Brighton avenue from said former boundary line to Massachusetts avenue changed to Commonwealth avenue, March 1, 1887.

Avery lane, B., 1820; from Rainsford's lane (now Harrison avenue,) east; closed.

Avery place, B., 1828; from Avery street, north.

Avery place, Chsn.: from Russell street, nearly opposite Oak street, north-east to Auburn avenue.

***Avery street**, B., 1826; from Washington street to Mason street; called Sheaf's lane in list of 1732, from Newbury (now Washington) street west to the Common; same extent and called Sheaf's lane in Selectmen's list, 1788; Sheaf's lane in Edes list, 1800; Sheafe lane or Sheafe's lane from Newbury street to Common street in 1817, including part of the present Mason street; name of Sheafe lane changed to Avery street, Oct. 21, 1826; also called Colburn's lane at an early date.

Avery's corner, B., 1800; cor. Newbury (now Washington) street and Sheafe's lane (now Avery street,) then so called.

Aves's corner, B., 1732; cor. Lynn (now Commercial) street, and Henchman's lane (now Henchman street) then so called.

***Avon place**, B., 1824; from Washington street to Chauncey street; called D'Emmings court, also Central court (from Newbury [now Washington] street, east), 1806; named Avon place, 1824; extended to Chauncey street, Sept. 25, 1868; name of Avon street given to Temple place and Avon place, March 30, 1869; making one street from Tremont street to Chauncey street; part of Avon street, from Washington street to Chauncey street, renamed Avon place, June 9, 1869. L 388, L 429, L 430.

†**Avon place**, Rox.; from Ruggles street north, between B. & P. (now N.Y., N.H. & H.) R.R. and Parker street; shown as an unnamed place in 1835; shown as Avon place or street, 1843–49; laid out, June 19, 1877; name changed to Leon street, March 1, 1894. L 1244.

Avon place, Chsn.; from Sullivan street south-east, south-west from Bunker Hill street.

***Avon street**, B., 1869; from Tremont street to Chauncey street; Temple place and Avon place together named Avon street, March 30, 1869; parts renamed as before, June 9, 1869.

Avon street, Rox., 1837; from Heath street, north-east, then south-east, then south to Heath street again; now called Lawn street.

Avon street, Rox., 1851; from Commonwealth (formerly Brighton) avenue, south, to B. & A. R.R. (formerly Boston & Worcester R.R.): shown from Brighton avenue, south, across said railroad to Beacon street; part south of the railroad closed.

***Avon street**, W. Rox., 1845; from Pond street to Brookline line; accepted, March 28, 1870

Avondale place, Dor., at the Lower Mills; from Richmond street, north, between Washington street and Dorchester avenue.

Ayr road, Bri., 1896; from Beacon street to Orkney road; authority to open given by Street Commissioners, July 30, 1896.

B street, B., 1828; from A (now River) street to D (now Brimmer) street parallel with and 140 feet south from Chestnut street; named Byron street, 1830.

†**B street**, So. B., 1804; from W. Seventh st. at junction Dorchester avenue across Eastern avenue (now Congress street) on South Boston flats; projected "from the boundary line to the sea" Oct. 4, 1804; laid out and named, Feb. 27, 1805; laid out from Seventh (now W. Seventh) street to low-water mark, Nov. 17, 1868. Vol. 31, page 48. L 27, L 654.

B street, Rox., 1872; leads south-east from unnamed street (now Mechanic street) leading south-west from Ruggles street, near Parker street; called B street court, 1883, and shown as Antwerp street in 1886; near where Willis street now is.

B street, Rox.; from Norfolk avenue to Proctor street.

B street, W. Rox., 1868; from Boylston street to Spring Park avenue; laid out with the name of Burr street, April 25, 1877. L 1230.

B street, W. Rox., 1877; from Williams street, south-west, across A street.

B street court, Rox, 1883; from continuation of Mechanic street, south of Ruggles street, south-east; called B street in 1872, and Antwerp street in 1886; near where Willis street now is.

B street, Dor., 1892; from Pleasant street to F (now Bakersfield) street; authority to open given by Street Commissioners, May 4, 1892; now called Morrill street.

Babcock court, Chsn., 1838; from Main street, north, opposite Sullivan square.

Back Bay Fens, Rox., 1887; Back Bay Park named Back Bay Fens, Dec. 30, 1887; entrances from Beacon street, Boylston street, Westland avenue, Huntington avenue and Brookline avenue.

Back lane, Chsn., 1638; another name for Back (now Warren) street.

Back lane, Chsn., 1788; from Middlegate (now Prescott) street to Bow (now Devens) street; possibly the same as later Prescott-street avenue.

Back street, B.; from 67 Brimmer street, west; 30-foot passageway running along by the Charles river.

Back street, B., 1708; from "Stanbury's Corner" at Middle (now Hanover) street to Prince street, May 3, 1708; included in Salem street, July 6, 1824.

***Back street**, Rox. and W. Rox., 1796; called "Back street, Road to the Great Lots," 1796; from Warren street to South street named Back street, May 9, 1825; name changed to Walnut street, Nov. 20, 1843; part of Walnut street from former corner of Walnut avenue and Forest Hills street to South street, included in Forest Hills street, June 26, 1848; part of same from present corner of Forest Hills street and Morton street to South street, made part of Morton street, Dec. 5, 1859; rest of Walnut street, named Walnut avenue,

April 21, 1868; part south of Sigourney street now in Franklin Park.

***Back street,** Dor. and W. Rox., 1840; from Blue Hill avenue to Hyde Park line; after annexation of Dorchester, westerly line of Back street made boundary line between Boston and West Roxbury by chapter 146, Acts of 1870; probably in early times this street and the present Harvard street in Dorchester formed a continuous way; shown as town road in 1835; street from turnpike by Samuel Capen's and Mrs. Floyd's to Trescott's lane named Back street, March 11, 1840; name changed to Mount Hope street, Sept 18, 1861; no record of renaming Back street; name of Back street, from Blue Hill avenue to Hyde Park line changed to Harvard street, March 1, 1896.

***Back street,** Chsn., 1638; down to 1831 extending from junction of Hepburne's or Hepburn's lane or street (now part of Henley street) and Streeter's or Phillips' lane (later part of Salem turnpike or Turnpike street, later part of Back street, now part of Park street) north-west to Broad street (later Market street, now Main street); called also Back lane, 1638, and at various times later shown as an unnamed street; street leading from City square to Main street being Back street and a part of the late Salem turnpike named Back street, Oct. 3, 1831; said "part of the late Salem turnpike" called Streeter's lane, 1670; Streeter or Phillips' lane, 1768; Phillips' lane, 1780; included in Salem turnpike or Turnpike street, 1803-4; Back street named Warren street, March 3, 1834; part from City square to Henley street (being part formerly Streeter's or Phillips' lane) named Park street, Dec. 29, 1868.

Bacon place, B., 1844; from Carver street, east, between Eliot street and Townsend place; shown on maps as late as 1861; now closed.

Badger place, Chsn., 1874; from Green street, north-west, between Bartlett street and Hancock street.

Bagnal street, Bri., 1894; from Holton street to Aldie street; authority to open given by Street Commissioners, April 14, 1894.

***Bailey street,** Dor., 1870; from Washington street to Dorchester avenue; laid out, June 29, 1877. L 1246, L 1247.

Bailey's court, Rox., 1852; from Albany street, south-east, near Yeoman street; now called Bailey court.

Baily street, W. Rox., 1887; from Washington street, north-west, near and south of Keyes street; laid out as Burnett street, March 29, 1890. L 2215.

Bainbridge street, E. B., 1836; from Porder street, south-east, to Chelsea street; shown on plan dated June 2, 1836, north-east of and parallel with Decatur street.

***Bainbridge street,** Rox., 1845; from Walnut avenue to Dale street and bounding on Washington park; part from Walnut avenue (then street) to land (now said park) shown as part of Hull street at one time; no record of laying out has been found. L 740.

***Bainbridge street,** Chsn., 1848; from Chelsea street to Moulton street; Selectmen directed to open a road from Salem turnpike to the rope-walks through Ebenezer Breed's land, June 8, 1807; agreement with Mr. Breed to build same 30 feet wide, May 3, 1813; deed of land from Mr. Breed to Town, Feb 8, 1814; shown as an unnamed street in 1818; first named Bainbridge street in 1848; called Brooks street in 1844-52.

Baker avenue, } **Baker court,** } Dor., 1873; from Washington street, east; formerly Baker avenue and Brandon street; laid out as Brent street, from Washington street to Carlisle street, Nov. 12, 1885. L 1896.

Baker court or } **Baker place,** } Dor., from Willow court, north-east.

Baker, (or Baker's) court, Dor., 1870; from Washington street, west, at Lower Mills, almost adjoining Neponset river.

Baker court, W. Rox., 1884; from Germania street, south-west; called Baker street in 1884 from Boylston street; part near Boylston street included in the laying out of Germania street.

Baker park, Dor., 1895; from East Cottage street, south, near New England R.R; authority to open given by Street Commissioners, Feb. 5, 1895.

Baker place, or Baker court, Dor., 1884; from Willow court, north-east.

Baker place, Dor., 1872; from Bird street, north, adjoining and west of N. E. R.R.

Baker place, W. Rox.; from Baker street; south-west, near and north-west of Gardner street.

***Baker street,** W. Rox., 1825; from Centre street to Newton line; named, May 9, 1825; probably a public highway some time previous; straightened from Centre street to Spring street, March, 1872. L 1647, L 1648, L 1649, L 2407.

Baker street, W. Rox., 1874; from Boylston street, near Washington street, south-west, crossing end of Germania street; part of included in the laying out of Germania street; also called Baker court.

Baker's alley, B., 1844; from North street, west, between Richmond street and Prince street.

Baker's alley, B., 1848; from Broad street, west, south of Batterymarch street; included in Sturgis street 1869, and Sturgis street, included in Franklin street, 1873. L 460.

Baker's alley, B., 1866; from South Margin street, south, between Prospect street and Norman street.

Bakersfield street, Dor., from Stoughton street to Willis street; authority to open under name of F street given by Street Commissioners, May 4, 1892.

Baldwin court, Chsn., 1854; from Main street, north-east, between Salem street and School street; Beckford court (now Linwood place), so called in 1854.

Baldwin place, B., 1829; from Salem street, west, between Prince street and Cooper street.

Baldwin place, So. B., 1874; from Baldwin street, south.

Baldwin place, Bri., 1874; from Washington street, south-west, near and west of Chestnut Hill avenue.

Baldwin street, B., 1878; from Northampton street to Camden street; laid out as Watson street, May 10, 1886. L 1904.

***Baldwin street,** So. B., 1851; from Granite street to A street; laid out Nov. 17, 1868. L 256.

Baldwin street, Rox., 1833; from Massachusetts avenue (formerly West Chester park) to Parker street; formerly from Parker street, east, to the channel in empty basin a few feet west from present location of B. & P. (now N.Y., N.H. & H.) R.R.; Baldwin street, from Massachusetts avenue to Parker street, laid out as Norway street, July 10, 1896.

***Baldwin street,** Chsn., 1850; from Rutherford avenue to Bunker Hill street, and from latter street to Medford street, the two parts not continuous; part from Bunker Hill street to Mystic river called Coggin street in 1837 and 1843; same part called Linden street in 1844; Baldwin street, from Main street to Bunker Hill street, laid out and accepted, Feb. 14, 1853; Linden street made a continuation of Baldwin street, Oct. 8, 1867; altered, etc., between Main street and Bunker Hill street and accepted, Feb. 28, 1870; laid out from Main street to Rutherford avenue, Oct. 9, 1891. L 2344.

Baldwin's lane, Dor.; from River street, near Hyde Park line; sometimes called Bird's lane.

Balfour street, Dor.; from Dalkeith street to Wayland street.

***Ball street,** Rox., 1860: from Washington street to Shawmut avenue, laid out, June 29, 1870. L 527.

Ballantine's corner, B., 1708; corner of Hanover street and Marshall's lane (now Marshall street), then so called.

Ballard place, B., 1831; from Bromfield street, south, then turning east; not given in directory later than 1849; probably now an arched passageway without name.

Ballard place, W. Rox., 1886; east from Ballard street.

***Ballard street,** W. Rox., 1884; from Centre street to Custer street; at one time known as Addison avenue; laid out Oct. 3, 1891. L 2340.

Ballard way, W. Rox., 1896; from Jamaica street, north-easterly, near Woodman street.

Ballard's corner, B., 1800; corner Newbury (now Washington) street, and West street, then so called.

Ballinakill avenue, W. Rox., 1874; from Baker street, north-east; also another portion crossing end of first and running south-easterly, crossing end of Ashland street; part of laid out as Johnson street, Jan. 6, 1888.

Ballou avenue, Dor., 1874; from Lauriat avenue to Norfolk street, near N. E. R.R.; authority to open part from Norfolk street, near R.R. bridge, north-west, then north-east, to beyond Mascot street, given by Street Commissioners, July 20, 1893.

Ballou place, Dor.; from Norfolk street, near Milton avenue, to Ballou avenue.

Ball's alley, B.; a name for North Centre street prior to 1708.

Baltic street, E. B., 1884; from Cottage street to Front street, crossing end of Swift street (proposed street).

Baltimore street, Dor.; from Beaumont street to Elm road.

Bancroft place, B., 1868; from 33 Hawkins street, east.

Bang's alley, B., 1803; from Kilby street, east; Marshall's alley, 1784–1800; Bangs alley, 1803–25; the alley way next south of Doane street.

Banister's lane, B.; Winter street was sometimes so called prior to 1708; first called Blott's lane, later Willis's lane, or Banister's lane, and sometimes Bolt's lane.

Bank Top road, B., 1794; a passageway 12 or 15 feet wide leading from the counting-room of Sears & Gosley on Sears (now Fort Hill) wharf, north-east then north-west to Purchase street; part now built over and parts now in Oliver street and Atlantic avenue. See deed Suffolk Reg. L 179, Fol. 85; altered so as to be parallel with Broad street, 1834.

Barbara street, W. Rox., 1896; from Centre street, westerly, near corner of Perkins street; authority to open given by Street Commissioners, June 25, 1896.

Barber's alley, B., 1868; from North street, north-west, between Fleet street and Clark street; shown on plan as an unnamed way in 1848.

Barlow street, W. Rox.; from Wachusett street, near Weld Hill street; authority to open given by Street Commissioners, July 19, 1893.

Barnan place, So. B., 1884; from East Third street, north, between Emmett street and K street; generally called Barnard place.

Barnard place, So. B., 1869; from East Third street, north, between Emmott street and K street.

Barnard place, So. B., 1884; from East Second street, south, between I street and Emmett street.

Barnard's corner, B., 1800; corner North street and Love lane, (now Tileston street), then so called.

Barnes street, Dor.; from 1817 Dorchester avenue, west.

Barnes street, W. Rox., 1895; from Amesbury street to Durant street; authority to open given by Street Commissioners, May 3, 1895.

Barque Warwick street, Dor., 1810; from Neponset street, south-east, to bridge on Mill-pond; sometimes written Bark Warwick street; street does not now exist.

Barrack lane, B., 1788; name given by Selectmen to Bury lane or street, from Federal street (formerly Long lane) to Atkinson (now Congress) street, but apparen'ly never used; called Berry street, 1803, and named Channing street, July 14, 1845.

Barre place, B., 1826; from 53 Eliot street, north, near Tremont street; sometimes called Barry place.

Barrett's corner, B., 1800; corner Middle (now Hanover) street and Bell alley (now Prince street), then so called

***Barrett street,** B., 1831; from North street to Fulton street; from Ann (now North) street, east, called Wentworth's lane, 1732; accepted and named Barrett street (conditionally) from Ann street to New street (now Fulton street) in rear of Commercial street, June 7, 1831; laid out and named, Oct. 24, 1842. L 112.

Barrill's corner, B., 1732; corner of Newbury (now Washington) street and Sheafe's lane (now Avery street), then so called.

***Barrington street,** Dor., 1889; from Bowdoin street to Columbia street; known as Hamilton avenue from 1872 to 1889; laid out as Barrington street, Oct. 21, 1889; shown as a proposed street from Bowdoin street to Holmes avenue, 1894; authority to open part of this given by Street Commissioners, Aug. 29, 1893. L 2181, L 2182.

Barry's corner, Bri.; at the junction of Western avenue and North Harvard street.

Barry / Barry's court, B., 1859; from Washington street, east, between Savoy street and Cottage place.

Barry place, B., 1826; from Eliot street, near Tremont street, north; sometimes called Barre place.

Barry street, Dor., 1872; from Quincy street to Clarkson street; authority to open portion from Barrington street to Clarkson street given by Street Commissioners, Oct. 13, 1896.

Barstow street, Bri., 1888; west from 36 Saunders street.

Barstow street, E. B. (proposed); from Cottage street to Georgia street, Wood Island.

Bartlett court, Rox., 1874; from 170 Norfolk avenue, north-east; sometimes called Bartlett street.

Barton's point, B., 1712; at the foot of Leverett street; called Blackstone's point, 1708.

† **Bartlett place,** B., 1837; apparently T shaped, first part from Salem street, west, opposite Parmenter street, second part from Cooper street to North Margin street, across end of first part; portion from Salem street, west, then north to Cooper street, called Salem place, 1828–36; part 50 feet north of Salem street, laid out as an extension of Richmond (now Parmenter) street, in 1845.

Bartlett place, Chsn., 1854; from near Bartlett street, south-west, between Sullivan street and Walker street; not in Charlestown directory after 1858, where it is described as "near 112 Bartlett street."

* **Bartlett street**, B., 1826; from Hanover street to Ann (now North) street: called White Bread alley, 1708; named Bartlett street, 1826; name changed to Harris street, April 21, 1868.

Bartlett street, Rox., 1884; from 170 Norfolk avenue, north-east; also called Bartlett court.

* **Bartlett street**, Rox., 1825; from Dudley street, at Eliot square to Washington street; so named, May 9, 1825; originally this street and the part of Washington street, from the present easterly end of Bartlett street, to Dudley street formed one street, such part being included in location of Norfolk and Bristol turnpike (otherwise Dedham turnpike) in 1804; Bartlett street at some time before it was so named called Perrin's lane; the present Bartlett street was called Cottage street; the street (now part of Washington street) commencing on Washington street, at City Hotel (which stood where Zeigler street now is) and running south to the present Bartlett street, also named Bartlett street July 31, 1848, making a continuous street from Washington street across Dudley street around to Dudley street again at Eliot square; the part of same from Dudley street, north, to Washington street named Guild row, and the part from Dudley street, south, to present easterly end of Bartlett street included in Shawmut avenue, Dec. 28, 1857, leaving Bartlett street as it now is: said Guild row and Shawmut avenue south of Dudley street included in Washington street, June 16, 1874.

* **Bartlett street**, Chsn., 1810; from Monument square to Walker street; from Elm street, north-west, to Pleasant (now Pearl) street nearly parallel with Summer street conveyed to the Town by Oliver Holden, July 17, 1810: shown in 1818 from Elm street to Sullivan street; from Elm street, north-west, to Walker street accepted, Nov. 28, 1831: continued south-east to Concord street, Sept. 1845; laid out to Concord street (now Monument square), May 4, 1847.

Bartlett terrace, Rox., 1896; from Washington street, north-west, near corner of Bartlett street.

* **Barton court**, B., 1868; from Barton street to Brighton street; shown as a passageway on Hale's plan, 1820; called Short Second street, 1849, and later Little Napier street; latter name changed to Barton court, April 21, 1868.

* **Barton street**, B., 1825: from Milton street, north-east, across Leverett street to Lowell street; part from Leverett street, north-east, shown as extending 250 feet therefrom and called Barton street or court in 1825, and as extended to Lowell street in 1836; this part probably nearly in position of a "40-feet highway" shown as extending from another "40-feet highway" (Leverett street) to the river on plan made in 1725, and said "40-feet highway" probably same as Bury (or Berry) lane on Osgood Carleton's plan, dated 1800, and afterward closed and included in Alms-House estate; other part of Barton street from Leverett street, south-west, originally Second street, 1809; from Leverett street, opposite Alms-House yard, south-west, to point 33½ feet beyond 18-feet passageway (Barton court) on Hale's plan, 1820; accepted and recorded as a public street, May 12, 1828; confirmed as such, Sept. 15, 1834; name changed to Napier street, April 25, 1855; Napier street extended, south-west, to Milton street, Oct. 5, 1863; name changed to Barton street, April 21, 1868. L 268.

Barton-street place, B.; from Barton street, south-east; Second-street court or place, 1835; Napier-street place, 1855; Napier place, 1868; greater part included in the extension of Chambers street, June 7, 1893.

Barton's point, B., 1712; at the foot of Leverett street; called Blackstone's point, 1708.

Basto place, W. Rox., 1860; from Washington street (formerly Shawmut avenue), near junction of Poplar street, north-west; extended to Brandon street and name changed to Corinth street, Nov. 25, 1882. L 1666.

* **Batavia street,** Rox., 1883; from St. Stephen (formerly Falmouth) street, to Parker street; laid out, May 11, 1893. L 2507, L 2508.

* **Batchelder street,** Dor., 1883; from Clifton street to Pontine street; laid out from Clifton street to Marshfield street, Oct. 29, 1884; extension from Marshfield street to Pontine street laid out, Aug. 10, 1894. L 1828, L 1829, L 2611.

Bateman place, So. B., 1876; from N street, west, between East Seventh street and East Eighth street.

Bates place, B., 1863; from Kneeland street, south, between Washington street and Whitmore street (formerly Kneeland place).

Bates place, Rox., 1848; from Roxbury (formerly Washington) street near Eliot square, north; formerly called Washington court; now called Roxbury terrace.

* **Bates street,** Chsn., 1854; from Bunker Hill street to Ferrin street; laid out, Jan. 2, 1878. L 1295.

Bath avenue, Dor., 1845; from Savin Hill avenue (part formerly part of Glenway) to Springdale street; laid out as Denny street, April 21, 1892.

* **Bath street,** B., 1806; from Post Office square, south-east, then south to Post Office square again; originally from Water street, south-east, then south to Milk street; called Tanner's lane, 1708; Horn lane, 1795; at one time called Horse lane and then "Bath street or Horn lane;" a portion included in extension of Pearl street to Water street, afterwards Post Office square, Dec. 27, 1873. L 1121.

Batterman place, B., 1822–37; from Essex street, opposite Lincoln street; included in Lincoln street, wholly or in part, upon the extension of Lincoln street, south of Essex street, 1836; mentioned until 1848, and a narrow opening shown and so named upon maps as late as 1851; now closed.

* **Battery alley,** B., 1708; from North (now Hanover) street to Ship (now Commercial) street; originally from Charter street to the North Battery, and part from Charter street to North (now Hanover) street discontinued before 1708; name written also Battrey alley; sometimes called Daggett's alley or lane, 1789–1823; named Battery street, Nov. 7, 1825.

Battery lane, Chsn., 1714; from Maudlin street to Battery (now Water) street; called Carriggs court in 1854; called Carey street, 1875, and Carey court, 1883. Name of Carriggs court given to another passageway leading north-west from Water street, north-east of Carey court or street in 1883.

* **Battery street,** B., 1825; from Hanover street to East Boston North Ferry, crossing Commercial street; part from North (now Hanover) street to Ship (now Commercial) street, called Battery alley, 1708; also sometimes Daggett's alley or lane, 1789–1823; named Battery street, Nov. 7, 1825; part from Commercial street to North Ferry called People's Ferry avenue, 1854, and also later North Ferry avenue; Battery street extended to include same, Aug. 3, 1880. L 100, L 144, L 207, L 551, L 559, L 1474.

Battery street, Chsn., 1714; from the swing-bridge near foot of Maudlin or Mardling street or lane (point now foot of Foss street), east, crossing Wapping street and Henley street, called also "way to battery from swing-bridge," 1785; part east of Wapping street discontinued on establishment of Navy Yard, Jan. 14, 1801; remainder included in Water street, 1802; latter part probably also at times called Water street, from 1780, when Water street and Battery street were straightened and improved.

***Batterymarch street**, B., 1708; from Liberty square to High street, also branch to Broad street, opposite Custom House street; from Liberty square across Milk street to northerly end of Hamilton street, thence northeasterly to Broad street opposite Custom House street, 1895; from Hallaway's or Hallowell's corner, Milk street, corner of present Batterymarch street, south-east by the South Battery, then south-west through part of the present Purchase street to the lower end of Gibb's lane (now Oliver street), 1708; from Liberty square, including Crab alley or lane, to Foster's wharf, near the South Battery, corner of present Purchase street and Broad street, 1800; part from present terminus in Broad street to Foster's wharf included in Broad street, 1808; name of Hamilton street changed to Batterymarch street, March 1, 1896. L 332, L 333, L 458, L 853.

Battle street, Chsn., 1878; from Medford street, north, nearly opposite Lexington street.

Bauch street, W. Rox.; from end of Augustus avenue, south-east.

Baxter place, B., 1857; from Harvard street, south, near Harrison avenue.

Baxter square, So. B., 1873; from E street, south-east, between West Seventh street and West Eighth street.

***Baxter street**, So. B.; from C street to E street; laid out from D street to E street, Nov. 17, 1868; laid out from D street to C street, Sept. 9, 1887. L 200, L 1097, L 2017.

Baxter's corner, B., 1708; corner Summer street and South street, then so called.

Bay street, B., 1816; from Washington street, east, near the present Rollins street; closed.

Bay street, B., 1833; across Fayette street and Knox street, parallel with Church street; described in 1846, "from Tremont street to rear of Knox street." L 387, L 391.

Bay street, Dor., 1869; from Dorchester avenue to N.Y., N.H. & H. R.R.; originally from westerly line land of Lewis Leeds, across end of Leeds street, Midland street, and Spring street to O.C. (now N.Y., N.H. & H.) R.R.

Bayard street, Bri., 1890; from Kenneth street to North Harvard street.

Bay State place, So. B., 1872; from East First street, south, between I street and K street.

***Bay State road**, Rox., 1889; from Beacon street to Essex street at Brookline line; laid out from Beacon street to street now called Deerfield street, Oct. 22, 1889; laid out from Deerfield street to Sherborn street, June 7, 1893; laid out from Sherborn street to Granby street, Aug. 15, 1895. L 2184, L 2517, L 2518, L 2716.

Bayswater street, E. B., 1875; from Saratoga street, at B., R. B. & L. R.R., south-east, then east and north, to Saratoga street, near Belle Isle inlet.

Bay-View place, So. B., 1872; from East Eighth street, near I street, north, then east and west, T shaped.

Bay-View place, Rox., 1875; from Rogers avenue, south-west, between Huntington avenue and Ruggles street.

Beach place, Chsn., 1872; from Beach street, south-east; sometimes called Beach-street place. L 1193.

***Beach street,** B., 1708; from Washington street to Federal street; from Orange (now Washington) street, east, to the water, 1708; from Orange street across Rainsford lane (later Front street, now Harrison avenue), 1817; extended east from Front street to Lincoln street conditionally, Sept. 5, 1836; same part accepted, Oct. 16, 1837; extended from Lincoln street to Broad (now Federal) street, Oct. 31, 1837. L 13, L 380, L 616, L 760, L 1021, L 1447.

Beach street, B., 1804; the eastern extremity of Essex street, then so called.

***Beach street,** Dor., 1857; from Commercial (now Freeport) street, to Park street; accepted July 20, 1857. L 651.

***Beach street,** W. Rox.; Beech street, sometimes so called.

***Beach street,** Chsn., 1870; from Medford street to the railroad; called lane to Johnson's wharf in deed, March 27, 1820; called "town-way to river" on plan dated 1837; no record of naming same; name first appears in 1870. L 1193.

†Beacham street, Chsn., 1870; from south-west of West street to Mystic river; laid out and accepted, from about 100 feet south-west of West street to Arlington avenue, June 24, 1872.

***Beachmont avenue,** E. B., 1888; from Ashley avenue to Revere line; formerly Butler avenue and later Atlantic avenue; laid out from Ashley avenue to Revere line, July 25, 1888. L 2042, L 2043, L 2044, L 2081, L 2082.

Beacon hill, B., the present site of the State House; formerly Centry, Centuary, or Sentry hill; on Dec. 28, 1752, the Selectmen, having searched the town records, find that the hill on which the beacon stands and which is the property of the Town, is six rods square, and the highway leading up to it from the Common between land of John Alford and of Thos. Hancock is 30 feet in width the whole length; recorded in town records, Jan. 16, 1753.

Beacon-hill place, B., 1847; from Bowdoin street to Mt. Vernon street.

Beacon-hill street, B.; called Bowdoin place, 1820.

***Beacon street,** B. and Rox., 1708; from Tremont street over Beacon hill, passing the Common and over the former Mill-dam of the Boston and Roxbury Mill Corporation and through the marshes formerly part of Brookline to boundary line of Brookline at St. Mary's street; "from near present corner of Beacon and Somerset streets, westerly, through the upper side of the Common and so down to the sea," 1708; the part of the present Beacon street, from Tremont street to a point near corner of Beacon street and Somerset street, formed part of School street, 1708; School street called South Latin School street, 1789; said part of School street included in Beacon street, 1803 (no record of such change); the Mill-dam from Charles street to Sewall's point, in Brookline, projected in 1813; Boston and Roxbury Mill Corporation incorporated and authorized to build same in 1814; Mill-dam begun in 1818, completed and opened to travel, July 2, 1821, road over same being called Western avenue; part of Western avenue from Charles street, west, about 690 feet to channel accepted, Sept. 19, 1831, but no record of naming this part of Beacon street; land covered by the Mill-dam released by the Boston and Roxbury Mill Corporation to the Commonwealth by indenture of June 9, 1854, "to be forever kept open as a public highway;" other parts of Western avenue have been accepted from time to time, usually upon condition, and deeds to comply with condition, all recorded in Suffolk Registers, have been given as follows: Part from part accepted, Sept. 19, 1831, to (Otter) street accepted and named Beacon street, conditionally, April 21, 1857, deed L 716, f. 227; part of Beacon street, between Otter street and avenue A (not identified) accepted conditionally, June 23, 1857; part between Otter street and "west end of new block of freestone front houses" (a point about 343 feet west from Otter street) accepted and named Beacon street, conditionally, May 27, 1858, deed L 738, f. 82; part between (George P.) Upham's house (west corner thereof 342 feet west from Otter street) and a point distant 140 feet westerly from the south-west corner of Berkeley street accepted, conditionally, and named Beacon street, Oct. 30, 1861, deed L 829, f. 3; part between Berkeley street and Clarendon street accepted, conditionally, Dec. 23, 1862, deeds L 829, f. 3. and L 867, f. 239; same part accepted and named Beacon street, May 26, 1863; part between Clarendon street and Dedham (now Dartmouth) street accepted, conditionally, and named Beacon street, July 3, 1865, and Oct. 31, 1865, deed in compliance with latter order, L 867, f, 239; "part of Mill-dam road known as Beacon street between east line of Clarendon street and division line between Brookline and Boston where it crosses Mill-dam road" (about 990 feet west from West Chester park, now Massachusetts avenue) laid out, Dec. 7, 1868; no record of laying out or naming the part of the Mill-dam formerly in Brookline from crossing of former Brookline boundary line (about 990 feet west from West Chester park), west to its end at junction of the three roads, Brookline avenue, Beacon street and Commonwealth (formerly Brighton avenue); part of Beacon street in Brookline from Harvard street, east, to the Mill-dam laid out by Norfolk County Commissioners. June, 1851; part thereof thrown into Boston by annexation to Boston of part of Brookline, east of westerly line of St. Mary's street, by chapter 374 of Acts of 1870 accepted, Nov. 4, 1870; boundary line between Brookline and Boston changed from westerly to easterly line of St Mary's street in 1872. L 374, L 416, L 417, L 647, L 862, L 1194, L 1802, L 1803, L 1804, L 1805, L 1964, L 1981, L 1982, L 1983, L 2184, L 2505, L 2759, L 2760.

***Beacon street**, Bri., 1860; from Brookline boundary line (distant about 440 feet [formerly 520 feet], east, from Chestnut Hill avenue, formerly Rockland street), west, across said avenue and skirting the Chestnut Hill reservoir to Newton boundary line, being a continuation through south part of Brighton of Beacon street from Boston through Brookline: "highway ——— from Centre village in Newton leading easterly through the towns of Newton and Brighton to the line of the town of Brookline" established by Middlesex County Commissioners, June 4, 1850; the part in Brighton of said County way named Beacon street, March 5, 1860; part of said way discontinued and relocated on account of construction of said reservoir. L 2102.

***Beacon street**, Bri., 1846-1860; name of Avenue street, being part in Brighton of the Brighton branch of the Mill-dam road, namely, from Brookline boundary line to Watertown boundary line, changed to Beacon street Nov. 10, 1846; said road shown as Brighton avenue or road to Mill-dam on plan dated 1825; lines of said road. part being called "Brighton branch or road" and part "Watertown turnpike," defined and established by indenture between the Commonwealth and Boston and Roxbury Mill Corporation, dated Dec. 30. 1856; name of Beacon street changed to North Beacon street, March 5, 1860; name of part of North Beacon street from former boundary line between Brookline and Brighton, west, to Cambridge street at Union square changed to Brighton avenue, Jan. 28, 1884; name of part of Brighton avenue from said former boundary line, west, to Massachusetts avenue at Malvern street changed to Commonwealth avenue, Jan. 24, 1887.

† **Beale street**, Dor., 1871; from Dorchester avenue to Carruth street; laid out from Dorchester avenue to the Shawmut Branch of the O. C. (now N. Y., N. H. & H.) R. R., Nov. 30, 1891. L 2369.

Bear lane, B., 1796; Beer lane from Middle (now Hanover) street to Back (now Salem) street so called, and also Bridge lane and Bur lane; name of "Beer lane or Bridges lane" changed to Richmond street, Jan. 22, 1800; name of that part of Richmond street changed to Parmenter street, Dec. 31, 1870.

Beard's corner, B., 1708; corner of Cow lane and Long lane, now High street and Federal street, then so called.

Bearse avenue, Dor., 1881; from River View avenue, north-east, across Butler street to the marsh; sometimes called Bearse street.

Bearse street, Dor., 1884; sometimes called Bearse avenue.

Beaumont avenue, Bri., 1886; from Washington street, south, next west of Lake street.

Beaumont street, Dor., 1877; from Adams street to Carruth street.

***Beaver street,** B., 1857; from Beacon street, nearly opposite Arlington street, north, to unnamed 30-foot street; accepted, conditionally, from Beacon street, north, to the water (Charles river), July 1, 1857.

Beaver street, W. Rox., 1874–9; from Eliot street to Burroughs street; probably another name for Brewer street.

Becket street, Dor.; from Van Winkle street at Dorchester avenue to Codman street; authority to open given by Street Commissioners Nov. 18, 1896.

Beckford court, Chsn., 1856–74; from Main street, north-east, between Salem street and School street; same given Baldwin court in 1854; same called Bickford place on plan 1872; name changed to Linwood place, 1874.

***Beckler avenue,** So. B., 1872; from K street, east, between East Fifth street and East Sixth street; laid out, Feb. 23, 1878. L 1298.

Bedford avenue, B., 1826–42; from Bedford street, south-west, near Rowe place (now Chauncey street); closed.

Bedford court, B., 1844–82; from Bedford street, south, between Columbia street and Kingston street, now closed.

Bedford court, } B., 1821–56; from Bedford street, north-east, toward
Bedford place, } Chauncey place; called Bedford court, 1821; Bedford place, 1822; laid out with Chauncey place as a continuous highway from Bedford street to Summer street, Jan. 3, 1856, and this new street named Chauncey street, Jan. 5, 1856. L 62.

Bedford place, B.; from Bedford street, nearly opposite Harrison avenue, north-east.

***Bedford street,** B., 1821; from Washington street to Summer street: part from Newbury (now Washington) street to Short (now Kingston) street, called Pond street 1708; Pond street called Rowe's lane, 1803; other parts from lower end of Pond street (*i.e.*, from Short [now Kingston] street), north-east, into Church Green by Summer street called Blind lane, 1708; Blind lane called also Pond lane and Rowe's lane; same included in Pond street, 1803; name of Pond street changed to Bedford street, Feb. 7, 1821. Volume 31, page 53. L 286, L 306, L 320, L 598, L 1455, L 1555, L 2201.

***Beech street,** W. Rox., 1825; from Centre street across Washington street to Poplar street; shown as an unnamed lane on plan 1815; named from Centre street near Dr. Draper's by the west end of Poplar street to Clapboard Hill at Dorchester line, May 9, 1825, and so shown on Hale's map of Roxbury, 1832; probably laid out as a highway some time previous; part from Poplar street to Dorchester (now Hyde Park) line discontinued before 1843, at least in part, and now wholly discontinued; sometimes written Beach street. L 2395.

Beech street, Rox., 1857; from Fort avenue to Highland street, a part adjoining the south side of Highland park; name changed to Beech Glen avenue, April 21, 1868; laid out and name changed to Beech Glen street, Oct. 24, 1882.

Beech Glen avenue, } Rox.; from Fort avenue to Highland street, a
***Beech Glen street,** } part adjoining the south side of Highland park; name of Beech street changed to Beech Glen avenue, April 21, 1868; same laid out as Beech Glen street, Oct. 24, 1882. L 1660, L 1661.

Beer lane, B., 1708; from Middle (now Hanover) street to Back (now Salem) street; called also Bear lane, 1708, and Bridges lane, 1796; "Beer lane or Bridges lane" changed to Richmond street, Jan. 22, 1800; named Parmenter street, Dec. 31, 1870.

***Beethoven street,** W. Rox., 1869; from Washington street to Arcadia street; accepted as a town way, Sept. 27, 1871; laid out, Sept. 29, 1874. L 967.

***Belcher lane,** B., 1826; from High street, Fort Hill square, to Atlantic avenue; originally laid out in 1667 from Fort Hill to the water; and said lane extended to low-water mark; prior to 1708 called the "Town way to the Town slip;" called Sconce lane, 1708; also Sconce street, 1784; upper part from Fort Hill to Purchase street called Belcher lane, 1826; confirmed as a public street, Sept. 15, 1834; lower part from Purchase street to Broad street (now Atlantic avenue) called Sconce lane or street as late as 1860, but called Belcher lane from 1848. L 218.

Belcher's lane, B., 1708; from Summer street to Gibbs lane (now Oliver street); on Bonner's plan, 1722, called Belcher's lane from Summer street to Batterymarch street; according to Price's plan, 1769, the part near Summer street called Purchase street and the part near and west of Gibbs lane called Belcher's lane; on Carleton's plan, 1800, included in Purchase street which runs from Summer street to Batterymarch (now Broad) street, including also part of Batterymarch street east of Gibbs lane.

Belcher street, B., 1834; from Fort Hill to Purchase street; another name for Belcher lane.

Belden court, Dor.; from Belden street, east, between Dudley street and Hamlet street; formerly Berkeley court.

***Belden street,** Dor., 1884; from Dudley street, north-east, crossing end of Hamlet street; Berkeley place laid out as Belden street, Sept. 2, 1884. L 1813.

†Belfort street, Dor., 1875; from Dorchester avenue to Saxton street; laid out from Dorchester avenue to Sagamore street, April 4, 1890. L 2218.

Belgrade avenue, W. Rox.; from Brandon street to Beech street.

Belgrade street, W. Rox., 1848; from Canterbury street to Dorchester (now Hyde Park) line at end of Largo (now a discontinued) street; included in Hyde Park avenue as laid out Dec., 1859.

Belknap place, B., 1847; from Joy (formerly Belknap) street, west, south of Hoyt's place.

***Belknap street,** B., 1734; from Cambridge street to May (now Myrtle) street; laid out as an unnamed passageway 30 feet wide in 1734; called Belknap street same year; also Belknap's lane at times down to 1800; extended, south, to Beacon street, including Clapboard (sometimes called George) street, 1803; confirmed as a public street, Sept. 15, 1834; named Joy street from Beacon street to Myrtle street, Jan. 20, 1851; name given to whole street in 1855; named Joy street, from Beacon street to Cambridge street, Feb. 26, 1855.

Belknap's alley, B., 1744; from Court street to Brattle square; called also Hiller's or Hillier's alley or lane and Gay alley; discontinued, conditionally, but probably not actually, Sept. 10, 1817; Brattle street extended through it, 1820.

Belknap's lane, B., 1787; from May (now Myrtle) street to Cambridge street; Belknap street (now Joy street) so called at times down to 1800.

Belknap's yard, B., 1788; between Court street and Brattle street; the present Cornhill made through it in 1816.

Bell alley, B., 1708; from Middle (now Hanover) street to Clark's (now North) square opposite the North Church; Prince street extended through, July 11, 1833; all that part not coming within the lines of the extension of Prince street discontinued, Dec. 30, 1833.

Bell court, So. B., 1872; from D street, north-west, to O. C. (now N.Y., N. H. & H.) R.R.; called Bells court in 1884.

***Bell street**, W. Rox., 1888; from Chestnut avenue to Lamartine street; formerly called Cedar avenue; laid out as Bell street, Oct. 23, 1888. L 2098, L 2168.

Bella Vista, W. Rox., 1849; from South street, near junction of Forest Hills (now Morton) street, north-west; now an unnamed way over grounds of the Arnold Arboretum.

Belle avenue, W. Rox., 1870; from Baker street, south, adjoining the west side of West Roxbury Branch of B. & P. (now N.Y., N. H. & H.) R.R.

Bellevue, So. B., 1837; City lands, commonly known as the Farm, on which Houses of Industry, Correction and Reformation were situated, named Bellevue, Feb. 27, 1837.

Bellevue avenue, W. Rox., 1872; from junction Washington street and Beech street to Dudley avenue; called Bellevue street in 1874; and Bellevue avenue in 1890.

Bellevue avenue, W. Rox., 1860; name of Lyon street in westerly part of town (from Centre street by Lyon's) changed to Bellevue avenue, April 2, 1860; commonly called Bellevue street.

Bellevue park, W. Rox., 1874; from Robin street to Adelaide terrace; Bellevue street extended over, June 21, 1887.

***Bellevue street**, Dor., 1848; from Columbia street, at Glendale street, across Quincy street to Barrington street; formerly from Bowdoin street (at Eaton square) to Columbia street; located Feb. 21, 1848; name of part from junction with Quincy street, which is a continuation of said Quincy street, to Bowdoin street, changed to Quincy street, March 1, 1886; part between Quincy street and Kane street laid out (over a part of Bellevue terrace) June 19, 1889; authority to open from Kane street to Barrington street, given by Street Commissioners, Oct. 13, 1896. L 790, L 1558, L 2137.

***Bellevue street**, W. Rox., 1860; from Centre street to Adelaide terrace; street from Centre street by Lyon's named Lyon street, May 9, 1825; same shown as Bellevue street in 1848; name of Lyon street changed to Bellevue avenue, April 2, 1860, but street commonly called Bellevue street thereafter; extended from Oriole street to a private way called Adelaide terrace, in part over a private way called Bellevue park, June 21, 1887; part now included in Parkway, West Roxbury. L 1054, L 2805.

***Bellevue street**, Rox., 1862; from Longwood (now Francis) street to Brookline avenue; from Pilgrim street (now Longwood avenue), south-west, 1849; called Cedar street from Francis (formerly Longwood) street to Elm street (now Longwood avenue), 1850–1857; same part called Bellevue avenue, 1862; accepted, conditionally,

Sept. 28, 1863; Bellevue street extended from Longwood avenue to Brookline avenue, over private way called Maple avenue, Feb. 14, 1887. L 1976, L 1977.

Bellevue street, W. Rox.; from junction Washington street and Beech street to Dudley avenue; now called Bellevue avenue. L 1996, L 1997.

Bellevue street, W. Rox., 1848; from Spring street.

Bellevue terrace, Dor., from Quincy street; laid out as Stanley street, Kane street and Bellevue street, June 19, 1889.

***Bellflower street,** Dor., 1884; from Dorchester avenue to Boston street; laid out, May 8, 1894. L 2613.

Bellingham place, B., 1885; from Revere street, north, between West Cedar street and Revere-street place; called Sherman place, 1847; May-street court, 1849; Revere-street court 1858; Hill place or Hill court, 1867.

Bellows place, Dor., 1851; from Dorchester avenue, west, between Richmond street and Codman street.

Bellows place, Chsn., 1854; from 20 Walnut street, north-west; formerly called Dennis place.

Bells court, So. B.: from D st., north-west, to O.C. (now N.Y., N. H. & H.) R.R.; sometimes called Bell court.

Belmont avenue, B.; from Clinton street, north, to Richmond street; between Essex avenue and Revere avenue; now built over.

Belmont avenue, W. Rox., 1849; from Florence street, at Mt. Hope station, to Poplar street; called Alpine avenue in 1847; Belmont avenue in 1848–49; Brown's avenue in 1855; accepted as Brown avenue, March 29, 1869.

Belmont court, B., 1857; from Belmont (now Oliver) street, north-east, between High street and Purchase street, nearly opposite Lane place; not in directory after 1868, and apparently now a court without a name.

Belmont place, E. B., 1863; from Everett street, north-east, between Cottage street and Lamson street.

***Belmont square,** E. B., 1833; between Seaver, Sumner, Webster and Lamson streets; laid out and accepted as a public square, April 4, 1853, and deed passed April 5, 1853.

Belmont street, B., 1844; from Washington place (now Fort Hill square) to Broad street (now Atlantic avenue); called Gibbs lane, 1708; name changed to Belmont street, Sept. 23, 1844; included in and name changed to Oliver street, April 21, 1868. L 298, L 299, L 300, L 301.

Belmont street, Rox., 1848; from Ruggles street to Vernon street, near Cabot street; called Suffolk street, 1830; laid out as Haskins street, July 31, 1886. L 1925.

***Belmont street,** Chsn., 1845; from Bunker Hill street to Medford street, between Webster street and North Mead street; laid out, July 23, 1861.

†**Belvidere street,** Rox.; from West Chester park (now Massachusetts avenue) to West Newton street, near junction of Falmouth street; a small part east of Dalton street, on land of B. & A. R.R. Co., being a proposed street; laid out from West Chester park to Dalton street, June 7, 1890. L 2230, L 2311.

***Bendall's lane,** B., 1882; from Faneuil Hall square to North street; a public footway: City Solicitor decided, Sept. 23, 1870, that it was public; named, Feb. 27, 1882. L 2707.

Benevento street, E. B., 1895; from Wauwatosa avenue to Waldemar street.

***Benedict street,** Chsn., 1887; from Rutherford avenue to Lawrence street; Edmands court laid out from Rutherford avenue, and extended to Lawrence street with name of Benedict street, July 2, 1887. L 1999.

Bennet avenue, B., 1839; from North Bennet street to Prince street: School alley, 1732; Grammar alley, 1795; Prince-street avenue, 1833; called Bennet avenue, 1839.

Bennet place, B., 1816; from Bennet (or South Bennet) street, north, near Harrison avenue; was sometimes called South Bennet place.

Bennet place, B., 1834; from North Bennet street, south-west, near Hanover street; called North Bennet place, 1858.

Bennett place, E.B., 1875; from 24 White street, north, nearly opposite Marion street.

***Bennet street,** B., 1708; from Middle (now Hanover) street to Back (now Salem) street; commonly called North Bennet street.

***Bennet street,** B., 1732; from Washington street to Harrison avenue; from Orange (now Washington) street, opposite Harvard (now Hollis) street to the sea, 1732; named by Selectmen, July 4, 1788; extended to Front street (now Harrison avenue), 1805; sometimes called South Bennet street.

***Bennett street,** Bri., 1858; from Market street, west, crossing Parsons street; laid out from Market street to Parsons street, Feb. 19, 1858; accepted, March 8, 1858; named, March 5, 1860; extended west from Parsons street, July 16, 1885. L 1871, L 2015.

Bennet-street avenue, B., 1846; now Bennet avenue.

Bennington place, E.B., 1848–9; from Bennington street; not identified.

†Bennington street, E. B., 1834; from Central square to Walley street, on Breed's Island; laid out from Chelsea street to a point about 260 feet from south-east line of land of Eastern R.R. Co. (now B. & M. R. R.), Aug. 7, 1848; to Swift street, Aug. 7, 1848; accepted from Central square to Chelsea street, April 26, 1858; triangle at junction of Chelsea street, Nov. 1, 1858; at junction of Bremen street, July 23, 1862; extended from Swift street to Wordsworth street, Sept. 2, 1885; extended from Wordsworth street to Saratoga street, on Breed's Island, Nov. 8, 1886; extended from Saratoga street to Ashley avenue, now Walley street, July 3, 1888. L 639, L 690, L 691, L 692, L 971, L 1880, L 1881, L 1882, L 1960, L 1961, L 2072.

Bentley street, Bri.; from Henshaw street to Sparhawk street; authority to open given by Street Commissioners, June 12, 1893.

Benton street, Rox., 1859; from Tremont street to Berlin street (now Columbus avenue); shown as an unnamed street in 1849.

Berkeley court, Dor., 1874; from Belden street (formerly Berkeley place) near Dudley street, south-east; now Belden court.

Berkeley place, Dor., 1868; from Stoughton (now Dudley) street, north east, crossing end of Hamlet street; laid out as Belden street, Sept. 2, 1884. L 1813.

Berkeley square, B.; parts of Boylston street and Newbury street, between Berkeley street and Clarendon street in front and rear of grounds of Institute of Technology and Natural History Rooms, so called at one time.

***Berkeley street,** B., 1858; from Tremont street, opposite Dover street, to Beacon street: called avenue I. on plans of Back Bay land dated 1854; laid out from Tremont street to Chandler street, April 7, 1868; laid out from Chandler street to land of Boston & Prov. (now N.Y., N.H. & H.), R.R. Corporation, Oct. 27, 1868; laid out from Stanhope street to Providence street, Nov. 17, 1868; laid out from Providence street to Beacon street, July 24, 1873. L 189½, L 354, L 374, L 410, L 447.

Berkshire street, Dor.; from Westmoreland street to Beaumont street.

Berkshire street, B.; shown on Hale's map of 1814, parallel, and west of, Shawmut avenue.

Berlin street, B., 1843; from East Canton street to Hamburg street; made a part of Mystic street, 1845.

Berlin street, B., 1857; from Pleasant street to Church street; called Pleasant-street court, 1829; named Berlin street, 1857; name changed to Tennyson street, April 20, 1869. L 387, L 397.

Berlin street, Rox, 1858; from Columbus avenue, a short distance north of Davenport street, to Walpole street; part of included in the extension of Columbus avenue, Jan. 4, 1895.

Bernard street, Dor., 1884; from Cemetery lane or street, to Harvard street; probably extended through Cemetery lane or street, or Burying-place lane, to Norfolk street; part south of Harvard street shown as Warner avenue at one time.

Bernice street, Dor.; from Preston street to Ashland street.

Bernier square, Rox.; junction Bernier street, Bellevue street, Woodstock street and Plymouth street.

Bernier street, Rox., 1874; from Brookline avenue, crossing end of Plymouth street to Brookline line; part between Brookline avenue and Plymouth street, called Leyden street in 1849.

Berry lane, B, 1733; from Leverett street, east. (Closed by erection of the almshouse in 1803.)

Berry street, B., 1803: from Federal street to Atkinson (now Congress) street; called Bury street, 1732; sometimes called Bury lane; named Barracks lane by Selectmen in 1788, but name not used; called Berry street, 1803; name changed to Channing street, July 14, 1845.

***Berry street,** Dor. and W. Rox., 1840; from Canterbury street to Sutton street; formerly from Ashland street by Calvary and Mt. Hope cemeteries to Canterbury street nearly opposite Mt. Hope avenue; named in Dorchester from Back (now Harvard) street to Roxbury line, March 11, 1840; part in West Roxbury called South Short street in 1849; part of, in Dorchester, near Roxbury line, which runs north-easterly, called Pain's lane in 1855; part from Back street running north-westerly to beginning of Pain's lane included in Oakland street, Sept., 1856; date of naming of present street which comprises Pain's lane and South Short street, unknown; part between Sutton street and entrance to Calvary cemetery discontinued, July 6, 1892. L 1325, L 2409, L 1686, L 2489.

Berry street, W. Rox., 1872; from Central avenue (now Cornell street), north, crossing Brook street, between Orange street and Hill street; authority to open extension to Aldrich street given by Street Commissioners, Dec. 1, 1891.

Bertram street, Bri.: from North Harvard street to Rena street.

Bertram street, Dor.: from Neponset avenue, east and then north, between Freeport street and Tolman street.

***Berwick park,** B., 1869; from Columbus avenue, west, to B. & P. (now N.Y., N. H. & H.) R.R; portion of Pembroke street lying west of Columbus avenue named Berwick park, Dec. 21, 1869. L 502, L 516, L 536, L 992.

Berwick road, Bri.; from Commonwealth avenue to Chiswick road.

Berwick street, W. Rox., 1895; from Baker street to Barnes street; authority to open given by Street Commissioners, May 3, 1895.

Bessom court, E. B., 1848; from Webster street, north-east, between Cottage street and Orleans street.

Bethel place, B., 1843–49; from north side of Sun-court street.

Bethel court, } B.; from Anderson street, west, on north side of **Bethel place,** } Bethel church; called Bethel court, 1864; Bethel place, 1867.

Bethune's corner, B., 1732; corner of Summer street and Newbury (now Washington) street, then so called.

***Beverly street,** B., 1807; from Charlestown street to Warren bridge; laid out and named from Charlestown street to Causeway street, Aug. 3, 1807; extended to Warren bridge by Fitchburg R.R. Co., in pursuance of Act of Legislature, passed April 20, 1847; accepted and named by City, July 30, 1849. Vol. 31, p. 102. L 1710.

Bickford avenue, Rox., 1875; from 105 Heath street, north-west, between Parker street and Lawn street.

Bickford place, Chsn., 1872; from Main street, north-east, between Salem street and School street; formerly Beckford court; now Linwood place.

***Bickford street,** Rox., 1872; from Heath street to Centre street; laid out from Heath street to Bromley park, Sept. 20, 1876; extended to Centre street, July 24, 1883. L 1183, L 1574, L 1721.

Bicknal avenue, Rox., 1878; from Roxbury street, between Shawmut avenue and Washington place; also called Bicknell place and Bicknell avenue.

Bicknal } **Bicknell** } **avenue,** Dor., 1875; from Harvard street to White (now Bradshaw) street; formerly from Harvard street, north, and parallel with Sanborn avenue; laid out as Bicknell street, from Harvard street to White street, Dec. 14, 1894.

Bicknell place, Rox., from Roxbury street, north, between Shawmut avenue and Washington place; also called Bicknal avenue and Bicknell avenue.

* **Bicknell street,** Dor., 1894; from Harvard street to Bradshaw street; Bicknell avenue laid out as Bicknell street, Dec. 14, 1894. L 2674.

† **Bigelow street,** Bri., 1858; from Newton street to Washington street at Oak square, with branch running south-east to Brooks street across end of Dunboy (formerly Everett) street; from Newton street to Faneuil street at Oak square with above branch, 1858; laid out so as to intersect the new County road (Faneuil street) proposed by Commissioners, July 8, 1872; accepted, Aug. 14, 1873; laid out, Dec. 18, 1873; accepted, conditionally, Dec. 30, 1873; extended from Faneuil street at Oak square to Washington street at Oak square, Aug. 14, 1882; extended from a point south of Webster street to Brooks street, Nov. 2, 1891. L 1632, L 2353, L 2354.

Bill and Smith's corner, B., 1732; corner Sudbury street and Hawkins street, then so called.

***Billerica street,** B., 1837; from Causeway street to Minot street; accepted, conditionally, Nov. 18, 1844, and finally, 1851.

Billings court, B., 1849, from Friend street, north-east, near Hanover street; included in the extension of Washington street to Haymarket square, Nov., 1872.

Billings place, Rox., 1869; from Parker street, north-west, near Alleghany street; Hillside street extended to Parker street in part over Billings place, April 27, 1882. L 1607.

Billings place, W. Rox., 1849; from Centre street, north-west, near Mt. Vernon street; included in La Grange street as laid out Oct. 1869.

† **Billings street,** W. Rox., 1888; from Spring street to south-east of Prospect street; known as Franklin avenue, 1870 to 1888; laid out from Spring street to Hamilton street, Sept. 28, 1888. L 2095.

Billings street, W. Rox., from Centre street, north-west, to Elmwood street, near Baker street.

Bills corner, B., 1732; corner Ship (now North) street, and White-bread alley (now Harris street), then so called.

Bills court, Rox., 1848; from Ruggles street, north, between Mechanic street and Field street

Binford street, S. B., 1897; from A street between Richards street and Congress street, south-east; authority to open given by Street Commissioners Jan. 17, 1897.

Binney place, Rox., 1848; from Albany street, south-east, between Yeoman street and Hampden street.

Binney street, Rox., 1850; from Francis street between Vila street and Brookline avenue, north-east, crossing Longwood avenue.

† **Birch street**, W. Rox., 1876; from South street at junction of Brandon street to Dudley avenue, crossing end of Prospect (now Penfield) street; name of Maple street (from South street to Prospect street) changed to Birch street, Dec. 5, 1876; laid out from South street to Prospect (now Penfield) street, Nov. 24, 1879; extended as a private way from Prospect street to Dudley avenue, 1886. L 1405.

Birch street, Dor.; from Lauriat avenue to Chapman avenue.

Bird lane, S. B., from G street, east, between E. Fifth street and E. Sixth street, called Story street, 1873; laid out as Story street from G street to H street, June 30, 1890.

Bird / **Bird's** } **lane**, Dor., 1874; from River street, north-west, towards Oakland street, crossing N.E. R.R. near Hyde Park line; sometimes called Baldwin's lane; shown as Randolph road in 1894.

Bird place, / **Bird-street place**, } Dor., 1871; from Bird street, south-east; called Bird place, except in the order to include in extension of Glendale street, Dec. 19, 1878, where it was called Bird-street place. L 1340.

* **Bird street**, Dor., 1854; from Magnolia street to Columbia street, crossing the N.E. R.R.; laid out, March 1, 1869. L 1552, L 2019.

Bird's avenue, W. Rox., 1874; from Centre street, north-west, opposite Bellevue street.

* **Bishop street**, W. Rox., 1871; from Newbern street to Call street, crossing Everett street; laid out, April 16, 1877. L 1229.

Bishop's alley, B., 1708; from Summer street to Milk street; called Board alley, 1792; Bishop's lane in 1796; named Hawley street, Dec. 10, 1799; called Bishop's alley as late as 1807.

Bishop Stoke street, B., 1732; a 25-foot street from Beacon street, north, 160 feet west of Belknap (now Joy) street; discontinued before 1800, part of being now within the limits of Walnut street.

Bismarck street, Rox., 1871; from Blue Hill avenue, east, south and south-west, to Blue Hill avenue again; name changed to Rand street, Dec. 30, 1871; southerly part of Rand street, near Blue Hill avenue, included in Brookford street, July 6, 1883.

Bismarck street, Dor., 1872; from Hersey street, south-west, crossing Oakland street between Favre street and Haven avenue.

Bismarck street, W. Rox., from Boylston street, south-west, parallel with Brookside avenue and crossing end of Germania street.

Blaban place, Chsn., 1852; from Pearl street, north-west, near Medford street, sometimes called Blavan place.

Black Horse lane, B., 1698; from Middle (now Hanover) street towards Charlestown Ferry; extended as a highway 24 feet wide from lower end to Charlestown Ferry, Jan. 25, 1702; called Prince street, 1708.

* **Blackinton street**, E. B., 1895; from Walley street to Leyden street; laid out June 7, 1895. L 2704.

Black Jack Alley, B.; an early name for part of Devonshire street, between Water street and Milk street.

Blackstone square, B., 1832; between Washington street, Brookline street, Shawmut avenue and Newton street

***Blackstone street**, B., 1834; from junction of Fulton street and Clinton street to Haymarket square crossing Ann (now North) street and Hanover street; portion near Hanover street mentioned in City Records, May 3, 1708; from Clinton street to North street Aug. 10, 1824, laid out from Fulton street and Clinton street over the entire length of the Mill creek to Cross street and Charlestown street at Haymarket square, Oct., 1833; named, Sept. 22, 1834; after laying out and previous to naming sometimes called Creek street and Canal street; easterly part from Ann (now North) street, east previously called Royall's alley. L 130.

Blackstone's point, B., 1708; at the foot of Leverett street; called Barton's point 1712.

Blackwell street, Dor.; from Neponset avenue to Bowman street.

***Blackwood street**, Rox., 1880; from St. Botolph street, between Cumberland street and Albermarle street, to B. & P. (now N.Y., N.H. & H.) R R.; laid out, Jan. 19, 1880. L 1427.

***Blagden street**, B., 1889; from Huntington avenue to Exeter street; this part of St. James avenue named Blagden street, March 1, 1889. L 410, L 862, L 1266, L 1699.

Blaine avenue, Bri., south from Braintree street, near and east of Everett street; laid out as Blaine street, July 14, 1891.

***Blaine street**, Bri., 1891; south from Braintree street, near and east of Everett street; formerly Blaine avenue; laid out, July 14, 1891. L 2314.

Blake street, So. B., 1872; from Boston street to Dorchester avenue, opposite Kemp street.

***Blakemore street**, W. Rox., 1880; from Hyde Park avenue to junction of Brown avenue and Florence street near Mt. Hope station; laid out, with bridge over B & P. (now N.Y., N.H. & H.) R.R., July 1, 1880. L 1467.

Blake's court, B., 1831; from Washington street, east, between Malden street and Waltham street; reaching to Front street (now Harrison avenue) on extension of the latter in 1834; accepted, conditionally, June 27, 1853; accepted and named Union Park street, Oct. 16, 1860. L 180, L 181.

***Blakeville street**, Dor.; from Bowdoin street to Olney street; laid out, June 19, 1890. L 2231.

Blanchard court, B., 1849; from Washington street, west, between Groton street and Dover street; called Hawthorn place after 1842.

Blanchard court, B., 1849–53; from Washington street, west, near Warren or Pleasant street.

***Blanchard place**, } Rox.; from Bartlett street to Norfolk street; called
***Blanchard street**, } Blanchard place, 1848; laid out, July 20, 1875; named Blanchard street, Aug. 17, 1875. L 1060.

Blanche court, B., 1844; from Tyler street, east, south of and near Kneeland street; called Munroe place, 1857.

***Blanche street**, Dor., 1885; from Greenhill street, north, then at a right angle, east, to Capen street; Harrison street laid out with name of Blanche street, July 21, 1885. L 1873.

Blandford street, Rox., 1894; from Commonwealth avenue opposite Sherborn street to B. & A. R.R.

Blavan place, Chsn.; from Pearl street, north-west, near Medford street; Blaban place sometimes so called.

Bleiler court, Rox., 1881; from Heath place, east.

Blind lane, B., 1708; from the lower end of Pond street at Short (now Kingston) street, north-east, to Church green, Summer street; sometimes also called Pond lane and Rowe's lane; Pond street extended through it to Summer street, 1803; Pond street named Bedford street, 1820.

Bloomfield street, Dor.; from Geneva avenue to Greenbrier street.

Bloomington street, Dor.; from Tolman street, north, and then east to Eaton street.

Blossom court, B., 1826; from Blossom street, east, between Cambridge street and Emmett place.

Blossom place, B., 1826; from Blossom street, east, between Emmett place and Parkman street.

***Blossom street,** B., 1803; from Cambridge street to Allen street; from Cambridge street, north, across Vine (now Parkman) street, 1803; laid out from Cambridge street to North Allen (now Allen) street, Dec. 10, 1817. L 1754.

Blossom street, Chsn., 1828; from Bunker Hill street to Vine street; now a part of Decatur street.

Blossom-street place, B., 1843; from Blossom street, east, opposite Fruit street; called Seabury place, 1844.

Blott's lane, B., 1690; from Newbury (now Washington) street to the Common; probably so called prior to 1708; called Willis' lane, Banister's lane, and Bolt's lane; named Winter street, 1708.

Blue Hill avenue, E. B., 1870; from Orient avenue to Washburn avenue (now Walley street) between Water avenue and Farrington street; now Overlook avenue.

***Blue Hill avenue,** Rox., Dor. and W. Rox., 1870; from Dudley street to Milton line; part in Roxbury from present Quincy street, north-west as far as junction of present Dennis street and said avenue named as a part of Dennis street, May 9, 1825; part from Warren street to Dudley (formerly Eustis) street including above part of Dennis street named as a part of East street, Aug 29, 1842; East street from Warren street to Dudley (formerly Eustis) street, named Grove Hall avenue, Dec. 8, 1851; part from Warren street to Milton line cons ructed by Brush Hill Turnpike Corporation, location being filed Sept., 1805, and called Brush Hill turnpike, sometimes also avenue; this turnpike laid out over a part of Canterbury street, near Roxbury and Dorchester line; part in Dorchester from Milton line to highway near s'ore of George L. Fisher laid out as a public highway, Dec., 1849; franchise relinquished by proprietors of the corporation, Oct. 13, 1856; remainder of street as far as Warren street in Roxbury, not before public, laid out as a public highway, Dec., 1856; name of Grove Hall avenue extended over part in Roxbury from Warren street to West Roxbury line at Seaver street, Jan. 28, 1867; Grove Hall avenue (from Dudley street to Seaver street) and Brush Hill avenue (from Seaver street to Mattapan) named Blue Hill avenue, Oct. 25, 1870; relocated at a width of 120 feet, from Washington street at Warren street to River street, Mattapan, Nov. 5, 1894. L 489, L 490, L 491, L 809, L 889, L 890, L 1085, L 1283, L 1400, L 1401, L 1410. L 1435, L 1494, L 1995, L 2345. L 2380, L 2478, L 2621, L 2622, L 2623, L 2624, L 2625, L 2626, L 2627, L 2628, L 2629, L 2630, L 2631, L 2632, L 2748, L 2749.

Board alley, B., 1769; from Milk street, nearly opposite Oliver street; called Parrott's alley in list of 1800; now closed, being part of land occupied by the Mason building.

Board alley, B., 1792; from Summer street to Milk street; called Bishop's alley, 1708; called Board alley, 1792; Bishop's lane, 1796; called Hawley street, 1800.

Board alley, B., 1833; from Charter street to Commercial street, between Lime alley and Foster street; named Jackson avenue, 1837.

Board alley, B., 1848; from Cow lane (now High street) opposite and slightly east of end of Long lane (now Federal street) to Belcher's lane (now Purchase street); called Crooked alley, 1708; Brick alley, 1788; Board alley in 1848; shown as Board alley on plans as late as 1870, but now closed.

***Board alley,** B., from Hanover street to North street, between Richmond street and Mechanic street; called Gallop's alley, 1708; Board alley, 1834.

Bodwell park, } Dor., 1879; from Columbia street to Bird street;
***Bodwell street,** } Bodwell park shown as a private street 24 feet wide extending about 430 feet south from Bird street in 1879; extended as a private way to Columbia street in 1882: laid out as a public street with name of Bodwell street, July 31, 1884. L 1797.

Bog lane, B., 1788; part of Distill-house square or Still-house square, leading north-west from Sudbury street, sometimes so called; same part of said square named Adams street, Sept. 9, 1850; widened and name changed to Bowker street, April 20, 1868.

Bolster street, Rox., 1887; from Wyman street, to Mozart street.

Bolton avenue, E. B., 1876; from Ashley avenue, between Jones street and Brimmer avenue, north-east, to Revere line; called Bolton street in 1896.

Bolton court, S. B., 1874; from Bolton street to W. Third street, between A street and N. E. R.R.

Bolton place, So. B., 1873; from Bolton street, north-east, north-west of N. E. R.R.

Bolton place, Chsn., 1861; from High street, opposite Franklin street, north-east; shown as part of Bolton street in 1818.

***Bolton street,** So. B., 1846; from Dorchester street., between W. Second street and W. Third street, to W. Second street, crossing N. Y. & N. E. (now N. E.) R.R.; laid out from C street to D street, July 1, 1862; from D street to E street, May 5, 1873; from B street to C street, April 11, 1874; from C street to D street, apparently a second time, Oct. 22, 1874; from E street to F street, May 31, 1875; from F street to Dorchester street, June 9, 1879; from B street to N. Y. & N. E. R.R., Aug. 23, 1880; from W. Second street to N. Y. & N. E. R.R., Dec. 26, 1884. L 246, L 855, L 921, L 979, L 1047, L 1355, L 1476, L 1842.

***Bolton street,** Chsn., 1818; shown in 1818 as extending from Main street to unnamed street in position of present Russell street; part from Main street to High street accepted, April 5, 1874, and then "known as Franklin street;" from High street to Russell street never accepted and the only part now existing known as Bolton place.

Bolt's lane, B.; before 1708 from Newbury (now Washington) street to the Common; another name for Blott's lane; also called Banister's lane and Willis' lane; now Winter street.

Bond avenue, W. Rox.; laid out as Sylvia street, from Washington street to Forest Hills street, July 17, 1891.

Bond street, Chsn., 1863; a part at junction of Heath street shown on plan; not identified.

***Bond street,** B. 1846; from Milford (formerly South Lowell) street to Hanson street; laid out May 5, 1868. L 379.

***Border street,** E. B., 1833; from Condor street along the west side of Central square across Sumner street to the North Ferry; accepted, conditionally, from Condor street to Sumner street, June 14, 1852;

extended from Sumner street to East Boston North Ferry, over street formerly known as People's Ferry avenue, Aug 3, 1880. Vol. 31, p. 23. L 207, L 1472, L 1616, L 1864.

Borland's corner, B., 1708; corner Milk street and Long lane (now Federal street), then so called.

Boston avenue, Dor., 1854; Dorchester avenue, so called on plan of laying out.

Boston avenue, W. Rox., 1837; from Willow (now Green) street, north-east, to land of N. D. Williams; but shown in 1849 under name of Lamartine street, as extended only to Boylston street; called Lamartine street, 1848.

***Boston avenue**, Chsn., 1836; from City square to Warren bridge; Warren avenue laid out, accepted, and named Boston avenue, May 2, 1836; no record of change to Warren avenue again, which name it now bears, but given in directories until 1854 as Boston avenue.

Boston Common, B.: bounded by Tremont, Boylston, Charles, Beacon, and Park streets.

Boston place, So. B., 1856; from Dorchester street, near Jenkins street, south-east, to O. C. (now N. Y., N. H. & H.) R.R.

Boston road, Rox., 1833; Centre street, so called.

***Boston street**, Dor. and So. B., 1840; from Dorchester avenue at Swett street to Dudley street junction of Hancock street; named in Dorchester from South Boston line (which then crossed the junction of present Dorchester street and Telegraph street) to the burying-place (Upham's corner), March 11, 1840, but probably commonly so called earlier than 1810; after annexation of Washington Village to South Boston (chapter 468, Acts of 1855) part of, in the territory annexed as far as Dorchester line named as a part of Dorchester street, July 3, 1855; Boston street laid out and variously altered at same time with Hancock street, forming a continuous highway from Meeting-House Hill to Boston, April, 1860; from Dudley street (at Upham's corner) to old Boston line, 1869; part of Dorchester street from Dorchester avenue, south-west, to Boston street, named as a part of Boston street, Oct. 7, 1873. L 195, L 683, L 716, L 865, L 866, L 867, L 1072, L 1073, L 1134, L 1135, L 2288, L 2485, L 2533.

Boston Theatre place, B., 1858; from Washington street, west, south of West street; a passageway in front of and leading to Boston Theatre one block south of Harlem (now an unnamed) place; discontinued some time before 1874.

Boston Wharf streets, So. B., 1855; seven streets laid out in 1855 on South Boston Flats, but never constructed. Two other streets were laid out in 1868, between Mt. Washington avenue and Eastern avenue (now Congress street), but also never constructed. L 27, L 58.

***Bosworth street**, B., 1883; from Tremont street to Chapman place; called Montgomery place, 1825; part of Montgomery place, from Tremont street to Chapman place extended, laid out and named Bosworth street, May 14, 1883; there is a part between the extension of Chapman place and Province street not yet laid out, although used as a way. L 1703, L 1712.

***Bothnia street**, Rox., 1889; from Boylston street to Belvidere street; laid out, Aug. 21, 1889. L 2153.

***Botolph street**, B., 1733; from Cambridge street to Myrtle street, between Garden street and South Russell street; confirmed as a public street, Sept. 15, 1834; named Irving street, April 25, 1855; called also Butolph, Buttolph, or Buttolf.

Bound lane, B., 1788; from Atkinson (now Congress) street to Federal street; probably an error in the list of 1788 for Round lane (now Matthews and formerly Williams street).

***Bourne street,** W. Rox., 1825; from Walk Hill street in a curved line to Canterbury street, at junction with Neponset avenue; named May 9, 1825; probably a public highway some time previous.

Bourneside street, Dor., 1891; from Melville avenue to Park street; authority to open given by Street Commissioners, Oct. 1, 1891.

Boutwell avenue, } Dor.; from Neponset turnpike (now avenue) west,
***Boutwell street,** } north of Ashmont street; called Boutwell avenue in 1858, and shown as crossing Train street; called Carter street in 1869; laid out from Neponset avenue to Train street and named Boutwell street May 31, 1882. L 1613.

***Bow street,** Chsn., 1670; from City square to Washington street; from City square across Rope or Rope-maker's lane (later Arrow street, now part of Washington street) to Town Hill (now Harvard) street at junction with Main street, being semi-circular in form, 1670; name of part extending north-east from Washington street to Harvard street at junction of Main street, changed to Devens street, March 1, 1882. L 1046.

Bow-street court, Chsn., 1852; from Devens street (formerly Bow street), north-west.

Bowditch court, } Rox.; from Warren street, north-west, nearly op-
Bowditch park, } posite Edgewood street; called Bowditch park,
Bowditch street. } 1874; Bowditch court, 1875; Bowditch street, 1884.

†**Bowdoin avenue,** Dor., 1836; from junction Washington street and Bowdoin street to Eldon street, with branch northerly to junction Rosseter street and Union avenue (now Bullard street); a part not contiguous to above from N. Y. & N.E. (now N.E.) R.R., opposite end of Rosseter street, at Eldon street, north-west, then north to junction Columbia street and Geneva avenue; originally projected as extending from Bowdoin street to Columbia street, dividing into two branches near Bowdoin street, as at present, and uniting again near junction of present Hawes avenue and Bowdoin avenue; the construction of the N. Y. & N. E. (now N. E.) R.R. across the two branches without building bridges severed communication between the north and south portions, and later that part of westerly branch between said railroad and junction of present Hawes avenue was discontinued; part of the easterly branch from Bullard street (formerly Maple Grove avenue) north, laid out as a part of Union avenue, Dec. 28, 1869; part from Bowdoin street, north and north-west, to Eldon street, near the railroad, laid out as Bowdoin avenue, Jan. 28, 1880; part of easterly branch from Union avenue (now Olney street) to Eldon street, laid out and named Rosseter street, Sept. 26, 1882; part formerly Union avenue, between Olney and Bullard streets, named Rosseter street, March 1, 1889; also called Mt. Bowdoin avenue. L 1282, L 1432, L 1433, L 1643, L 1781, L 2350.

Bowdoin block, B., 1845–48; Milk street, corner of Hawley street.

Bowdoin court, } B., 1834; from Bowdoin street, west, near Beacon
Bowdoin place, } Hill place; attempt made to close Bowdoin place, 1844, when it was reported to have been used for many years and to be a private way; called also Bowdoin court; taken by Commonwealth in 1893, for State House grounds.

Bowdoin place, B., 1820; from Bowdoin street to Mt. Vernon street; called in directory (1820–45), "south end Bowdoin street," (1846), "south end Bowdoin street to Mt. Vernon street;" in 1843 reduced to an 8-foot passageway and soon thereafter called Beacon Hill place.

Bowdoin place, B., 1818; Bowdoin st., was so called.

Bowdoin row, B., 1825-29; Court street, near Bowdoin square, so called.

***Bowdoin square,** B., 1788; the space between Cambridge, Green, Chardon, Court, and Bulfinch streets. L 11, L 74.

Bowdoin square, Dor., 1870; from Westville street north and south, near Geneva avenue; formerly from Westville street, south, then east at a right angle, then north at a right angle crossing Westville street; shown as a 40-foot street and a contemplated 33-foot street running east from Bowdoin street to said 40-foot street with branch running south and then east to said 40-foot street in 1853: Westville street extended to Bowdoin street through part extending from Bowdoin street, east, Dec. 29, 1880; part south of Westville street shown on atlas 1894 as going to Tonawanda street. L 1513.

***Bowdoin street,** B., 1805; from Cambridge street to Beacon street; part from Cambridge street to near present Derne street laid out as a 40-foot street in 1727, and later known as Middlecott street; part from Middlecott street to Beacon street opened in 1800; called Bowdoin street, 1805; laid out as Bowdoin street from Derne street to Beacon street, Sept. 13, 1816; name extended over Middlecott street to Cambridge street, July 6, 1824.

***Bowdoin street,** Dor., 1801; from Washington street to junction Adams street and Hancock street at Eaton square, forming three sides of the square; accepted March 2, 1801; named from Four Corners (at Washington street) to the Meeting House (Eaton square) April 6, 1801; named again from Captain Eaton's (Eaton square), to the Four Corners, March 11, 1840; the part now forming the south side of Eaton square named as a part of Church street, 1840, was changed to Bowdoin street, March 1, 1882. L 765, L 1006, L 1007, L 1008, L 1009, L 1010, L 1056, L 1057, L 1058, L 1059, L 1414.

Bowdoin's corner, B., 1732: cor. of Tremont row and Southack's court (now Howard street), then so called.

Bowe street, Rox. and W. Rox., 1871; from Centre street between Sheridan avenue (now street) and Wyman street, southwest to Forbes place; included in the laying out of Forbes street, July 28, 1890. L 2174, L 2252, L 2253.

Bowen court, B., 1846-60; from Belknap (now Joy) street, west, opposite Mt Vernon place; closed.

†**Bowen street,** So B., 1868; from Dorchester street across C street between West Fifth street and West Sixth street; private way called Quincy street named Bowen street, April 21, 1868; laid out from D street to E street, May 5, 1873; from F street to Dorchester street, June 22, 1875; from C street to D street, Sept 23, 1882; laid out for 128 feet west of C street, May 27, 1887; part from E street to F street not yet laid out. L 854, L 1050, L 1640, L 1991.

***Bower street,** Rox., 1844; from Warren street between Lansing street, and Monroe street, to Walnut avenue; accepted and named conditionally, April 1, 1844. L 698, L 1020, L 2120, L 2501.

Bower park, Rox.; from 18 Bower street.

Bower place, Rox.; from 30 Bower street.

Bower terrace, W. Rox.; from 78 South street.

***Bowker street,** B., 1868: from Sudbury street to Chardon street; from end of Hawkins street, north, to the Mill-pond, then southeast to Sudbury street; called Distill square, Distiller's square and Distill-House square; same street named Distill-House square, July 4, 1788; called Still-House square in 1795 and 1800; part from Sudbury street, north-west, called also sometimes Bog lane, 1788; this part named Adams street, Sept. 9, 1850; Adams street widened and name changed to Bowker street, April 20, 1868. L 351, L 552, L 2139, L 2167.

Bowling green, B., 1722; the space between Cambridge street, and Sudbury street and the Mill-pond.

Bowman street, Dor.; from Blackwell street.

Bow's corner, B., 1708; corner Union street and Salt lane, then so called.

***Boyle street,** Chsn., 1891; from Cordis street to Pleasant street; formerly Cordis-street place; laid out, Sept. 28, 1891. L 2338.

***Boylston avenue,** W. Rox., 1858; from Boylston street to Green street; probably first extended from Boylston street only to Stony Brook; called Boylston street in 1868; constructed and continued to Green street, including Glen street, March 29, 1872; accepted April 5, 1872. L 2740.

Boylston court, B., 1831–34; from north side of Boylston street, between Washington street and Tremont street; exact situation not identified.

Boylston court, } B.; from Boylston street, south, opposite the burial
Boylston place, } ground extending nearly to Eliot street, opposite end of Warrenton street; called Boylston court, 1820; Boylston place, 1826; now Boylston place.

Boylston Market place, B., 1820; from Washington street, west, then north to Boylston street adjoining Boylston market (now Boylston building); called also Boylston square and part also called Boylston place.

Boylston place, B., 1828–30; "from west side of Washington street, near Boylston market" (now Boylston building), there were two parallel passageways on land of the Boylston market, both running west from Washington street to the passageway leading north to Boylston street; the southerly one of these probably called as above, but usually both known as part of Boylston square or Boylston Market place; the northerly passage way was formerly the larger, but southerly one only is now open.

Boylston place, W. Rox., 1884; from Boylston street, north-east, near and east of Amory street.

Boylston square, B., 1820; from Washington street, west, then north to Boylston street; the south and west sides of the Boylston market (now Boylston building) laid out in 1809 as a 20-foot passageway; part of called Boylston place, 1828–30; called also Boylston Market place.

***Boylston street,** B. and Rox., 1809; from Washington street by south side of the Common and Public Garden to Back Bay Fens, and then from the west side of the Fens to Brookline avenue; part from Orange (now Washington) street to the sea (near southwest corner of the Common) called Frog lane, 1708; but in 1800 said lane extended only as far as the burying-ground on the Common; Frog lane from South Market place to the south end of the Mall called Boylston street, 1809; called Boylston street from Boylston Market (now Boylston building) to Pleasant street (south-west corner of Common), 1813; extended from Pleasant street to the Back Bay Basin (at present Arlington street), 1843; part from Arlington street, west to Cross-dam (now Parker street) projected as Avenue H. in 1853; projected as Avenue H. to Brookline line, 1855; from Arlington street to Berkeley street accepted, conditionally, May 8, 1865, and finally Aug. 22, 1865; laid out from Berkeley street to Clarendon street, Feb. 8, 1870; from Clarendon street to Dartmouth street May 19, 1873; from Parker street to West Chester park (now Massachusetts avenue) and about 140 feet easterly of said park, Aug. 26, 1878; from Dartmouth street to Hereford street June 8, 1883, from Hereford street to the part leading east from West Chester park, already public, crossing the B & A. R.R., July 6, 1886; part from Berkeley street to Clarendon street, sometimes called part of Berkeley square; extended from west side of Back Bay Fens to

Brookline avenue, Oct. 4, 1894. Vol. 31, p. 3. L 148, L 239, L 282, L 310, L 356, L 374, L 862, L 1296, L 1316, L 1553, L 1585, L 1699, L 1705, L 1706, L 2002, L 2008, L 2606, L 2620.

*__Boylston street__, W. Rox., 1825; from Centre street to Washington street; from Centre street, south-east to present junction of Boylston avenue and Boylston street, then east to School street, named Boylston street May 9, 1825; extended from junction of Boylston avenue, south-east to Shawmut avenue (now Washington street), Sept. 8, 1873; name of part from junction of Boylston avenue, east to School street changed to Amory street, March 1, 1882. L 1919, L 2219, L 2676.

Boylston street, W. Rox., 1868; Boylston avenue, so called on plan 1868.

Boylston terrace, W. Rox.; from 426 Centre street, between Boylston street and Paul Gore street.

Boylston's alley, B., 1734; a passageway from the end of that part of Corn hill now a part of Washington street to Brattle street; after 1816, when a new street (called Market street, 1817, and Cornhill, 1828) was laid out from Court street to Cornhill, said alley extending from junction of said street and Cornhill to Brattle street; called also Draper's alley; included in the extension of Washington street to Haymarket square, 1872.

*__Boynton street__, W. Rox., 1870; from South street to Call street; laid out, April 15, 1890. L 2220.

*__Bradbury street__, Bri., 1891; from Franklin street to Mansfield street; laid out, Aug. 14, 1891. L 2322.

Bradford place, B., 1826; from Mason street, east, between Mason-street place and rear of Boston Theatre building; called Hogg alley, 1708; built over with Keith's Theatre, 1894.

*__Bradford place__, Rox., 1846; from East (now Hampden) street, opposite Proctor (now Eustis) street to Magazine street; so called in 1843–49; accepted as a public street, June 19, 1867; name changed to Eustis street, April 21, 1868.

*__Bradford street__, B., 1846; from Waltham street, north, to end of Medford court, then west to Shawmut avenue (formerly Suffolk street); named, May 14, 1849; accepted, conditionally, 1855.

Bradford's corner, B., 1800; cor. of Dock square and Union street, then so called.

*__Bradlee street__, Dor., 1891; from Washington street to School street, authority to open given by Street Commissioners, June 24, 1891; laid out June 22, 1894. L 2603.

Bradlee's corner, B., 1800; cor. of Dock square and Pierce's alley (now Change avenue), then so called.

Bradley court, } B., 1839–61; from Endicott street, east, between
Bradley place, } Cooper street and Thacher street; closed.

†**Bradshaw street**, Dor., 1896; from Glenway street to Sanborn avenue; White avenue laid out as Bradshaw street, from Glenway street to beyond Bicknell street, Jan. 3, 1896; authority to open portion from end of present public street to Sanborn avenue given by Street Commissioners June 16, 1896. L 2752.

Bradstreet, W. Rox., 1860; north-west end of Mt. Hope street, from near Mt. Hope station, south-east; called Bradstreet previous to 1871, when it was laid out as a part of Mt. Hope street.

Bradstreet avenue, W. Rox., 1884; from Mt. Hope avenue or street, south-west; formerly called Weld street by old deed.

Bradstreet court, Chsn., 1868; from Park street, west, nearly opposite end of Joiner street.

Bragdon street, Rox., 1871; from Washington street to Amory street; named from Shawmut avenue (now Washington street) to Amory street, April 28, 1871.

Brahms street, W. Rox., from Washington street, near West Roxbury way to beyond Nikisch avenue.

***Braintree street,** Bri., 1885; from Everett street to Franklin street (formerly Harvard avenue) parallel with and next south of B. & A. R. R.; laid out as a public street, Sept. 6, 1886. L 1944.

Branch avenue, } B., from Charles street to Spruce street, between
***Branch street,** } Beacon street and Chestnut street; called Kitchen street, 1824; called Branch avenue, 1849; accepted conditionally, Dec. 15, 1863, but never finally till it was laid out as a public street and named Branch street, July 26, 1884. L 1795.

Branch avenue, Dor.; from Arcadia street, south, then west to Ditson street.

Branch street, Dor., 1881; from Butler street to Riverview avenue (now Medway street); at north side of Milton Branch R. R.

Branch avenue, } Dor.; from Arcadia street, south-east, then south-
Branch street, } west to Ditson street; shown as an unnamed street in 1874; sometimes called Branch avenue; called Branch street in 1884.

Brandon street, Dor.; from Washington street to Carlisle street; part from Washington street, east, called Baker court or avenue in 1873, and shown as an unnamed court in 1874; later extended east to Carlisle street; also called by abutters Brandon street; laid out and named Brent street, Nov. 12, 1885.

†**Brandon street,** W. Rox., 1881; from South street to Dudley avenue; formerly from South street at junction with Birch street, crossing Dudley avenue and Aldrich street; parallel with and south from B. & P. (now N. Y., N. H. & H.) R.R.; shown as extending from South street westerly, and called Williams street in 1871; shown as Williams street from South street to Dudley avenue in 1874; part from South street to Cottage (now Amherst) street laid out as Brandon street, Sept. 14, 1881; remainder of street after this date called Brandon street; authority to open part from Dudley avenue to near Colberg avenue given by Street Commissioners, Dec. 1, 1891; later, a portion of Brandon street, from Dudley avenue to Belgrade avenue, called Belgrade avenue. L 1557.

Brattle alley, } B., 1708; from Mr. Coleman's church (now corner of
Brattle lane, } Brattle street and Brattle square) to Queen (now Court) street; that part of Brattle street above described, sometimes so called at an early time; called also Dassett's or Dorsett's lane or alley as early as 1755; called Franklin avenue, 1815.

***Brattle square,** B., 1737; from Elm street to Brattle street; a part of Brattle street, 1708; as early as 1737 names of Brattle street and Brattle square used interchangeably for street from Wing's lane (now Elm street) to the church (cor. of present Brattle street and Brattle square), then east to Dock square; same street called Brattle-street square in list of 1800; name of Brattle square restricted to part from Elm street to the church, and name of Brattle street given to other part and to Hillier's lane, 1820.

***Brattle street,** B., 1694; from Washington street at Adams square to Court street at Scollay square, from the middle of Wing's lane (now Elm street) to Mr. Coleman's church (cor. of present Brattle square and Brattle street), thence two ways, easterly to Dock square and southerly to Queen (now Court) street, 1708; on Price's map 1769 and Page's map 1775 represented as running from Wing's lane to Queen street across Hillier's lane, the part from the church to Dock square being made a part of Hillier's lane; the part from the church to Queen street called also at an early time Brattle alley or lane; called Dassett's or Dorsett's alley, 1755–1817; called Franklin avenue, 1817; the part from Wing's lane to the church called also at times Brattle square, as early as 1737, and Brattle-street square 1800; now called Brattle square; the part from the church to Dock square besides being called Hillier's lane (see above), called at times (with the part from Wing's lane to the church) Brattle square, 1737, and Brattle-street square on Edes' list of 1800, but shown as Cooper's alley on Carleton's map of 1800, and sometimes so called as late as 1818; this part commonly, however, called Brattle square or Brattle street till 1820, when name of Brattle street was extended over whole street from Court street to Dock square, the part leading west to Court street being previously called Hillier's lane (1708) and sometimes also Belknap's alley (1744) and Gay alley; the easterly end near Dock square included in the extension of Washington street, 1872. L 65, L 818, L 949.

Brattle-street square, B., 1800; from Wing's lane (now Elm street) to the church (corner present Brattle street and Brattle square) then east to Dock square; Brattle street or square (now part of Brattle street and Brattle square) sometimes so called; part running east to Dock square also called Cooper's alley about same time, and Hillier's lane on maps of 1769 and 1775.

Brazer's corner, B., 1800; corner Dock square and Exchange lane (now street), then so called.

***Bread street**, B., 1808; from Broad street to India street, between Wharf street and Custom-House street; conveyed to City for a public way, March 9, 1808, by deed, and shown as Bread street in 1808; confirmed as a public street, Sept. 15, 1834; name changed to Franklin street, March 1, 1896.

***Breck street**, Bri., 1871; from Warren street to Washington street; laid out, Dec. 16, 1873; included in the laying out of Massachusetts avenue (now Commonwealth avenue) Nov. 6, 1883.

†**Breed street**, E.B., 1875; from Ford street to Terrace avenue (now Gladstone street); laid out, Aug. 23, 1886; authority to open part between Ford street and Bennington street, given by Street Commissioners, April 21, 1893. L 1936, L 1937.

Breen place, B., 1870; from Livingston street, south, between Charles street and the river; called Livingston place, 1844; named Breen place May 10, 1870; obliterated by the construction of the Charles River Embankment (now Charlesbank), authorized 1881, completed 1887.

Bremen place, E. B., 1859; from Bremen street, north-west, between Sumner street and Maverick street.

†**Bremen street**, E. B., 1833; from Sumner street to Addison street; accepted from Sumner street to Porter street, May 29, 1857; accepted from Porter street to Curtis street, July 29, 1861; accepted at junction of Bennington street, July 23, 1862. L 891, L 892, L 893, L 894.

***Brent street**, Dor., 1885; from Washington street to Carlisle street; private way heretofore known as Baker avenue and later as Brandon street, laid out with name of Brent street, Nov. 12, 1885. L 1896, L 2537.

Brenton street, Dor.; from Glenway street to Greenwood street.

***Brentwood street**, Bri., 1889; from Franklin street to Everett street; laid out by Selectmen as Pearl street, Dec. 16, 1873; laid out as Brentwood street, Aug. 13, 1889. L 2150.

Brewer avenue, Rox., 1872; from Dudley street to George street, between Magazine street and Clarence street; changed in same year to Woodward avenue; laid out as Woodward avenue, May 7, 1877.

***Brewer street**, W. Rox., 1855; from Burroughs street to Eliot street; shown as a street without name in 1849; laid out, March 19, 1875; called Beaver street, 1874–79. L 1030.

Brewer's hill, B., 1800; from Charter street to Lynn (now Commercial) street, parallel with and south-west of Henchman's lane (now street); called Sliding alley, 1708, 1732 and 1769; called Foster's lane, 1741 and as late as 1819 or later; called also Fuller street on Carleton's map of 1795, and called Brewer's hill by Edes' list of 1800; called Foster street on Carleton's map of 1800, which name it now bears.

Brewery court, Chsn., 1831–40; from 45 Salem turnpike (now Chelsea street.)

***Brewster street**, S. B., 1861; from East Seventh street to East Eighth street, between Springer street and I street; laid out Oct. 29, 1877. L 1284.

Brewster street, Rox.; 1864, from Eustis street, south-west, then south-east across Harrison avenue to Winslow street; name changed to Renfrew street, April 20, 1869.

Brick alley, B., 1788; from Cow lane (now High) street, opposite end of Long lane (now Federal street) to Belcher's lane (now Purchase street); called Crooked alley, 1708; Brick alley, 1788; Board alley, 1848; erroneously called Broad alley, 1864; shown as Board alley on plans as late as 1870 and extending from High street near and east of junction of Federal street to Purchase street, but now closed.

Brick alley, B., 1848; from North street to Fulton street; near Ferry street; from Ann (now North) street, east, 1848.

Bridge court, B., 1833; from George (now West Cedar) street, west, between Cambridge street and Stetson's place; called Gilson's court or place, 1867.

Bridge court, } B; from North Anderson street, east, between
Bridge-street court, } Parkman street and Adams place; called Bridge court in 1828, 1830–35, 1869–87; Bridge-street court in 1829.

***Bridge street**, B., 1803; from Cambridge street, north, across Vine (now Parkman) street, west of Blossom street; from Cambridge street to South Allen street, 1809; so much of street as fell within the lands of the Massachusetts General Hospital discontinued, Nov. 19, 1817, Blossom street to be substituted therefor; formally extended from Vine (now Parkman) street to land of Massachusetts General Hospital, Oct. 31, 1831; accepted as a public street, Sept. 15, 1834; name changed to North Anderson street, April 21, 1868.

Bridge street, W. Rox., 1872; from Canterbury street, east, crossing end of Brook street.

Bridge street, Chsn., 1714; from Fish street (now Charles-River avenue), east, to "the swing bridge" (near south end of present Gray street); described as "New Fore street, what is now called Water street," and laid out 40 feet wide, 1780; Water street as thus laid out probably included Bridge street and Battery street.

Bridge-street avenue, B., 1832; from Bridge (now North Anderson) street to Blossom street; named Adams place, 1845, but given in directories as above until 1849.

Bridges' lane, B, 1796; from Middle (now Hanover) street to Salem street; name used late in the 18th century for street commonly known as Beer lane, 1708–1800; same street also called Bear lane, 1708; "Beer lane or Bridges' lane" named Richmond street, Jan. 22, 1800; named Parmenter street, Dec. 31, 1870.

Brigden's lane, Chsn., 1670; from Bow street, next west of Grave street to the river, 12 feet wide; called Jenner's lane, 1767; shown as Cook's lane in 1818; new street laid out over Cook's lane from Bow street to Front street, and called Jenner street, Sept. 17, 1866.

Brigg's court, Rox., 1847; from Orange (now Elmwood and Hampshire) street.

Brigg's place, B., 1849; from Shawmut avenue, south-east, between Bradford street and Groton street; called New court, 1845; named Briggs place, 1849.

***Brigham street,** E. B., 1892; from Webster street to a point south-east of Ida street, formerly part of Terrace place; laid out, Nov. 26, 1892. L 2460, L 2461.

***Brighton avenue,** Rox. and Bri., 1825; from Commonwealth avenue to Cambridge street; an early name sometimes given to the Mill-dam road from Brookline line to Watertown line, and same name used at times down to 1875; said road named Avenue street, June 15, 1840; named Beacon street, Nov. 10, 1846; North Beacon street, March 5, 1860; name of part of North Beacon street, from the former boundary line of towns of Brighton and Brookline to Cambridge street at Union square, changed to Brighton avenue, March 1, 1884; name of part of Brighton avenue from Beacon street to Massachusetts avenue (now Commonwealth avenue) at Malvern street changed to Commonwealth avenue, being a continuation of the same, March 1, 1887; sometimes described as Brighton branch of the Mill-dam, Brighton road and road to the Mill-dam. L 649, L 1799, L 2726, L 2727, L 2728.

Brighton court, B., 1848; from Brighton street, south-east, between Allen street and Poplar street, extending to junction of Kennard court and Lovell place; Brighton-street court, 1860; Elder court, 1863; Elder place since 1868.

Brighton road, Rox. and Bri.; see Brighton avenue.

Brighton road, Bri., 1847; from junction of Newton road (now part of Washington street) and Brookline road (now part of Washington street), north-east; called Cambridge street.

Brighton square, Bri.; at intersection of Chestnut Hill avenue and Rockland street.

***Brighton street,** B., 1816; from end of Lowell street across Leverett street and Poplar street to Allen street; from Leverett street to Poplar street called Copper street, 1803; changed to Brighton street, 1816; Brighton street extended from Poplar street to North Allen (now Allen) street, 1826; extended north on Barton point, March 15, 1828; confirmed as a public street, Sept. 15, 1834; part from Leverett street, north, extended to the flats and sometimes called North Brighton street, 1834; Lowell street extended in 1842 to Brighton street, and part from Leverett street to Lowell street, accepted, May 1, 1848. L 560.

†Brighton street, Chsn., 1852; from Cambridge street, north-east, across Perkins street, then north by B. & M. R.R., then north-west to Caldwell (formerly Columbia) street; laid out from Cambridge street to Perkins street, Oct. 25, 1852; remainder shown as Brookline street in 1858; called Brighton street from Cambridge street to Columbia street, 1868.

Brighton street, Bri; part of Washington street, from junction of Tremont street, west, so called in 1871.

Brighton-street avenue, B., 1844; from Brighton street, north-west, to Auburn street, between Livingston (now Chambers) street and Poplar street; called Derby avenue, 1841; Brighton-street avenue, 1844.

Brighton-street court, B., 1860; from Brighton street, south-east, between Allen street and Poplar street, extending to junction Kennard court and Lovell place; called Brighton court, 1848; Brighton-street court, 1860; Elder court, 1863; Elder place since 1868.

Brighton-street place, B., 1859; from Brighton street, south-east, between Leverett street and Chambers street.

Brimmer avenue, } B., 1822-26; from Liberty square to Broad street;
Brimmer's avenue, } another name for street called Liberty street on Hale's map of 1814 and at various times till 1826; Liberty street included in Water street, March 20, 1826.

Brimmer avenue, } B., 1842; from Essex street, north, opposite end
Brimmer place, } of Harrison avenue; called Essex place, 1816; Essex court, 1818; Brimmer avenue or place, 1842; Harrison avenue extended from Essex street to Bedford street, over Brimmer place, part of Chickering place and part of Norfolk place, July 6, 1881.

Brimmer avenue, E. B., 1876; from Ashley avenue, north-east, to Revere line.

Brimmer place, B., 1884; from North street, south-east, near Richmond street; also called North Brimmer place.

***Brimmer street,** B., 1866; from Pinckney street to Beacon street; part between Chestnut street and Beacon street called D street, 1828; this part named Messenger street, Jan. 5, 1856; part from Pinckney street, south, to Mt. Vernon street, laid out as Brimmer street, Dec. 19, 1866; extended from Mt. Vernon street to Chestnut street, Oct. 9, 1868; name of Messenger street changed to Brimmer street, April 20, 1869. L 266, L 297, L 346.

Brimmer's corner, B., 1800; corner Marlboro' (now Washington) street and School street, then so called.

Brinton street, Rox.; from Washington street, nearly opposite Marcella street, south-east, abandoned.

Briscow's corner, B., 1708; corner Marlboro' (now Washington) street and Rawson's lane (now Bromfield street), then so called; also written Brisco's corner.

***Bristol street,** B., 1869; from Albany street to Harrison avenue, between Dover street and Thayer street; laid out parallel with and 250 feet distant south-west from Dover street, March 12, 1869. L 431, L 444, L 2336.

Broad alley, B., 1722; from Orange (now Washington) street, west; called Hollis street, 1732.

Broad alley, B., 1864; from High street, near and east of junction of Federal street to Purchase street; Board alley (earlier called Crooked alley and also Brick alley) erroneously so called in 1864; now closed.

***Broad street,** B., 1805; from State street, between Kilby street and India street, to Atlantic avenue; from State street to Batterymarch street (*i.e.*, to present junction of Batterymarch street and Broad street) laid out 70 feet wide and named, June 26, 1805; name of Broad street extended over part of Batterymarch street, running easterly from former end of Broad street to Foster's wharf, 1808; 50-foot street laid out from Sconce (now Belcher) lane (termination of Broad street, near Foster's wharf) through part of Flounder alley to Sea street, at present termination of Summer street, and said street included in Broad street, Oct. 17, 1833; name of Sea street from easterly end of Summer street to South Boston bridge discontinued, and entire street leading from State street to South Boston lower (free) bridge called Broad street, Jan. 3, 1834; name of part from Summer street to North Free bridge changed to Sea street again, April 4, 1842, and named Federal street, April 30, 1856; name of part from Rowe's wharf to Federal street changed to Atlantic avenue, March 17, 1874. Volume 31, page 76. Volume 31, page 82. L 186, L 339, L 466, L 586, L 622, L 788, L 810, L 874, L 875, L 876.

Broad street, Chsn., 1670; early name for the street leading from the north-east side of the Market-place (now City square), north; same street called Market street, 1714, and Main street, 1769.

***Broadway,** B., and So. B., 1804; from Washington street, opposite Pleasant street, across Fort Point channel to Dorchester avenue, opposite West Broadway; laid out and named from the north end of Dorchester street in South Boston, south-east to the sea, and north-west to the line of the Turnpike (now Dorchester avenue) Feb. 27, 1805, plan dated Oct. 4, 1804; laid out from Federal street (now Dorchester avenue) north-westerly to low water mark, Nov. 17, 1868; extended across Fort Point channel to Albany street crossing and over a part of Way street, May 3, 1869; part east of Dorchester street named East Broadway and part west of said street named West Broadway, Feb. 18, 1873; extended from Albany street to Washington street, opposite Pleasant street, over part of Curve street and including Vinal place, July 3, 1880. L 8, L 125, L 154, L 361, L 362, L 363, L 367, L 368, L 473, L 632, L 1465, L 1466, L 1532, L 2117.

***Broadway,** Chsn., 1858; part of Main street from Columbia street, near Somerville line, south-east; the continuation of Main street in Somerville is called Broadway.

***Broadway bridge,** B. and So. B., 1869; over Fort Point channel; Broadway extended over channel and bridge built, May 3, 1869.

Broadway court, So. B., 1863; from junction East Broadway and Emerson street, south-east of, and parallel with, I street.

Brodbine avenue, Rox., 1894; from Dudley street to Forest street; authority to open given by Street Commissioners, Dec. 26, 1894.

Broderick alley, B., 1885; from Commercial street, south-west, between Jackson avenue and Commercial court.

Bromfield place, B., 1828–48; from Bromfield street, north (closed).

***Bromfield street,** } B.; from Washington street, between School street
Bromfield's lane, } and Winter street, to Tremont street; called Rawson's lane, 1708; Bromfield's lane, 1796; named Bromfield street, Nov. 10, 1828. Volume 31, page 21. L 453.

***Bromley park,** Rox., 1872; from Bickford street to B. & P. (now N.Y., N. H. & H.) R.R.; laid out, May 15, 1874. L 928.

†**Bromley street,** Rox., 1872; from New Heath street, between Parker street and B. & P. (now N.Y., N. H. & H.) R.R., south-west, crossing Heath street and Bromley park; laid out from New Heath street to Bromley park, May 15, 1874. L 927.

***Brook avenue,** Dor., 1855; from Dudley street, south-west, south and north-east to Dudley street again; called Brook street in 1856; laid out from Stoughton (now Dudley) street crossing West Cottage street to Stoughton (now Dudley) street, Aug. 12, 1869. L 880, L 1511.

Brook-avenue place, } Dor ; from Brook avenue, west, between Dud-
Brook court, } ley street and West Cottage street; shown as an unnamed place in 1855; called Brook court in 1860; called Leavitt place in 1873; Brook-avenue place in 1884.

Brook place, Dor., 1875; from Dudley street, nearly opposite north end of Brook avenue, north-east.

Brook street, Dor., 1856; from Dudley street, south-west, south and north-east to Dudley street again; Brook avenue so called in 1856.

Brook street, } Dor., 1874; from Howe street, north, across Gibson
Brooks street, } street to Teneau creek; shown as an unnamed street in 1852; shown as a proposed street in 1874.

Brook street, } Dor., 1874; from Dorchester avenue, opposite the
Brooks street, } south cemetery, east, crossing Patterson street to Hutchinson street.

Brook street, W. Rox., 1872; from Paine (formerly Sargent) street, north, to Bridge street.

Brook street, W. Rox., 1872; from Bellevue avenue to Hill street, crossing Orange street and Berry street.

Brook street, W. Rox., 1874; from Mt. Hope street, north of Lawn street, east, to Stony Brook; shown as an unnamed street in 1853.

Brook street, W. Rox., 1882; from Florence street, south-west, then north-west, to Sycamore street; shown as an unnamed street in 1874.

Brook street,) W. Rox., 1882; from Newbern avenue to Stony brook, **Brooks street,**) between Canterbury street and Hyde Park line; shown as an unnamed street in 1874 and as proposed street in 1884.

Brook Farm avenue, W. Rox., 1874; from Baker street to Newton line, but shown in 1874 and later as from Baker street, west, in an irregular line on land, and to buildings of, Martin Luther Orphan Home.

***Brookfield street,** W. Rox.; from South street to S. Fairview street; laid out, Dec. 27, 1893. L 2577.

***Brookford street,** Rox. and Dor., 1883; from Blue Hill avenue, opposite Woodbine street to Howard avenue at Hartford street; laid out, July 6, 1883, the part near Blue Hill avenue being laid out over the southerly portion of Rand (earlier Bismarck) street. L 1715, L 2677.

Brookledge street, Rox., 1889; from Humboldt avenue east.

***Brookline avenue,** Rox. and B., 1849; from Beacon street, at Commonwealth avenue, south-west, to Brookline line; called road to the Punch Bowl Tavern in 1828; Punch Bowl road on map 1845; Brookline street in 1845, and by directories until 1868; road over Mill-dam on plan dated 1850, called Brookline Branch of Western avenue, or Punch Bowl road, and by those names located by indenture between Commonwealth and Roxbury Mill Corporation, dated Dec. 30, 1856, from the Mill-dam (now Beacon street) to Washington street, Brookline; laid out as Brookline avenue Dec. 7, 1868. L 416, L 417, L 648, L 735, L 736, L 1800, L 1801, L 2505.

Brookline road, Bri., 1847; leading south-east from junction of Newton road (now Washington street) and Brighton road (now Cambridge street); now part of Washington street.

Brookline street, B., 1834; from Tremont street to Front street (now Harrison avenue; from Tremont street to Washington street, seems to have been called both Brookline street and Dorchester street previous to 1834, from Tremont street to Front street named Brookline street, Sept. 15, 1834, reaching to Albany street on the extension of that street to Roxbury line, April 21, 1855; accepted, Dec. 7, 1857; part west of Tremont street to line of Boston Water Power Company, accepted, Dec. 21, 1859; whole street accepted, Oct. 30, 1860; laid out from Tremont street to Warren avenue and accepted, May 21, 1867; part from Washington street to Albany street named East Brookline street, and part from Washington street to Warren avenue, named West Brookline street, April 21, 1868. L 138.

Brookline street, Rox., 1845; Brookline avenue, so called on plan, and by directory until 1868.

Brookline street, Chsn., 1858; from Perkins street, north-east, to and along B. & M. R.R., then north-west to Columbia (now Caldwell) street; by directory 1868 and thereafter considered as a part of Brighton street.

Brooklyn street, W. R.; from Sycamore street to Florence street.

Brook's corner, B., 1708; cor. Marshall lane (now street) and Creek lane (now square), then so called.

Brooks place, B., 1861; from Cambridge street, south, next east of Anderson street.

Brooks place, Rox., 1854; from Brooks (now Conant) street, south, between Phillips street and Parker street; called Brooks street place, 1860–68; now called Conant street place or court.

Brooks place, Bri., 1883; from Washington street, north, near Oak square.

Brooks street, E. B., 1835; from Bremen street, between Putnam street and Marion street, to Condor street (with extension north of Condor street to the water, and proposed extension south from Bremen street to Front street); extended from Condor street to Harbor Commissioners' line (for water-pipes), Aug. 31, 1850; accepted from Chelsea street to Condor street, June 3, 1856; accepted from Chelsea street to Bremen street, Nov. 26, 1861. L 606, L 641, L 673, L 2154.

Brooks street, Rox., 1845; from Parker street, north-east of Smith street, north-west, 780 feet; shown as extending to Bumstead lane, now St. Alphonsus street, in 1867, named Conant street, April 21, 1868.

Brooks street, Chsn., 1848–52; from Moulton street to Chelsea street; Bainbridge street, so called.

Brooks street, Chsn., 1831; from Morton street, near Edward Adams' ropewalk (now corner of Moulton street and Bainbridge street) to Mystic river in 1846; shown as a part of Morton street in 1818; this street was accepted as Moulton street by selectmen June 9, 1826; but names of Brooks street, Morton street and Moulton street were applied to it subsequently and simultaneously; now called Moulton street.

*__Brooks street__, Bri., 1858; from Faneuil street to Faneuil station, B. & A. R.R.; resolve that said street be laid out so as to intersect the new county way (Faneuil street) proposed by commissioners, July 8, 1872; laid out, Dec. 18, 1873; accepted conditionally, Dec. 30, 1873; laid out by City from Faneuil street to B. & A. R.R., April 22, 1876. L 1152, L 1153.

Brooks-street place, Rox., 1860–68; from Brooks (now Conant) street, south, between Phillips street and Parker street; called Brooks place, 1854–60; now Conant-street place.

*__Brookside avenue__, W. Rox., 1868; from Green street to Boylston street, between Boylston avenue and Washington street; called "Brookside, or Chemical, avenue," in 1870; laid out from Green street, north-east to land of heirs of William H. Sumner (*i.e.*, to present junction with Chemical avenue), Feb. 27, 1871; extended to extension of Boylston street, Sept. 8, 1873. L 1654, L 1655.

*__Brown avenue__, / __Brown's avenue__, } W. Rox., 1848; from Florence street, at Mt. Hope station, south-west, to Poplar street; called Alpine avenue in 1847; Belmont avenue in 1843–49; Brown's avenue in 1855; laid out and accepted as Brown avenue, March 29, 1869. L 1467.

Brown's court, Chsn., 1856; from Lawrence street, nearly opposite Johnson avenue, south-west.

Brown court, Bri., 1876–82; from Webster avenue, near Union square.

Brown place, W. Rox., 1875; from Seaverns avenue, south, near Centre street; shown but not named in 1874.

Brown street, B., 1828; that part of Hull street, from Snowhill street to Lynn (now Commercial) street, so called.

Brown street, Rox., 1872; from Hunneman street, between Harrison avenue and Fellows street, north-east.

Browning avenue, Dor., 1872; from Bernard street, south-west, between Kingsdale street and Talbot avenue.

Brown's corner, B., 1732; corner of Milk street and Bishop's alley (now Hawley street), then so called.

*__Bruce street__, Dor., 1894; from Ashmont street to Dracut street; laid out as Wrentham street, from Ashmont street to Dell (now Dracut) street, March 27, 1890; name changed to Bruce street, March 1, 1894. L 2214.

Bruce street, W. Rox.; from Ricker street to Joy street; near Brookline line.

Brunswick avenue, Rox. and West Roxbury, 1883; from Centre street, opposite junction of Pynchon street (now Columbus avenue) and Heath street to West Walnut park; shown as a proposed street in 1884; part of included in the extension of Columbus avenue, Jan. 4, 1895.

Brunswick street, Dor.; from Dorchester avenue, east, then south, nearly opposite Fuller street.

†**Brunswick street,** Rox. and Dor., 1884; from Elm Hill avenue, opposite Wenonah street, to Columbia street; from Elm Hill avenue to Warren street shown as an unnamed street in 1884; authority to open part between Warren street and Blue Hill avenue given by Street Commissioners, June 14, 1892, and laid out, Oct. 15, 1892; authority to open part east of Blue Hill avenue given by Street Commissioners, Dec. 5, 1893; authority to open portion from Columbia street, north-westerly, given by Street Commissioners, Dec. 7, 1895. L 2450.

***Brush Hill turnpike or avenue,** Rox., Dor , and W. Rox., 1805; from Warren street to Milton line; location as above filed by the Brush Hill Turnpike Corporation, Sept., 1805, the part south of Seaver street near Roxbury and Dorchester line being laid out over a part of the old Canterbury street; laid out by County Commissioners as a public highway from junction of highway in Milton to junction of highway in Dorchester at or near store of George L. Fisher, Dec., 1849; proprietors relinquished franchise of corporation, Oct. 13, 1856; remainder of street as far as Warren street, in Roxbury, not before made public, laid out, Dec., 1856; part from Warren street to West Roxbury line at Seaver street included in Grove Hall avenue, Jan. 28, 1867; Grove Hall avenue and Brush Hill avenue named Blue Hill avenue, Oct. 25, 1870.

* **Bryant street,** Rox., 1884; from Huntington avenue to Parker street; part of Rogers avenue lying north of Huntington avenue laid out with name of Bryant street, May 21, 1884. L 1777.

Buchanan court, W. Rox., 1873; from South street, west, between White avenue (now Custer street) and Jamaica street.

Buchanan place, Rox., 1858; from Parker street, west, between Conant street and Smith street.

Buckingham place, B., 1873; from Buckingham street, south, laid out with name of Burbank street, Oct. 20, 1894. L 2660.

***Buckingham street,** B., 1872; from Columbus avenue, opposite Clarendon street, west, to Dartmouth street; named, Oct. 22, 1872; laid out, Oct. 25, 1873. L 901.

Buckley avenue, Rox.; at rear of 310 Centre street; from near Lowell school, east, across the end of Johnson avenue.

Bucknam street, Rox., 1895; from Fisher avenue to Lawn street; authority to open given by Street Commissioners, Sept. 19, 1895.

Buena Vista avenue, ***Buena Vista street,** Rox., 1867; from Warren street, opposite Montrose avenue, (now Montrose street) to Walnut avenue; called Buena Vista street in 1869-76; laid out with the name of Buena Vista street, April 30, 1894. L 2590.

Buffalo street, B., 1839; from Beach street, south, between Front street (now Harrison avenue) and Hudson street; name given in 1839 to street then and now known as Tyler street.

Buffalo street, Bri., 1882; from Market street, east, south of and parallel with B. & A. R.R., leading to cattle yards.

Bulfinch place, B., 1805; from Bulfinch street to Bowdoin street; called "Clap's building" in 1807.

***Bulfinch street**, B., 1800; from Court street at Bowdoin square to Allston street; from Cambridge (now Court) street, south, to the present Allston street, thence to Middlecot (now Bowdoin) street, 1800; called "a new street from Bowdoin square to Middlecot street" in 1801; part running west to Middlecot street considered a part of Somerset place as early as 1821; Somerset place named Allston street, Dec. 19, 1842; Bulfinch street erroneously called Middlecot street on Hale's plan of Bowdoin square, 1819; confirmed as a public street, Sept. 15, 1834.

***Bullard street**, Dor.; from Bowdoin avenue to Bowdoin street; part from Bowdoin avenue to Union avenue (now Rosseter street), and formerly called Maple Grove avenue laid out as Bullard street, March 21, 1888; part from Bowdoin avenue (now Rosseter street) to Bowdoin street, and formerly called Union avenue, named Bullard street, March 1, 1889. L 1650, L 2059.

Bullock street, So. B.; (proposed street) from the proposed extension of B street to the proposed extension of E street on the so-called Commonwealth flats.

Bull's corner, B., 1708; corner of Summer street and Sea (now Federal) street, then so called.

Bumstead court, B., 1825; from Boylston street, north, between Washington street and Head place.

Bumstead lane, Rox., 1863; from Huntington avenue to Tremont street; formerly from Ward street to and across Tremont street; laid out from Tremont street to Huntington avenue with name of St. Alphonsus street, Dec. 20, 1893.

Bumstead place, B., 1807-1868; from Common (now Tremont) street, east, then north to Bromfield's lane; now closed except the portion leading into Bromfield street, which is now unnamed.

Bunker Hill court, Chsn., 1842; from Bunker Hill street, south-west, near Mead street.

Bunker Hill terrace, Chsn., 1893; from Tufts street, near Bunker Hill street; authority to open given by Street Commissioners, June 9, 1893.

***Bunker Hill street**, Chsn., 1714; from Chelsea street, north-west, over Bunker Hill to Main street, at junction with Medford street; early called "road over Bunker's Hill," and "road to brick kilns;" from road to Moulton's point (at present junction Bunker Hill street and Moulton street), north-west, over Bunker Hill to Market (now Main) street, 1714; staked out by Eben Breed's land to the brick kilns, Aug 7, 1809; laid out from the Neck to Salem turnpike 60 feet wide, March, 1825; south-east end of Morton (also called Moulton) street, from Bunker Hill street to Salem turnpike, named Bunker Hill street, being a continuation of the same, Dec. 15, 1834; extended from Tufts street to Vine street, July 10, 1854. L 2156, L 2255, L 2591.

Bur lane, B.; see Beer lane and Bridges lane (now Parmenter street).

***Burbank street**, B., 1894; from Buckingham street, south-east, and then north-east; formerly called Buckingham place; laid out as Burbank street, Oct. 20, 1894. L 2660.

Burbank street, Dor., 1895; from Washington street to Merrill street, authority to open given by Street Commissioners, March 27, 1895; laid out under the name of Fenelon street, June 2, 1896.

***Burgess street**, Dor., 1888; from Dudley street to Clifton street; formerly called Taylor street; laid out as Burgess street, July 12, 1888. L 2076.

Burgoyne street, Dor.; from Beaumont street to Elm road.

***Burke street,** Rox., 1860; from Tremont street to Berlin street (now Columbus avenue), between Benton street and Coventry street; shown as an unnamed street in 1849; laid out, May 18, 1891. L 2292.

Burke's court, E. B.; from Everett street, north-east, near Cottage street; sometimes called Burke court.

Burley street, W. Rox., 1884; from Metropolitan avenue to Dale street.

Burlington avenue, B., 1872; from Brookline avenue, south of Butler street, to Brookline Branch R.R.; by directories, from 1876, from Brookline avenue to Beacon street, but part from railroad to Beacon street called Munson street in 1875 and 1884.

Burlington street, B., 1864; name given without authority to part of Dedham (now Dartmouth) street, west from Tremont street; order given to remove signs bearing this name, Aug. 30, 1864.

Burlington street, B., 1874; from Beacon street to Mountfort street; now included in proposed Audubon road.

Burmah street, Dor., 1896; from Edgewater drive, northerly; near Hyde Park line; authority to open given by Street Commissioners, Feb. 24, 1896.

***Burnett street,** W. Rox., 1890; from Washington street, north-west, near and south of Keyes street; called Baily street, 1887-90; laid out as Burnett street, March 29, 1890. L 2215.

***Burney street,** Rox., 1871; from Tremont street, south, across end of Delle avenue; laid out, May 6, 1892. L 2396.

***Burnham street,** So. B., 1883; from Lowland (now Mercer) street, between Vale street and Newman street, north-east, to East Ninth street; laid out, July 13, 1883. L 1719.

***Burr street,** W. Rox., 1877; from Boylston street to Spring Park avenue; called B street in 1868; laid out with name of Burr street, April 25, 1877. L 1230.

Burrill place, So. B., 1870; from I street, west, between East Sixth street and East Seventh street.

Burroughs place, B., 1848; from Hollis street, north, between Hollis place and Washington street.

***Burroughs street,** W. Rox., 1825; from Centre street to Pond street; named from Centre street near Joshua Seaver's, to Pond street, May 9, 1825; probably a public highway some time previous. L 1595, L 2312.

Burt avenue, Dor., 1885; from Washington street, nearly opposite Rockwell street, east, to Ashmont street; part beginning a short distance east from Washington street, and running toward Ashmont street, previously called, in part, Tolman lane.

Burton avenue, Rox., 1876; from Copeland street, near Waverly street, south-east; called Copeland court in 1873.

Burton street, Bri., 1891; from Washington street to the proposed extension of Newton street; authority to open given by Street Commissioners, Oct. 22, 1891.

Bury lane, B.; from Leverett street, north-east, to the water north-west of Cart lane (now Minot street); another name for Berry lane (now Barton street).

Bury lane, } **Bury street,** } B., 1732; from Long lane (now Federal street) to Atkinson (now Congress) street; shown but not named in 1722; called Bury street, 1732; named Barracks lane by Selectmen, 1788, but name not used; called Berry street, 1803; name changed to Channing street, July 14, 1845.

Burying-place lane, Dor., 1806; from Norfolk street along east side of Catholic cemetery; widened, May 12, 1806; called also Cemetery lane or street; probably included in Bernard street.

Bush street, B., 1873; from East Canton street, north-east, between Thorn street and Andrews street; named April 1, 1873.

***Bushnell street**, Dor.; from Dorchester avenue to Beale street; laid out from Ashmont street to Rowena street, Aug. 29, 1889; extended from Rowena street to Beale street, June 21, 1890; extension from Ashmont street to Dorchester avenue laid out, Aug. 10, 1893. L 2159, L 2232, L 2523.

Bussey place, B., 1842; from Arch street, west, midway between Franklin street and Summer street; called Summer place for short time previously.

Butland place, So. B.; from O street between East Fifth street and East Sixth street, westerly; shown in 1873.

***Bussey street**, W. Rox., 1832; from South street to Walter street along the south-west side of the Arnold Arboretum.

Butler avenue, E. B., 1875; from Ashley avenue at Beachmont avenue, south-west to flats across Saratoga street, parallel with the railroad. L 2042, L 2043, L 2044.

Butler place, B., 1886; from Prince street, south-west, near Lafayette avenue.

Butler row, B.; Chatham row, so called previous to 1848.

***Butler square**, B., 1836; from Butler's row to Chatham street; construction authorized by filling up dock and wharves to form a street from Butler's row to Green's wharf, June 13, 1804; called Butler square, 1836; named as a part of Butler street, March 7, 1842; Butler street called Butler square in 1848; name later confined to part running into Chatham street, the remainder being called Butler's row.

***Butler street**, B., 1842; a street leading from State street, north, then east, then north again to Chatham street; so named, March 7, 1842; part parallel with State street formerly known as Butler's row and part running into Chatham street called Butler square, 1836; whole street called Butler's square, 1848, and later in part Butler's row and in part Butler square.

Butler street, B., 1874; from Brookline avenue, between Burlington avenue and Depot street, north-west, to Brookline Branch R.R.

†**Butler street**, Dor., 1874; from Richmond street to Riverview avenue; laid out from Adams street to Richmond street, May 9, 1874; part from Adams street to Riverview avenue first shown in 1881. L 923.

Butler's corner, B., 1708; corner King (now State) street and Merchant's row, then so called.

***Butler's row**, 1789; from State street, north, then east, to Chatham row; from Merchant's row, east, to Spear's wharf originally; so shown on Carleton's map of 1800, and so described in list of 1817; soon after the laying out of Chatham street, in 1825, parallel with and slightly north of said row, the part near Merchant's row was probably built over and there was an exit instead at that end south into State street, such exit being shown on Carleton's map as an unnamed passageway; Butler's row ordered to be discontinued, Feb. 25, 1828, and again, April 23, 1832, on condition that a way 20 feet wide parallel with State street and along the north side of the buildings fronting southerly on State street be kept open, and on condition also that a way 18 feet wide from said 20-foot way north to Chatham street be conveyed to City for a street; by this order the old Butler's row was practically moved south a little distance, the south side of the old street being near the north side of the new 20-foot one; the 18-foot way to Chatham street above mentioned was opened in 1804 as a passageway from the old Butler's row to Green's wharf (vote authorizing above dated June 13);

this new 20-foot street having an opening at the end near Merchant's row south into State street, as above noted, and another at the other end (the 18-foot street), north into Chatham street, named Butler street, the whole length, from State street to Chatham street; March 7, 1842, the part running into Chatham street having been previously called Butler square in 1836–42; whole street called Butler square on map 1848; later the name Butler square restricted to part running into Chatham street and part from State street, north, then east, including a passageway to Chatham row, called Butler's row.

***Buttolph street**, B., 1733; from Cambridge street, south, to May (now Myrtle) street, between South Russell street and Garden street, 1800; confirmed as a public street, Sept. 15, 1834; name changed to Irving street, April 25, 1855; called also Botolph and Butolf street.

Buttonwood court, Dor., 1871; from Buttonwood street, east.

***Buttonwood street**, Dor., 1864; from Locust street to Crescent avenue; laid out from Mt. Vernon street to Grafton street (formerly Garden street), March 27, 1882; laid out from Mt. Vernon st eet to Locust street, Aug. 14, 1891; authority to open from Grafton street to Crescent avenue given by Street Commissioners, May 20, 1892; laid out from Grafton street to Crescent avenue, Dec. 23, 1893. L 1592, L 2323, L 2575.

Buttrick place, B.; 1847 from North Margin street east.

Bynner street, Rox., 1896; from Day street to Jamaica-way; authority to open given by Street Commissioners, March 18, 1896.

Byrnes place, E. B.; from Havre street, north-west, between Maverick street and Decatur street; called Conologue court in 1882 and 1885; not shown on late atlas.

Byron court, W. Rox., 1848; from School street, south, between Erie place and Ellsworth place.

Byron street, B., 1830; from River street to Brimmer street, between Beacon street and Chestnut street; shown as B street in 1828; "from River street to the water, 1830;" proviso in chapter 58, Acts of 1844, that City shall have the right to extend same to the channel over wharf to be built by Boston and Roxbury Mill Corporation; order for City to release such right, passed, Sept. 27, 1847.

†**Byron street**, E. B., 1838; from Coleridge street, north, then west to Chelsea street, near the bridge; laid out from Saratoga street to Coleridge street, July 24, 1889; laid out from Saratoga street to Pope street, Dec. 1, 1891. L 1851, L 2145, L 2146, L 2370.

C street, B., 1828; from River street to Brimmer street, between Mt. Vernon street and Chestnut street; from A (now River) street, west, 280 feet, nearly to the water, 1828; called Lime street, 1845.

***C street**, So. B., 1804; from end of Baxter street at O C. (now N. Y., N. H. & H.) R R. to low-water mark (with proposed extension to Eastern avenue, now Congress street); projected "from the boundary line to the sea," Oct. 4, 1804; laid out and named, Feb. 27, 1805; laid out from old line between Boston and Dorchester to low-water mark, Nov. 17, 1868.

C street, Dor., 1892; from Bakersfield street to Stoughton street; authority to open from F (now Bakersfield) street to Stoughton street given by Street Commissioners, May 4, 1892; now Mayfield street.

C street, W. Rox., 1868; from Boylston street south-west, to Spring Park avenue between Burr (formerly B) street and Nelson street; laid out under the name of Clive street; July 17, 1888. L 2077.

Cable street, W. Rox., 1895; from Merriam street to Minton street authority to open given by Street Commissioners March 20, 1895.

Cabot place, Rox.; from Cabot street to Warwick street; shown in 1860, but not named.

Cabot street, B., 1828; from Pleasant street to West Castle (now Castle) street, included wholly or in part in extension of Tremont street, 1832.

***Cabot street,** Rox., 1841; from Tremont street, near junction with Hammond street, to Linden park, now Linden Park street, near Roxbury street; part from present junction with Ruggles street, south, to Worcester turnpike (later Washington, now Roxbury street) including small portion of present Linden park named as a part of Ruggles street, May 9, 1825; part from Ruggles street north to Tremont street not constructed till later; acceptance of Cabot street (probably this part) recommended by Selectmen, March 8, 1841; shown in 1843 as extending from Tremont street to Washington (now Roxbury) street, but part from present Ruggles street, south, commonly called a part of Ruggles street, till much later; street from Tremont street to Washington street by Linden park, part of what has been called Cabot street and part Ruggles street, named Cabot street, Aug. 9, 1858 (no record of the change of portion now called Linden park to that name).

Calder place, W. Rox.; from Chestnut avenue, near corner of Green street, north-west.

Calder street, W. Rox., 1872; from Blue Hill avenue to Canterbury street, opposite Franklin Park.

***Caldwell street,** Chsn., 1887; from Main street to Perkins street parallel with and near Somerville line; same street called Columbia court in 1866, but usually known as Columbia street; private street called Columbia street laid out as a public way and named Caldwell street June 7, 1887. L 1992.

Caledonia street, Rox.; from Massachusetts avenue to Huntington avenue; laid out from Falmouth street to Huntington avenue as Norway street, Dec. 22, 1891; laid out as Norway street between Massachusetts avenue and Falmouth street, Sept. 14, 1894.

Calef street, Bri., 1895; from Garden street, south-west; authority to open given by Street Commissioners Nov. 13, 1895.

***Call street,** W. Rox., 1877; from Gordon street at Jamaica Plain station, B. & P. (now N.Y., N.H. & H.) R.R. to Hall street; laid out as a new street from said station near Gordon street to Starr street (*i.e.*, present corner of Call street and Everett street), March 10, 1873; no record of any name given, but commonly called Union avenue and Starr street; "street from Gordon street to Keyes street, part of which has been called Starr street and part Union avenue," named Call street, Dec. 4, 1877; Call street laid out from Keyes street to Hall street, May 7, 1891. L 1028, L 1029, L 1891, L 2291.

***Call street,** Chsn., 1842; from Park street, near junction of Henley street and Warren street, to Chelsea street, mentioned as a town dock, July 31, 1822; shown as town way from Warren (now Park) street to Chelsea street on plan of burnt district, 1836; street leading by Leonard Tufts' shop to Chelsea street, named Call street, Feb. 18, 1842; laid out by metes and bounds, June 16, 1848.

Call-street place, Chsn.; from Call street to Henley street.

Calvert place, B., 1878; from Dover street, between Harrison avenue and Albany street, north, then west.

†**Calumet street,** Rox.; from Tremont street, at its junction with Huntington avenue, south-west, then south-east, crossing Hillside street and Harleston street to Parker Hill avenue near Parker street; laid out between Tremont street and Hillside street, Sept. 19, 1887; authority to open from Parker Hill avenue to Hillside street, given by Street Commissioners, Nov. 8, 1894. L 2025, L 2026.

***Cambria street**, Rox.; from Dalton street to Bothnia street, laid out, May 14, 1890. L 2224.

***Cambridge road**, 1681; from the Main street, at the neck, west to Cambridge (Chsn. land records): the old way to Cambridge from Charlestown, known also as Cambridge way, and road to Cambridge; shown in 1818; called Cambridge road as late as 1859; called also Cambridge street as early as 1847; now Cambridge street.

***Cambridge street**, B., 1708; from Bowdoin square to Cambridge bridge; from Sudbury street, at present junction of Court street, west, to the water, 1708; from Sudbury street, west, to the water, then south by the water to the Common 1733; from Sudbury street to the water at about the present line of W. Cedar street, 1784; part from Sudbury street to Bowdoin square included in Court street, 1807; laid out westerly about 450 feet near the bridge and accepted July 28, 1828; part formerly owned by the Bridge Corporation confirmed as a public street, Sept. 15, 1834; part from junction with West Cedar street to stone abutment of Hancock free bridge, then lately filled in and formerly the easterly part of said bridge, deeded by Hancock Free Bridge Corporation to City, accepted as a public street and named Cambridge street, Oct. 28, 1850; extended to the bridge again, Oct. 25, 1854. L 18, L 312.

Cambridge street, B., 1774; Castle street, so called.

***Cambridge street**, Chsn., 1847; from Main street at Sullivan square to Somerville line; the old way from Charlestown to Cambridge; called Cambridge road, 1681; and from an early time also Cambridge way and road to Cambridge; laid out and accepted, Dec. 28, 1857; altered from Brighton street to Somerville line and lines established, April 25, 1859. L 1245, L 1357, L 1358, L 1359, L 2198.

***Cambridge street**, Bri., 1840; from Washington street, nearly opposite Winship street to Cambridge line; shown as "road to Cambridge," 1815; "road from Brighton to Cambridgeport," 1835; named (from Washington street to Cambridgeport), June 15, 1840; called Brighton road, 1847. L 2266, L 2267, L 2294, L 2295, L 2389, L 2530; L 2675, L 2721, L 2735, L 2784.

Cambridge-street avenue, B., 1857; from Cambridge street, near North Grove street, north, then west by south side of County jail lot to Charles street.

Cambridge-street place, B., 1857; between Cambridge street and Cambridge-street avenue and parallel with both.

Cambridge terrace, Bri.; from Cambridge street, between Allston Heights and Webster avenue, south-east to Webster place; authority to open given by Street Commissioners, May 15, 1893.

Cambridge way, Chsn.; see Cambridge road.

Camden place, B., 1847; from Washington street, between Northampton street and Flagg street, south-east.

***Camden street**, B 1826; from Washington street, opposite Camden place, to B. & P. (now N. Y., N. H. & H.) R.R., from Washington street to Tremont street called Davis street, 1810; laid out on the Neck, July 24, 1826; named Camden street, Sept. 15, 1834; accepted Dec. 7, 1857; accepted west of Tremont street, Dec. 2, 1867; laid out from B. & P. R.R., to Falmouth street, Oct. 7, 1878; name of part west of B. & P. R.R., to Falmouth street changed to Gainsborough street, March 1, 1886. L 30, L 118, L 119, L 532, L 1296, L 1321.

Cameron street, Rox., 1894; from Heath street, north; present Wensley street in about the same location.

Campbell place, Rox.; from Eustis street, south-west, between Hampden street and Adams street.

Canal Bank, Chsn.; from Beacham street to Dorrance street; shown as Temple street, 1884.

Canal bridge, B., 1809; from foot of Leverett street to Lechmere's point (East Cambridge); called also Central bridge and Craigie's bridge.

***Canal street,** B., 1807; from Haymarket square to Causeway street laid out across the Mill pond from Union street to Causeway street, Aug. 3, 1807; part of, near Union street, laid out as part of Haymarket square, April 21, 1845.

Canal street, B., 1834; from Fulton street and Clinton street over the Mill creek to Charlestown street and Cross street at Haymarket square; laid out, October, 1833; named Blackstone street, Sept. 22, 1834; called also Creek street the same year previous to naming; part from Ann (now North) street, east, previously called Royall's alley.

Canal street, Rox., 1858; from Swett street at junction with East Chester park (now Massachusetts avenue), north-east; name changed to Hilton street, April 21, 1868.

Canal street, Chsn., 1847; from Cambridge street, at Sullivan square, south, to Middlesex street, then south-east to Main street at Hancock square, 1847; part from Middlesex street to Hancock square laid out and named Essex street, Dec. 31, 1855, laid out 60 feet wide from Richmond street (which then terminated at a point near the present junction of Rutherford avenue and Dunstable street) to Cambridge street, Sept. 9, 1867; "the north-east line of which public street will be a continuation from Cambridge street to Richmond street of the south-west line of the place or way known as Canal street;" this 60-foot street laid out on a continuation of Richmond street, Sept. 30, 1867, but name of Richmond street appears not to have been commonly used; Canal street as laid out Sept. 9, 1867, discontinued Sept. 7, 1868, and laid out again by slightly altered plan, Oct. 26, 1868: name of Canal street extended over the portion of Richmond street between Austin street and former termination of Canal street June 16, 1874, both Richmond street and Canal street named Rutherford avenue, May 28, 1878. L 1216, L 1217, L 1218, L 1219.

Cannon street, Chsn., 1878; from Medford street, north, nearly opposite Monument street.

Canny place, B., 1883; from Webster avenue, north-east, between Unity street and Washington place; Webster court (1857–83), now so called.

***Canterbury street,** W. Rox., 1825; from Blue Hill avenue opposite Abbot street in an irregular line to Poplar street; named from Brush Hill turnpike, (now Blue Hill avenue) to Poplar street May 9, 1825; probably a public highway sometime previous, and Brush Hill avenue or turnpike, between Canterbury street and Seaver street, probably laid out over a part of the old street. L 2308, L 2500.

***Canton street,** B., 1826; laid out on the Neck from Tremont street to Washington street, July 24, 1826; named from Tremont street to Front street (now Harrison avenue), Sept. 15, 1834; reaching to Albany street on the extension of that street to Roxbury line, April 21, 1855; accepted Dec. 7, 1857; from Tremont street about 170 feet west to Water Power Company's line, accepted Dec. 21, 1859; laid out from Harrison avenue to Albany street, Oct. 30, 1860; whole street accepted, Oct. 30, 1860; part west of Tremont street called (without authority), Hawthorne street and signs bearing that name ordered to be removed, Aug. 30, 1864; laid out from Tremont street to Warren avenue, May 21, 1867; from Washington street to Albany street named East Canton street and from Washington street to Warren avenue named West Canton street, April 21, 1868. L 50.

Canton-street court, B., 1840; from West Canton (formerly Canton) street, north, between Washington street and Shawmut avenue.

Canton-street place, B., 1844; from West Canton (formerly Canton) street, south, between Washington street, and Shawmut avenue, nearly opposite Canton-street court.

Capen place, B., 1846–57; from Hanover street, south, between Elm street and Union street, closed.

Capen street, Dor., from Freeport street to Preston street; shown in 1870, authority to open from Ashland street to Freeport street, given by Street Commissioners, Dec. 7, 1895.

†**Capen street**, Dor., 1871; from Norfolk street to Fairmount street; laid out from Norfolk street to Evans street Nov. 6, 1890. L 2268.

Cardington street, Rox., 1893; from Cobden street, north-east, to an unnamed passageway; authority to open given by Street Commissioners, Feb. 6, 1893.

Carey court, Chsn., 1893; from Maudlin street to Water street; called Battery lane, 1714; described as running from Maudlin street and called Carriggs court, 1854; called Carey street, 1875.

Carey place, Chsn., from High street, north-east, then south-east, between Bolton place and Sullivan street; shown as an unnamed place, 1861; sometimes called Cary place.

***Carey street**, Chsn., 1875; from Maudlin street to Water street; Carriggs court (early called Battery lane, and now Carey court), so called in 1875.

Carl street, W. Rox.; from Corey street, south-west, to and beyond Park street; laid out and extended to Mount Vernon street under the name of Montview street, Nov. 17, 1893; part of at an earlier date known as Walnut avenue.

Carleton avenue, } **Carleton place,** } Dor.; from Harvard street to Park street; Carleton street (formerly Carleton avenue), so called, 1874; now Kilton street.

Carleton street, B., 1868; adjoining and parallel with the B. & P., now N. Y., N. H. & H. R.R., from Yarmouth street to West Chester park (now Massachusetts avenue), except where the streets running north-west from Columbus avenue to the railroad cross and intercept it; laid out from West Chester park to West Newton street, Dec. 31, 1870, but order for laying out afterwards declared defective; portion of part between Wellington street and West Chester park now built over. L 502, L 516.

Carleton street, } **Carlton street,** } Dor.; from Crescent avenue to Mount Vernon street. at crossing of O. C. (now N. Y., N. H. & H.) R.R; shown as an unnamed street, 1860; laid out and name changed to Carson street, Jan. 5, 1887. L 1970.

***Carlisle street**, Rox., 1883; from Warren street, east, between Gaston street and Holborn (formerly Hayward) street; private way called Roslin street laid out as Carlisle street, Sept. 20, 1883. L 1732.

Carlisle street, So. B., 1877; from Locust street to Mount Vernon street between Von Hillern street and Richardson avenue (proposed); shown without name in 1874.

Carlisle street, Dor.; from Welles avenue to Centre street; shown as extending from Welles avenue, north, in 1874; extended about 204 feet to Centre street, 1880.

Carlos street, Dor.; from Lauriat avenue to Chapman avenue; authority to open given by Street Commissioners, Sept. 14, 1894.

Carlton avenue, Dor., 1860; from Harvard street to Park street; called Carleton avenue, and Carleton place, in 1874; Carleton street, 1884; now Kilton street.

Carlton court, Rox.; from Vernon street, opposite Simmons street, north-east.

Carlton place, B., 1838; from Eliot street, south, between Warren (now Warrenton) street and Tremont street; called Eliot court, 1829–38; now built over.

Carlton street, Dor., 1884; from Harvard street to Park street; called Carlton avenue, 1860; Carleton avenue and Carleton place, 1874; now Kilton street.

Carnes court, B., 1767; from Ann street.

Carnes court, } B., from Hawkins street, south-west; called Carnes
Carnes place, } court, 1820; Carnes place, 1836.

Carnes street, Chsn., 1870; from Alford street, east, to Everett line; opened on old almshouse estate, April 24, 1850; laid out through portion of almshouse estate from the highway to Everett line and named Carnes street, Oct. 25, 1870; called Dexter street, 1896.

***Carney place**, B., 1831; from Washington street to Shawmut avenue; laid out Oct. 1, 1870; name changed to Waterford street, Nov. 8, 1871. L 545, L 562.

†**Carolina avenue**, W. Rox., 1849; from South street, crossing Call street to B. & P. (now N. Y., N. H. & H.) R.R. opposite Williams street; from South street to Roanoke avenue over what are now Carolina avenue and Newbern street; part from junction with Newbern street to Starr (now Call) street called Child street, 1850; part of Newbern street so called, 1861; altered, extended and constructed from South street to B. & P. R.R., including Child street, March 10, 1873.

Carolina place, W. Rox.; from Carolina avenue, nearly opposite John A. Andrew street, south-west.

***Carpenter street**, So. B.; from Preble street to Hyde street; formerly called Ceylon street; laid out, Nov. 28, 1887. L 2039.

Carriggs court, Chsn., 1854–83; from Maudlin street to Water street; called Battery lane, 1714; called Carey street, 1875; called Carey court, 1883.

Carriggs court, Chsn., 1883; from Ice court, north-east; shown in 1884 as extending from Water street, north-west, between Carey court and Wapping street in position of court called Ice court.

Carroll place, 1834; from Salem street, west, between Baldwin place and Cooper street.

Carroll's court, Chsn., from Beacham street, near corner of Arlington avenue, north-west.

***Carruth street**, Dor., 1869; from Ashmont street to Codman street; laid out, Aug. 12, 1869. L 976.

***Carson street**, Dor., 1887; from Crescent avenue to Mt. Vernon street at crossing of O. C. (now N. Y., N. H. & H.) R. R. called Carleton or Carlton street, 1860; laid out as Carson street, Jan. 5, 1887. L 1970.

Cart lane, B., 1733; from Leverett street, east; called Minot street, 1825.

Carter place, B., 1874; from Charter street, north-east, between Jackson avenue and Foster street; called Dillaway place, 1840; Carter place, 1874.

Carter street, Dor., 1869; from Neponset turnpike (now avenue), west, crossing Train street; called Boutwell avenue, 1858, and shown as extending to Train street; called Boutwell street, 1874; laid out from Neponset avenue to Train street, and named Boutwell street, May 31, 1882.

Carter street, Chsn., from Cambridge street, near Somerville line, and nearly opposite Parker street, southerly, to Roland street; shown in 1884.

Carver place, [illegible] 1855; [illegible]m Carver street, east, south of and near Eliot street.

***Carver street**, B., 1803; from Boylston street to Pleasant street; part from Eliot street to Pleasant street called Haskins street, 1803–14; whole street from Pleasant street, north, to the burial-ground (Boylston street), 1817; confirmed as a public street, Sept. 15, 1834.

Cary place, Chsn.; from High street, north-east, then south-east, between Bolton place and Sullivan street; shown as unnamed place, 1861; sometimes called Carey place.

***Cary street**, Rox., 1875; from Ruggles street at junction with Culvert street to Tremont place (now Terry street); laid out, Dec. 20, 1875; discontinued, Jan. 4, 1895. L 1120, L 1291, L 2684.

Cary street, W. Rox., 1866; from Forest Hills avenue to Union terrace.

Caspar street, Dor., from Weld street to Lasell street; authority to open given by Street Commissioners, April 20, 1894.

†**Cass street**, W. Rox., 1849; from Centre street to Spring street, near Spring-street station; called "Granite (formerly Cass) street;" Granite street between Centre street and Powell street laid out and name changed to Cass street, Dec. 10, 1883. L 1748.

Castle Court, E. B.; from Everett street, north-east, between Lamson street and Doherty court.

***Castle street**, B., 1722; from Washington street to Tremont street; from Orange (now Washington) street, east to the harbor, and west to Cambridge bay, formed the part, from Charles river to Front street (now Harrison avenue), "which goes through the dock," built in the manner of a timber wharf covered with gravel and railed at both sides, in 1817; parts on corresponding sides of Orange street seem to have been called also East and West Castle streets from an early date; West Castle street (from Washington street to Tremont street) named Castle street, June 23, 1874; East Castle street named Motte street, June 23, 1874. L 524, L 546, L 547, L 563, L 566, L 727, L 837, L 838, L 1349.

Castle Rock street, Dor., 1895; from Grampian way to Woodland avenue; authority to open given by Street Commissioners, Oct. 7, 1895.

***Castle square**, B., 1894: open space at the junction of Chandler street with Ferdinand street and Tremont street; named Castle Square, June 8, 1894.

Castleton street, W. Rox., 1895; from Jamaicaway to point 100 feet south-east of Catalpa street; authority to open given by Street Commissioners, Jan. 5, 1895.

Catalpa street, W. Rox., 1895; from Perkins street, north, crossing Castleton street; authority to open given by Street Commissioners, Jan. 5, 1895.

***Catawba street**, Rox., 1854; from Laurel street to Sherman street; laid out, Sept. 7, 1871. L 686.

***Catherine street**, W. Rox., 1893; from Bourne street to Florence street; formerly called Spruce street; laid out, Dec. 28, 1893. L 2579.

Cathedral court, Rox.; from Washington street, south-east, then south-west to and beyond Cathedral street, 1884.

Cathedral street, Rox.; from Fenwick street, north-west, to Cathedral court, 1884.

***Causeway street**, B., 1807; from Leverett street to Charles-River bridge at Prince street; from Leverett street to the causeway, shown, 1722; called Mill alley, 1733; Mill street, 1788; part near Leverett street also at times called Walder street; called Causeway street and laid out into the Mill pond, 1807; extended to the foot of Charlestown street, 1819; the portion near Leverett street called Merrimac street by Hale's plan, 1819; accepted, Dec. 11, 1826. Vol. 31, p. 68. L 165, L 280, L 2535.

***Cazenove place,** } B., 1871; from Chandler street to Columbus
***Cazenove street,** } avenue; leading from Chandler street towards B. & A. R.R., named Cazenove place, Sept. 12, 1871; laid out, Oct. 15, 1874; extended to Columbus avenue, Sept. 23, 1878; named Cazenove street, March 1, 1882. L 973, L 1318.

Cedar avenue, Dor., 1836; from Bowdoin street to Union avenue (now Olney street, formerly Love Lane avenue).

Cedar avenue, W. Rox., 1870; from Lamartine street to Oakdale street; shown from Lamartine street to Nebraska street (now Chestnut avenue), but not named in 1848; part from Lamartine street to Oak place (now Oaklale street) shown in 1870; part from Chestnut avenue to Lamartine street laid out with name of Bell street, Oct. 23, 1888. L 2098.

Cedar lane, B., 1826; from Chestnut street, north, near Charles street; from Chestnut street to Mt. Vernon street, 1830; called Chestnut place, 1839; Chestnut avenue, 1863.

Cedar park, Rox.; from Cedar street, near corner of Highland street, south-west, to meet Highland Park street.

***Cedar place,** Dor.; from junction Monadnock street and Bird street, westerly, 1884. L 1552, L 2208.

Cedar place, Dor., 1869; from Quincy street to Lawrence avenue; called also Cedar street; now called Mascoma street.

Cedar square, Rox.; the enclosure between Cedar street, Thornton street, an unnamed street and Juniper street; formerly the name was applied to a private way of irregular shape and as new streets were extended through it, the name was applied to the enclosure.

Cedar square, Rox., formerly a private way running north-east from Cedar street by two branches, one either side of the square, so called, the westerly of which extended past the square with a branch to the east along the north side of the square; the easterly branch from Cedar street extended northward with an opening into Shawmut avenue (now Washington street) and another opening into Guild street; shown but not named, 1835–44; part of same included in extension of Thornton street to Guild street, Dec. 10, 1881, and part in Juniper street, same date. L 1578, L 1580.

Cedar-square avenue, Rox., 1870; from Shawmut avenue (now Washington street) westerly about 150 feet, then southerly towards Cedar square and parallel with Shawmut avenue (now Washington street); part parallel with Washington street now part of Juniper street.

Cedar street, B.; see South Cedar street and West Cedar street.

***Cedar street,** Rox., 1835; from Washington street to Pynchon street (now Columbus avenue), and from N. Y., N. H. & H. R.R. to Terrace street; from Dedham turnpike (now Washington street) to Centre street, 1835; road from Centre street, opposite Cedar street, to Lowell street (afterward Pynchon street, now Columbus avenue), accepted and named Cedar street, Sept. 13, 1844; from Highland street to Centre street accepted, conditionally, Sept. 3, 1855; same part accepted, June 28, 1858; from Shawmut avenue (now Washington street) to Highland street accepted, conditionally, Sept. 27, 1858; whole street accepted, July 30, 1860; formerly extended across the B. & P. (now N.Y., N.H. & H.) R.R., to Terrace street, but was not a public way and is now discontinued.

Cedar street, Rox.; from Francis (formerly Longwood) street to Elm street (now Longwood avenue); Bellevue street, so called, 1850–57.

Cedar street, Dor.; from Quincy street to Lawrence avenue; Cedar place sometimes so called; now Mascoma street.

†Cedar street, Dor., 1853; from River street, north-west, to Manchester street, accepted, June 15, 1853. L 1587.

Cedar street, W. Rox., 1872; from Washington street, near corner of Beech street to Bellevue avenue.

***Cedar street**, Chsn., 1862; from High street to Bartlett street; shown as an unnamed street in 1839; accepted, Oct. 20, 1862; laid out and widened, June 29, 1863; continued and laid out between Laurel street and Bartlett street, March 29, 1870.

Cedar street, Bri., 1840; from Cambridge street to Brookline, crossing Avenue (now Beacon) street; named, June 15, 1840; name changed to South Harvard street, Nov. 10, 1846; called Harvard avenue, Dec. 30, 1873.

Cedar-street court, } **Cedar-street place,** } B., 1831, from South Cedar (now Winchester) street east; called Cedar-street court, 1831; Cedar-street place, 1840; South Cedar-street place, 1857.

Cemetery lane or street, Dor.; from Norfolk street, north, along the east side of the Catholic cemetery; shown as an unnamed lane, 1838; called Cemetery street, 1872; at one time connected with Warner avenue, and late a part of, probably made a part of Bernard street; also called Burying-place lane.

Center street, } **Centre street,** } B., 1773; from Hanover street to North street; from Ann (now North) street, north-west, called Ball's alley and Penaway's alley previous to 1708; Paddy's alley, 1708; Center street, 1773; named by Selectmen from Ann street, north of the bridge, into Middle (now Hanover) street, 1788; called North Centre street, but no record of naming.

Central avenue, Rox., 1855; from junction of Blue Hill avenue and Warren street, east; sometimes called Centre avenue; now built over.

***Central avenue**, Dor., 1875; from River street to Neponset river; laid out to meet street of like name in Milton, Nov. 13, 1875. L 1092.

Central avenue, W. Rox., 1872; from Washington street, near Cedar street, north-west; laid out as Cornell street, Aug. 7, 1890. L 2256.

Central bridge, B., 1809; Craigie's bridge, sometimes so called.

Central court, B., 1805; from Washington street, east, near Summer street from Newbury (now Washington) street, east, then south, then west to Newbury street, 1816; the southerly entrance from Newbury street was called Deming's, Demming's, or D'Emming court, 1806–16; Avon place, 1824; built over.

Central court, Bri.; at junction of Market street; given as one of the bounds of Lincoln street in order for acceptance of that street, June 13, 1873.

Central place, B., 1842; from Winter street to Music Hall; name changed to Music Hall place, Feb. 25, 1874.

Central place, Chsn.; from Main street, near Devens street, south-west.

***Central square**, E. B., 1833; at junction of Border street, Meridian street, Saratoga street, Bennington street, Porter street, Meridian street and Liverpool street; accepted, laid out according to metes and bounds in deed from East Boston Company to City of Boston and named, Nov. 10, 1851; part accepted, July 12, 1852. Vol. 31, p. 34. Vol. 31, p. 43.

Central square, Rox., 1860; open space lying between the P. O., Guild's buildings, Soren's block and land formerly of Amos Stevens; so named, Dec. 31, 1860.

***Central street**, B., 179–; from Kilby street to Atlantic avenue; existed as a 40-foot passageway from Kilby street down what was then known as Central wharf nearly to the present Broad street, 179–; extended by Broad street, east, across Broad street to India street, 1806; confirmed as a public street, Sept. 15, 1834; opened by Central Wharf and Wet Dock Corporation along south side of State-street block, 18—; accepted, conditionally, for a distance of 458 feet, east, from street running between Custom House and State-street block, April 13, 1858; part from India street to west end of State-street block accepted, conditionally, June 1, 1858; extended to Atlantic avenue, Aug. 16, 1876. L 134, L 853, L 1163.

Central street, W. Rox.; from Centre street to Central station of N.Y., N. H. & H. R.R., 1884.

Central street. Bri.; Centre (now Lincoln) street; so called in 1851 and 1872.

Central wharf, B.: from India street, easterly, across Atlantic avenue; from the east side of Atlantic avenue there are two entrances to the wharf proper, the northern one being in continuation of Central street. L 1001.

Centre avenue, Rox.: from junction of Blue Hill avenue and Warren street; Central avenue, sometimes so called; now built over.

*__Centre avenue__, Dor., 1869; from Dorchester avenue to Centre street; laid out, Aug. 12, 1869.

Centre court, Dor.; from Centre street, near Adams street, north.

Centre place, So. B.; from Preble street, nearly opposite Ward street, south; to Hyde street, 1884.

Centre place, Rox., 1867; from Centre street, near Gardner street, north-west.

Centre place, Dor.; from Centre street, north, near junction with Remington street.

Centre place, W. Rox.; from Centre street, near Green street, south-east, to Warren square.

Centre street, B., 1800; from Cambridge street, crossing May (now Myrtle) street to the rope-walks; extended to Pinckney street, 1833; name changed to Anderson street, May 21, 1861; also called West Centre street.

Centre street, E. B., 1864; from Orleans street to Marginal street; accepted, conditionally, Jan. 25, 1864; name changed to Haynes street, April 21, 1868.

Centre street, So. B.; from Dorchester street to Preble street; name changed to Ward street, Aug. 7, 1855.

*__Centre street__, Rox. and W. Rox., 1825; from Eliot square to Dedham line; that part of this street lying in Roxbury, and to South street in West Roxbury, laid out, Jan. 19, 1662; called the Middlepost-road from Boston to Hartford; altered from Colonel Draper's through Dedham to Dover line, May, 1795; called "Old road to Dedham," 1823; "Road from the parting stone by J. Riley's store, by Rev. Mr. Gray's meeting-house, by Captain Winchester's to Rev. Mr. Flagg's meeting-house, and on to Dedham line;" named Centre street, May 9, 1825; called Boston road, 1833; name of part in West Roxbury changed to Austin street, May 3, 1852; name of Austin street changed to original name of Centre street, Dec. 2, 1861. L 373, L 1041, L 1138, L 1145, L 1588, L 1595, L 1757, L 1758, L 1955, L 2037, L 2140.

*__Centre street__, Dor., 1837; from Washington street, opposite Norfolk street, to Adams street; mistake in location (road from Plymouth road to Lower road) rectified, April, 1804; named from Upper road (now Washington street) to Lower road (now Adams street), March 11, 1840. L 584, L 969, L 2758, L 2787, L 2788.

Centre street, Bri., 1846; from Cambridge street to Everett street; called Central street, 1851 and 1872; now Lincoln street.

Centry Field, B.; the Common for a long time so called; called also Training field.

Centry or Sentry hill, B., 1708; Beacon hill, then so called; also Century or Centuary Hill.

Centry street, } B., 1708; the highway leading north from Beacon
Centrey street, } street, between Captain Alford's land and Madam Shrimpton's pasture to Centry hill (to the head of the former Temple street), laid open and named Centrey street, May, 1708; an order for continuance to lie open was passed, April 25, 1709; called Century street in list, 1732; from Common (now Tremont) street to Beacon hill, 1784; from Granary on Common street to almshouse on Beacon street, 1800; the part north-west from Beacon street called Sumner (now Mt. Vernon) street, 1800; the part from Common street to Beacon street named Park street, 1803; a part of Sudbury street and a part of Court street once so called; also spelled Sentry.

Centurie-hill street, B., a part of Queen (now Court) street was once so called.

Century street, B.; Centry street, so called in list of 1732.

Cerwithy's corner, 1708; corner Prince street and Salem street was then so called.

Ceylon street, So. B.; from Preble street to Hyde street; from Preble street, south, 1874; laid out and name changed to Carpenter street, Nov. 28, 1887. L 2039.

***Ceylon street**, Dor., 1873; from Quincy street to Bird street; laid out, Nov. 22, 1873. L 912.

Chadwick court, Rox.; from Chadwick street, near Orchard park, south-east.

Chadwick place, Rox., 1872; from Chadwick street, north-west.

***Chadwick street**, Rox., 1868; from Hampden street to Hartopp place (now Ambrose street) at junction with Trask place (now Orchard-park street); name of Eaton street from Hampden (formerly East) street to Yeoman street changed to Chadwick street, April 21, 1868; laid out through Trask place from Yeoman street to Orchard Park, May 24, 1870; extended to Hartopp place (now Ambrose street), Dec. 31, 1870. L 529.

Chair alley, B.; from Cross street to Richmond street, between Fulton street and Commercial street.

***Chamberlain street**, Dor.; from Algonquin street, north, to Harvard street, nearly opposite Harvard avenue; authority to open given by Street Commissioners, March 24, 1893; laid out July 10, 1896. L 2776.

***Chambers street,** } B.; from Cambridge street to Charles street; the
Chamber street, } third of three streets leading from Cambridge street to Green street, so called in 1732; from Cambridge street, northerly, by the marsh to Mr. Allen's house; so named by Selectmen, July 4, 1788; from Cambridge street to Green street, 1800; extended over Wiltshire street to Poplar street, Sept. 18, 1811; portion formerly called Wiltshire street together with Gravel street (from Poplar street to Leverett street) accepted and named Chambers street, May 26, 1828; part formerly Gravel street named Ashland street, Feb. 22, 1845; but the name Ashland street has been commonly applied only to the part running at right angles to Leverett street; extended to Spring street, through Spring-street place, Jan 6, 1872; extended from Spring street to Brighton street, June 7, 1893; name of Livingston street from Brighton street to Charles street, changed to Chambers street, March 1, 1894. L 579, L 732, L 2519, L 2765.

***Chambers street**, Chsn., 1780; from City square to Water street; laid out 30 feet wide from Russell's and Odin's land to New Fore (now Water) street, 1780; laid out by a committee by order of Town after the fire, Dec. 23, 1835. L 1974.

Chambers-street court, B., 1828; from Chambers street, west, near Cambridge street.

Chamblet street, Dor.; from Hartford street to Magnolia street; formerly called Robert avenue; authority to open from Magnolia street to Hartford street given by Street Commissioners, Nov. 17, 1892.

Champney court, } B., 1834; from Anderson street, near Revere street,
Champney place, } west.

Champney court, So. B.; from Champney street, south-west, to N.Y., N. H. & H. R.R.

Champney place, Rox.; from Madison street south-west, then south-east, parallel with Madison street, nearly to Washington street.

Champney street, So. B., 1859; from Lowland (formerly Highland, now Mercer) street, north-west, to O. C. (now N. Y., N. H. & H.) R.R., then north-east to Newman street; shown on plan, 1860.

Champney street, Bri.; from Washington street to Stratton street.

***Chandler street**, B., 1866; from Tremont street to Columbus avenue; called avenue H on plan Back Bay lands; H street from Tremont street to Berkeley street conditionally accepted, Nov. 24, 1865; accepted and name changed to Chandler street, April 28, 1866; laid out from Berkeley street to Columbus avenue, Nov. 3, 1869. L 307, L 354.

***Change alley,** } B.; from State street to Market (now Faneuil Hall)
Change avenue, } square; called Pierce's alley, 1708; Change alley 1788; Fitche's alley, 1796; Flagg alley, 1828; named Change avenue, March 22, 1841. L 242, L 1765.

Channel street, Dor.; from Walnut street, south-east, to Neponset river (Neponset).

Channing place, B., 1852; from Leather square (formerly Sister street), east.

***Channing street**, B., 1845; from Federal street to Congress street; called Bury street, from Long lane to Atkinson street, 1708; Barrack lane, 1788; Berry street, 1803; named Channing street, July 14, 1845. L 834, L 835.

Chapel place (North), B., 1844; from Friend street, north, near Travers street.

Chapel place, B., 1859; from Albany street, west, near Harvard street.

Chapel place, B., 1837; from Washington street to Marlboro' chapel; Gillam or Gilman place, 1809; Chapel place, 1837; closed.

Chapel place, B.; from Friend street, between Travers street and Market street, north-east.

***Chapel street**, Rox.; from Milford place (now Sarsfield street) to Weston street; laid out, July 16, 1885; included in the extension of Columbus avenue, Jan. 4, 1895; a small portion not included in Columbus avenue discontinued on same date. L 1872, L 2683.

Chapel street, Rox. and W. Rox., 1867; from Boylston street to Wyman street, between Curtis street (now Chestnut avenue) and Lamartine street; shown as an unnamed street, 1856; name changed to Curtis street, June 22, 1878; named Danforth street, Sept. 12, 1881.

Chapin avenue, W. Rox., 1869; from La Grange street, north-east.

Chapman avenue, Dor.; from Blue Hill avenue, north-east, to Tucker street; parallel with Lauriat avenue.

***Chapman place**, B., 1841; from School street to Bosworth street; called Cook's court, 1733; Chapman place, 1841; reported to have been a public highway for many years, Dec. 24, 1846; extended to Montgomery place (now Bosworth street), Dec. 22, 1882. L 182, L 1675, L 1712.

Chapman place, Chsn.; from Chapman street, between Rutherford avenue and Washington street, south-east; shown but not named in 1846.

***Chapman street,** B., 1852; from Washington street to Tremont street; laid out, including Killam place, Jan. 3, 1852; named, May 24, 1852; extended from Tremont street to Chandler street, Aug. 20, 1860; same portion discontinued (except the part taken by the extension of Appleton street), Sept. 16, 1872; name of part between Tremont street and Washington street changed to Compton street, March 1, 1895. Vol. 31, pp. 18, 19. Vol. 19, p. 124. L 56, L 190, L 197, L 544, L 545, L 720, L 728, L 764.

***Chapman street,** Chsn., 1846; from Main street to Washington street at junction with Austin street; shown but not named, 1844; shown from Washington street to Richmond street, May 2, 1846; laid out from Main street to Lawrence street, Jan. 2, 1851; laid out and accepted from Lawrence street to Austin street, Dec. 18, 1854; widened over lands and flats of Commonwealth, June 29, 1863.

Chardon court, B., 1874; from Chardon street, south-east; called Chardon-street place, 1841; Grant place, 1866; Chardon court, 1874.

Chardon court, } **Chardon place,** } B.; from Chardon street, north; called Chardon place, 1840; Chardon court, 1842; Chardon-street court, 1849; closed.

***Chardon street,** B., 1821; from Bowdoin square to Merrimac street at junction with Portland street; from Bowdoin square to the present Hawkins street was a part of Hawkins street in 1743; called Chardon's lane in 1795 and probably in 1784; Chardon street in 1821; made part of Ivers street (which then extended from Bowdoin square to Merrimac street), Dec. 30, 1859; whole street renamed Chardon street, May 21, 1860. Vol. 31, p. 81–89. L 92.

Chardon-street court, B., 1849; from Chardon street, north; called Chardon place, 1840; Chardon court, 1842; Chardon-street court, 1849; closed.

Chardon-street place, B.; from Chardon street, north-west, now built over.

Chardon-street place, B., 1841; from Chardon street, south-east; Grant place, 1866; Chardon court, 1874.

Chardon's lane, B., 1795; from bottom of Hawkins street, southerly, to Lyman's (*i.e.*, corner Cambridge street); part of Hawkins street prior to 1795; called Chardon's lane in 1795, and probably as early as 1784; called Chardon street (from Hawkins street to Bowdoin square), 1821.

Charles place, So. B.; from Foundry street, near Swan street, south-east; closed; in territory taken by O. C. R.R. by authority of Acts of Legislature of 1893.

Charles place, Chsn.; from Charles street, south-east; shown but not named in 1844; also called Charles-street place.

***Charles street,** B., 1805; from Boylston street, opposite Park square to Leverett street; permission to form and complete 100 feet of new street from Pleasant street to Beacon street parallel with the rope-walks granted, July 6, 1803; laid out from Beacon street to Cambridge bridge, 1805; from Boylston street to Cambridge street, 1809; in 1817 said street extended from the west end of Beacon street to West Boston bridge; accepted as a public street, Sept. 15, 1834; from Livingston street, south-west, 1841; extended from jail land to Allen street, July 31, 1855; North Charles street extended from Allen street to bend in street north of Poplar street, June 12, 1857; extended from Livingston street to Leverett street, Nov. 5, 1858; the street extending from Cambridge street to Leverett street, laid out in 1855 and 1857 in parts as "Charles street extended" and "North Charles street;" named Charles street, Feb. 13, 1866. L 45, L 97, L 170, L 175, L 178, L 202, L 278, L 935, L 1439.

Charles street, Rox.; from Bumstead lane (now St. Alphonsus street) to B. & P. (now N. Y., N. H. & H.) R.R.; name changed to Ward street, April 21, 1868.

***Charles street,** Dor., 1874; from Dorchester avenue to Geneva avenue; laid out from Dorchester avenue to Ditson street, Aug. 3, 1874; extended to Geneva avenue, Aug. 27, 1884. L 954, L 1809.

Charles street, W. Rox.; from Spring street, near Dedham line, south-east, then south.

Charles street, W. Rox., 1872; from Poplar street, nearly opposite Dale street to Kittredge street; included in the laying out of Cornell street, from Poplar street to Washington street, June 24, 1892.

***Charles street,** Chsn., 1850; from Main street to Bunker Hill street; name of School-house street changed to Charles street, Sept 30, 1850.

Charlesbank, B., 1889; the name of the park between Craigie's bridge and W. Boston bridge from Charles street, west, to Charles river; named, Aug. 9, 1889; previously called Charles-river Embankment.

Charlesgate, B.; the name of the parkway south-west of Massachusetts avenue, extending from Charles river to Back Bay Fens.

Charlesgate, east, B., 1887; name of the street extending from Charles river to B. & A. R.R. along the easterly side of the Charlesgate; named, Dec. 30, 1887; at one time it was proposed to name this street Ipswich street. L 1515.

Charlesgate, west, B., 1887; name of the street extending from Charles river to Boylston road along the westerly side of the Charlesgate; named, Dec. 30, 1887; at one time it was proposed to name this street Jersey street. L 1515.

***Charles-river avenue,** Chsn.; from City square to Charles-river bridge; shown, but not named, 1841.

***Charles-river bridge,** B. and Chsn., 1785; from foot of Prince street at Causeway street to Charles-river avenue, 1839; called also Charlestown bridge; this was the first bridge built in Boston.

Charles-river Embankment, B.; former name of the park between Craigie's bridge and West Boston bridge from Charles street, west, to Charles river; now called Charlesbank.

Charles-street place, Chsn., 1843; from Charles street, south; also called Charles place.

Charlestown bridge, B. and Chsn., 1785; from foot of Prince street to Charles-river avenue; called also Charles-river bridge.

Charlestown ferry, B. and Chsn.; upon nearly the same site as the bridge until 1786. (The date of the bridge was 1785.)

Charlestown square, Chsn., 1803; in front of City Hall; name changed to City square, Jan. 17, 1848.

***Charlestown street,** B., 1806; from Haymarket square to Causeway street; laid out from Charles-river bridge across Mill-pond and to Middle (now Hanover) street, May 26, 1806; street accepted, Dec. 11, 1826; said to have extended from Haymarket square to Causeway street in 1840; part of included in Haymarket square, April 21, 1845. L 1039.

Charlotte street, Dor., 1896; from Blue Hill avenue to Bradshaw street; authority to open from Old Road to Bradshaw street given by Street Commissioners, June 16, 1896.

***Charter street,** B., 1708; from Hanover street, north-west, to Commercial street; from North (now Hanover) street running by the north side of Copp's hill burying-ground towards Charlestown ferry, 1708; to the ferry-way, 1732; to Lynn (now Commercial) street, 1803. Vol. 31, p. 60. Vol. 31, p. 71.

***Chatham row**, B., 1829; from State street to Chatham street; laid out, May 9, 1827; called Portland street, 1842; named Chatham row, March 18, 1829; at some time called Butler row; renamed Chatham row, July 3, 1848.

***Chatham street**, B., 1827; from Merchant's row to Commercial street; part of called Butler's row, 1789; laid out from Merchant's row to Commercial street, March, 1825; named, Jan. 15, 1827.

***Chaucer street**, E. B., 1838; from Pope street to Moore street; accepted, Dec. 10, 1861. L 247.

Chauncey place, B., 1809; in front of First church, Summer street, 1809; street laid out from Summer street to Bedford street, through Chauncey place and Bedford place, Jan. 3, 1856; same named Chauncey street, Jan. 5, 1856. L 62.

Chauncy place, W. Rox., 1857; from Washington street, opposite Boylston street, south-east.

Chauncy place, Chsn.; from Decatur street to Moulton street, shown but not named, 1850; shown from Decatur street to Fremont place, 1892.

***Chauncey street**, B., 1856; from Summer street to Essex street; continuous highway laid out from Summer street, through Chauncey place and Bedford place, to Bedford street, Jan. 3, 1856; same named Chauncey street, Jan. 5, 1856; extended through Rowe street to Essex street, April 15, 1856. L 62, L 72, L 430, L 840, L 1598, L 1973, L 2202, L 2203.

Cheapside, B., 1816; from Tremont street to Brattle alley; laid out and so named, March 5, 1816; street from Court street to the market named Market street, June 11, 1817; sometimes called New Cornhill from Court street to Washington street; named Cornhill, May 6, 1829.

Checkley's entry, B., 1732; corner Ann street and Scottow's alley; then so called.

Cheever court, E. B.; from Sumner street, near Webster avenue, south-west.

Cheever's corner, B., 1800; corner Cambridge street and Staniford street, then so called.

Chelsea avenue, E. B. (Breed's Island); from Saratoga street, at junction with Ford street, to Eastern division of B. & M. R.R.

Chelsea bridge; from Chelsea street, Charlestown, to Broadway, Chelsea.

Chelsea court, E. B.; from Chelsea street, between Porter street and Marion street, north-west.

Chelsea ferry, B , from foot of Hanover street to Chelsea; called also Winnisimmet ferry.

Chelsea Free bridge; formerly from East Boston to Chelsea; at an early date belonged to "Proprietors of Chelsea Point bridge;" so much as lay in Boston laid out, July 1, 1851.

Chelsea place, E. B.; from Chelsea street between Porter street and Decatur street, north-west.

***Chelsea place**, Chsn., 1860; from Chelsea street to Water street; formerly a private way; portion from Water street about half-way to Chelsea street, laid out, May 22, 1860; remainder laid out, Nov. 25, 1867; name changed to Hudson street, Feb. 6, 1871.

***Chelsea street**, B., 1826; from Shawmut avenue to Tremont street; laid out west of Tremont street, July 24, 1826; named from Tremont street to Suffolk street (now Shawmut avenue), Sept. 15, 1834; name changed to Upton street, April 2, 1857.

***Chelsea street**, E. B., 1833; from Maverick square to Chelsea bridge; from Maverick street to Decatur street, laid out and accepted, May 6, 1850; from Decatur street to Chelsea Free bridge, one-half the width, accepted, May 27, 1850; so much as was not accepted in 1850, laid out as a public highway, Nov. 29, 1852; from Decatur street to Chelsea Free bridge, whole width accepted, June 3, 1856; accepted at junction Bennington street, and at junction Princeton street, Nov. 1, 1858; at junction Saratoga street, Sept. 13, 1859. L 971, L 1653.

***Chelsea street**, Chsn., 1833; from City square to Chelsea bridge; known as Salem turnpike, 1818; laid out as a new street, near site of the fire, to take the place of Gill street (Gill street discontinued) from south-east corner of the square to Joiner street, Dec. 7, 1835; laid out by County Commissioners, March 1, 1836; to be laid out, etc., by Town before May 1, 1837; laid out as a public highway from junction with Mt. Vernon street to Vine street, Sept. 7, 1863. L 2156.

Chelsea-street bridge; from Chelsea street, East Boston, to Marginal street, Chelsea.

Chemical avenue, W. Rox., 1870; from Washington street, between Boylston street and Green street to Brookside avenue; shown in 1843–49, from Dedham turnpike (now Washington street) to Laboratory, but not named; shown on plan in 1870 as "avenue," and in accompanying deed called "Brookside or Chemical avenue;" laid out as a public street and name changed to Cornwall street, June 24, 1886. L 1913.

***Cheney street**, Rox., 1882; from Blue Hill avenue to Elm Hill avenue; private way called Mt. Seaver avenue laid out from Elm Hill avenue to Montana street, as Cheney street, June 26, 1882; extended to Blue Hill avenue, April 11, 1883. L 1617, L 1697.

Cherokee street, Rox.; from Hillside street north-east, then north-west to Pontiac street.

Cherry court, Rox.; from Cherry street, south-east; shown, but not named, 1884.

Cherry place, Rox.; from Tremont street, north-east, between Phillips street and Faxon street; now Sherbrooke place.

***Cherry street**, B., 1837; from Washington street, near Chapman street, to Shawmut avenue; laid out, Dec. 16, 1870. L 545, L 562, L 728.

***Cherry street**, Rox., 1853; from Quincy street, north-east, crossing Dove street; laid out, Sept. 29, 1874; name of Cherry street changed to Dacia street, March 1, 1892. L 964, L 2358.

***Cheshire street**, W. Rox., 1881; from Green street, north-east, near Lamartine street; private way, called Walnut place, laid out as Cheshire street, May 2, 1881. L 1521, L 2210.

Chessman place, B., 1842; from Hanover street, north-west, near Parmenter (formerly Richmond) street.

Chester avenue, B.; see East and West Chester avenue.

***Chester park**, B., 1858; from Washington street to Albany street; from South Bay to Boston Water Power Company's land named Chester Park, June 22, 1858; part east of Harrison avenue named East Chester park, Nov. 16, 1858; from Shawmut avenue to Tremont street named Chester square, Dec. 29, 1858; from Tremont street, west, to Boston Water Power Company's land called West Chester park and so accepted, Dec. 21, 1859; from Washington street to Shawmut avenue named Chester square, March 3, 1864; from Washington street to Albany street named East Chester park, April 27, 1869; East Chester park named East Chester avenue, July 13, 1869, and East Chester avenue named Chester park, April 5,

1870; name of East Chester park, Chester park, Chester square, and West Chester park changed to Massachusetts avenue, March 1, 1894. Vol. 31, p. 1.

Chester place, B., 1860; from Shawmut avenue, near Chester square, east, then south to Northampton street.

***Chester square,** B., 1857; from Washington street to Tremont street; the part of Chester street called Chester square accepted, Dec. 29, 1857; Chester street named Chester park, June 22, 1858; "so much of the street now known in the records of the City as Chester park between Shawmut avenue and Tremont street" named Chester square, Dec. 29, 1858; part of Chester park from Washington street to Shawmut avenue named Chester square, March 3, 1864; Chester square included in West Chester avenue, July 8, 1869; part of West Chester avenue from Tremont street to Shawmut avenue named Chester square, Oct. 5, 1869; part of West Chester avenue from Washington street to Shawmut avenue named Chester square, April 5, 1870; name of East Chester park, Chester park, Chester square, and West Chester park changed to Massachusetts avenue, March 1, 1894. Vol. 31, p. 1. L 98.

***Chester street,** B., 1826; from Washington street, west, 1826; named, Sept. 15, 1834; extended from south-east side of Harrison avenue to creek formerly the boundary line between Boston and Roxbury, with mall through same, April 11, 1853; part of Chester street incorrectly named Chester square in 1857; Chester street accepted, Dec. 7, 1857; name of Chester street from South Bay to Boston Water Power Company's land changed to Chester park, June 22, 1858; name of East Chester park, Chester park, Chester square, and West Chester park changed to Massachusetts av., March 1, 1894.

Chester street, Dor.; from Oakland street, near N. E. R.R., north-east, to near Blue Hill avenue.

***Chester street,** Bri., 1841; from Brighton avenue (formerly North Beacon street) to Ashford street; accepted, conditionally, Dec. 30, 1873; accepted, Sept. 16, 1876. L 1169.

Chesterfield street, Rox.; from Massachusetts avenue to Allerton street.

Chestnut avenue, B., 1863; from Chestnut street, near Charles street, to Mt. Vernon street; called Cedar lane, 1826; Chestnut place, 1839, Chestnut avenue, 1863; laid out as Malcom street, Dec. 16, 1891.

***Chestnut avenue,** W. Rox., 1877; from Green street to Centre street; part from Green street to Boylston street called Nebraska street, 1848; Chestnut street, 1857; part from Boylston street to Wyman street called Curtis street, 1852; both laid out as one street, and named Chestnut avenue, Dec. 26, 1877; Gilbert street, from Wyman street to Centre street, made part of Chestnut avenue, Feb. 6, 1886. L 1128, L 1499.

Chestnut court, Chsn.; from Chestnut street, near Chelsea street, north-west.

Chestnut grove, W. Rox.; from Centre street, opposite Pond street, south-east.

Chestnut knoll, Bri.; from Englewood avenue.

Chestnut park, Bri., 1870; private way, shown on plan Middlesex So. Reg. Lib. 1134, f. 641, but not named.

Chestnut place, B. 1839; from Chestnut street, near Charles street, to Mt. Vernon street; called Cedar lane, 1826; Chestnut place, 1839; Chestnut avenue, 1863.

Chestnut place, So. B., 1871; from B street, between West Fifth street and West Sixth street, to N. E. R.R.; named June 20, 1871.

Chestnut place, W. Rox.; 1870; from Chestnut avenue, near Spring Park avenue, north-west.

Chestnut square, W. Rox.; from Chestnut avenue, nearly opposite Chestnut place, south-east, then north-east; authority to open given by Street Commissioners August 26, 1896.

†**Chestnut street,** B., 1800; from Walnut street, parallel with Beacon street, across Brimmer street, nearly to Charles river; from Walnut street, west, to the water, 1800; extended to Charles street, Dec. 2, 1822; accepted, Dec. 31, 1827; extended toward Charles river, bounding west on a passageway, March 11, 1833; part west of Charles street accepted, conditionally, Aug. 7, 1855; from Charles street to Messinger (now Brimmer) street accepted, Aug. 25, 1857; recommendation for acceptance to sea-wall when street should be extended and graded by abutters and offered to the City, March 4, 1867. L 114, L 266, L 276.

***Chestnut street,** Rox., 1833; from Elm avenue (now Mt. Pleasant avenue), near junction of Dudley street and Dearborn street, to same at a point near Blue Hill avenue; accepted, May 11, 1840; name changed to Forest street, April 20, 1868.

Chestnut street, Dor.; from Eben I. Andrews to Dorchester turnpike, probably near Cottage street, and through land of Andrews; named, March 11, 1840; discontinued, March 14, 1853.

***Chestnut street,** W. Rox., 1860; from Perkins street, north, to Brookline line; laid out over part of Chestnut street and Pond lane from Perkins street to Washington, later Tremont street, and now Huntington avenue, Nov. 20, 1867; street laid out from point in Perkins street, near gate-house of Jamaica Pond Aqueduct, and running northerly to boundary line between West Roxbury and Brookline, at point where Chestnut street in Brookline meets the boundary, following nearly the same path or private way then existing, and same named Chestnut street, Nov. 20, 1867; shown as Pond avenue, 1874.

Chestnut street, W. Rox., 1852; from Green street to Boylston street; shown as Nebraska street, 1843–49; no record of change of name; laid out by Selectmen as Chestnut street (that evidently being its established name) and accepted by the Town, July 25, 1868; together with Curtis street, named Chestnut avenue, Dec. 26, 1877.

***Chestnut street,** Chsn., 1845; from Monument square to Chelsea street; part from Monument square, south-east, shown but not named, 1839; laid out from Adams street to Lexington street (Monument square), May 5 1845; name of Townsend street (from Adams street to Chelsea street) changed to Chestnut street, June 20, 1846. L 2492.

***Chestnut Hill avenue,** Bri., 1872; from Washington street, opposite Market street, to Brookline line; shown as "road" in 1843; named Rockland street from near Parish house, south, to South street and continued to Brookline line, 1840; name changed to Chestnut Hill avenue, Dec. 27, 1872. L 1573, L 1630, L 2720.

Chestnut Hill driveway, Bri.; from Commonwealth avenue, around the Chestnut Hill reservoir, to Beacon street.

***Chickatawbut street,** Dor.; from Neponset avenue to Glide street; from Neponset turnpike to Baptist meeting-house located, May 2, 1853; extended from the church to Plain street, March 2, 1868; extended again, March 1, 1869.

Chickering place, B., 1855; from Washington street, opposite Avery street to Harrison avenue; from Washington street, east, called Sweetser's alley, 1798; Sweetser's court, 1809; Chickering place, 1855; part included in extension of Harrison avenue, July 6, 1881.

***Child street,** W. Rox.; from South street to Call street; the Eastern end of Carolina avenue, from Newbern street to Starr (now Call) street, called Child street, 1850, and part of Child street, from Lee street to Starr street, called Jamaica street; latter street called

Child street, 1860; Carolina avenue extended to railroad over street formerly Child street, previous to 1873; Child street laid out from Call street to Leo street, Dec. 12, 1881: laid out from Leo street to South street, June 22, 1892. L 1582, L 2406.

Chilson place, B., 1844; from Lyman street, north; included in extension of Staniford street, May 11, 1886.

Chip street, Chsn.; from Moulton street to Medford street; laid out and accepted and name changed to Corey street, May 23, 1853.

Chipman street, Dor., 1870; from Norfolk street, opposite the cemetery, to Torrey street.

***Chiswick road,** Bri.; from Chestnut Hill avenue to Englewood avenue, laid out Nov. 13, 1895. L 2720, L 2742, L 2743, L 2744.

Choate street, B., 1846–53; from Pleasant street, near the Common; supposed to be what is now called Providence street.

Christian court, B., 1848; from Canal street, near Market street, southwest; now built over.

Church avenue, So. B.; from West Broadway, near E street, to Silver street.

Church court, Chsn; from Warren street, at Thompson square, northeast.

Church green, B ; vacant space at intersection of Bedford street and Summer street; early so called and sold to religious society in 1715. L 306.

Church lane, Bri.; from Cambridge street to Brighton avenue, near Union square.

Church place, B., 1844; from Church street, east, next south of Madison place; called Moore place, 1840; Church place, 1844; now closed.

Church place, B., 1896; from North Grove street, west; formerly called Davis court.

Church place, Rox., 1868; from Cabot street, nearly opposite Culvert street, south-east.

Church place, Dor.; from Washington street, near Centre street, east.

Church square, B., 1708; from Cornhill (now Washington street), nearly opposite King (now State) street, round the old meeting-house, or old brick church, 1708–1800; called Cornhill square, 1817; Cornhill court, 1834; now a part of Court avenue.

***Church street,** B , 1835; from Tremont street to Columbus avenue, and from Providence street to Boylston street; from Fayette street, north, across the B. & P. (now N. Y., N. H. & H.) R.R., with proposed extension to meet proposed extension of Boylston street, in 1835; extended north to Boylston street, 1846; accepted, May 24, 1852; extended from Fayette street, south, to Tremont street, through Lincoln court, June 24, 1852; portion adjoining estate of B & P. R.R. Corporation from Providence street to proposed extension of Columbus avenue discontinued, Nov. 10, 1871. Vol. 31, p. 40. Vol. 31, p. 49. Vol. 31, p. 52. L 60, L 387, L 391, L 392, L 393, L 394, L 613.

***Church street,** Dor., 1840; from Adams street at Eaton square to High street; from Captain Eaton's by Dr. Thaxter's and Mr. Colyer's so named, March 11, 1840; from Bowdoin street to Winter street, the rest of the street being called Highland street, 1874; part west of Adams street named Bowdoin street, March 1, 1882; laid out from Winter street to High street, Oct. 16, 1891. L 765, L 1010, L 1414, L 2349.

***Church street,** W. Rox., 1830; from Centre street, opposite South street, to Brookline line.

Church street, Bri., 1863; from Washington street to Mt. Vernon street; called also Cochran lane; called Worcester street in 1875; laid out with name of Eastburn street, June 11, 1886. L 1911.

Churchill place, Dor., from Washington street at Lower Mills, nearly opposite Richmond street, south-west.

Circuit place, Rox.; from Circuit street, south-west; Fenwick street laid out through it to Hulbert street, Jan. 14, 1884.

Circuit square, Rox.; from Circuit street, near corner of Regent street, south-west.

***Circuit street**, Rox., 1845; from Walnut avenue, westerly, to Regent street, thence northerly to Washington street; first shown running from Dedham turnpike (now Washington street) to Warren street; extended to Walnut street (now avenue) previous to 1858; laid out between Walnut avenue and Shawmut avenue (now Washington street), July 1, 1871; Walnut avenue afterwards opened through a part of Circuit street. L 634, L 635, L 636, L 637.

City court, B., 1822; from Fish (now North) street, west; called Mechanic street, 1825.

***City Hall avenue**, B., 1861; from School street to Court square; east side of City Hall; named, Dec. 31, 1861. L 1350.

City Point court, So. B.; from East First street, near O street, south.

City Point park, So. B.; east of Q street, between said street and the water; now called Marine Park.

***City square**, Chsn., 1848; at junction of Main, Park, Chelsea and Chamber streets, Charles-river avenue, Warren avenue, Bow and Harvard streets; shown but not named, 1838; formerly called Charlestown square; named City square, Jan. 17, 1848. L 1549, L 1815.

City wharf, B., 1855; from Commercial street, opposite South Market street, to the water; accepted, Aug. 6, 1855; named City wharf, Sept. 10, 1855; included in extension of South Market street to Atlantic avenue, April 2, 1872. Vol. 31, p. 47. L 46, L 1000.

Claflin place, B., 1834; from Pleasant street, west, near London (now Kirkland) street; a portion included in the extension of Shawmut avenue in 1870; the remainder later built over. L 549.

Claflin street, So. B.; from B street to E street, north-east of, and parallel with Mt. Washington avenue.

Clapboard street, B., 1795; from Olive (now Mt. Vernon) street, opposite Hancock street (now south part of Joy street), north, about to the present Pinckney street; Belknap (now Joy) street extended south from May (now Myrtle) street through Clapboard street across Olive street and thence through George (earlier Hancock) street to Beacon street, 1803; named Joy street, 1851.

Clapp place, Dor., 1851; from Boston street, south-east.

Clapp street, So. B., 1866; from West Seventh street to West Eighth street; laid out as a public street with name of Loring street, Aug. 27, 1884. L 1808.

†**Clapp street**, Dor. and Rox., 1870; from Boston street, north-west, then west crossing Oak street nearly to N. E. R.R.; laid out and accepted from Boston street to East Chester park (now Massachusetts avenue), Sept. 13, 1883. L 1730.

Clapp's building, B., Bulfinch place, so called in 1807.

Clap's corner, B., 1800; corner of Fish (now North) street and Proctor's lane (now Richmond street) then so called.

***Claremont park**, B., 1870; from Columbus avenue to B. & P. (now N. Y., N. H. & H.) R.R.; part of Worcester street, from Columbus avenue to B. & P. R.R., named Claremont park, Nov. 22, 1870. L 502, L 516.

Claremont street, B.; from Claremont park to West Rutland square; probably a part of Carleton street.

Clarence place, Rox., 1870; Clarence street from George street, south-west, so called.

Clarence place, Dor.; from Washington street to Whitfield st.

***Clarence street,** Rox., 1871; from Dudley street to George street; named, Jan. 2, 1873; laid out, Nov. 28, 1879. L 1406.

Clarence street, Rox., 1873; from Bartlett street to Marie avenue.

Clarence street, W. Rox., 1870; from Spring street (near Dedham line) to Belle avenue; portion between Spring street and Hamilton street laid out with name of Gould street, Sept. 28, 1888. L 2094.

Clarendon avenue, W. Rox., 1869; from junction of Roslin avenue and Kittredge street, southerly and westerly, crossing Metropolitan avenue; at its intersection with Poplar street the two join for a distance and again separate; called also Clarendon street, 1887; Clarendon avenue extended only to Poplar street, the part from Poplar street to Metropolitan avenue bearing no distinct name, while the part formerly extending westerly from Metropolitan avenue is carried through to Dale street and called Burley street; street between Poplar street and Metropolitan avenue laid out as Maynard street, Oct. 17, 1887; portion of Clarendon avenue between Augustus avenue and Kittredge street laid out as Whitford street, Oct. 23, 1888. L 2099.

Clarendon avenue, W. Rox.; from Metropolitan avenue, south-west, opposite Maynard street.

Clarendon avenue, W. Rox.; from Beech street to Hauteville street, called also Clarendon street.

Clarendon park, W. Rox., 1870; from Poplar street, south-west, to Metropolitan avenue, crossing Clarendon avenue.

Clarendon place, B., 1868; from Berkeley street to Clarendon street; laid out and name changed to Gray street, Oct. 11, 1870.

***Clarendon street,** B., 1860; from Tremont street to Columbus avenue, and from B. & P. (now N. Y., N. H. & H.) R.R. to Beacon street; called Avenue B on plan of Back Bay lands, 1855; called Clarendon street from Beacon street to B. & P. R.R., 1860; from Tremont street to Boylston street, 1863; laid out from Appleton street to Warren avenue, May 21, 1867; from Warren avenue to Tremont street, Oct. 16, 1867; from Appleton street to Chandler street, April 12, 1870; from Chandler street to Columbus avenue, July 19, 1870; from Beacon street to B. & P. R.R., Nov. 6, 1870. L 354, L 374, L 410, L 543.

Clarendon street, W. Rox., from junction of Roslin avenue and Kittredge street, south and west, across Metropolitan avenue; Clarendon avenue sometimes so called.

Clarendon street, W. Rox., 1871; from Beech street to Hauteville street; called also Clarendon avenue.

Clark court, } W. Rox.; from Lamartine street, near Lamartine court,
Clark place, } south-east, to the railroad.

Clark court, Chsn.; from Bunker Hill street, south-west, opposite burying ground.

Clark }
Clark's } square, B., 1708; " the Square liing on ye Southly side of the
Clarke's }
North Meeting House including ye wayes on each side of ye watch-house " 1708; shown in 1722 as Clarke's square; in 1729 as Clark's square and was the enclosure between Moon street, Garden court, Sun court and Fleet street; named North square, 1788.

***Clark**
Clark's } **street**, B., 1788; from Hanover street to Commercial street,
Clarkes
called Foster street, from Ship (now Commercial) street, to North (now Hanover) street in list of 1732; named Clarkes street, July 4, 1788; shown as Foster's lane, 1800; called Clark street in Edes list, 1800; called Clark street, in list, 1817; widened and laid out from Ann (now North) street, to Commercial street, May 2, 1836. Vol. 31, p. 58. L 12, L 1149.

Clark street, Rox., from Ruggles street, north-east, to Sudbury (now Weston) street; opened by William Clark through his land; named Windsor street, April 21, 1868.

Clark street, Dor., 1872; from Bellevue street, south-west, crossing Hamilton avenue (now Barrington street); laid out from Quincy street to Barrington street, with the name of Clarkson street, May 28, 1890. L 2226.

***Clark's alley**, B., 1824; from Hanover street to Ann (now North) street, south of Richmond street; confirmed as a public way, Sept. 15, 1834; a portion near Hanover street now built over and the remainder called Keith's alley, 1868.

Clark's (Jonas) corner, B., 1708; corner of Middle (now Hanover) street and Bennet street then so called.

Clark's corner, B., 1732; corner of Common (now Tremont) street and School street then so called.

Clark's corner, B., 1732; corner of Cornhill (now Washington street) and Spring lane then so called.

Clark's corner, B., 1732; corner Summer street and Bishop's alley (now Hawley street) then so called.

Clark's (Dr.) corner, B., 1732; corner Fish (now North) street and Gallop's alley (now Board alley) then so called.

†Clarkson street, Dor., 1890; from Draper court to and beyond Barrington street; called Clark street from Bellevue (now Quincy) street, south-west, crossing Hamilton avenue (now Barrington street), 1872; laid out from Quincy street to Barrington street, May 28, 1890. L 2226.

Clay place, Rox., from Clay (now Linden-park) street, opposite Simmons street, south-west.

***Clay street**, Rox., 1839; from Tremont street, south-east, to Simmons street; accepted, Dec. 10, 1861; shown in 1884 as extending past Simmons street to Stony brook sewer; name of Clay street from Tremont street to Simmons street changed to Linden-park street, March 1, 1885.

Clay street, Dor.; from Neponset avenue to Commercial street, at Pope's Hill station; laid out and named Pope's Hill street, Dec. 8, 1882. L 1069.

Clayton place, Rox., 1850; from Magazine street, south-east.

Clayton place, Dor.; from Clayton street, south-easterly, toward railroad.

†Clayton street, Dor., 1870; from Park street to Greenwich street, at its junction with Commercial (now Freeport) street; laid out from Greenwich street to Dickens street, May 19, 1882. L 1611.

Clearview street, Dor., 1894; from Blue Hill avenue, opposite Fessenden street, to Back street, nearly parallel with Walk Hill street; authority to open from Blue Hill avenue, near Walk Hill street, given by Street Commissioners, Dec. 26, 1894; abandoned; Ponemah street is in about the same location as a part of this street.

Clement avenue, W. Rox.; from end of Farrington street, west, parallel with West Roxbury branch of B. & P. (now N. Y., N. H.

& H.) R.R. to Park street; authority to open, from Park street to Flora street, given by Street Commissioners, Nov. 17, 1883.

Clement street, Dor.; from Gorham street to Nixon street, near Centre street.

***Cleveland place,** B., 1846; from Snowhill street to Margaret street; called Margaret alley, 1814; Margaret avenue, 1837; Cleveland place, 1846.

Cleveland avenue, Bri.; from Everett street, near North Beacon street, south-east; also called Cleveland place.

Cleveland place, Bri.; from Everett street, near North Beacon street, south-east; also called Cleveland avenue.

***Cleveland street,** Rox., 1854; from Winthrop street to Moreland street, opposite Greenville street; laid out, June 24, 1875. L 1053.

Cleveland street, E. B.; from Putnam street, north-east, to parkway leading to Wood Island Park; authority to open given by Street Commissioners, April 21, 1893.

Cliff place, Rox.; from Cliff street, south-east, nearly opposite Glenwood street.

***Cliff street,** Rox., 1844; from Warren street, near Circuit street, to Washington street; shown as an unnamed 30-foot passageway in 1840; shown as Cliff street, 1843–49; from Warren street to Dedham turnpike (now Washington street) subsequently called Cottage street, 1857–63; name changed from Cottage street to Cliff street, April 21, 1868; laid out to Shawmut avenue (now Washington street), Dec. 16, 1870. L 594, L 595, L 596.

Clifford place, B., 1854; from Fleet street, north-east.

***Clifford street,** Rox., 1845; from Warren street, opposite Dale street, to Blue Hill avenue; laid out, March 8, 1872. L 501.

Clifford street, W. Rox.; from Canterbury street to Grew avenue, near B. & P. (now N. Y., N. H. & H.) R.R., and parallel with railroad for part of the way.

Clifton avenue, B., 1840; from Suffolk street (now Shawmut avenue) to Middlesex street; closed.

Clifton park, Rox.; from Clifton street, between Shirley street and Hudson street, south-east, connecting with Brook place; also called Clifton place.

Clifton place, B.; from Washington street, north-west, nearly opposite Newcomb street.

***Clifton street,** Dor., 1862; from Dudley street to Shirley street, opposite George street; laid out from Cottage (now East Cottage) street to Hudson street, Aug. 12, 1869; extended from Hudson street to Shirley street, at George street, Sept. 1, 1875; from Cottage street, to Dudley street, in part through private way called Taylor avenue, June 15, 1883. L 1074, L 1707, L 1708.

Clifton street, W. Rox., 1852; from Norfolk street to Kittredge street (formerly Roslin avenue), crossing Albano street.

Clinton court, Chsn., 1870; from Cambridge street, west of B. & M. R.R., north; also called Clinton place.

Clinton place, Chsn., 1870; from Cambridge street, west of B. & M. R.R., north; also called Clinton court.

***Clinton street,** B., 1824; from Merchant's row to Atlantic avenue; from Merchant's row, east, 1824; laid out (as a new street) from Merchant's row to Commercial street, parallel with North Market street March 10, 1828; same named, April 8, 1829; having become obstructed near Commercial street, "continued to Commercial street and laid out" again, Oct. 10, 1831; laid out again, extended to (Mercantile street) and discontinued in part, July 7, 1854; to Mercantile street, 1856; extended to Atlantic avenue, Oct. 8, 1875. Vol. 31; p. 104. L 20, L 614, 1042, L 1081, L 2751.

Clinton street, Dor.; from Waterlow street to Faxon street; a part of what was formerly called Waterlow street.

***Clive street**, W. Rox., 1888; from Boylston street to Spring Park avenue; called C street in 1868; laid out, July 17, 1888. L 2077.

Clough street, B., 1733; from Frog lane (now Boylston street) to Hollis street, 1733; later to Dr. Byle's at corner of present Common street, to Orange (now Washington) street, through Walker lane or street (now Common street), 1743; from Orange street to Dr. Byle's house at present corner of Tremont street and Common street, 1750, from Dr. Byle's to Frog lane being called Holyoke street; from Orange street to Frog lane, including Clough and Holyoke streets, named Nassau street, July 4, 1788; same included in Common street, 1824; Common street named Tremont street, 1829; part of Tremont street, from Miss Byle's to Washington street, named Common street again, 1836.

Clough street, B., 1756; Unity street, from Charter street to Love lane (now Tileston street), so called.

***Clyde street**, E. B., 1869; from Marginal street, south-west, to Cunard S.S. wharf; laid out, Aug. 17, 1869; named, Sept. 14, 1869. L 110, L 476.

***Cobb street**, B., 1870; from Washington street, near Castle street to Shawmut avenue; laid out, Dec. 16, 1870. L 547, L 563.

Cobb street, B., 1840; from Washington street to Harrison avenue; name changed to Florence street, 1842.

***Cobden street**, Rox., 1871; from Walnut avenue, near Westminster avenue to Washington street; laid out, Sept. 23, 1871. L 693.

Coburn court, B., 1867; from Phillips street, south, near Anderson street.

Coburn place, B., 1875; from Reed street, near Northampton street, north-west.

Cochran lane, Bri., 1863; from Washington street, south-west; Church street, so called.

Codman avenue, Rox., 1871; from Washington street to Amory street; laid out as a public street, with name of Dimock street, Oct. 20, 1884. L 1826.

Codman hill, Rox.; from Washington street, near Codman street, south-east to Codman park; formerly called Codman park.

Codman park, Rox., 1870; from Townsend street, south to Codman place, and west from about middle point in T form to Washington street; from Shawmut avenue (now Washington street), between Townsend street and Cobden street named, June 8, 1870; portion from Townsend street laid out, July 16, 1877; portion from Washington street now called Codman Hill. L 1254.

Codman place, Rox.; from Washington street, near Cobden street, south-east, to Codman park.

***Codman street**, Dor., 1859; from Adams street to Morton street; from Adams street to Washington street located; March 28, 1859.

Coffee court, } **Coffee place**, } Dor.; from Washington street, near School street, west.

Coffey street, Dor.; from Newhall street to Neponset avenue, between Newhall avenue and Ashmont street.

Coffin's field, B., 1775; between Essex street, Summer street, Short street and South street.

Coggin street, Chsn., 1837; from Bunker Hill street to Mystic river; later called Linden street; now part of Baldwin st.

†**Cohasset street,** W. Rox., 1889; from Corinth street to Dudley avenue; formerly called Salem street, between Corinth street (formerly Basto place) and Albano street; laid out between Corinth street and Albano street, Oct. 30, 1889. L 2186.

Colberg avenue, W. Rox.; from Beech street to Belgrade avenue.

Cold lane, } B., 1708; from Hanover street, north-west, to the Mill-
Cole lane, } pond; called Cole lane on Carlton's map, 1800; also in order for filling in Mill-pond, 1807; included in Portland street about 1809.

Coleburn's lane, } B.; Avery street, so called at one time, probably
Colburne's lane, } between 1709 and 1732.

***Coleman street,** Dor., 1872; from Bellevue (now Quincy) street, near Bowdoin street to Hamilton street (or avenue, now Barrington street); laid out, April 18, 1881. L 1520.

†**Coleridge street,** E. B., 1838; from Rice street to Swift street; from Rice street across Short street to the water, with proposed extension to Baltic street in 1838; laid out from Wordsworth street to Short street, Aug. 6, 1889. L 2147.

Cole's place, B., 1839; from Pleasant street to Church street; Hamlen place, 1844; now closed.

Collamore place, B., 1857; from Salem street, near Parmenter street, south-east, then north-east.

College court, B , 1849; from Fruit street; probably included in North Grove street in 1855.

Collins street, Dor., 1872; from Blue Hill avenue, opposite Mattapan station, north-west.

Collins street, E. B. (Breed's Island); from Bayswater street to Riverside avenue, parallel with Saratoga street.

Colonnade row, B., 1811; a uniform range of 24 brick buildings, each with row of freestone columns, upon Common (now Tremont) street, south of West street; called Fayette place, 1824.

Colonial avenue, Dor.; from Talbot avenue to New England avenue.

Colonial road, Bri.; from Commonwealth avenue to Chestnut Hill avenue.

Colony place, Rox.; From Albany street, near Hunneman street, to Fellows street.

***Colony street,** So. B., 1849; from Swan street, near Dorchester avenue, to Foundry street; accepted, conditionally, Oct. 29, 1849; laid out between Sixth (now Foundry) street and Swan street, Oct. 12, 1869; closed; taken by O. C. R.R. Co. by authority of the Acts of Legislature of 1893. L 483, L 555.

Colson's lane, B., 1746; "near the great trees at the south end."

***Colton street,** So. B., 1888; from West First street to West Second street; Green alley between West First street and West Second street; laid out, Dec. 31, 1888. L 2110.

Columbia court, Chsn., 1866; Columbia street so called.

Columbia court, Chsn., 1880; from rear 662 Main street, 1880–87.

Columbia place, Dor., 1846; from Columbia street, near Geneva avenue, to Vaughan avenue; closed.

Columbia place, Dor.; from Columbia street, near Quincy street, north-west.

***Columbia street,** B., 1809; from Bedford street to Essex street; confirmed as a public street, Sept. 15, 1834.

***Columbia street,** Rox. and Dor., 1840; from Hancock street at Upham's corner to Blue Hill avenue; named from Payson's shop by Wales' to Brush hill, March 11, 1840. L 561, L 790, L 955, L 1282, L 1308, L 1402, L 1979, L 2536.

Columbia street, Chsn.; from Main street to Perkins street; shown but not named, 1858; called Columbia court, 1866; laid out as a public street, and named Caldwell street, June 7, 1887. L 1992.

Columbia terrace, Dor.; from Columbia street at junction with Richfield street, south-east.

***Columbus avenue**, B. and Rox., 1860; from Park square to Walnut avenue, opposite Franklin park; in 1860 projected from Park square to Roxbury line, over land of Boston Water Power Co.; laid out from Church street to Ferdinand street, Oct. 9, 1868; order authorizing Mayor and Aldermen to contract with Boston Water Power Co. for transfer to City of Columbus avenue and streets between it and B. & P. (now N. Y., N. H. & H.) R.R., Nov. 18, 1868; laid out from Ferdinand street to Northampton street, Oct. 16, 1869; from Church street to Park square, Dec. 29, 1871; from Northampton street, south-west, to near old Roxbury line, Dec. 30, 1881; extended from near old Roxbury line, through Berlin street, Chapel street, Windsor street, a portion of Tremont street, Pynchon street, a portion of Brunswick avenue, and through that part of Seaver street, between Washington street and Walnut avenue, Jan. 4, 1895. L 354, L 398, L 410, L 452, L 515, L 516, L 569, L 613, L 745, L 878, L 1448, L 1584, L 2680, L 2681, L 2682, L 2683, L 2684, L 2685, L 2686, L 2687, L 2688, L 2689, L 2690, L 2691, L 2692, L 2693, L 2694, L 2695, L 2696, L 2697.

Columbus place, B., 1869; from Eliot street, near Carver street, north; named, Sept. 13, 1869.

***Columbus square**, B., 1876; between Warren avenue, and Columbus avenue; part of Warren avenue bounded by Pembroke street, West Newton street and Columbus avenue; named Columbus square, April 4, 1871.

Colwell place, Bri; from Chestnut Hill avenue, near South street, north-west; called also Colwell avenue.

Comins terrace, Rox.; from Bower street, nearly opposite Sherman street, south-east; laid out June 14, 1895. L 2706.

***Commerce street**, B., 1853; from Commercial street to Atlantic avenue; from Commercial street, east, in 1853; accepted, conditionally, Nov. 26, 1866; extended to Atlantic avenue, Dec. 24, 1874. L 614, L 1002.

Commercial avenue, B., 1834; from Ann (now North) street, at head of Union wharf; continued to Commercial street, March 10, 1834; named Commercial avenue, April 28, 1834; discontinued March 13, 1835.

Commercial avenue, Chsn., 1870; from Alford street, north-west, to Somerville line; Arlington avenue, so called.

Commercial court, B., 1836–41; from Commercial street, near Fulton street; closed.

Commercial court, B., 1849; from Commercial street, between Jackson avenue and Foster street, south-west; called Commercial-street avenue, 1839; Commercial court, 1849; called Commercial place, 1875; Commercial court, 1883.

Commercial place, B., 1849; from Commercial street to Charter street, with branch north-west to Foster street; from Commercial street, near Henchman street, 1849.

Commercial place, B.; Commercial court, so called 1875.

Commercial point, Dor.; from Freeport street, opposite foot of Washington street and Union street.

Commercial street, B., 1817; that part of Milk street, from Batterymarch street to the water, named Commercial street, May 29, 1817; renamed Milk street, July 6, 1824.

***Commercial street**, B., 1828; from State street to Prince street; a marginal street 65 feet wide projected from North Market street to Lewis wharf, April 17, 1826; order for erection of bridge over Mill creek connecting Marginal street, so called, with the 65-foot street leading to Long wharf, July 28, 1828; the marginal street above described accepted and named Commercial street, Dec. 22, 1828; the 65-foot street leading from Long wharf to southerly end of Commercial street considered continuation of same and named Commercial street, June 17, 1829; extended to Clark street, July 15, 1833; from present terminus to Hanover street, Oct. 17, 1833; Lynn street, from Prince street to Hanover street, and part of Ann (now North) street, from Hanover street to Commercial street, named Commercial street, Feb. 17, 1834. Vol. 31, p. 47. L 17, L 33, L 134, L 1384, L 1385, L 1386, L 1387, L 1388, L 1392, L 1393, L 1394, L 1395, L 1396, L 1947.

***Commercial street**, Dor., 1810; from Hancock street to Neponset avenue; road from Quincy turnpike (now Neponset avenue) to Commercial point, with bridge over Mill creek and draw, originally built by authority of the General Court in or about 1809; having become unsafe and impassable, the same were rebuilt by the Tenean Free Bridge Co., 1833, and again laid out by County Commissioners, 1844; called old Plymouth road, between Dorchester almshouse and Commercial point; same named Commercial street, March 11, 1840; name changed to Freeport street, March 1, 1892. L 710, L 721, L 1840, L 1862.

Commercial-street avenue, B., 1839; from Commercial street, opposite Ripley's wharf; called Commercial court, 1849.

Common, The, B.; between Park street, Beacon street, Charles street, Boylston street, and Tremont street; early called Centry field and Training field.

***Common street**, B., 1824; from Washington street to Tremont street; called Walker's lane or Walker's street, 1741; a part of Clough street, 1743; a part of Nassau street, 1788; called Common street and considered a part of the continuous street, from corner of Harvard street to Washington street, 1824; the whole named Tremont street, 1829; part from Washington street to present Tremont street, named Common street again 1836.

Common street, B., 1708; from School street through the Common to Frogg lane (now Boylston street), 1708; from the corner of Howard street, over Pemberton Hill, through Tremont street and Nassau street to Washington street, 1824; part from Washington street to Court street, named Tremont street, and part from junction with Court street to Howard street named Pemberton Hill, April 22, 1829; last-mentioned part named Tremont street, Nov. 4, 1844; parts of Common street called Colonnade row, Fayette place and Long acre at different times.

***Common street**, Chsn., 1831; from Winthrop street to Adams street, on south-west and south-east sides of Winthrop square; streets leading round the Training field on south-west and south-east sides named Common street, March 14, 1831.

***Commonwealth avenue**, B., Rox. and Bri., 1862; from Arlington street to Newton line; laid out as Avenue Five, from Avenue I. (now Berkeley street) to Cross-dam (now Parker street), 120 feet wide by indenture between Commonwealth and Boston Water Power Company, dated June 9, 1854; laid out by another indenture between same, parallel with Beacon street, 200 feet wide, from Arlington street to Punch Bowl road (now Brookline avenue) with park, etc., Dec. 27, 1856; called Avenue V. on plan of Back Bay land, 1860; conditionally accepted from Arlington street to Berkeley street, July 28, 1862, and deed satisfying condition accepted, Feb, 15, 1864; laid out from Berkeley street to Clarendon street,

Dec. 15, 1868; from Clarendon street to Dartmouth street, May 31, 1871; from Dartmouth street to Exeter street, May 19, 1873; from Exeter street to West Chester park (now Massachusetts avenue), Nov. 4, 1875; extended to Beacon street July 8, 1879; extended over Brighton avenue to Massachusetts avenue, Jan. 24, 1887; extended over Massachusetts avenue to Chestnut Hill avenue, March 1, 1887; extended from Chestnut Hill avenue through grounds at Chestnut Hill reservoir and over a portion of South street to Newton line, Jan. 5, 1895; part from Arlington street to Charlesgate west, included in Park system, June 29, 1894. L 374, L 649, L 862, L 1105, L 1106, L 1296, L 1362, L 1742, L 1743, L 1744, L 1745, L 1799, L 1964, L 2050, L 2051, L 2052, L 2053, L 2054, L 2055, L 2476, L 2505, L 2583, L 2593, L 2594, L 2595, L 2650, L 2651, L 2652.

***Compton street,** B., 1895; from Washington street to Tremont street; name of Chapman street changed to Compton street, March 1, 1895.

Compton street, Dor.; from Boston street parallel with Dorchesterway to Dorchester avenue; now Roseclair street.

Conant court, } **Conant place,** } Rox.; from King street, north-east; called Conant court and Conant place.

Conant place, } **Conant-street place,** } Rox.; from Conant street, near Parker street, south-west; called Brook's place, 1854–60; Brooks-street place., 1860–68; no record, but name probably changed at same time Brooks street was named Conant street, 1868; called Conant place and Conant-street place.

***Conant street,** Rox., 1868; from Parker street, near Longwood avenue, to Huntington avenue, shown as Brook street, from Bumstead lane (now St. Alphonsus street), south-east, 1845; named Conant street, April 21, 1868; laid out from Parker street to land of Thos. Wigglesworth, Oct. 4, 1870; extended to Huntington avenue, March 22, 1883. L 575, L 576, L 1696.

Concord avenue, B., from Clinton street, north-east, to Arlington avenue, over land of Mercantile Wharf Corporation.

Concord avenue, Chsn.; from Jefferson avenue to and crossing Lexington street; shown as an unnamed street in 1839; part between Lexington street and Monument street at one time called Monument lane.

Concord place, B., 1876; from Worcester street, near Tremont street, to Concord square.

***Concord square,** B., 1866; from Tremont street to Columbus avenue; part of Concord street from Tremont street to a point 135 feet east of Columbus avenue accepted and named Concord square, July 10, 1866; remainder to Columbus avenue laid out, June 23, 1868. L 329.

***Concord street,** B., 1826; from Washington street, west; laid out on the Neck, July 24, 1826; from Tremont street to Front street (now Harrison avenue) named Concord street, Sept. 15, 1834, to Albany street, 1854; accepted, Dec. 7, 1857; portion west of Tremont street, accepted Dec. 21, 1859; street accepted, Oct. 30, 1860; part from Tremont street to a point 135 feet east of Columbus avenue, named Concord square, July 10, 1866; name of part from Washington street to Albany street changed to East Concord street and from Washington street to Tremont street to West Concord street, April 21, 1868. L 212.

Concord street, Chsn., 1837; from Bunker Hill street, north-west, to Mystic river, 1837 and 1843; discontinued.

***Concord street,** Chsn., 1839; from Monument square to Bunker Hill street; part from Tremont street to High street, shown as an unnamed street, 1834; from Monument square to Bunker Hill street, 1839; laid out 50 feet wide Dec. 21, 1844; accepted Dec. 23, 1844; name of part from Tremont street to High street changed to Monument square, Feb. 2, 1860.

***Condor street**, E. B., 1852; from Border street to Glendon street; accepted from Border street to Knox (now Glendon) street, Oct. 4, 1852. L 1616.

Conduit, B., 1788; in Dock square.

Conduit alley, B., 1825; from Market square to Ann (now North) street; built over.

Conduit street, B.; part of Ann (now North) street from Conduit in Dock square to Cross street, originally so-called.

Coney's lane, B.; Cross street was so called prior to 1708.

Confirmation place, } Chsn.; from Rutherford avenue, north-east;
Confirmed place, } called Confirmation place, 1885.

Congress court, B., 1826; from Congress street, east, near State street; called Post Office avenue, 1849.

Congress place, B., 1861; Congress street, east, nearly opposite Matthews street; called Congress-street place, 1877.

†**Congress square**, B., 1821; from State street, south, then east to Congress street, and from Devonshire, east, to Congress street; called Half-square court from King (now State) street, south, 1708; same from Maccarty's corner into Pudding lane (now Devonshire street), 1732; same was called Court square and Half-court square in 1798; same "round the buildings back of the post office," 1800; no mention of it in list of 1817; called Salter's court, 1808; Exchange square (rear of Congress street and State street), 1818; Congress square, 1821, and the part from State street, west, called Story place, 1845; but in 1810 the records appear of it as Half-square court and at that date the area leading east to Congress street was laid out making a direct way from Devonshire street to Congress street; name Congress square again given to part from State street, south, then east to Congress street, some time prior to 1874; name Exchange place given in 1854 to part from Devonshire street, east, to Congress square; Exchange place, "from Devonshire street to Congress st," made part of Congress square, Oct. 17, 1873. L 16, L 497, L 2587.

†**Congress street**, B., and So. B., 1800; from State street to Reserved Channel, near foot of L street, So. B.; from King (now State) street to Water street called Leverett's lane, 1708; called Quaker lane in 1800; from Water street to Milk street called Dalton's row, 1769–88, and Dalton street, 1788–1800; from Milk street to Cow lane (now High street) including Green or Green's lane, and to Purchase street, including Gray's lane, called Atkinson street, 1732; Dalton street and Quaker lane, from State street to Milk street, named Congress street, 1800; name of Atkinson street, from Milk street to Broad street (now Atlantic avenue) changed to Congress street, Aug. 4, 1854; part from Water street to Milk street named Post Office square, April 18, 1873; Eastern avenue, laid out from Broad street (now Atlantic avenue) to Harbor Commissioners' line, Jan. 3, 1874; extended across Fort Point Channel to C street extended May 14, 1879; name of Eastern avenue from Atlantic avenue to C street extended changed to Congress street, March 1, 1881. Vol. 31, pp. 5, 10, 12, 13, 22, 26, 32, 55, 88, 97. Vol. 19, pp. 70, 129. L 1, L 28, L 68, L 87, L 279, L 283, L 439, L 834, L 844, L 845, L 846, L 853, L 856, L 918, L 1199, L 2205, L 2587.

Congress street, B.; King street frequently so called before the present name of State street was settled on in 1784.

***Congress-street bridge**, B.: from Altantic avenue, opposite Congress street, across Fort Point Channel.

Congress-street place, B., 1877; from Congress street, east, nearly opposite Matthews street; called Congress place, 1861; Congress-street place, 1877.

Congreve street, W. Rox.; from South street, near Dudley avenue.

Connecticut lane, Rox., 1662; laid out Jan. 19, 1662; laid out two rods wide to Brookline line, Aug. 5, 1762; now Perkins street.

Connell street, Dor.; from Bellevue street, near junction of Trull street, south-east.

Connolly street, Rox.; from Fellows street, north-west, between East Lenox street and Orange court.

Conologue court, E. B.; from Havre street, between Decatur street and Maverick street, north-west; called also Byrnes place; not now shown.

***Conway street**, W. Rox, 1885; from South street to Fairview street; private way called Skinner street laid out and named Conway street, July 21, 1885. L 1875.

Cook place, B., 1868; from Commercial street, north of Battery street; shown but not named, 1874 and 1884.

Cook street, Dor.; from Washington street, near Harvard street, south-west; laid out under name of Gaylord street to Chamberlain street, July 10, 1896.

***Cook street**, Chsn., 1838; from Bunker Hill street to Medford street; report accepted recommending acceptance of street under certain conditions, June 20, 1838; laid out and accepted, Oct. 4, 1854.

Cook-street court, Chsn.; from Cook street, near Bunker Hill street, north-west, crossing Sheafe street; shown as an unnamed court, 1845.

Cook-street place, Chsn.; from Cook street, near Medford street, to Sheafe street.

Cook's corner, B., 1800; corner Orange (now Washington) street and Beach street; then so-called.

***Cook's court**, B., 1800; the way back of Hunt's grammar school-house in School street, 1800; confirmed as a public street, Sept. 15, 1834; called Chapman place, 1841; reported by committee to be an old established public way, Dec. 24, 1846.

Cook's court, Dor.; from Norfolk street, south-east, to Fremont place.

Cook's lane, W. Rox., 1870; from Brush Hill turnpike (now Blue Hill avenue) to Walnut street; now Williams street.

Cook's lane, Chsn.; from Bow street to Front street; laid out and widened, July 2, 1866; name changed to Jenner street, Sept. 17, 1866.

Cooledge avenue, Dor.; see Coolidge avenue.

Coolidge avenue, B., 1841; from Cambridge street, south, then west, to Temple street, with opening into Bowdoin street.

Coolidge avenue, Dor., 1872; from Standish street to Warner avenue, and from Bernard street, south-west, to unnamed street; not shown to exist between Warner avenue and Bernard street; first part called Cooledge avenue in 1884; second part called Coolidge avenue; laid out as Kingsdale street, Nov. 23, 1895.

Coolidge place, So. B.; from West Second street, near C street, to Bolton street.

***Coolidge street**, Bri., 1892; from Mansfield street to North Harvard street; formerly called Coolidge road; laid out as Coolidge street; Aug. 24, 1892. L 2429.

***Cooper street**, B., 1807; from Salem street to Charlestown street, opposite Beverly street; laid out across the Mill-pond, Aug. 3, 1807; extended to Salem street, 1838. Vol. 31, p. 96. L 1221.

Cooper street, W. Rox., 1856; from Green street to Stony brook; not now shown.

Cooper-street court, B., 1837; from Cooper street, south-east, between Endicott street and North Margin street; also called Cooper court; not now shown.

Cooper's alley, B., 1708; the "alley leading from ye end of Water street through Mr. Oliver's land into Milk street;" the third of the ways from Milk street to Water street, 1732; called Kilby street, 1769; Miller's lane previously to 1784; named Adams street, July 4, 1788; Kilby street again, 1825.

Cooper's alley, B., 1819; the easterly end of Brattle street, so called; included in Brattle street in 1820.

Cooper's court, B., 1837; from Cooper street, south-east, between Endicott street and North Margin street; also called Cooper-street court; not now shown.

Copeland court, Rox., 1873; from Copeland street, near Waverly street, south-east; now called Burton avenue.

Copeland place, Rox.; from Copeland street, near Moreland street, south-east.

Copeland street, Rox., 1835; from Cedar street to Highland street; Hawthorne street so called in 1835 and 1843.

***Copeland street**, Rox., 1851; from Warren street to Moreland street; accepted, conditionally, May 26, 1851; laid out and extended from Warren street to Moreland street, June 15, 1869; this street appears to have been formerly Mt. Warren avenue by a plan dated 1869; L 449.

Copeland's alley, B., 1824; from Court street, east, near Hanover street; closed.

Copeland's lane, B., 1820; from Court street to Sudbury street; called Alden's lane, 1732; Copeland's lane, 1820; Alden's lane again, 1829; named Alden street, 1846.

***Copley square**, B., 1883; junction of Dartmouth street, Boylston street, Huntington avenue, Trinity place and St. James avenue; lot bounded by Huntington avenue, Dartmouth and Boylston streets purchased for a public square named Copley square, Feb. 21, 1883 Trinity triangle, a triangular area bounded by Huntington avenue; Trinity place and St. James avenue, included in Copley square, April 21, 1885.

***Copley street,** } **Copley terrace,** } Rox. and W. Rox.; from School street near Arcadia street, north-east; Copley terrace laid out and named Copley street, Aug. 27, 1886; shown in 1884. L 1941.

Copper street, B., 1803; from Leverett street to Poplar street; named Brighton street, 1816.

Copp's Hill, B.; between Snowhill street, Charter street and Lynn (now Commercial) street.

Copp's Hill avenue, B., 1849; from Prince street to Snowhill avenue; released to Boston Gaslight Company, in exchange for land to widen Prince street, Dec. 8, 1866; now covered by Boston Gas Works. L 151.

Coral court, } **Coral place,** } B.; from Anderson street, west; called Coral court, 1844; Coral place, 1846; closed by erection of Phillips schoolhouse in 1861.

Coral place, Chsn.; from Pearl street, between Pearl-street place and Blaban place, north-west.

***Corbet street**, Dor., 1871; from Forest Hills avenue (now Morton street) to Norfolk street; laid out, Aug. 15, 1889. L 2152.

Cordage court, So. B.; from East Seventh street to East Sixth street, between N street and O street.

Cordis court, Chsn.; from Cordis street to Pleasant street; also called Cordis-street place; laid out as Boyle street, Sept. 28, 1891. L 2338.

***Cordis street**, Chsn., 1799; from Warren street to High street; accepted, April 7, 1817.

***Cordis-street avenue**, Chsn.; from Cordis street to Pleasant street; shown as Cross street, 1799.

Cordis-street place, Chsn.; from Cordis street to Pleasant street; shown as Cross street, 1808, when land was given to lay out the street; called also Cordis court; laid out as Boyle street, Sept. 28, 1891. L 2338.

Corey avenue, B., 1846; from Ash street, east, then north-east to Bennet street.

Corey avenue, W. Rox.; from Weld street to Corey street; laid out with name of Ruskin street, April 1, 1890. L 2216.

Corey court, Chsn.; from Corey street, west, near Medford street.

†**Corey road**, Bri.; from Washington street to Brookline line; formerly called Dean avenue; by change of the Brookline boundary line, a portion of the street became public.

***Corey street**, W. Rox., 1853; from Weld street at junction with Arnold street to Park street; part from Austin (now Centre) street, north-west, shown as Garden street, 1852; laid out from Weld street to Centre street and accepted, March 20, 1865; extended from Centre street to Park street, Dec. 12, 1874; laid out from Centre street and extended to Weld street, July 30, 1875. L 999, L 1069, L 1070, L 1071.

***Corey street**, Chsn., 1853; from Medford street to Moulton street, near Bunker Hill street; shown as an unnamed street, 1850; Chip street laid out, accepted and name changed to Corey street, May 23, 1853.

***Corinth street**, W. Rox., 1882; from Washington street at Poplar street to Brandon street; Basto place laid out, extended to Brandon street and named Corinth street, Nov. 25, 1882. L 1666, L 2580.

***Corn court**, B., 1708; from Faneuil Hall square, southerly and easterly in irregular form to Merchant's row; from the Corn Market, south, 1708.

Cornauba street, W. Rox.; from Brown avenue, between Poplar street and Ashland street, north-west, then north-east.

†**Cornell street**, W. Rox., 1890; from Poplar street to north-west of Aldrich street; portion between Washington street and Orange street called Central avenue in 1872; laid out as Cornell street, Aug. 7, 1890; Cornell street extended from Washington street over private land and through Charles street to Poplar street, June 24, 1892. L 2256, L 2413, L 2414.

Corn Hill, B.; Fort Hill was so called previous to 1632; afterwards Fort Field.

Cornhill, B., 1708; from School street to Dock square, 1708; line of street laid down and established Nov. and Dec., 1711, and Feb., 1712; name changed to Washington street, 1824.

***Cornhill**, B., 1829; from Washington street to Court street; laid out from Tremont street at Scollay's building across Court street to Cornhill (now Washington street), near Brattle alley including Belknap's yard, and named Cheapside, March 5, 1816; named Market street, June 11, 1817; part between arch leading to Brattle street and Dock square named Market row, Oct. 1, 1817; from Court street to Washington street named Cornhill, May 6, 1829; sometimes called New Cornhill; part between Tremont street and Court street named Pemberton square, Feb. 19, 1838, and Scollay square, June 25, 1838. L 817.

***Cornhill court**, B., 1814; from Washington street, west, then south, to Court avenue; called Church square, in rear of the First church, 1708; same around old brick church, 1800; Cornhill square, 1809; Cornhill court from Cornhill (now Washington street) nearly opposite State street, 1814; the portion between Young's Hotel and Washington street on the southerly side of Rogers' building called Suffolk Inns, 1812; Suffolk avenue, 1820; Court avenue, 1839.

Cornhill square, B., 1809; from Cornhill (now Washington street), nearly opposite State street; called Church square, 1708; Cornhill square, 1809; Cornhill court, 1814.

***Corning street**, B., 1895; from Tremont street to Washington street; formerly Indiana place; name changed to Corning street, March 1, 1895.

Corn Market, B., 1708; the present south side of Faneuil Hall (then along the side of the dock), so called in 1708; from the Sun Tavern in Dock square to Merchant's row, 1732; called Corn Market street, 1762; Market square, 1784; included in Faneuil Hall square, 1855.

Corn Market street, B., 1762; Corn market so called at one time; enlarged on south side of Faneuil Hall market, April 14, 1762; later a part of Market square, and now a part of Faneuil Hall square.

***Cornwall street**, W. Rox., 1886; from Washington street to Boylston avenue; Chemical avenue laid out from Washington street to Brookside avenue and name changed to Cornwall street, June 24, 1886; extended to Boylston avenue, Aug. 12, 1891. L 1913, L 2320.

Corona street, Dor.; from Bowdoin street near Westville street, to Geneva avenue; authority to open given by Street Commissioners, Nov. 8, 1894.

***Cortes street**, B., 1863; from Ferdinand street to Berkeley street; laid out, July 26, 1875. L 1061.

Cosmos street, E. B.; from Wauwatosa avenue to Benevento street.

***Corwin street**, Dor , 1890; from Westville street to Arcadia street; formerly called Westville street; laid out, Sept. 10, 1890. L 2260.

Cottage avenue, Dor., 1836; from Geneva street (now avenue), northerly and north-westerly, to Green (now Olney) street; name changed to Everton street, Dec. 30, 1876.

Cottage avenue, W. Rox., 1851; from Centre street, south-east, near La Grange street; called Cottage place, 1843–44–49, and in 1884; named Cottage street by Town in 1825.

Cottage court, Rox.; from Julian street to Gayland avenue.

Cottage place, B , 1833; from Washington street, near Perry street, to Harrison avenue.

Cottage place, Rox., 1844; from Tremont street, north-west, to B. & P. (now N. Y., N. H. & H.) R.R.; Columbus avenue extended across it, Jan. 4, 1895; formerly School court.

Cottage place, Rox.; from Tremont street, south-east; name changed to Howe court, April 21, 1868.

Cottage place, W. Rox., 1844; from Centre street, south-east; shown in 1843–49; also called Cottage avenue and Cottage street.

Cottage row, Chsn.; from Medford street, opposite Lexington street.

Cottage side, Dor.; from East Cottage street to Willis street; formerly Turpin court.

†**Cottage street,** E. B., 1833; from Marginal street to Parkway leading to Wood Island Park; laid out from Marginal street to Maverick street, Oct. 25, 1852; a foot-bridge 25 feet wide extends across the water from Maverick street to Prescott street; authority to open from Prescott street to Parkway leading to Wood Island Park given by Street Commissioners, April 21, 1893. L 1354.

Cottage street, So. B.; from West Ninth street, south-west, to N. Y., N. H. & H. R.R.

Cottage street, Rox.; from Warren street to Shawmut avenue (now Washington street), near Dudley street; used before Dedham turnpike was made for carting wood from Muddy Pond woods; Town Surveyor recommended closing this street, April 7, 1845; name changed to Cliff street, April 21, 1868; called Cliff street, from Warren street to Dedham turnpike, 1843–49; on plan dated 1863 called "Cottage street, formerly Cliff street."

Cottage street, Dor., 1799; from Dudley street crossing Five Corners (now Edward Everett square) to Pleasant street; named from Boston street to Old road (now Dudley street), March 11, 1840; name of Myrtle street from Boston street to Pleasant street changed to Cottage street, March 1, 1847; name of Cottage street, between Dudley street and Pleasant street, and Pond street between Pleasant street and Dorchester avenue, changed to East Cottage street, March 1, 1893. L 811, L 812, L 813, L 814, L 815, L 858, L 859, L 860, L 861, L 2547.

Cottage street, W. Rox., 1825; from Centre street, near La Grange street, south-east; named "from Centre street by Howe's place," May 9, 1825; called Cottage place, 1844, also on Whitney's map of Roxbury, 1843–49, and again in 1884; called Cottage avenue, 1851, and in 1874.

Cottage street, W. Rox., 1849; from Pond street to Perkins street; called so in 1843–49–51; now called Prince street.

Cottage street, W. Rox., 1871; from Williams (now Brandon) street to Prospect (now Penfield) street, near Birch street; laid out with name of Amherst street, Sept. 14, 1881. L 1556.

***Cottage street,** Chsn., 1855; from Bunker Hill street to Medford street; laid out, April 8, 1878. L 1301.

Cottage-street place, E. B.; from Cottage street between Webster street and Sumner street, south-east.

Cottage terrace, Dor.; from East Cottage street, between Batchelder street and N. E. R.R., north-east, to Marshfield street; authority to open given by Street Commissioners, April 11, 1895.

Cotting court, B., 1848; from Cotting street; included in Wall street, when extended to Causeway street in 1852.

Cotting place, B., 1835; from Chambers street, near Cambridge street, north-west.

***Cotting street,** B., 1843; from Lowell street to Leverett street; called Leverett court, 1822; Cotting street, 1843; accepted from Lowell street to Wall street, Oct. 10, 1853; accepted from Wall street to Leverett street, Aug. 27, 1855. L 51.

Cotton alley, } B.; from Atlantic avenue (formerly Broad street) to **Cotton place,** } Purchase street; called Cotton alley, 1826; Cotton place, 1828; and since by both names.

Cotton Hill, B.; anciently so called and as late as 1733; named after residence of Rev. John Cotton; subsequently called Pemberton hill after James Pemberton.

†**Court avenue,** B., 1837; from Washington street to Court square called Suffolk Inns, 1812; Suffolk avenue, 1820; Court avenue, 1837; part from Washington street to Cornhill court at one time a part of that court.

Court square, B., 1798; from State street to Congress street; called Half-square court, 1708; Court square, 1798; now a part of Congress square.

Court square, B., 1815; from School street to the new court-house; laid out on land appertaining to the school-house in School street, May 20, 1812; named Court square, Sept. 27, 1815; now included in site of City Hall.

***Court square,** B., 1841; from Court street, south-west, around the old court-house to Court street again; the present east entrance probably called Prison lane, 1722; laid out on east and west sides of new court-house, Dec. 7, 1835; street on west side discontinued, Aug. 15, 1836; street laid out around new court-house, Nov. 5, 1838; square in which court-house is situated named Court square, Aug. 30, 1841. L 222, L 1350.

***Court street,** B., 1784; from Washington street to Bowdoin square, from Washington street to the head of Hanover street, called Queen street, and from Sudbury street to Bowdoin square, called Cambridge street, 1708; name of Queen street changed to Court street, July 4, 1788; extended to Bowdoin square through a part of Cambridge street, 1807; area between Court street and Tremont street named Pemberton square, Feb. 19, 1838, and Scollay square, June 25, 1838; part from Sudbury street to Bowdoin square called Green street, 1850, and later in the same year again called Court street, part once called Centry or Sentry street, Century or Century Hill street. L 3, L 11, L 37, L 74, L 580, L 1702.

Court street, Dor.; from Minot street, south; so called in 1874; shown as an unnamed place in 1868; called Minot place, 1884.

Courtland street, Rox., 1871; from Parker street, crossing Huntington avenue to Rogers avenue.

Cove, The, B., 1708; where Faneuil Hall (sometimes called Quincy) market now stands; then so-called.

Cove place, B., 1845; from Cove street, east, then south to Furnace street; from Cove street, east, 1845.

†**Cove street,** B., 1842; from East street, near Federal street, to Furnace street; from East street to Kneeland street, 1842; to Lehigh street, 1846; accepted and laid out from East street to Kneeland street, Aug. 23, 1852. Vol. 31, p. 101.

Coventry street, B., 1733–91; about the same as the easterly half of Walnut street.

Coventry street, Rox., 1849; from Tremont street to Columbus avenue.

***Cow lane,** B., 1708; from Fort Hill to Summer street; extended by abutters to Sconce street and accepted by Town, 1741; named High street, May 24, 1797, but called Cow lane in list of 1800.

Cow lane, Bri., 1837; see plan, book 365, p. 554, Middlesex South District Deeds.

Cowell's corner, B., 1708; corner Newbury (now Washington) street and West street then so-called.

Cowing street, W. Rox.; from La Grange street, opposite Martin street, south-west, then south-east, across Partridge street.

†**Cowper street,** E. B., 1838; from Rice street to Moore street (with proposed extension to Swift street); laid out from Moore street to Short street, July 25, 1881. L 1544.

Coy's lane, Rox.; an old road or cartway from Norfolk and Bristol turnpike (now Washington street) to St. James street; shown in 1844.

Crab alley, B.; from Batterymarch street to Broad street.

Crab alley, B., 1708; from Batterymarch street to the foot of Water street, opposite Mackerel lane; included in Batterymarch street, 1803; sometimes called Crab lane.

Crab alley, B., 1800; from Liberty square to Broad street; called Brimmer avenue, 1822–26.

Crab lane, B., 1708; from Macril lane (now Kilby street) to the sea, 1708; also called Crab alley; included in Batterymarch street, 1803.

Craddock street, Dor.; from Neponset avenue, near junction of Walnut street, south-westerly.

Craft street, Rox., 1872; from Heath street near Tremont street (now Huntington avenue), to Jamaicaway.

Crafts street, Chsn.; from Cambridge street, south-east, to Roland street, near and west of Boston & Maine R.R.

Craigie's bridge, B., 1786; from the foot of Leverett street to Lechmere's point, Cambridge; called also Canal bridge and Central bridge.

***Cranston street**, W. Rox., 1890; from Sheridan street, south-west, then north-west, over Terrace avenue to another part of Terrace avenue; laid out Nov. 11, 1890. L 2272.

***Crawford street**, Rox., 1872; from Warren street to Walnut avenue; laid out from Warren street to point included in present Elm Hill avenue, Oct. 16, 1877; extended through Llewellyn avenue to Walnut avenue, Dec. 4, 1879. L 1280, L 1408, L 1409.

Crawshaw place, Rox.; from Hampshire street, north-west, between Vernon street and Clay (now Linden park) street.

Creek lane, B., 1708; from Marshall's lane (now Marshall street) to Scottow's (now Scott) alley; south part called Creek square, 1803; called Hatter's square, 1823; the part leading from Marshall street or lane called Hancock row, 1826; whole called Creek square, 1855.

***Creek square**, B., 1803; from Marshall street to Blackstone street; formerly Creek lane; the name was applied to part of same, 1803; called Hatter's square, 1823; part called Hancock row, 1826; previous name again applied, 1855.

Creek street, B., 1831; from Fulton street and Clinton street to Charlestown street and Cross street; Ann (now North) street widened near Creek street, 1831; laid out, Oct. 23, 1833; sometimes called Canal street; discontinued; seems to be in same place as present Blackstone street.

***Creek street**, Dor., 1840; from Pleasant street to Dorchester avenue, near Commercial (now Freeport) street; named "from Sam'l Downers to Dorchester turnpike and Wales creek," March 11, 1840; called Swan street in 1854.

***Creighton street**, Rox., 1856; from Centre street, north-westerly, to Day (formerly Cross) street; laid out from Centre street to Day street, Sept. 10, 1889. L 2104.

Crescent, The, B., 1798; part of the present Franklin street between Bishop's alley (now Hawley street) and Federal street; laid out with an oval enclosure 300 feet long in the centre, on one side of which was Franklin place, and on the other the Tontine crescent, a block of sixteen dwelling-houses; made part of Franklin street, 1858.

Crescent avenue, Chsn.; from Cambridge street, near Somerville line, southerly, to unnamed street; Crescent street.

***Crescent avenue**, Dor., 1810; from Dorchester avenue, opposite Pond (now East Cottage) street, to O. C. (now N. Y., N. H. & H.) R.R., at Crescent-avenue station; located May 14, 1810; laid out by Selectmen, Nov. 10, 1868; accepted by Town, April 5, 1869.

Crescent avenue, Bri.; from Washington street, southerly and south-westerly to Newton line; shown but not named in 1846.

Crescent court, B., 1844; from Friend street, south-west, near Causeway street; called Crescent place, 1884.

Crescent place, B.; Crescent court, so called in 1884.

Crescent place, B. 1822; from Green street, north, near Pitts street.

Crescent street, Chsn.; from Roland street, near Somerville line, north, across Cambridge street, then north-east, beyond Hadley street to unnamed street opposite Pearl street, in Somerville; also called Crescent avenue.

Crest avenue, Dor.; from Riverview avenue, at Bearse street, south-east, to Riverview avenue again.

Crest street, W. Rox.; from Kirk (formerly Oak and later Short) street, south-west, to and beyond Houston street.

Crestwood park, Rox.; from Townsend street, between Humboldt avenue and Harold street, north-east.

Crestwood terrace, Rox.; from Townsend street.

Crimmen place, Chsn.; from Corey street, east, between Moulton street and Medford street.

Crocker place, B., 1857; from Albany street, east, rear of East Orange (now Way) street.

Crofts street, B., 1732; at north end of Ann (now North) street; from the sea north-west to the Mill-pond; probably same as Cross street.

Cromwell street, Rox.; from Massachusetts avenue to Dalton street; laid out as St. Germain street, Sept. 14, 1894. L 2618.

Crooked alley, B., 1708; from Cow lane (now High street) to Belcher's lane (now Purchase) street; in 1834 it existed as a narrow passageway opposite head of Federal street, but had no name; called Brick alley, 1788; Board alley, 1847; Broad alley by plan, 1864; shown as Board alley as late as 1870, but now built over.

Crooked lane, B., 1708; from Dock square to King (now State) street, name changed to Wilson's lane, May 12, 1712; included in extension of Devonshire street, 1872.

Crosby place, B., 1859; from West Canton street, between Newland street and Ivanhoe street, south-west.

Crosby place, B., 1876; from Reed street.

Crosby place, Rox.; from Adams street, between Hampden street and Yeoman street, north-west.

Crosby place, W. Rox.; from Call street, near Carolina avenue, south-west; also called Crosby square.

Crosby street, Bri., 1870; from Brooks street, east, near B. & A. R.R. at Faneuil; shown as part of Parkman street in 1874; location changed and called Crosby street in 1884.

Cross-dam, Rox.; Parker street, anciently and for a long time so called. L 862.

***Cross street**, B., 1708; from Haymarket square to Commercial street; from the Mill-pond, south-east, to the sea, 1708; called at the same time "the highway to Breeden's wharf;" probably same as Crofts street, 1732; Coney lane and Drum lane continued into the Mill-pond, Sept. 30, 1807; in 1817 it crossed Middle (now Hanover) street, Back (now Salem) street and Fish (now North) street, extended to Commercial street, 1830. Vol. 31, pp. 11, 37. L 14, L 2209.

Cross street, B., 1802; the part of Lyman street running east from Leverett street was then so called.

Cross street, E. B., 1833; from Border street to New street. L 241.

Cross street, Rox., 1825; from Centre street to Heath street; probably laid out Jan. 19, 1662; named May 9, 1825; name changed to Day street, April 21, 1868.

Cross street, Dor., 1840; from Columbia street, near Quincy street to Hancock street; located, May 18, 1807; named, March 11, 1840; name changed to Glendale street, May 31, 1870.

Cross street, W. Rox.; from Augustus avenue to Hillside avenue, near Poplar street.

***Cross street**, Chsn., 1823; from Cordis street to Pleasant street; accepted, June 6, 1823; probably now Cordis-street place (or Cordis court.)

***Cross street**, Chsn., 1839; from High street to Bartlett street, opposite Trenton street; laid out, Oct. 29, 1839; accepted, Nov. 11, 1839.

Coss-street avenue, Chsn.; from Cross street to Cedar street.

Cross-street court, Chsn.; from Cross street to Cedar street.

Crossin place, Rox.; from King street, south-west, near Elmwood street.

Crossland place, Bri.; from Winship street, south-east.

Crossman street, Dor.; from junction of Norfolk street and Delhi street, north-east, then south-east across West Selden street.

Cruft place, B., 1841-52; from Pearl street, east, near Milk street; closed.

Crystal place, Chsn.; from Mead street, north-west, near Main street.

Culbert place, Rox.; from Columbus avenue (formerly Pynchon street), near Cedar street, south-east, to N. Y., N. H. & H. R.R.

Culvert place, Rox.; from Culvert street, south-west, toward Vernon street; laid out as a public street and named Downing street, Aug. 29, 1884. L 1812.

***Culvert street**, Rox.; from Cabot street to Ruggles street; part from Tremont street to Ruggles street laid out, July 29, 1867; Columbus avenue was extended across Culvert street, Jan. 4, 1895. L 1015, L 1115.

***Cumberland street**, Rox., 1880; from Huntington avenue, to N.Y., N. H. & H. R.R.; laid out, Jan. 19, 1880. L 1425, L 2191.

Cummings road, Bri.; from Commonwealth avenue, south, then south-east to Dean (now Corey) road near Brookline; authority to open road No. 4 (Cummings road) given by Street Commissioners, May 13, 1892.

Cummington street, Rox., 1893; from Avon street to Blandford street.

***Cumston place**, B., 1861; from Shawmut avenue to Cumston street; laid out as a public street, May 21, 1867. L 352.

***Cumston street**, B., 1847; from West Concord street to Rutland street; new street from Concord street to Rutland street, named Cumston street, 1847; accepted May 21, 1867. L 352.

***Cunard street**, Rox., 1849; from Columbus avenue to Cabot street; from Tremont street to Berlin street laid out, Oct. 15, 1877; from Tremont street to Cabot street laid out, Oct. 4, 1894. L 1277, L 2656.

***Cunningham street**, Dor.; from Howard avenue to Hartford street; laid out, June 28, 1892. L 2418.

Curlew street, W. Rox.; from Cottage avenue, south-west.

Curtis court, Rox.; from Vernon street, near Downing street, north-east.

***Curtis street**, E.B., 1859; from Chelsea street to Saratoga street; laid out from Chelsea street to Pope street, Dec. 27, 1859; extended to Saratoga street, Dec. 31, 1875. L 1125.

***Curtis street**, Rox. and W. Rox., 1852; from Boylston street, opposite Chestnut street, north; laid out from Boylston street to Wyman street, Jan. 31, 1876; street from Wyman street to Green street, part of which has been called Curtis street and part Chestnut street, named Chestnut avenue, Dec. 26, 1877; Curtis street together with Chestnut street included in one street and named Chestnut avenue, Dec. 26, 1877. L 1128.

Curtis street, W. Rox., 1878; from Boylston street to Wyman street, near Chestnut avenue; shown as an unnamed street, 1856; called Chapel street, 1867; name of Chapel street changed to Curtis street, June 22, 1878; laid out as Danforth street, Sept. 12, 1881. L 1551.

***Curtis street**, W. Rox., 1825; from Norfolk and Bristol turnpike (now Washington street) to Walnut street; named Dedham turnpike south of Independent spring to Back street (now Walnut avenue), May 9, 1825; formerly known as Jube's lane, and probably a public highway some time previous to 1825; Curtis street and that part of Walnut street from its junction with Curtis street to South street named Forest Hill street, June 26, 1849; called Forest Hills street, Nov. 5, 1860.

***Curve street**, B., 1840; from Albany street to Broadway; from Harrison avenue to Lincoln street, 1840; to Albany street, 1846; accepted, conditionally, Dec. 17, 1849; accepted Jan. 5, 1856; Broadway extended to Washington street through part of Curve street, July 3, 1880. L 435, L 1530.

***Cushing avenue**, Dor., 1881; from Sawyer avenue, westerly, northerly and Westerly to Hancock street; Thacher avenue laid out and extended to Hancock street, including part of Upham avenue and name changed to Cushing avenue, Oct. 28, 1881. L 1562, L 1563, L 1564, L 2206.

Cushing street, W. Rox.; from Baker street to Barnes street; authority to open given by Street Commissioners, May 3, 1895.

Cushman avenue, B., 1855; from Leverett street to Wall street between Minot street and Cotting street; called Leverett lane, 1831; Cushman avenue, 1855.

Cusson place, B., 1871; from South Margin street, near Norman street, south-west.

***Custer street**, W. Rox., 1881; from South street, west, crossing Ballard street and Goldsmith street; White avenue from South street to Woodman street laid out and name changed to Custer street, May 19, 1881. L 1522.

***Custom-House street**, B., 1804; from Broad street to India street; confirmed as a public street, Sept. 15, 1834. L 15.

Cypher street, So. B.; from B street to E street, north-east of and parallel with West First street.

Cypress place, B., 1840; from Cypress street, east, near Vine (now Parkman) street; called Cypress-street place in 1848; built over.

Cypress place, B.; Cypress street from Cambridge street to Parkman street; so called in 1883.

Cypress road, Bri.; from George street to Dustin street, between Spring street and Garden street; also called Cypress street.

Cypress street, B., 1840; from Cambridge street to Parkman street; called Cyprus place, 1883.

Cypress street, W. Rox., 1872; from Beech street to Bellevue avenue, opposite Cedar street. L 1949.

***Cypress street**, W. Rox.; from Baker street to Spring street; laid out, Sept. 28, 1886.

Cypress-street place, B., 1848; from Cyprus street, near Vine (now Parkman) street; called Cypress place, 1840; now built over.

***D street**, B., 1828; from Mill-dam (now Beacon street), north, to the water; established in 1828; from Western avenue (now Beacon street) to Chestnut street accepted, Aug. 7, 1855; same named Messinger street, Jan. 5, 1856; name changed to Brimmer street, 1869.

***D street**, So. B., 1804; from Dorchester avenue to low-water mark with proposed extension to Eastern avenue (now Congress street); projected "from the boundary line to the sea," Oct. 4, 1804; laid out and named Feb. 27, 1805; laid out from point 46 feet south of Baxter street to O C. (now N. Y., N. H. & H.) R.R., Sept. 17, 1867; laid out, 50 feet wide, from O. C. R.R. to low-water mark ("502 to 509 feet from E street"), Nov. 17, 1868; extended to Dorchester avenue across location of O. C. R.R., passing under the tracks, March 29, 1882. L 183, L 369, L 1593.

D street, Dor., 1892; from Pleasant street to F (now Bakersfield) street; authority to open given by Street Commissioners, May 4, 1892; now called Hinckley street.

D street, W. Rox., 1868; from Spring Park avenue, south-west; laid out and extended to Green street under name of Rockview street, May 26, 1880. L 1459, L 1478.

Dabney place, Rox., 1868; from Regent street, near Fountain street, south-east.

***Dacia street**, Rox.; from Quincy street to Brookford street; laid out from Dalmatia street to Dewey street, Nov. 10, 1891; laid out from Dewey street to Brookford street, Dec. 31, 1891; Cherry street, from Quincy street to Dalmatia street, named Dacia street, March 1, 1892; for laying out of this part see Cherry street. L 964, L 2357, L 2358, L 2381.

Dacia place, } Rox.; from Dacia street, near corner Quincy street, south-
Dacia court, } east.

Dacia terrace, Rox.; from Dacia street, nearly opposite Dove street, south-east.

D'Acosta's pasture, B.; the space between Milk, Summer, Federal, and Hawley streets as spoken of in early records.

Dafforne's corner, B., 1708; corner of Milk street and Cooper's alley (now Kilby street); then so-called.

Daggett's alley or lane, B., 1789–1823; from North (now Hanover) street to Ship (now Commercial) street; Battery alley sometimes so called from 1789 to 1823; Battery street since 1806.

Dakota street, Dor.; from Geneva avenue to and across Bowdoin square.

Dale avenue, Rox.; from Dale street, north; Sherman street extended from Dale street to Rockland street, including Dale avenue, Oct. 10, 1882. L 1646.

***Dale street**, Rox., 1844; from Warren street to Washington street; petition that a new street from Warren street to Walnut street (now avenue) be accepted and named Dale street, reported favorably on certain conditions, April 1, 1844; and report accepted by Town; accepted from Shawmut avenue (now Washington street) to Walnut street, Oct. 14, 1867; accepted from Walnut street to Warren street, Oct. 28, 1867. L 638, L 907, L 908, L 1099.

***Dale street**, W. Rox., 1849; from Poplar street, south-east, to Hyde Park line; laid out, Nov. 12, 1877. L 1289.

Dalkeith street, Dor.; from Howard avenue, near and north of Quincy street; authority to open given by Street Commissioners, May 25, 1893.

Dallas place, Rox.; from Cabot street, near Ruggles street, south-east.

***Dalmatia street**, Rox. and Dor., 1891; from Blue Hill avenue to Howard avenue; laid out, Dec. 8, 1891. L 2373.

Dalrymple street, W. Rox.; from Egleston street to Georgianna street.

***Dalton street**, B. and Rox., 1878; from Falmouth street to B. & A. R.R.; laid out Oct. 7, 1878. L 1296, L 1320, L 2311, L 2373.

Dalton street, B., 1788; from Water street, opposite Leverett's lane, to Milk street; opened May 30, 1763, but no name then officially given; called Dalton's lane or row until 1788, when it was named Dalton street; name changed to Congress street, Jan. 22, 1800.

Dalton's lane or row, B., 1769; opened from Water street, at end of Leverett's lane, into Milk street, May 30, 1763, but not then named; so called prior to 1788; named Dalton street, 1788; Congress street, Jan. 22, 1800.

Damascus street, Dor.; from Blue Hill avenue to Howard avenue; laid out as Dewey street, May 13, 1889. L 2131.

Damon place, B., 1876; from Bennet street, south, to unnamed place leading from Ash street.

Dana court, Rox.; from 16 Dana street, south-east.

Dana place, Rox., 1849; from Dudley street, south-west, with branch to the west and another south-east; laid out and extended to Cliff street with name of Dana street, Nov. 26, 1884.

Dana place, Rox.; from 26 Dana street, south-east.

Dana street, So. B.; from West Ninth street, near Dorchester street, south-west to O. C. (now N. Y., N. H. & H.) R.R.; at one time called Watti court; laid out and named Mitchell street, Aug. 12, 1885. L 1877.

***Dana street**, Rox., 1884; from Dudley street to Cliff street: Dana place laid out from Dudley street and extended to Cliff street with name of Dana street, Nov. 26, 1884. L 1836.

Danby street, So. B.; (proposed street) from the proposed extension of B street to the proposed extension of E street, on the so-called Commonwealth flats.

Danforth place, Rox.; from St. James street, south, near Alpine street.

***Danforth street**, Rox., and W. Rox., 1881; from Boylston street to Wyman street; Curtis street laid out as Danforth street, Sept. 12, 1881. L 1551.

Daniel street, Rox., 1895; from Webber street to Mall street; authority to open given by Street Commissioners, March 27, 1895.

***Danube street**, Dor.; from Brookford street to Dewey street; laid out, March 21, 1890. L 2211.

Danville street, W. Rox.; from Bellevue street to Wren street.

Darling's lane, W. Rox., 1871; from Blue Hill turnpike (now avenue), near Williams street, north-west, then south-west; now included in Franklin Park.

Darling street, Dor.; from Norfolk street, opposite Wentworth street, to Southern avenue.

***Dartmouth place**, B., 1874; from Dartmouth street, north-east, to an unnamed place or way between Warren avenue and Appleton street; laid out from Dartmouth street, May 9, 1877. L 1233.

***Dartmouth street**, B., 1866; from Tremont street to Beacon street; shown as Avenue A in 1855; from the Mill-dam across the Back Bay to Tremont street, opposite Dedham street in 1856; called Dedham street to 1866, with exception of short time about 1864 when the name of Burlington street was used; portion of Dedham street, between Tremont street and the line of the Boston Water

Power Company's land (Beacon street) named Dartmouth street, Jan. 23, 1866; laid out from Tremont street to Warren avenue, Dec. 3, 1867; laid out from Warren avenue to Columbus avenue, Oct. 20, 1868; laid out from Columbus avenue to St. James avenue, April 27, 1869; laid out from Beacon street to the former boundary line between land of the Commonwealth and of the Boston Water Power Company (near where Huntington avenue now is), April 15, 1871. L 309, L 354, L 374, L 410, L 516, L 526, L 862, L 1699.

Dassett's } **alley**, B., 1789; from Brattle square to Court street; some-
Dorsett's } times, but rarely, so called; called Brattle street, 1708; Brattle's alley or lane, 1722; Dassett's alley, 1789; Franklin avenue, 1818; properly Dassett's alley was the easterly end of Brattle street leading to Dock square; called Cooper's alley, 1819; included in Brattle street, 1820.

Davenport avenue, Dor.; from Columbia street, near Hancock street, north-west, to Virginia street.

Davenport place, Rox.; from 23 Davenport street, north-east.

Davenport street, Rox., 1859; from Tremont street to Columbus avenue.

Davenport square, Dor.; shown on atlas of 1894 as between Rocky Hill avenue and Arion street near junction Columbia street and Hancock street.

Davenport's lane, Dor., 1805; mentioned, May 13, 1805; straightened, April 1, 1816; relocated, Nov. 11, 1839; now Marsh street (from Adams street, near Minot street.)

Davenport's lane, Dor., 1840; from Bowdoin street, west; the street from Bowdoin street through Davenport's lane named Green street, according to recommendation of committee, March 11, 1840; now Olney street.

Davidson avenue, Dor.; from Richfield street, opposite Norton street.

Davies lane, B., 1708; from Beacon street at the corner of the present Mt. Vernon street, across the State-house grounds, past the beacon to Walnut street (then Allen's orchard), 1708; shown on Bonner's plan, 1722; on Burgess' 1729; is in list of 1732; but is not shown on Price's map, 1733.

Davis court, B., 1869; from North Grove street, near Cambridge street, west; changed to Church court in 1896.

Davis court, E. B.; from London street near Marion street, south-east.

Davis place, Rox.; from Webber street, near Fellows street, north-east.

Davis place, Dor.; from Cottage street, near Sumner street, south-west; called also Turpin court.

***Davis street**, B., 1853; from Washington street to Harrison avenue, opened from Washington street to Harrison avenue, Dec. 20, 1852; named Davis street, Feb. 28, 1853. Vol. 19, p. 123; vol. 31, pp. 56 and 70.

Davis street, B., 1810; from Washington street to Tremont street, 1810; called Camden street, 1826.

Davis street, Rox., 1825; from Northampton street to Eustis street; prior to 1800 this street led from town landing on Roxbury canal to Eustis street (then Mall street); later Eustis street changed south of Mall street and Davis street extended across New Eustis street to Dudley street; named, May 9, 1825; certain alterations in June, 1842; extended to Dudley street opposite Elm street (now Mt. Pleasant avenue), April 2, 1855; City Government of Boston request that of Roxbury to lay out Davis street to meet Albany street, at Roxbury creek, April 21, 1855; name changed to Albany street, April 21, 1868.

Davis street, Rox., 1845; from Parker Hill avenue, east; from High street (Parker Hill avenue) east, 1849; name changed to Hillside street, April 21, 1868.

***Day street**, Rox., 1868; from Centre street to Heath street; named Cross street, May 9, 1825; probably laid out Jan. 19, 1662; name changed to Day street, April 21, 1868. L 381, L 2187.

Day street, Bri.; from junction Washington street and Cambridge street; included in the laying out of Henshaw street, Nov. 6, 1891.

Day's alley or **lane**, B.; Henchman street, from Charter street to Lynn (now Commercial) street, so called prior to 1708.

Dayton avenue, Rox.; from 30 Mall street, north-east.

***Deacon street**, B., 1871; from West Concord street to Worcester street; named Nov. 14, 1871; laid out, Sept. 29, 1875. L 1077.

Deacon street, B., 1788; from Friends (Friend) street to Cold lane (Portland street), 1788; extended from Friend street to Merrimac street, Oct. 3, 1831; name of Deacon street discontinued and Sudbury street extended to Merrimac street, Sept. 2, 1839; name of Deacon street again discontinued and part from Portland street to Merrimac street made part of Sudbury street, April 14, 1851.

Dean avenue, Dor.; from Howard avenue; laid out as Dean street, and extended to Judson street, Oct. 14, 1892.

***Dean street**, Dor., 1892; from Howard avenue to Judson street; Dean avenue laid out as Dean street, Oct. 14, 1892. L 2447.

Dean street, Bri., 1871; from Warren street to Brock street; closed; Massachusetts (now Commonwealth) avenue having been laid out parallel with and a few feet from it.

***Dearborn place**, Rox., 1857; from Dearborn street, near Eustis street to Dearborn grammar school; laid out, June 27, 1871. L 627.

***Dearborn street**, Rox., 1857; from Albany street to Dudley street; part north of Eustis street called Abney place, 1850; westerly-line established from Davis (now Albany) street to Eustis street, June 22, 1857. L 1314.

Dearborn's avenue, B., 1823; from Federal street to Theatre alley (Devonshire street), 1823–45; closed.

***Deblois street**, B., 1871; from Shawmut avenue to Deacon street; named, Nov. 14, 1871; laid out, May 6, 1876. L 1146.

Decatur avenue, Rox.; first street south of Roxbury street running west from Columbus avenue.

Decatur court, Chsn.; from Decatur street, near Bainbridge street, north-west; shown as an unnamed court on plan, 1850; called also Decatur-street court.

***Decatur street**, B., 1842; from Washington street to Harrison avenue, near Dover street; laid out, Aug. 13, 1877. L 1258.

***Decatur street**, E. B., 1833; from Border street to Orleans street (with proposed extension to Lamson street); accepted, conditionally, from Border street to Meridian street, Aug. 16, 1852, and from Meridian street to Bremen street, May 17, 1856; accepted from Bremen street to Orleans street, April 5, 1859; part from Meridian street to Bremen street named Gove street, March 1, 1893. L 2502.

Decatur street, W. Rox., 1872; from Beech street, north-east, between Anawan avenue and West Roxbury branch R.R.; shown only on plan of Anawan land Co., dated June, 1872.

***Decatur street**, Chsn., 1850; from Bunker Hill street to Medford street; portion from Vine street to a new street laid out and accepted, Dec. 30, 1852; extended and laid out from Perry street to Medford street, Dec. 14, 1859; extended and laid out of uniform width from Vine street to Bunker Hill street, March 15, 1869.

Decatur-street court, Chsn.; from Decatur street, north-west; Decatur court, sometimes so-called.

Decher avenue, W. Rox.; from 198 Lamartine street.

Declination passage, B.; Henchman street, from Charter street to Lynn (now Commercial) street, so called at some time prior to 1708; also called Day's alley or lane.

Dedham court, B., 1850; from Dedham street, east, 1850; included in Meander street, 1851.

***Dedham street**, B., 1826; from Washington street, west, 1826; the seventh of new streets at South End, from Tremont street to Front street (now Harrison avenue), named Dedham street, Sept. 15, 1834; extended to Albany street, 1854; order for purchase of land for extension to Beacon street, Nov. 8, 1856; street accepted, Dec. 7, 1857; accepted again, Oct. 30, 1860; portion west of Tremont street unofficially called Burlington street for a long time, and this name ordered removed from sign in 1864; from Tremont street to line of Boston Water Power Co.'s land named Dartmouth street, Jan. 23, 1866; from Washington street to Albany street named East Dedham street, April 21, 1868; from Washington street to Tremont street, named West Dedham street, April 21, 1868. L 295, L 372.

Dedham turnpike, Rox. and W. Rox., 1808; from Dudley street to Dedham line; Norfolk and Bristol turnpike sometimes so called; see map of 1849; called also Dedham and Providence turnpike, Dedham road, Dedham old road, road to Dedham, etc., Norfolk and Bristol turnpike; later called Shawmut avenue and now Washington street.

Dedham and Providence turnpike, Rox., 1843; now Washington street.

***Deerfield street**, Rox., 1893; from Commonwealth avenue to Charles river; laid out and construction ordered, June 7, 1893. L 2516.

Deering's corner, B., 1708; corner Cornhill (now Washington street) and Queen (now Court) street, then so-called.

Delaware street, Rox.; from Tremont street to Calumet street; authority to open given by Street Commissioners, Feb. 27, 1894; St. Alphonsus street extended through Delaware street to Calumet street, Sept. 23, 1895. L 2734.

Delay's court, Chsn.; from Walnut street, north-west.

Delhi street, Dor.; from Norfolk street, north-east, near and parallel to N. E. R.R.

Dell avenue, So. B.; from East Seventh street, near I street, north; now called Linden place.

Dell street, Dor.; from Dorchester avenue to Wrentham (now Bruce) street; laid out as Dracut street, April 19, 1890. L 2221.

***Delle avenue**, Rox., 1871; from Parker street, near Tremont street, to Burney street; laid out from Parker street, July 9, 1879. L 1363.

Deming's court, B., 1806; from Newbury (now Washington) street, south of Central court, 1806; called Central court, 1816; spelled also Demming's and D'Emming's court; see Avon place.

Demisa square, B.; from Reed street, west, about 225 feet; included in East Lenox street, 1874. L 957.

D'Emming's,
Demming's, } court, B.; see Deming's court.
Denning's,

Dennis place, Chsn.; from Walnut street, near Bunker Hill street, north-west; now called Bellows place.

***Dennis street**, Rox.; from Dudley street to Woodville street; formerly from Dudley street to Blue Hill avenue; laid out Jan. 19, 1662; confirmed, May 17, 1797; named from Eustis street to Warren street, including present Dennis street, part of Blue Hill avenue and part of South Dennis street, May 9, 1825; laid out by County Commissioners from Warren street to Eustis (now Dudley) street, near Elm street (now Mt. Pleasant avenue) Sept., 1840; alterations in June, 1842; part now Blue Hill avenue shown on plan dated 1849 as East street, and part now Quincy street as South Dennis street; relocated from Dudley street to Woodville square (now street), June 4, 1886; name of that part between Woodville square and Blue Hill avenue changed to Woodville street, March 1, 1890. L 1085, L 1755, L 1909.

***Denny street**, Dor., 1892: from Savin Hill avenue to Springdale street; Bath avenue laid out as Denny street, April 21, 1892. L 2393.

†**Dent street**, W. Rox., 1872; from Mt. Vernon street to West Roxbury Branch R.R. at West Roxbury Station; portion from Jordan street to Ivory street laid out, Sept. 28, 1876; authority to open part between Lasell street and Weld street given by Street Commissioners, March 5, 1895. L 1173.

Denvir street, Dor.; from Edwin street, north, near Dorchester avenue.

Depot square, Dor., 1858; from Walnut street, south-east.

Depot square, W. Rox.; from Green street to Gordon street; at Jamaica Plain station.

Depot street, Rox.; from Brookline avenue, near Brookline Branch R.R., north-west, to same.

Derby avenue, B., 1841; from Brighton street to Auburn street, 1841; called Brighton-street avenue, 1844.

Derby court, So. B.; from East Second street, near H street, north.

Derby place, B., 1853; from Washington street, near Woodbury street, north-west, to unnamed place.

***Derne street**, B., 1806; from Bowdin street to Hancock street; called Hill street, from Middlecot (now Bowdoin) street to Hancock street in Selectmen's list, 1788; named Derne street, June 25, 1806. L 1505, L 2105.

Desmond place, Rox.; from 90 Fellows street.

***Devens street**, Chsn., 1882; from Washington street to Main street; formerly a part of Bow street; name changed to Devens street, March 1, 1882.

Devens-street place, Chsn.; from Devens street, between Rutherford avenue and Washington street.

Dever street, Dor.; from Bowdoin street, between Olney street and Blakeville street, north-west.

†**Devon street**, Rox., 1880; from Warren street to Columbia street; laid out from Blue Hill avenue to Warren street, Oct. 6, 1880; authority to open part east of Blue Hill avenue given by Street Commissioners, Dec. 5, 1893; authority to open portion from Columbia street north-westerly, given by Street Commissioners, Dec. 7, 1895. L 1496.

Devon street, Bri.; from Third street to Fifth street; shown on atlas of 1882; now in Brighton cattle yards.

***Devonshire street**, B., 1766; from Dock square to Summer street; from King (now State) street to Water street called Pudden or Pudding lane, and from Water street to Milk street called Joyliff's or Joylieff's lane, 1708; at one time called Black Jack alley from Water street to Milk street; Pudden lane was, after the fire, enlarged into a street, named Devonshire street, April 20, 1766, in honor of a merchant of Bristol who generously contributed to aid the sufferers by the fire; so called also in list of 1788; extended from Milk street to Franklin street through Theatre alley and Odeon avenue, June 22, 1857; from Franklin street to Otis and

Winthrop places, June 26, 1858, and Sept. 3, 1858; to Summer street through Winthrop place, April 23, 1861; same part accepted, Oct. 16, 1861; extended, June 25, 1862, and Dec. 30, 1862; extended 50 feet wide through Wilson's lane across Dock (now Adams) square to Washington street, June 6, 1872. L 101. L 105, L 133, L 163, L 205, L 375, L 376, L 399, L 400, L 767, L 772, L 831, L 832, L 834, L 852, L 982.

Dewerson court, So. B.; from Silver street, near C street, north-east.

***Dewey street**, Dor., 1889; from Blue Hill avenue to Howard avenue; Damascus street laid out as Dewey street, May 13, 1889. L 2131.

***DeWolf street**, Dor., 1880; from Commercial (now Freeport) street to Downer avenue; laid out, June 21, 1880; formerly Austin street, but with no record under that name. L 1464.

Dexter court, Dor., 1874; from Boston street, opposite Clapp place, west, then north.

Dexter row, Chsn.; on Thompson square, between Green street and Five Cents Savings Bank.

***Dexter street**, So. B., 1855; from Dorchester avenue, near Swett street, to Ellery street; name of Howard street changed to Dexter street, Aug. 7, 1855; laid out from Dorchester avenue to Ellery street, June 5, 1875. L 1048.

Dexter street, Chsn., 1896; from Alford street to Everett line, formerly called Carnes street.

***Dickens street**, Dor., 1879; from Adams street, near Dorchester avenue, east, to Clayton street, at Harrison square; laid out and widened, Aug. 25, 1879. L 1374, L 2124.

***Dighton place**, Bri.; south, from Washington street, between Chestnut Hill avenue and Eastburn street; formerly called Winship place; laid out as Dighton place, Dec. 19, 1889. L 1850, L 2177, L 2195, L 2196.

Dillaway place, B., 1840; from Charter street, north-east, nearly opposite Washburn place; called Carter place, 1874.

***Dillon street**, B., 1887; from Lenox street to Sawyer street; formerly known as Trainer court and Winfred court; laid out as Dillon street, Oct. 24, 1887. L 2034.

***Dimock street**, Rox., 1884; from Washington street, opposite Codman park, to Amory street; Codman avenue laid out as Dimock street, Oct. 20, 1884. L 1826.

†**Dingley place**, B., 1872; from Fayette street, east of Church street, north-west, past hose-house, then east, then south-east to Fayette street; part to hose-house formerly a part of Knox street, as laid out Sept. 29, 1868; part of Knox street from Church street, north, built over, and balance north of Church street included in Dingley place, 1869. L 387, L 392, L 404.

Dindale's alley, B.; from Milk street to Franklin street; so called prior to 1796, when it was called Theatre alley; included in Devonshire street in 1859.

Distill-House square, B., 1743; from Sudbury street, north-west, to Mill-pond, then south-west to the bottom of Hawkins street; also called Distillers square; called Still-house square in Selectmen's list, 1788; a portion known as Bog lane at one time; part included in Ivers street, 1820; name of remaining part changed to Adams street, Sept. 9, 1850, and to Bowker street, 1868.

Distill-House street, B., 1826; from Washington street to Harrison avenue, 1826; called Indiana street, 1844.

†**Ditson street**, Dor., 1882; from Charles street across Westville street; laid out, Nov. 4, 1882, from Charles street to Westville street. L 1662, L 2194.

Division street, B., 1869; from Northampton street to Chester park (now Massachusetts avenue), with arm at right angle extending to Harrison avenue, with three openings into Northampton street, named Division street, July 26, 1869.

***Division street**, So. B., 1873; from Dorchester avenue at its junction with Broadway, west, to Foundry street; laid out, Oct. 1, 1873. L 898, L 900.

Dix avenue, Bri., 1875; from Union street, south-west, near Madison avenue.

***Dix place**, B., 1846; from Washington street, north-west, opposite Harvard street; called Dutch lane prior to 1823: Orange court, 1823; Orange court, from Washington street towards Johnson school-house; accepted and laid out as Orange court, Sept. 1, 1845; name changed to Dix place, March 30, 1846. L 321.

***Dix street**, Dor., 1877; from Adams street, near Centre street, to Dorchester avenue; laid out from Adams street, May 21, 1877; extended to Dorchester avenue, including Luelner place, Oct. 2, 1877. L 1239, L 1267.

***Doane street**, B., 1806; from Kilby street to Broad street; Doane's wharf prior to 1806: by request of abutters, Selectmen record same as a public street with name of Doane street, June 11, 1806.

***Dock square**, B., 1708; between Adams square and Faneuil Hall square; the square between the houses of Eliakim Hutchinson and Mr. Pemberton on one side, and Kenney's shops and Meer's corner on the other, near the Town Dock, 1708; committee report that Town Dock belonged to Town, and recommended that Town fill up same and lay out suitable way, 1775; between Cornhill, west end of Faneuil Hall, then Market square, and King's Tavern, including the block of stores in the centre, 1800; portion discontinued, 1852; westerly end called Adams square, 1879. Vol. 31, p. 57. L 65.

Doherty court, E. B.; from Everett street, near Lamson street, north-east.

Dolan court, Rox.; from Norfolk avenue, near N. E. R.R., south-west; included in laying out of Marshfield street, July 5, 1890. L 2241.

Don street, Dor.; from Lauriat avenue to Chapman avenue; authority to open given by Street Commissioners, Sept. 14, 1894.

Donovan's court, Chsn.; from Mead street, near Bunker Hill street, south-east.

Doody's court, Dor.; from Geneva avenue, near Columbia street.

Doolin place, So. B.; from West Third street, south-west, between D street and E street.

***Dorchester avenue**, So. B. and Dor., 1854; from Federal-street bridge to junction Adams street and Washington street at Lower Mills; shown as an unnamed avenue on plan dated, 1811; formerly called Dorchester turnpike and sometimes, though improperly, South Boston turnpike, and the part from dividing line between Boston and Dorchester to Federal-street bridge called Turnpike street; Turnpike street from Federal-street bridge to dividing line between Boston and Dorchester named Dorchester avenue, March 27, 1854; part in Dorchester laid out and located, April, 1854; lines changed in neighborhood of Crescent avenue and Pond (now East Cottage) street, Sept. 8, 1865; name of part formerly Turnpike street and Dorchester avenue to dividing line between Boston and Dorchester changed to Federal street in continuation of that street, Feb. 13, 1866; same renamed Dorchester avenue, March 1, 1870; relocated from Commercial (now Freeport) street to Adams street, Aug. 18, 1881; relocated from Field's corner to the Lower Mills, May 12, 1884. Vol. 31, p. 79. L 39, L 79, L 85, L 245, L 360, L 446,

L 474, L 603, L 632, L 683, L 725, L 881, L 1122, L 1123, L 1214, L 1215, L 1231, L 1285, L 1415, L 1510, L 1546, L 1771, L 1772, L 1773, L 1774, L 1865, L 2093, L 2223, L 2227, L 2436, L 2468, L 2469, L 2470, L 2471, L 2472, L 2473, L 2474, L 2475, L 2614.

Dorchester road, Dor., 1809; see plan, L 33, f. 177, Norfolk Registry.

Dorchester square, Dor, 1872; between Church, Winter, Adams, and Bowdoin streets; Meeting House Hill, called Dorchester square, Dec. 28, 1872.

Dorchester street, B.; from Washington street to Tremont street; Boookline street, so called previous to 1826; named West Brookline street, 1868.

***Dorchester street,** So. B., 1804; from junction Sweet, Boston, and Preble streets and Dorchester avenue (now Andrew square) to West First street (with proposed extension to I street); shown on plan dated Oct. 4, 1804, beginning on line which divides South Boston from Dorchester at the place "where the present road over the marsh and causeway crosses division line, thence running north, 63 degrees, 42 chains and 20 links; and 80 feet wide;" on annexation of part of Dorchester with name of South Boston, the principal street from the dividing line, north-easterly, named Dorchester street, Feb. 27, 1805; committee authorized to complete so much "as they may think expedient," May 19, 1819; completed from Broadway to First street, Nov. 7, 1821; street "running from Dorchester line to the water, in a north-easterly direction, formerly called Dorchester street, and recently Mather street and Boston street," named Dorchester street throughout, July 3, 1855; lines defined between Eighth street and O. C. (now N. Y., N. H. & H.) R.R., Dec. 15, 1863; laid out from I street to line between Boston and Dorchester, Nov. 17, 1868; part between Dorchester avenue and Boston street (at Mt. Vernon street) named Boston street, Oct. 7, 1873. Vol. 31, p. 16 L 53, L 140, L 195, L 253, L 263, L 265, L 267, L 335, L 353, L 363, L 683, L 716, L 865, L 866, L 879, L 1209, L 1415, L 1508.

Dorchester turnpike, Dor., 1805; from Milton bridge to Nook point; see stat. March 4, 1805; "Turnpike to Boston:" laid out and located as public way, April 22, 1854: called Dorchester avenue.

Dorchesterway, Dor., 1892; part of Parkway, from Edward Everett square, to the water in Old Harbor; named, 1892.

Dorr street, So. B., 1864; from 448 Dorchester avenue, near D street, south-east, crossing Ames street; shown as an unnamed street on plan, 1854.

***Dorr street,** Rox., 1833; from Highland street to Ascension street (now Lambert avenue); laid out and accepted, Dec. 8, 1871. L 723.

***Dorrance street,** Chsn., 1863; from junction Mystic avenue and Main street to Arlington avenue; from Main street, laid out and accepted, Dec. 24, 1868.

***Dorset street,** Dor.; from Boston street to Dorchester avenue, opposite Locust street; laid out Aug. 8, 1888. L 2086.

***Dorsett's alley,** B.; opinion of town advocate that the way was a townway Nov. 11, 1807; same as Dassett's alley; included in Brattle street in 1820.

Douglas street, So. B., 1860; from East Eighth street, near G street, to East Ninth street.

Douglass avenue, Rox.; from Mall street, between Dayton avenue and Harrison avenue, to Webber street; called also Mall-street place in 1873.

Douglass court, B., 1872; from Endicott street, east; called Endicott-street place, 1837; Douglass court, 1872.

Dove court, Rox.; from Dove street, south-west.

***Dove street**, So. B., 1862; from Dorchester street, between West First street and West Second street, to E street; report recommending acceptance from Dorchester street to F street, on certain conditions, July 28, 1862; same laid out and accepted Sept. 11, 1878; laid out from E street to F street, July 2, 1885. L 1317, L 1867.

***Dove street**, Rox., 1853; from Blue Hill avenue to Cherry (now Dacia) street; laid out and accepted, July 29, 1879. L 1731.

Dover place, B., 1848; from Dover street, south, then east to Harrison avenue, called Granite place, 1844; Dover place, 1848; Dover-street place, 1861; laid out with name of Fay street, Nov. 9, 1877. L 1288.

***Dover street**, B., 1834; from Tremont street to N. Y., N. H. & H. R.R.; laid out from Orange (now Washington) street to South bridge on Front street (now Harrison avenue), but not named, July 11, 1804; extended to Tremont street and named Dover street, Nov. 10, 1834; from Washington street to South Boston bridge, including South Bridge street (sometimes called Bridge street and also East Dover street), 1839; laid out over tide-water, from Albany street to location of O. C. (now N. Y., N. H. & H) R.R., Aug. 16, 1876. L 26, L 185½, L 408, L 544, L 545, L 639, L 724, L 837, L 1164, L 1184, L 1349.

***Dover-street bridge**, B., 1839; from Front street (now Harrison avenue) to South Boston; called South bridge and South Boston bridge, 1805; made part of Dover street, Aug. [illegible] 1876.

Dover-street place, B., 1861; from East Dover street, south, then east to Harrison avenue; called Granite place, 1844; Dover place, 1848; Dover-street place, 1861; laid out with name of Fay st., Nov. 9, 1877. L 26, L 1288.

†**Downer avenue**, Dor., 1871; from Pleasant street, near Hancock street, to Sawyer avenue; laid out from Pleasant street 284 feet crossing end of De Wolf street, Dec. 13, 1879. L 729, L 1413.

Downer court, Dor.; from 253 Hancock street, near Draper court, north-west.

Downer place, Dor.; from Hancock street, near Adams street.

***Downer street**, Rox.; 1866; from Tremont street (now Huntington avenue), north-east, near Brookline line, and parallel with Muddy river; laid out, Nov. 9, 1877; included in Riverway, April 30, 1890. L 1286.

Downing place, Rox.; from 159 Vernon street.

***Downing street**, Rox., 1884; from Culvert street to Vernon street; Culvert place, laid out and named Downing street, Aug. 29, 1884. L 1812.

***Dracut street**, Dor., 1890; from Dorchester avenue to Wrentham (now Bruce) street; Dell street laid out as Dracut street, April 19, 1890. L 2221.

Drake street, E. B., from 96 Chelsea street to Paris street.

***Draper court**, Dor., 1807; from Eaton square near Quincy street, north-west; located, May 18, 1807.

†**Draper street**, Dor., 1871; from Arcadia street, north-west, crossing Westville street and Robinson street; laid out from Robinson street to Arcadia street, Nov. 10, 1871; authority to open part between Homes avenue and Bowdoin street given by Street Commissioners, Aug. 2, 1894. L 713, L 1538.

Draper street, W. Rox., 1872; from Beech street, north-east, between Anawan avenue and West Roxbury Branch R.R.; shown only on plan of Anawan Land Co., dated June, 1872.

Draper's alley, B., 1734; from Brattle square to Cornhill; called also Boylston's alley; included in extension of Washington street, 1872.

Draper's lane, B., from Newland street to Ivanhoe street.

Draw-Bridge, B.; over the Mill creek, in Ann (now North) street; rebuilt about 1688.

Draw-Bridge street, B.; Ann (now North) street was at one time so called.

Drew place, Rox.; from Ruggles street, near Windsor street, north-east.

Drisko street, Rox., 1871; from Parker street, crossing Huntington avenue, south-east.

Dromey avenue, Dor.; from Judson street, south-east, then south-west to Brookford street; formerly from Brookford street, crossing end of Judson street, and to Brookford street again. Judson street extended over a portion of Dromey avenue to Brookford street, Dec. 12, 1896. L 2800.

Druid street, Dor.; from Morton street to Codman street; authority to open part given by Street Commissioners, May 5, 1893, and June 7, 1893.

Drum lane, B.; from the Mill-pond, east, to the sea; now Cross street.

Drury place, Rox., 1874; from Parker street, nearly opposite Delle avenue, to Terrace street; laid out as a public street with name of Oscar street, Aug. 19, 1881. L 1548.

Duck lane, Bri.; from Western avenue, north-east, to Smith street, near and parallel with North Harvard street.

Dudley avenue, W. Rox., 1871; from Washington street (formerly Shawmut avenue) across B. & P. (now N. Y., N. H. & H., R.R. to South street; called in 1867 Dudley avenue, and described as leading from South street to Shawmut avenue.

Dudley place, Rox , 1855; from Dudley street, north, near Putnam street, then both east and west.

Dudley square, Rox.; junction Washington and Dudley streets and Guild row.

***Dudley street**, Rox. and Dor., 1662; from Eliot square in Roxbury, to junction of Hancock, Boston, and Stoughton streets, in Dorchester, and a piece in Roxbury, now called Dearborn street, running north from a point opposite Mt. Pleasant avenue, to Eustis street; located from Guild row to Dorchester brook, Jan. 19, 1662; part in Roxbury, from Guild row to Roxbury street at Eliot square, opened and called Dudley street, prior to 1825; named "from parting stone by James Riley's store, through Dudley street by Samuel Weld's to Eustis street," May 9, 1825; straightened, etc., near Greenville street, Oct. 26, 1846; part of Eustis street, from what is now Dearborn st. to Dorchester line named Dudley street, April 21, 1868; name of part of Stoughton street, "from Brooks avenue to Upham's corner," changed to Dudley street, June 30, 1874; part in Dorchester sometimes called Lower road to Boston. L 628, L 701, L 702, L 703, L 704, L 705, L 706, L 782, L 783, L 784, L 880, L 882, L 902, 1369, L 1541, L 1788, L 1791, L 2290, L 2755.

Duke street, Dor., 1895; from Ponemah street to Ormond street; authority to open given by Street Commissioners, May 20, 1895.

Dumas street, Dor.; from Willowwood street to Mascot street.

Dummers' corner, B., 1708; cor. of King (now State) street, and Mackerel lane (now Kilby street) then so-called.

Dummers' corner, B., 1732; cor. School street and Governor's alley (Province street) then so-called.

Dunbar avenue, Dor.; from Washington street nearly opposite Roslin street, to Gordon street.

Dunbar street, W. Rox.; from Westover street, north-east, to Brookline line.

Dunboy avenue, Bri.; from Faneuil street to Bigelow street; known as Everett street in 1858; laid out as Dunboy street, Aug. 13, 1889. L 2151.

***Dunboy street**, Bri., 1889; from Faneuil street to Bigelow street; known as Everett street in 1858; Dunboy avenue in 1889; Dunboy avenue laid out as Dunboy street, Aug. 13, 1889. L 2151.

Duncan place, Dor.; from Duncan street, opposite Fenton street, south-west.

Duncan street, Rox., 1873; from Ruggles street, opposite Leon street to Halleck street; authority to open given by Street Commissioners Oct. 5, 1895.

***Duncan street**, Dor., 1870; from Leonard street to Greenwich street, near Field's corner; laid out, Dec. 14, 1893. L 2572.

***Dundee street**, Rox.. 1891; from Massachusetts avenue to Dalton street; laid out from West Chester park (now Massachusetts avenue) to Dalton street, Nov. 2, 1891. L 2355.

Dunford street, Rox.; from Cobden street; authority to open given by Street Commissioner, Feb. 6. 1893.

Dunham park, So. B.; from 65 West Fifth street; formerly Webster place.

***Dunham street**, So. B., 1885; from angle in East Ninth street, south-east of Lowland street to Old Harbor street; name of part of East Ninth street changed to Dunham street, March 1, 1885. L 191, L 192, L 751, L 1789.

Dunkeld street, Dor.; from Quincy street to Phipps avenue.

Dunlow place, Rox.; from Dunlow street near Elmwood street.

Dunlow street, Rox., 1868; from Roxbury street to Elmwood street; name of High street changed to Dunlow street, April 21, 1868.

***Dunmore street**, Rox., 1884; from Dudley street to Magazine street; part of Magazine street, from St. Patrick's church to Dudley street, at Hampden street, named Dunmore street, March 1, 1884. L 1972.

Dunreath place, Rox.; from Warren street, near Montrose avenue (now street), east; laid out as Dunreath street, from Warren street, May 10, 1889. L 2130.

***Dunreath street**, Rox., 1889; from Warren street, near Montrose street; laid out, May 10, 1889. L 2130.

***Dunstable street**, Chsn., 1881; from Main street to Rutherford avenue; private way called Winchester street, laid out from Rutherford avenue, and extended to Main street, and named Dunstable street, Nov. 11, 1881. L 1565.

Dupee place, B., 1839; from Friend street, north, near Hanover street; 1839; part included in extension of Washington street, 1872, and the remainder built over.

***Dupont street**, Chsn., 1890; from Chelsea street to Decatur street; part of Perry street laid out as Dupont street, Aug. 29, 1890. L 2258.

Durant street, W. Rox., 1895; from Baker street to Barnes street; authority to open given by Street Commissioners, May 3, 1895.

***Durham street**, B., 1880; from St. Botolph street to B. & P. (now N. Y., N. H. & H.) R.R.; laid out Jan. 19, 1880. L 1424.

***Dustin street**, Bri., 1890; from Cambridge street to North Beacon street; Gramercy street laid out as Dustin street, Feb. 20, 1890. L 2207.

Dutch lane, B.; from Washington street, west, near Eliot street; so called prior to 1823; called Orange court, 1823; named Dix place, 1846.

Dutton place, B., 1857; from Phillips street, near Grove street, north.

***Dwight street**, B., 1859; from Shawmut avenue to Tremont street; a part of Groton street, 1826; named Dwight street, April 19, 1859.

Dwinell street, W. Rox.; from Weld street, near Arnold street, to beyond Worley street.

Dyer avenue, Dor., 1872 (proposed); from Blue Hill avenue, near Tileston avenue, north-west.

Dyer avenue, So. B.; from West Third street to Athens street, near F street.

Dyer street, Dor., 1871; from Capen street, east, then south-east, to Evans street.

Dyke road, Rox., 1832; from Tide Mill road, south-east, to boundary line between Boston and Roxbury; part of Dyke street, Boston, and now part of Harrison avenue.

Dyke street, B.; ordered to be repaired, etc., from Dedham (now East Dedham) street, to the east end of the Dyke, June 2, 1835; Front street (now Harrison avenue) continued, spoken of as "lately Dyke street," Oct., 1835; now a part of Harrison avenue.

†**E street**, So. B., 1804; from O.C. (now N. Y., N. H. & H.) R.R. to low-water mark with proposed extension to Eastern avenue (now Congress street): projected "from the boundary line to the sea;" laid out 50 feet wide by Town of Dorchester, from North (now West Eighth) street 62 feet to South Boston line, April 11, 1849; laid out from Sullivan (now West Ninth) street to low-water mark, Nov. 17, 1868; laid out from West Ninth street to the O. C. R.R., Oct. 12, 1892. L 2443.

E street, W. Rox., 1868; from Spring Park avenue, south, then east to D (now Rockview) street; laid out from Spring Park avenue to Hazel street under name of Enfield street, Aug. 28, 1880; and from Rockview (formerly D) street to Enfield street, under name of Hazel street, Aug. 28, 1880. L 1477, L 1478.

E street, Dor., 1892; from Pleasant street to F (now Bakersfield) street; authority to open given by Street Commissioners, May 4, 1892; afterwards called Willis street, and laid out under that name from Pleasant street to Sumner street, Aug. 10, 1893. L 2527.

E street — D street, W. Rox., 1868; street so called connecting D (now Rockview) street, and E (now Enfield) street, and about 190 feet long; laid out as Hazel street, Aug. 28, 1880. L 1478.

Eagle-Mill place, Dor.; from River street, opposite Cedar street, south.

Eagle pass, Chsn.; from Mead street, north-west, near Russell street, shown on atlas of 1892.

Eagle square, E. B., 1858; space enclosed by Eagle street, Sumner street and Chelsea street, so-called, Nov. 1, 1868.

Eagle street, W. Rox.; from Cottage avenue to Willet street.

***Eagle street**, E. B., 1835; from Border street to Brooks street, and from Reservoir lot, west of Putnam street, in continuation of part first described to Eagle square; land accepted as public highways, at junction of Trenton street and Eagle street, Lexington street and Eagle street, and Princeton street and Eagle street, Nov. 1, 1858; accepted between Border street and Brooks street, and between Reservoir lands and Chelsea street, April 5, 1859; sometimes called East Eagle street and West Eagle street. Vol. 31, p. 23. L 448, L 755.

Earl street, So. B., 1849; from Dorr street to O. C. (now N. Y., N. H. & H.) R.R., and thence to West Ninth street.

***East street**, B., 1735; from South street to Federal street; called Sea street in 1819; for date 1735, see Pub. Stats.; from South street to Sea (now Federal) street, 1822. Vol. 31, p. 25.

East street, Rox., 1842; in two parts, viz.: (Blue Hill avenue) from Warren street, near Grove Hall, to Eustis (near Dudley) street, at Elm street (now Mt. Pleasant avenue), over part of Dennis street and (Hampden street) from Eustis street at Magazine street to the Lead Works, at corner of Davis (now Albany) street, Northern place and Swett street; named, Aug. 29, 1842; name of part from Eustis street to Warren street changed to Grove Hall avenue, Dec. 8, 1851; bounds altered, March 14, 1853, to correspond with laying out by County Commissioners, as shown on plan of Dec. 15, 1852; name of part from Davis street to Eustis street changed to Hampden street, April 21, 1868.

***East street**, Dor., 1840; from Adams street at Meeting-House Hill to Dorchester avenue; named from Mrs. Saunders' to Mr. Glover's store; March 11, 1840. L 791, L 2310.

East street, W. Rox., 1871; from Adams street to High street; abandoned.

East-street place, B., 1835; from East street, south. L 1674.

***East Broadway**, So. B., 1873; from Dorchester street, opposite West Broadway, to Q street (City Point); part of Broadway from Dorchester street to low-water mark called East Broadway, Feb. 18, 1873; all that portion east of Q street adjoining land of City of Boston discontinued, Aug. 20, 1885. Vol. 31, p. 94. L 8, L 125, L 154, L 363, L 2056.

***East Brookline street**, B., 1868; from Washington street to Albany street; part of Brookline street between Washington street and Albany street named East Brookline street, April 21, 1868.

Eastburn place, Bri.; from 25 Eastburn street.

***Eastburn street**, Bri., 1886; from Washington street to Mt. Vernon street; private way heretofore known as Worcester street and as Church street laid out with name of Eastburn street, June 11, 1886. L 1911.

***East Canton street**, B., 1868; from Washington street to Albany street; the part of Canton street east of Washington street named East Canton street, April 21, 1868. L 50.

East Castle street, B., 1732; from Orange (now Washington) street, east, to the water in 1732; to Front street (now Harrison avenue), 1805; name changed to Motte street, June 23, 1874. L 434.

East Chester avenue, B., 1869; from Washington street to Albany street; East Chester park, that is between Washington street and Albany street, named East Chester avenue, July 13, 1869; same named Chester park, April 5, 1870; named Massachusetts avenue, March 1, 1894.

***East Chester park**, B., 1858; from Washington street to Albany street; the part of Chester park lying east of Harrison avenue, that is, between Harrison avenue and South Bay, named East Chester park, Nov. 16, 1858; same accepted, Oct. 30, 1860; extended to Albany street, Nov. 17, 1865; Chester park from Washington street to Harrison avenue included in East Chester park, April 27, 1869; East Chester park, that is, between Washington street and Albany street, named East Chester avenue, July 13, 1869, and same named Chester park, April 5, 1870; all of East Chester park named Massachusetts avenue, March 1, 1894. L 261, L 303, L 1331, L 1512, L 2299.

***East Chester park**, B., Rox. and Dor., 1874; from Albany street to Boston street at Five Corners (now Edward Everett square); part from Albany street across the Ox-Bow, extended, Nov. 17, 1865; extended by laying out part from Swett street to Boston street, Dec. 13, 1878; part from Albany street to Swett street laid out, Jan. 4, 1879; named Massachusetts avenue, March 1, 1894. L 1327, L 1328, L 1329, L 1330, L 1331, L 1352, L 1701, L 2485, L 2546, L 2547.

East Chester street, B.; the part of Chester street east of Washington street; sometimes so called prior to 1858.

East Clinton street, B., 1856; part of Clinton street, from Commercial street to Mercantile street, so called in 1856.

***East Concord street**, B., 1868; from Washington street to Albany street; the part of Concord street between Washington street and Albany street, so named April 21, 1868. Vol. 31, p. 1. L 1770.

***East Cottage street**, Dor., 1893; from Dudley street to Dorchester avenue; part between Dudley street and Pleasant street formerly called Cottage street, and part between Pleasant street and Dorchester avenue formerly called Pond street; both parts named East Cottage street, March 1, 1893. L 811, L 812, L 813, L 814, L 815, L 858, L 859, L 860, L 861, L 2547.

***East Dedham street**, B., 1868; from Washington street to Albany street; the part of Dedham street between Washington street and Albany street so named, April 21, 1868. L 1442.

East Dover street, B., 1834; the part of Dover street from Washington street to South Boston bridge (now Dover-street bridge), sometimes so called 1834-1839.

***East Eagle street**, E. B.; part of Eagle street from Reservoir grounds west of Putnam street to Eagle square sometimes so called.

***East Eighth street**, So. B., 1873; from Dorchester street to O street; the part of Eighth street from Dorchester street to O street so called, Feb. 18, 1873. L 109, L 2118.

***Eastern avenue**, B., 1843; from Commercial street to East Boston South Ferry; laid out, Aug. 3, 1880. L 207, L 1473.

***Eastern avenue**, B. and So. B., 1868; laid out 100 feet wide from Fort Point channel to land or flats of Boston Wharf Co., 1,150 feet northeast from Mt. Washington avenue, Nov. 17, 1868; from Broad street (now Atlantic avenue) to Harbor Commissioners' line in Fort Point channel in continuation of Congress street, Jan. 3, 1874; extended by existing bridge across Fort Point channel to C street, extended, March 14, 1879; name changed to Congress street, from Atlantic avenue to C street, July 12, 1880, taking effect March 1, 1881. L 27, L 918, L 1109.

***East Fifth street**, So. B., 1873; from G street to Q street (City Point); the part of Fifth street from G street to low-water mark so called, Feb. 18, 1873; part east of Q street adjoining land of City of Boston discontinued, Aug. 20, 1885. L 8, L 509, L 1614, L 1920.

***East First street**, So. B., 1873; from H street to low-water mark (east of P street, but not beyond Q street); part of First street so named, Feb. 27, 1805; the part east of H street so named, Feb. 18, 1873; part east of Q street adjoining land of City of Boston discontinued, Aug. 20, 1885. L 215, L 228, L 229, L 1444.

***East Fourth street**, So. B, 1873; from Dorchester street to Q street (City Point); the part of Fourth street between Dorchester street and low-water mark so called, Feb. 18, 1873; part east of Q street adjoining land of City of Boston discontinued, Aug. 20, 1885. L 8, L 145, L 258, L 604, L 1154.

East High street, B.; that part of High street from Fort Hill square to junction of Broad street and Purchase street sometimes so called.

***East Lenox street**, B. and Rox., 1851; from Washington street to Fellows street; called Shawmut place from Washington street, east, 1849; East Lenox street, 1851; laid out and extended to Harrison avenue, Sept. 25, 1874; to Fellows street, including Demisa square, Dec. 8, 1874. L 957, L 958, L 991, L 1353.

Eastman place, Dor.; from Eastman street.

***Eastman street**, Dor., 1888; from Boston street to Elder street; laid out, Nov. 9, 1888. L 2104.

***East Newton street**, B., 1868; from Washington street to Albany street; the part of Newton street between Washington street and Albany street so named, April 21, 1868. L 1770, L 2491.

***East Ninth street**, So. B., 1873; from Dorchester street to N street, with proposed extension to O street; the part of Ninth street from Dorchester street to Old Harbor street, and from G street to N street so called Feb. 18, 1873; extended from H street to Lowland (now Mercer) street Dec. 29, 1882; laid out as a public street from the angle south-east of Lowland street to H street, Oct. 6, 1883, and part between Lowland street and said angle laid out as Burnham street, July 13, 1883; name of part of street as originally laid out from angle south-east of Lowland street to Old Harbor street paralleled by the extension of said East Ninth street to H street, changed to Dunham street, March 1, 1885. L 52, L 191, L 192, L 751, L 1693, L 1719, L 1720, L 1789.

East Northampton street, Rox., 1873; from junction of Island street and Gerard street, south-easterly, parallel with Allerton street; shown since 1873 only on directory map for 1884.

Easton street, B., 1849; from corner of Malden street, extended, and Albany street, to a dock in South Bay; named, May 14, 1849; see plan of Neck lands February, 1848; abandoned.

†**Easton street**, Bri., 1889; from Franklin street to east of Mansfield street; formerly called Hill avenue; laid out from Franklin street to Mansfield street, Sept. 10, 1889. L 2165.

***East Orange street**, B., 1840; from Washington street, east, in 1840; probably Orange lane in 1827; to Lehigh street, 1843; between Harrison avenue and Lehigh street, called on many old plans, Orange street; accepted from Harrison avenue to Albany street, Sept. 27, 1852; accepted, May 26, 1857; name changed to Way street, Dec. 21, 1857; named East Orange street again, Dec. 30, 1857; named Way street from Harrison avenue to Lehigh street, March 21, 1864; the part between Washington street and Harrison avenue has been discontinued, or is now part of Orange lane. L 95.

***East Second street**, So. B., 1873; from Dorchester street to Q street (City Point); the part of Second street, from Dorchester street to low-water mark, so called, Feb. 18, 1873; part east of Q street adjoining land of City of Boston discontinued, Aug. 20, 1885. L 8, L 216, L 265, L 1445, L 2229.

***East Seventh street**, So. B., 1873; from G street to the water, east of O street; the part of Second street as above so called, Feb. 18, 1873; part east of Q street, adjoining land of City of Boston, discontinued, Aug. 20, 1885. Vol. 31, pp. 35, 48.

***East Sixth street**, So. B., 1873; from G street to Q street (City Point); part of Sixth street so called, Feb. 18, 1873; part between G street and H street laid out, Oct. 22, 1874; part east of Q street, adjoining land of City of Boston, discontinued, Aug. 20, 1885. L 7, L 980.

***East Springfield street**, B., 1861; from Washington street to Albany street; so called on plan dated 1861; part of Springfield street as above so called, April 21, 1868, part between Harrison avenue and Albany street, discontinued, July 10, 1891. L 176, L 261, L 303, L 1512, L 2299.

East Tenth street, So. B. (proposed); from proposed extension of F street to the water east of M street; included in the Strandway.

***East Third street**, So. B., 1873; from Dorchester street to west side of Independence square, and from east side of same to Q street (City Point); part of Third street, east of Dorchester street, to low-water mark so called, Feb. 18, 1873; part east of Q street adjoining land of City of Boston discontinued, Aug. 20, 1885. L 8, L 123, L 143, L 155, L 157, L 2049, L 2490.

East Waltham street, B.; part of the present Waltham street, from Washington street to Harrison avenue; so called in 1850, crossing and including part of what was formerly Adams court.

East Windsor street, Rox.; Windsor street, from Cabot street to Shawmut avenue, sometimes so called.

East Worcester street, B., 1834; from Washington street to Front street (now Harrison avenue); named Worcester square, 1851; from Harrison avenue to Albany street, 1854, but abandoned in 1861 for site for the new City Hospital.

Eaton court, B., 1846; from North Bennet street, near Hanover street, south-west; Eaton place, sometimes so called.

Eaton court, B., 1844; from Gouch (now Norman) street, near Green street, west; now called Eaton place.

Eaton court, Rox., 1869; from Cedar street, near Pynchon street (now Columbus avenue), to Merton place; called also Eaton street; laid out as Newark street, July 22, 1892. L 2416.

Eaton place, B., 1844; from Gouch (now Norman) street, near Green street, north-west; called also Eaton court.

Eaton place, B., 1846; from North Bennet street, near Hanover street, south-west; more commonly called Eaton court.

Eaton square, Dor., 1880; enclosure bounded by Adams, Bowdoin, Church, and Hancock streets; laid out and named Percival square, April 7, 1879; named Eaton square, June 1, 1880; the street now forming the south side of Eaton square, named as a part of Church street, 1840, was changed to Bowdoin street, March 1, 1882. L 1010.

***Eaton street**, B., 1795; from Chambers street to North Russell street, 1795; named about 1802; confirmed as a public street, Sept. 15, 1834.

Eaton street, Rox.; from Cedar street, near Pynchon street, to Merton place; Eaton court sometimes so called; laid out as Newark street, July 22, 1892. L 2416.

†**Eaton street**, Rox., 1849; shown on map, 1849, as extending from East (now Hampden) street, south-west, across Yeoman street; afterwards continued south-east, by a bend past Orchard street to Adams street; accepted from Yeoman street to East street, and named, May 28, 1855; same accepted again according to a new plan, June 30, 1856; that part of Eaton street from Orchard street to Adams street accepted and made part of Orchard street, Nov. 12, 1860; later part from Yeoman street to Orchard street called Trask place; part from East street to Yeoman street, named Chadwick street, April 21, 1868; Trask place from Yeoman street to Hartopp place (now Ambrose street) laid out as Chadwick street, May 24 and Dec. 31, 1870; part from Orchard street to Hartopp place laid out as Orchard Park street, Feb. 19, 1876.

Eaton street, Dor.; from Tolman street, north-west; between Bloomington street, and Norwood street.

Eddy place, B., 1848; from Tyler street, near Curve street, west.

Eden place, Chsn.; from Eden street, near Eden-street court, south-east.

***Eden street**, Chsn., 1826; from Main street, at Hancock square, to Russell street; accepted, April 4, 1826.

Eden-street court, Chsn.; from 19 Eden street, south-east, to an open space.

***Edge Hill street**, Rox.; from Gay Head street to Round Hill street; laid out, Nov. 1, 1893. L 2545.

Edgerly place, B., 1841; from Winchester street, between Ferdinand street and Church street, south.

Edgewater drive, Dor., 1896; from River street to Hyde Park line; authority to open given by Street Commissioners, Feb. 24, 1896.

***Edgewood street,** Rox., 1868; from Warren street to Blue Hill avenue; name of Park street changed to Edgewood street, April 21, 1868; laid out April 9, 1875. L 1033, L 1034.

Edgeworth place, E. B.; from Paris street, between Sumner street and Maverick street, north-west.

***Edgeworth street,** Chsn., 1845; from Bunker Hill street to Prospect street; laid out and accepted from Bunker Hill street to Jay (now Tremont) street, Dec. 14, 1859; extended and laid out from Tremont street to Prospect street, under the same name, April 26, 1870.

***Edinboro' street,** B., 1839; from Essex street to Beach street; laid out, May 18, 1872. L 759.

Edinboro' street, Rox., 1846; from Cedar street, south-west, parallel with Norfolk and Bristol turnpike (sometimes called Dedham turnpike, and now Washington street), and then south-east to the turnpike; accepted, conditionally, from Cedar street to Ellis street, Sept. 3, 1855; named Thornton street, April 21, 1868; at one time also called Wiggin street.

Edison Green, Dor., 1895; from Dorchester avenue to Pond street; authority to open given by Street Commissioners, Sept. 19, 1895.

Edmands court or place, Chsn.; from Rutherford avenue to Lawrence street; formerly from Rutherford avenue, north-east, connecting with Brown court; shown as an unnamed street in 1851; called Edmunds place, 1863 and 1878; called Edmunds court in 1884; laid out from Rutherford avenue to Lawrence street, with name of Benedict street, July 2, 1887. L 1999.

Edmund place, B., 1863; from North Russell street, west, between Parkman street and Russell place.

Edna street, Dor., 1894; from Walk Hill street to Clearview street; authority to open given by Street Commissioners, Dec. 26, 1894; abandoned.

***Edson street,** Dor., 1888; from Norfolk street to Milton avenue; Prospect street laid out as Edson street, Sept. 6, 1888. L 2091.

Edward street, Chsn.; from Mishawum street to Gibbs court.

***Edward Everett square,** Dor., 1894; junction Massachusetts avenue, Boston street, East Cottage street, and Dorchesterway; Five Corners named Edward Everett square, Jan. 24, 1894.

Edward's corner, B., 1732; corner of Fish (now Hanover) street, and Wood's lane (now Richmond street) then so called.

Edwards place, Rox.; from 37 Adams street (Directory); maps and atlases show same as Travers place.

Edwin street, Dor.; from Dorchester avenue to Shawmut park extended; laid out May 7, 1896. L 2763.

***Egleston square,** Rox. and W. Rox., 1866; from Walnut avenue to Washington street; laid out from Walnut street (now Walnut avenue) to Shawmut avenue (now Washington street), March 26, 1866; name changed to Seaver street, being a continuation of that street, March 1, 1882; included in extension of Columbus avenue, Jan. 4, 1895. L 930.

***Egleston street,** W. Rox., 1890; from School street to Boylston street; laid out, June 5, 1890. L 2228.

Egmont street, So. B. (proposed street); from the proposed extension of B street to the proposed extension of E street, on the so-called Commonwealth flats.

Eighth street, B., 1866; Hereford street so called on plan.

***Eighth street**, So. B., 1804; shown on Badlam's plan, 1804; parallel with Broadway from Dorchester street easterly to the sea; part west of Dorchester street, crossing end of E street, formerly called North street; laid out as per said plan and named, Feb. 27, 1805; accepted "as extended by deed of Taylor and Mullay to City," Dec. 22, 1857; extended to D street, Dec. 31, 1857; accepted as extended 60 feet west of D street, Jan. 29, 1861; name of Goddard street (from D street to Dorchester street) changed to Eighth street, being properly a continuation of same, April 9, 1867; narrow street from D street to E street, "heretofore improperly called Eighth street," named Baxter street, April 9, 1867; portion 75 feet east of D street, accepted Sept. 17, 1867; laid out from D street to Dorchester street and thence to low-water mark, Nov. 17, 1868; extended north-west from D street, May 4, 1869; named East and West Eighth streets, Feb. 18, 1873. L 109, L 201, L 257, L 273, L 369.

Elbow alley, B., 1708; from Ann street, north and east, to Cross street; closed.

Elbow street, E. B.; from Meridian street, east, then south-east, to Chelsea street, near Maverick square.

Elder court or **place**, B.; from Brighton street, south-east, between Poplar street and Allen street; called Brighton-street court, 1860; Elder court, 1863; Elder place, 1868.

Elder street, Dor.; from Humphrey's street, east, near East Cottage street.

***Eldon street**, Dor., 1880; from Washington street to Rosseter street; laid out from Washington street to Bowdoin avenue, Jan. 28, 1880; extended from southerly part of Bowdoin avenue to northerly part of Bowdoin avenue (now Rosseter street), Sept. 5, 1881. L 1431, L 1550, L 1897.

***Eldora street**, Rox.; from Hillside street to Sunset street; laid out, March 30, 1891. L 2285.

Eldredge street, W. Rox., 1871; from Metropolitan avenue, near Poplar street, south-west.

Eldridge road, W. Rox., 1896; from Hyde Park avenue, near Walk Hill street, to beyond Nathan street; authority to open given by Street Commissioners, Aug. 5, 1896.

***Eleanor street**, Bri.; from Cambridge street to Ridgemont street; authority to open given by Street Commissioners, Feb. 2, 1893; laid out, Dec. 14, 1894. L 2670.

Elgin street, W. Rox.; from Centre street, near La Grange street.

Eliot court, B., 1829; from Eliot street, south; called Carlton place, 1838; now built over.

Eliot place, B., 1845; from Eliot street, near Tremont street, north.

Eliot place, Rox.; from Roxbury street, near Gay street, north; name changed to Malbon place, April 21, 1868.

Eliot place, W. Rox.; from 39 Eliot street, north-east.

***Eliot square**, Rox., 1849; unenclosed space between Roxbury, Dudley, Bartlett, Highland, and Centre streets; named, Dec. 17, 1849.

***Eliot street**, B., 1740; from Washington street to Columbus avenue, at Park square; laid out by owners, 1740; across Holyoke (now Tremont) street, east and west, 1750; from Orange (now Washington) street, to Pleasant street, 1788, and then called Eliot street; Kneeland street named Eliot street, so that the avenue running from side to side of city might bear the same name, July 16, 1838; same part called Kneeland street again, June 2, 1840; extended from Pleasant street to Columbus avenue, July 23, 1873. L 103, L 153, L 411½, L 412, L 413, L 517, L 518, L 878, L 1448.

***Eliot street**, W. Rox., 1802; from Centre street to Pond street; laid out by Selectmen and accepted, Aug. 17, 1802; named, May 9, 1825. L 1043, L 1044.

Eliot terrace, Rox., 1896; from Centre street, near corner of Roxbury street, south.

Eliot's corner, B., 1708; corner of Orange (now Washington) street and Essex street then so called.

Eliot's (Samuel) corner, B., 1784; corner Dock square and Wilson's lane (now Devonshire street) then so called.

Eliot's pasture, B.; near Pleasant street and Eliot street in former times.

***Elizabeth street**, Dor.; from Norfolk street, south-east, to Astoria street; laid out, July 10, 1896. L 2778.

***Elko street**, Bri., 1893; from Cambridge street to Sparhawk street; Sparhawk avenue, laid out as Elko street, Aug. 10, 1893. L 2526.

Ellery court, So. B., 1872; from Ellery street, near Swett street, north-east.

***Ellery street**, So. B., 1855; from South Bay, north of Dexter street, south-east then west to Boston street; name of Oak street changed to Ellery street, Aug. 7, 1855; laid out from Dexter street to Swett street, March 18, 1876; laid out from Swett street to Boston street, Dec. 24, 1879. L 1136, L 1416.

Ellery terrace, So. B., 1896; from Ellery street, near the bend, south-west, formerly called Abbott's place; also Abbott's block.

***Ellet street**, Dor.; from Dorchester avenue to Adams street; laid out, Nov. 18, 1896. L 2798.

***Ellicott street**, W. Rox., 1856; from Walnut street (later Walnut avenue) to Morton street, near Forest Hills street; laid out as a public street, Dec 15, 1880; now included in Franklin Park. L 1507.

Ellingwood street, Rox., 1895; from Lawn street, north-east, then north-west; authority to open given by Street Commissioners, Sept. 19, 1895.

Ellis corner, B., 1708; corner of Newbury (now Washington) street and Winter street then so called.

***Ellis street**, Rox., 1843; from Thornton street (formerly Edinboro' street) to Hawthorne street; shown in 1849 as extending from Copeland street (now Hawthorne street) to Edinboro' street; accepted, conditionally, from Highland street to Edinboro' street, Sept. 3, 1855; part near Highland street included in Hawthorne street, Dec. 19, 1859.

Elliston's corner, B., 1708; corner Cross street and Ann (now North) street then so called.

Ellits street, B., 1733; from Charter street to Love lane (now Tileston street); called Unity street, 1795.

Ellswood street, W. Rox., 1895; from Baker street, nearly opposite Mt. Vernon street, to Farragut street; authority to open given by Street Commissioners, May 3, 1895.

Ellsworth place, W. Rox.; from School street, near Walnut avenue, south-west.

Ellsworth street, Dor.; from Dorchester avenue, opposite Leeds street, to Commercial (now Freeport) street.

***Ellwood street**, Chsn., 1887; from Putnam street, north-east; Mechanic street laid out as Ellwood street, Sept. 13, 1887. L 2018.

Elm avenue, Rox., 1833; from Eustis street (now Dudley street at Blue Hill avenue), west, then north-west, then north-east to Dudley street (at Dearborn street); usually called Elm street and that name changed to Mt. Pleasant avenue, April 21, 1868.

Elm avenue,
Elm road, } Dor.; from Adams street to Carruth street.

Elm avenue, Bri.; from Commonwealth avenue to Brookline line; afterwards called Argyle road; now Strathmore road.

Elm place, B., 1850; from 34 Portland street, near Sudbury street, south-west.

Elm place, Rox.; Elmwood court from Elmwood street, north-west, so called in 1868 and 1873.

***Elm street,** B., 1800; from Hanover street to Union street at Dock square; called Hudson's lane, 1658; Wing's lane, 1708; Elm street, May 26, 1800. L 796.

Elm street, E. B.; from Breed street to Washburn avenue (now Walley street); laid out with name of Leyden street, Aug. 23, 1886. L 1938, L 1939.

Elm street, Rox., 1850; from Brookline avenue to Longwood street (Longwood street now in Riverway); later called Pilgrim street, and now included in Longwood avenue.

Elm street, Rox., 1835; road on Mt. Pleasant called Elm street; accepted, provisionally, April 6, 1835; name changed to Mt. Pleasant avenue, April 21, 1868;c alled also Elm avenue.

***Elm street,** Dor., 1851; from Exchange street to Everett street; located, April 7, 1851; accepted, April 21, 1851.

Elm street, W. Rox.; from Granite (now Cass) street, near railroad toward Ballanakill avenue (now Johnson street); Elm street now known as Oak avenue.

***Elm street,** W. Rox., 1847; from Green street to Sedgwick street (formerly Walker street); part from Revere street to Seaverns avenue laid out as part of Roanoke avenue, on plan dated 1847; on map 1849 part from Green street to Revere street shown as part of Roanoke avenue; Elm street from Revere street to Walker street accepted as a public way, Feb. 3, 1868; again accepted and Selectmen recommended that Hillside avenue (from Revere street to Seaverns avenue), with extension to Green street, be laid out and called Elm street, July 25, 1868.

***Elm street,** Chsn., 1810; from High street to Medford street; land for said street, from High street to Bunker Hill street, conveyed to Town by Oliver Holden, July 17, 1810, said street having been laid out some years before by Selectmen; called Washington street prior to this date; continuation from Bunker Hill street to Medford street to be accepted by Town when laid out by owner of land satisfactorily to Selectmen, Sept. 15, 1837. L 2801.

Elmer place, B., 1867; from Salem street, near Prince street, east; part of now included in Hancock school-house yard.

***Elm Hill avenue,** Rox., 1852; from Warren street to Seaver street; laid out, June 26, 1882. L 1619, L 1620, L 2166.

Elm lawn, Dor., 1888; from Centre street, north-west, near Dorchester avenue.

Elm road,
Elm avenue, } Dor.; from Adams street to Carruth street.

Elmhurst street, Dor., 1896; from Norfolk street to Southern avenue.

***Elmira street,** Bri., 1893; from Murdock street to George street; part of Hill street laid out from Murdock street to George street as Elmira street, Nov. 10, 1893. L 2550.

***Elmo street,** Dor., 1871; from Blue Hill avenue to and across Erie avenue (now Erie street), then turning and crossing back to the latter street near N.Y. & N.E. (now New England) R.R.; part from

Blue Hill avenue to Erie avenue crossing "Old Road" laid out as a public street, Oct. 2, 1885; all that part south-east of Erie street laid out, Nov. 29, 1892. L 1888, L 2464.

Elmont street, Dor.; from Waterlow street to Faxon street.

***Elmore street,** Rox., 1868; from Washington street to Walnut avenue; laid out, Nov. 6, 1879. L 1398.

Elmore park, Rox.; from 17 Elmore street.

Elmwood Court, Rox.; from Elmwood street, north-west, then north-east to Leutman place; sometimes called also Elm place.

Elmwood place, Rox., 1868; from Elmwood street, south-east.

†Elmwood street, Rox., 1868; from Roxbury street to Linden Park street; name of Orange street between Washington (now Roxbury) street and Pearl (now King) street changed to Elmwood street, April 21, 1868; part between Pearl and Clay (now Linden Park) street, now also called Elmwood street, but not public.

Elmwood street, W. Rox.; from Baker street, south, near railroad.

***Elton street,** Dor.; from Dorchester avenue to Sagamore street; laid out, Dec. 28, 1888. L 2108.

***Emerald street,** B., 1831; from Dover street to Castle street; from Dover street, north, 1831; opened and extended, Dec. 8, 1858; extended to Castle street, Dec. 16, 1870. L 54, L 544, L 545, L 546, L 547, L 566, L 838.

Emerson place, Chsn., 1863; from Hanley street to Warren street extended (probably led to manufactory of Charles Emerson, and was closed on extension of Warren street, or soon after).

Emerson place, Chsn., 1869; way leading from Park street to Charles Emerson's place of business, 42 and 46 Park street; so called by Emerson and authorized by City, Dec. 27, 1869.

***Emerson street,** So. B., 1864; from Dorchester street crossing East Fourth street at K street to M street and East Fourth street; name of "Old Road" from Third street to Fourth street changed to Emerson street, March 22, 1864; name of Emerson street between M and N streets changed to Fourth street, April 21, 1868; laid out from Third street between G street and H street to M street at junction with Fourth street, Nov. 17, 1868; extended from East Third street to West Second street at Dorchester street, May 7, 1872. L 754, L 1154.

Emery place, B., 1841; from Warrenton street, near Eliot street, east; closed.

Emery street, Dor.; from Washington street, opposite Bailey street, to Milton avenue; laid out with name of Stockton street, Dec. 10, 1886. L 1965.

Emmet place, B., 1873; from 9 Blossom street, near Cambridge street, east.

Emmet place, E.B.; from 17 Everett street near Orleans street, south-west.

Emmet street, So. B.; from East Second street to East Third street between I street and K street.

Emmon's corner, B., 1708; corner of Cambridge (now Court) street and Sudbury street then so called.

Empire street, Bri., 1896; from North Harvard street, near Cambridge street, north-east; authority to open given by Street Commissioners, Nov. 18, 1896.

Endicott court, B., 1843; from 178 Endicott street, near Thacher street, west.

***Endicott street,** B., 1836; from Hanover street, at junction with Salem street, to Causeway street; part called Mill lane, 1805, and part Mill Pond street, 1807; known as Pond street, from Hanover street to Charlestown bridge, that is, at Prince street, 1814; name changed to Endicott street, June 13, 1836.

Endicott-street place, B., 1737; from Endicott street, east, near Thacher street, north of Pond-street place; called Douglass court, 1872.

Endicott terrace, Dor.; from 1653 Dorchester avenue.

Endleigh street, Dor.; from northerly part of Savin Hill avenue, north-east.

***Enfield street**, W. Rox., 1880; from Spring Park avenue to Hazel street; part of E street laid out as Enfield street Aug. 28, 1880. L 1477.

***Englewood avenue**, Bri., 1872; from Chestnut Hill avenue (formerly Rockland street), easterly, to former Brookline line (between Strathmore road and Beacon street); accepted, Dec. 27, 1872. L 2383.

Englewood street, Dor.; from Hillsdale street, at Adams street, west.

Emsella terrace, W. Rox., 1896; from Lamartine street to New York, New Haven & Hartford R.R., authority to open given by Street Commissioners, Nov. 11, 1896.

Episcopal avenue, W. Rox.; from Centre street, north-west, near Myrtle street; shown in 1882, but not named, north-east of engine-house, and leading from Centre street towards parsonage of St. John Episcopal Church; now built over.

Ericsson street, Bri., 1895; from Lincoln street to Adams street; authority to open given by Street Commissioners, Nov. 4, 1895.

Ericsson street, Dor., 1856; from Walnut street to Fulton street; laid out, April 5, 1858, at Port Norfolk (Neponset).

Erie avenue, Dor., 1871; from Washington street to McLellan avenue (now McLellan street); laid out with bridge over N. E. R.R. and named Erie street, Aug. 12, 1885. L 1878.

Erie place, W. Rox.; from School street, near Washington street, south-west.

Erie street, B., 1844; from Harrison avenue to Albany street; called Seneca street, 1849.

Erie street, E.B.; proposed street from Cottage street, south-east, to Shirley street (Wood Island).

***Erie street**, So. B., 1868; street laid out 50 feet wide from south-west side of street 550 feet north-east of Mt. Washington avenue to south-east side of flats of Boston Wharf Co., Nov. 17, 1868; not shown on public maps and apparently never built.

***Erie street**, Dor., 1885; from Washington street to McLellan avenue (now McLellan street); Erie avenue laid out as a public street crossing N. E. R.R., with name of Erie street, Aug. 12, 1885; relocated at entrance to Washington street, July 2, 1886. L 1878, L 1897.

Erie terrace, So. B.; from 162 West Fourth street; formerly Humphrey court.

Erin alley, E.B.; from Liverpool street to Border street, near Maverick street.

Esmond street, Dor., 1896; from Blue Hill avenue to Bradshaw street; authority to open given by Street Commissioners, June 16, 1896.

Essex avenue, B.; from Clinton street, near Atlantic avenue, to Richmond street.

Essex court, 1818. }
Essex place, 1816. } B.; from Essex street, opposite Front street (now Harrison avenue); called Essex place, 1816; Essex court, 1818; Brimmer avenue or place, 1842; included in extension of Harrison avenue, July 6, 1881. L 1526.

***Essex place**, B., 1809; from Essex street, opposite Columbia street, to Tufts street, laid out from Essex street to south of where Tufts street now is, Aug. 17, 1880; part south of Tufts street discontinued, Aug. 26, 1893. L 1475, L 2170.

***Essex street**, B., 1708; from Washington street to Federal street; from Newbury (now Washington) street, at Eliot's corner to Windmill point, 1708; called also Auchmuty street, 1775; the eastern end was also called Beach street, 1804; extended from South street, through South-street court, to Federal street, May 5, 1880. L 73, L 624, L 873, L 1450, L 1451, L 1526, L 1598, L 1951, L 1973, L 2126, L 2441, L 2514, L 2515, L 2596, L 2597.

***Essex street**, Chsn., 1847; from Hancock square to Rutherford avenue at Middlesex street; formerly part of Canal street; laid out and accepted (from Main street to Middlesex street), Dec. 31, 1855.

Essex street, Bri.; from Brighton (now Commonwealth) avenue (at Cottage farm), northerly to Charles River.

Estes avenue, } Dor., from Wales place, north-east, near Puritan
Estes place, } avenue.

Estes place, B.; from Summer street to Congress street.

***Etna street**, Bri., 1893; from North Beacon street to Elmira street; part of Lucas street laid out with name of Etna street, Nov. 10, 1893. L 2551, L 2552.

***Euclid street**, Dor., 1872; from Washington street to Withington street, near Norfolk street; laid out, Oct. 21, 1882. L 1656.

Eugene street, W. Rox.; from Forest Hills street to Peter Parley street; later called Olmstead street; authority to open under name of Olmstead street, given by Street Commissioners, May 24, 1893.

Eulalie street, Bri., 1896; from Winship street.

Eulita terrace, Bri., 1894; from Union street, near Chestnut Hill avenue, to Eulalie street; authority to open given by Street Commissioners, June 6, 1894.

Eustis place, Rox.; from Eustis street, near Harrison avenue, south-west; see plan 1849.

Eustis place, Rox.; from 259 Eustis street (directory).

***Eustis street**, Rox., 1825; from Washington street to Magazine street; laid out Jan. 19, 1662; shown as "Road to Dorchester" in 1796; formerly extended over present location of Mall street; named from Washington street by burying-ground to Dorchester line, May 9, 1825; name of Eustis street between what is now Dearborn street (opposite Mt. Pleasant avenue) and Dorchester line changed to Dudley street, April 21, 1868; name of Orchard street, between Dearborn street and Adams street, of Proctor street from East (now Hampden) street, north-west, and of Bradford place, from East street, south-east, changed to Eustis street, April 21, 1868; extended to Magazine street, Dec. 15, 1873. L 719, L 909, L 1212.

Euston street, Rox.; from Ivy street to St. Mary's street (now closed).

Eutaw place, E. B.; from Marion street, near Eutaw street, south-west; called also Marion court.

***Eutaw street**, E. B., 1834; from Border street to White street; first projected from White street to Meridian street; extended to Border street, accepted and laid out as public highway, May 31, 1852; accepted at junction of Eutaw street and White street, Nov. 1, 1858. Vol. 31, p. 36. L 42.

Evandale terrace, Dor.; from Savin Hill avenue, east.

***Evans street**, Dor., 1871; from Milton avenue to Morton street; laid out from Milton avenue to Nelson street, Nov. 23, 1883; extended from Nelson street to Forest Hill avenue (now Morton street), Dec. 1, 1884. L 1740, L 1741, L 1838.

Evelyn avenue, Dor.: from Blue Hill avenue to Norfolk street; laid out as Evelyn street, June 15, 1892. L 2402

***Evelyn street,** Dor., 1892; from Blue Hill avenue to Norfolk street; Evelyn avenue laid out as Evelyn street, June 15, 1892. L 2402.

***Everett avenue,** Dor., 1866; from Stoughton street to Jerome street; formerly from Stoughton street to Hancock street; laid out in part from Stoughton street towards Hancock street, Nov. 9, 1877; part leading from Hancock street to part already public laid out as Jerome street, March 22, 1883. L 1287, L 1695.

Everett court, B.; from 322 North street, near Clark street, north-west; apparently an archway; called also Everett place.

Everett court, E. B.; from 250 Everett street, north-west of, and near Jeffries street, north-east.

Everett court, Chsn.; from 45 Everett street, near Medford street, south-east.

Everett place, B., 1853; from 322 North street, west, near Clark street; called also Everett court, which see.

Everett place, E. B.; from Everett street, north-west of Everett court, north-east.

Everett place, E. B.; from Everett street, near Emmett place.

Everett place, }
Everett square, } Bri.; from Vernon (now Raymond) street, near Everett street, north; laid out with name of Westford street, May 18, 1891. L 2293.

Everett square, Bri.; from Westford street, north.

Everett street, B., 1866; Exeter street, so called.

***Everett street,** E. B., 1836; from Orleans street to Jeffries street; order to lay out and accept on fulfilment of certain conditions, April 10, 1854. L 36, L 1139, L 1417.

***Everett street,** Dor., 1851; from Park street to Mill street; shown as an unnamed street in 1841; located, April 7, 1851; the report of Selectmen, recommending acceptance of said street accepted, April 21, 1851.

***Everett street,** W. Rox., 1871; from Elm street to Call streets, called on plan dated 1871, "Everett street formerly Starr's lane;" street from Gordon street at junction with Elm street to Starr (now Call) street, formerly known as Starr lane, named Everett street, Dec. 4, 1877. L 1029.

***Everett street,** Chsn., 1837; from Bunker Hill street, opposite Concord street to Medford street, accepted, March 22, 1841.

***Everett street,** Bri., 1846; from North Beacon street to Western avenue; projected from River street (now Western avenue) to North Beacon street, July 22, 1867; accepted, April 26, 1869.

Everett street, Bri., 1858; from Faneuil street to Bigelow street; laid out by Selectmen, Dec. 18, 1873; known as Dunboy avenue, in 1889; laid out as Dunboy street, Aug. 13, 1889. L 2151.

***Evergreen street,** Rox.; from 89 Day street, north-west; Atwood avenue; laid out as Evergreen street, Aug. 10, 1894. L 2612.

Everton street, Dor., 1876; from Olney street, south-easterly and southerly to Geneva avenue; name of Cottage avenue (from Geneva street) (now avenue) to Green (now Olney) street, changed to Everton street, Dec. 30, 1876.

Everton's corner, B., 1708; Ship (now North) street, near Scarlett's wharf then so called.

Ewer street, So. B., 1849; from West Ninth street to Dorr street.

Exchange court, Chsn.; from Main street, south-west, between Frothingham avenue and Dunstable street.

Exchange lane, B., 1809; from King (now State) street to Dock square; called Shrimpton's lane, 1708; also sometimes Royal Exchange lane; Exchange lane, 1800; Exchange street, 1870.

***Exchange place,** B., 1873; from Congress street to Kilby street; name of Lindall street, changed to Exchange place, Oct. 14, 1873. L 203, L 822, L 853.

Exchange place, B., 1854; from Devonshire street to Congress square; made part of Congress square, Oct. 14, 1873. L 497.

Exchange square, B., 1818; rear of Congress street and State street; called Half-square court, 1708; Salter's court, 1808; Exchange square, 1818; Congress square, 1821.

***Exchange street,** B., 1817; from State street to Dock square; called Shrimpton's lane, 1708; Royal Exchange lane sometime previous to 1800; Exchange lane, 1800; Exchange street, 1817.

Exchange street, Dor., 1853; from Park street, south-east, parallel with O. C. (now N. Y., N. H. & H.) R.R., nearly to Tenean creek. L 1182.

Exeter court, Chsn.; from Sullivan street, near Bartlett street, south-east, with branch north-east to Exeter place.

***Exeter place,** B., 1848; from Harrison avenue to Chauncey street; from Chauncey street, opposite Rowe place, 1848; accepted, May 7, 1849.

Exeter place, Chsn.; from Sullivan street, near Bartlett street, south-east, parallel with Exeter court.

***Exeter street,** B., 1863; from Beacon street to Huntington avenue; called Avenue Four in 1866; Exeter street in 1863; then Everett street; Exeter street, 1866; laid out as a public street from Beacon street to southerly side of Commonwealth avenue, July 24, 1873; from Newbury street to Commonwealth avenue, Dec. 6, 1875; from Newbury street to Boylston street, Oct. 7, 1884; from Boylston street to Huntington avenue, July 27, 1886. L 862, L 1111, L 1825, L 1923.

Exeter street, B., 1809; from Pond (now Bedford) street to Essex street; see directory, 1809, and accompanying map upon which the south end of Exeter street coincides with the south end of the present Chauncey street, and the street extends in a nearly straight line about to the site of the Latin School-house; on Hale's map, 1820, the north end coincides with the present line of Chauncey street; called Rowe place, 1825; Rowe street, 1837; Chauncey street, 1856.

Export street, B., 1868; from Broad street, near India square to India street; shown on maps of 1848, but not then named.

***F street,** So. B., 1804; from West Eighth street to low-water mark; laid out and named, Feb. 27, 1805; extended to Eighth street, Nov. 20, 1855; laid out from Eighth street to low-water mark, Nov. 17, 1868. L 53, L 225.

F street, Dor., 1892; from Stoughton street to Willis (formerly E) street; authority to open given by Street Commissioners, May 4, 1892; later called Bakersfield street.

***Fabin street,** B., 1839; from Newland street to Ivanhoe street; laid out, May 13, 1871. L 477, L 539, L 605.

Fabyan street, Dor., 1894; from Blue Hill ávenue to Harvard street; authority to open given by Street Commissioners, Nov. 8, 1894.

Factory street, Rox., 1839; from Tremont street to Stony brook; Vernon street extended through, May 16, 1842, but shown on plan as Factory street as late as 1866. L 440.

***Fairbanks street,** Bri., 1892; from Washington street to Faneuil street; laid out, Oct. 19, 1892. L 2448.

***Fairbury street,** Rox., 1894; from Blue Hill avenue to Rand street; laid out, Dec. 14, 1894. L 2602.

Fairfax street, Dor.; from Carruth street, north-east, between Minot street and Beaumont street.

Fairfield place, B., 1853; from Harris street, north.

***Fairfield street**, B., 1863; from Beacon street to Boylston street; from Beacon street to Commonwealth avenue, 1871; same laid out, May 15, 1874; extended to Boylston street, Sept. 29, 1876; also called Sixth street. L 862, L 929, L 1167.

Fairhaven street, Rox.; from Brookline avenue to Audubon road, parallel with Brookline Branch R.R. (Proposed.)

***Fairland street**, Rox., 1846; from Mt. Pleasant avenue to Moreland street; laid out, Nov. 18, 1878. L 1332.

Fairmount street, Dor.; from Washington street to Forest Hill avenue (now Morton street).

Fairmount street, W. Rox.; from Walnut avenue, south-east, near Scarborough street; also called Fairmount avenue; now included in Franklin Park.

Fairmount avenue, W. Rox., 1860; from Walnut avenue, south-east, near Scarborough street; also called Fairmount street; now included in Franklin Park.

Fairview street, Dor.; from Train street to Frost avenue.

†**Fairview street**, W. Rox.; from South street to Mendum street; laid out from South street to beyond Proctor street, Nov. 12, 1886. L 1963.

Fairweather street, B.; from Harrison avenue, opposite Randall street to Reed street; authority to open given by Street Commissioners, Oct. 4, 1895.

Fairwether's corner, B., 1708; corner School street and Tremont street then so called.

***Falcon street**, E. B.; from Border street to Glendon street; laid out from Meridian street to Border street, Aug. 28, 1880; from Glendon street to Putnam street, Oct. 15, 1888; and from Meridian street to Putnam street, Aug. 25, 1891. Vol. 31, p. 23. L 1479, L 2097, L 2328, L 2329.

***Falmouth street**, B. and Rox., 1878; from Massachusetts avenue to West Newton street; laid out from Camden (now Gainsborough) street to Dalton street, Oct. 7, 1878; extended from Dalton street to West Newton street, June 9, 1882; extended south from Gainsborough street, May 7, 1889; name of part south of West Chester park (now Massachusetts avenue) changed to St. Stephen street, March 1, 1892. L 1296, L 1322, L 1615, L 2129.

***Faneuil street**, Bri., 1840; from Market street to Washington street, at Oak square; named, June 15, 1840. L 1632, L 1884.

***Faneuil Hall square**, B., 1855; from Merchants' row, on north and west sides of Faneuil Hall, to Merchants' row, on south side; in 1708 the north side was called the Fish Market; the south, the Corn Market, and the west, the Sheep Market; the north, south, and west sides of Faneuil Hall called Market square, about 1784; from Merchants' row, on north side of Faneuil Hall, to Merchants' row, on south side, named Faneuil Hall square, April 25, 1855. Vol. 31, p 61. L 242.

Faneuil's corner, B., 1732; corner King (now State) street and Merchants' row then so called.

Fargo street, So. B.; proposed street from the proposed extension of B street to the proposed extension of E street, on the so-called Commonwealth flats.

Farmgate street, Rox.: from Fisher avenue to Parker Hill avenue.

†**Farnham street**, Rox., 1867; from Hampden street, south-east, crossing Reed (now Reading) street and Gerard street; part from East (now Hampden) street to Reed street; formerly called Foundry street and name changed to Farnham street, April 20, 1869.

Farnsworth street, So. B.; from Congress street to N. E. R.R. piers.

Farnum place, Rox.; from Rogers avenue, west, near Ruggles street.

Farquhar street, W. Rox.; from Centre street, near Weld street, to South street.

Farragut street, W. Rox., 1895; from Baker street, south-west, opposite Keith street; authority to open given by Street Commissioners, May 3, 1895.

Farragut street, E. B. (Breed's Island); from Washburn avenue to Riverside avenue; shown on atlas, 1892.

Farrell place, So. B.; from West First street, south-west, between F street and Dorchester street.

***Farrington avenue**, Bri., 1879; from Harvard avenue to Linden street; laid out, Sept 6, 1879. L 1376.

Farrington avenue, W. Rox., 1874; } south-west from and parallel with
Farrington street, W. Rox., 1872; } Beech street, from a point south-east of Anawan avenue, crossing Anawan avenue and Oak (now Kenneth) street to Clement avenue; called Farrington street, 1872; called Farrington avenue, 1874.

Farrington street, W. Rox.; from Beech street to Rockland street, south-east of and parallel with Washington street; sometimes called Farrington avenue.

Farrington street, W. Rox.; from Park street to Bellevue street; laid out as Rutledge street, June 15, 1877. L 1243.

Farrington street, E. B. (Breed's Island); from Orient avenue to Walley street.

Farwell avenue, B.; from Poplar street, near Spring street, to Pike's alley; the westerly end of Pike's alley, 1879.

***Faulkner street**, Dor., 1887; from Dorchester avenue to Freeman street; laid out, July 28, 1887; formerly Foster street. L 2006.

Favre street, Dor., 1872; from Hersey street, crossing Oakland street.

Faxon place, Rox., 1869; from Tremont street, north-east, near Parker street; laid out, widened and extended to Smith street, with the name of Faxon street, Aug. 25, 1877. L 1263.

***Faxon street**, Rox., 1877; from Tremont street to Smith street; Faxon place from Tremont street, north-easterly, laid out, widened and extended to Smith street, with name of Faxon street, Aug. 25, 1877. L 1263.

Faxon street, E. B. (Breed's Island); from Butler avenue to Riverside avenue; Bromley's atlas, 1892.

***Fay street**, B., 1877; from Dover street, south, then east, to Harrison avenue; Granite place, 1844-48; Dover place 1848; Dover-street place, 1861; laid out as Fay street, Nov. 9, 1877. L 26, L 1288.

Fayette avenue, B., 1825; from Prince street to Pond (now Endicott) street; called La Fayette avenue, 1828.

Fayette court, B., 1825; from Washington street, west, south of Avery street.

Fayette place, B., 1824; block of houses on Tremont street, between West street and Boylston street; called Colonnade row some time after 1824, but without official sanction.

***Fayette street**, B., 1824; from Pleasant street to Ferdinand street; South Allen street called Fayette street, 1824; laid out from Pleasant street to the water, May 29, 1848. L 69½, L 387, L 391, L 392, L 2278.

Federal court, B., 1817; from Union and Hanover streets to the Mills; called North Federal court in 1817; discontinued in 1857, and closed and built over in 1860.

Federal court, B., 1817; from Federal street, opposite Williams (now Matthews) street to Milton place: called South Federal court in 1817.

Federal place, Bri., 1850: from Federal street, west, near East street; also called Federal-street place.

*__Federal street__, B. and So. B., 1788: from Milk street to Federal-street bridge; called Long lane from Milk street to Cow lane (now High street), 1708: named Federal street, 1788; extended to Purchase street, May 5, 1836; extended by the foot of Purchase street to the South Boston North Free Bridge including Sea street, April 30, 1856; part of Dorchester avenue, formerly called Turnpike street, from Federal-street bridge to line between Boston and Dorchester, named Federal street, Feb. 13, 1866: laid out from bridge to Dorchester avenue and Sea street, Nov. 17, 1868; same part renamed Dorchester avenue, March 1, 1870. Vol. 31. pp. 12, 13, 28, 54, 100, 101. L 32, L 44, L 55, L 71, L 79, L 108, L 129, L 135, L 243, L 339, L 357, L 358, L 359, L 360, L 364, L 446, L 451, L 474, L 834, L 835, L 847, L 848, L 849, L 853, L 2296.

*__Federal-street bridge__, B. and So. B.; from Federal (formerly Sea) street to Turnpike street on Dorchester avenue, South Boston; called Sea street, or South Boston North Free Bridge, when opened in 1828. L 1599.

Federal-street place, B.; from Federal street, near corner of Kneeland street, south-west.

Feiling place, Rox.; from Tremont street, south, between Sterling street and Weston street.

Fellows court, B. and Rox.; north-west from Fellows street, between Northampton street and Lenox street.

Fellows place, Rox.; from Fellows street, north-west, between Hunneman street and Randall street. L 1195, L 1491.

†__Fellows street__, Rox., 1849; from Northampton street to Webber street; laid out from Northampton street to Hunneman street, Nov. 23, 1874. L 984, L 985, L 1195, L 1491.

Felton place, Rox.; from Washington street, south-east, between Palmer street and Eustis street.

Fenelon street, Rox., 1896; from Washington street to Merrill street; Burbank street laid out under name of Fenelon street, June 2, 1896. L 2771.

Fenner street, Rox., 1893; from Rochdale street to Cardington street.

Fenno place, Dor.; from Dorchester avenue, east, near Adams street.

*__Fenno street__, Rox., 1894; from Buena Vista street to Rockland street; authority to open given by Street Commissioners, May 10, 1894; laid out, June 11, 1895. L 2705.

Fenton place, Dor., 1870; from Fenton street to Greenwich place.

Fenton street, Dor., 1870; from Duncan street to Clayton street.

Fenway, Rox.; the way bordering the Back Bay Fens upon the east and south extending from Boylston street to Riverway; so named, Dec. 30, 1887.

*__Fenwick street__, Rox., 1845; from Circuit street to Hulbert street; laid out in part upon a private way known as Circuit place, Jan. 14, 1884. L 1752.

Fenwick road, Bri., 1891; from Chiswick road to Strathmore road; authority to open given by Street Commissioners, Oct. 1, 1891.

***Ferdinand street,** B., 1863; from Columbus avenue to Tremont street; laid out from Chandler street to Columbus avenue, Oct. 26, 1869. L 387, L 391, L 392, L 393, L 394, L 485, L 2279.

Fern place, Bri.; on Rockland street and High-school place; sometimes called Academy Hill.

***Fern street,** Bri.; from Franklin street to Holton (formerly Pleasant) street; laid out Aug. 30, 1887. L 2014.

Ferndale street, Dor., 1896; from Norfolk street, opposite Laurel street.

***Ferrin street,** Chsn., 1845; from Bunker Hill street to Chelsea street; laid out from Bunker Hill street to Edgeworth street, June 6, 1853; south-east of Edgeworth street, June 2, 1878; extended to Chelsea street, June 16, 1884. L 1294, L 1784.

Ferry court, B., 1857; from Ferry street.

***Ferry street,** B., 1842; from North street to Fulton street; called Persia street, 1831; laid out and named Ferry street, Aug. 1, 1842.

Ferry way, B., 1708; from Hudson's point to the Mill stream; from the west end of Lyn street round the beach to Ferry wharf, 1732; to Charlestown ferry, 1784; made part of Lynn street, 1784; now part of Commercial street.

Fessenden court, E. B.: from Webster street, north, between Cottage street and Orleans street; also called Fessenden place.

Fessenden place, E.B., from Webster street, north, between Orleans street and Cottage street; also called Fessenden court.

.**Fessenden street,** Dor.; from Norfolk street to Blue Hill avenue.

Fessenden street, W. Rox.; from Chestnut avenue, west, near Green street.

Field court (or **Field's court**), Dor.; from Willow court, north-easterly.

***Field street,** Rox., 1887; from Ruggles street to Madison court; formerly Russell court; laid out with the name of Field street, Jan. 5, 1887. L 1971.

***Field's corner,** Dor.; junction of Dorchester avenue and Adams street.

Fifth street, Bri., 1882; from Devon street to Texas street; now in Brighton cattle yards.

***Fifth street,** So. B., 1805; laid out parallel with Broadway, and named Feb. 27, 1805; laid out from A street to Dorchester street, and from H street to low-water mark, Nov. 17, 1868; from G street to H street, Dec. 30, 1869; called East and West Fifth streets, Feb. 18, 1873. L 8, L 509.

Fifth street, Chsn., 1838; from Lynde street to the railroad; laid out from Lynde street to Front street, Nov. 13, 1860; discontinued and part taken by the Eastern (now B. & M.) R.R. by authority of an act of the Legislature.

Fifth-street place, So. B.; from West Fifth street, south-west, between Dorchester avenue and N. E. R.R.; also called West Fifth-street place.

Fillmore court, B., 1857; from High-street place; partly built over, and the remainder called High-street place.

Fillmore place, B., 1859; from Hanover street, east, near Commercial street; now built over.

***First street,** So. B., 1805; laid out parallel with Broadway and named, Feb. 27, 1805; laid out north-west from Dorchester street, about 530 feet, Oct. 5, 1840; completed from K street to a point 500 feet west therefrom, Sept. 14, 1847; accepted 500 feet from Dorchester street, towards F street, previous to May 1, 1848; completed from a point 538 feet north-west from Dorchester street to E street, Sept. 16, 1850; portions between A street and B street and between E street and C street completed, Sept. 15, 1851; laid out from Foundry street to Dorchester street, and from H street to low-water mark, Nov. 17, 1868; called East and West First streets, Feb. 18, 1873. L 122, L 126, L 128, L 215, L 228, L 229.

First street, Chsn., 1838; from junction Austin street and Lynde street to the railroad; laid out from Lynde street to Front street, Feb. 14, 1848; discontinued as public street and part taken by the Eastern (now B. & M.) R.R., by authority of an act of the Legislature.

Fish lane, B., 1789; from the Town dock to Ann (now North) street; called Roebuck alley, or passage, 1815; included in Merchant's row, 1825.

Fish Market, B., 1708; north side of Dock square; part of Market square in 1784; now part of Faneuil Hall square.

***Fish street**, B., 1708; from Cross street to Fleet street; laid out, Feb. 27, 1730; from Cross street to Ship (now Commercial) street, 1817; made part of Ann (now North) street, July 6, 1824; North street, 1853.

Fish street, Chsn.; now Charles River avenue.

†**Fisher avenue**, Rox., 1868; from Parker street to Parker Hill avenue; from Parker street to High street (now Parker Hill avenue) called Prospect street, 1849; laid out from Parker street to Hayden (formerly Short) street, June 28, 1886. L 1915, L 1916.

Fisher's court, B., 1846; from Washington street, east; now closed.

Fitche's alley, B., 1796; from King (now State) street to Corn market (now Faneuil Hall square); called Pierce's alley, 1708; Change alley, 1788; Fitche's alley, 1796; Flagg alley, 1828; Change avenue, 1841.

Fitche's corner, B., 1708; corner Union street and Marshall's lane then so called.

Fitche's corner, (Capt.), B., 1708; corner King (now State) street and Peirce's alley (now Change avenue) then so called.

Fitche's lane, B., 1788; from Cambridge (now Court) street to Southack's court (now Howard street); called Stoddard's alley, or lane, in 1722, and again in 1800; Stoddard street in 1829.

Fitzgerald court, Chsn.; from Rutherford avenue near corner of Chapman street, north-east.

Flagg alley, B., 1828; from State street to Market square (now Faneuil Hall square); called Pierce's alley, 1708; Change alley, 1788; Fitche's alley, 1796; Flagg alley, 1828; Change avenue, 1841.

Flagg street, B., 1895; from Washington street to Reed street; Flagg street laid out over Walnut place, to Reed street, June 5, 1895. L 2703.

Flagg street, Bri.; from Lake street, east, opposite Kenrick street.

***Fleet street**, B., 1708; from Hanover street to Commercial street; from Middle (now Hanover) street to the water, 1708; from the Universal-Meeting House to Fish (now Commercial) street, 1817; portion from Ann (now North) street to Hanover street, once called Scarlett's wharf. L 1947.

Fleet's corner, B., 1800; corner Cornhill (now Washington street) and Water street then so called.

Fletcher street, W. Rox.; from South street, opposite Dudley avenue to Montclair avenue; authority to open southwardly from Centre street, given by Street Commissioners, July 30, 1896.

Flint place, So. B.; from East Ninth street, north, between L street and M street; called East Ninth-street place in Bromley's atlas of 1891.

***Flint street**, Dor., 1889; from Norfolk street to N. E. R.R.; laid out, June 11, 1889. L 2136.

Flora street, W. Rox., 1893; from Kenneth street to Clement avenue; authority to open given by Street Commissioners, Nov. 17, 1893.

Floral place, B., 1867; from Washington street, west, between Warrenton street and Common street.

***Florence street,** B., 1842; from Washington street to Harrison avenue; called Cobb street, 1840; name changed to Florence street, 1842; accepted, conditionally, April 17, 1843; laid out, Oct. 21, 1878. L 1323.

†**Florence street,** W. Rox., 1848; from Poplar street to Mt. Hope station, and from Hyde Park avenue to Bourne street; part from railroad to Bourne street also called Stony Brook avenue; part adjoining west side of location of B. & P. (now N. Y., N. H. & H.) R.R., near Blakemore street, at Mt. Hope, discontinued, May 26, 1884. L 1467, L 1780.

Flounder alley (or lane), B., 1708; from the foot of Summer street, north-east, by the water; from Bull's wharf to Adams' wharf; thence west to Belcher's lane, 1722; a portion included in Broad street, 1833; the remainder discontinued, 1856. L 69.

***Follen street,** B., 1882; from St. Botolph street to B. & P. (now N. Y., N. H. & H.) R.R.; laid out, Dec. 27, 1882. L 1680.

Folsom avenue, Rox.; from Parker street, west, between Hillside street and Alleghany street.

Folsom place, Rox., 1868; from Conant street to end of Whitney street; laid out as part of Whitney street, July 15, 1876. L 1160.

Folsom street, W. Rox., 1873; from Neponset avenue to Mt. Hope street.

***Folsom street,** Dor., 1884; from Dudley street, south-west, between Howard avenue and Magnolia street; Woodward park laid out with name of Folsom street, Aug. 5, 1884. L 1798.

Forbes avenue or place, W. Rox.; from Chestnut avenue to end of Bowe street; formerly a part of Bowe street; laid out as part of Forbes street, July 28, 1890. L 2253.

***Forbes street,** Rox. and W. Rox., 1890; from Centre street to Chestnut avenue; Bowe street and a part of Forbes place laid out as Forbes street, July 28, 1890. L 2174, L 2252, L 2253.

***Ford street,** E. B. (Breed's Island), 1886; from Saratoga street to Breed street; laid out, Aug. 23, 1886. L 1931.

†**Ford's Run,** B., 1854; from South Market street to Clinton street; 65 feet of north end laid out, July, 1854; from South Market street to Clinton street, 1860.

Fore street, B., 1789; probably Fish street, so called; the earliest name by which what is now North street was called; was also at one time called Front street.

Forest avenue, Rox., 1850; from Warren street, east, between Rockville place and Montrose street; included in Whiting street, March 19, 1884. L 1762.

Forest place, Rox.; from Forest street, north-east.

Forest place, Chsn.; from Eden street, north-west, near Russell street.

***Forest street,** Rox., 1868; from 14 to 144 Mt. Pleasant avenue; formerly called Chestnut street, and as such laid out, March 11, 1840; named Forest street, April 21, 1868. L 2029.

***Forest Hill avenue,** Dor. and W. Rox., 1852; from River street (Lower Mills) to Norfolk street; laid out from northerly end of Neponset street, crossing Norfolk street, through Madison street, crossing Back (now Harvard) street, to a point on Canterbury street opposite Morton street, August, 1852; part from Norfolk street to Canterbury street called Madison street and Austin street; name changed to Morton street, March 1, 1888. L 823, L 1667.

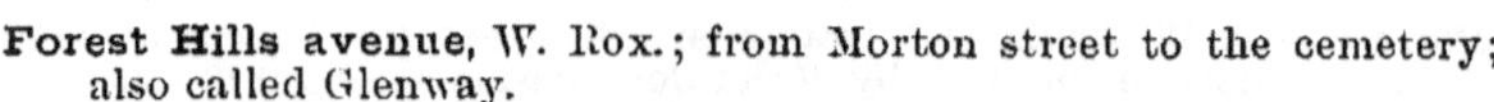

Forest Hills avenue, W. Rox.; from Morton street to the cemetery; also called Glenway.

***Forest Hills street,** W. Rox., 1848; from Washington street to Morton street; called Curtis street previous to 1848; earlier called Jube's lane or road leading to Rocky swamp, or Rocky Swamp road. This, with Amory (formerly School) street in Roxbury and West Roxbury, formed a continuous road sometimes called the road leading to Gamblin's end, a part of which was discontinued or abandoned at the time of the laying out, in 1804, of the Norfolk and Bristol turnpike (later Shawmut avenue, now Washington street); named Forest Hill street, June 26, 1848; part of, from Washington street to Scarboro' street, named Morton street, Dec. 5, 1859; Forest Hill street, named Forest Hills street, Nov. 5, 1860. L 970.

Forster's Court, Chsn.; from Union street, south-west, between Main street and Rutherford avenue; also called Foster's court.

Fort avenue, B., 1847; from Harrison avenue, north-west, between Fay street and Ashland place.

***Fort avenue,** Rox., 1825; from Highland street to Centre street; laid out, Nov. 4, 1875. L 1102, L 1103, L 1104.

Fort Field, B.; an early name for Fort Hill.

Fort Hill, B., 1632; an eminence in the eastern part of the town, previously Corn Hill and Fort Field, levelled, 1868. L 922

Fort street, B.; an early name for Milk street.

***Fort Hill square,** B., 1875; between Oliver street and High street, where Fort Hill formerly stood; Washington place, 1808; Washington square, 1837; park in the centre of Washington square, between Oliver street and High street, named Fort Hill square, Dec. 15, 1875. L 348. L 626.

Forty-foot passage, B., 1800; Allen's lane or street, along the front of the ropewalks to Blanchard's wharf then so called.

***Foss street,** Chsn., 1869; from Chelsea street to Water street; laid out and named, Aug. 18, 1869.

Foster court, B., 1826; from Tremont street, west, between Boylston street, and Eliot street; called Foster place, or South Foster place, 1831; Van Rensselaer place, 1852.

Foster court, B.; from Foster street.

Foster place, B., 1823; from Foster street, south-east, near Charter street; named Foster place, July 8, 1829.

***Foster street,** B., 1800; from Charter street to Commercial street; called Sliding alley, 1708; Foster lane, 1741; Fuller street, 1795; Brewer's Hill, 1800; Foster street, 1800; from Lynn street to low-water mark staked out by Town, May 22, 1807; same part confirmed as a street, in continuation of Foster's lane, March 17, 1819; north end of Foster street, from Commercial street to the dock, discontinued, Jan. 3, 1856. L 1389.

Foster street, Dor.; from Dorchester avenue to Freeman street; laid out, with name of Faulkner street, July 28, 1887. L 2006.

Foster street, Bri., 1848; from Commonwealth avenue, crossing Washington street to Surrey street; Proprietors Way 1814; laid out as Seaver lane by Selectmen, Aug. 1, 1842; named Foster street, Nov. 20, 1848; laid out (straightened, etc.), April 29, 1853; accepted Sept. 5, 1853; extended from Washington street to Surrey street, Sept. 4, 1884. L 1017, L 1018, L 1019, L 1818, L 2280.

Foster's lane, B., 1732; from North street to Ship (now Commercial) street; named 1732; called Clark street in 1788 and 1789, 1795 and 1800, and thereafter.

Foster-street slip, B., 1819; from Commercial street to the water; discontinued in 1856.

Foundry avenue, So. B.; from Foundry street, east, between West Fourth street and Swan street; discontinued and taken into the property of the O. C. (now N. Y., N. H. & H.) R.R. by authority of an act of the Legislature of 1893.

Foundry square, So. B.; between Swan, Foundry, and West Fourth streets, entered from southerly side of West Fourth street; discontinued and taken into property of the O. C. (now N. Y., N. H. & H.) R.R. by authority of an act of the Legislature of 1893.

***Foundry street**, Rox., 1865; from East (now Hampden) street to Reed (now Reading) street; accepted, Dec. 30, 1867; name changed to Farnham street, April 20, 1869.

***Foundry street**, So. B., 1854; from Dorchester avenue to West Fourth street; formerly from Dorchester avenue, south, then curving east to Dorchester avenue again; accepted from Fourth (now West Fourth) street to Swan street, Dec. 18, 1854; accepted and laid out from Swan street to about 150 feet from southerly line of Sixth (now West Sixth) street, Nov. 20, 1855; laid out from Federal street (now Dorchester avenue) to O. C. (now N. Y., N. H. & H.) R.R.; Nov. 17, 1868; name of Foundry street extended over street leading from Fourth (now West Fourth) street, to Dorchester avenue, near Sixth (now West Sixth) street, March 11, 1873; part south of West Fourth street discontinued and taken into property of O. C. (now N. Y., N. H. & H.) R.R., by authority of an act of the Legislature of 1893. L 39, L 336, L 355.

Fountain place, Rox., 1872; from Fountain street, easterly.

Fountain place, B., 1853; from Hanover street, west, near Charter street.

Fountain square, Rox., 1852; public square bounded by Walnut avenue, and Townsend, Harold, and Munroe streets; laid out and dedicated to public use, Jan. 26, 1852.

Fountain square, Rox.; from Fountain street, westerly.

***Fountain street**, Rox., 1845; from Circuit street to Regent street, laid out, April 2, 1875. L 1032.

Fountain Hill place (or **Fountain Hill**), Rox.; from Fountain street, easterly.

***Fourth street**, So. B., 1805; laid out parallel with Broadway, and named, Feb. 27, 1805; finished, acceptance and laying out, April 25, 1831; name of Emerson street, between M street and N street, changed to Fourth street, April 21, 1868; laid out from Dover-street bridge to Dorchester street, and thence to low-water mark, Nov. 17, 1868; called East and West Fourth streets, Feb. 18, 1873. L 8, L 145, L 258, L 604, L 779.

Fourth street, Chsn., 1838; from Lynde street to Front street; one of the boundaries of Lynde street, mentioned as "Union street, otherwise called Fourth street," but shown on plan of Eastern R.R. property in 1874; part taken by the Eastern (now B. & M.) R.R., by authority of an act of the Legislature.

Fourth street, Bri., 1882; from Devon street to Texas street; now in Brighton cattle yards.

Fourth-street court, So. B.; from West Fourth street, north-easterly, near B street.

Fourth-street place, So. B.; from East Fourth street, southerly, near G street.

Fowler street, Dor., 1894; from Glenway street to Greenwood street; authority to open given by Street Commissioners, Oct. 24, 1894.

Fox avenue, Dor., 1861; from Adams street to Percival avenue (now Percival street); laid out with the name of Fox street, March 21, 1888. L 2061.

***Fox street**, Dor., 1888; from Adams street to Percival street (formerly Percival avenue); formerly Fox avenue; laid out, March 21, 1888. L 2061.

Fox hill, B., 1722; on the Back Bay shore, about opposite the centre of the Common; levelled.

Francis place, B., 1851; from Hanover street, near Cross street.

***Francis street**, Rox., 1833; from Tremont street, at its junction with Huntington avenue, crossing Brookline avenue, to Bellevue street; laid out north-west of Brookline avenue, from said avenue over a way called Longwood street, to the angle therein at which it turned towards Longwood avenue, by the Street Commissioners, Oct. 19, 1874; part north-west of Bellevue street taken into the Riverway. L 977, L 2096, L 2213

Francis street, Rox.; shown on old plans as a 50-foot street, parallel with and 390 feet east of Parker street, running from an unnamed street 40 feet wide to another unnamed street near the canal, nearly in line of Camden street extended.

Francis street, W. Rox.; from Mt. Vernon street, between Temple street and Baker street, to Keith street.

Frankfort street, E. B., 1893; from Prescott street to the Parkway; authority to open given by Street Commissioners, April 21, 1893.

Frankfort street, E. B., 1845; from Maverick street to Bennington street, at its junction with Swift street.

***Franklin avenue**, B., 1817; from Court street to Brattle street; called Brattle street, 1708; Brattle's alley or lane, 1722; Dassett's or Dorsett's alley, 1789; from the court-house to Brattle square called Franklin avenue, 1817.

Franklin avenue, W. Rox., 1851; from Centre street, opposite the Arnold Arboretum, north-west, then curving northerly; called "Franklin avenue or Allendale street," on plan dated 1857. L 2095.

Franklin avenue, W. Rox., 1870; from Spring street, south-east, near Charles river; called also Franklin street; laid out as Billings street, Sept. 28, 1888. L 2095.

Franklin court, Dor.; from Norfolk avenue, near East Cottage street, north-easterly.

Franklin Park, W. Rox.; between Seaver street and Morton street, and Blue Hill avenue and Canterbury street and Walnut avenue and Forest Hills street.

Franklin Park, W. Rox., 1870; parallel with and south-east of Spring street, near Charles River, and bounded by Franklin (now Billings), Prospect, Washington and Hamilton streets.

Franklin Park terrace, W. Rox., 1893; from Walnut avenue, near and north of Peter Parley street; authority to open given by Street Commissioners, May 24, 1893; called Park lane, 1894; laid out as Park Lane street, Nov. 23, 1895.

Franklin place, B., 1792; from Franklin street to Federal street: one side of the present Franklin street, the other side being originally called "The Tontine Crescent;" from Bishop's alley (now Hawley street) to Federal street, 1800; made part of Franklin street, Sept. 21, 1858. L 139.

Franklin place, Rox., 1848; from Tremont street, north-west, between Cunard street and Milford place (now Sarsfield street); laid-out as Walpole street, Nov. 16, 1881. L 1570.

Franklin place, W. Rox., from Washington street near Stony brook, south, to N. Y., N. H. & H. R.R.

Franklin square, B., 1845; open space bounded by Washington, East Brookline, James and East Newton streets; laid out, 1834; name of

Shawmut square changed to Franklin square, April 21, 1845; called Shawmut square, 1847–49; Franklin square, 1849.

Franklin square, Bri.; square at junction of Franklin street and Fern street.

***Franklin street**, B., 1798; from Washington street to India street; called Vincent's lane, from Marlboro' (now Washington) street to Bishop's alley (now Hawley street), 1777; called Franklin street, 1798, and part from Bishop's alley to Federal street laid out the same year with an oval enclosure 300 feet long in the centre, on one side of which was Franklin place, and on the other the Tontine Crescent, a block of sixteen dwelling houses; confirmed as a public street, Sept. 15, 1834; Franklin place and enclosure made part of Franklin street, Sept. 21, 1858; part formerly called Franklin place, from Hawley street to New Devonshire street including centre of Franklin street, heretofore enclosed, accepted, May 31, 1859; extended to Pearl street, at Sturgis street, April 18, 1873; name of Sturgis street, from Oliver street to Broad street, changed to Franklin street, Sept. 30, 1873; the part called Sturgis street included a part of Hamilton court and the whole of Sturgis place and Baker's alley; Bread street, from Broad street to India street, changed to Franklin street, March 1, 1896. Vol. 31, pp. 31, 100. L 101, L 133, L 139, L 163, L 220, L 459, L 460, L 461, L 462, L 600, L 834, L 835, L 851, L 853.

***Franklin street**, Chsn., 1824; from Main street to High street; Bolton street, from Main street to High street, accepted, May 5, 1824; and "now known as Franklin street" (1824), but no record of change of name.

***Franklin street**, Dor., 1845; from Roxbury line to Cottage (now East Cottage) street; accepted, conditionally, May 2, 1853; laid out by County Commissioners, July, 1854; name changed to Norfolk avenue, being a continuation of same, Dec. 21, 1875.

Franklin street, Dor., 1854; from Fulton street to Taylor street.

Franklin street, Dor., 1850; from Adams street to Milton street; Malvern street, supposed to have been so called.

***Franklin street**, Bri., 1847; from Cambridge street to North Harvard street; known as "Road to Roxbury" in 1815; laid out from Cambridge street to Harvard street (now North Harvard street), Jan. 15, 1855; accepted and named, May 28, 1855; laid out from Central or Centre (now Lincoln) street to Cambridge street, opposite South Harvard street (now Harvard avenue), in 1859; accepted, Oct. 22, 1879; part between Lincoln street and Cambridge street named Lincoln street, being a continuation of the same, April 25, 1876; footway over B. & A. R.R., connecting northerly and southerly parts of street laid out, July 10, 1883; footway under B. & A. R.R. connecting same parts of street laid out, April 21, 1894; overhead bridge taken down, 1894. L 983, L 1718, L 2592.

Franklin street, W. Rox., 1870; from Spring street, south-east, near Charles River; called also Franklin avenue; laid out as Billings street, Sept. 28, 1888. L 2095.

Frank's court, B., 1874; From South May (now Savoy) street, south.

Frary's corner, B., 1708; corner Orange (now Washington) street and Frog lane (now Boylston street) then so called.

Fred street, Chsn., 1870; from Sherman street, crossing Arlington avenue, to George street, near and parallel with Somerville line.

***Frederick street**, So. B., 1875; from West Ninth street, south-west, nearly to O. C. (now N. Y., N. H. & H.) R.R.; laid out, Oct. 7, 1875. L 1079.

Frederick terrace, Dor., 1896; from Hartford street, opposite Cunningham street.

*__Frederika street__, Dor., 1884; from Adams street to Minot (sometimes called New Minot) street; laid out, Dec. 24, 1884. L 1841.

Fredonia street, Dor.; from Westville street, south-east, between Iowa street and Head street.

Freedom court, Chsn.; from Main street, westerly, near Middlesex street.

Freeland street, Dor.; from Standard street, near Manchester street, north-east.

Freeman place, B., 1846; from Beacon street, north, between Somerset street and Bowdoin street.

Freeman street, Dor., 1871; from Charles street to beyond Faulkner street; authority to open southwardly from Faulkner street, given by Street Commissioners, May 23, 1896.

Freeman's corner, B., 1800; corner Ann (now North) street and Cross street then so called.

*__Freeport street__, Dor., 1892; from Hancock street to Neponset avenue; the name of Commercial street was changed to Freeport street, March 1, 1892. L 710, L 1840, L 1862, L 2452.

Fremont avenue, Rox., 185; from Mall street, north-easterly.

Fremont court, Chsn.; from Fremont place, east, near Medford street.

Fremont place, Chsn.; from Medford street to Chauncy place.

Fremont place, Rox.; from Dudley street, south-westerly, between Pevear street and Greenville street.

Fremont place, B., 1859; from Pleasant street, east, nearly opposite Clafleu place; built over, 1873.

Fremont place, Dor.; from Fremont street to Cook court.

†**Fremont street**, Dor., 1869; from River street to Blue Hill avenue; extension from Norfolk street to Brush Hill (now Blue Hill) avenue laid out, Aug. 12, 1869.

French place, B., 1844; from Essex street, south, near Harrison avenue; built over, 1869–70.

French square (or **French's square**), So. B.; from (59) West Fourth street, southerly; discontinued and taken into property of O.C. (now N.Y., N.H. & H.) R.R. by authority of an act of the Legislature of 1893.

French street, Dor.; from Delhi street, near Norfolk street, east.

Fresno street, W. Rox.; from Dudley avenue to Alder street.

*__Friend street__, B., 1733; from Union street to Causeway street; from Hanover street to the Mill-pond called Separate lane in 1722; named Friend street, 1733; extended across the Mill-pond to Causeway street, 1807; extended to Dock square, over part of Scott's (formerly Minot's) court, 1854–55. L 40.

Friend-street court, B., 1833; from Friend street, west, near Hanover street; closed in 1849.

Friend-street court, B., 1855; from Friend st., north-east, near Traverse street.

Friend-street court, B., 1828; } from Friend street, west, near Cause-
Friend-street place, B., 1833; } way street.

Frizzell's corner, B., 1708; in Garden court.

Frizzell's square, B.; North square, at one time so called.

Frobisher's corner, B., 1800; corner Hanover street and Link alley (afterwards North Federal court) then so called.

Frog lane, B., 1708; from Orange (now Washington) street, west, by the Common, to the water; from Orange street, opposite the old Liberty tree, west, to the new burying-ground, 1800; from Orange street to the mall called Boylston street, 1809; from the mall to the water called Boylston street, 1812.

Front street, B.; the oldest name of the present North street; called also at the same time Fore street.

Front street, B., 1805; from Beach street to South Boston bridge (now Dover street); extended to Essex street, through Rainsford lane or street, July 6, 1824; continuation to the dike laid out conditionally, June 3, 1834; street next the dike (sometimes called Dyke street), extending from Joshua Davis' land to Northampton street, named Front street, Sept. 15, 1834; new street from South Boston bridge to connect with street lately made from Northampton street, over City land to easterly end of the dike opened for travel, June, 1836; from Northampton street to Roxbury line accepted and known as continuation of Front street, June, 1836; name of Front street changed to Harrison avenue, April 26, 1841.

***Front street,** Chsn., 1838; from Warren avenue to Austin street; laid out from Austin street to Boston (now Warren) avenue; named and accepted, March, 1845.

Front street, E. B. (proposed); from proposed part of Porter street to proposed part of Putnam street, parallel with and next east from B., R. B. & L. R.R.

Frost avenue, Dor.; from Boutwell street to Fairview street.

***Frothingham avenue,** Chsn., 1869; from Main street to Rutherford avenue; laid out, Oct. 15, 1877. L 1278.

Fruean place, Dor.; from Highland street, near High street, north-east.

***Fruit street,** B., 1822; from Blossom street to Charles street; from Blossom street to Bridge (now North Anderson) street, 1822; across Bridge street, 1831; accepted, conditionally, Aug. 8, 1831; confirmed as a public street, Sept. 15, 1834; to Grove street, 1852; extended from North Grove street to Harbor Commissioners' line, May 7, 1860. L 170, L 278.

Fruit street, Chsn., 1828; from Bunker Hill street to Vine street.

***Fruit street,** W. Rox., 1867; extended to Weld street and whole street, from Weld street to Centre street, accepted, March 25, 1867; now Maple street.

Fruit-street court, B., 1833; from Fruit street, northerly, near the hospital.

Fruit-street place, B., 1840; from Fruit street, northerly, near the Medical College.

***Fulda street,** Rox., 1889; from Highland street to Ellis street; formerly Nopper street; laid out, Aug. 27, 1889. L 2157, L 2309.

Fuller street, B., 1795; Foster street, from Charter street to Lynn (now Commercial) street; so called on Carleton's map.

Fuller street, B., 1840; from Church street, west; name changed to Grenville place, 1860.

†**Fuller street,** Dor., 1870; from Morton street to Bushnell street; formerly from Forest Hill avenue (now Morton street) to Dorchester avenue, then, after an interval, continued across Shawmut branch, O. C. (now N. Y., N. H. & H.) R.R. to Carruth street; laid out, from Washington street to Dorchester avenue, June 29, 1877; part from Carruth street to Bushnell street, laid out as Rowena street, Aug. 29, 1889; part of Fuller street, near and west of Washington street, at one time known as Warren place. L 1252, L 1253.

Fullerton street, Rox., 1896; from Brookline avenue to Fairhaven street; Miner street, laid out under the name of Fullerton street, Oct. 12, 1896. L 2790.

Fulton court, B., 1834; from Cross street to North street; formerly from Cross street, rear of Ann (now North) street, and Fulton street.

***Fulton place**, B., 1848; from Fulton street to North street; laid out, Oct. 11, 1864. L 269.

***Fulton street**, B., 1827; from Clinton street to Lewis street; from Clinton street to Richmond street, 1827; probably what was called Second street when laid out from Clinton street to Cross street, Feb. 22, 1828; from Clinton street to Richmond street named Fulton street, Dec. 10, 1832; extended to Lewis street, Nov. 8, 1838; doubts of legality having arisen, extension to Lewis street, laid out again, Oct. 2, 1842.

Fulton street, Dor., 1854; from Ericsson street to Franklin street.

Furbush court, Chsn., 1867; from Main street to Rutherford avenue.

Furnace street, B., 1846; from Federal street to Cove street; from South street to Sea (now Federal) street, 1846; part between South street and Cove street in 1883 occupied by O. C. (now N. Y., N. H. & H.) R.R. passenger station.

Fussell avenue, Rox.; from Day street, westerly; abandoned; part of Bynner street now in about same location.

***G street**, So. B., 1805; from Dorchester street to East Ninth street, with proposed extension to line in Old Harbor; laid out from salt water, on the south, to the harbor of Boston on the north, and named, Feb. 27, 1805; laid out from Dorchester street to harbor line in Dorchester bay, Nov. 17, 1868. L 142, L 174, L 879, L 1890.

†**Gainsborough street**, Rox., 1886; from B. & P. (now N.Y.,N. H. & H.) R.R., opposite Camden street, to Parker street; name of part of Camden street changed to Gainsborough street, March 1, 1886. L 1296, L 1321.

***Galena street**, Rox., 1892; from Elmore street to Kingsbury street; formerly Grainger street; laid out, July 6, 1892. L 2408.

Gallatin street, Rox.; from Blue Hill avenue to Maple street; authority to open under the name of Nazing street given by Street Commissioners, Feb. 24, 1896.

Gallatin street, Dor.; from Codman street, parallel with Shawmut Branch of N.Y., N. H. & H. R.R., to extension of Milton street at Cedar Grove station.

Gallop's alley, B., 1708; from Fish (now North) street to Middle (now Hanover) street; named Board alley, 1850.

***Gannett street**, Rox., 1893; from Holborn street to Gaston street; laid out, May 22, 1893; formerly Galena street. L 2513.

Garaux place, B., 1839; from Portland street, east, near Hanover street; built over about 1883.

Garden court, B., 1708; from Bell alley (now Prince street) to Fleet street; changed to Garden-court street, from North square to Fleet street, some time later than 1817, but no record of change.

Garden place, Chsn., 1860; from Eden street to Mead street; laid out with the name of Ludlow street, June 30, 1884. L 1786.

***Garden street**, B., 1733; from Cambridge street to Myrtle street; laid out from Cambridge street to the Mount, beginning near the rope-walks at West Boston, 1800; from Cambridge street to Myrtle street, 1817.

Garden street, Rox., 1845; from Tremont street (now Huntington avenue) to Davis street (now Hillside avenue); later called Hillside avenue and Wait street.

Garden street, Dor., 1864; from Dorchester avenue to Buttonwood street; laid out with the name of Grafton street, March 27, 1882.

Garden street, W. Rox., 1870; from Brown avenue to Hancock (now Sherwood) street.

Garden street, W. Rox.; from Maple street to Corey street.

Garden street, W. Rox., 1852; from Austin (now Centre) street, north-west; afterwards Corey street.

Garden street, Bri., 1874; from Market street to Murdock street.

***Garden-court street**, B.; from North square to Fleet street; called Garden street, 1709; no record of naming.

Garden-street arch, B., 1859; from Garden street, west, near Cambridge street.

Garden-street court, B., 1840; from Garden street, west.

Gardiner street, B., 1845; from Tremont street to Emerald street; name changed to Paul street, April 21, 1868; sometimes called Gardner street.

***Gardiner street**, Chsn., 1858; from Broadway (now Main street) to Sever street; also called Gardner street.

Gardner avenue, Rox., 1855; from Central avenue, south-west, then south-east, near Warren street and Blue Hill avenue.

Gardner avenue, Rox.; from Roxbury street, between Gardner street and Pynchon street (now Columbus avenue), south, then east.

Gardner court, Rox., 1867; from Washington (now Roxbury) street, near Gardner street, south-west, then south-east; sometimes called Gardner avenue.

Gardner place, So. B.; from West Broadway, north-easterly, between B street and C street.

Gardner street, B.. 1845; from Tremont street to Emerald street; name changed to Paul street, April 21, 1868; called sometimes Gardiner street.

***Gardner street**, Chsn., 1858; from Main street to Sever street; also called Gardiner street.

***Gardner street**, Rox.; from Roxbury street to Centre street; name of Smith street changed to Gardner street, Oct. 29, 1860; this street was regarded as public by the Roxbury authorities at the time of annexation and has been taken care of by the City since; no record of laying out can be found. L 420.

†**Gardner street**, Bri., 1841; from Harvard avenue across Malvern street; from Harvard avenue to Malvern street, laid out Dec. 17, 1873; accepted, conditionally, Dec. 30, 1873; laid out, Sept. 16, 1876; authority to open part east of Malvern street to Babcock street, extended across Commonwealth avenue, given by Street Commissioners, Sept. 7, 1892. L 1177, L 1178, L 1179.

†**Gardner street**, W. Rox.; from Spring street to High street; laid out from Spring street to Baker street, March 6, 1871; from Baker street to Cow Island, Nov. 29, 1876; extended to Morrison street, Nov. 11, 1881. L 1203, L 1204, L 1205, L 1566, L 2319, L 2407.

Gardner's corner, B., 1732; corner Fish (now North) street and Sun court then so called.

Garfield avenue, W. Rox.; from Corey street to Mt. Vernon street.

Garfield avenue, W. Rox.; from Washington street, south-easterly, near Greenwood avenue; also called Garfield street.

Garfield place, Rox.; from Washington street, near Ball st.

Garland place, B., 1826; from Washington street, westerly; extended to Suffolk street (now Shawmut avenue) and named Garland street, Sept. 12, 1836.

Garland place, B.; from Garland street, south-westerly, near Washington street.

***Garland street,** B., 1831; from Washington street to Shawmut avenue; Garland place, from Washington street, west, laid out as Garland street and extended to Suffolk street (now Shawmut avenue), Sept. 12, 1836; laid out conditionally from Suffolk street to Tremont street, Dec. 12, 1836, but conditions never complied with; laid out from Washington street to Shawmut avenue, Sept. 5, 1870. L 545, L 562, L 720.

***Garrison street,** B., 1882; from Huntington avenue, south-easterly, crossing St. Botolph street; laid out, Dec. 27, 1882. L 1681.

***Gaston street,** Rox., 1871; from Warren street to Blue Hill avenue; named, March 7, 1871; laid out, June 20, 1871. L 621.

***Gates street,** So. B., 1863; from Dorchester street to East Eighth street; laid out, Nov. 17, 1868.

Gawain street, Dor.; from Park street to Harvard street.

Gay alley, B.; Hillier's lane, from Queen (now Court) street to Brattle street, sometimes so called; called also at same time Belknap's alley; Brattle street extended through it to Court street in 1820.

***Gay street,** Rox.; from Roxbury street to Linden park (now Linden Park street); orders for acceptance in 1859 and 1861 not concurred in.

Gay street, Rox., 1856; Woodville square, from West Cottage street to Dennis street, so called.

***Gay Head street,** Rox.; from Centre street to Minden street; laid out, June 23, 1890. L 2200.

Gayland avenue, Dor.; from Judson street to West Cottage street.

Gaylord street, Dor., 1896; from Washington street to Chamberlain street: Cork street, laid out and extended to Chamberlain street, under the name of Gaylord street, July 10, 1896. L 2775.

Gee's corner, B., 1708; corner Prince street and Back (now Salem) street then so called.

***Genesee street,** B., 1844; from Harrison avenue to Albany street; accepted, Jan. 5, 1856. L 209, L 2679.

***Geneva avenue,** Dor. and Rox., 1876; from Blue Hill avenue to Dorchester avenue; from Blue Hill avenue to Bowdoin street in Directory of 1884: street from Columbia street to Bowdoin street, part of which was called Green street and part Geneva street, named Geneva avenue, Dec. 30, 1876; extended from Columbia street to Blue Hill avenue, at its junction with Warren street, including Marston avenue, May 26, 1880; extended from Bowdoin street to Charles street, Aug. 27, 1884. L 1461, L 1462, L 1810, L 1811, L 1979, L 2350, L 2729, L 2730.

Geneva street, E.B. (proposed); from Maverick street to proposed part of Putnam street.

Geneva street, Dor.; from angle in Green street to Bowdoin street; with part of Green street, forming continuous street from Columbia street to Bowdoin street; named Geneva avenue, Dec. 30, 1876.

Geneva street, Dor.; proposed extension of Geneva avenue, from Westville street to Charles street; so called by Bromley, 1884.

George street, B., 1732; from Beacon street, north, then east, then north, to Cambridge street; from Cambridge street to Olive (now Mt. Vernon) street called Hancock street, 1788; this part also at one time called Turner street; from Hancock street to Clapboard (now Joy) street, called Sumner (now Mt. Vernon) street, 1800; from Beacon street to Sumner street, called Belknap (now Joy) street, 1803.

***George street,** B., 1810; from Cambridge street, near the bridge, to Chestnut street 1810; a part of Southac street from 1729; from Chestnut street, to Sumner (now Mt. Vernon) street called West

Cedar street 1828; from Sumner street to Pinckney street, called West Cedar street, 1833; confirmed as a public street, Sept. 15, 1834; from Pinckney street to Cambridge street called West Cedar street, April 1, 1839.

*__George street__, Rox., 1865; from Hampden street to Shirley street, accepted, July 31, 1865; laid out from Magazine street to Shirley street, Nov. 28, 1879. L 1407, L 2263.

George street, W. Rox.; from Billings street to North avenue.

George street, Chsn.; from Hamblen street to Fred street.

George street, Bri.; from North Beacon street, south-westerly, towards Whitney street.

Georgia avenue, Rox.; from Elm Hill avenue to Blue Hill avenue; part from Elm Hill avenue to Montana street, laid out as Georgia street, June 26, 1882; from Montana street to Blue Hill avenue, laid out as Georgia street, June 23, 1884.

*__Georgia street__, Rox., 1882; from Elm Hill avenue to Blue Hill avenue; Georgia avenue, from Elm Hill avenue to Montana street, laid out as Georgia street, June 26, 1882; relocated and extended over remainder of Georgia avenue, from Montana street to Blue Hill avenue, June 23, 1884. L 1618, L 1782.

Georgia street, E. B. (proposed); from Putnam street to Neptune street (Wood Island) (abandoned).

Georgianna street, W. Rox.; from Boylston street to Dalrymple street.

*__Gerard street__, Rox., 1865; from Massachusetts avenue to George street; accepted, June 31, 1865; laid out from East Chester park (now Massachusetts avenue) at its junction with Swett street to Norfolk avenue, Dec. 8, 1882. L 794, L 1670, L 1671.

Germain street, Rox.; from near Norfolk avenue to Sherwood street, parallel with N. E. R.R.

*__German street__, W. Rox.; from Washington street to Grove street; laid out, Sept. 10, 1891. L 2334.

Germania avenue, W. Rox., 1871; from Bismarck street to Baker street, later called Germania street. L 2534.

*__Germania street__, W. Rox.; from Bismarck street to Boylston street; laid out, from Bismarck street, and over a part of Baker street, or court, to Boylston street, Aug. 24, 1893; formerly called Germania avenue. L 2534.

Gerrish street, So. B. (proposed); from Dorchester avenue, across Washington avenue (proposed), to Richardson avenue (proposed).

Gerrish street, Bri.; from Brooks street, west, then south-west to Bigelow street.

Gibbons court, B.; Gibbons place, from Washington street, west, next north of Boylston street, sometimes so called.

Gibbons place, B., 1784; from Washington street, west, next north of Boylston street; from Newbury street, west, 1784; called Gibbons court, 1800; called Market place, 1818; since by both names.

Gibbs court, Chsn.; from Main street, westerly, nearly opposite Charles street.

Gibbs lane, B., 1708; from the upper part of Cow lane (now High street) to the sea; from Belcher's lane to Cow lane, 1732; called Gibson's lane by the 1796 Directory; from Purchase street into Cow lane, 1800; from Washington place to Fort Hill wharf, 1817; name changed to Belmont street, from Washington place to Broad street, Sept. 23, 1844; named Oliver street in 1865.

†__Gibson street__, Dor., 1849; from Dorchester avenue, crossing Adams street, to Tenean creek; laid out and built across to the school pasture from Adams street to Dorchester turnpike (now avenue) in 1849; named, April 1, 1850.

Gibson's lane, B., 1796; Gibbs lane, from Purchase street, into Cow lane (now High street), so called by Directory of 1796; now Oliver street.

Gifford court, } So. B., 1859; from Ward street, northeasterly, between
Gifford place, } Dorchester street and Ward court.

Gilbert avenue, Chsn.; from Hamblen street to Fred street.

Gilbert place, B.; from the end of the extension of Summer street beyond Atlantic avenue, to Congress street.

***Gilbert street,** Rox., 1874; from Centre street to Wyman street; laid out from near Roys street to Hoffman street, Oct. 6, 1880; from near Roys street to Centre street, Sept. 7, 1881; from Hoffman street to Wyman street, Oct. 7, 1882; name changed to Chestnut avenue, March 1, 1886. L 1499.

Gilbert's alley, B.; from Summer street to Milk street; called Bishop's, alley, 1708; Broad alley, 1792; also Richardson's alley and Wybourne's lane; named Hawley street in 1800.

Gill street, Chsn.; mentioned in 1827 as "Austin's lane or Gill street;" new street (Chelsea street), laid out from City square to Joiner street, to take the place of Gill street, Dec. 7, 1835; Gill street discontinued, March 28, 1836; Town's rights relinquished to adjacent proprietors, May 2, 1836.

Gillam place, B., 1809; from Washington street to Marlboro' chapel; changed to Chapel place, 1837; also called Gilman, or Gillman place; built over.

Gill's alley or **lane,** Chsn., 1761; from Back street (now Warren avenue), south-west; later probably same as Gill street; from Charlestown square to Joiner street; a portion taken by Chelsea street and remainder discontinued.

Gilman place, B., 1834; from Friend street, south-west, next northwest from Traverse street; enclosed.

Gilman place, B.; Gillman place, from Washington street to Marlboro' chapel, sometimes so called; called Chapel place in 1837; built over.

Gilman street, W. Rox.; from Canterbury street to Sutton street.

Gilson court, B., 1867; from West Cedar street, north-westerly, near Cambridge street; called Bridge court, 1833; name changed to Gilson court, 1867.

†**Gladstone street,** E. B. (Breed's Island), 1886; from Walley street (formerly Washburn avenue) to the junction of Waunatosa avenue and Cosmos street; laid out from Breed street to Washburn avenue (now Walley street), Aug. 23, 1886; formerly Terrace avenue. L 1933, L 1934, L 1935.

***Gleason street,** Dor.; from Harvard street to Bradshaw street; laid out, Dec. 30, 1889. L 2197.

Glen avenue, Dor., 1871; from Blue Hill avenue, crossing Erie avenue (now Erie street) to Read avenue or street; made part of Glen road, later Glenway street; called also Glenn avenue.

Glen avenue or **street,** Dor., 1872; from Glenway street (formerly Glen road) to Greenwood street.

***Glen road,** W. Rox. and Dor., 1853; from Washington street to Franklin Park, formerly from Washington street, opposite Green street, to Harvard street, opposite Warner avenue; laid out from Forest Hills street to Walnut avenue; thence extended to Blue Hill avenue, near Columbia street, March, 1872; name of Green street, between Forest Hills street and Washington street, changed to Glen road, March 1, 1888; part of Glen road from Sigourney street to Blue Hills avenue, included in Franklin Park; part from Old road (Blue Hill avenue) to Glen avenue laid out as Glenway street, July 31,

1893; part from Glen avenue to Harvard street, laid out as Glenway street, Aug. 10, 1894; this last part is shown on early atlas as Warner avenue. L 1469, L 2192.

***Glen street**, Dor., 1873; from Glendale street to Trull street; laid out, Dec. 10, 1875. L 1113.

Glen street, W. Rox., 1856; from Green street, north, 1,003 feet, next to B. & P. (now N. Y., N. H. & H.) R.R.: Boylston avenue extended to Green street over it, April 5, 1872.

Glen way, W. Rox.; from Centre street, east, nearly opposite Lake Ville (now Lakeville) place.

***Glenarm street**, Dor., 1882; from Washington street to New Seaver (now Seaver) street: Miller street, from Washington street to Merrill street, laid out and name changed to Glenarm street, July 3, 1882; name of part of Merrill street, from angle in same at Glenarm street to New Seaver street, changed to Glenarm street, March 1, 1883. L 1545, L 1631, L 1657.

Glenbrook street, Rox. and Dor.; from Dewey street to Dalmatia street.

***Glendale street**, Dor., 1870; from Bird street to Hancock street; name of Cross street (from Hancock street to Columbia street) changed to Glendale street, May 31, 1870; extended from Columbia street to Bird street in part over a private way known as Bird-street place, Dec. 19, 1878. L 1340.

Glendon avenue, Bri., 1887; from Commonwealth avenue to Kinross road; from Englewood avenue to Massachusetts (now Commonwealth) avenue, on plan in 1887; part from Englewood avenue to Selkirk road now called Chiswick road; part from Chiswick road to Kinross road abandoned.

Glendon place, E. B.; from Bremen street to Chelsea street.

***Glendon street**, E.B.; from Eagle street, opposite Trenton street, to Condor street; laid out, April 20, 1869; late Knox street. L 441, L 816.

Glenham street, W. Rox., 1893; from Baker street to La Grange street; authority to open given by Street Commissioners, March 5, 1895.

Glenmore street, Dor.; from standard street to Groveland street.

Glenside avenue, W. Rox.; from Glen road, south-westerly, nearly opposite Sigourney street.

Glenvale terrace, W. Rox.; from Lamartine street, north-west, between Spring lane and Bell street.

Glenway, Dor., 1845; a part of curvilinear driveway through Savin Hill. from Grampian way to Indian way (now Savin Hill avenue); name changed to Grampian way, Aug. 12, 1869; also called Glenway avenue.

Glenway, W. Rox., 1849; from Scarboro' street (part of present Morton street), southerly, curving easterly to Scarboro' street again; now included in Forest Hills avenue.

Glenway, Rox.; from Seaver street, south; now in Franklin Park.

***Glenway street**, Dor.; from Blue Hill avenue (Old road) to Harvard street, opposite Warner avenue; formerly Glen road; laid out and named Glenway street, from the Old road (Blue Hill avenue) to Glen avenue, July 31, 1893, and from Glen avenue to Harvard street, Aug. 10, 1894; part near Harvard street shown on early atlas as Warner avenue. L 2528, L 2529, L 2609, L 2610.

Glenwood avenue, W. Rox., 1856; from Dedham turnpike (now Washington street) to proposed avenue; plan, book 3, No. 57, Middlesex, South District Deeds.

Glenwood place, Rox.; from Glenwood street, south-east, near Cliff street.

*__Glenwood street__, Rox., 1868; from Warren street to Cliff street, name of Myrtle street changed to Glenwood street, April 21, 1868; laid out, Dec. 22, 1870. L 583.

__Glenwood terrace__, Rox.; from Glenwood street, near Warren street, north-west.

†__Glide street__, Dor., 1869; from Chickatawbut street to Marsh street; from Chickatawbut street to Minot street, laid out and named, March 1, 1869.

__Glines avenue__, W. Rox.; from School street, south-east, between Byron court and Erie place.

__Globe court__ or __alley__, B., 1862; from Commercial street, south-west, near Hanover street.

__Gloucester place__, B., 1863; from Harrison avenue, west, next north of Dover street.

*__Gloucester street__, B., 1867; from Boylston street to 30-foot street on bank of Charles River; at one time called Seventh street on plans; laid out from Beacon street to Commonwealth avenue, Aug. 3, 1874; extended from Commonwealth avenue to Boylston street, April 12, 1880; laid out from Beacon street to 30-foot street, May 3, 1895. L 862, L 951, L 1443, L 2701.

__Glover court__, So. B., 1863; from Woodward street, south-west.

__Glover place__, Dor.; from Highland street, north-east; also called Glover's court.

*__Glover's corner__, Dor.; at the junction of Dorchester avenue, East street, and Commercial (now Freeport) street.

__Goddard street__, So. B., 1855; from Dorchester street to D street; accepted, conditionally, Sept. 13, 1859; name changed to Eighth (now West Eighth) street, April 9, 1867. L 201, L 257.

__Goddard street__, Bri., 1891; from North Harvard street to Seattle street; authority to open given by Street Commissioners, July 10, 1891.

*__Gold street__, So. B., 1852; from A street, near Dorchester avenue, to Dorchester street; accepted and laid out, Nov. 29, 1852; extended from E street to D street, Nov. 22, 1859; extended from C street to D street, Sept. 9, 1862; laid out from B street to C street, Oct. 18, 1870; laid out from D street to E street, Feb. 29, 1872; laid out from F street to Dorchester street, May 9, 1874; laid out from C street to D street, Sept. 23, 1882; laid out from E street to F street, May 21, 1884; laid out from A street to N. Y. & N. E. (now N. E.) R.R., June 23, 1884; laid out from B street to N. E. R.R., March 26, 1891; laid out over location of N. E. R.R., March 14, 1895. L 168, L 183, L 558, L 744, L 924, L 1642, L 1776, L 1783, L 2616.

__Goldsmith place__, W. Rox.; from Centre street, east, near Spring Park avenue.

__Goldsmith place__, Rox.; from Ruggles street, south-west, between Washington street and Shawmut avenue.

*__Goldsmith street__, W. Rox.; from Centre street to Custer street; laid out, Sept. 11, 1891. L 2333.

__Goldthwait street__, Rox.; from Parker street to Halleck street.

__Gooch lane__ or __street__, B.; same as Gouch lane or street; now Norman street.

__Goodenough street__, Bri., 1893; from North Beacon street to Faneuil street; authority to open given by Street Commissioners, Oct. 24, 1893.

__Goodridge's alley__, B.; from Charter street, north, at an early date.

__Goodwin court__, So. B.; from Ward street, north-easterly, near Preble street.

Goodwin place, B., 1859; from Revere street, north, near Grove street.

Gordon place, Dor.; from Adams street, north-east, near its junction with Dorchester avenue.

***Gordon street**, W. Rox., 1865; from Elm street to Jamaica Plain station; laid out, May 7, 1872.

Gordon street, Dor.; from Torrey street to Dunbar avenue.

***Gordon street**, Bri., 1876; from North Beacon street to Cambridge street; laid out, Feb. 5, 1876. L 1129.

Gore avenue, Rox., 1863; from Parker street to Terrace street; formerly from Parker street to Tremont street; accepted, conditionally, May 11, 1863; laid out in part (from Tremont street), April 17, 1875; name of last-mentioned part changed to Terrace street, Sept. 23, 1875; part between Terrace street and Parker street laid out as Gore street, Aug. 25, 1886. L 1040.

***Gore street**, Rox., 1886; from Parker street to Terrace street; laid out, Aug. 25, 1886; formerly Gore avenue. L 1040.

Gore street, W. Rox.; from Centre street to Lamartine street; Paul Gore street sometimes so called.

Gorham place, B., 1835; from Washington street, north-west, near Waltham street.

Gorham street, Bri.; from Holmes avenue to Commonwealth avenue.

Gorham street, Chsn., 1810; Oliver Holden conveys to Town for public highway a parcel of land called Gorham street, being a continuation of High street, terminating at west corner of Baptist meeting-house, July 17, 1810; later made a part of High street.

Gorham street, Dor.; from Centre street to Clement street.

Gosnold street, E.B., 1893; from Prescott street to the Parkway; authority to open given by Street Commissioners, April 21, 1893.

***Gouch lane or street**, B., 1732; from Green street to the Mill-pond, called Gouch lane, 1732; Merrimac street filled in across foot of, 1807; from Green street to Merrimac street called Gouch street, 1822; name changed to Norman street, Dec. 18, 1877.

Gouch-street place, B., 1849; from Norman street (formerly Gouch street), north-west.

Gould avenue, W. Rox.; from Weld street to Agassiz avenue.

†**Gould street**, W. Rox., 1888; from Spring street, near the Charles river, to Belle avenue; formerly Clarence street, of which the part between Spring street and Hamilton street was laid out, with the name of Gould street, Sept. 28, 1888. L 2094.

Gould's court, E. B.; from Orleans street, near Decatur street, north-westerly, to land of E. (now B. & M.) R.R.

Gouldville terrace, Dor.; from Brook avenue, south-west, then west, between Victor street (formerly Grenville place) and West Cottage street.

***Gove street**, E. B., 1893; name of that part of Decatur street, between Meridian street and Bremen street, changed to Gove street, March 1, 1893. L 2502.

***Governor's alley**, B., 1732; named from Dummer's corner in School street, south-west, to Rawson's lane (now Bromfield street), 1732; called Montgomery street, 1833; named Province street, June 17, 1833; confirmed as a public street, Sept. 15, 1834.

Grace avenue, Dor.; from Robinson street to Arcadia street; laid out as Montello street, Nov. 16, 1894. L 2671.

Grace court, So. B.; from East Third street, northerly, between O street and P street.

Grace street, Dor.; from Walton street to Roslin street; authority to open given by Street Commissioners, Jan. 11, 1895.

***Grafton street**, Dor., 1882; from Dorchester avenue to Buttonwood street; private way, called Garden street, laid out with the name of Grafton street, March 27, 1882. L 1592.

Graham court, Dor.; from Graham street to Clapp street.

Graham street, Dor.; from south of Clapp street, crossing it and Massachusetts avenue (formerly East Chester park) to Graham court.

Grainger street, Rox., 1890; from Elmore street to Kingsbury street; laid out as Galena street, July 6, 1892. L 2408,

Gramercy street, Bri.; from Cambridge street to North Beacon street; laid out with the name of Dustin street, Feb. 20, 1890. L 2207.

Grammar alley, B. 1795; from North Bennet street to Prince street; called School alley, 1732; called Grammar alley, 1795; Prince-street avenue in 1833; Bennet avenue in 1839.

***Grampian way**, Dor., 1845; curvilinear driveway through Savin Hill, from Savin Hill avenue to Savin Hill avenue; laid out, including Glen way, and accepted, Aug. 12, 1869.

***Granby street**, Rox., 1895; from Commonwealth avenue to Charles river; laid out, Aug. 15, 1895. L 2713.

Granby street, So. B.; proposed street from the proposed extension of B street to the proposed extension of E street, on the so-called Commonwealth flats.

Grandview street, W. Rox.; from Beech street, nearly opposite Kitredge street.

Granger place, Dor.; from Duncan street, opposite Granger street.

***Granger street**, Dor., 1870; from Duncan street to Clayton street; laid out, June 18, 1891. L 2300.

***Granite avenue**, Dor.; Granite street, from Adams street to Neponset river; so called in County Commissioners' records.

Granite street, Dor.; from Adams street, at junction with Marsh street, to Neponset river; called Granite turnpike on a plan in 1846; called Granite bridge road in 1847, and previously turnpike, bridge, etc.; laid out by County Commissioners, September, 1865; called Granite avenue in Commissioners' records.

***Granite street**, So. B., 1855; from West Second street to Mt. Washington avenue and beyond; from First street, now West First street, to Mt. Washington avenue, accepted, conditionally, April 30, 1855: laid out from Second (now West Second) street to Mt. Washington avenue, and from street 550 feet north-east of Mt. Washington avenue to limit of solid structures, Nov. 17, 1868; part north of Mt. Washington avenue now abandoned. L 27, L 41, L 58, L 80.

Granite place, B., 1844; from Dover street to Harrrison avenue; called Dover place, 1848; Dover-street place, 1861; Fay street, 1877.

Granite street, W. Rox., 1870; from Centre street to Spring street, near Spring-street station; in same year called Cass street on a plan; part from Centre street to railroad laid out as Cass street, Dec. 11, 1883. L 1748.

Grant avenue, Bri.; from Wilton street.

Grant place, B., 1866; from Camden street, south-west, next north of Washington street.

Grant place, B., 1866; from Chardon street, south; called Chardon-street place, 1841; Grant place, 1866; Chardon court, 1874.

Grant place, Dor.: from Washington street (at Lower Mills), westerly near Sanford street.

Grant place, } **Grant street,** } Bri.; from Upton court, near Western avenue, southerly.

***Grant street,** Dor.; from Crescent avenue to Harbor View street; laid out, July 22, 1887. L 2003.

Grant's court, Chsn.; from North Mead street, south-easterly.

Grant's corner, B., 1800; corner Union street and Minot's court at one time so called.

Granville street, W. Rox.; from Beech street, opposite Kittredge street.

Granville place, Dor., 1871; from Brook avenue, southerly; laid out as a public street, with the name of Victor street, from Brook avenue to Dean street, July 26, 1894.

Granville street, Dor.; from Adams street, near Granite avenue to Milton street.

Grape place, B., 1851; from Spring street, north-west, between Leverett street and Milton street; near corner of Chambers street.

Graphic court, B., 1827–61; from Washington street, opposite Franklin street; closed and built over.

***Grave street,** Chsn.; from Main street to Bunker Hill street; from Main street to Bartlett street, accepted, Nov. 28, 1831; continuation to Bunker Hill street laid out, Oct. 6, 1834, and accepted, Nov. 10, 1834; called also Graves, Greave and Greaves streets; no record of change of name, but soon after called Sullivan street.

Gravel street, B., 1733; from Leverett street to Wiltshire (now Chambers) street; from Leverett street to Poplar street, 1803; accepted and included in Chambers street, May 26, 1828; that part of Chambers street formerly called Gravel street named Ashland street, Feb. 22, 1845.

Gravelly Point road, Rox., 1662; from Ruggles street across B. & P. (now N.Y., N. H. & H.) R.R. to the marsh; located, Jan. 19, 1662 and 1694; portion east of Sudbury (now Weston) street discontinued, Nov. 30, 1863.

Graves lane, Chsn., 1803; from Charlestown square, south-west.

Gray place, B., 1841–57; from Portland street, west, near Hanover street; closed.

***Gray street,** B., 1870; from Berkeley street to Clarendon street; Clarendon place laid out and name changed to Gray street, Oct. 11, 1870. L 354, L 568.

***Gray street,** Chsn., 1842; from Chelsea street to Water street; laid out, March 28, 1842.

Gray's alley or lane, B., 1722; from Belcher's lane (now Purchase street) to Cow lane (now High street), shown on a plan in 1722; named, 1732; from Cow lane to Milk street, 1788; part included in Atkinson (now Congress) street, between 1788 and 1795; laid out from Atkinson street to Milk street, Aug. 25, 1795; Atkinson street laid out through remainder, 1816.

Greave street, Chsn.; from Main street to Bunker Hill street; also called Grave street.

Green and Walker's corner, B., 1732; cor. Queen (now Court) street, and Hillier's lane (now Brattle street), then so called.

Green alley, So. B.; from West First street to West Second street; laid out as Colton street, Dec. 31, 1888. L 2110.

Green lane, B., 1803; Allen's lane, from Wiltshire street, west, to the water, so called.

Green lane, B.; Atkinson (now Congress) street, from Milk street to Cow lane (now High street), so called previously to 1788.

Green lane, B., 1708; from Well's corner (now Bowdoin square) to the water; called Green street, from Well's corner, north-west, to Barton's point, 1732; from Bowdoin square to Chambers street, 1784.

Green lane, B., 1789; Pearl (formerly Hutchinson) street, from Milk street to Cow lane (now High street), so called by a plan of 1789.

Green lane, B.; Salem street, from Prince street to Charter street, so called at one time.

Green place, W. Rox.; from Centre street, opposite Green street; now a part of Myrtle street.

***Green street**, B., 1732; from Bowdoin square to Chambers street; called Green lane, from Well's corner (Bowdoin square) to the water, 1708; called Green street, from Well's corner, north-west, to Barton point, 1732; from the present Bowdoin square to Chambers street, 1784. Vol. 31, p. 74. L 11, L 75, L 271, L 579.

Green street, B., 1850; Court street from Bowdoin square to Sudbury street, so called in 1850, and later in same year changed back to original name.

***Green street**, Chsn., 1799; from Main street to Bunker Hill street; laid out from corner of Green's lane to Bunker Hill lane, March 4, 1799; continuation to Bunker Hill street accepted, April 6, 1840.

Green street, Dor., 1840; from Bowdoin street to Columbia street; street leading from Bowdoin street, through Davenport's lane, named Green street, March 11, 1840; called Love lane on a plan dated 1859; name of part from Columbia street to Geneva street changed to Geneva avenue, Dec. 30, 1876; name of part from Geneva street to Bowdoin street changed to Olney street, Dec. 30, 1876. L 1191.

***Green street**, W. Rox., 1837; from Centre street to Forest Hills street; new road from Jamaica Plain to Dedham turnpike (now Washington street) named Green street, Aug. 14, 1837; laid out from Shawmut avenue (now Washington street) to Forest Hills street, to connect with Glen road, Dec. 15, 1870; accepted, Dec. 15, 1870; name of part between Washington street and Forest Hills street changed to Glen road, March 1, 1888. L 1698, L 2210, L 2739.

Green-street court, Dor.; from Olney street, northerly.

Green-street place, B., 1874; from Green street, south, opposite Crescent place.

Green-street place, Dor., 1868; from Green street (now Geneva avenue), north-east, then north-west, to Columbia street; part north-east from Geneva avenue, now called Vaughn court or avenue.

†**Greenbrier street**, Dor.; from Park street, north-west, near Washington street, crossing Bloomfield street; laid out from Bowdoin street to Bloomfield street. Sept. 19, 1895. L 2731.

Green Dragon lane, B., 1708; from Hanover street to the Mill-Pond; opened to width of 40 feet, Sept. 16, 1828; laid out from corner of Hanover street and Union street, to Merrimac street, as a continuation of and named Union street, Sept. 26, 1828.

Green's block, Chsn.; from Walnut street, north-west.

Green's lane, Chsn.; laid out from Main street to High street, March 4, 1799; no other record.

Greenhalge street, Dor.; from Roseclair street to Dorchesterway.

Green Hill avenue, W. Rox., 1851; from Centre street, north-west, near Allandale street.

***Green Hill street**, Dor.; from Mill street to Blanche street; laid out, July 21, 1885. L 1874.

***Greenheys street**, Dor., 1893; from Magnolia street to Mascoma street; authority to open given by Street Commissioners, July 19, 1893; laid out, Dec. 5, 1893. L 2555.

Greenleaf street, Rox., 1871; from Huntington avenue to Rogers avenue; formerly from Parker street, near its junction with Huntington avenue, easterly; authority to open portion from Rogers avenue west and north-west; given by Street Commissioners, Jan. 7, 1897.

***Greenough avenue**, W. Rox., 1853; from Centre street to Elm street; accepted, March 7, 1864; laid out by Selectmen by the new High school-house to Elm street, and accepted by the Town, July 25, 1868. L 1148, L 1955.

Greenock street, Dor., 1894; from Blue Hill avenue to Harvard street; authority to open given by Street Commissioners, Nov. 8, 1894.

Greenough place, W. Rox., 1872; from Greenough avenue, north-east.

Greenough's avenue, B., 1848; from Charter street to Commercial street; called Greenough's alley, 1708; Greenough's lane, 1732; Greenough's avenue, 1848; Greenough lane, 1858.

Greenough alley, B., 1708; the alley leading from Charter street, down through Mr. Greenough's building yard into Lynn (now Commercial) street; called both alley and lane after 1732.

***Greenough lane**, B., 1732; from Charter street to Commercial street; Greenough's alley called Greenough's lane in 1732; called Greenough's avenue in 1848; called Greenough lane in 1855. L 23, L 1391.

Greenville park, Rox.; from Greenville street; also called Greenville place.

Greenville place, Rox.; from Greenville street, westerly; also called Greenville park.

***Greenville street**, Rox., 1845; from Dudley street to Winthrop street; accepted from Dudley street to East street (now Blue Hill avenue), Jan. 28, 1850; Winthrop street laid out over part of from Grove Hall (now Blue Hill avenue), north-westerly, April 2, 1855.

***Greenwich park**, B., 1870; from Columbus avenue to B. & P. (now N. Y., N. H. & H.) R.R.; part of West Concord street, from Columbus avenue to the railroad named Greenwich park, March 29, 1870. L 502, L 516.

Greenwich place, Dor., 1870; from Dorchester avenue to Commercial (now Freeport) street.

***Greenwich street**, Dor., 1870; from Dorchester avenue to Commercial (now Freeport) street; laid out, Dec. 3, 1877. L 1293.

***Greenwich street**, Rox., 1866; from Warwick street to Westminster street; laid out, Sept. 1, 1871. L 382, L 659, L 661.

Greenwood avenue, W. Rox., 1857; from Washington street, south-easterly, near Garfield avenue.

Greenwood park, Dor.; from Park street, near Dorchester avenue, north.

Greenwood street, Dor., 1872; from Glen road (now Glenway street) or Warner avenue, easterly, then northerly, parallel with N. E. R.R.; part from Glenway street, easterly, now known as Roxton street; Greenwood street now runs from Harvard street, northerly, parallel with N. E. R.R., to beyond Glenway street.

Greenwood street, Dor., 1893; from Harvard street to Elmo street; authority to open from Harvard street to Roxton street given by Street Commissioners, March 28, 1893; authority to open across the end of Fowler street, from near Glen street to near Elmo street given by Street Commissioners, Oct. 24, 1894.

***Greenwood street**, Rox., 1872; from Marcella street to Brunswick (now Columbus) avenue; accepted from Marcella street to Stony brook, Sept. 24, 1872; named, Oct. 11, 1872; location altered, Dec. 27, 1879; discontinued, July 23, 1881; given in Directory, 1884, and on chart, 1884; Ritchie street laid out over part of former location of, from Marcella street to Centre street, Dec. 31, 1888. L 1456, L 2111.

Greims place, Rox.; from Longwood avenue, south, between Parker street and Phillips street.

***Grenville place**, B., 1860; from Columbus avenue to Church street; called Fuller street, from Church street, west, 1840; name changed to Grenville place, 1860; laid out between Church street and line of proposed extension of Columbus avenue, Sept. 14, 1868. L 387, L 394, L 397.

Grew avenue, W. Rox.; from Canterbury street, opposite Poplar street, to Hyde Park line.

***Gridley street**, B., 1825; from High street to Purchase street; called Tilley's lane, 1708; Gridley's lane, 1795; Gridley street, 1825. L 82.

Gridley's lane, B., 1708; from Cow lane (now High street) to the rope-walk; called Griffin's lane in 1795 or 1800, and both names seem to have been used until it was included in the extension of Pearl street, in 1821.

Gridley's lane, B., 1795; from Cow lane (now High street) to Belcher's lane (now Purchase street); called Tilley's lane, 1708; Gridley's lane, 1795; Gridley street, 1825.

Gridley's lane, B., 1857; from Grove street, west, near Cambridge street; probably same as Grove place, with same description.

Griggs place, Bri.; from Allston street, south-west, opposite Hollis place.

Griggs street, Bri., 1857 (from Commonwealth avenue to Holmes avenue, formerly); from Washburn street to Holmes avenue; part of taken into Massachusetts (now Commonwealth) avenue.

Griffin court, Dor.; from Clayton street, opposite Granger street.

Griffin's lane, B.; from Cow lane (now High street) to Belcher's lane (now Purchase street); called Gridley's lane from 1708 to 1795 or 1800; from which time both names seem to have been used until the lane was included in the extension of Pearl street in 1821.

***Grimes street**, So. B.; from West Seventh street to West Eighth street; laid out, April 8, 1878. L 1300.

Grinnell street, Rox., 1848; from Columbus avenue to Walpole street.

Grosvenor place, Rox., 1868; from Washington street to Cliff street; name of Lincoln place changed to Grosvernor place, April 21, 1868.

Groton court, B., 1841; from Shawmut avenue, east; extended to Washington street, and called Groton street, 1842.

***Groton street**, B., 1826; from Washington street to Shawmut avenue; from Tremont street to Suffolk street (now Shawmut avenue), 1826; accepted, 1826; named, Sept. 15, 1834; extended to Washington street through Groton court, 1842; accepted, Dec. 7, 1857; part between Shawmut avenue and Tremont street named Dwight street, April 19, 1859. L 2372.

Grotto glen, Rox., 1871; from Day street, westerly.

Grouse street, W. Rox.; from Washington street to Huron street.

Grove court or **place**, B., 1846; from Myrtle street, at the head of Grove street; called Grove square, 1856.

Grove place, B., 1848; from Grove street, west, near Phillips, formerly Southac street.

***Grove place**, B., 1851; from May (now Revere) street to Myrtle street; accepted and laid out as a highway, Oct. 27, 1851; no other record; same as Myrtle court, through which Myrtle street was extended to Revere (then May) street in 1851.

Grove place, B., 1857; from Grove street, west, near Cambridge street.

Grove place, Dor.; from Lawrence avenue.

***Grove street**, B., 1729; from Cambridge street to Myrtle street; from Cambridge street, southerly, across Southac (now Phillips) street and May (now Revere) street, 1729; near the new bridge from Cambridge to the Mount, 1800; from Cambridge street to Pinckney street, 1807; confirmed as a public street, Sept. 15, 1834; from Cambridge street to Myrtle street, 1851.

Grove street, Rox. and Dor., 1846; from Blue Hill avenue to Lawrence avenue.

***Grove street**, W. Rox.; from Centre street to Dedham line; from Norfolk and Bristol turnpike (now Washington street) to Mill Village, Dedham; laid out, September, 1829; from Norfolk and Bristol turnpike, opposite new road to Mill Village, Dedham, to old post road to Boston; laid out and confirmed as a public highway, April, 1833. L 1567.

Grove street, W. Rox., 1871; from Gardner street; laid out with the name of Morrison street, Nov. 11, 1881.

***Grove square**, B., 1856; from Myrtle street, southerly, opposite Grove street; called Grove court or place in 1846.

Grove terrace, B., 1879; from Grove street, west, between Phillips street and Cambridge street.

Groveland street, Dor., 1895; from River street to Manchester street, authority to open given by Street Commissioners, May 20, 1895.

***Grove Hall avenue**, Rox. and Dor., 1851; from Dudley street to Seaver street; part of East street, from Eustis (now Dudley) street, to Warren street, called Grove Hall avenue, Dec. 8, 1851; name of Brush Hill turnpike changed to Grove Hall avenue, Jan. 28, 1867; Grove Hall avenue from Dudley street to Seaver street, and Brush Hill avenue from Seaver street to Mattapan, named Blue Hill avenue, Oct. 25, 1870. L 489, L 490, L 491.

Grover avenue, W. Rox.; from Neponset avenue, near Canterbury street to Florence street.

Guernsey street, W. Rox.; from Centre street, crossing South street, to Central Station.

Guild row, Rox., 1857; from Dudley street to Washington street; part of Bartlett street named Guild row, Dec. 28, 1857; same made a part of Washington street, June 16, 1874. L 504.

***Guild row**, Rox., 1874; from Roxbury street to Dudley street; early called Winslow street, and Shawmut avenue extended through, Dec. 28, 1857; named Guild row, June 16, 1874. L 2222.

***Guild street**, Rox., 1865; from Washington street to Lambert avenue; laid out and extended to Lambert avenue, Dec. 6, 1870. L 582.

***Guilford street**, Bri., 1886; from Saunders street to Pomeroy street; laid out from Saunders street to Orchard (now Pomeroy) street, Oct. 15, 1886. L 1954.

***Gurney street**, Rox., 1870; from Tremont street to Parker street; laid out, Sept. 11, 1882. L 1637.

***Gustin street**, So. B.; from West Ninth street to O. C. (now N.Y., N. H. & H.) R.R.; Morni court laid out as Gustin street, Oct. 13, 1891. L 2348.

Gustine avenue, Dor.; from King street to Rosemont street.

***H street**, B., 1863; from Tremont street to Berkeley street; accepted, conditionally, Nov. 24, 1865; accepted finally and name changed to Chandler street, April 28, 1866.

***H street**, So. B., 1805; from East First street to East Ninth street, with proposed extension to line in "Old Harbor;" laid out from the salt water on the south to the harbor of Boston on the north and named, Feb. 27, 1805; laid out from First (now East First) street to Harbor line in Dorchester Bay, Nov. 17, 1868. Vol. 31, p. 48.

H-street place, So. B.; from H street, west, between Emerson street and East Broadway.

Haberstrohe place, W. Rox.; from Lamartine street, south-east, near Boylston street.

***Hadley street**, Chsn., 1880; from Parker street to Somerville line; shown as an unnamed street on a plan dated 1878; laid out, Oct. 11, 1880. L 1500.

Hadwin way, W. Rox.; from Hyde Park avenue, near Ashland street.

***Hagar street**, W. Rox.; from Eliot street to Thomas street; laid out, Oct. 26, 1887. L 2035.

Halborn street, Dor.; from Delhi street to West Selden street.

Hale's court, Dor.; from Adams street, north-east, between Linden street and East street; also called Hall's court; laid out from Adams street to Dorchester avenue with the name of Hecla street, Aug. 30, 1892. L 2426.

Half-court square, B.; Half-square court, from King (now State) street, south, so called in 1798.

Half Moon place, B., 1848; from Broad street, west, nearly opposite Wharf street; Humphrey place laid out and extended through Half Moon place to Broad street and name changed to Wendell street, Dec. 30, 1870. L 460.

Half-Moon street, Dor., 1895; from Magnolia street to Hooper avenue; authority to open given by Street Commissioners, Aug. 7, 1895.

Half-square court, B., 1708; the way leading from King (now State) street to Pudding lane (now Devonshire street) in 1708; called also Half-court square in 1798, the way round the buildings back of the Post-Office, 1800; called Salter's court, 1808; extended east to Congress street, 1810; called Exchange square, 1818; a part called Congress square, 1821; parts discontinued, 1832, 1842; a part called Story place, 1845; all named Congress square, 1873.

Half place, B., 1849; from Hanover street, south-easterly, near Cross street.

Hall place, B.; from Hanover street, south-east, between Richmond street and Board alley.

Hall place, So. B.; from East Fifth street, south, between L street and Pickering place.

***Hall street**, W. Rox., 1870; from South street, east, to near B. & P. (now N. Y., N. H. & H.) R.R.; laid out, Dec. 1, 1887. L 2041.

***Halleck street**, Rox.; from Station street to Ruggles street; shown as an unnamed street on a plan dated 1856; laid out from Station street to Ward street, Dec. 30, 1869; from Ward street to Ruggles street, Sept. 4, 1871. L 505, L 672, L 690, L 1889.

Hallowell's corner, B., 1732; corner Milk street and Batterymarch street then so called; called Hollawaye's corner, 1708.

Hall's (Dr.) corner, B., 1800; corner Dock square and Wing's lane (now Elm street) then so called.

Hall's court, Rox.; from Washington street, north-westerly, opposite Warren street.

Hall's court, Dor.; from Adams street, north-east, between Linden street and East street: shown as an unnamed court on a plan dated 1861; also called Hale s court; laid out from Adams street to Dorchester avenue with the name of Hecla street, Aug. 30, 1892. L 2426.

Hamblen street, Chsn.; from Temple street, north-easterly, nearly to Mystic River; shown as an unnamed street on plan dated 1851; from Arlington avenue, near Dorrance street, by Directory.

***Hamburg street**, B., 1843; from Mystic street to Harrison avenue; accepted, conditionally, Nov. 4, 1857; laid out, July 10, 1861; accepted, finally, Sept. 25, 1861. L 224, L 231.

Hamburg street, E. B.; from Decatur street to proposed part of Marion street; shown as from Maverick street to Bennington street on a plan dated 1845.

***Hamerton street**, Rox.; from Crawford street to Humboldt avenue; laid out from Crawford street to Harold street, Dec. 1, 1892; from Harold street to Humboldt avenue, Oct. 12, 1893. L 2466, L 2549.

Hamilton alley, B., 1820; from Batterymarch street to Wendell street.

Hamilton avenue, B., 1823; from Broad street to Hamilton (now Batterymarch) street; called Quincy lane in 1822; closed.

Hamilton avenue, Dor., 1872; from Bowdoin street to Columbia street; also called Hamilton street; laid out with the name of Barrington street, Oct. 21, 1889. L 2181, L 2182.

Hamilton court, B., 1827; from Hamilton street, near Wendell street; formerly called Hamilton lane; a part included in Franklin street, and the remainder built over.

Hamilton court, Chsn.; from Main street, westerly, nearly opposite Albion place.

Hamilton lane, B., 1820; from Hamilton street to Broad street; the south part closed in 1827; the part opening from Hamilton street called Hamilton court; a part later included in Franklin street and the remainder built over.

Hamilton place, B., 1806; from Common (now Tremont) street, easterly, opposite Park street.

***Hamilton street**, B., 1807; from Batterymarch street to High street; called Sconce lane, 1708; Sconce street, 1784; Hamilton street, 1807; confirmed as a public street, Sept. 25, 1834; name changed to Batterymarch street, March 1, 1896. L 332, L 333, L 457, L 458, L 922.

Hamilton street, W. Rox., 1870; from Clarence (now Gould) street to Charles street, near Charles river.

Hamlen place, B., 1844; from Pleasant street, near Tennyson street, west; called Cole's place, 1839; and then extended to Church street; called Hamlen place, 1844.

Hamlet street, Dor., 1871; from Boston street to Belden street.

Hamlin street, So. B., 1860; from East Eighth street to East Ninth street, between G street and H street.

Hammatt road, W. Rox.; from Hyde Park avenue to Ashland street.

***Hammett street**, Rox.; from Grinnell street to Sarsfield street; formerly Hammett avenue; laid out, Nov. 15, 1892. L 2457.

***Hammond avenue**, B., 1850; from Chambers street to Leverett street; a passageway four and one-half feet wide, pronounced a public way, Oct. 18, 1847; laid out again, Oct. 30, 1848; called Steele's court, 1849; Hammond avenue, April 1, 1850.

Hammond park, B. and Rox., 1867; from Shawmut avenue to Tremont street; later called Hammond street. L 189.

Hammond square, B. and Rox., 1865; from Shawmut avenue to Tremont street; later called Hammond park and Hammond street.

*__Hammond street__, B. and Rox., 1868; from Shawmut avenue to Tremont street; called Hammond square, 1865; Hammond park, 1867; laid out, July 28, 1868. L 189, L 382, L 442, L 659, L 1711.

__Hammond terrace__, B.; from Hammond street, north-east, then north-west, to Smith avenue.

__Hampden place__, Rox., 1876 from Hampden street, westerly, between Prescott street and Norfolk avenue; name of Perry court changed to Hampden place, May 9, 1876.

*__Hampden street__, B. and Rox., 1868; from Albany street to Dudley street; probably laid out by County Commissioners in April, 1830; named East street, August, 1842; Hampden street, April 21, 1868. L 719.

__Hampshire court__, Rox.; from Hampshire street, south-east, then south-west, to Vernon street.

__Hampshire place__, Rox.; from Hampshire street.

*__Hampshire street__, Rox., 1868; from junction of Cabot street and Ruggles street to Clay (now Linden Park) street; name of Orange street, between Clay street and Cabot street, changed to Hampshire street, April 21, 1868; laid out from Clay street to Vernon street, July 15, 1871; from Vernon street to Culvert street, July 31, 1886. L 630, L 1924.

__Hampstead road__, W. Rox., 1895; from Arborway, northerly, then westerly, near South street; authority to open given by Street Commissioners, Nov. 13, 1895, and June 20, 1896.

__Hampton court__, B., 1870; from Northampton street, south-westerly, between Washington street and Shawmut avenue; named, June 14, 1870.

__Ham's court__, Chsn.; from Main street, westerly, towards Rutherford avenue; shown as an unnamed street on a plan dated 1849; laid out from Main street to Canal street (now Rutherford avenue), Dec. 6, 1869; discontinued, July 21, 1871; laid out from Main street to Rutherford avenue, with the name of Mishawum street, July 26, 1894.

*__Hancock avenue__, B., 1828; from Beacon street by the west side of the State House to Mt. Vernon street; same in 1827; named Jan. 21, 1828; also called State House avenue.

*__Hancock bridge__, B., 1793; from the foot of Cambridge street to Cambridge; called also West Boston bridge.

__Hancock place__, B., 1823; from Belknap (now Joy) street, east; between Beacon street and Mt. Vernon street; name changed to Mt. Vernon place in 1829.

__Hancock place__, B.; from Blossom street, west, between Cambridge street and Parkman street.

__Hancock row__, B., 1826; from Marshall street to Creek square.

*__Hancock square__, Chsn., 1870; junction Main, Essex, Eden, and South Eden streets, and Tibbet's Town way; named, Nov. 15, 1870.

__Hancock street__, B., 1788; from Cambridge street to Mt. Vernon street; called Davis lane and Turner street at some time previous to 1732; called George street, 1732; street from Beacon street in the Common by Governor Hancock's, running northward over the hill from his garden down to Cambridge street, called Hancock street, 1788. L 1505, L 2105.

*__Hancock street__, Dor., 1840; from Dudley street, at Upham's corner, to Eaton square, at junction of Adams street and Bowdoin street. L 737, L 1788, L 2206, L 2536.

__Hancock street__, W. Rox., from Ashland street to Florence street; laid out with the name of Sherwood street, Oct. 25, 1886. L 1956, L 1957.

***Hancock street,** Chsn., 1854; from Green street to Elm street; laid out and accepted, Nov. 28, 1854.

***Hanley square,** Rox.; at the junction of Roxbury street and Pynchon street (now Columbus avenue) so named, March 5, 1891.

†**Hano street,** Bri.; from Braintree street to Cambridge street; laid out, July 14, 1891, from Braintree street, south-westerly, about 500 feet. L 2313.

***Hanover avenue,** B., 1829; from Hanover street to North street; called Methodist alley from North (now Hanover) street to Ship (now North) street, 1796; name changed to Hanover avenue, Aug. 24, 1829. L 1022, L 1149.

Hanover court, B., 1825–48; from Hanover street, north-west, between Friend street and Union street; closed.

Hanover place, B., 1827; from Hanover street, north-west, between Cross street and Parmenter street; called Robinson's court, 1821; Robbin's court, 1822; North Hanover court or place, 1825; Hanover place, 1827.

***Hanover square,** B.; corner Newbury (now Washington) street and Essex street; so called previous to 1765.

***Hanover street,** B., 1708; from Court street to Chelsea ferry; the part from Queen (now Court) street to Wing's lane (now Elm street) called Orange Tree lane previous to 1708; called Hanover street, from Court street to the Mill bridge, 1708; the street running from Court street through Hanover, Middle, and North streets, to the ferryways, named Hanover street throughout, July 6, 1824; discontinued from Commercial street to Winnisimmet ferry, 1836; laid out again from Commercial street to Chelsea ferry, April 5, 1886. Vol. 31, p. 37. L 9, L 14, L 37, L 66, L 86½, L 89, L 100, L 326, L 421, L 422, L 479, L 480, L 481, L 482, L 531, L 533, L 559, L 591, L 797, L 978, L 1149, L 1903, L 2209.

***Hanson street,** B., 1834; from Shawmut avenue to Tremont street; laid out on the Neck, July 24, 1826; third of new cross streets at southerly part of the city, extending from Tremont street to Suffolk street (now Shawmut avenue); called Hanson street, Sept. 15, 1834, accepted and laid out, Oct. 17, 1855. Vol. 31. pp. 66, 86.

†**Harbor View street,** Dor., 1870; from Dorchester avenue, crossing the O. C. (now N.Y., N. H. & H.) R.R. to the pumping station; laid out from Dorchester avenue to Sydney street, July 6, 1892. L 2410, L 2411.

Harbor view, E. B.; Coleridge street, between Byron street and Harmony street; Coleridge street, between Moore street and Wordsworth street.

***Harcourt street,** B., 1882; from St. Botolph street to B. & P. (now N. Y., N. H. & H.) R.R.; laid out, Dec. 27, 1882. L 1682.

Harding court, So. B.; from Gold street, south-westerly, near D street, to West Fifth street.

Harlaem or **Harlem place,** B., 1822; from Newbury (now Washington) street, west, near and south of West street: rear part now discontinued, and remainder apparently now without name.

Harlem street, Dor., 1895; from Blue Hill avenue to Norfolk street; between Hosmer street and Evelyn street; authority to open given by Street Commissioners, Nov. 23, 1895.

Harleston street, Rox.; from Parker Hill avenue to Hillside street.

***Harley street,** Dor., 1873; from Welles avenue to Roslin street; laid out, July 31, 1873. L 886.

Harlow street, Dor., 1873; from Woodward park (now Folsom street), north-westerly, crossing Howard avenue; street leading south-easterly from Howard avenue, named Harlow street, Nov. 26, 1873.

Harmony court, B., 1841; from Canal street, south-west, near Market street; built over about 1872.

Harmony place, E. B.; from Lexington street, south-easterly, between Meridian street and Marion street.

Harmony street, E. B.; from Bennington street to Auburn street, with proposed extension to proposed part of Coleridge street; shown as an unnamed street on a plan dated 1838.

†**Harold street**, Rox., 1886; from Walnut avenue to Seaver street; part between Crawford street and Homestead street formerly called Naseby street, laid out and named Harold street, March 10, 1886; part between Homestead street and Hutchings street laid out, April 20, 1888; between Townsend street and Harrishof street, June 21, 1890; between Townsend street and Munroe street, Oct. 7, 1890; between Crawford street and Harrishof street, June 12, 1891; authority to open from Monroe street to Walnut avenue given by Street Commissioners, Oct. 1, 1895. L 1901, L 2068, L 2176, L 2234, L 2264, L 2297, L 2298.

Harriet street, Bri.; from Parsons street, westerly, near Arlington street.

Harrington avenue, Rox.; from Centre street, north-westerly, near Gardner street; shown as an unnamed court on a plan dated 1867.

***Harris avenue**, W. Rox., 1852; from Centre street to Alveston street; called Harris place on a map of Roxbury dated 1843–49; accepted, Oct. 31, 1854; laid out from Austin (now Centre) street, easterly, Nov. 13, 1854.

Harris corner, B., 1708; cor. Hanover street and Cold lane (now Portland street) then so called.

Harris place, W. Rox.; from Centre street to Alveston street; Harris avenue, so called on a map of Roxbury dated 1843–49.

***Harris street**, B., 1868; from Hanover street to North street; called Whitebread alley, 1708; Bartlett street, 1826; Harris street, April 21, 1868.

†**Harrishof street**, Rox.; from Walnut avenue to Warren street; laid out from Walnut avenue to Harold street, June 21, 1890; from Harold street to Humboldt avenue, Dec. 23, 1893; authority to open part between Humboldt avenue and Warren street given by Street Commissioners, May 4, 1892. L 2233, L 2574.

***Harrison avenue**, B. and Rox., 1841; from Bedford street to Warren street; part from Essex street to the sea called Rainsford lane, 1708; part from Beach street to South Boston bridge (now Dover street) called Front street, 1805; Front street extended to Essex street, through Rainsford's lane, 1825, and from South Boston bridge to Northampton street, 1834; name of Front street changed to Harrison avenue, April 26, 1841; Plymouth street, from Northampton street to Roxbury line, accepted and name changed to Harrison avenue, Aug. 9, 1859; extended to Warren street, Nov. 11, 1870; extended from Essex street to Bedford street, over Brimmer place, part of Chickering place and part of Norfolk place, July 6, 1881. Vol. 19, p. 123; Vol. 31, p. 56. L 150, L 162, L 173, L 173½, L 212, L 214, L 260, L 432, L 456, L 571, L 572, L 573, L 587, L 868, L 1021, L 1195, L 1331, L 1353, L 1447, L 1491, L 1492, L 1512, L 1517, L 1526, L 1527, L 1554, L 1555, L 1598, L 1729, L 1951, L 2117, L 2520, L 2558, L 2584.

Harrison park, Dor.: from Beach street, easterly.

Harrison place, B., 1840; from Friend street, south-west, near Causeway street; now built over.

Harrison place, Chsn.; from Russell street, north-easterly, near Walker street.

Harrison street, Dor., 1846; from Lawrence street, north-east, crossing Quincy street; called "Myrtle street, formerly Harrison street," on plan dated 1869.

Harrison street, Dor.; from Ashland street, crossing Greenhill street; laid out from Greenhill street to Capen street, and name changed to Blanche street, July 21, 1885. L 1873.

Harrison street, W. Rox.; from Florence street, north-easterly to the B. & P. (now N. Y., N. H. & H.) R.R.

Harrod's corner, B., 1782; corner Prince street and Salem street then so called.

Hart place, So. B.; from East Eighth street, northerly, between K street and L street.

Hart street, W. Rox.; from Baker street to Prospect street.

Hartford place, B., 1819; from High street, south-east, near Pearl street.

Hartford place, Dor.; from Washington street, westerly, to land of N. E. R.R., near Mt. Bowdoin station; now Lynnville terrace.

***Hartford street,** B., 1869; from Purchase street to Wendell street; laid out between Purchase street and High street, including Purchase place, July 23, 1869; name of Quincy place, from High street, in continuation of Hartford street to Pearl place (now Wendell street), changed to Hartford street, March 1, 1882. L 464, L 465, L 836, L 922, L 2283.

***Hartford street,** Dor., 1869; from Howard avenue to Wayland street (formerly Howard place); laid out, Aug. 12, 1869. L 1835, L 2283.

Hartford terrace, Dor.; from Hartford street, north-easterly, near Howard avenue.

***Hartland street,** Dor.; from Saxton street to Sydney street; laid out, June 5, 1895. L 2702.

***Hartopp place,** Rox., 1850; from Albany street, at its junction with Dearborn street, to Chadwick street, at Orchard park; laid out from Dearborn street to Orchard park, Dec. 13, 1870; called Hartopp street in an atlas dated 1884; name changed to Ambrose street, March 1, 1886. L 535.

Hart's avenue, Bri., 1857; from Allston street, south-easterly, curving to Harvard street (now Harvard avenue); closed.

Hart's yard, Chsn.; from Lawrence street, south-westerly, between Austin street and Benedict street.

***Hartwell street,** Rox.; from Schuyler street to Georgia street (formerly Georgia avenue); laid out, July 28, 1892. L 2419.

Harvard alley, B., 1820–27; from School street, westerly, by the Universalist church, to Harvard place; closed.

Harvard avenue, Dor.; from Harvard street, northerly, near Washington street.

***Harvard avenue,** Bri., 1873; from Cambridge street, opposite Franklin street, to Brookline line; previous to 1846 called Cedar street; named South Harvard street, Nov. 10, 1846; name changed to Harvard avenue, Dec. 30, 1873. L 2664.

Harvard court, B., 1831; from Harvard street, southerly, between Washington street and Harrison avenue; built over.

Harvard place, B., 1820; from Washington street, westerly, opposite the Old South church.

Harvard place, Chsn.; from Harvard street, westerly, between Bow street and Washington street.

Harvard place, Bri., 1873; from Washington street, southerly, between Chestnut Hill avenue and Dighton place.

***Harvard square,** Chsn.; from Harvard street east, then south, then west to Harvard street again.

***Harvard street,** B , 1732; from Washington street to Albany street; called Hollis street (from Orange street. east, to the sea) in 1731; called Harvard street in 1732; extended east to Lincoln street, and probably included Thaxter place, 1836; accepted between Harrison avenue and Albany street, July 10, 1848.

Harvard street, B., 1732; from Orange (now Washington) street, running north-westerly by the new church; soon after and now called Hollis street.

***Harvard street,** Dor., 1840; from Washington street, opposite Bowdoin street, to Hyde Park line, named from Four corners, by Samuel B. Pierce's to Brush Hill turnpike (now Blue Hill avenue), March 11, 1840; Back street, from Blue Hill avenue to Hyde Park line, changed to Harvard street, March 1, 1896. L 1677, L 1731, L 2022, L 2325, L 2446.

***Harvard street,** Chsn., 1836; from City square to Main street, name of Town Hill street changed to Harvard street, Nov. 7, 1836.

***Harvard street,** Bri., 1825; from Cambridge street to Brookline line; at one time called Old Road to Cambridge; called South Harvard street, 1846; name changed to Harvard avenue, Dec. 30, 1873.

Harvard Hill, Chsn., 1875; between Harvard street, Main street, and City square.

***Harvest street,** Dor.; from Boston street to Dorchester avenue; laid out, Aug. 25, 1891. L 2327, L 2717.

Harvest street, Dor.; from Willowwood street, west, near Lauriat avenue; shown on atlas of 1894.

***Harwich street,** B., 1879; from Dartmouth street to Yarmouth street; laid out Nov. 6, 1879. L 1399.

Harwood street, W. Rox., 1893; from Weld street to Lasell street; authority to open given by Street Commissioners, March 5, 1895.

Harwood street, Dor.; from Willowwood street, west, near Lauriat avenue; shown on atlas of 1894.

***Haskell street,** Bri.; from Coolidge street to Holland road (now Hooker street); Haskell road laid out with the name of Haskell street, Aug. 24, 1892. L 24, L 27.

Haskins street, B., 1803–14; Carver street, from Eliot street to Pleasant street then so called.

***Haskins street,** Rox., 1886; from Ruggles street to Vernon street; Belmont street laid out, with the name of Haskins street, July 31, 1886. L 1925.

***Hastings street,** W. Rox.; from Centre street to Carl (now Montview) street; Henshaw street laid out with the name of Hastings street, June 13, 1892. L 2401.

Hathaway street, B.; from Summer street extended to Congress street.

Hathaway street, Bri.; from Market street, easterly, towards Sparhawk street; included in the laying out of Henshaw street.

Hathaway street, W. Rox.; from South street to Centre street.

Hathon square, Chsn., 1878; from Main street, south-easterly, near School street; name of Main-street court changed to Hathon square, April 24, 1878.

Hatter's square, B., 1823; a part of Creek square at one time.

Haugh's corner, B., 1708: corner Marlboro' (now Washington) street and School street then so called.

Hautvale street, W. Rox., 1871; from Poplar street, north-westerly near Beech street.

Haven avenue, Dor.; from Blue Hill avenue to Oakland street.

Haven place, B., 1860; from Shawmut avenue, west, between Rutland street and Newton (now West Newton) street; closed.

***Haven street,** B., 1847; from Shawmut avenue, easterly, then southerly, to Rutland street; located, Oct. 28, 1861. L 233.

Haven street, E. B. (Breed's Island); from Ashley avenue to Riverside avenue; Bromley's atlas, 1892.

***Haverhill street,** B., 1807; from Haymarket square to Causeway street; laid out over the Mill-pond, Aug. 3, 1807; extended to Warren bridge in 1829; the causeway leading from Causeway street to Warren bridge accepted and declared a public highway and continuation of Haverhill street, Oct. 8, 1838. L 277.

***Haverhill street,** Chsn., 1858; from Main street to Perkins street; laid out, Dec. 24, 1868.

Havey street, W. Rox.; from Dudley avenue.

***Haviland street,** Rox.; from West Chester park (now Massachusetts avenue) to Parker street; laid out, May 2, 1889. L 2127.

Havre court, E. B.; from Havre street, north-westerly, near Sumner street.

***Havre street,** E. B., 1833; from Sumner street to Bennington street; part between Meridian street and Porter street accepted and laid out, conditionally, June 14, 1852; street accepted, Nov. 22, 1852; between Marion street and Bennington street accepted, April 23, 1861. L 675, L 2123, L 2502, L 2718.

Hawes avenue, Dor., 1836; from Washington street to Bowdoin avenue.

***Hawes street,** B., 1828; from Congress street to Kilby street; an unnamed lane shown in same place on Bonner's map of 1722; street near the Post-Office named Hawes street, Dec. 15, 1828; confirmed as a public street, Sept. 15, 1834.

Hawkins place, B., 1857; from Hawkins street; cannot be identified.

***Hawkins street,** B., 1732; from Sudbury street to Chardon street; from Cambridge street, north, then east, to Sudbury street, 1732; sometimes called Tattle street, 1756–84, and, according to Drake, commonly so called in 1800; from Sudbury street, west, "round to Chardon's." 1784; from Bowdoin square, easterly, to Nath. Hall's house, and from thence to Sudbury street, 1788; the part running north from Cambridge street (Bowdoin square), called Chardon lane, 1795; from Sudbury street, west, to Distill-House square (now Bowker street), 1800. Vol. 31, pp. 81, 89. L 34, L 92.

Hawley place, B., 1821–52; from Hawley street to Marlboro' (now Washington) street, opposite Bromfield lane (now Bromfield street); closed.

Hawley place, B.; from Hawley street to Arch street, between Franklin street and Milk street.

***Hawley street,** B., 1799; from Milk street to Summer street; called Bishop's alley in 1708; Board alley in 1792; called also Gilbert's alley, Richardson's alley and Wybourne's lane at an early date; name of Bishop's alley changed to Hawley street, Dec. 10, 1799. L 631, L 819.

Hawthorn place, B., 1852; from Washington street, north-westerly, near Dover street.

***Hawthorn street,** Rox., 1855; from Cedar street to Highland street; shown as Copeland street on a plan dated 1843; accepted, conditionally, from Cedar street to Ellis street, Sept. 3, 1855; accepted and named, from Cedar street to Highland street, Dec. 19, 1859. L 499.

Hawthorne avenue, Rox., 1857; from Washington street, south-easterly, between Cliff street and St. James street.

†**Hawthorne street,** W. Rox , 1851; from Florence street to Sycamore street, south-east of Heathcote street; laid out from Florence street to Albion (now Sycamore) street, Oct. 14, 1875; authority to open part south-east from Sycamore street given by Street Commissioners, Sept. 6, 1894. L 1082.

Hawthorne street, B.; name given without authority to Canton street, west of Tremont street, in 1864.

Hayden place, Rox.; from Cottage place, south-westerly; included in the extension of Columbus avenue, Jan. 4, 1895.

Hayden place, So. B.; from Silver street, south-westerly, between B street and C street; part of what was formerly Parker's alley.

*__Hayden street,__ Rox., 1886; from Fisher avenue to Lawn street: Short street laid out and named Hayden street, July 28, 1886. L 1914.

Hayden terrace, Rox.; from Washington street, north-westerly, near Bartlett street.

Haydn street, W. Rox.: from Washington street to Nikisch avenue.

Haymarket, The, B., 1789; on Tremont street, between West street and Mason street.

Haymarket place, B., 1806; from Sheafe's lane (now Avery street), southerly.

*__Haymarket square,__ B., 1839; at the junction of Merrimac, Canal, Haverhill, Charlestown, Cross, Blackstone, Union, and Washington streets; at junction of Merrimac, Charlestown, Blackstone, and Union streets, in 1839; parts of Canal, Market, and Charlestown streets and land of B. & M. R.R. Co. laid out as part of Haymarket square, April 21, 1845.

Haynes park, Rox.; from Warren street, opposite Woodbine street.

*__Haynes street,__ E.B., 1868; from Orleans street, south-easterly, then southerly, then south-westerly, to Marginal street; accepted as Centre street, Jan. 25, 1864; name of Centre street changed to Haynes street, April 21, 1868; laid out, June 20, 1873. L 870.

*__Hayward place,__ B., 1822: from Washington street to Harrison avenue; from Newbury (now Washington) street, between Essex street and Bedford street, east, in 1822; laid out from Washington street, Nov. 15, 1875; Harrison avenue laid out, by easterly end of, July 6, 1881. L 1094.

Hayward place, Dor.; from Minot street, nearly opposite Sheridan street, to Chickatawbut street.

Hayward street, Rox., 1867; from Warren street to Blue Hill avenue; laid out and named Holborn street, Aug. 21, 1883. L 1725.

Hazel place, Rox.; from Maywood street, easterly; also called Hazel park.

*__Hazel street,__ W. Rox., 1880; from Rockview street to Enfield street; part of E street, from Rockview (formerly D) street to Enfield street, laid out and named Hazel street, Aug. 28, 1880. L 1478.

*__Hazelwood street,__ Rox.; from Munroe street to Townsend street; laid out, Dec. 5, 1893. L 2568.

Head place, B., 1825; from Boylston street, northerly, near Tremont street.

Head street, Dor.; from Westville street, south-east, between Bowdoin street and Fredonia street.

Heath avenue, Rox.; from Heath street, southerly, then easterly, crossing Heath place.

Heath avenue, E. B. (Breed's Island); from Ashley avenue, at junction with Leverett avenue, crossing Jenkins avenue, to Belle Isle Inlet; shown on atlas, 1892.

***Heath place**, Rox., 1860; from Heath street to Minden street; laid out from Heath street and extended to Walden street, Dec. 15, 1875; part from westerly termination of Minden street, about 115 feet, called Minden street, Aug. 10, 1881; part from Minden street laid out as Poson street, Nov. 16, 1881; part laid out as Arklow street, Nov. 16, 1881; from westerly terminus of Arklow street to Walden street called Arklow street, Nov. 25, 1881; from Minden street to Arklow street, called Ulmer street, Nov. 25, 1881. L 1117, L 1118, L 1404, L 1568, L 1569.

***Heath street**, Rox., 1825; from Centre street to Tremont street (now Huntington avenue); north branch from Parker street, east, to Centre street, called New Heath street; south branch from Parker street, east, to Pynchon street (now Columbus avenue) called Heath street. L 478, L 493, L 534, L 617, L 618, L 700, L 1143, L 1524, L 2160, L 2161, L 2162, L 2163, L 2444, L 2504.

Heath street, Chsn., 1863; from Bond street, east; not identified.

Heathcote street, W. Rox., 1894; from Poplar street, to proposed extension of Hawthorne street; authority to open given by Street Commissioners, Sept. 6, 1894.

Heavey place, Rox.; from Pynchon street (now Columbus avenue), easterly, near New Heath street.

***Hecla street**, Dor., 1892; from Adams street to Dorchester avenue; Hall's court laid out with the name of Hecla street, Aug. 30, 1892. L 2426.

Hedge place, W. Rox., 1849; from Dedham turnpike (now Washington street), north-westerly, parallel with Chemical avenue (now Cornwall street).

Hefferan place, Bri.; from No. 152 North Harvard street.

Helen street, Dor., 1896; from Talbot avenue to Bernard street; authority to open given by Street Commissioners, May 6, 1896.

Helena street, W. Rox.; from Lamartine street, south-easterly, between Clark place and Lawndale terrace.

Hemlock street, W. Rox., 1872; from Washington street to junction Roslindale avenue and Bellevue avenue.

Hemman street, W. Rox.; from Poplar street to Kittredge street.

Henchman's lane, B., 1709; the way leading from Charter street, down by Mrs. Buckley's, into Lynn street, 1708; previously called Declination passage and Day's alley or lane; name changed to Henchman street in 1850.

***Henchman street**, B., 1850; from Charter street to Commercial street; Henchman's lane, from Charter street to Lynn street, 1708; formerly known as Declination passage or Day's alley or lane; name changed to Henchman street, in 1850. L 281, L 1390.

Hendee street, E. B. (proposed); from Cottage street to Shirley street (Wood Island). (Abandoned.)

Henderson avenue, So. B.; from East Sixth street, north, between H street and I street.

Henley's lane, Chsn.; from Monument square to Warren street; laid out in place of and named Soley street, Dec. 24, 1850.

Henley place, Chsn., 1859; from Chelsea street to the Navy Yard; now Henley street.

***Henley street**, Chsn., 1831; from Harvard square to the Navy Yard; laid out 40 feet wide, 1780; laid out from Main street to Meeting House hill, May 7, 1787; same approved by Town, Sept. 24, 1787; altered, June 23, 1788; continued to Navy Yard, Oct. 5, 1829; named Henley street, from Main street to the Navy Yard, Oct. 3, 1831.

***Henry street**, E. B.; from Maverick square to Paris street; shown as an unnamed street on a plan dated 1833; accepted, June 4, 1851; formerly called Hotel street.

Henry street, Chsn.; from Main street, north-east; plan Middlesex So. Dist. Reg., Book 11, No. 61.

Henshaw street, W. Rox.; from Centre street to Carl (now Montview) street; laid out under the name of Hastings street, June 13, 1892. L 2324.

***Henshaw street**, Bri.; from Market street to Cambridge street; part of formerly Hathaway street; laid out, including Day street, Nov. 6, 1891. L 2356, L 2539, L 2791.

Henshaw terrace, W. Rox.; from Corey street, near Centre street, south-west.

Herbert street, Dor.; from Clarence place to Park (sometimes called West Park) street.

†**Hereford street**, B., 1871; from 30 foot street on bank of Charles River, to Boylston street; called Eighth street, on a plan dated 1866; street west of and parallel with Gloucester street from Beacon street to B. & A. R. R., named Hereford street, Nov. 14, 1871; laid out between Beacon street and Marlborough street, June 24, 1875; laid out between Marlborough street and Commonwealth avenue, April 9, 1877; extended from Commonwealth avenue to Boylston street, Feb. 19, 1878. L 862, L 1052, L 1297, L 1585.

***Herman street**, Rox., 1888; Summit street; laid out from Circuit street to Regent street with the name of Herman street, Dec. 28, 1888. L 2109.

Heron avenue, E. B. (Breed's Island); from Ashley avenue, crossing Riverside avenue to the water, shown on atlas, 1892.

Heron street, W. Rox.; from Washington street, north-westerly, near La Grange street.

***Herrick street**, Bri., 1884; from North Beacon street to Hichborn street; laid out, Dec. 26, 1884. L 1844.

Hersey place, B., 1845; from Essex street, southerly, near Washington street.

Hersey street, Dor., 1872; from Haven avenue, north-westerly, crossing Bismarck street and Favre street.

Hestia park, Rox.; from Walnut avenue, north-westerly, between Circuit street and Rockland street.

***Hewes street**, Rox., 1884; from Regent street to Rockland street; laid out, Jan. 14, 1884. L 1751.

***Hewlett street**, W. Rox., 1893; from Centre street to Walter street; laid out, May 17, 1893; part near Walter street, formerly called Union avenue. L 2511, L 2512, L 2736.

Hewins street, Dor.; from Columbia street to Erie street.

†**Hichborn street**, Bri., 1884; from North Beacon street, north-easterly, easterly, and southerly, to North Beacon street again; laid out from North Beacon street, north-easterly and easterly, to beyond Arthur street, Aug. 27, 1884. L 1806.

Hickory avenue, Chsn.; from Jackson street to Ferrin street.

***High street**, B., 1797; from Summer street and around Fort Hill square to Broad street; called Cow lane from Summer street to Fort Hill, 1708; name of Cow lane changed to High street, May 24, 1797; name of Washington square (around Fort Hill square) and Washington avenue (from Washington square to Purchase street) changed to High street, Dec. 15, 1875. Vol. 19, p. 69; vol. 31, pp. 6, 65. L 25, L 82, L 283, L 343, L 344, L 364, L 365, L 466, L 467, L 626, L 657, L 820, L 844, L 883, L 922, L 2283.

High street, Rox., 1845; from Washington street (later Tremont street and now Huntington avenue), southerly, then south-easterly; later called Highland place, and named Parker Hill avenue, May 3, 1870.

High street, Rox., 1842; from Washington (now Roxbury) street to Orange (now Elmwood) street; name changed to Dunlow street, April 21, 1868.

***High street,** Dor., 1856; from Water street to Ericsson street; laid out as a townway, April 2, 1866.

***High street,** Dor., 1804; from Highland (now Church) street to Commercial (now Freeport) street; laid out from Highland street, north, by Town, March 27, 1804; named from Meeting House hill by Mr. Stone's to the gun-house, March 11, 1840. L 620.

High street, W. Rox.; from Parkway, near and parallel with Rockland street.

High street, W. Rox., 1871; from East street, south-westerly, towards Charles River.

***High street,** Chsn., 1799; from Monument square to Walker street; laid out by Selectmen from Green's lane to the Training Field, March 4, 1799; Oliver Holden conveys to Town for public highway, a parcel of land called Gorham street, being a continuation of High street terminating at the west corner of Baptist Meeting House, July 17, 1810; continued to Bolton (now Franklin) street, June 7, 1827; accepted between Franklin street and Walker street, Nov. 28, 1831; laid out and altered, Aug. 21, 1848; name of part from Pleasant street to Monument court changed to Monument square, Feb. 2, 1860; name of part from Monument court to junction of Winthrop street and Adams street changed to Winthrop street, Feb. 2, 1860. L 1211, L 1490, L 2005, L 2434.

High street, Bri.; from Dunboy street to Bigelow street.

High-street court, Rox., 1865; see plan Norfolk Reg., L. 338, f. 59.

High-street court, B., 1825; from High street, north-west, between Federal street and Atkinson (now Congress) street; called High-street place, 1828.

High-street court, B., 1844; from High street, south-east, near Washington square, 1844; at some time previous to 1879 called High-street place, between Hartford street and Oliver street.

High-street place, B.; from High street, south-easterly, between Hartford street and Oliver street; called High-street court in 1844.

***High-street place,** B., 1828; from High street to Matthews street; called High-street court (from High street, north-westerly) in 1825; name changed to High-street place, 1828; laid out and extended to Matthews street, Sept. 1, 1871. L 365, L 718, L 774.

***Highgate street,** Bri., 1893; from Cambridge street to Farrington avenue; Highland avenue laid out from Cambridge street, and extended to Farrington avenue, with the name of Highgate street, Nov. 23, 1893. L 2553.

***Highland avenue,** Rox., 1859; from Centre street to Lewis park; laid out, Nov. 16, 1869. L 494, L 495.

Highland avenue, Bri., 1871; from Cambridge street, south, between Linden street and Harvard avenue; laid out and extended to Farrington avenue with the name of Highgate street, Nov. 23, 1893, L 2553.

Highland avenue, W. Rox.; from Walnut street to Blue Hill avenue; shown on atlas, 1874; now included in Franklin Park.

Highland avenue, W. Rox., 1851; from Centre street, north-west, near Allandale street; now closed.

Highland avenue, Dor.; from Minot street, south-easterly, opposite Narragansett street; shown as an unnamed court on a plan dated 1868.

Highland park, Rox., 1863; from Fort avenue, south-westerly, near Highland street.

***Highland Park avenue,** Rox., 1871; from Fort avenue to Highland Park street; laid out, Nov. 23, 1878. L 1337.

†**Highland Park street,** Rox., 1871; from Fort avenue, north-easterly, crossing Highland Park avenue; laid out from Fort avenue to Highland Park avenue, Nov. 23, 1878. L 1337.

Highland place, Rox.; from Highland street, east, between Eliot square and Norfolk street.

Highland place, Rox.; from Tremont street (now Huntington avenue), southerly; called High street on a map of Roxbury dated 1843–49; name changed to Parker Hill avenue, May 3, 1870.

Highland Spring square; junction of Parker street and Heath street; named, June 8, 1894.

***Highland street,** So. B., 1860; from Eighth (now East Eighth) street to Jenkins street; accepted, July 5, 1860; name changed to Lowland street, April 21, 1868; name of Lowland street changed to Mercer street, March 1, 1888. L 191, L 192.

***Highland street,** Rox., 1825; from Eliot square, south-westerly, then north-westerly, to Centre street; accepted, July 15, 1850. L 373.

Highland street, Dor.; from High street, opposite Church street, to East street; acceptance from East street to Church street left with Selectmen, April 5, 1852. L 787.

Highland street, W. Rox., 1849; from Farrington (now Rutledge) street to Martin street; called so in an atlas dated 1874; called Wren street, 1884.

Highland terrace, Rox.; from Highland avenue, near Lewis park, south-west.

High rock avenue, Bri.; from Webster street, westerly; also called High Rock way.

Hilburn street, W. Rox., 1870; from Poplar street to Metropolitan avenue.

Hildreth place, B.; from Washburn place, south-east, between Charter street and Hull street; from 1846–74 a part of Washburn place.

Hildreth street, Dor.; from Norfolk street, at junction with Morton street, to north-west of Alma street.

Hill avenue, Bri.; from Franklin street, near Pleasant (now Holton) street; given in an atlas of 1875 as a part of Otis street; no record of change of name; shown as an unnamed street on a plan dated 1869; laid out from Franklin street to Mansfield (formerly Otis) street with the name of Easton street, Sept. 10, 1889. L 2165.

Hill place, So. B.; from East Third street, near corner of L street, south.

Hill street, B., 1733; from May (now Revere) street, south, between Grove street and Southac (now West Cedar) street; laid out on the land at West Boston, near the new bridge, running north and south to the Mount and near the Ropewalks, 1800; since closed.

Hill street, B., 1788; from Middlecot (now Bowdoin) street round the bottom of Beacon Hill into Hancock street, opposite Mr. Austin's Ropewalk, 1788; name changed to Derne street in 1806.

Hill street, B.; the westerly end of Myrtle street was so called on Hale's plan in 1814.

***Hill street,** Chsn., 1848; from Webster (now Sackville) street, to Sheafe street, in Bromley's atlas of 1885; laid out from Sackville street and extended to Cook street, July 5, 1890. L 2240.

Hill street, W. Rox., 1872; from Cornell street, north, between Berry street and Newbury street.

Hill street, Bri.; from Market street to Murdock street; part from Murdock street to George street laid out with the name of Elmira street, Nov. 10, 1893.

Hill's court, B., 1867; from Revere street, northerly, opposite Myrtle street; probably formerly Sherman place; now Bellingham place.

Hill's lane, B., 1733; from Essex street, south, about where Lincoln street now is; shown on Price's map, 1769.

Hillcrest street, W. Rox.; from Elgin street, south-westerly, across Temple street.

Hiller's lane, } B., 1708; the new way leading from Mr. Pollard's corner
Hillier's lane, } in Brattle street (now square) through Mr. Belknap's yard into Queen (now Court) street; called also Gay alley and Belknap's alley; Brattle street extended through it to Court street, 1820.

Hillsdale street, Dor.; from Adams street, north-westerly, opposite Cedar Grove Cemetery.

Hillside avenue, Rox., 1845; from Tremont street (now Huntington avenue) to Hillside street; on a plan in Norfolk Registry it is spoken of as a street "formerly Garden street;" laid out with the name of Wait street, Oct. 24, 1882. L 1659.

Hillside avenue, Rox., 1845; from High street (now Parker Hill avenue), east; Hillside street so called on a plan in Norfolk Registry.

Hillside avenue, W. Rox., 1870; from Poplar street to Clarendon avenue.

***Hillside avenue,** W. Rox., 1865; from Revere street to Seaverns avenue; accepted "as laid out by Selectmen;" extended to Green street and named Elm street, July 25, 1868.

Hillside avenue, W. Rox.; from Wenham street, south-east, to near Leland street.

Hillside avenue, Bri., 1856; from Winship avenue (now Wexford street) to the railroad; formerly from Winship avenue to North Beacon street; part from the railroad to North Beacon street laid out, with Lyman avenue, as Wicklow street, Dec. 5, 1881. L 1577.

Hillside place, E. B.; from Haynes street, east, near Marginal street.

Hillside place, Chsn.; from Bunker Hill street, south, near Main street.

***Hillside street,** Rox., 1868; from Parker street to Parker Hill avenue; called Hillside avenue on a plan dated 1845; name of Davis street changed to Hillside street, April 21, 1868; laid out and extended to Parker street, in part over a private way called Billings place, April 27, 1882. L 1605, L 1606, L 1607.

Hillside terrace, Dor.; from Fuller street to Bailey street.

Hilton street, Rox., 1868; from junction of Swett street and East Chester park (now Massachusetts avenue), opposite Gerard street, north-easterly; name of Canal street changed to Hilton street, April 21, 1868.

Hinckley street, Dor., 1892; from Pleasant street to Bakersfield (formerly F) street; also called D street; authority to open given by Street Commissioners, May 4, 1892.

***Hingham street,** B., 1831; from Shawmut avenue to Emerald street. L 250, L 545, L 715, L 720, L 1349.

Hinsdale street, Rox., 1894; from Commonwealth avenue to Cummington street.

***Hobart street,** Bri., 1888; from Brooks street to Faneuil street; laid out, July 20, 1888. L 1832, L 2079.

Hodges court, Dor.; from Norfolk street, east, near River street.

Hog bridge, Rox.: over Stony Brook at Centre street, near Pynchon street (now Columbus avenue).

***Hoffman street**, Rox., 1880; from Lamartine street to Chestnut avenue; laid out from Lamartine street to Gilbert street (now Chestnut avenue), Oct. 6, 1880. L 1498.

Hoffman street, So. B.; proposed street from the proposed extension of B street to the proposed extension of E street, on the so-called Commonwealth flats.

Hogarth street, E. B., 1838; from Addison street to Trumbull street.

Hogg alley, B., 1708; from Newbury (now Washington) street, west, between Sheafe's lane (now Avery street) and West street; from Newbury street to Common (now Tremont) street, on map dated 1722; since closed in part and the west end included in Bradford place; Bradford place built over by Keith's Theatre, 1894.

Holborn park, Rox.; from 28 Holborn street.

***Holborn street**, Rox., 1883; from Warren street to Blue Hill avenue; formerly Hayward street; laid out and named Holborn street, Aug. 21, 1883. L 1725.

Holborn terrace, Rox.; from 9 Holborn street.

Holbrook avenue, Dor.; from Neponset avenue, north-east, near Walnut street.

Holbrook place, Bri.; from North Beacon street, south-west, between Saunders street and Dustin street.

***Holbrook street**, W. Rox., 1877; from Centre street to Eliot street; Monument street laid out and named Holbrook street, May 21, 1877. L 1238.

Holden court, B., 1859; from Commercial street, westerly, between Hanover street and Battery street.

Holden place, B., 1834; from Belknap (now Joy) street, west, between Cambridge street and Myrtle street.

Holden place, Dor., 1871; from Dudley street, north-east, near Humphreys street.

Holden street, Dor.; from Boston street, north-east, then south-east, then north-east to Humphreys street.

Holden row, Chsn., 1878; from Wesley street to Salem Hill court; named, March 12, 1878.

Holiday street, Dor., 1893; from Bowdoin street to Topliff street; authority to open given by Street Commissioners, March 22, 1893.

Holland place, B., 1857; from Tyler street, east, near Harvard street.

Holland street, Rox.; from Crawford street to Humboldt avenue; laid out from Crawford street to Harold street, Dec. 28, 1892, and from Harold street to Humboldt avenue, Oct. 12, 1893, with the name of Hollander street. L 2481, L 2541.

Holland road, Bri.; from North Harvard street to Royal street (formerly Royal road); also called Holland street; laid out as Hooker street, Aug. 26, 1892. L 2430.

***Hollander street**, Rox., 1892; from Crawford street to Humboldt avenue; Holland street laid out from Crawford street to Harold street with name of Hollander street, Dec. 28, 1892; from Harold street to Humboldt avenue, Oct. 12, 1893. L 2481, L 2541.

Hollaway's corner, B., 1708; corner of Milk street and Battree March then so called; called Hallowell's corner, 1732.

Holley square, B., 1854; from Hollis street, south, near Washington street.

Hollingsworth street, Dor.; from Oakland street, south-west, near N. E. R.R.; authority to open given by Street Commissioners, Nov. 14, 1895.

Hollis place, B., 1847; from Hollis street, northerly, near Tremont street.

Hollis place, Bri.; from Allston street, south-east, near Brighton avenue; shown as an unnamed place from Allston street to Harts avenue, on a plan dated 1856.

Hollis place, Rox.; from Roxbury street to Vernon street; laid out with the name of Kent street, Nov. 19, 1888. L 2106.

***Hollis street,** B., 1732; from Washington street to Tremont street; called Broad alley, 1722; March 2, 1730, it had not received a name; called Harvard street, from Orange (now Washington) street running north-westerly by the new church, 1731; named Hollis street, 1732; by Price's map, 1743, extended across Clough (now Tremont) street.

Hollis street, B., 1731; from Orange (now Washington) street, east, to the sea; named Harvard street in 1732.

Holly street, Rox., 1871; from Ruggles street, south-westerly, between Halleck street and Duncan street.

***Holman street,** Bri., 1892; from Coolidge street to Hooker street; Homer road laid out from Coolidge street to Holland road (now Hooker street), Aug. 26, 1892. L. 2431.

Holmes avenue, Bri., 1872; from Harvard avenue, westerly, towards Warren street, crossing Gorham street and Griggs street.

Holmes street, Bri., from Raymond street, northerly, between Franklin street and Riverdale street.

Holmes place, Dor.; from Mill street, south-easterly, between Neponset avenue and Tenean creek; called Mill-street place on plan dated 1884; included in Houghton street, Nov. 27, 1891. L 2365, L 2366.

Holmes' alley, B., 1822; in the rear and west of Belknap (now Joy) street, between Cambridge street and Myrtle street; given in the Directory of 1880 as "rear of Joy, from Smith court;" not given later than 1880.

***Holton street,** Bri., 1887; from Franklin street to Everett street; Pleasant street laid out and name changed to Holton street, Aug. 2, 1887. L 2007.

Holton street, Bri.; from Brooks street, south-easterly, between Hobart street and Crosby street.

***Holworthy street,** Rox., 1892; from Walnut avenue to Humboldt avenue; laid out from Walnut avenue to Harold street, Dec. 2, 1892, and from Harold street to Humboldt avenue, Nov. 1, 1893. L 2467, L 2543.

***Holyoke street,** B., 1868; from Columbus avenue to B. & P. (now N. Y., N. H. & H.) R.R.; laid out, Dec. 7, 1869. L 502, L 516.

Holyoke street, B., 1740; laid out by owners from Frog lane (now Boylston street) to Hollis street; called Clough street in 1733; from Walker or Common street to Frog lane, 1750; made part of and named Nassau street, 1788; called Tremont street, 1824.

Home avenue, Bri., 1891; from North Harvard street, near Cambridge street, north-easterly; authority to open given by Street Commissioners, July 10, 1891; laid out, with the name of Hopedale street, April 29, 1892. L 2394.

Homer place, Rox.; from Moreland street to Winthrop street, between Cleveland street and Fairland street; Whiting street laid out through Homer place to Winthrop street, May 29, 1896. L 2770.

Homer road, Bri.; from Coolidge street to Holland road (now Hooker street); laid out with the name of Holman street, Aug. 26, 1892. L 2431.

Homer street, Dor., 1871; from Washington street to Milton avenue; laid out and named Rockwell street, Feb. 2, 1880. L 1434.

†**Homer street**, E. B.; from West street, south-westerly, crossing B., R. B. & L. R.R., and the Jewish cemetery, to Moore street, with proposed extension to proposed part of Harmony street; laid out from Byron street to Moore street, June 23, 1891. L 2305.

Homes avenue, Dor., 1893; from Bowdoin street to Adams street; authority to open portion from Bowdoin street to Topliff street given by Street Commissioners, March 22, 1893.

Homes avenue, Dor., 1868; from Adams street, opposite Linden street, westerly, southerly, and again westerly.

Homes place, Chsn.; from Main street, south-west, between Gardner street and Haverhill street.

Homes street, Dor.; from Homes avenue to Fox street.

Homestead avenue, Dor.; from Magnolia street to Hartford street; now Robinhood street.

Homestead place, Chsn.; from Main street, south-west, between Austin street and Chapman street.

†**Homestead street**, Rox., 1878; from Walnut avenue to Elm Hill avenue; laid out from Walnut avenue to Humboldt avenue, July 5, 1887. L 2001, L 2176.

Honcheu's corner, B., 1708; the north end of Queen (now Court) street and Hanover street then so called.

***Hooker street**, Bri., 1892; from North Harvard street to Royal street; Holland road laid out with the name Hooker street, Aug. 26, 1892. L 2430.

Hooper avenue, Dor.; from Magnolia street to Hartford street; authority to open given by Street Commissioners, Aug. 7, 1895.

***Hooper street**, Dor.; from Melville avenue to Tremlett street; laid out, Sept. 16, 1885. L 1887.

Hooten court, E. B.; from Everett street, south-westerly, near Lamson street.

Hope place, B., 1870; from North Russell street, west, near Cambridge street.

***Hopedale street**, Bri., 1892; from North Harvard street to a point near and north-east of Windom street; Home avenue laid out with the name of Hopedale street, April 29, 1892. L 2394.

Hopestill avenue, Dor.; from Northern avenue to Southern avenue.

Hopkins place, Dor.; from Fremont place, south-east.

***Hopkins street**, Dor.; from Evans street to Corbet street; laid out, Oct. 7, 1892. L 2439.

***Horace street**, E. B., 1891; from Moore street to Byron street; part of Milton street, between Moore street and Byron street, laid out with the name of Horace street, July 2, 1891. L 2307.

Horn lane, B., 1795; from Milk street to Water street; previously called Tanner's lane; at one time called Horse lane; name changed to Bath street, 1807.

Horse lane, B.; Horn lane from Milk street to Water street at one time so called; now Bath street.

Hosmer street, Dor., 1896; from Blue Hill avenue to Norfolk street between Woolson street and Harlem street; authority to open given by Street Commissioners, Feb. 14, 1896.

Hotel street, E. B., 1833; from Hotel (now Maverick) square to Paris street; accepted as Henry street, June 4, 1851.

***Hotel square**, E. B., 1833; from Sumner street to Maverick street; laid out, Aug. 7, 1848; now Maverick square.

Houghton place, Rox., 1868; from Centre street, southerly, near Wyman street; name of Irving place changed to Houghton place, April 21, 1868; included in Mozart street, May 19, 1887. L 1988.

***Houghton street,** Dor.; from Pope's Hill (formerly Clay) street to Mill street; laid out, including Holmes place, Nov. 27, 1891. L 2365, L 2366.

Houston place, Rox., 1866: from Tremont street (now Columbus avenue), southerly, near Texas avenue (now street) crossing Texas court: part at Tremont street now built over.

Houston street, W. Rox; from Amherst street to Metcalf street.

Houston street, W. Rox.; from Montview street to Crest street; formerly crossing Montview (formerly Carl) street, from north-west to south-east; part south-east of Montview street now called Park street; authority to open from Montview street to Crest street given by Street Commissioners, Oct. 1, 1896.

Hovey avenue, Dor.; from Blue Hill avenue to Franklin Field; formerly from Blue Hill avenue, north-easterly, towards the Catholic cemetery, crossing Lyons street; part included in Franklin Field; has probably been known at some time as Noyes avenue, and is so called in Bromley's atlas of Dorchester of 1889.

Hovey avenue, Chsn.; from Main street, south-westerly, nearly opposite Baldwin street; called also Hovey's court.

Hovey's court, Chsn.; rear of 444 Main street; called Hovey avenue, from 444 Main street to Rutherford avenue on chart, 1885.

***Howard avenue,** Dor.; from Dudley street to Quincy street; laid out, Aug. 12, 1869. L 679, L 680, L 681, L 2362, L 2363.

Howard place, Chsn.; from Elm street, south-easterly, between High street and Bartlett street.

†**Howard place,** Bri., 1872; from Union street to Commonwealth (formerly Massachusetts) avenue: part of, now included in Union street; shown as an unnamed passageway on a plan dated 1871; accepted from Washington street to a point about 100 feet southwest of the present angle in Union street, July 8, 1872.

Howard place, Dor.; from Howard avenue, north-east, near Dudley street.

***Howard street,** B., 1821; from Court street to Bulfinch street; called Southack's court from Court street, opposite Hanover street, westerly, 1732; to Dr. Bulfinch's pasture, 1788; to Bulfinch street, 1817; name changed to Howard street, April 11, 1821. Vol. 31, p. 83.

Howard street, Dor., 1857; from Howard avenue to Magnolia street; also called Howard place; laid out, Aug. 12, 1869; name changed to Wayland street, March 1, 1888. L 550.

***Howard street,** Rox., 1865; from Hampden street to Magazine street; from Hampden street, south-easterly; crossing Gerard street, 1865; extended to Magazine street, May 16, 1893. L 793, L 2510.

Howard street, So. B., 1854; from Dorchester avenue, west, north of and near Swett street; name changed to Dexter street, Aug. 7, 1855.

Howes avenue, So. B.; from H street, west, between East Sixth street and East Seventh street.

Howe court, Rox., 1868; from Tremont street, south-east, between Ruggles street and Weston street; name of Cottage place changed to Howe court, April 21, 1868.

Howe place, Chsn.; from Quincy street, north-west.

Howe street, Dor.; from junction Neponset avenue and Adams street, opposite Parkman street, to Tenean creek; shown as an unnamed street on a plan dated 1852.

Howe street, Dor.; from Hancock street, south-west, near Rill street.

Howe street, E. B. (Breed's Island); from Riverside avenue to the water; shown on atlas, 1892.

***Howell street**, Dor.; from Dorchester avenue to Boston street; shown as Newell street on atlas, 1884; laid out, Dec. 28, 1892. L 2486.

Howes avenue, So. B.; from H street, west, between East Sixth street and East Seventh street.

Howes street, Dor.; from Dorchester avenue, west, between East Cottage street and Mayfield street.

***Howland street**, Rox., 1880; from Warren street across Humboldt avenue; laid out from Warren street, westerly, Jan. 28, 1880; extended to Elm Hill avenue, May 19, 1882; from Elm Hill avenue to Humboldt avenue, Oct. 13, 1887; west of Humboldt avenue, June 8, 1892. L 1430, L 1612, L 2030, L 2399.

Hoyt place, B., 1857; from Joy street, west, near Cambridge street.

Hubbard street, Bri.; from Western avenue, near North Harvard street, south, to Rena street.

Hubbard terrace, Rox.; from Eustis street, north-east, between Hampden street and Magazine street.

Hubbardston street, Dor.; from Boston street, north-west, opposite Dorset street; shown on atlas of 1884.

Huckins avenue, Rox., 1858; from Blue Hill avenue to Dennis street; laid out with the name of Huckins street, June 26, 1882. L 1621.

***Huckins street**, Rox., 1882; from Blue Hill avenue to Dennis street; Huckins avenue laid out and named Huckins street, June 26, 1882. L 1621.

Hudson place, B., 1844; from Hudson street, westerly, near Kneeland street.

***Hudson street**, Dor., 1862; from Dudley street to Clifton street; from Dudley street to George street, at junction Clifton street, 1862; laid out, Aug. 12, 1869. L 1213.

***Hudson street**, Chsn., 1871; from Chelsea street to Water street; name of Chelsea place changed to Hudson street, Feb. 6, 1871.

***Hudson street**, B., 1846; from Beach street to Curve street; part from Beach street to Kneeland street accepted, Sept. 21, 1846; part from Kneeland street, 253 feet towards Harvard street, accepted, Oct. 18, 1847; from Harvard street to Oak street, accepted, July 10, 1848; from Harvard street to Kneeland street and from Oak street to Curve street, accepted, Jan. 5, 1856. L 1534.

Hudson's lane, B., 1658; from Orange-tree lane, east; Wing's lane, 1708; Elm street, 1800.

Hudson's point, B., 1708; the extreme north-east point of the town, on Charles river; called Mylne point in 1635.

Huff place, B., 1848; from Tyler street to Curve street; closed.

***Hulbert street**, Rox.; from Washington street to Regent street; laid out, Nov. 6, 1882. L 1664.

***Hull street**, B., 1701; from Salem street to Commercial street; granted to Town by Samuel Sewall, May 20, 1701; from Salem street to the North Burial Ground, 1708; from Salem street to Snow street, 1733; extended across Snow street or Snow-Hill street to Lynn (now Commercial) street, 1828, which part was also called Brown street.

Hull street, Chsn.; from Bunker Hill street to Vine street.

Hull street, Rox., 1845; from Walnut street (now Walnut avenue) to Bainbridge street; shown on plans to 1860; probably included in Washington park, except part included in southerly end of Bainbridge street.

Hull-street court, B., 1837; from Hull street, south-westerly, near Salem street.

Hull-street place, B.; from Hull street, south-westerly, near Snow-Hill street.

Hull's row, Chsn.; from Mill street, southerly.

***Humboldt avenue**, Rox., 1882; from Seaver street to Walnut avenue; Williams avenue, laid out from Seaver street and extended to Munroe street, and name changed to Humboldt avenue, Dec. 30, 1882; extended from Munroe street to Walnut avenue, Sept. 15, 1886. L 1688, L 1689, L 1690.

Humboldt park, Rox.; from Bower street, south-westerly, between Humboldt avenue and Warren street.

Humboldt place, So. B., 1871; from Dorchester avenue, westerly, near Dexter street; named, Nov. 27, 1871.

Humphrey court, So. B.; from West Fourth street, north-easterly, adjoining N. E. R.R.

Humphrey place, B., 1825; from Hamilton street, east, 1825; laid out and extended to Broad street, including part of Half Moon place and name changed to Wendell street, Dec. 30, 1870. L 460.

Humphreys place, Dor.; from Humphreys street, north-west, near Dudley street.

Humphreys square, Dor.; from Dudley street, north-easterly, to Iona street.

***Humphreys street**, Dor., 1840; from Dudley street to East Cottage street; road by Deacon Humphreys' (Stoughton, now Dudley street) altered and new lane laid out from same to another lane (Cottage, now East Cottage street), April, 1800; street from Deacon Humphreys' to Mr. Bridgham's named Humphreys street, March 11, 1840. L 1733.

Hunneman court, Rox.; from Harrison avenue, north-westerly; now Plymouth court.

Hunneman place, Rox.; from Washington street, south-easterly, between Hunneman street and Eustis street; shown as Hunneman court on city map, 1891, and Bromley atlas, 1890.

***Hunneman street**, Rox., 1864; from Washington street to Albany street; accepted, conditionally, from Washington street to Harrison avenue, May 30, 1864; laid out from Harrison avenue to Albany street, Nov. 27, 1874; from Harrison avenue to Washington street, Dec. 1, 1891. L 990, L 1195, L 2371.

Hunnewell court, Rox.; from Culvert place (now Downing street), north-westerly, to Hampshire street; now called Salvisberg avenue.

Hunnewell place, E. B.; from Marion street, south-westerly, between Princeton street and Saratoga street.

Hunter street, Dor.; from Morton street to Norfolk street, opposite Ballou avenue.

***Huntington avenue**, B. and Rox., 1864; from Boylston street, at Copley square, to Brookline line; laid out from Boylston street to Camden (now Gainsborough) street, Nov. 1, 1875; extended from Camden street to Parker street, May 24, 1881; from Parker street to Tremont street, Dec. 29, 1882; over a part of Tremont street, from Francis street to the Brookline line, Jan. 5, 1895. L 747, L 748, L 749, L 1089, L 1525, L 1684, L 1685, L 1699, L 1831, L 2096, L 2213, L 2637, L 2638, L 2639, L 2640, L 2641, L 2642, L 2643, L 2644, L 2645, L 2646, L 2647, L 2648, L 2649.

Huntington avenue, W. Rox.; from Canterbury street, near Hyde Park avenue, to Hyde park line.

Huntoon street, Dor.; from Medway street (formerly Riverview avenue), north-easterly, crossing Butler street.

Hunt's corner, B., 1800; corner Fish (now North) street, and Sun court then so called.

Huron street, E. B. (proposed); from Cottage street to Georgia street (Wood Island); abandoned.

†**Hutchings street,** Rox., 1878; from Elm Hill avenue to Harold (formerly Naseby) street; laid out from Humboldt avenue to Harold street, April 20, 1888. L 2067.

Hutchins avenue, Rox.; from Day street, north-west.

Hutchinson lane or street, B., 1732; from Milk street to Cow lane (now High street); shown in 1722; named in 1732; called Palmer street in 1788; by plan of 1789 called Green lane; name of Hutchinson street changed to Pearl street, Jan. 22, 1800.

Hutchinson street, Dor.; from Codman street, south, across Brook street.

Hyde street, So. B., 1872; from Dorchester avenue, easterly, to O. C. (now N. Y., N. H. & H.) R.R.

***Hyde Park avenue,** W. Rox.; from Washington street to Hyde Park line; from Canterbury street to Dorchester line laid out as Belgrade street on a map of Roxbury dated 1843–49; laid out from River street, Dorchester, nearly parallel with B. & P. (now N. Y., N. H. & H.) R.R. to new road from Mattapan to West Roxbury (now Ashland street), December, 1859; extended from Mattapan road to Walk Hill street, running nearly parallel with the railroad, May, 1869; location changed from Walk Hill street to land of Bussey heirs, January, 1870; extended through a portion of Walk Hill street to Washington street, Dec. 27, 1878. L 1344, L 1403.

Hyde square, W. Rox.; junction of Centre, Perkins, and Day streets so called.

***I street,** So. B., 1805; from north of East First street to south of (proposed) East Tenth street, with proposed extensions, northerly, to proposed extension of Eastern avenue (now Congress street), and southerly to line of Old Harbor (1884); from salt water on the south to the Harbor of Boston on the north laid out and named, Feb. 27, 1805; laid out from low-water mark north of First street to harbor line in Dorchester bay, Nov. 17, 1868; southerly portion of that part south of East Ninth street now included in the Strandway. Vol. 31, p. 93.

Ice court, Chsn.; from Water street, north-west, between Foss street and Wapping street.

Ida street, E. B., 1892; from Ruth street to Brigham street; laid out, including a part of Terrace place, Nov. 26, 1892. L 2459.

Idaho street, Dor.; from River street, northerly, to Manchester street.

Iffley road, W. Rox., 1895; from Washington street, near Forest Hills street, to Walnut avenue; authority to open given by Street Commissioners, Sept. 19, 1895.

Inches corner, B., 1784; corner Orange (now Washington) street and Eliot street then so called.

***Independence square,** So. B., 1859; between East Second and N streets, East Broadway and M street; laid out, Dec. 31, 1857; named, May 10, 1859; accepted, Oct. 1, 1860.

†**India square,** B., 1873; from Broad street, north-easterly, to India street, and from India square, easterly, to Atlantic avenue; passageway from Broad street to India street, accepted and named India street, Aug. 8, 1842; part of India wharf between Broad street and Atlantic avenue called India square, Feb. 12, 1873.

***India street,** B., 1804; from State street to India wharf; from Long wharf to India wharf, 1817; laid out around the Custom House, Oct. 2, 1837; laid out, named and accepted to India wharf, April 11, 1842; passageway from Broad street to India street accepted, and named

India street (now India square), Aug. 8, 1842; laid out from India square to Atlantic avenue, Dec. 8 1884. L 134, L 262, L 1839, L 2199, L 2700.

India wharf, B.; from Atlantic avenue, easterly, opposite India square; part of India wharf, between Broad street and Atlantic avenue, called India square, Feb. 12, 1873. L 1000.

Indian lane, Bri.; Nonantum street, from Washington street to Newton line formerly so called.

Indian way, Dor., 1855; laid out as a part of Savin Hill avenue, Aug. 12, 1869.

***Indiana place,** B., 1843; from Washington street to Tremont street; from Washington street, west, 1843; accepted "as at present laid out" from Washington street to Tremont street, Oct. 11, 1852; extended to Tremont street in 1859; name changed to Corning street, March 1, 1895. Vol. 31, p. 87. L 210, L 522, L 548, L 549, L 724, L 756, L 762, L 838, L 1349.

Indiana street, B., 1844; from Washington street to Harrison avenue: called Distill-House street, 1826: name changed to Indiana street in 1844; accepted, conditionally, May 21, 1849.

Ingersoll place, B., 1847; from Purchase street, south-east, near Belmont (now Oliver) street; name changed to Quiet place in 1849; built over.

***Ingleside street,** Rox., 1892; from Blue Hill avenue to Dacia street; laid out, Nov. 3, 1892. L 2454.

Inner temple, B., 1727; in Prison lane, Queen (now Court) street.

Institute avenue, B., 1867; from Endicott street to North Margin street; built over.

Intervale park, Dor., 1891; from Bourneside street to Upland avenue.

†**Intervale street,** Rox., 1892; from Warren street to south east of Blue Hill avenue; laid out, Oct. 15, 1892; authority to open south-east of Blue Hill avenue given by Street Commissioners, Dec. 5, 1893. L 2449.

Iona street, Dor.; from Humphreys street to Humphreys square.

Iowa street, Dor.; from Westville street to Dakota street.

Ipswich place, E. B.; from Everett street, south-westerly, between Jeffries street and Lamson street.

Ipswich street, Rox.; from Beacon street to B. & A. R.R.; included in the Back Bay Fens and called Charlesgate-east, Dec. 30, 1887. L 1515.

Irving place, B., 1859; from Irving street, west, near Cambridge street.

Irving place, Rox.; from Centre street; name changed to Houghton place, April 21, 1868.

Irving place, Chsn., 1872; from Main street, north-easterly, between Albion place and Baldwin street.

***Irving street,** B., 1855; from Cambridge street to Myrtle street; called Butolph or Buttolf street, 1733; name changed to Irving street, April 25, 1855.

Irving street, W. Rox., 1870; from Anawan avenue, near Park street, south-easterly, nearly to Pelton street, and from Pelton street, south-easterly.

***Irvington street,** B., 1884; from Huntington avenue to B. & P. (now N. Y., N. H. & H.) R.R.; laid out from Huntington avenue to St. Botolph street, April 10, 1884; from St. Botolph street to the railroad, July 23, 1889. L 1767, L 2141.

Irwin avenue, Rox.; from Blue Hill avenue, north-west, opposite Woodville street.

***Isabella street**, B., 1863; from Ferdinand street to Columbus avenue; laid out, Dec. 22, 1876. L 1208.

Island street, E. B., 1845; from Cottage street to proposed part of Orleans street; from Frankfort street to Cleveland street, 1895, with proposed extension north-west to a proposed part of Orleans street.

Island road, } Rox., 1832; from Hampden street to Magazine street;
†**Island street**, } laid out from Hampden street to Gerard street, Aug. 5, 1876. L 1161.

***Isleworth street**, Bri., 1887; from Chestnut Hill avenue to Englewood avenue: Roxbury avenue laid out as a public street and named Isleworth street, May 11, 1887; name changed to Sutherland road, March 1, 1892. L 1985.

†**Ivanhoe street**, B., 1868; from Upton street to West Brookline street; name of Waverly street changed to Ivanhoe street, April 21, 1868; laid out from West Canton street to West Brookline street, Nov. 9, 1870; from West Canton street to West Dedham street, May 13, 1871. L 477, L 541, L 581, L 605.

Ivers street, B., 1820; from Hawkins street, north, to the Mill-pond; sometimes called Ivers lane; from Bowdoin square to Merrimac street, including Chardon street, Dec. 30, 1859; name of same changed to Chardon street, May 22, 1860. Vol. 31, pp. 81, 89. L 92.

***Ivory street**, W. Rox., 1872; from Temple street to Dent street; laid out, Sept. 28, 1876. L 1172.

***Ivy street**, B. and Rox.; from Mountfort street to St. Mary's street, the Brookline line; laid out, June 12, 1894. L 2605.

Jackson avenue, B., 1837; from Charter street to Commercial street; called Board alley in 1833; named changed to Jackson avenue, in 1837.

Jackson avenue, Bri.; from Chestnut Hill avenue to Rockland street.

Jackson court, B., 1836; from North Margin street, west; built over.

Jackson place, B., 1827; from Winter street, south-westerly, near Washington street.

Jackson place, Dor.; from School street, south-westerly; Athelwold street, laid out over Jackson place, May 6, 1896. L 2761.

Jackson square, Bri.; at junction Chestnut Hill avenue, Union street, and Winship street.

Jackson square, Bri., 1871; at junction of Everett (now Dunboy) street and Webster street.

†**Jackson street**, So. B., 1875; from Boston street to Dorchester avenue; portion laid out, eastwardly from Boston street, Dec. 24, 1875; laid out with the name of Rawson street from Boston street to Dorchester avenue, Dec. 29, 1892. L 1072, L 2484.

***Jackson street**, Chsn., 1864; from Bunker Hill street to Ferrin street; laid out, July 25, 1864.

Jackson's corner, B., 1732; at the head of the Town Dock, Dock square.

Jackson's corner, B., 1732; at the Mill-creek, Ann (now North) street.

Jamaica place, W. Rox.; from Jamaica street, westerly.

Jamaica street, Dor., 1802; from Norfolk street to Back (now Harvard) street, opposite Walk Hill street; laid out from road leading from Boies' mill to Dr. Jasper Baker's to old road leading to Meeting House, Jamaica Plain, April, 1802; located from Samuel Cox's to Roxbury (now West Roxbury) line, April 2, 1804; named from Cox's corner to Back street and Roxbury line, March 11, 1840; name changed to Walk Hill street, being a continuation of that street, May 9, 1876.

***Jamaica street,** W. Rox., 1851; from South street, westerly, southerly, westerly, northerly, and easterly, back to Jamaica street; laid out from South street to Woodman street, Dec. 9, 1878; extended, July 3, 1882. L 1338, L 1623, L 1624, L 1625.

Jamaica street, W. Rox., 1850; easterly part of Child street, from Leo street to Starr (now Call) street called so on a plan in Norfolk Registry, 1850.

Jamaicaway, Rox. and W. Rox.; from Tremont street (now Huntington avenue) to Prince street.

James avenue, So. B.; from G street, westerly, near East Eighth street.

James place, B., 1839; from Anderson street, westerly, between Phillips street and Revere street.

***James street,** B., 1857; from East Brookline street to East Concord street; named, Dec. 8, 1857. L 1770.

James street, Rox., 1799; from land of Joel Gay to the road to the salt marsh (plan l. 13, f. 183, Norf. Reg.); laid out as a new road 50 feet wide and called in deed James street; shown on plan l. 17, f. 57. Norf. Reg.

James street, W. Rox., 1872; from Poplar street, north-westerly, parallel with Charles (now Cornell) street and Beech street to Kittredge street.

Jarvis place, Rox., 1870; from George street, easterly, between Magazine street and Langdon street, named, May 10, 1870.

Jarvis row, B., 1805; from Newbury (now Washington) street, east, south of Suffolk place; name changed to Norfolk place in 1823.

Jarvis's corner, B., 1800; corner of Newbury (now Washington) street and Summer street then so called.

Jasper place, B., 1849; from North street, south-east, near Langdon place; same as City slip.

Jay street, So. B.; from East Fourth street to East Fifth street, between I street and K street.

Jay street, W. Rox., 1848; from Martin street, south-east, to La Grange street.

Jay street, Chsn., 1818; from Chelsea street to Edgeworth street; laid out, May 23, 1859; name changed to Tremont street, Oct. 29, 1866.

Jeannette place, W. Rox.; from Washington street, south-east, between Ashland street and Poplar street.

Jefferson avenue, Chsn.; from Bunker Hill street to Bartlett street; shown as an unnamed street on plan dated 1839.

Jefferson place, B., 181–; from Bennet street, southerly, between Harrison avenue and Ash street.

***Jefferson street,** B., 1824; from Fayette street to Tremont street; from Fayette street, 1824; extended to Tremont street, 1834; accepted, conditionally, Sept. 19, 1842; decided to have become public by dedication, Dec. 20, 1880. L 387, L 392.

***Jeffries street,** E. B., 1836; from Marginal street to Maverick street; laid out and accepted, April 10, 1854.

Jenkins avenue, E. B. (Breed's Island); from Beachmont avenue, easterly, to a junction with Ashley avenue at Belle Isle inlet; Bromley's atlas, 1892.

Jenkins place, B., 1834; from Commercial street; included in the North End park.

***Jenkins street,** So. B., 1855; from Dorchester street to Lowland street; name of Lewis street changed to Jenkins street, Aug. 7, 1855; laid out from Dorchester street to O. C. (now N. Y., N. H. & H.) R.R., Nov. 2, 1876. L 1187.

***Jenner street,** Chsn., 1866: from Bow street to Front street; "recently" laid out over Cook's lane; named Jenner street, Sept. 17, 1866.

Jennings place, Chsn.; from Medford street, south-westerly, between Polk street and Elm street.

Jephson's corner, B., 1732; corner of Marshall lane and Creek lane then so called.

Jerome place, Chsn.; from Bunker Hill street, northerly; laid out from Bunker Hill street to Princeton street, with name of Sprague street, Aug. 11, 1892. L 2482.

***Jerome street,** Dor., 1883; from Hancock street to Everett avenue; part of Everett avenue, from Hancock street to the part already public, laid out as Jerome street, March 22, 1883. L 1605.

Jersey street, Rox.; from Beacon street to B. & A. R.R.; included in Back Bay Fens and called Charlesgate-west, Dec. 30, 1887. L 1515.

Jersey street, Bri., 1882: from Third street to Fifth street; now in Brighton cattle-yards, near B. & A. R.R.

***Jess street,** W. Rox.; from Porter street, south-westerly; laid out, Dec. 13, 1876. L 1206.

Jewel place, Rox.; from Ottawa street, northerly, near Sherman street.

Jewett street, W. Rox.; from Neponset avenue to Mt. Hope street.

***John street,** B., 1869; from Fulton street to North street; called Shoe and Leather street in 1842; laid out as John street, Feb. 2, 1869. L 428.

***John A. Andrew street,** W. Rox., 1871; from Newbern street to Carolina avenue; laid out, Dec. 5, 1881. L 1576.

Johnson avenue, Rox.; from Centre street, southerly, nearly opposite Wyman street, to Buckley avenue.

Johnson avenue, Chsn., 1846: from Main street to Lawrence street; named Miller street, Sept. 2, 1844; name changed to Johnson's avenue, March 9, 1846, now called Johnson avenue.

Johnson place, Dor.; from River street, north-westerly, between Morton street and River court.

†**Johnson street,** W. Rox., 1888; from Baker street to Ashland street; Ballanakill avenue, from Baker street to Ashland street, also portion, north-westerly, towards railroad, laid out with name of Johnson street, Jan. 6, 1888. L 2047.

Johnson's avenue, see Johnson avenue.

Johnston park, Rox.; from Warren street, near corner of Dale street, westerly.

Johnston street, W. Rox.: from Jamaica street, south, then west.

Johnswood road, W. Rox., 1896; from Prospect avenue, south-west, between Sherwood street and Brown avenue; authority to open given by Street Commissioners, Feb. 24, 1896.

***Joiner street,** Chsn., 1827: from Park street to Water street; laid out opposite O. W. Preston's lot to Deacon Thos. Miller's house, May 21, 1827; laid out near site of fire, Dec. 23, 1835; laid out as far as practicable and accepted, March 28, 1836.

Joiliff's lane, B., 1708; called also Joliff's, Jolliff's, Joyliff's, and Joylieff's lane; at one time called Black Jack alley; from Water street to Milk street: called Devonshire street, 1784; by Edes list, 1800, called Jolliff's lane and also by Carleton's map of 1800; called Devonshire street.

Jones avenue, Dor.; from Mascot street to Ballou avenue.

Jones street, W. Rox.: from Walter street to Fairview street; authority to open given by Street Commissioners, April 21, 1894.

Jones street, E. B. (Breed's Island); from Ashley avenue crossing Jenkins avenue, to Belle Isle inlet; shown on atlas, 1892.

***Jordan street,** W. Rox., 1872; from Dent street to La Grange street, near West Roxbury station; laid out, Sept. 28, 1876. L 1174.

Josephine street, Dor.; from Ditson street to Geneva avenue; laid out, Sept. 7, 1895. L 2722.

Joy place, B., 1834; rear of west side of Belknap (now Joy) street, near Beacon street; closed.

***Joy street,** B., 1851; from Beacon street to Cambridge street; part from Cambridge street to May (now Myrtle) street; called Belknap's lane, 1787; same called Belknap street, 1789; extended south to Beacon street through Clapboard street and George street, 1803; Belknap street, between Myrtle street and Beacon street called Joy street, January, 1851; Belknap street, from Beacon street to Cambridge street, named Joy street, Feb. 26, 1855. Vol. 31, p. 69.

Joy street, W. Rox.; from Brookline line, south-west, crossing Raymond, Bruce and Walker streets.

Jubes lane, W. Rox.; an early name for Curtis (now Forest Hills) street; shown on plans dated 1845.

***Judson street,** Dor., 1892; from West Cottage street to Brookford street; laid out from West Cottage street to Dromey avenue, Feb. 26, 1892; laid out over Dromey avenue to Brookford street, Dec. 12, 1896. L 2384, L 2800.

***Julian street,** Rox., 1892; from Blue Hill avenue to Howard avenue; name of part of Rand street changed to Julian street, March 1, 1892; extended over Rand square to Howard avenue, Sept. 7, 1895. L 1591, L 2733.

***Juniper street,** Rox., 1881; from Cedar street to Thornton street; laid out from Cedar street, in part upon a portion of private way known as Cedar square, to Thornton street extended to Guild street, Dec. 10, 1881. L 1578, L 1579.

Juniper terrace, Rox.; from Washington street to Juniper street, between Cedar street and Guild street.

***K street,** So. B., 1805; from north of East First street, south, to the Strandway; laid out and named from salt water on the south to the Harbor of Boston on the north, Feb. 27, 1805; laid out from the low-water mark north of First (now West First) street to harbor line in Old Harbor, Nov. 17, 1868; portion of K street from harbor line in Old Harbor to East Ninth street now included in the Strandway. L 146, L 217.

K-street place, So. B.; from K street, east, between East Broadway and East Third street.

Kaine street, Dor.; from Richardson avenue between Locust street and Story street, west, to end of Buttonwood street.

Kalada park, Rox.; from Holborn street; authority to open given by Street Commissioners, July 20, 1893.

***Kane street,** Dor.; from Bellevue street to Stanley street; formerly called Bellevue terrace; laid out, June 19, 1889. L 2137.

***Kearsarge avenue,** Rox., 1868; from Warren street to Winthrop street; name of Mt. Vernon place having been changed to Mt. Warren place, Oct. 30, 1865; named Kearsarge avenue, April 21, 1868.

Kearsarge place, Rox.; part of Kearsarge avenue from Winthrop street in a general northerly direction, to angle in same, so called in 1873.

Keith avenue, W. Rox.; from Baker street near Mt. Vernon street, to La Grange street; also called Keith street.

Keith's alley, B., 1865; from North street, near Richmond street, northwest; a portion of what was called Clark's alley, 1824; called Keith alley on plan dated 1865.

Keith street, W. Rox.; from Baker street, near Mt. Vernon street, to La Grange street; also called Keith avenue.

Kellam place, B., 1837; near Lucas place and street; included in Chapman (now Compton) street, which was laid out from Washington street to Tremont street in 1852.

Kelley court, Chsn.; from Cook street to Sheafe street; same given "Kellies block" on chart, 1875.

Kelley court, Bri.; from Western avenue, south-easterly, towards Waverly street; same called Kelly's lane, 1884.

Kelley's lane, Bri.; from Western avenue, south-easterly, towards Waverly street; same called Kelley court in 1875.

Kellies block, Chsn.; from Cook street, north-westerly, 1875; same called Kelley court, from Cook street to Sheafe street, 1884.

Kemble place, So. B.: from P street, near corner East Second street, west; also called Kimball place.

†**Kemble street**, Rox., 1865; from Hampden street, east, then southeast, parallel with Norfolk avenue to Magazine street; part from Hampden street, east, to Reed (now Reading) street once shown as part of Reed street; laid out from Hampden street to Magazine street, Aug. 6, 1889. L 2143, L 2144.

Kemp street, So. B.: from Dorchester avenue, east, to O. C. (now N. Y., N. H. & H.) R.R.

***Kendall street**, B., 1845; from Shawmut avenue to Tremont street; accepted, conditionally, Dec. 3, 1860; laid out, Nov. 3, 1868; laid out, Aug. 3, 1869. L 189, L 382, L 414, L 415.

***Kenilworth street**, Rox., 1847; from Dudley street, south-easterly, then north-easterly, to Dudley street; accepted, June 21, 1847; laid out, June 14, 1852. L 2803.

***Kenmore street**, Rox.; from Commonwealth avenue to Newbury street; laid out, Dec. 29, 1893. L 2581.

Kenna place, B., 1860: from Grove street, easterly, near Revere street.

***Kennard avenue**, B., 1833; from Allen street to Poplar street; same in 1833; accepted and laid out as public street, June 14, 1852; called Kennard street on plan, 1883. L 2382.

Kennard court, B., 1846; from Kennard avenue, north-westerly, to junction of Lovett place and Elder place; from Kennard avenue, near Poplar, 1846.

Kennard street, B.; Kennard avenue, from Allen street to Poplar street; so called on plan, 1883.

Kennedy's corner, B., 1784; corner of Dock square and Shrimpton's lane (now Exchange street), then so called.

Kenneth street, Bri.; from Franklin street, nearly opposite Brentwood street, south-east, to and beyond Bayard street.

†**Kenneth street**, W. Rox.; from Beech street to Stratford avenue; formerly called Oak street; laid out from Beech street to Farrington street, July 24, 1891; authority to open part between Stratford avenue and Farrington street given by Street Commissioners, Nov. 17, 1893. L 2318.

Kenney street, Rox.; from Day street, north-west.

Kenny's corner, B., 1709; in Dock square.

***Kenrick street**, Bri., 1856; from Lake street, north-east, to Newton line; laid out by Commissioners, Jan. 2, 1856; named, March 5, 1860.

Kensington park, Rox.; from Warren street, near Dale street, northwesterly.

***Kensington street,** Rox.; from Kingsbury street to Elmore street; laid out, Oct. 22, 1885. L 1894.

Kensington street, Bri.; from extension of Foster street to Parsons street; laid out as a public street and named Surrey street, Sept. 4, 1884. L 1817.

***Kent street,** Rox., 1888; from Roxbury street to Vernon street; formerly Hollis place; laid out as Kent street, Nov. 19, 1888. L 2106.

Kentle street, B., 1848-51; from Suffolk street (now Shawmut avenue), near Rutland street; cannot be now identified.

***Kenwood street,** Dor.; from Allston street to Washington street; laid out, Oct. 4, 1894. L 2663.

Kerwin street, Dor., 1896; from Talbot avenue to Bernard street; authority to open given by Street Commissioners, May 6, 1896.

Keyes place, W. Rox., 1860; from Keyes street, north-west; part now in Call street; also called Keyes-street court.

***Keyes street,** W. Rox., 1850; from South street to Forest Hills street; laid out as a town way, March 31, 1859; relocated between Washington street and B. & P. (now N. Y., N. H. & H.) R.R., Nov. 6, 1883; extended south-easterly from Washington street to Stony brook, Nov. 6, 1883; extended to Forest Hills street, Aug. 4, 1890. L 1734, L 1735, L 2254.

Keyes-street court, W. Rox.; from Keyes street, near Call street, south; portion taken by extension of Call street, May 7, 1891; also called Keyes place.

Keyes-street place, W. Rox.; from Keyes street on north-easterly side of Stony Brook, north-easterly.

***Kilby street,** B., 1769; from State street to Milk street; called Mackerel lane from King (now State) street to Water street, and Cooper's alley from Water street to Milk street, 1708; called Kilby street from King street to Milk street, 1769; sometime prior to 1784, part from Water street to Milk street called Miller's lane; from State street to Liberty square, 1788; part from Liberty square to Milk street called Adams street, 1788–1824; called Kilby street in Edes' list, 1800; from the Bunch of Grapes tavern running by Mr. Coolidge's new stores to Miller's in Milk street; street from State street across Liberty square to Milk street called Kilby street, and Adams street named Kilby street, throughout, July 6, 1824. L 839, L 853, L 2113.

Kilsyth road, Bri.; from Lanark road to Brookline line; authority to open Road No. 1 (Kilsyth road) given by Street Commissioners, May 13, 1893.

Kilton street, Dor.; from Washington street to Talbot avenue; portion between Harvard street and Park street called Carlton avenue, 1860; Carleton avenue and Carleton place, 1874; Carlton street, 1884; authority to open part from Harvard street, a short distance northerly, given by Street Commissioners, Aug. 13, 1895; authority to open from Washington street to Faxon street, under the name of Tilton street, given by Street Commissioners, May 15, 1895.

Kimball place, So. B.; from P street, near East Second street, westerly; also called Kemble place.

Kimball street, Rox., 1872; from Tremont street (now Huntington avenue) near junction of Heath street, to Crafts street; now in Jamaicaway.

Kineo street, Dor.; from end of Idaho street to Cedar street; now called Manchester street.

King street, B., 1708; from Cornhill (now Washington street) on each side of the Town House easterly to the sea; continued to low-water mark, 1711; from west end of Town House, east, to Long wharf,

1732; name changed to State street, 1784, having been called Congress street for a short time before new name was settled on.

***King street**, Rox., 1868; from Roxbury street to Elmwood street, name of Pearl street changed to King street, April 21, 1868; laid out, July 16, 1877. L 1255.

***King street**, Dor., 1858; from Dorchester avenue to Neponset avenue; laid out from Dorchester avenue to Adams street, Dec. 8, 1871; laid out, from Adams street to Train street, Oct. 21, 1878; laid out from Train street to Neponset avenue, April 27, 1880. L 722, L 1324, L 1510, L 2125, L 2712.

King terrace, Rox.; from King street near the bend, south-west; formerly called King-street court.

King-street court, Rox., 1874; from King street, south-westerly; now called King terrace.

***Kingsbury street**, Rox.; from Washington street to Bainbridge street; laid out, March 21, 1874. L 920.

Kingsdale street, Dor., 1895; from Standish street to west of Bernard street; Coolidge avenue laid out with name of Kingsdale street, Nov. 23, 1895. L 2747.

Kingsley street, Bri.; from North Harvard street, to Rena street.

Kingston court, B.; from Kingston street, easterly, near Essex street; called Short-street court, 1827; named Kingston court or place in 1847; now built over.

Kingston place, B.; from Kingston street, easterly, near Beach street; included in extension of Tufts street, from Lincoln street to Kingston street, Sept. 28, 1889.

Kingston place, Chsn., 1871; from Kingston street, easterly, then south-easterly.

***Kingston street**, B., 1800; from Summer street to Beach street; from Summer street to Short street, and Pond street, 1800; called Plymouth street in Edes' list, 1800; extended through Short street to Beach street, April 1, 1839. L 221, L 305, L 598, L 599, L 623, L 2201, L 2441.

***Kingston street**, Chsn., 1858; from Cambridge street to Sever street; laid out and accepted, Aug. 18, 1869.

Kinross road, Bri.; from Sutherland road to Commonwealth avenue.

Kirk street, W. Rox.; from Carl (now Montview) street to Crest street; formerly called Short street.

***Kirkland street**, B., 1858; from Pleasant street to Indiana place (now Corning street); called London street, from Pleasant street, 1838; extended to Indiana place (now Corning street), 1853; accepted and named Kirkland street, 1858. Vol. 31, pp. 75, 87. L 140½, L 548, L 838.

Kitchen street, B., 1824; from Charles street to Spruce street, name changed to Branch avenue in 1849; laid out as Branch street, July 26, 1884.

Kittredge place, B., 1860; from Washington street, south-westerly, near junction Friend street; from Friend street, south-westerly, 1860; portion included in the extension of Washington street, Nov. 6, 1872.

***Kittredge street**, W. Rox., 1882; from Washington street to Beech street; part of Roslin avenue, from Washington street to Norfolk street, laid out as Kittredge street, Dec. 22, 1882. L 1672, L 1673.

Kittredge terrace, W. Rox.; from Kittredge street near Washington street, westerly.

***Knapp street**, B., 1879; from Beach street, southerly, then easterly to Harrison avenue; Newton place, from Beach street, south, and

Plymouth place, from Harrison avenue, west, laid out and named Knapp street, May 14, 1879. L 1351.

Kneeland place, B., 1834; from Kneeland street, south-west, near Washington street; laid out as a public street named Whitmore street and extended to Harvard street, June 12, 1886. L 1910.

***Kneeland street**, B., 1800; from Washington to Federal street; from Orange (now Washington) street, east, 1732; from Orange street east to the water called Kneeland's lane by Selectmen's list of 1788; same called Kneeland street, 1800; continued to Front street (now Harrison avenue), 1805; extended from Front street to Lincoln street, 1835; name changed to Eliot street, July 16, 1838; renamed Kneeland street, June 2, 1840; extended to sea (now Federal) street, 1843; accepted conditionally from Harrison avenue to Lincoln street, Nov. 4, 1844; part which crosses track of B. & W. (now B. & A.) R.R. closed, as dangerous for public travel, Sept. 21, 1846; same rescinded, Nov. 16, 1846; part east of Harrison avenue called Marginal street in 1855; part between Albany street and Lincoln street discontinued, Dec. 17, 1855; same reopened, Dec. 30, 1856; accepted between Lincoln street and South street, Dec. 4, 1865. L 38, L 86, L 193, L 574, L 607, L 1626, L 1627, L 1628, L 1629.

Kneeland's lane, B., 1788; Kneeland street so called by Selectmen's list.

Kneller street, E. B., 1838; from Addison street to Trumbull street.

Knights' avenue, W. Rox.; from Green street, opposite Jamaica Plain station, north-east, then north-west, to Oakdale street; also called Knights' court.

Knoll street, W. Rox.; from Centre street, near Hewlett street, to Walter street.

Knower place, Rox., 1869; from Washington street, south-easterly, near Zeigler street.

***Knowlton street**, So. B.; from Telegraph street to East Eighth street; laid out, Nov. 17, 1868. L 1016.

***Knox street, B.**, 1830; from Church street to Ferdinand street; from Lincoln court (now Church street) to the water, 1830; part of laid out from Church street to Ferdinand street, Dec. 13, 1870. L 387, L 391, L 404, L 585.

Knox street, E. B.; no record; Condor street bounded it in 1852; laid out as Glendon street, April 20, 1869.

Kuhn place, B., 1833; from Tremont street, west, south of Eliot street; now built over.

***L street**, So. B., 1805; from Reserved Channel, near end of Congress street, to the Strandway; from harbor, north of East First street, to Old Harbor, south of East Ninth street, with proposed extensions northerly to proposed extension of Eastern avenue (now Congress street) and southerly to line in Old Harbor, 1805; from salt water on the south to the Harbor of Boston on the north, laid out and named, Feb. 27, 1805; laid out from low-water mark north of First (now East First) street to Harbor line in Dorchester Bay, Nov. 17, 1868. L 158.

L-street bridge, So. B.; from foot of L street across Reserved Channel to foot of Summer street extension.

***Laconia street**, B., 1896; from Washington street to Harrison avenue; Ashland place laid out with the name of Laconia street, Feb. 15, 1896. L 2757.

***La Fayette avenue**, B., 1828; from Prince street to Endicott street; called Fayette avenue (from Prince street to Pond street) in 1825; name changed to La Fayette avenue in 1828; confirmed as public street, Sept. 15, 1834.

La Fayette place, Rox.; from Julian street, northerly, near Blue Hill avenue.

La Fayette square, Chsn., 1875; at junction of Main street and Warren street; named La Fayette square, June 22, 1875; name changed to Thompson square, July 19, 1875.

La Fayette street, E. B. (Breed's Island); from Orient avenue, north-east, then south-east to Orient avenue again.

La Grange place, B., 1828; from Washington street, west; extended to Tremont street, Oct. 14, 1864; name changed to La Grange street, Oct. 24, 1865. L 275 L 296.

La Grange place, Rox.; from Blue Hill avenue, north-westerly, between Winthrop street and Mt. Pleasant avenue.

***La Grange street,** B., 1865; from Washington street to Tremont street, near Boylston street; name of La Grange place changed to La Grange street, Oct. 24, 1865. L 275, L 296.

***La Grange street,** W. Rox., 1849; from Washington street, near Beech street, to Newton line; laid out from Centre street across West Roxbury Branch R.R. to Weld street, October 1869; laid out from Weld street to Newton line, July, 1871; extended to Shawmut avenue (now Washington street), Aug. 21, 1873, and Sept. 8, 1873. L 2037, L 2805.

***Lake street,** Bri., 1847; from Washington street to Commonwealth avenue; laid out, April 27, 1847; accepted, conditionally, May 17, 1847; by the Town in 1854 and 1859; named by the Town, March 5, 1860; called "Lake street or Foster street" on plan dated 1866. L 2243, L 2244, L 2245, L 2280.

Lake-Hill avenue, W. Rox., 1851; from Cottage street, south-west, north-west, and north, to Cottage street again; shown on Plan L. 220, f. 321, Norf. Reg.

Lakeville avenue, W. Rox., 1846; from Centre street, north-west, towards Jamaica park; called Lakeville place.

Lamartine court, W. Rox.; from Lamartine street, south-easterly, to railroad, between Boylston street and Clark court.

Lamartine place, W. Rox.; from Green street to Lamartine street; Lamartine square so called, 1874.

Lamartine place, W. Rox.; from Lamartine street, easterly, to railroad, between Oak place and Lawndale terrace; shown as an unnamed place on plan.

Lamartine square, W. Rox.; from Green street, north-easterly, then north-westerly, to Lamartine street; called Lamartine place, 1874.

***Lamartine street,** Rox. and W. Rox., 1848; from Green street to Centre street; formerly known as Boston avenue; laid out from Green street to Boylston street, Dec. 19, 1859; laid out from Centre street to boundary line between Boston and West Roxbury, Dec. 10, 1869; laid out from boundary line to Boylston street, March 10, 1873. L 503.

Lamartine terrace, W. Rox.; from Lamartine street, north-west, opposite Lamartine place.

***Lambert avenue,** Rox., 1845; from Kenilworth street to Cedar street; early called Ascension street, and later, Walnut street; by deed dated 1835 abutters agree to call Ascension street Lambert avenue; conditional acceptance recommended by Selectmen, April 7, 1845; extended from Bartlett street to Kenilworth street, Nov. 28, 1881. L 1572.

***Lambert street,** Rox., 1833; from Highland street to Lambert avenue; accepted, conditionally, April 25, 1864; accepted, finally, April 29, 1867.

***Lamont street**, Rox., 1887; from Linden Park street to Vernon street; Linden avenue laid out as a public street and named Lamont street, June 23, 1887. L 1098.

Lamson court, E. B.; from Lamson street, near Everett street, north-east.

***Lamson street**, E. B., 1871; from Webster street to Maverick street, with proposed extension to proposed part of Putnam street; proposed extension of Lamson street is now occupied in part by the location of the B., R. B. & L. R.R. L 1418, L 2172.

Lanark road, Bri.; from Kinross Road to Brookline line.

Lancaster court, } B.; from Lancaster street, south; called Lancaster
Lancaster place, } place, 1837; Lancaster court, 1839; built over about 1860.

***Lancaster street**, B., 1807; from Merrimac street to Causeway street; laid out from Merrimac street over the Mill-pond, Aug. 3, 1807; to Causeway street, 1841.

Land's court, B., 1852; from North street, nearly opposite Sun-Court street, south-east.

Landseer avenue, Rox.; from Seaver street nearly to Waumbeck street; called Landseer street on plan dated June 1, 1881; abandoned.

***Landseer street**, W. Rox.; from La Grange street to Bellevue street; laid out, June 13, 1892. L 2400.

Lane place, B., 1834; from Gibbs lane (now Oliver street), west, near Washington (now Fort Hill) square.

Langdon court, B., 1840; from Langdon place, west.

Langdon place, B., 1820; from North street, near Richmond street; south.

***Langdon street**, Rox., 1867; from Dudley street, north-easterly, to beyond George street, parallel with Shirley street; laid out from Dudley street to George street, July 8, 1871. L 629, L 1791.

Lansdowne street, Rox.; from Massachusetts avenue to Allerton street.

***Lansing street**, Rox., 1869; from Warren street to Sherman street; laid out, March 13, 1882. L 1589.

Larch place, W. Rox.; from Hyde Park avenue, opposite Florence street, to the railroad.

Largo street, W. Rox.; from Belgrade street (now Hyde Park avenue) to Newbern street, at Hyde Park line; see Charles Whitney's map of Roxbury dated 1843–49; now closed.

***Lark street**, So. B., 1868; from West Eighth street, south-westerly, to O. C. (now N. Y., N. H. & H.) R.R.; laid out from Eighth (now West Eighth) street to Sullivan (now West Ninth) street, Nov. 17, 1868; laid out from West Ninth street to O. C. (now N. Y., N. H. & H.) R.R., June 16, 1876. L 1158.

Lark street, W. Rox., 1874; from La Grange street to Bellevue street.

La Rose place, Bri.; from Union street, north-west, near Washington street.

Lasell street, W. Rox ; from Baker street, north-east, to beyond Caspar street; authority to open from La Grange street to a point north-east of Caspar street given by Street Commissioners, April 20, 1894; authority to open from Baker street to La Grange street given by Street Commissioners, March 5, 1895.

Lathrop place, B., 1836; from Hanover street, south-easterly, between Prince street and Richmond street.

***Laurel street**, Rox.; from Dale street to Humboldt avenue; name of Seneca street changed to Laurel street, May 10, 1870, but called

Laurel street on plan dated 1869; laid out, Sept. 7, 1871. L 634, L 2121.

Laurel street, Dor.; from Norfolk street, near the cemetery, south-easterly.

***Laurel street**, Chsn.; from Monument square to Cedar street; shown as an unnamed street on plan dated 1839; laid out and accepted from Concord street to a lane running from High street to Bartlett street, Sept. 8, 1856.

†**Lauriat avenue**, Dor.; from Norfolk street, westerly, to Blue Hill avenue; from Norfolk street crossing railroad and Ballou avenue to Blue Hill avenue; shown in 1874 and 1884; laid out from Blue Hill avenue to Tucker street, Sept. 7, 1895. L 2723, L 2724, L 2725.

Lauriat street, Dor.; from Lauriat avenue to Chapman avenue.

Lauten place, So. B.; from East Second street, north, between O street and P street; also shown as Simpson's court.

***Lawn street**, Rox., 1850; from Heath street, northerly, north-westerly, and south-westerly to Heath street; laid out from Heath street to Hayden street, June 16, 1892; laid out from Hayden street to Heath street, Dec. 14, 1893. L 2404, L 2573.

Lawn street, W. Rox., 1859; from Mount Hope street, north-easterly, near Canterbury street.

Lawndale terrace, W. Rox.; from Lamartine street, south-west, between Lamartine place and Helena street to N. Y., N. H. & H. R.R.

Lawrence avenue, Chsn.; from Lawrence street, north-east, nearly opposite Benedict street.

***Lawrence avenue**, Rox. and Dor.; from Blue Hill avenue to Magnolia (formerly Myrtle) street; called Lawrence street, 1846; seems to have been called Lawrence street until 1869, in which year it is shown on plans as both street and avenue; laid out as Lawrence avenue, Sept. 27, 1879. L 1381, L 1382, L 1946.

Lawrence court, So. B.; from West Third street, between B street and C street, south-west.

Lawrence court, Chsn.; from Lawrence street, south-west, between Benedict street and Austin street.

Lawrence place, B., 1844; from Cambridge street, northerly, between Blossom street and North Anderson street.

Lawrence place, Dor.; from Lawrence avenue, south-west, near Grove street; also called Lawrence place.

Lawrence place, Bri.; from Market street, south-east, near North Beacon street.

Lawrence park, Dor.; from Lawrence avenue; also called Lawrence place.

***Lawrence street**, B., 1866; from Berkeley street to Dartmouth street; laid out, Dec. 7, 1869. L 354.

Lawrence street, Rox. and Dor.; from Blue Hill avenue to Myrtle (now Magnolia) street; called Lawrence avenue.

***Lawrence street**, Chsn., 1824; from Union street to Phipps street; accepted, March 1, 1824; continuation from Austin street to Miller street accepted, May 4, 1837; continued to Phipps street, Nov. 25, 1844.

Lawrence-street place, Chsn.; from Lawrence street, south-westerly.

Lawrence-street place, Chsn.; from Lawrence street, south-easterly, between Chapman street and Austin street; shown in directory only.

Learnard street, Dor., 1870; from Norfolk street, opposite the cemetery, to Torrey street.

***Leather square**, B., 1867; from Channing street to Matthews street; called Sister street in 1732; name changed to Leather square, Sept. 24, 1867 L 77, L 330, L 455, L 834.

Lebanon street, Rox.; from Magnolia street to N. E. R.R.

Leavitt place, Dor.; from Brook avenue, north-west; shown as an unnamed place on plan dated 1855; later called Brook court; Leavitt place, 1873; Brook-avenue place, 1884.

Lee place, B., 1849; from Phillips street, northerly, between West Cedar street and Grove street.

Lee street, W. Rox., 1850; from Carolina avenue to Keyes street.

Leeds court, B; from Washington street, west, before 1840; supposed to have been included in Indiana place (now Corning street) or taken for the Worcester (now B. & A.) R.R.

Leeds street, So. B.; from Woodward street, south-westerly.

Leeds street, Dor., 1869; from Savin Hill avenue to Bay street.

Leeds street, Dor.; from Adams street to Dorchester avenue; shown as an unnamed street on plan dated 1861.

***Lehigh street**, B., 1843; from Albany street to South street; accepted and laid out as a public street, Nov. 8, 1852; extended to Sea (now Federal) street, April 30, 1856; order for extension rescinded, May 9, 1856.

Leicester street, Rox.; from Ivy street to Mountfort street; now closed.

***Leicester street**, Bri.; from Washington street to Arlington street; laid out from Bennett street to Arlington street, Aug. 16, 1893; laid out from Washington street to Bennett street, Oct. 12, 1896. L 2532, L 2791.

Leighton park, B.; in the rear of Dartmouth street, Truro street, Yarmouth street and Columbus avenue.

Leighton street, B.; from Truro street, southerly.

Leland place, B., 1856; from Washington street, north-westerly, near Waltham street.

Leland street, W. Rox.; from Wachusett street, south-east, to cemetery, and from Wachusett street, north-west, towards Wenham street; authority to open given by Street Commissioners, July 19, 1893.

Leman place, B.; from High street, north-west, between Broad street and Batterymarch street.

Lendall's lane, B., 1733; from Leverett's lane (now Congress street), opposite the Quakers' meeting-house, to Kilby street; same as Lindall's lane.

Lenox court, B.; from East Lenox street, north-easterly, near corner Harrison avenue.

***Lenox street**, B., 1833; from Washington street, opposite East Lenox street, to Tremont street; from Washington street to Suffolk street (now Shawmut avenue), 1833; to Tremont street, 1851; accepted, conditionally, "as at present laid out," July 6, 1853; accepted, finally, from Washington street to Shawmut avenue, Oct. 9, 1854; accepted, conditionally, from Shawmut avenue to Tremont street, Aug. 4, 1857. L 22, L 264, L 500.

***Leon street**, Rox., 1894; formerly Avon place; name changed to Leon street, March 1, 1894. L 1244.

Leonard court, Dor.; from Leonard street, south-east, near Leonard place.

Leonard place, Dor.; from junction of Leonard street and Duncan street, south.

Leonard place, So. B.; from East Fourth street, near N street, south-east.

***Leonard street,** Dor., 1870; from Duncan street to Clayton street; laid out, Nov. 2, 1896. L 2795.

Le Roy street, Dor.; from Geneva avenue to Ditson street.

Leslie park, Rox.; from Walnut avenue, north-westerly, near corner Dale street.

Lester place, W. Rox.; from Centre street, east, between Green street and St. John street.

Letterfine terrace, Dor.; from Howard avenue, south-east, nearly opposite Dewey street.

Leutman place, Rox.; from Texas street, south-westerly, near Elmwood street; also called Luteman place.

Levant street, Dor.; from Geneva avenue to Topliff street; shown in 1894.

Leveret's lane, B., 1708; from King (now State) street to Water street; also called Quaker's lane, from State street by Dalton's row to Milk street, 1784; from Water street to Milk street called Dalton street, 1788; from State street to Milk street called Congress street, 1800.

Leverett alley, B., 1812; from Leverett street, east; called also Leverett place, previously to 1812; called New Prince street, Cross street and Tucker street; name changed to Lyman place in 1834, and Lyman street in 1856.

Leverett avenue, B., 1859; from Leverett street, south-westerly, nearly opposite Minot street; called Phillips court, 1843; Leverett avenue, 1859.

Leverett court, B., 1822; from Leverett street north; named Cotting street, 1843.

Leverett court, B., 1852–59; from Leverett street, west, near Hammond avenue.

Leverett lane, B., 1831; from Leverett street to Wall street, 1831; named Cushman avenue, 1855.

Leverett place, B., 1812; from Leverett street, east; called also Leverett alley; previously called New Prince street, Cross street and Tucker street; name changed to Lyman place, April 14, 1834; called Lyman street, 1856.

***Leverett street,** B., 1733; from Green street, north-westerly, to Craigie's bridge; from Green lane to Barton's point, 1733; from Tucker's corner to the new alms-house, 1800; extended to Central or Craigie's bridge, 1809; from westerly end of street "as now laid out" to Canal bridge accepted, conditionally, Aug. 19, 1856. Vol. 31, pp. 68, 74. L 935, L 988.

***Lewis park,** Rox., 1864; from Highland street, near Linwood street.

Lewis place, Rox., 1869; from Dudley street, south-westerly, opposite Clarence street.

***Lewis street,** B., 1831; from Commercial street to Moon street; laid out as a new street opposite Mercantile wharf, Oct. 19, 1831; street near head of Lewis wharf named Lewis street, March 26, 1838; laid out from North street, through Moon-street court, to Moon street, March 25, 1893. L 81, L 2506.

***Lewis street,** E. B.; from Sumner street to East Boston South Ferry; Maverick square to South Ferry, June 12, 1848. L 207.

Lewis street, So. B.; name changed to Jenkins street, Aug. 7, 1855; Jenkins street, by chart, 1874, from Dorchester street, south-easterly, to O. C. (now N. Y., N. H. & H.) R.R.

Lexington avenue, Chsn.; from Bunker Hill street to Concord avenue; shown as an unnamed street on plan dated 1830.

Lexington avenue, Bri.; from Washington street, south-westerly, crossing Union street and Cushman street; shown as an unnamed street in 1873; laid out between Washington street and Union street as Shannon street, July 8, 1892; portion from Union street, south-westerly, now closed.

Lexington place, E. B.; from Lexington street, south-east, near corner Marion street.

***Lexington street,** E. B., 1834; from Border street to Eagle street; from Meridian street to Eagle street accepted, April 28, 1873; accepted at junction Lexington street and Eagle street, Nov. 1, 1858. L 107, L 1383.

†**Lexington street,** Chsn., 1839; from Monument square to Medford street; formerly from Monument square to Bunker Hill street; shown as an unnamed street on plan dated 1834; accepted from Monument square to Bunker Hill street; Dec. 23, 1844; extended to Medford street, March 15, 1848; name of part from Wallace court to Tremont street changed to Monument square, Feb. 2, 1860.

***Leyden street,** E. B. (Breed's Island), 1886; from Wauwatosa avenue to Beachmont avenue; Elm street, laid out from Breed street to Washburn avenue (now Walley street) as Leyden street, Aug. 23, 1886; extended from Walley street to Atlantic (now Beachmont) avenue, July 3, 1888; extended from Breed street, over Elm street, to Chelsea avenue, July 30, 1889. L 1938, L 1939, L 2080, L 2148, L 2149, L 2171.

Leyden street, Rox., 1849; from Brookline avenue to Plymouth street; now portion of Bernier street.

***Leyland street,** Dor.; from East Cottage street to Burgess street; laid out, Dec. 22, 1891. L 2378.

***Liberty square,** B., 1793; at the junction of Kilby street, Water street and Batterymarch street; named, Jan. 24, 1793; confirmed as a public way, Sept. 15, 1834. L 850.

Liberty street, B., 1820; from Liberty square to Broad street; made part of Water street, March 20, 1826.

Liberty street, So. B.; from Preble street, southerly, near N. Y., N. H. & H. R.R.

Libby street, W. Rox.; from Mt. Vernon street, near La Grange street to Keith street.

Lilly street, So. B.; from Tudor street to West Seventh street, between E street and F street.

***Lime alley,** B., 1708; from Charter street to Commercial street; from the burying-place in Charter street to Adkins' lime kiln in Lyn street, 1708; from Alley's ship-yard at Hudson's point to the north burying-place, 1800.

***Lime street,** B., 1845; from River street to Brimmer street; called C street, 1830; name changed to Lime street, 1845; laid out, Dec. 29, 1875; extended to Brimmer street, May 13, 1881. L 1124.

Lime-street alley or place, B., 1860; from Lime street, south-east; formerly called Allen place.

Limerick place, B., 1847; from Hanover street, east, near Commercial street; cannot be now identified.

Linck alley, B.; same as Link alley.

Lincoln court, B., 1829; from Fayette street; Church street extended to Tremont street through Lincoln court, June 24, 1852. Vol. 31, p. 40

Lincoln park, So. B.; from East Third street, south, between I street and K street.

Lincoln place, B.; from Winchester street, southerly, near Church street.

***Lincoln place**, B., 1863; from Worcester street to West Springfield street; laid out, Oct. 9, 1877. L 1276.

Lincoln place, B.; from 9 Salutation street, south.

Lincoln place, Rox., 1861; from Weston street, formerly Sudbury street, north-east.

Lincoln place, Rox.; name changed to Grosvenor place, April 21, 1868. (Grosvenor place extends from Washington street to Cliff street.)

Lincoln place, Chsn ; from Elm street, south-easterly, between High street and Bartlett street.

Lincoln square, So. B.; between East Fourth street M street and Emerson street.

***Lincoln street**, B., 1795; from Summer to Kneeland street; from Summer street to Essex street, 1795: from Church square to Essex street by Carleton's map, 1800; confirmed as a public street, Sept. 15, 1834; extended southerly from Essex street through Batterman place to the passenger depot of the B. & W. (now B. & A.) R.R. Sept. 5, 1836; accepted, Oct. 16, 1837; part between Harvard street and Ontario street relocated to the westward of present location, 1844; to Lehigh street, 1846; now to Station and land of B. & A. R.R. at Kneeland street. L 61, L 73, L 85½, L 833, L 2515.

***Lincoln street**, Dor., 1869; from Dorchester avenue to Adams street; shown as an unnamed street in 1867; laid out as a town way, Dec. 28,1869. L 771.

Lincoln street, Chsn., 1869; from Main street to Rutherford avenue; name of Walker's avenue or West Walker street leading from westerly side of Main street changed to Lincoln street, Dec. 27, 1869. L 1220.

***Lincoln street**, Bri., 1846; from Market street to Cambridge street, where it is called "Lincoln street (formerly Centre street);" accepted from Market street to Franklin street, near Allston station, June 13, 1883; portion of Franklin street between Lincoln street and Cambridge street called Lincoln street being a continuation of the same, April 25, 1876. L 2390.

Lindall alley, } B.; from Phillips street, northerly, then easterly, to
Lindall court, } Lindall place; called Lindall alley, 1868; Lindall court, 1870.

Lindall place, B., 1831; from Cambridge street, near West Cedar street, south-westerly.

Lindall street, B., 1821; from Congress street to Kilby street; name of Lendell's lane changed to Lindall street, Sept. 19, 1821; named Exchange place, Oct. 14, 1873. L 203, L 822, L 853.

Lindall street, W. Rox., 1895; from Washington street to Ashland street; authority to open given by Street Commissioners, March 26, 1895.

Lindall's lane, B.; called also Lyndall's Lindal's, Lendall, and Lendell's lane; from Leveret's lane (now Congress street), opposite the Friend's meeting-house, to Oliver's dock, 1733; from Leveret's lane to Kilby street, 1788; to Oliver's dock, 1800; called Magnor's row in 1801; renamed Lindall's lane the same year; from Congress street to Kilby street, 1817; name changed to Lindall street, Sept. 19, 1821; called Exchange place in 1873.

Linden avenue, Rox.; from Linden-Park street to Lamont street; also called Linden park.

Linden avenue, Rox.; from Linden park to Vernon street; laid out as a public street and named Lamont street, June 23, 1887. L 1998.

Linden court, Dor.; from Linden street, near Dorchester avenue, south.

Linden park, Rox.; from Linden-Park street to Lamont street; also called Linden avenue.

***Linden park**, Rox., 1836; from Roxbury street, west, crossing Linden avenue and Gay street, curving northerly and easterly to Linden avenue, where the part from Main (now Roxbury) street to Ruggles (now Cabot) street is called Ruggles street; accepted from Ruggles street to Gay street, July 7, 1852; extended from Gay street, including a part of Clay street, to Simmons street, Nov. 8, 1884; named Linden-Park street, March 1, 1885, name of Clay street, from Simmons street to Tremont street (now Columbus avenue) changed to Linden Park street, March 1, 1885. L 1833.

Linden place, B., 1852; from Allen street, north, between Spring street and Chambers street.

Linden place, Rox ; from Linden Park, northerly, parallel with Cabot street; now Prentiss place.

Linden place, So. B.; from East Seventh street between I street and K street.

***Linden street**, So. B.; from East Fourth street to Thomas park; dedicated (conditionally) as a public way, Oct. 30, 1861; laid out, Nov. 17, 1868. L 235, L 259.

***Linden street**, Rox., 1863; from Grove Hall (now Blue Hill) avenue to Elm Hill avenue; accepted, Oct. 24, 1864; name changed to Wayne street, April 21, 1868. L 1778.

***Linden street**, Dor.; from Adams street to Commercial (now Freeport) street; from Adams street to Dorchester avenue accepted, April 4, 1853; continuation to Commercial street, accepted, March 5, 1855.

Linden street, W. Rox., 1870; from Montgomery street to Webster street, parallel with Pleasant street.

Linden street, W. Rox., 1872; from Beech street to Bellevue street or avenue.

Linden street, W. Rox., 1871; from Brandon (formerly Williams) street to Birch (formerly Prospect) street, and from Dudley avenue, south-east, to near Birch street.

***Linden street**, Chsn., 1844; from Bunker Hill street to Medford street; laid out and accepted, June 26, 1865; made a continuation of Baldwin street, Oct. 8, 1867.

***Linden street**, Bri., 1850; from Cambridge street to Commonwealth avenue: laid out from Cambridge street to Gardner street, Dec. 17, 1873; accepted conditionally, Dec. 30, 1873: laid out, Sept. 16, 1876; extended to Brighton avenue, May 26, 1884; extended to Massachusetts (now Commonwealth) avenue, June 2, 1885. L 1170, L 1778, L 1860, L 2388.

***Linden-Park street**, Rox., 1885; from Roxbury street to Tremont street (now Columbus avenue); name of part of Linden Park, from Roxbury street to Clay street, at Elmwood street changed to Linden-Park street, March 1, 1885; name of Clay street, from Simmons street to Tremont street, changed to Linden-Park street, March 1, 1885.

Link alley, B., 1708; from the junction of Union street and Hanover street, north-east, to the Mill-pond; called North Federal court, 1806; discontinued in 1857, and built upon and closed in 1860.

†**Linnet street**, W. Rox., 1848; from Bellevue street to La Grange street, also from Martin street to Linnet street; laid out from Bellevue street to La Grange street, Aug. 16, 1878. L 1315.

Linsey street, Dor., 1893; from Waldeck street, south-west, near Park street; authority to open given by Street Commissioners, Jan. 18, 1893.

Linwood park, Rox.; part of Linwood street, near its junction with Centre street.

Linwood place, B., 1836; from South street, near Summer street, east. L 1471.

Linwood place, Rox., 1859; from Linwood street, north-west, to Centre street; now part of Linwood street.

Linwood place, Chsn.; from Main street, north-east, between Salem street and School street.

†**Linwood square,** Rox., 1868; from Centre street to Linwood street; name of part of Linwood street changed to Linwood square, April 21, 1868; laid out, June 6, 1873. L 494, L 864.

***Linwood street,** Rox.: from Centre street to Highland street; also formerly from Linwood street to Highland street; part shown as an unnamed street on plan dated 1859; name of part changed to Linwood square, April 21, 1868; laid out from Centre street to Highland street, Nov. 16, 1869. L 494, L 496.

Lisbon street, E. B., 1834; from Sumner street to Maverick street; shown on plan dated 1836; discontinued.

Liszt street, W. Rox.; from Washington street to West Roxbury Parkway.

Litchfield court, E. B.; from Sumner street, north-east, near Cottage street.

Litchfield street, Bri.; from Lincoln street, north-east, to Avenue place; authority to open given by Street Commissioners, Oct. 14, 1892.

Lithgow street, Dor., 1895; from Washington street, near Brent street, north-east, crossing Talbot avenue; authority to open given by Street Commissioners, Oct. 18, 1895.

Little alley, B., 1836; near Prince street.

Little Napier street, B.; from Napier street to Brighton street; named Barton court, April 21, 1868.

Liverpool avenue, E. B.; from Liverpool street to Border street, between Maverick street and Decatur street; formerly called Erin alley.

***Liverpool street,** E. B., 1833; from Sumner street to Central square; accepted, Nov. 22, 1852.

Livingston place, B., 1844; from Livingston street; name changed to Breen place, May 10, 1870; included in Charles river embankment (now Charlesbank).

†**Livingston street,** B., 1838; from Brighton street to Charles river; from Brighton street, west, 1838; to the river, 1842; accepted and named from Brighton street to Charles street, June 4, 1844; across North Charles street, 1859; portion from Charles street to Charles river now included in Charlesbank; name of, from Brighton street to Charles street, changed to Chambers street, March 1, 1894.

Llewellyn avenue, Rox., 1853; from Walnut street (now Walnut avenue), southerly, to Williams (now Humboldt) avenue extended; Crawford street extended through it, Dec. 4, 1870. L 1408, L 1409.

Lochstead street, W. Rox.; from Centre street to Jamaicaway; authority to open given by Street Commissioners, Jan. 30, 1895.

Locke place, So. B.; from East Fourth street, north, between H street and I street.

Locksley street, W. Rox.; from Enfield street; authority to open given by Street Commissioners, Dec. 28, 1892.

Locust street, Dor., 1864; from Dorchester avenue, easterly, to O. C. (now N. Y., N. H. & H.) R.R.

***Logan street,** Rox.; from Thornton street to Lambert avenue; laid out, Nov. 27, 1888. L 2107.

Lombard place, B., 1856; from Prince street, south-westerly, then north-westerly, to Thacher street; from Prince street, west, near Salem street, 1856.

Lombard place, So. B.; from Ellery street, north-easterly.

Lombard street, Dor.; from Carruth street to Bushnell street.

London court, E. B.; from London street, between Porter street and Marion street, south-easterly.

London street, B., 1838; from Pleasant street; extended to Indiana place (now Corning street), May 16, 1853; accepted and name changed to Kirkland street, Nov, 16, 1858. Vol. 31, p. 75. L 140½.

***London street,** E. B., 1833; from Sumner street to Bennington street at junction with Marion street; accepted, Nov. 22, 1852. L 677.

Long acre, B., 1777; the wall on the west side of Common (now Tremont) street, between Winter street and School street; called also Paddock's Mall.

Longfellow street, Dor.; from Topliff street to Draper street; authority to open given by Street Commissioners, July 20, 1892.

Long lane, B., 1708; from Milk street to Cow lane (now High street); called Federal street in 1788.

***Longmeadow street,** Dor.; from Clifton street to Batchelder street; laid out, June 19, 1891. L 2303.

Long wharf, B., 1809; from Atlantic avenue, easterly, opposite State street; agreement as to building wharf, highways and cartways on same, etc., March 13, 1809; so called as it is supposed to be the longest on the continent, being 1,700 feet in length and above 100 feet in breadth; street on Long wharf running at right angles to North and South Market streets, continued in southerly direction to southerly front of stores on Long wharf, July 28, 1825. Vol. 31, p. 47. L 1001.

***Longwood avenue,** Rox., 1857; from Parker street to Brookline line; from Brookline avenue, through Pilgrim street to Beacon street, Brookline; laid out by County Commissioners as a highway, June, 1857; named from Punch Bowl road to Longwood creek or Muddy river, Dec. 7, 1857; accepted and named from Parker street to Brookline Branch of the Western avenue (Brookline avenue), July 29, 1867.

Longwood-avenue court, Rox.; from Longwood avenue, south-west, near Parker street.

Longwood park, Rox.; between Bellevue street, Austin street, Brookline avenue and Park street.

Longwood street, Rox., 1850; from Brookline avenue, opposite Francis street, to Longwood avenue; part west of Brookline avenue to angle in said street laid out as Francis street, Oct. 19, 1874; remainder of street now in Riverway.

Lonsdale street, Dor., 1895; from Dorchester avenue to Adams street; authority to open given by Street Commissioners, April 30, 1895.

Lorenzo street, Dor.; from Walnut street to Wood street; formerly called Wood-street court.

Lorette street, W. Rox.; from Centre street opposite Cottage avenue, north-westerly, to beyond Hillcrest street.

Loretto street, W. Rox.; from Spring street, north-west, near Baker street.

***Loring street,** So. B., 1884; from West Seventh street to West Eighth street; Clapp street laid out as a public street and named Loring street, Aug. 27, 1884. L 1808.

Lorraine street, Dor., 1895; from Stanwood street to Brunswick street; authority to open given by Street Commissioners, Dec. 7, 1895.

Lorraine street, W. Rox.; from Colberg avenue to Belgrade avenue.

Lothrop place, B.; from Hanover street, south-east, between Prince street and Richmond street; also called Lathrop place.

Lotus avenue, W. Rox., 1856; from Lotus street to Williams street; now closed.

Lotus place, W. Rox.; from Washington street, south-easterly, nearly opposite Burnett street, to Stony Brook.

Lotus street, W. Rox., 1856; from Forest Hills street to Williams street; portion from Williams street, south-west, abandoned.

Louisburg square, B., 1826; from Pinckney street to Mt. Vernon street.

Louisiana place, E. B.; from Princeton street, near Marion street, south-east.

Love lane, } B., 1708; from North street to Salem street; called
Love street, } North Writing School lane, 1789; Love lane, from North street by the North writing school to Salem street, 1800; name changed to Tileston street, June 20, 1821.

Love lane, Dor., 1836; from Wales lane (now Geneva avenue) south-east, to Love lane avenue (now part of Olney street).

Love-lane avenue, Dor., 1836; from Bowdoin avenue (now Rosseter street) north-east, to Love lane (Green street, now Geneva avenue); now a part of Olney street.

Lovedeed court, Rox.; from Chadwick street, north-west, near corner of Hampden street.

Lovell place, B.; from Poplar street, south-west, to the junction of Kennard court and Elder place; Lovett place so called in 1883.

Lovering place, B., 1855; from Washington street to Harrison avenue, near Asylum street.

Lovett place, B., 1836; from Poplar street, south, near Brighton street; called Lovell place, 1883.

Lovis street, So. B.; from West Fifth street to Gold street near E street.

***Lowder's lane**, W. Rox., 1849; from Centre street, near May street, south-westerly, then westerly; see Charles Whitney's map of Roxbury dated 1843–49; also called Louder's lane.

Lowe street, W. Rox., 1892; from Woodside avenue to Sylvia street; authority to open given by Street Commissioners, Aug. 10, 1892.

Lowell court, } B; from Boylston street, near Common (now Tremont)
Lowell place, } street, south; Lowell court, 1806; later to La Grange street; laid out and named Tamworth street, April 28, 1880. L 1452.

Lowell court, B., 1847; from Tamworth street (formerly Lowell place) east.

Lowell square, B., 1852; on Cambridge street and Lynde street; public square in front of the West church in Cambridge street named Lowell square, Aug. 30, 1852.

***Lowell street**, B., 1834; from Causeway street to Brighton street; from Causeway street, west, 1834; from Causeway street to Brighton street, accepted, laid out and named, July 18, 1842.

Lowell street, B., 1826; laid out over the Neck, July 24, 1826; second of new cross streets, at southerly part of city, extending from Tremont street to Suffolk street (now Shawmut avenue) named Lowell street, Sept. 15, 1834; called South Lowell street in 1848; name changed to Milford street, May 14, 1849.

***Lowell street**, Rox., 1833; laid out as a new public highway from road near Guy Carlton's factory, in a southerly direction to old Boston & Providence road, near Hog bridge, September, 1833; road from Carlton's to Heath street named Lowell street, Sept. 23, 1834; name changed to Pynchon street, April 21, 1868.

Lowell street, Chsn., 1837; from Bunker Hill street, north-east, to Mystic river.

Lower road; from Roxbury to Milton; old name of Adams street; also a part of Dudley street.

Lowland place, E. B.; from Everett street, between Cottage street and Lamson street, south-westerly.

***Lowland street**, So. B., 1868; from East Eighth street to Jenkins street; name of Highland street changed to Lowland street, April 21, 1868; laid out from Eighth (now East Eighth) street to Jenkins street, Nov. 17, 1868; name changed to Mercer street, March 1, 1888. L 191, L 192.

Lubec street, E. B., 1845; from Swift street to Maverick street; authority to open between Parkway and Prescott street given by Street Commissioners, April 21, 1893.

†Lucas place, / **Lucas street,** } B.; from Washington street to Tremont street; from Washington street, west, called Lucas place, 1828; Lucas street, 1851; extended to Tremont street, 1855; Lucas street laid out from Middlesex street to Shawmut avenue, Oct. 13, 1891. L 544, L 545, L 546, L 547, L 724, L 2346.

Lucas street, Bri.,; from North Beacon street to Mapleton street, laid out from North Beacon street to Elmira street as Etna street, Nov. 10, 1893.

***Ludlow street**, Chsn., 1884; from Eden street to Mead street; Garden place laid out as a public street and named Ludlow street, June 30, 1884. L 1786.

Luelner place, Dor.; from Dorchester avenue, east, parallel with Centre street; shown as an unnamed court in 1867; included in Dix street upon its extension to Dorchester avenue, Oct. 2, 1877.

Luke street, Bri.; near Washington street in 1859; no record.

Luteman place, Rox.; from Texas street, south-westerly; called also Lentman place.

Luther place, B., 1868; from Commercial street, near Henchman street, south-west.

Lyd's corner, B., 1708; corner of Hanover street and Wing's lane (now Elm street) then so called.

Lyman avenue, Bri., 1856; from Market street, north-westerly, to railroad; then parallell with it to Hillside avenue; laid out with a part of Hillside avenue, as Wicklow street, Dec. 5, 1881. L 1577.

Lyman place, B., 1869; from Lyman street, south-westerly, towards Green street.

Lyman place, B., 1834; from Leverett street, east; previous to 1812 called New Prince street, Cross street, Tucker street; called Leverett place or alley in 1812; Lyman place, April 14, 1834; changed to Lyman street, July 23, 1856.

***Lyman street**, B., 1856; from Staniford street to Leverett street; part from Leverett street, east, called New Prince street, at times previous to 1788; Cross street, 1802; Tucker street, 1803; Leverett place or alley, 1812; named Lyman place April 14, 1834; name changed to Lyman street, July 23, 1856; Staniford street extended over part of, May 11, 1886. L 1905.

Lynde avenue, Chsn., 1852; from Main street, south-westerly, then south-easterly to Austin street.

Lynde court, / **Lynde place,** / **Lynde-street place,** } B.; from Lynde street, westerly; called Lynde place, 1837; Lynde court, 1874; also Lynde-street place.

***Lynde street**, B., 1732; from Cambridge street to Green street.

***Lynde street**, Chsn., 1838; from Arrow street to Austin street at junction of First street; accepted from Arrow street to Union street, March 27, 1843; accepted from Union street to Austin street, March 27, 1849.

Lyndeboro' place, B., 1838; from Carver street at its junction with Pleasant street, north-easterly.

***Lyndeboro' street**, Chsn., 1847; from Essex street to Middlesex street; laid out and accepted, Dec. 21, 1857; entrance from Essex street enlarged, May 14, 1866.

***Lyndhurst street**, Dor.; from Washington street to Allston street; laid out, May 8, 1894. L 2598.

Lynn street, B., 1708; from the North Battery, north-westerly, to the ferry-way by Hudson's point; laid out after the "great desolations" of the war, March 5, 1787; from Winnisimmet ferry to Charles River bridge, 1800; the part from North Battery to Winnisimmet ferry being included in Ship street; together with part of Ann street, named Commercial street, Feb. 17, 1834.

***Lynn street**, B., 1884; from Cooper street to Thacher street; Thacher avenue laid out as a public street and named Lynn street, Sept. 10, 1884. L 1819.

Lynnville terrace, Dor.; from Washington street, south-west, nearly opposite Eldon street; formerly called Hartford place.

Lyon place, Rox.; from Shawmut avenue, near corner Camden street, south-east.

***Lyon street**, Dor.; from Dorchester avenue to Adams street; laid out, Aug. 10, 1893. L 2524.

Lyon street, W. Rox., 1825; from Centre street by Lyon's; named, May 9, 1825; name changed to Bellevue avenue, April 2, 1860.

Lyons street, Dor.; from Lauriat avenue to Franklin Field.

***M street**, So. B., 1805; from East First street to East Ninth street, with proposed extensions northerly to Harbor, and southerly to line in "Old Harbor;" from salt water on to south, to Harbor of Boston on the north; laid out and named, Feb. 27, 1805; laid out from low-water mark north of First street to Harbor line in Dorchester Bay, Nov. 17, 1868; portion south of location of proposed East Tenth street included in the Strandway. L 7, L 2078.

M-street place, So. B.; from M street, west, between East Fifth street and East Sixth street.

Maccarty's corner, B., 1708; corner of King (now State) street and Leveret's lane (now Congress street) then so called.

Mackerel, Macril, Mackrill, lane, B., 1708; from King (now State) street to Water street; called Kilby street, 1769.

Mackin street, Bri.; from Western avenue to Waverly street. L 2782.

Madison avenue, Dor., 1874; from Madison (now Morton) street to Willowwood (formerly Shreve) street.

Madison avenue, Chsn., 1875; from Tremont street to Ferrin street.

Madison avenue, Bri., 1875; from Washington street, south-westerly, crossing Union street, Cushman street, and Ames street; shown as a contemplated street from Washington street to Union street.

Madison court, Rox., 1853; from Parker street, easterly, near Huntington avenue.

Madison park, Rox.; between Marble, Warwick, Westminster and Sterling streets; same called Madison square, 1884.

Madison place, B., 1826; from Pleasant street, near Eliot street, west; afterwards to Church street; closed on extension of Columbus avenue; 1872. L 393, L 613.

Madison place, B., 1868; from Washington street, east, near Dover street, parallel with Washington street between Dover street and Decatur street, opening through an arch into Washington street.

Madison square, Rox.; between Marble, Warwick, Westminster and Sterling streets; at one time called Madison park. L 659.

***Madison street,** Rox., 1868; from Washington street to Shawmut avenue, called Webster street; name changed to Madison street, April 21, 1868; laid out, July 21, 1876. L 530.

Madison street, Dor., 1840; from Norfolk street, opposite Forest Hills avenue (now Morton street), to Back (now Harvard) street (West Roxbury line), opposite Morton street; same named, March 11, 1840; new road from Lower Mills in Dorchester to Jamaica Plain laid out by County Commissioners, September, 1852, including parts of Forest Hills avenue, Madison street, and Morton street; part from Back street to Canterbury street named Morton street; name of Madison street, from Norfolk street to Back street, changed to Morton street, March 1, 1888. L 2074.

Magazine lane, Rox.; from junction Hampden street and Dudley street to Magazine street, north of St. Patrick's church; part of Magazine street, from end of present Dunmore street to Dudley street, so called after Magazine street was straightened to Dudley street; named Dunmore street, Jan. 28, 1884.

Magazine road, Rox.; Magazine street sometimes so called.

***Magazine street,** Rox., 1662; from Dudley street, opposite Blue Hill avenue and Mt. Pleasant avenue, to Swett street; Town way from Dudley street to Pine Island laid out, Jan. 19, 1662; called Magazine lane, Magazine road and Magazine street; extended from end of present Dunmore street in a straight line to Dudley street, Dec. 15, 1873, remainder of old street to Dudley street being called Magazine lane and named Dunmore street, March 1, 1884; relocated from East Chester park (now Massachusetts avenue) to Norfolk street, July 17, 1886. L 936, L 937, L 1921, L 2263.

Magdala street, Dor.; from Codman street to Van Winkle street; Bromley atlas, 1894.

Magnolia square, Dor.; from Magnolia street, north-west, near Chamblet street.

***Magnolia street,** Dor., 1882; from Dudley street to Lawrence avenue; from Dudley street to Quincy street located and accepted as Myrtle street, March 2, 1853; extended to Lawrence avenue, Sept. 16, 1876; named Magnolia street, March 1, 1882. L 1168, L 2169.

Magnolia street, W. Rox.; from Washington street opposite Burnett street, south-east.

Magnor's row, B.; boards placed at corner of lane leading from Kilby street, with name of Magnor's row upon them, removed and replaced by others bearing the former name of Lindall's lane, June 24, 1801.

Magog place, Rox.; from Albany street, north-west, near Hunneman street.

Mahan avenue, Rox.; from Hampshire street to Downing street.

Mahan place, B., 1839; from Pleasant street, east, near Eliot street.

Mahn's terrace, W. Rox.; from Amory street, north-west, near Boylston street.

Maiden lane, Rox.; from Hampden street to Reed (now Reading) street.

Main street, Rox.; the present Roxbury street so called on plan dated 1836.

***Main street,** Chsn.; from City square to Somerville line; altered and straightened from corner of Water street nearly to the Neck or Canseway, 1780; alteration of the road at the Neck and at junction of road leading to Cambridge approved, May 12, 1800; lands conveyed for purpose in 1801 and 1804; laid out on or near land when vacant by fire, Dec. 23, 1835; laid out anew from Charlestown square to southerly side of railroad, in direction of Charles River bridge, Oct. 6, 1845; from Bunker Hill street to Cambridge street accepted and laid out as a public way, Sept. 4, 1865; laid out and accepted, Dec. 31, 1867; straightened and laid out between Eden street and Mead street, July 20, 1868. L 1086, L 1787, L 1898, L 2255.

Main street, Bri.; Washington street so called on plan dated 1843.

Main-street court, Chsn.; from Main street, north-east, then north-west; name changed to Hathon square, April 24, 1878.

Maitland street, Rox.; from Beacon, south-easterly, to Brookline Branch of B. & A. R.R.

Malbon place, Rox., 1868; from Roxbury street, north, parallel with Gay street; name of Eliot place changed to Malbon place, April 21, 1868.

***Malcolm street,** B., 1891; from Chestnut street to Mt. Vernon street; Chestnut avenue laid out with name of Malcolm street, Dec. 16, 1891. L 2376.

Malcom street, W. Rox.; from Colberg avenue to Central station.

Malden court, B., 1859; from Malden street, north, near Harrison avenue.

Malden place, B., 1843; from Malden street, north, near Harrison avenue.

Malden road, Chsn.; an old name of Alford street, from Main street to Malden bridge.

***Malden street,** B., 1826; from Washington street to Albany street; laid out on the Neck, July 24, 1826; named from Washington street to Front street (now Harrison avenue), Sept. 15, 1834; to Albany street, 1854; extended from Harrison avenue to Albany street, Dec. 14, 1859. L 150.

Mall, The, B.; on the east side of the Common, about 1790; extended to the end of "Foster's pasture, lately so called," May 13, 1795.

***Mall street,** Rox., 1825; from Eustis street to Dearborn street; from Davis (now Albany) street to Eustis street, north-east of the Mall, named Mall street, May 9, 1825; line changed, July 16 and Sept. 3, 1860; line established, Nov. 27, 1865. L 1517.

Mall-street place, Rox.; from Mall street to Webber street; now Douglass avenue.

Mallett street, Chsn., 1837; from Bunker Hill street to Mystic river, near present location of Walnut street.

Malone block, } **Malone place,** } B., 1855; a block of buildings on the east side of Washington street, between Concord street and Worcester street (now Worcester square), 1855; called Malone place in 1859.

Malta street, Dor., 1896; from River street, near Hyde Park line, to Edgewater drive; authority to open given by Street Commissioners, Feb. 24, 1896.

Malvern street, Dor.; from Adams street to Milton street.

Malvern street, Bri., 1841; from North Beacon street (now Brighton avenue), to Ashford street; laid out by Selectmen, Dec. 17, 1873; accepted, conditionally, Dec. 30, 1873.

Man place, Rox.; from Yeoman street, north-easterly, between Chadwick street and Adams street; so shown in an atlas dated 1884; now Yeoman place.

Manchester street, Dor., 1895; from Cedar street, westerly.

Manning street, W. Rox.; from Gilman street to Berry street.

Manning's yard, Rox.; from No. 18 Fellows street.

Manor street, Rox.; from Farmgate street to an unnamed street leading to Reservoir, and parallel with Fisher avenue.

Mansfield place, Chsn.; from Tremont street, south-west, near Chelsea street; formerly Arlington place.

***Mansfield street,** Bri., 1882; from Cambridge street to Hill avenue (now Easton street); part of Otis street laid out, from Cambridge street to Hill avenue, with name of Mansfield street, April 17, 1882. L 1600, L 2387.

***Mansur street,** Rox.; from Day street to Schiller street; laid out, July 16, 1891. L 2315.

Mansur street, W. Rox: from Metropolitan avenue to Hyde Park line.

Maple avenue, Bri.; from Market street to Murdock street, between Elmira street and Garden street.

Maple avenue, Rox.; from Brookline avenue, westerly, then curving south-westerly, to Longwood avenue, opposite Bellevue street; part of formerly Appleton place; accepted, conditionally, June 29, 1863; Bellevue street extended over Maple avenue, from Longwood avenue to Brookline avenue, Feb. 14, 1887. L 1976, L 1977.

***Maple-avenue court,** Rox.; accepted conditionally with Bellevue street and Appleton place, June 29, 1863; conditions do not appear to have been complied with or street built (and not given in directories or on chart).

Maple park, Rox.; from Dale street, south-west, between Laurel street and Sherman street.

Maple place, B., 1837; from Harrison avenue, west, then north, to Oak street; from Harrison avenue, west, next south of Oak street, 1837.

Maple place, E. B.; from Havre street, south-east, near Porter street, to an unnamed place; same called Model place in 1884.

Maple place, W. Rox.; from Starr lane, south, crossing Seaverns avenue.

Maple place, W. Rox.; from Canterbury street, north-west; shown on a map of Roxbury dated 1849; now a part of Mount Hope avenue. L 2503.

Maple street, B., 1822; from Chestnut street to Olive (now Mount Vernon) street; name changed to Willow street in 1823.

***Maple street,** Rox.; from Seaver street to Georgia street; accepted, Oct. 24, 1864; shown from Seaver street to and across Schuyler street in 1874 atlas; laid out from Schuyler street to Georgia avenue (now street), Oct. 2, 1877. L 1269.

Maple street, Dor.; from Norfolk avenue, north-east, nearly to Willow court, crossing Clapp street and East Chester park (now Massachusetts avenue).

***Maple street,** W. Rox.; from Centre street to Weld street, shown as an unnamed street on plans dated 1851.

Maple street, W. Rox.; from South street, near Roslindale station, to Prospect (now Penfield) street; name changed to Birch street, Dec. 5, 1876.

Mapleton street, Bri.; from Market street to Murdock street; Whitney street now so called.

Maple Grove avenue, Dor.; from Bowdoin avenue to Union avenue (now Rossetor street); laid out as Bullard street, March 21, 1888. L 2059.

Marbury terrace, Rox., 1895; from Amory street to N. Y., N. H. & H. R.R.; authority to open under the name of Radcliffe terrace given by Street Commissioners, July 15, 1895; authority to change name to Marbury terrace given by Street Commissioners, Sept. 17, 1895.

Marble court, B., 1859; from Lynde street, west.

***Marble street**, Rox.; from Westminster street to Warwick street; shown but not named on plan dated 1860; laid out, Sept. 1, 1871. L 660.

***Marcella street**, Rox.; from Washington street to Centre street; shown but not named on plan dated 1845; on Charles Whitney's map of Roxbury, 1849, from Dedham turnpike to Highland street; plan dated 1860, shows contemplated continuation of Marcella street from Highland street, north, then north-west; lines of Marcella street and Highland street changed, Dec. 22, 1862; accepted, Dec. 27, 1864. L 981.

***March avenue**, W. Rox.; from Bellevue street to Park street; laid out, Nov. 2, 1876. L 1188.

***Margaret alley**, B., 1814; from Snowhill street to Margaret lane (now street); confirmed as a public street, Sept. 15, 1834; named Margaret avenue, 1837; called Cleveland place, 1846.

***Margaret avenue**, B., 1837; from Snowhill street to Margaret lane (now street); called Margaret alley, 1814–1837; named Cleveland place, 1846.

Margaret lane, B., 1733; from Prince street, north; called Margaret street, in 1796; given as Margaret Lane on Carleton's map, 1800, and in Edes' list, 1800.

***Margaret street**, B., 1796; from Prince street to Sheafe street; Margaret lane, 1733–1796; confirmed as a public street, Sept. 15, 1834. L 1539.

Marginal street, B., 1824; from South Market street to Clinton street; included in Commercial street in 1825.

Marginal street, B., 1832; including Commercial street, Sea street and part of Front street, and laid out between these to make a continuous street from north to south part of city, May, 1832; now Commercial street, Atlantic avenue, Federal street, from Summer street to Kneeland street, Kneeland street to Harrison avenue, and Harrison avenue to Northampton street.

***Marginal street**, E. B., 1833; from Lewis street to Harbor; accepted and laid out from Lewis street to Cottage street, May 10, 1852; extended south-east from Jeffries street to the water, Feb. 1, 1897. L 110, L 187, L 188, L 2812

Marie avenue, Rox.; from Lambert avenue, east, opposite Lambert street.

Marine park, So. B.; at City Point, South Boston.

Mariner place, B., 1859; from Purchase street, west, south of Belcher's lane; also shown as Mariner's place; built over.

Marion court, E. B.; from Marion street, south-west, between Havre street and Paris street; Directory gives it Marion place.

Marion court, E. B.; from Marion street, south-west, between Eutaw street and Monmouth street; same given Eutaw place in Directory, and on Bromley's atlas of East Boston dated 1892.

Marion place, E. B.; from Marion street, south-west, between London street and Havre street; so given in Bromley's atlas of East Boston, dated 1892; Directory of 1894 gives Marion court; called Appian place in 1896.

***Marion street**, B., 1825; from Pleasant street, west, to the Back Bay; from Pleasant street to Church street laid out and named, Oct. 24, 1862; name changed to Melrose street, April 20, 1869. L 387, L 395.

***Marion street**, E. B.; from Meridian street, at junction with White street, to Bremen street, with proposed extension to proposed part of Front street; from White street to Bennington street shown on plan dated 1834; to Cottage street on plan dated 1845; accepted from Chelsea street to White street, June 3, 1856; accepted from Chelsea street to Bremen street, Dec. 4, 1861; laid out. Sept. 15, 1868; extended from White street to Meridian street, Jan. 15, 1872. L 21, L 678, L 775, L 1126, L 1653.

Marion street, W. Rox.; from Florence street, north-east, to B. & P. (now N. Y., N. H. & H.) R.R.

***Marion street**, Chsn.; from Bunker Hill street to Princeton street; laid out, Oct. 27, 1851.

Mark street, Rox., 1896; from Day street, south-east; authority to open given by Street Commissioners, Nov. 11, 1896.

Market place, B., 1788; near the Town dock; called Corn Market, 1708, and Market square about 1784; a part of Faneuil Hall square in 1855.

Market place, B., 1818; from Newbury (now Washington) street, west, next north of Boylston street, 1818; Gibbon's place, 1784; now Gibbon court; called Gibbon place in Directory, 1884 and 1894.

Market place, Rox.; from Tremont street, south-east, between Vernon street and Clay (now Linden Park) street.

Market row, B., 1818; the name given to buildings between Market street and Dock square, to avoid confusion of numbers on Cornhill, Oct. 1, 1817; now Cornhill.

Market square, B., 1784; north, south, and west sides of Faneuil Hall market; changed to Faneuil Hall square in 1855. Vol. 31, p. 61.

Market street, B., 1817; from Court street to Cornhill (now Washington) street; new street from Court street to the Market, named Market street, June 11, 1817; name changed to New Cornhill, Jan. 29, 1827; same named Cornhill, May 16, 1829.

***Market street**, B., 1807; from Portland street to Canal street; laid out over the Mill-pond, Aug. 3, 1807; named in 1829; extended to Charlestown street, 1836; part across B. & M. R.R. discontinued, April 7, 1845; part of laid out as part of Haymarket square, April 21, 1845; discontinued between Canal street and Haverhill street in 1848.

***Market street**, Bri., 1840; from Washington street to Western avenue; road leading to Cambridge widened, 1826; named from "near Unitarian Meeting-house, north-east, to River street" (now Western avenue), June 15, 1840.

Marlboro' place, B., 1813; from Washington street, about opposite Bromfield street, to Hawley street; closed in 1848.

Marlboro' row, B., 1816–25; Marlboro' street, opposite Old Province House; same as Province House row.

***Marlboro' street**, B., 1856; from Washington street to Bradford street; called Washington court, 1845; accepted conditionally, and when accepted to be named Marlboro' street, Oct. 27, 1856; no record of fulfilment of conditions, but Marlboro' street accepted, Oct. 4, 1859; name changed to Acton street, Feb. 29, 1864.

Marlborough street, B. 1708; from Summer street to School street; made a part of Washington street, June 6, 1824.

***Marlborough street**, B. and Rox., 1858; from Arlington street to Ipswich street, now Charlesgate-east; from Arlington street, west, on Back Bay land, 1858; from Arlington street to Berkeley street dedicated as a public highway, Dec. 21, 1864; from Berkeley street to Dartmouth street laid out, Dec. 7, 1869; from Dartmouth street to Exeter street laid out, July 24, 1873; from Exeter street to Gloucester street laid out, Aug. 3 1874; from Gloucester street to Hereford street laid out, Feb. 19, 1876; from Hereford street to West Chester park (now Massachusetts avenue) laid out, June 13, 1879; from West Chester park to Ipswich street, Dec. 28, 1882. L 374, L 862, L 952, L 953, L 1131, L 1356, L 1683.

Marlou terrace, W. Rox.; from Lamartine street, north-west, between Green street and Bell street.

Marlowe street, Dor.; from Park street to Vinson street.

Marmion street, W. Rox.; from Cornwall street, north-east, near Brookside avenue.

***Marsh lane**, B., 1708; from Union street, east, to Creek square; the way leading from Creek lane (now square) to Mr. Webb's corner in Union street, 1708; from Odiorne's, east, to Creek lane, 1800; from Union street to Creek square, 1817.

†**Marsh street**, Dor., 1840: from junction Adams street and Granite avenue, generally easterly and south-easterly towards Neponset river; laid out previous to 1805 and called Davenport's lane; road to the landing-place by Daniel Pierce's straightened, etc., and named Marsh street, March 11, 1840.

Marshall place, B., 1846; from Charter street, south-west, next to Copp's Hill Burying-Ground.

Marshall place, Chsn.; from Walnut street, north-west.

***Marshall street**, B., 1822; from Union street, to Hanover street, called Marshall's lane, 1708; named Marshall street, April 3, 1822. Vol. 31, p. 44.

Marshall street, W. Rox.; from Spring street, near Gardner street, north.

Marshall's alley, B., 1784; from Kilby street, east; from Kilby street, east, to the water, 1800; called Bangs alley, 1803-1825; probably the alley-way next south of Doane street.

Marshall's court, Chsn.; from Bow street, east.

Marshall's lane, B., 1708; from Hanover street to Union street; named Marshall street, April 3, 1822.

***Marshfield street**, Dor., 1886; from Clifton street to Norfolk avenue; from Clifton street to Batchelder street laid out, Aug. 13, 1886; from Batchelder street, including Dolan court, to Norfolk avenue, July 5, 1890. L 1929, L 2241.

Marston avenue, Dor.; from Blue Hill avenue, at junction Warren street, east included in extension of Geneva avenue, May 26, 1880. L 1462.

Marston place, B., 1828; from Chambers street to Leverett street, with two openings into Leverett street; from Chambers street, east, 1828.

Martin street, W. Rox., 1848; from La Grange street, across Park street.

***Marvin street**, Rox., 1885; from Washington street to Shawmut avenue; laid out May 11, 1885. L 1858.

Mascoma street, Dor.; from Quincy street to Lawrence avenue.

Mascot street, Dor.; from Mountain avenue to Ballou avenue; authority to open given by Street Commissioners, July 20, 1893.

Mason court, B., 1825–29; from Elm street, north; now a private passage.

Mason court, B., 1857; from Mason street, east, later Mason place; now built over.

Mason court, Chsn.; from Sullivan street, south-east, between Bartlett street and Russell street.

Mason place, B.; from Mason street, east (called Mason-street place on chart, 1884); formerly called Mason court; now built over.

***Mason street,** B., 1809; from West street, south-west, to Avery street, then west, to Tremont street; shown on Carleton's map, 1795; from West street to Sheafe's lane (now Avery street) named, 1809; included a part of Sheafe's lane, 1834; confirmed as a public street, Sept. 15, 1834; the site of the Haymarket. Vol. 31, p. 78. L 1084.

***Mason street,** Chsn.; from Bow street to Front street. L 1622.

Mason-street place, B.; from Mason street, east; called Mason place in Directory and records; now built over.

***Massachusetts avenue,** Bri.; from Brighton avenue, at Malvern street, to Chestnut Hill avenue, opposite entrance to Chestnut Hill reservoir; laid out, Nov. 5, 1883, including Washburn street from Harvard avenue, south-westerly, towards Warren street; name changed to Commonwealth avenue, March 1, 1887. L 1742, L 1743, L 1744, L 1745.

***Massachusetts avenue,** B., Rox. and Dor., 1894; from Charles river at Harvard bridge to Cottage street, at Boston street; the names of West Chester park, Chester square, Chester park, and East Chester park, changed to Massachusetts avenue, March 1, 1894. Vol. 31, p. 1. L 98, L 261, L 303, L 452, L 502, L 516, L 805, L 805½, L 862, L 1140, L 1327, L 1328, L 1329, L 1330, L 1331, L 1352, L 1512, L 1585, L 1701, L 2133, L 2299, L 2485, L 2493, L 2546, L 2547.

Massasoit avenue, Dor.; from Talbot avenue to New England avenue; Bromley atlas, 1894.

Matchett street, Bri.; from Washington street, near Newton line, to Richards street.

Mather court, Dor.; from Dorchester avenue, west, now Mather street.

***Mather street,** Dor.; from Dorchester avenue to Allston street; called Mather court on plan dated 1854; laid out, Aug. 12, 1869. L 1201, L 1202, L 1307.

Mather street, So. B.; with part of Boston street named Dorchester street, July 3, 1855.

Mattapan street, Dor.; from Tileston and Blue Hill avenues, near Walk Hill street, north-west, to Tileston avenue again.

Mattapan street, W. Rox.; from Shawmut avenue (now Washington street) to Dorchester line; named, April 2, 1860; called Ashland street before and since.

***Matthews street,** B., 1868.; from Federal street to Congress street; called Round lane, 1732; Williams street, 1821; name changed to Matthews street, April 21, 1868. L 350, L 365, L 455. L 718, L 844.

***Maudlin street,** Chsn.; from Wapping street to Foss street; "March 2, 1767," continuation 14 feet wide from Water street to Charles river restored to original width, Nov. 28, 1831; no record of discontinuance from Foss street to the river.

***Maverick square,** E. B., 1833; from Sumner street, opposite Lewis street, to Maverick street, opposite Meridian and Chelsea streets; laid out as Hotel square, Aug. 7, 1848; no record of change of name.

***Maverick street,** E. B., 1833; from New street to Jeffries street; laid out from Orleans street to Hotel square, Aug. 7, 1848; laid out from Hotel square to New street, Dec. 16, 1850; street accepted, Nov. 22, 1852.

Maxfield street, W. Rox.; from Bellevue street to La Grange street.

***Maxwell street**, Dor.; from Nelson street to Milton avenue; laid out, June 8, 1891. L 2301, L 2302.

May place, B., 1833; from Oak street, northerly, by two exits to Nassau street.

May place, Rox.; from Ruggles street, north, between Field street and Leon street (formerly Avon place).

May place, W. Rox.; from end of May street, north-east; so called in deed.

***May street**, B., 1733; from Butolph (now Irving) street, west, to the water, 1733; by Carleton's maps, 1795 and 1800, from Hancock street to the water; leading to the powder-house, 1800; the portion from Hancock street to Butolph street called Myrtle street, 1806; from South Russell street to Charles street, 1817; laid out and continued through to Belknap (now Joy) street, June 9, 1834; confirmed as a public street, Sept. 15, 1834; discontinued as a public street, March 17, 1835; name changed to Revere street (from South Russell street to Charles river) Aug. 7, 1855.

May street, Dor.; from Glen road (now Glenway street) to Greenwood street.

***May street**, W. Rox.; from Centre street to Pond street; named, May 9, 1825; probably a public highway some time previous; shown on plan dated 1845; May's lane named May street, May 7, 1855. L 1678.

May-street court, B., 1849; from May (now Revere) street, near West Cedar street; named Revere-street court, 1858.

May-street place, B., 1844; from May (now Revere) street, near Grove street; named Revere-street place, 1857.

***Mayfair street**, Rox., 1882; from Elmore street to Bainbridge street; name of Wilmont street changed to Mayfair street, March 1, 1882. L 1470.

***Mayfield street**, Dor.; from Dorchester avenue to Bakersfield (formerly F) street; part between Dorchester avenue and Pleasant street laid out, Nov. 25, 1882; authority to open part between Pleasant street and Bakersfield street, which was then called C street, given by Street Commissioners, May 4, 1892; laid out from Pleasant street to Bakersfield street, July 23, 1895. L 1665, L 2715.

***Maynard street**, W. Rox., 1887; from Metropolitan avenue to Poplar street; laid out, Oct. 17, 1887. L 2033.

***Mayo street**, B.; from Castle street to Cobb street, near Washington street; laid out, Sept. 21, 1886. L 1948.

Mayo street, W. Rox.; from Washington street to Kittredge street.

May's court, B., 1812; from Belknap (now Joy) street, west; named Smith court, 1848.

May's lane, W. Rox.; May street, from Centre street to Pond street, so called at one time.

Maywood place, Rox.; from Maywood street, north-east, near Blue Hill avenue.

***Maywood street**, Rox.; from Warren street to Blue Hill avenue; laid out, April 9, 1875. L 1035, L 1036.

Maywood terrace, Rox.; from Maywood street, south-west, near Warren street.

McGee street, Rox.; from Norfolk avenue to Sherwood street, near Germain street.

McLean court, B., 1829; from McLean street, south-westerly, then north-westerly, south-westerly, and southerly, to Seabury place, and south-easterly, towards Chambers street, and southerly, to Eaton street; called South Allen court, 1822; McLean court (from McLean street, south), 1829.

***McLean street,** B., 1828; from Chambers street to Blossom street; called "Thirty-foot passage," 1784; from Wiltshire (now Chambers) street, westerly, Carleton's map, 1800; called South Allen street, 1806; accepted, recorded as a public street and named McLean street, Dec. 22, 1828; from Chambers street to Blossom street, 1829; confirmed as a public street, Sept. 15, 1834.

McLellan avenue, Dor.; from Blue Hill avenue, south-west, near Glen road (now Glenway street); laid out, with the name of McLellan street, from the Old road to Erie street, Dec. 29, 1892, and from Erie street to White (now Bradshaw) street, Oct. 16, 1894. L 1469.

***McLellan street,** Dor., 1892; from Blue Hill avenue, to Bradshaw street; McLellan avenue laid out, with the name of McLellan street, from the Old road to Erie street, Dec. 29, 1892, and from Erie street to White (now Bradshaw) street, Oct. 16,1894; extended by relocation, to Blue Hill avenue, Nov. 27, 1896. L 2483, L 2673, L 2799.

McLellan street, B ; from Reed street, near corner of East Lenox street, north-west.

McManus court, Chsn.; from Quincy street, north-westerly.

†**Mead street,** Chsn., 1844; from Main street to Bunker Hill street; laid out from Main street to Russell street, Aug. 4, 1851.

Mead street, Bri.; from Raymond street near Franklin street north-east.

Mead-street court, Chsn.; from Mead street, north-west, opposite Ludlow street.

***Meander street,** B.; from East Dedham street to Malden street, between Washington street and Harrison avenue; laid out by City prior to 1834; named by City in 1850; accepted, July 23, 1862. L 1704.

Mechanic court, B.; from Mechanic street.

Mechanic court, B., 1844-46; from Washington street, west, north of Winter street; closed.

Mechanic court, B., 1855; from Hawley street between Franklin street and Milk street; closed.

Mechanic court, So. B.; named on plan dated 1855.

Mechanic place, B., 1823; from Orange (now Washington) street, west, near Pleasant street; called Ohio place, 1843, and Ohio street (from Washington street to Shawmut avenue), 1872.

Mechanic place, Bri., 1856; from Mill-dam road (now North Beacon street), south-west; plan in Middlesex Reg. South District, 17 A, No. 1; part of now included in Mechanic street.

Mechanic street, B., 1825; from Hanover street to North street; called City court; from Fish (now North) street, west, in 1822; called Mechanic street in 1825.

Mechanic street, So. B.; name changed to Rogers street, Aug. 7, 1855 (Rogers street from Dorchester street to Preble street).

†**Mechanic street,** } **Mechanics street,** } Rox., 1844; from Willis street, crossing Ruggles street to Madison court; whole street shown on plan dated 1853; accepted and named, from Ruggles street to Madison court, June 27, 1864; previously called Mechanicks court or place and Mechanics street. L 939, L 2242.

Mechanic street, Rox., 1843; from Dedham and Providence turnpike (now Washington street), north-west, then north-east, to Cedar street; the first part is now part of Oakland street, and the second, part of Thornton street.

Mechanic street, Chsn.; from Putnam street to Adams street; same in 1875; laid out from Putnam street with the name of Ellwood street, Sept. 13, 1887. L 2018.

Mechanic street, Bri., 1860; from North Beacon street (now Brighton avenue), south, then east to Allston street; part of sometimes called Mechanic avenue; part of formerly called Mechanic place.

†**Mechanicks court or place**, Rox.; from Willis street, crossing Ruggles street, to Madison court; called also Mechanic and Mechanics street; accepted and named Mechanic street, from Ruggles street to Madison court, June 27, 1864.

Mechanics place, So. B.; from East Seventh street, south, between L street and M street; same given Pleasant place in Directory, 1884.

Mechanics row, B.; from Washington street, east, between Savoy (formerly South May) street and Cottage place; known as Sands place, 1859; Ottawa place, 1873; and as Temple Park, 1879.

Medfield street, Rox.; from Audubon road to St. Mary's street, formerly Monmouth street.

Medford court, B.; from Medford street, south-west, near Charlestown street; enclosed.

Medford court, B., 1844; from Washington street to Bradford street; from Washington street, west, 1844.

Medford road, Chsn., 1834; from West Cambridge road (plan in south Middlesex Reg., 349 end).

***Medford street**, B., 1807; from Charlestown street to Causeway street; laid out over the Mill-pond, Aug. 3, 1807.

***Medford street**, Chsn., 1837; from junction of Main street, and Bunker Hill street to Chelsea street; new street laid out on north-east side of Bunker Hill from the Neck to Salem turnpike (now Chelsea street), Dec. 7, 1835; laid out and named Medford street, from town way leading to Johnson's wharf to a cross street contemplated to connect with Bunker Hill street (Main street to Everett street), March 27, 1837; continued towards Salem turnpike "so far as deemed expedient for interest of Town," Nov. 25, 1844; continuation from Everett street to Tufts street laid out, April 26, 1845; continuation from Everett street to Lexington street laid out, July 21, 1848; extended from Lexington street to Chelsea street, Jan. 3, 1852. L 934.

Medford turnpike, Chsn.; from Main street to Somerville line; laid out by County Commissioners, June 26, 1807; name of so much as lies within limits of Charlestown changed to Mystic avenue, April 13, 1869.

Medford-street court, B.; from Medford street, north-east; enclosed.

***Medway street**, Dor., 1889; from Adams street to Milton Branch of N. Y., N. H. & H. R.R., Riverview avenue laid out from Adams street with the name of Medway street, Oct. 21, 1889. L 2183.

Meer's corner, B., 1708; south side of Dock square, corner of the Corn Market then so called.

Melbourne street, Dor.; from Centre street to Welles avenue.

Mellen street, Dor.; from Ocean street to Montague street; authority to open from Waldorf street to Montague street given by Street Commissioners, July 19, 1893.

Melrose place, B., 1849; from Poplar street, north-east, between Chambers street and Spring street; same called Parris place in 1845–49.

***Melrose street**, B., 1869; from Pleasant street to Ferdinand street; from Pleasant street, west to the Back Bay called Marion street, 1825; laid out from Pleasant street to Church street and named Marion street, 1862; name changed to Melrose street, April 20, 1869. L 387, L 391, L 392, L 395.

Melton road, Bri., 1895; from Wallingford road to the junction of Colonial road and Nottingham road; authority to open given by Street Commissioners, Jan. 1, 1895.

***Melville avenue,** Dor.; from Washington street to Dorchester avenue; shown from Washington street to Allston street on plan dated 1863; laid out from Washington street, and extended to Dorchester avenue, Dec. 28, 1869. L 553, L 554, L 1141, L 1142.

Melville place, B.; from Spring street, north-west, near Milton street; same in 1840.

Melynes corner, B., 1708; the northerly termination of Common (now Tremont) street.

Melzer street, W. Rox.; from Catherine street.

Mendelssohn street, W. Rox.; from Washington street to Nikisch avenue, near corner of Beech street.

Mendum street, W. Rox.; from Walter street to Fairview street; authority to open given by Street Commissioners, April 21, 1894.

***Menlo street,** Bri., 1891; from Henshaw street to Sparhawk street; laid out, Nov. 13, 1891. L 2360.

Mennig court, Rox.; from Hampshire street, south-east, near Culvert street.

Menton street, Dor., 1895; from Groveland street to Standard street; authority to open given by Street Commissioners, May 20, 1895.

***Mercantile street,** B.; from South Market street to Richmond street; from Clinton street to 90 feet north of Richmond street, 1856; street leading from Clinton street to Richmond street in rear of Mercantile wharf. Buildings named Mercantile street, July 1, 1857; portion north of Richmond street extended; discontinued, Oct. 8, 1875; extended from Clinton street to South Market street, Dec. 19, 1879. Vol. 31, p. 104. L 20, L 1042, L 1412.

Mercantile wharf, B.; from Atlantic avenue, south-east, next south of Commercial wharf. L 1001.

***Mercer street,** So. B., 1863; from Dorchester street to Jenkins street; laid out from Dorchester street to East Eighth street, Nov. 17, 1868; name of Lowland street, from East Eighth street, opposite Mercer street, to Jenkins street, changed to Mercer street, March 1, 1888. Vol. 31, p. 95. L 191, L 192.

Merchants hall, B., 1817; in Water street.

***Merchants' row,** B., 1708; from State street to North street; from King (now State) street north, to the Town Dock, 1708; from Faneuil's corner round to Woodmansie's wharf, 1732; from State street across the east end of Faneuil hall, 1784; from State street to Ann (now North) street, including part of Roebuck passage, 1825; Roe Buck passage from the Town Dock to Ann street laid out as a continuation of Merchants' row, Oct. 9, 1826; continued to Blackstone street, Dec. 8, 1834; angular piece, between estates of Moses Pond and George B. Richardson, discontinued, March 31, 1851; the portion between North Market street and North street was formerly called Swing-Bridge lane, Fish lane, and Roebuck passage.

Meridian place, E. B.; from Central square, near Meridian street, east.

***Meridian street,** E. B., 1833; from Maverick square to Meridian-street bridge north of Condor street; accepted at junction of Paris street, Aug. 12, 1836; accepted from Hotel (now Maverick) square to Paris street, Aug. 27, 1849; laid out, accepted and named from Paris street to Saratoga street, Dec. 30, 1850; same laid out and named, July 28, 1851; remaining portion not accepted (from Saratoga street to Condor street) laid out as a public highway, May 10, 1852; laid out from Condor street to low-water mark on south side of Chelsea creek, Sept. 10, 1884. Vol. 31, p. 23. L 342, L 1820.

Merlin street, Dor.; from Park street to Athelwold street.

Merlin street, W. Rox.; from Centre street to Weld street.

Merrau's alley, B., 1744; from South street, east; see deed l. 69, f. 252, Suffolk Registry.

Merriam place, Rox.; from Thornton street, south-east, near Marcella street.

Merriam street, W. Rox.; from Brookside avenue to Stony brook, near corner of Germania street.

***Merrill street**, Dor.; from Glenarm street to Erie avenue (now Erie street); from New Seaver (now Seaver) street to Erie avenue, 1874; laid out from New Seaver street to Erie avenue, August, 1881; altered, Oct. 21, 1882; name of part from angle at Glenarm street to New Seaver street changed to Glenarm street, March 1, 1883. L 1545, L 1657.

Merrimac place, B., 1857; from Merrimac street, south, near Norman street; called Paris place, 1848; named Merrimac place, 1857.

***Merrimac street**, B.; from Haymarket square to Causeway street; laid out over the Mill-pond, from Union street to Causeway street, Aug. 3, 1807; accepted in 1813. L 280.

Merry's point, B., prior to 1666 the site of the North Battery; now Battery wharf.

Merton place, Rox.; from Centre street to Newark street (formerly Eaton court).

Messenger street, B., 1856; from Chestnut street to Beacon street; called D street, 1828; named Messenger street, Jan. 5. 1856; name changed to Brimmer street, April 20, 1869. L 266.

Messinger street, Dor.; from Rockville street, north-westerly, crossing N. E. R.R., Haven avenue, Bismarck and Favre streets.

Metcalf street, W. Rox.; from Dudley avenue, north-east, crossing Houston street.

Methodist alley, B., 1796; from North (now Hanover) street to Ship (now North) street; named changed to Hanover avenue, Aug. 24, 1829.

***Metroplitan avenue**, W. Rox.; from north-west of Washington street to Hyde Park line; laid out from Shawmut avenue (now Washington street) through Hyde Park to Brush Hill road (now Blue Hill avenue), Milton, March, 1872.

Metropolitan place, B.; 1859; from Washington street, west, near Arnold street; laid out and extended to Shawmut avenue and named Woodbury street, March 29, 1882. L 1594.

Meyer street, W. Rox.; crossing Catherine (formerly Spruce) street, north and south, between Florence street and Bourne street.

***Michigan avenue**, Dor.; from Columbia street, near Blue Hill avenue, to Erie avenue (now Erie street); laid out, Dec. 15, 1875. L 1116.

Middle street, B., 1708; from the Mill bridge to Jonas Clark's corner at the end of Bennet street; from the Mill bridge to the Rev. Mr. Murray's Meeting-house, 1800; from Mill creek to North street, 1817; made a part of Hanover street, July 6, 1824.

***Middle street**, So. B.; from Dorchester street to Dorchester avenue; extended to Dorchester avenue, Dec. 17, 1861; accepted from Dorchester street to Dorchester avenue, May 23, 1865; laid out from Dorchester street to Federal street (now Dorchester avenue), Nov. 17, 1868. L 240, L 322.

Middle street, Chsn., 1810; from Bartlett street to Bunker Hill street; Oliver Holden conveys to Town for a public highway a parcel of land now used as a road called Middle street, running from Bartlett street, north-easterly, to Bunker Hill street, nearly parallel with Pleasant street, July 17, 1810; same later part made a part of School street.

Middle street, Bri., 1882; from Third street to Fifth street; now in Brighton cattle-yards, near B. & A. R.R.

Middlecot street, B., 1769; from Cambridge street, south, to Beacon Hill; laid out as a 40-foot street from Cambridge street to near the present Derne street, 1727; included in Bowdoin street, July 6, 1824.

Middlegate street, Chsn.; existed previous to 1831; name changed to Prescott street, Dec. 5, 1836.

Middlesex place, B., 1826; from Washington street, west, south of Bedford street; closed in 1845.

Middlesex place, B., 1851; from Middlesex street, near West Castle (now Castle) street; built over in 1861.

***Middlesex street,** B.; from Castle street to Dover street; from West Castle (now Castle) street to Hingham street, 1831; extended from Hingham street to Dover street, Oct. 10, 1870. L 251, L 545, L 547, L 566, L 567, L 715, L 720, L 724, L 838, L 1349.

***Middlesex street,** Chsn.; from Main street to Rutherford avenue at junction Essex street; laid out from Main street to Essex street and accepted, Dec. 21, 1857.

Middleton avenue, Dor.; from Norfolk street, north-west, near Morton street.

Midland street, So. B.; from First street, north-east; laid out over land and flats of Boston Wharf Company from First (now West First) street towards Eastern avenue (now Congress street) Dec. 17, 1855; name changed to A street, April 21, 1868.

***Midland street,** Dor., 1869; from Savin Hill avenue to Bay street; laid out, July 13, 1874. L 947.

Midway street, So. B., 1897; from Richards street to Binford street; authority to open given by Street Commissioners, Jan. 18, 1897.

Milford place, Rox., 1848; from Tremont street to Grinnell street; laid out, with name of Sarsfield street, Dec. 10, 1887. L 2046.

***Milford street,** B., 1849; from Shawmut avenue to Tremont street; laid out over the Neck, July 24, 1826, and named Lowell street, Sept. 15, 1834; called South Lowell street, 1848; named Milford street, May 15, 1849; accepted Dec. 7, 1857. L 19, L 117.

***Milk street,** B., 1708; from Washington street to India street, opposite Central wharf; called Fort street prior to 1708; from the South Meeting-house down to the sea, 1708; way staked out by Selectmen at foot of Milk street to low-water mark, agreeable to ancient order of July 1, 1673, Aug. 6, 1724; from the Old South Church eastward to the late Mr. Hallowell's ship-yard, 1800; to India street, 1804; easterly part of Milk street from Batterymarch street to the water named Commercial street, May 29, 1817; street leading from the main street (Washington street) easterly by the Old South Meeting-house to India street and called Milk and Commercial streets, named Milk street throughout, July 6, 1824; the northerly side of Milk street from Congress street to Bath street, included in Post Office square, 1874. Vol. 31, p. 46. L 375, L 842, L 843, L 853.

Milk-row road, Chsn.; voted, inexpedient to alter, April 18, 1814; Selectmen to straighten part leading from the school-house to Cambridge road, May 2, 1825.

Mill alley, B., 1733; from Leverett street to the Causeway; shown in 1722; named in 1733; called Mill street in 1788; later included in Causeway street.

Mill creek, B.; from the Harbor to the Mill-pond, nearly upon the line of the present Blackstone street.

Mill-dam, B. and Rox.; from Charles street to Sewall's point in Brookline; projected in 1813; Boston and Roxbury Mill Corporation incorporated and authorized to build same in 1814; begun in 1818;

completed and opened to travel, July 2, 1821, the road over same being called Western avenue; shown from Charles street to Side Mill road on plan dated 1832; land covered by the Mill-dam released by the Boston and Roxbury Mill Corporation to the Commonwealth by indenture of June 9, 1854, "to be forever kept open as a public highway;" parts laid out as Western avenue at different times and later (1865) all included in Beacon street. L 416, L 417.

Mill-dam road, Bri.; formerly road from Brookline to Watertown line; named Avenue street, June 15, 1840; named Beacon street, Nov. 10, 1846; North Beacon street, March 5, 1860; name of part of North Beacon street from the former boundary line of towns of Brighton and Brookline to Cambridge street at Union square changed to Brighton avenue, March 1, 1884; sometimes described as Brighton branch of the Mill-dam, Brighton road, and road to the Mill-dam.

Mill field, B.; on what is now Copp's Hill.

Mill lane, B., 1805; from Middle (now Hanover) street by Mill creek to the mills; also called Mill-pond street, 1807–12; called Pond street in 1812 or 1814; Endicott street, 1836.

Mill-pond, B.; extended from near Prince street on the east, and Salem street on the south-east to south-west of Merrimac street, to the present South Margin street.

Mill street, B., 1788; from Leverett street by Mr. Pierce's distill-house to the Causeway; called Mill alley, 1733; included in Causeway street, 1807.

Mill street, E. B.; from Sumner street to north wharf of National Dock and Warehouse Company.

***Mill street,** Dor., 1800; from Commercial (now Freeport) street to Adams street; laid out from Tileston's mill to Preston's gate, March 3, 1800; named from Commercial street by Tide mill to Lower road (now Adams street), March 11, 1840. L 1182, L 1292.

***Mill street,** Chsn.; from Essex street to Rutherford avenue; laid out as a public highway, Dec. 27, 1864.

Mill-pond street, B., 1807; from the mills near Middle street across the Mill pond to the mills near Prince street; called Mill lane from 1805; called Pond street, 1812 or 1814; Endicott street, 1836.

Mill-street court, Chsn.; from Mill street, south; shown as an unnamed passageway on plan dated 1867.

Mill-street place, Dor.: from Mill street, south-easterly, parallel with and near Neponset avenue; same called Holmes place in directories 1880 and 1884; as Holmes place, included in Houghton street, Nov. 27, 1891.

Miller park, Dor., 1897; from Dudley street, south-west, between Dennis street and Brook avenue.

Miller street, Dor.; from Washington street to Merrill street; laid out as Glenarm street, July 3, 1882. L 1631.

***Miller street,** Chsn.; from Main street to Rutherford avenue; shown but not named on plan dated 1844; accepted conditionally "as laid out" from Main street to Lawrence street, May 4, 1846; laid out from Main street to Richmond street (now Rutherford avenue), July 13, 1863.

Miller street, Chsn.; from Main street to Lawrence street; named, Sept. 2, 1844; named Johnson's avenue, March 9, 1846.

Miller's lane, B.; from Water street to Milk street, previous to 1784; called Cooper's alley, 1708; Kilby street, 1769; Adams street, 1788; and Kilby street again, 1825.

Millers lane, Dor.; from Washington street near its junction with Dorchester avenue, south-west to Baker street.

***Millet street**, Dor.; from Park street to Talbot avenue; laid out, Dec. 14, 1893. L 2571.

***Mills street**, Rox.; from Rockland street to Dale street; laid out, March 29, 1879. L 1348.

***Millmont street**, Rox., 1868; from Lambert avenue to Highland street; name of Porter street changed to Millmont street, April 21, 1868.

Milner place, B., 1844; from Washington street, east, between Bennet street and Harvard street.

***Milton avenue**, Dor.; from Lauriat avenue to Fairmount avenue; laid out from Norfolk street to Fuller street, Sept. 6, 1879; extended from Fuller street to Fairmount avenue, July 5, 1881; laid out from Norfolk street to Lauriat avenue, March 17, 1884. L 1378, L 1379, L 1537, L 1759.

Milton place, B., 1825; from Federal street, west, to Summer street, near High street.

Milton road, Dor., 1847; Blue Hill avenue so called on plan.

***Milton street**, B., 1821; from Spring street to Brighton street; opened conditionally, April 25, 1821; confirmed as a public street, Sept. 15, 1834.

Milton street, E. B., 1838; from Harmony street to Trumbull street; part for Moore street to Byron street laid out with name of Horace street, July 2, 1891. L 2307.

***Milton street**, Dor., 1850; from Adams street to Granite avenue; laid out as a town way, April 2, 1866.

Minchen's court, Dor.; from Geneva avenue, south-west, near N. E. R.R.

***Minden street**, Rox.; from Bickford street to Day street; laid out from Heath place to Bickford street (including a part of Heath place), Nov. 10, 1879; part of Heath place now from Heath place to Ulmer street named Minden street, March 1, 1882; extended to Walden street, Aug. 19, 1881; from Walden street to Day street, Nov. 9, 1885. L 1117, L 1404, L 1547, L 1895, L 2276.

***Mindoro street**, Rox.; from Prentiss street to Station street; shown but not named on plan dated 1856; laid out, Dec. 30, 1869. L 506.

†**Miner street**, B.; from Beacon street, opposite Arundel street, to Brookline avenue, on both sides of Brookline Branch R.R.; laid out from Beacon street to Brookline Branch R.R., May 15, 1893; laid out from Brookline avenue to Fairhaven street under the name of Fullerton street, Oct. 12, 1896. L 2509, L 2790.

Minnie court, So. B.; from I street, east, between East Fourth street and East Fifth street.

Minot place, Dor.; from Minot street, south, near Narragansett street.

***Minot street**, B., 1825; from Leverett street to Nashua street; called Cart lane, 1733; named Minot street from Leverett street east, 1825; confirmed as a public street, Sept. 15, 1834; to Andover street, 1844; Andover street closed in the same year. Vol. 31, p. 39. L 111.

†**Minot street**, Dor., 1805; from Neponset avenue crossing Adams street to Carruth street; located from John Minot's barn to the road leading over Neponset bridge (now Neponset avenue), May 13, 1805; from Neponset Village to Lower road (now Adams street) named, March 11, 1840; part from Adams street to Carruth street called New Minot street in Directory, 1884.

Minot's court, B.; from Union street, west, towards Hanover street, 1708; called Scott court, 1796, but given as Minot's court in Edes' list, 1800; included in extension of Friend street, 1855.

Minton street, Dor.; from Savin Hill avenue, south-west, near Dorchester avenue.

Minton street, W. Rox.; from Brookside avenue to Stony brook.

***Mishawum street**, Chsn., 1894; Ham's court, laid out from Main street to Rutherford avenue, with the name of Mishawum street, July 26, 1894; formerly called Harris court. L 2607.

Mistick road, Chsn.; from Mistick River on the north, curving slightly south-east, nearly to Monotomy road; surveyed in October, 1732.

***Mitchell street**, So. B., 1885; Dana street (formerly Watti court), laid out from West Ninth street, near Dorchester street, with the name of Mitchell street, Aug. 12, 1885. L 1877.

Model place, B., 1857; from Pleasant street, east, opposite Piedmont street.

Model place, E. B.; from Havre street, south-east, near Porter street; same called Maple place on chart, 1884.

***Monadnock street**, Dor.; from Dudley street to Bird street; laid out, Sept. 12, 1881. L 1552.

***Monks street**, So. B.; from East Seventh street to East Sixth street; laid out, July 31, 1886. L 1926.

***Monmouth square**, E. B.; at junction of Monmouth, Brooks and White streets.

Monmouth street, Rox.; from Audubon road to St. Mary's street; now Medfield street.

***Monmouth street**, E. B., 1834; from Meridian street to White street, near Brooks street; accepted and laid out, July 19, 1852; altered at junction of Monmouth and White streets, Sept. 29, 1856; accepted at junction of Monmouth and White streets, Nov. 1, 1858. L 78.

Monotomy road, Chsn.; committee appointed to ascertain width of, Oct. 5, 1829; surveyed in 1732. See Lib. 33, f. 497, Middlesex South Dist. Reg.

Monroe street, Rox.; from Warren street to Walnut avenue; Munroe street, sometimes so called.

Monroe street, So. B.; named changed to Richards street, April 21, 1868 (Richards street, from Granite street to A street). L 255.

***Monson street**, Dor., 1890; Temple place, leading from Temple street, laid out with the name of Monson street, March 21, 1890. L 2212.

Montague street, Dor., 1893; from Roslin street to Ashmont street; authority to open given by Street Commissioners, July 19, 1893.

***Montana street**, Rox.; from Georgia street to Cheney street; laid out, April 24, 1889. L 2122.

Montclair avenue, W. Rox.; from Centre street, near South street, to Merlin street.

Montebello road, W. Rox., 1895; from Washington street to Walnut avenue; authority to open given by Street Commissioners, Sept. 19, 1895.

***Montello street**, Dor., 1894; Grace avenue laid out from Robinson street to Arcadia street, with name of Montello street, Nov. 16, 1894. L 2671.

Montello street, W. Rox.; from Colberg avenue to beyond Belgrade avenue.

Montgomery park, B.; from Montgomery street, between Montgomery street, Tremont street, Dartmouth street, and West Canton street.

Montgomery place, B., 1825; from Tremont street, east, to Governor's alley (now Province street); laid out from Tremont street to

Chapman place extended, and named Bosworth street, May 14, 1883; remainder of street to Province street not included in order for laying out. L 1703.

Montgomery square, B.; junction of Tremont, Clarendon and Montgomery streets; named in list of 1879, without date. L 206, L 354.

***Montgomery street,** B.; from Tremont street to West Canton street; from Tremont street, opposite Waltham street, to the extension of Dedham (now Dartmouth) street, 1860: called Avenue K on plan of Back Bay lands, 1860; laid out as a public street from Tremont street to Clarendon street, Oct. 16, 1867; laid out from Clarendon street to West Canton street, Nov. 17, 1868. L 206, L 354.

Montgomery street, B., 1833; from School street to Bromfield street; called Governor's alley, 1732; named Montgomery street, 1833; named Province street, 1834.

Montgomery street, W. Rox.; from Spring street, near Baker street, to Linden street.

Montmorenci avenue, Breeds Island; from Orient avenue, north-east, then south-east to Orient avenue again.

Montrose avenue, Rox.; from Warren street, east; included in Montrose street, Nov. 23, 1883. L 1739.

***Montrose street,** Rox.; from Warren street to Moreland str eet; laid out in part over private way called Montrose avenue, Nov. 23, 1883. L 1739.

***Montview street,** W. Rox., 1893; Carl street laid out from Corey street to Mt. Vernon street, with name of Montview street, Nov. 17, 1893; part of at one time known as Walnut avenue. L 2548.

***Monument avenue,** Chsn.; from Main street to Monument square; shown as an unnamed street on plan dated 1834; laid out from Warren street to High street, Aug. 23, 1852; named, Oct. 11, 1852; extended and laid out from Warren street to Main street, Nov. 19, 1866; formerly called High street, 1835; Suffolk Deeds Lib. 1399, f. 139; L 1457 f. 39; and Middlesex Deeds Lib. 338, f. 173.

Monument court, So. B.; from H street, between East Sixth street and East Seventh street.

***Monument court,** Chsn.; from Winthrop street, south-west, opposite Wallace court; laid out and accepted, Sept. 30, 1867.

Monument lane, Chsn.; from Bunker Hill street, south-west, between Concord street and Monument street to Concord avenue, 1885.

Monument lane, Chsn.; from Monument street to Lexington street, now a part of Concord avenue.

Monument place, Chsn.; from Monument street, east, near Bunker Hill street; also called Riordan place.

Monument square, W. Rox.; junction of Centre and South streets, at Jamaica Plain.

***Monument square,** Chsn., 1860; around Bunker Hill Monument grounds; shown but not named on plan dated 1839; streets around Monument square accepted, Dec. 11, 1843; names of Lexington street, from Wallace court to Tremont street, Tremont street to Concord street, Concord street to High street, High street to Monument court, changed to Monument square, Feb. 2, 1860.

Monument street, W. Rox.; from Centre street, north-westerly, then north-easterly to Eliot street; laid out as Holbrook street, May 21, 1877. L 1238.

***Monument street,** Chsn.; from Monument square to Medford street; laid out from Monument square to Bunker Hill street, Dec. 21, 1844; same accepted, Dec. 23, 1844; extended to Medford street, Nov. 10, 1868. L 1899.

Moon court, B., 1796; in Moon street.

***Moon street**, B., 1708; from North square to Fleet street; from the North Meeting-house, north, by the east side of Clarke (now North) square, to Sun-court street, 1708; to Fleet street, including part of Sun-court street, 1784; from the east side of North square to Fleet street, 1800. L 411.

Moon-street court, B., 1833; from Moon street, south-easterly; included in extension of Lewis street, from North street to Moon street, March 25, 1893.

Moorcock's buildings, B., 1708; in Corn court.

Moore place, B., 1840; from Church street, east, next south of Madison place; named Church place, 1844.

†**Moore street**, E. B., 1838; from Pope street to Cowper street, with proposed extension to proposed extension of Coleridge street; accepted from Pope street to Saratoga street, Dec. 10, 1861; extended from Saratoga street to Cowper street, July 25, 1881. L 1543.

Moore street, Bri.; from Washington street to Newton line; shown on plan of Brighton dated 1873; in 1875, by a change in boundary line, brought within the limits of Newton.

Mora street, Dor., 1894; from Washington street to Milton avenue; authority to open given by Street Commissioners, June 22, 1894.

Moreland place, W. Rox.; from Pond street, northerly, to ice-house, Jamaica pond; included in Jamaica park.

†**Moreland street**, Rox. and Dor., 1854; from Warren street to and across Blue Hill avenue and Dennis street; part from Cleveland street across end of Fairland street, shown and so named on plan dated 1854; part from Grove Hall (now Blue Hill) avenue, north-west, shown as part of Perrin street on plan dated 1856; laid out as a new street from Grove Hall avenue to Warren street, in part over Warren place, December, 1860; laid out from Blue Hill avenue to Dennis street, Aug. 28, 1891. L 2330.

Moreland street, W. Rox.; from Spring street to Belle avenue.

Moreland terrace, Rox.; from Blue Hill avenue, south-east, included in the extension of Moreland street to Dennis street, Aug. 28, 1891.

Morey's corner, B., 1708; corner of Summer street and Cow lane (now High street) then so called.

Morgan street, B., 1865; from Columbus avenue, north-westerly, to Stanhope street.

***Morley street**, Rox.; from Highland street; Walden park laid out from Highland avenue (now Highland street), with name of Morley street, Sept. 23, 1887. L 2027.

Morlock place, Rox.; from Longwood avenue, southerly, near Phillips street.

Morni court, So. B., 1849; from West Ninth street, near Dorchester street, south-westerly, to O. C. (now N. Y., N. H. & H.) R.R.; laid out as Gustin street, Oct. 13, 1891.

Morrill street, Dor., 1892; from Pleasant street to Bakersfield (formerly F) street; also called B street; authority to open given by Street Commissioners, May 4, 1892.

Morrill's or **Morrell's corner**, B., 1708; corner of Middle (now Hanover) street and Prince street, then so called.

***Morris street**, E. B.; from Marion street to Putnam street; laid out from Marion street to Putnam street, between Chelsea street and Paris street, July 10, 1883. L 1717.

***Morrison street**, W. Rox., 1881; from Gardner street, south-westerly, towards Charles river; private way called Grove street laid out as Morrison street, Nov. 11, 1881. L 1567.

Morse street, Dor.; from Washington street to Bowdoin avenue; authority to open given by Street Commissioners, Dec. 7, 1891; laid out June 2, 1896. L 2772.

Morton court, B., 1842; from the foot of Morton place; from Arch street to Hawley street, 1879; included in Hawley place.

Morton place, B., 1824; from Milk street, south, 1824; included in extension of Arch street, April 18, 1873. L 841.

Morton place, Rox.; from Tremont street, south, between Parker street and Terrace street.

***Morton street**, B., 1838; from Salem street to Endicott street; called Ritchie street, 1840–1844; since again called Morton street; accepted conditionally, Nov. 18, 1844; accepted finally, Oct. 25, 1847.

***Morton street**, W. Rox. and Dor.; from South street to River street; from Forest Hills street to South street previous to 1832; laid out, conditionally from Forest Hills avenue to Canterbury street, Oct. 7, 1850; street connecting Scarboro' street with Canterbury street, called Morton street, June 14, 1851; laid out by abutters over the "great fresh meadow" from Back (now Harvard) street, nearly to Canterbury street in 1853; street formerly known as Forest Hills street and Scarboro' street, called Morton street, Dec. 5, 1859; names of Madison street and Forest Hills avenue, from Back street to River street, changed to Morton street, March 1, 1888. L 823, L 1667, L 2074, L 2075.

Morton street, Chsn.; south-east end laid out 50 feet wide from Salem turnpike (now Chelsea street) to Bunker Hill street, Dec. 15, 1834; this part of Morton street, named Bunker Hill street, being a continuation of same, to avoid confusion, there being in that vicinity a street named Moulton street, Dec. 15, 1834.

Morton street, Chsn.; Moulton street, from Bunker Hill street to Vine street, sometimes so called, and so shown on plan dated 1828.

Moseley avenue, Dor.; from Crescent avenue to Mt. Vernon street; shown as an unnamed street on plan dated 1860; north-easterly end included in Dorchesterway.

Moss place, B., 1868; from Cambridge street, northerly, opposite Bowdoin street.

†**Moss Hill road**, W. Rox.; from junction of Pond and May streets, south, west, and north, to Pond street again, at latter's junction with Woodland road; authority to open part from junction Pond and May streets to easterly end of Woodland road given by Street Commissioners, June 20, 1892; same part laid out as a public street, Oct. 12, 1894. L 2636.

***Motte street**, B., 1874; from Washington street, opposite Castle street, to Harrison avenue; from Orange (now Washington) street, east, to the water; called East Castle street, 1732; to Front street (now Harrison avenue), 1805; name changed to Motte street, June 23, 1874; became public by use. L 434.

Moulton court, Chsn.; from Moulton street, near Bainbridge street, westerly, then northerly and southerly, parallel with Moulton street.

***Moulton street**, Chsn.; from Bunker Hill street to Mystic river; accepted and named from the river to head of Ropewalk, June 9, 1826; this street has been called by three different names, and estates purporting to bound on the same have been conveyed as bounding on Brooks, Morton, and Moulton streets, that section of the town formerly called Moulton's point being owned by a person of that name; part from Bunker Hill street to Vine street shown as Morton street on plan dated 1828; part shown on Moulton point as Brooks street on plan dated 1846; from Bainbridge street, north-easterly, being formerly Brooks street, by plan dated 1868; laid out and altered, Jan. 2, 1849. L 1986, L 2591, L 2738.

Moultrie avenue, Dor.; from Seaborn street to Church place; authority to open, with name of Moultrie street, given by Street Commissioners, Dec. 1, 1891.

Moultrie street, Dor.; north of and parallel with Centre street, near Washington street, crossing Seaborn street east and west; authority to open given by Street Commissioners, Dec. 1, 1891.

Mountain avenue, Dor.; from Ballou avenue to Lauriat avenue.

Mountain street, W. Rox., 1849; from Dedham turnpike (now Washington street) to Walk Hill street; see Charles Whitney's map of Roxbury, 1843–49; probably part from Walk Hill street changed to Walk Hill avenue and later to Wachusett street; the part from Washington street probably now called Weld Hill street.

***Mountfort street**, Rox.; from Beacon street to Brookline line; laid out from Beacon street to Ivy street, March 11, 1891; from Ivy street to Audubon road, June 12, 1894. L 2282, L 2604.

Mountfort's corner, B., 1708; corner of Dock square and Pierce's alley (now Change avenue) then so called.

Mountfort's corner, B., 1732; corner of Fish (now North) street and Moon street then so called.

Mountjoy's corner, B., 1708; corner of Fish (now North) street and Ann street (now part of same street) then so called.

Mt. Bowdoin avenue, Dor.; from Bowdoin street to Columbia street (Directory, 1880); now called Bowdoin avenue.

Mt. Bowdoin green, Dor.; on Bowdoin avenue. L 1781.

Mt. Bowdoin terrace, Dor.; from Eldon street, easterly, near Rosseter street.

***Mt. Everett street**, Dor.; from Hamilton avenue (now Barrington street) to Quincy street; laid out, Dec. 8, 1876. L 1200.

Mt. Hope avenue, Dor.; from Blue Hill avenue, north-west, near Mattapan station, N. E. R.R.; called Almont street in 1896.

Mt. Hope avenue, W. Rox.; from Hyde Park avenue to Canterbury street; Mt. Hope street often so called.

Mt. Hope street, Dor.; from Blue Hill avenue to Hyde Park line; name of Back street changed to Mt. Hope street, Sept. 18, 1861; afterwards Back street again.

***Mt. Hope street**, W. Rox.; from Hyde Park avenue to Mt. Hope cemetery; old way, part of which was called Bradstreet avenue and part Mt. Hope avenue or street, laid out as Mt. Hope street, June 13, 1871; extended from Canterbury street, through Weber street to Mt. Hope cemetery, July 22, 1892. L 1892, L 2417.

Mt. Ida street, Dor.; from Bowdoin street, near Adams street; not on chart, 1884; on chart, 1874, "Mt. Ida" given on land of Nahum Capen, but no street; same on chart, 1894, but street given in directory of that year.

***Mt. Pleasant avenue**, Rox.; from Dudley street (part formerly Eustis street), opposite Dearborn street, south-westerly, then south-easterly, then north-easterly, to Dudley street, opposite Magazine street; called Elm avenue on plan dated 1833, but generally Elm street; name of Elm street changed to Mt. Pleasant avenue, April 21, 1868.

Mt. Pleasant place, Rox.; from Dudley street, south-west, near Adams street.

Mt. Prospect street, Rox.; from Norfolk and Bristol turnpike (now Washington street), south-east; shown on plan of laying out of said turnpike dated 1857, Vol. 3, No. 279, Norfolk County Commissioners.

Mt. Seaver avenue, Rox.; from Elm Hill avenue to Blue Hill avenue; from Elm Hill avenue to Montana street, laid out as Cheney street,

June 26, 1882; remainder to Blue Hill avenue laid out as Cheney street, April 11, 1883. L 1617, L 1697.

Mt. Vernon, B., 1796; north of Beacon street and west of Belknap (now Joy) street; the buildings on the north side of Olive (now Mt. Vernon) street, 1805–1817.

Mt. Vernon avenue, B., 1846; from Mt. Vernon street to Pinckney street; called Pinckney lane, 1835; named Mt. Vernon avenue, 1846.

Mt. Vernon avenue, Rox.; from end of Roxbury place south; being continued to Warren place by an irregular 20-foot passageway; later made a part of Kearsarge avenue.

***Mt. Vernon avenue**, Chsn.; from Mt. Vernon street to Chestnut street.

Mt. Vernon avenue, Bri.; from Mt. Vernon street, south, then east to Rockland st.

***Mt. Vernon place**, B.; from Joy street to Hancock avenue; called Hancock place, 1823; named Mt. Vernon place, Jan. 28, 1828.

***Mt. Vernon place**, Rox.; from Warren place (now Winthrop street), north, then north-west, then north again to Warren street; accepted and named Mt. Warren place, Oct. 30, 1865; name of Mt. Warren place changed to Kearsarge avenue, April 21, 1868.

Mt. Vernon place, Chsn.; from Chelsea street, south, near the Navy Yard.

***Mt. Vernon street**, B., 1832; from Beacon street, north, then west to Charles river; from Beacon street to the head of former Temple street called Centry or Sentry street, 1708–95; from the present Hancock street to the present Joy street called George street, 1732–1800; from Beacon street to Joy street called Sumner street, 1795–1833; from Joy street to Charles street, called Olive street, 1796–1825; from Charles street to Temple street called Sumner street, July 6, 1824; Sumner street from Beacon street to Charles street named Mt. Vernon street, Aug. 27, 1832; confirmed as a public street, Sept. 15, 1834; extended west, across Charles street to River street, 1856; portion west of Charles street accepted, Aug. 19, 1856; extended from River street to Harbor Commissioners' line, April 6, 1866. L 297, L 1505, L 2105.

†**Mt. Vernon street**, Dor., 1860; from Boston street to Pumping Station, near Dorchester bay; laid out from Boston street to Dorchester avenue, Nov. 27, 1875; laid out from Dorchester avenue to O. C. (now N. Y., N. H. & H.) R.R., July 13, 1878. L 1096, L 1312.

***Mt. Vernon street**, W. Rox., 1849; from Centre street to Baker street; accepted, Sept. 27, 1871; extended from La Grange street to Baker street, Sept. 8, 1873.

Mt. Vernon street, W. Rox.; from Ashland street, opposite Albion street, to Roslin avenue; part from Poplar street to Roslin avenue shown as unnamed street on several plans, the earliest being dated 1852; same given as part of Sycamore street, 1884.

***Mt. Vernon street**, Chsn.; from Adams street, about northerly, nearly to Tremont street; see plan dated 1846; laid out and accepted, Jan. 2, 1849.

***Mt. Vernon street**, Bri.; from Rockland street to Foster street; part of laid out in continuation of Mt. Vernon street to road leading from Rockland street to Academy Hill, March 29, 1851; same accepted, Sept. 5, 1853; street named, Sept. 5, 1853; laid out, Dec. 16, 1873; extension to Foster street laid out, April 22, 1891. L 2286.

Mt. Walley avenue, W. Rox.; from Pond street to Brookline line.

Mt. Warren avenue, Rox.; from Warren street; formerly called Mt. Warren place; called Mt. Warren avenue, Oct. 30, 1865; extended to Moreland street and called Copeland street, June 15, 1869.

Mt. Warren place, Rox.; from Walnut avenue, northerly, near Warren street; same called Mt. Warren street in directories.

Mt. Warren place, Rox.; from Warren street called Mt. Warren avenue, Oct. 30, 1865; extended to Moreland street and called Copeland street, June 15, 1869.

***Mt. Warren place**, Rox.; from Warren place (now Winthrop street), north, then north-west, then north again to Warren street; Mt. Vernon place accepted and named Mt. Warren place, Oct. 30, 1865; name of Mt. Warren place changed to Kearsarge avenue, April 21, 1868.

Mt. Warren street, Rox.; from Walnut avenue, northerly, near Warren street; same as Mt. Warren place.

***Mt. Washington avenue**, B. and So. B.; from Federal street across Fort Point Channel to Granite street; accepted, conditionally, from Sea (now Federal) street across Fort Point Channel to Boston wharf, March 26, 1855; laid out from south-east side of Granite street to harbor line on east side Fort Point Channel, Nov. 17, 1868. L 537.

***Mt. Washington bridge**, B.; across Fort Point Channel; accepted, conditionally, with Mt. Washington avenue, March 26, 1855.

Mt. Washington place, So. B.; from East Eighth street, southerly, near G street.

Moylen street, Rox.; from Elm Hill avenue to Landseer avenue, parallel with and 210 feet north-east from Crawford street; shown on plan dated June 1, 1881; abandoned.

Mozart avenue, W. Rox., 1873; from Walter street, north-west, to Selwyn street; called Mozart street on city plan, 1891.

***Mozart street**, Rox., 1887; from Centre street to Lamartine street; laid out from Centre street, including Houghton place, to Chestnut avenue, May 19, 1887; from Chestnut avenue to Lamartine street, including Raymond street, Aug. 31, 1888. L 1988, L 2089.

Mulberry place, B., 1834; from Portland street, north-east, near Sudbury street.

Mulberry place. Rox., 1861; from Dudley street (part formerly Eustis street), south-west near Vine street.

Mulgrave street, Rox.; from Elm Hill avenue to Landseer avenue; shown on plan dated June 1, 1881; abandoned.

Mullaney street, Dor.; from Clarkson street to Barry street; now called Barry street.

Mulvey avenue, Rox.; from Heath street, south, near Bickford street.

Munroe place, B., 1857; in rear of 38 Tyler street, near Kneeland street; called Blanche court, 1844; named Munroe place, 1857.

Munroe place, Rox.; from Vernon street, south-west, between Washington street and Shawmut avenue.

***Munroe street**, Rox., 1852; from Warren street to Walnut avenue, opposite Elmore street; Munroe farm laid out into lots, and streets laid out in 1852; written also Monroe. L 799, L 800, L 801, L 2274, L 2501.

Munroe terrace, Dor.; from Neponset avenue to Train street.

Munson street, Rox.; from Beacon street to Brookline Branch railroad.

Murdock place, Bri.; from Murdock street.

***Murdock street**, Bri.; from Cambridge street to North Beacon street; shown on plan dated 1868, from Cambridge street to Sparhawk street, but not named; laid out from Cambridge street to North Beacon street, Nov. 3, 1888. L 2100, L 2101.

Murphy court, B., 1834; from North street to Commercial street, near their junction.

Murray avenue, Rox.; from Blue Hill avenue, opposite Dennis street, west; named, Oct. 1, 1878.

Murray court, E. B.; from Orleans street, between Webster street and Sumner street, south-easterly; spoken of as a private way in 1864.

Murray place, B., 1830; from Prince street, north-easterly, near Salem street; discontinued now in school-yard.

Music-hall place, B., 1874; from Winter street, north-east; called Central place, 1842; name changed to Music-hall place, Feb. 25, 1874.

Muzzy street, Dor., 1895; from Adams street at its junction with Centre street to King street.

The Mylne street, B.; an early name for Summer street previous to 1708.

Myrtle court, B., 1822; from West Centre (now Anderson) street, opposite the west end of Myrtle street; extended to Grove place and named Myrtle street, Sept. 15, 1851; accepted, laid out and named Myrtle street, Oct. 13, 1851. Vol. 31, p. 15.

Myrtle place, Rox.; from Glenwood street, west.

Myrtle place, Dor.; from Magnolia street, north-westerly.

Myrtle place, W. Rox.; from Stony Brook avenue (now Florence street), south-easterly; see Charles Whitney's map of Roxbury, 1843–49; no street now given.

***Myrtle street**, B., 1806; from Hancock street, west, then north, to Revere street; called Warren street (from Hancock street, southerly by Mr. Austin's ropewalk, and by the powder-house down to Cambridge bay), 1788; May street, leading to the powder-house, 1795; Myrtle street, from Hancock street to Butolph (now Irving) street, 1806; from Hancock street to West Centre (now Anderson) street, 1814; on Hale's plan, 1814, the westerly end of the present Myrtle street, was called Hill street; from Hancock street to Charles street 1817; confirmed as a public street, Sept. 15, 1834; extended through Myrtle court to Zone street, at Grove street and place, Sept. 15, 1851; Myrtle court accepted, laid out and called Myrtle street, Oct. 13, 1851; Zone street (from Grove street to rear of West Cedar street) named Myrtle street, Oct. 20, 1851; new street laid out from May (now Revere) street to Myrtle street, Dec. 19, 1853, and named Myrtle street, Dec. 29, 1853. Vol. 31, pp. 15, 99. L 1859.

Myrtle street, Rox.; from Warren street to Cliff street; name changed to Glenwood street, April 21, 1868 (formerly Adams street).

Myrtle street, Dor., 1840; from Five Corners (now Town Meeting square) to Pleasant street; street from Five Corners by Mr. Cassel's and Mr. Kettle's, named Myrtle street, March 11, 1840; name changed to Cottage street, March 1, 1847.

***Myrtle street**, Dor.; from Dudley street to Lawrence avenue; shown as Harris street on plan dated 1846; and on plans dated 1846, 1847, 1859, and 1860, as "Myrtle street, formerly Harrison street;" Harrison street, on plan dated 1847; Myrtle street, formerly Harrison street, on plan dated 1869; from Dudley street to Quincy street, located and accepted, March 2, 1853; laid out from Quincy street to Lawrence avenue, Sept. 16, 1876; name changed to Magnolia street, March 1, 1882. L 1168.

***Myrtle street**, W. Rox.; from Centre street (part formerly Austin street) opposite Green street, to Pond street; laid out, Sept. 2, 1876. L 1166.

***Mystic avenue**, Chsn.; from Main street to Somerville line; name of Medford turnpike changed to Mystic avenue, April 12, 1869.

Mystic place, Chsn.; from Cook street, north-west, near Hill street.

Mystic place, Chsn.; from Walnut street, north-west, near Medford street.

Mystic road, Chsn.; see Mistick road.

***Mystic street**, B., 1845; from Malden street to East Brookline street; called Berlin street (from East Canton street to Hamburg street), 1843; Mystic street, from East Dedham street to Brookline street, 1845; from Malden street to Brookline street, 1846; passageway between Washington street and Harrison avenue laid out by City prior to 1834, and named Mystic street in 1850; accepted, July 23, 1862.

***Mystic street**, Chsn.; from Bunker Hill street to Medford street; not named on plan dated 1848.

***N street**, So. B.; from East Second street to Strandway, formerly to Old Harbor south of East Ninth street, with proposed extension northerly to East First street; laid out and named "from salt water on the south to the Harbor of Boston on the north," Feb. 27, 1805; laid out from low-water mark north of East First street to harbor line in Dorchester bay, Nov. 17, 1868; House of Correction covers land north of East First street to water. L 7.

Nanney's buildings, B., 1708; in Elbow alley.

Nantasket avenue, Bri.; from Union street, near Madison avenue, north-east.

Napier place, B.; from Barton street, east; called Second-street court or place, 1835; Napier-street place 1855; Napier place, 1868; called Barton-street place on atlas, and Napier place in directories; greater part included in the extension of Chambers street, June 7, 1893. L 2765.

***Napier street**, B., 1855; from Leverett street to Copper (now Brighton) street; name of Second street changed to Napier street, April 25, 1855; from Leverett street through Short Second street (from Second street to Brighton street), to Brighton street, 1855; extended to Milton street, Oct. 5, 1863; name changed to Barton street, April 21, 1868. L 268.

Napier-street place, B., 1855; from Napier street, east; called Second-street court or place 1835; Napier street place, 1855; Napier place, 1868; called Barton-street place on atlas, and Napier place in directories; greater part included in the extension of Chambers street, June 7, 1893. L 2765.

Naples road, Bri.; from Commonwealth avenue near Malvern street south-west to Brookline line.

***Narragansett street**, Dor.; from Chickatawbut street to Minot street, located, May 2, 1853.

Naseby street, Rox.; from Crawford street to Hutchings street; laid out with name of Harold street from Crawford street to Homestead street, March 10, 1886; Harold street extended to Hutchings street, April 20, 1888. L 1901.

Nash court, So. B.; from West First street to Dove street, near Dorchester street.

Nash row, Chsn.; from 184 Main street, between Chapman street and Austin street.

Nashua court, B., 1844; from Nashua street, north, near Minot street; closed in 1871.

Nashua place, B., 1844; from Nashua street, north, near Causeway street; closed in 1871.

***Nashua street**, B., 1837; from Causeway street, north-westerly, to Minot street; accepted, May 12, 1851. Vol. 31, p. 39.

Nason place, Rox.; from 33 Conant street, northerly, between Phillips street and Parker street.

Nason place, Chsn.; from 7 Everett street, south-east, near Bunker Hill street.

Nason's court, B., 1833; from Pleasant street, west, at or near Hamlen place or Berlin (now Tennyson) street.

Nassau court, B., 1825; from Tremont street, west, nearly opposite Hollis street, 1825; named Seaver place, 1844.

Nassau place, B., 1859; from Nassau street, near Harrison avenue, northerly, to Corey avenue.

***Nassau street,** B.; from Harrison avenue to Ash street; shown by plan as early as 1816, but not named; on Hale's plan, 1820; called Ash street; accepted, conditionally, May 1, 1843; laid out March 1, 1875. L 1025.

Nassau street, B.; Clough street (from Orange [now Washington] street to Dr. Byle's house), and Holyoke street (from Dr. Byle's house to Frog lane, now Boylston street) called Nassau street, 1788; same called Common street, 1824; part from Orange street to Dr. Byle's house now called Common street, and part from Dr. Byle's house to Frog lane called Tremont street.

Nathan street, W. Rox., 1896; from Patten street to Eldridge road; authority to open given by Street Commissioners, Aug. 5, 1896.

***National street,** So. B.; from East Fourth street to Thomas park; laid out, Nov. 17, 1868. L 445.

Navy street, Chsn.; from Pear Tree street, south-east; these streets do not now exist, but are shown on plan near the present location of Bunker Hill street and Ferrin street.

Nawn court, Rox.; from King street, near Elmwood street, north-easterly.

Nawn place, Rox.; from Harrison avenue, north, near Nawn street.

Nawn street, Rox.; from Washington street to Harrison avenue, near Webber street.

Nazing street, Rox., 1896; from Blue Hill avenue to Maple street, between Wayne street and Seaver street; authority to open given by Street Commissioners, Feb. 24, 1896; formerly called Gallatin street.

Neal / **Neal's** } **court,** Chsn.; from Short street, south-easterly.

Nebraska street, W. Rox.; from Green street to Boylston street; on plan dated 1852, shown as Chestnut street and by that name accepted by Town, July 25, 1868; later a part of Chestnut avenue.

Neck alley, B.; mentioned in deeds, Sept. 6, 1755; no description or record.

***Nelson street,** Dor.; from Norfolk street to Selden street; laid out, June 18, 1885. L 1863.

Nelson street, W. Rox.; from Boylston street to Spring Park avenue.

***Neponset avenue,** Dor.; from Adams street to Neponset river; called Quincy turnpike on plan dated 1844, and Neponset turnpike on plan dated 1856; laid out as a public highway or control assumed by County, December, 1858. L 1063, L 1182, L 1785, L 1834.

***Neponset avenue,** W. Rox.; from Hyde Park avenue to Canterbury street; laid out by Selectmen, Sept. 27, 1871.

Neponset court, W. Rox.; from Neponset avenue, near Jewett street.

Neponset street, Dor.; from Freeport street to South street (Commercial Point); shown on plan dated 1810, from South street, north-west, crossing Plymouth, Washington, Union, Commercial, Barque Warwick, and Mill streets; same in 1835 and 1848.

***Neponset street,** Dor.; from River street to Sanford street; accepted March 3, 1845; shown on plan of new road from Lower Mills to

Jamaica Plain in 1852; later made part of Forest Hill avenue, and latter name changed to Morton street, March 1, 1888.

Neponset turnpike, Dor.; Neponset avenue so called on plan dated 1856.

Neptune avenue, } E. B.; from Bennington street to Wood Island park;
Neptune street, } now included in the Parkway.

Neva street, Dor.; from Preston street, opposite Capen street, to Tenean creek.

New lane, Rox.; part of Warren street, from Washington street to Dudley street, so called when laid out.

New road, W. Rox.; part of Centre street, from South street to Walter street, so called on plan in 1815; also part from Green street to Dedham turnpike, on plan in 1854.

***New street**, E. B.; from Sumner street to Maverick street; accepted, Nov. 22, 1852.

New street, Rox. and W. Rox.; several streets so called on plans when first laid out.

New street, Dor.; from Adams street to Commercial (now Freeport) street; Leeds street so called on plans dated 1861, 1864, and 1866.

New street, W. Rox.; part of Boylston avenue so called on plans dated 1858 and 1868.

New street, Chsn.; a street parallel with School-House court, leading from Charles street; so called on plan dated 1850.

***Newark street**, Rox., 1892; from Cedar street, south; Eaton court laid out with name of Newark street, July 22, 1892. L 2416.

***New Atherton street**, Rox.; from Amory street to Copley street; laid out, Aug. 27, 1886; name changed to Atherton street, March 1, 1889. L 1942.

New Way, Bri.; laid out from junction of Howard place and Union street to junction of Beacon street and Rockland street (now Chestnut Hill avenue), July 8, 1872 (no street shown on chart or map from junction Howard place and Union street to either Beacon street or Rockland street).

New Atlantic street, So. B.; from 374 East Eighth street; that part of Atlantic street south of Thomas park sometimes so called.

Newbern avenue, W. Rox.; from Roanoke avenue, southerly; now part of Newbern street.

Newbern court, Rox.; from 156 Sterling street, westerly.

Newbern, } **place**, B., 1834; from Carver street, between Eliot street
Newbern, } and Pleasant street, westerly, and then northerly and southerly.

***Newbern street**, Rox., 1868; from Sterling street to Weston street; formerly from Tremont street, south-east, then south-west, to Weston street; accepted, conditionally, as Oxford street, March 11, 1844; named Newbern street, April 21, 1868; part near Tremont street named Sterling street, March 1, 1884. L 926.

***Newbern street**, W. Rox.; from Carolina avenue to Elm street; shown but not named on plan dated 1850; named on plan dated 1867; laid out, Nov. 22, 1875. L 1095.

Newbern street, W. Rox.; from junction Canterbury street and Huntington avenue to Hyde Park line; from Canterbury street to Largo street on plan dated 1848; same given Newbern avenue 1884 and then Newbern street.

Newburg street, W. Rox., 1891; from Beech street to Brandon street: authority to open given by Street Commissioners, Dec. 1, 1891.

Newbury place, B., 1805; from Newbury (now Washington) street, east, next north of Essex street; built over by the Globe Theatre in 1866.

***Newbury street,** B.; from Arlington street to Charlesgate-east, and from Charlesgate-west to Brookline avenue; from Arlington street, west, on Back Bay land, 1860; deed of Newbury street, between Arlington and Clarendon streets, tendered by Public Lands Commissioners, Nov. 10, 1865; same accepted and laid out, May 6, 1867; same laid out, Dec. 9, 1869; laid out from Clarendon street to Dartmouth street, May 31, 1871; laid out from Dartmouth street to Exeter street, Dec. 6, 1875; laid out from Exeter street to Hereford street, Dec. 27, 1878; laid out from Hereford street to West Chester park (now Massachusetts avenue), May 5, 1880; laid out from West Chester park to Ipswich street, now Charlesgate-east, Aug. 31, 1883; West Newbury street, from Charlesgate-west to Brookline avenue, laid out with name of Newbury street and construction ordered, March 30, 1894. L 374, L 862, L 1110, L 1341, L 1342, L 1343, L 1437, L 1728, L 2585.

Newbury street, B., 1708; from Eliot's corner, Essex street, to Okes' corner, Summer street; made part of Washington street, July 6, 1824.

Newbury street, W. Rox.; from Canterbury street, near Ashland street, to Hyde Park line; Newbern street or avenue, so called.

Newcomb place, B.; from Eliot street, near Warrenton street, southerly.

***Newcomb street,** B.; from Washington street to Harrison avenue; from Washington street, east, named Prescott place, May 14, 1849; from Washington street to Reed street named Newcomb street, April 1, 1874; laid out and extended to Harrison avenue, Sept. 8, 1874. L 961, L 962, L 1078.

New Cornhill, B., 1828; from Court street to Washington street; called Market street, 1817; name changed to New Cornhill, 1828; commonly called Cornhill.

New County road, Dor.; part of River street so called on plan of new location dated 1865.

New County road, W. Rox.; Ashland street so called on plan dated 1862.

New Court, B., 1845; from Shawmut avenue, east, near Groton street; name changed to Briggs place, 1849.

New England avenue, Dor.; from Talbot avenue to Southern avenue at its junction with Bernard street.

Newell street, Dor.; (proposed) from Dorchester avenue to Boston street; laid out as Howell street, Dec. 28, 1892.

Newfield street, W. Rox., 1894; from Weld street to Lasell street; authority to open given by Street Commissioners, April 20, 1894.

New Fore street, Chsn.; laid out, 40 feet wide, 1780; now Water street.

New Gravelly Point road, Rox.; from Huntington avenue, southerly, to Rogers avenue.

***Newhall avenue,** / **Newhall street,** } Dor.; from Adams street to Neponset avenue; shown but not named on plans dated 1851 and 1859.

Newhall place, Dor.; from Newhall avenue near Newhall street, northwest.

***Newhall street,** Dor.; from Pierce avenue to Ashmont street; laid out, March 1, 1869. L 711, L 2786.

***New Heath street,** Rox.; from Heath street at junction Parker street and Heath street to Centre street; report of Committee on Streets recommending laying out passed, June 27, 1859; laid out from near junction Parker street across B. & P. (now N. Y., N. H. & H.) R.R. at grade to Centre street, Oct. 31, 1859; construction ordered, Nov. 14, 1859. L 534.

Newland place, B., 1860; from Newland street; cannot be identified.

***Newland street**, B., 1838; from Upton street to West Springfield street, between Shawmut avenue and Tremont street; laid out from West Dedham street to West Canton street, Sept. 14, 1869; laid out from West Canton street to West Brookline street, Nov. 9, 1870; laid out from West Concord street to Worcester street, June 30, 1873; laid out from West Dedham street to Upton street, Oct. 27, 1876; laid out from West Newton street to Rutland street, Aug. 25, 1879. L 477, L 542, L 581, L 605, L 871, L 1186, L 1373.

Newman block, B.; from Pleasant street, west, next north of Piedmont street; called Newman place, 1849.

Newman court, So. B.; from Champney street, south-westerly.

Newman place, B.; from Pleasant street, west, next north of Piedmont street, 1849; at some time previous to 1879 called Newman block.

Newman place, Rox.; from Dudley street, south-westerly, near and south of Vine street.

***Newman street**, So. B.; from Dorchester street to Lowland (now Mercer) street; laid out, Nov. 17. 1868. L 238, L 424.

New Minot street, Dor.; from Adams street to Carruth street; that part of Minot street sometimes so called.

New North alley, B.; from Middle (now Hanover) street, 1781.

***Newport street**, Dor.; from Harbor View street to Crescent avenue; laid out, Dec. 4, 1893. L 2554.

New Prince street, B.; previously to 1788, from Leverett street, east; called Tucker street, 1803; Leverett place, 1812; Lyman place, 1834; Lyman street 1856; part of Lyman street, near Green street, included in Staniford street, May 11, 1886.

***New Seaver street**, Dor. and Rox.; from Columbia street, opposite Seaver street, to Erie avenue (now Erie street); laid out, July 30, 1878; named Seaver street, March 1, 1889. L 1313.

Newton court, B., 1848; from Tyler street, westerly, near and south of Oak street.

Newton place, B., 1825; from Beach street, south, to Plymouth place: Newton place and Plymouth place laid out as Knapp street, from Beach street to Harrison avenue, May 14, 1879. L 1351.

Newton road, Bri.; Washington street, formerly so called.

***Newton street**, B., 1826; from Albany street to Columbus avenue; laid out on the Neck, July 24, 1826; named from Tremont street to Front street (now Harrison avenue); Sept. 15, 1834; to Albany street, 1834; accepted, Dec. 7, 1857; accepted, Oct. 30, 1860; portion west of Tremont street having been extended to line of Boston Water Power Company accepted, Aug. 13, 1861; accepted to a point 637 feet west of Tremont street, June 13, 1865; named East Newton street from Washington street to Albany, and West Newton street from Washington street, to Columbus avenue, April 21, 1868. L 198, L 354.

†**Newton street**, Bri.; from Brooks street, westerly, then south-westerly crossing end of Bigelow street; see plan dated 1871; laid out, Dec. 18, 1873: accepted conditionally, Dec. 30, 1873: laid out from Brooks street to a point about 200 feet east of Bigelow street, Nov. 10, 1876. L 1189.

New Walnut place, B.; from Reed street to Walnut place.

Nichols court, } **Nicholson court**, } Rox.; from Phillips street across the end of Smith-street court; called Nichols court in 1884; called Nicholson court on plans dated 1858, 1870, 1873, and 1888.

Nickerson street, Rox.; from Heath street, south-westerly, to Jamaica-way, near Craft street.

Nightingale street, Dor.; from Talbot avenue to Bernard street.

Nikisch avenue, W. Rox.; from Beech street to Parkway.

***Ninth street,** So. B., 1805; now East and West Ninth streets; laid out parallel with Broadway and named, Feb. 27, 1805; laid out from H street to low-water mark, Nov. 17, 1868; name of Sullivan street from D street to Old Harbor street, changed to Ninth street, Nov. 17, 1868; called East and West Ninth streets, Feb. 18, 1873. L 52, L 96, L 191, L 192, L 194, L 273, L 369, L 751.

Nixon avenue, Dor.; from Centre street to Mather street; laid out as Nixon street, May 26, 1884.

***Nixon street,** Dor., 1884; from Centre street to Mather street; Nixon avenue laid out as Nixon street, May 26, 1884. L 1779.

Noble court, E. B.; from Sumner street between Cottage street and Seaver street, south-easterly.

Noble's corner, B., 1800; corner of Dock square and Friend street, then so called.

Noddle's alley, B.; by Directory, 1796; from Newbury (now Washington) street.

Noddle's Island, B.; name of East Boston previous to 1832.

***Nonantum street,** Bri., 1840; from Washington street at Oak square, southerly, south-westerly, and westerly to Newton line, named, June 15, 1840; previously called Indian lane; altered, etc., Sept. 10, 1855. L 2487.

Nonquit street, Dor.; from Dudley street, south-west, between Monadnock street and N. E. R.R.

Nopper street, Rox.; from Highland street to Ellis street; laid out with name of Fulda street, Aug. 27, 1889. L 2157.

Norcross place, So. B.; from East Eighth street, north, between K street and L street.

Norfolk avenue, B., 1828; from Washington street, near Bromfield street, west, then north, to Province House court (now Province court); name changed to Ordway place, April 21, 1868.

***Norfolk avenue,** Rox. and Dor., 1850; from Hampden street to East Cottage street; from East (now Hampden) street to Dorchester line accepted and named, Nov. 25, 1850; street leading from Norfolk avenue (Rox.) to Cottage (now East Cottage) street (Dor.), heretofore called Franklin street, named Norfolk avenue, being continuation of same, Dec. 21, 1875; for laying out see Franklin street.

Norfolk place, B., 1823; from Washington street to Harrison avenue, south of Bedford street; called Jarvis row, 1805; named Norfolk place (from Washington street, east, south of Suffolk place), 1823.

Norfolk place, Dor.; from Washington street near corner Norfolk street, south-west to Norfolk street; now called Norfolk terrace.

***Norfolk street,** Rox.; from Highland street to Lambert avenue; accepted, July 2, 1860. L 781.

Norfolk street, Rox.; from Ruggles (now Cabot) street to Williams (now part of Vernon) street; accepted and extended to Washington street over a part of Williams street and name changed to Vernon street, May 16, 1842.

***Norfolk street,** Dor.; from Washington street to Blue Hill avenue, at Mattapan near River street; laid out from Dr. Baker's to James Tolman's shop, May 9, 1803, and April 2, 1804; formerly West street; located by County Commissioners, Dec. 15, 1835; from Upper Mills to the Town House altered, etc., December, 1838; same named, March 11, 1840; part between B. H. & E. (now N. E.) R.R. and Jamaica street relocated, February, 1866; altered near Washington street, May 20, 1878; altered at Blue Hill avenue, Feb. 14, 1880; part near River street included in Blue Hill avenue, Nov. 5, 1894. L 1306, L 1435, L 1501, L 1759, L 1975, L 2083, L 2103, L 2495, L 2496, L 2497, L 2498, L 2499.

Norfolk street, W. Rox.; from Washington street to Kittredge street (formerly Roslin avenue).

Norfolk terrace, Dor.; from Washington street near corner Norfolk street, south-west, to Norfolk street; formerly called Norfolk place.

Norfolk and Bristol turnpike, Rox. and W. Rox.; old County road, from Dudley street, Roxbury, to Dedham line; alteration of part over Smelt brook confirmed, April, 1808; called Dedham turnpike, 1849; laid out as a public highway, with extension to Boston line, to meet end of Shawmut avenue there, June, 1857; part in Roxbury, from West Roxbury line, with extension to Boston line, named Shawmut avenue, Dec. 28, 1857; part in West Roxbury named Shawmut avenue, Feb. 3, 1858; from Dudley street, Roxbury, to Dedham line named Washington street, June 16, 1874.

***Norman street,** B., 1877; from Green street to Merrimac street; called Gouch lane, 1732; Gouch street, 1822; named Norman street, Dec. 18, 1877.

***North avenue,** Dor.; from Dudley street to Brook avenue; see plan dated 1860; laid out from Stoughton (now Dudley) street to Brook avenue, Aug. 12, 1869. L 880, L 1511.

North avenue, W. Rox.; from Centre street near corner of Grove street, north-west, to N. Y., N. H. & H. R.R.

North row, B., 1803; on Fish (now North) street, corner of Cross street.

***North square,** B., 1788; between North, Sun court, Moon, Garden court and Prince streets; called Clark's square, 1708; North square 1788; called Garden square on Carleton's map, 1800, but no record as such. L 211, L 2367, L 2422.

***North street,** B.; from Dock square to Commercial street; part of Ann street, from Dock square to North square, named North street, Jan. 1, 1852; Ann street, from North square to Commercial street, named North street, April 10, 1854; at different times called also Ship street, Fish street, Drawbridge street, Conduit street,—1708 to about 1824; Ann street from Union street at Dock square to Fish street at Cross street; Fish street from Cross street to Ship street at Fleet street; Ship street from Fleet street to Lynn street at Battery street. Vol. 31, pp. 45, 51, 58, 77, 91. L 6, L 81, L 83, L 113, L 127, L 169, L 172, L 252, L 1149, L 1947, L 2013.

North street, B., 1708; from Bennet street to the sea; from Clark's corner (Bennet street) across Lynn street to the sea, 1732; to Winnisimmit Ferry, 1800; made a part of Hanover street, July 6, 1824.

†**North street,** Dor.; from Boston (now Dorchester) street, near former South Boston line, north-westerly, passing intersection of E street leading to South Boston; see plan dated 1844; accepted to intersection of E street, April 11, 1849; now part of West Eighth street.

***North street,** Chsn.; from High street, south-westerly, parallel with Salem street; from Gorham (now High) street, south-west, to end of Osgood's lane, by plan dated 1810; accepted, Dec. 15, 1834; laid out "per present bounds." Nov. 17, 1851; name changed to Salem-street avenue, July 21, 1869.

North Allen street, B., 1807; from Chambers street to Brighton street; named Allen street, April 1, 1829.

Northampton place, B.; from Northampton street, south-westerly, to Camden street; court on easterly side of Everett school-house named Northampton place, Oct. 19, 1871.

***Northampton street,** B. and Rox.; from Albany street, north-westerly, to the B. & P. (now N. Y., N. H. & H.) R.R.; order to open the street heretofore laid out over the land adjoining the Neck called Northampton street, and to extend the same from the Neck eastwardly to Roxbury line or Hill's dam, Sept. 8, 1819; laid out on the Neck, July 24, 1826; from Tremont street to Front street (now Harrison avenue), Sept. 15, 1834; certain alterations in June, 1842; street accepted, Dec. 7, 1857; part west of Tremont street, accepted, Dec. 2, 1867; part adjoining estate of Boston Water Power Company discontinued, Oct. 26, 1868. L 137, L 405, L 619, L 1195, L 1331, L 1353, L 1491, L 1700, L 2225, L 2708.

***North Anderson street,** B., 1868; from Cambridge street, northerly, to grounds of Massachusetts General Hospital; called Bridge street, 1803; name changed to North Anderson street, April 21, 1868.

***North Battery wharf,** B.; from Commercial street, north-easterly, between Hanover street and Battery street.

***North Beacon street,** Bri.; from Cambridge street at Union square to Watertown line; Beacon street called North Beacon street, March 5, 1860; highway over Mill-dam road and Watertown turnpike and connecting bridges, from line between Brighton and Brookline through town of Brighton to line at Arsenal grounds, accepted, Nov. 19, 1868. L 1112.

North Bennet place, B., 1858; from North Bennet street, south-westerly; called Bennet place, 1834; named North Bennet place, 1858.

***North Bennet street,** B., 1708; from Hanover street to Salem street; at different times known as North School street, North Grammar School street, North Latin School street and Bennet street.

North Brimmer place, B., 1867; from North street, south-easterly, near Richmond street; probably Trant's alley, 1849; called North Brimmer place, 1867; same called Brimmer place in 1884; North Brimmer place in 1890.

***North Centre street,** B ; from North street, north-westerly, to Hanover street; previous to 1708 called Ball's alley and Perraway's alley; Paddy's alley, 1708 ; called North Centre street from Ann (now North) street, north-west, about 1773; Centre street from Ann street north of the bridge into Middle (now Hanover) street, 1778; from Ann street, west, across Middle street and Back (now Salem) street to the Mill-pond, 1800; from Ann street to Middle street, 1817. L 130, L 978.

North Charles street, B.; from Cambridge street to Leverett street; from Livingston street, south-west, 1841; extended southerly to Charles street, in front of new jail, 1855; extended from Cambridge street to Allen street, by construction of a pier bridge, 1856; from Cambridge street to Leverett street, 1859; street extending from Cambridge street to Leverett street, portions of which were laid out in 1855 and 1857 as "Charles street extended," and a portion of which is known as "North Charles street," called Charles street, in extension of that street, Feb. 13, 1866. L 45, L 97, L 202, L 278.

North Chapel place, B.; from 167 Friend street, between Market street and Traverse street; Chapel place sometimes so called.

Northern avenue, So. B.; a proposed street crossing Fort Point Channel, in continuation of Oliver street, north of and parallel with Eastern avenue (now Congress street); shown on plan dated Dec. 27, 1880.

Northern avenue, Dor.; from Washington street to Talbot avenue.

North Federal court, B., 1806; from Union street at junction of Hanover street, north-east; called Link alley, 1708; North Federal court, 1806; to Mill-pond street, 1820; discontinued, Sept. 7, 1857; partly built upon and closed, 1860; shown in 1884 and 1888, from Blackstone street, south-west.

North Ferry, B.; from the end of Battery street, east, to East Boston. L 207.

North Ferry avenue, B.; from Commercial street to Ferry Landing; from Commercial street, opposite Battery street, 1870; sometimes called People's Ferry avenue; laid out as Battery street, Aug. 3, 1880.

North Ferry avenue, E. B.; from Sumner street to Ferry Landing; given also as extension of Sumner street.

***Northfield street,** B.; from Tremont street, south-easterly, then north-easterly, to Camden street; laid out from Tremont street between Camden street and Lenox street, 1856; named, Nov. 19, 1857; now from Tremont street to land of St. Vincent Orphan Asylum, then north-easterly by the same to Camden street.

North Grammar School street, B.; name given to North Bennet street, 1789.

***North Grove street,** B.; from Cambridge street, northerly, across Fruit street to Medical College buildings; from Cambridge street, north, 1818; to the Medical College, 1850; accepted, Oct. 30, 1855. L 57, L 70, L 278.

North Hanover court, } B.; from Hanover street, north-westerly,
North Hanover place, } opposite Board alley; called Robinsons' court, 1821; Robbins court, 1824; North Hanover place or court, 1825; Hanover place, 1827; North Hanover court, 1840.

***North Harvard street,** Bri.; from Cambridge street, north-westerly to Franklin street, then north-easterly to Charles river; named Harvard street from Cambridge street to Old Cambridge bridge, near the Colleges, June 15, 1840; altered, Nov. 24, 1857, at which date it was called Harvard street and there is no record of change to North Harvard street; called North Harvard street on plan dated 1866.

***North Hudson street,** B., 1838; from Hull street, north-easterly, to Snowhill street; laid out, March 1, 1875. L 1024.

North Latin School street, B.; name given to North Bennet street, about 1789.

North Margin place, B., 1844; from North Margin street, easterly between Thacher street and Cooper street.

***North Margin street,** B., 1807; from Stillman street to Lafayette avenue; formerly from Salem street, north-westerly, northerly, north-westerly to Lafayette avenue; laid out over the Mill-pond, Aug. 3, 1807; from Thacher street to the First Baptist Church, 1821; extended through Richmond street to Salem street, 1841; extended from angle near and south of Cooper street to Stillman street, Sept. 25, 1891; part leading north-west from No. 90 Salem street to the part extended to Stillman street was changed to Wiget street, March 1, 1894. L 366, L 1221, L 1827, L 2337.

North Margin-street court, B., 1868; from North Margin street, north-easterly, near and south of Lafayette avenue.

***North Market street,** B., 1825; from Commercial street to Merchants' row; laid out from Commercial street to Merchants' row, north side of Faneuil Hall Market, March 30, 1825; continuation to Dock square, which was staked out in 1826 as a continuation of North Market street and since used as a public street; laid out and established as a street of city, April 30, 1838.

North Mead street, Chsn.; from Medford street to Bunker Hill street; shown as an unnamed street on plan dated 1843.

North Mead-street court, Chsn.; from North Mead street, north-westerly.

North Munroe terrace, Dor.; from Neponset avenue nearly opposite Pope's Hill street to Train street.

North Pleasant street, Chsn.; from northerly end of Summer street, north-easterly, to Bunker Hill street; same conveyed to Town for public highway by Oliver Holden, July 17, 1810; name changed to Pearl street, July 7, 1845.

North Quincy place, Chsn.; from Quincy street, north-west between Medford street and South Quincy place.

Northrop street, Rox.; from Elm Hill avenue to Landseer avenue; now part of Ruthven street.

***North Russell street**, B., 1795; from Cambridge street to Eaton street; from Cambridge street northerly, 1800; on Carleton's map, 1800, from Cambridge street to Eaton street; named in 1802.

North School street, B.; name given to North Bennet street, 1789.

North Short-street place, Chsn.; from Short street, north-west, between Medford street and South Short-street place.

North Townsend place, B.; from 516 Commercial street; Townsend place sometimes so called; part of it included in Commercial street when widened in 1879; now included in park.

North Writing School street, B.; from Hanover street to Salem street, 1789; formerly called Love lane (called Love lane on Carleton's map, 1800, and Edes' list, 1800); lane formerly called Love lane named Tileston street, June 20, 1821.

†**Norton street**, Dor., 1887; from Richfield street to Speedwell street; laid out from Bowdoin street to Richfield street, April 23, 1887; authority to open part from Bowdoin street to Speedwell street given by Street Commissioners, Aug. 29, 1893. L 1980.

***Norway street**, B.; from Huntington avenue to Parker street; Caledonia street laid out from Huntington avenue to Falmouth street with name of Norway street, Dec. 22, 1891, and extended over the private way known as Caledonia street, from Falmouth street to Massachusetts avenue, Sept. 14, 1894; Caledonia street, from Massachusetts avenue to Parker street; laid out as Norway street, July 10, 1896. L 2379, L 2619, L 2779.

***Norwich street**, B.; from Mystic street, south-easterly, to Meander street; laid out between Washington street and Harrison avenue, prior to 1834; named, 1850; accepted, July 23, 1862. L 1704.

Norwood street, Dor.; north-westerly, from and parallel with O. C. (now N. Y., N. H. & H.) R.R., crossing Tolman street.

Notre Dame street, Rox.; from Dimock street (formerly Codman avenue) to Bragdon street; named, April 28, 1871.

Nottingham road, Bri., 1895; from the junction of Colonial road and Melton road, near Chestnut Hill avenue and Commonwealth avenue; authority to open given by Street Commissioners, Jan. 1, 1895.

Nottingham street, Dor., 1892; from Bowdoin avenue to Bullard street; authority to open given by Street Commissioners, Sept. 23, 1892.

Noyes alley, B., 1801; near Merchants' row and Corn court, 1801; probably the easterly part of Corn court.

Noyes place, B., 1825; from Salem street, westerly, near Prince street.

***O street**, So. B., 1805; from Reserved Channel north of East First street to Strandway; from salt water on the south to the harbor of Boston on the north laid out and named, Feb. 27, 1805; lines run and stakes or posts placed at corners of intersecting streets, Sept. 21, 1835; lines run and established, April 23, 1849; laid out from low-water mark north of First (now West First) street to Harbor line in Dorchester Bay, Nov. 17, 1868. L 7.

O-street place, So. B.; from O street to Cordage court, between East Sixth street and East Seventh street.

Oak avenue, Dor., from Adams street to Plain street; shown in 1867.

Oak avenue, W. Rox.; from Cass street, south-west, near West Roxbury Branch R.R.; formerly called Elm street.

Oak place, B.; from Oak street, southerly, opposite Ash street; Ash street completed, about 1820, across Oak street to near Pine street, and in 1834 the part south of Oak street called Oak place.

***Oak place,** W. Rox.; from Green street, north-east, then north-west, to Lamartine street, with a short piece from angle to B. & P. (now N. Y., N. H. & H.) R.R.; laid out from Green street to Lamartine street, Feb. 14, 1876; name changed to Oakdale street, March 1, 1884. L 1130.

Oak ridge, Dor.; from Morton street.

***Oak square,** Bri.; junction Faneuil, Washington; Tremont, and Nonantum streets; laid out, Sept. 10, 1855; named, March 5, 1860. L 1632.

***Oak street,** B., 1805; from Washington street to Albany street; from Orange (now Washington) street to Ash street, 1809; extended to Front street (now Harrison avenue), 1827; accepted, April 16, 1832; extended to Lincoln street, 1837; accepted from Harrison avenue to Albany street, Oct. 9, 1848; Oak street from Albany street and Lincoln street from Kneeland street discontinued on land of B. & A. R.R. Company at some time later than 1880; no record.

Oak street, So. B.; from Old road from Boston (now Boston street) to land of Boston Wharf Company; shown in 1846; name changed to Ellery street, Aug. 7, 1855.

Oak street, Rox.; from Massachusetts avenue to Norfolk avenue; same called Oakes street.

Oak street, Rox.; from Park street to Elm street (now Longwood avenue), 1850; laid out with name of Autumn street, 1871.

Oak street, Rox.; from Edinboro' (now Thornton) street to Norfolk and Bristol turnpike (now Washington street), 1844; shown as an unnamed 30-foot street on plan dated 1835; also called Mechanics street on plan dated 1843; accepted conditionally, Sept. 3, 1855; accepted finally Feb. 9, 1863; name changed to Oakland street, April 21, 1868.

Oak street, W. Rox.; from Beech street south-westerly, crossing Farrington avenue or street; shown in 1872; laid out from Farrington street to Beech street with name of Kenneth street, July 24, 1891.

***Oak street,** Chsn.; from Main street to Russell street; accepted, March 22, 1841.

Oak terrace, Dor.; from Birch street to Lyons street.

***Oakdale street,** W. Rox.; from Green street, north-east, then north-west to Lamartine street; formerly Oak place, and by that name laid out, Feb. 14, 1876; name of part of Oak place changed to Oakdale street, March 1, 1884. L 1130.

Oakdale place, W. Rox.; from Oakdale street, south-east, near Green street.

Oakdale square, W. Rox.; from Oakdale street, north-east.

Oakdale terrace, W. Rox.; from Oakdale street, north-west.

Oake's corner, B., 1777; corner of Summer street and Newbury (now Washington) street then so called.

Oakes street, Rox.; from Norfolk avenue to Massachusetts avenue; Oak street so called.

Oak Grove terrace, Rox.; from Ruggles street nearly opposite Westminster street south-west to Auburn place.

Oak Hill avenue, Dor.; from Delhi street south-east towards West Selden street.

Oakland avenue, Rox.; from Dudley street between Greenville street and Mt. Pleasant avenue, south-west; Albany avenue, 1874.

Oakland avenue, Bri.; from Oakland street, south-west.

Oakland avenue, Dor.; from Columbia street, south-east, parallel with Rosalinda street; shown on plan dated 1872 in about the location of present Hewins street.

Oakland park, Rox.; from Oakland street, south-west.

Oakland place, Dor.; from Blue Hill avenue, west, then south-west to Oakland street.

Oakland place, Bri.; from Oakland street.

***Oakland street,** Rox.; from Washington street to Thornton street; called Mechanic street on plan dated 1843; formerly also called Oak street and by that name accepted Feb. 9, 1863; named Oakland street, April 21, 1868.

***Oakland street,** Dor.; from River street to Harvard street; shown but not named on plan dated 1855; part in West Roxbury shown on plan without date; laid out from River street, Upper Mills, to Norfolk and Bristol turnpike (now Washington street), West Roxbury, by way of Berry street and Ashland street, September, 1856.

***Oakland street,** Bri., 1853; from Washington street, northerly, then westerly, then north-westerly, to Faneuil street; located, May 6, 1853; accepted and named, Sept. 5, 1853.

Oakley street, Dor., 1893; from Bowdoin street to Geneva avenue; authority to open given by Street Commissioners, March 22, 1893.

***Oakman street,** Dor., 1873; from Walnut street to Taylor street (Neponset); laid out, June 22, 1875. L 1051.

Oakridge street, Dor., 1893; from Codman street to Morton street; authority to open given by Street Commissioners, June 7, 1893.

Oakview avenue, Rox.; from Marcella street, north-east, then north-west.

Oakville avenue, Rox.; from St. James street, north-east, nearly opposite Alpine street.

Oakwood avenue, Dor.; from Capen street nearly opposite Dyer street, westerly.

***Ocean street,** Dor.; from Ashmont street to Welles avenue; laid out, July 31, 1873. L 888.

Odeon avenue, B., 1842; from Milk street to Franklin street; formerly called Dinsdale's alley and Theatre alley; the south part of Theatre alley called Odeon avenue, 1842; from Milk street to Franklin street, 1859; Devonshire street extended through, 1859; called also Odeon place. L 101.

Ohio place, B., 1843; from Washington street, west; called Mechanics place, 1823; name of Ohio place, leading from Washington street to Shawmut avenue, changed to Ohio street, May 30, 1872. L 549, L 726.

***Ohio street,** B.; from Washington street to Shawmut avenue; called Mechanics place from Orange (now Washington) street, west, 1823; Ohio place, 1843; name changed to Ohio street, May 30, 1872; laid out, Aug. 21, 1883. L 549, L 726, L 1724.

Oke's corner, B., 1708; in Newbury (now Washington) street.

Old Cambridge road; see Cambridge street, Chsn.

Old Harbor place, So. B.; from Old Harbor street, east, between Thomas park and East Eighth street; shown in 1873.

†**Old Harbor street,** So. B.; from Dorchester street to East Ninth street, with proposed extension to line in "Old Harbor;" laid out on land of Champney, Thos. Bird's heirs, and Mary Clap, Feb 27, 1805; laid out from Dorchester street to former dividing line between Dorchester and Boston, Nov. 17, 1868. Vol. 31, pp. 30, 85. L 752, L 1790.

Old road, So. B.; before annexation, part of Dorchester street; from angle in same north of Third street to the junction of M street and Fourth (now East Fourth) street, see plan dated 1837; name of part from Third (now East Third) street to Fourth (now East Fourth) street changed to Emerson street, March 22, 1864.

***Old road,** Dor.; from Columbia street to Elmo street; discontinued from Columbia street to Blue Hill avenue, Nov. 8, 1880; relocated from Michigan avenue to Blue Hill avenue, Oct. 29, 1889. L 1469, L 1503, L 2185.

Old road, W. Rox.; leading from Canterbury street to Boston, and lying between Blue Hill avenue and land of W. E. Abbott; discontinued, July 26, 1852.

Old road to Dedham, W. Rox.; from Centre street, opposite Third Parish Meeting-house; shown on plan dated 1815; now part of South street.

Old way, B.; from Cross street, north, by the Mill-pond, 1708–1732; closed.

Oleander street, Dor.; from Magnolia street to N. E. R.R.

Olive court, B.; from Washington street, east, 1837; called Olive pl., 1849.

Olive place, B.; from Washington street, south-easterly, to Waltham street, near its junction with Harrison avenue; called Olive court, 1837; Fisher's court, 1846; Olive place, from Washington street, east, afterwards to Harrison avenue.

Olive street, B.; north of J. Joy's to the water, 1796; from Belknap (now Joy) street to Charles street, 1817; Sumner street extended through Olive street, July 6, 1824; named Mt. Vernon street, Aug. 27, 1832.

Oliver court, B.; from Webster avenue, easterly; same in 1863.

Oliver place, B.; from Essex street to Beach street; same in 1825; sometimes called Oliver's avenue.

***Oliver street,** B.; from Kilby street to Atlantic avenue; the street where Mr. Daniel Oliver dwells, from Milk street to Fort Hill, 1708; from Milk street, south, to Cow lane (now High street) 1732; called Oliver's lane by Directory, 1789; from Milk street to Washington place (Fort-Hill square), 1817; the portion now from Fort Hill square to Atlantic avenue was called Gibbs or Gibson's lane from 1708, and named Belmont street, from High street to Broad street (now Atlantic avenue), 1845; Oliver street extended through Washington square and Belmont street, Sept. 6, 1865; name of Belmont street changed to Oliver street, April 21, 1868; portion discontinued, May 21, 1868; extended to Kilby street at Liberty square, April 18, 1873. L 298, L 299, L 300, L 301, L 378, L 492, L 850, L 853, L 883, L 922, L 2090.

Oliver's avenue, B.; Oliver place, from Essex street to Beach street, sometimes so called.

Oliver's bridge, B.; in Mackerel lane (now Kilby street), 1722.

Oliver's (Mrs.) corner, B.; at foot of Water street, 1708.

Oliver's lane, B., 1789; Oliver street so called.

Olmstead street, W. Rox., 1893; from Forest Hills street to Peter Parley street; authority to open given by Street Commissioners, May 24, 1893; formerly called Eugene street.

***Olney street**, Dor.; from Bowdoin street to Rosseter street; name of Green street between Bowdoin street and Geneva avenue changed to Olney street, Dec. 30, 1876; through Union avenue, extended from Geneva avenue to Rosseter street, March 1, 1888. L 1191, L 1727, L 1652, L 2020.

Olney-street place, Dor.; from Olney street to Wales place; formerly called Green-street court.

***Oneida street**, B.; from Harrison avenue to Albany street; from Harrison avenue, east, 1844; to Albany street, 1845; accepted, Jan. 5, 1856. L 234.

Onslow terrace, So. B.; from East Fifth street south between M street and N street.

Ontario street, B.; from Lincoln street to Lehigh street, 1855; closed. L 61.

***Ontario street**, So. B.; from Swan street to Foundry street; laid out between Sixth street and Swan street, Oct. 12, 1869; closed; taken by O. C. R.R. Co. by authority of the Acts of Legislature of 1893. L 483, L 514.

***Ophir street**, W. Rox., 1892; laid out from Washington street to Brookside avenue, Sept. 6, 1892. L 2433.

Orange avenue, B.; from West Orange street to West Castle street, nearly opposite Middlesex street, 1849; sometimes called Orange place; closed.

Orange court, B.; from Orange (now Washington) street, west, 1823; previously called Dutch lane; from Washington street, to Johnson school-house accepted, Oct. 1, 1838; accepted and laid out, Sept. 1, 1845; name changed to Dix place, March 30, 1846.

Orange court, Rox., 1850–59; from Fellows street, north-westerly.

Orange lane, B.; from Washington street, opposite Orange street, to Harrison avenue; same in 1827.

Orange place, B.; from Washington street, west, 1825; accepted from Washington street, westerly, as far as houses numbered 30 and 31 and named Orange street, Aug. 2, 1830.

Orange place, B.; from West Orange street to West Castle street, nearly opposite Middlesex street, 1849; same as Orange avenue; closed.

Orange street, B.; from Washington street to Shawmut avenue; Orange place, 1825; Orange place accepted from Washington street as far westerly as houses numbered 30 and 31, and named Orange street, Aug. 2, 1830; formerly a public street, but was discontinued in 1872; from Washington street next south of the B. & A. R.R., 1874. L 523, L 547, L 549, L 563, L 727.

Orange street, B.; from Beach street to Dover street, 1663; from Essex street to the fortifications (near Dover street), 1708; made a part of Washington street, July 6, 1824.

†**Orange street**, Rox.; from Washington (now Roxbury) street to Clay (now Linden-Park) street; also from Clay street to junction Ruggles and Cabot streets; laid out, etc., July 25, 1853; accepted, between Washington street and Pearl (now King) street, Sept. 7, 1857; accepted, conditionally, between Factory (now Vernon) street and Culvert street, Oct. 28, 1867; part between Washington street and Pearl street, named Elmwood street, April 21, 1868; between Clay street and Cabot street, named Hampshire street, April 21, 1868; remainder from Pearl street to Clay street, subsequently named Elmwood street; no record.

Orange street, W. Rox.; from Beech street, north-easterly, then northerly to West street; same in 1874.

Orange-Tree lane, B.; previously to 1708, from Queen (now Court) street to Hudson lane (now Elm street); called Hanover street in 1708.

Orchard avenue, W. Rox.; from Morton street near Washington street.

Orchard court, Rox.; from what is now Orchard street to a point opposite Proctor (now Eustis) street, and about 100 feet distant, northwesterly from Adams street; name changed to Orchard street, and extended to Adams street, May 27 and Sept. 10, 1867; called Eustis street, April 21, 1868.

Orchard park, Rox.; park at junction of Chadwick street and Orchard-Park street.

Orchard place, Dor.; from Boston street, south-easterly, opposite Clapp street.

†**Orchard street**, Rox.; from Yeoman street to Eustis street across Orchard park; also from Orchard street, opposite Trask place, to Adams street now Orchard-Park street; accepted, conditionally, Oct. 24, 1859; portion of Eaton street from Orchard street to Adams street, accepted and named Orchard street, Nov. 12, 1860; now Orchard-Park street; extended to Adams street, through Orchard court, May 27 and Sept. 10, 1867 (this part is now Eustis street); between Dearborn street and Adams street called Eustis street, April 21, 1868.

***Orchard street**, W. Rox.; from Centre street to Pond street; accepted, located and laid out, Oct. 1, 1866; accepted, March 25, 1867; laid out, 1873.

Orchard street, Bri.; from Saunders street to Gordon street; laid out as Pomeroy street, June 9, 1887. L 1994.

***Orchard-Park street**, Rox.; from Chadwick street at junction with Ambrose street to Adams street; that part of Eaton (now Orchard-Park) street to Adams street, accepted and made a part of Orchard street, Nov, 12, 1860; from Orchard street to Hartopp place (now Ambrose street) at junction with Chadwick street, laid out, Feb. 19, 1876; no record of change of name of part of Orchard street between Orchard street and Adams street to Orchard-Park street. L 1132.

Orchardale street, Dor.; from Westville street to Corona street.

Ordway place, B.; from Washington street, near Bromfield street, west, then north to Province court; called Norfolk avenue, 1828; named Ordway place, April 21, 1868.

***Oregon street**, Rox.; from Conant street to Smith street; laid out from Conant street, and extended to Smith street, Sept. 23, 1882. L 1641.

Organ-Park street, W. Rox.; from Catherine street, south-east, then north-east, near Bourne street.

Orient avenue, E. B. (Breed's Island); from Farrington street, west, to unnamed street near B. & M. R.R.

Orient Heights, E. B.; on Breed's Island.

Orienta place, Breed's Island; from Orient avenue to Gladstone street.

Oriental court, Rox.; from Phillips street, westerly, near Tremont street.

Oriole street, Rox.; from Walnut avenue to Humboldt (formerly Williams avenue); laid out as Ruthven street, Dec. 1, 1884. L 1837.

***Oriole street**, W. Rox.; from Park street to Bellevue street; same in 1874; laid out, Aug. 28, 1882. L 1634.

Orkney road, Bri., 1896; from Strathmore road to west of Ayr road; authority to open given by Street Commissioners, July 30, 1896.

†**Orleans street**, E. B.; from Marginal street to Bennington street; laid out from Maverick street to Marginal street, Aug. 7, 1848; portion between Maverick and Decatur streets accepted, April 5, 1859. L 1133.

Ormond street, Dor., 1895; from Blue Hill avenue, opposite Fessenden street, north-westerly to beyond Duke street; authority to open given by Street Commissioners, May 20, 1895.

Ormond terrace, B., 1896; from Harrison avenue, opposite Newcomb street; formerly sometimes called a part of Orange court.

Osborn place, B.; from Pleasant street to and crossing Shawmut avenue; from Pleasant street, south, between Washington street and Tremont street, 1845; a portion taken by the extension of Shawmut avenue in 1870. L 549, L 724, L 726, L 792.

***Oscar street,** Rox.; from Parker street to Terrace street; private way known as Drury place, laid out as Oscar street, Aug. 19, 1881. L 1548.

Osgood court, Rox.; from Washington street, north-westerly, parallel with Cedar street.

Osgood place, B.; from Poplar street to Pike alley; same in 1874.

Oswald street, Rox., 1894; from Hillside street to Calumet street; authority to open given by Street Commissioners, Sept. 20, 1894.

***Oswego street,** B.; from Harrison avenue to Albany street; from Harrison avenue, east, 1844; to Albany street, 1845; accepted, Jan. 5, 1856. L 208, L 2679.

Otis place, B.; from Brimmer street; westerly and southerly and northerly, to Mt. Vernon street.

Otis place, B.; from Summer street, opposite Kingston street, to rear of Franklin place; called Otis street from 1812 to 1816; Otis place, 1816 to 1861; renamed Otis street, April 23, 1861. L 105, L 133.

Otis place, Chsn.; from Main street; opposite Lincoln street, north-east.

Otis place, W. Rox.; from Norfolk street, south-west.

***Otis street,** B.; from Summer street, opposite Kingston street; to Winthrop square; from Summer street to rear of Franklin place, 1812; called Otis place, 1816; renamed Otis street, April 23, 1861; on petition for acceptance City Solicitor gives opinion that Otis street is a public highway, Nov. 11, 1861. L 338, L 832.

Otis street, Rox.; name changed to Townsend street, April 21, 1868; (Townsend street from Washington street to Warren street, 1884).

Otis street, Bri.; from Cambridge street, north-westerly, then westerly, to Franklin street; from Cambridge street to Hill avenue, laid out as Mansfield street, April 17, 1882; Hill avenue, which is the part from Franklin street, easterly, laid out as Easton street, Sept. 10, 1889. L 1600.

Otis wharf, B.; from Atlantic avenue, easterly, between High street and Oliver street

***Otisfield street,** Rox.; from Blue Hill avenue to Gaston street; formerly Otisfield avenue; laid out, March 5, 1895. L 2698.

Ottawa place, B.; from Washington street, east, near South May (now Savoy) street; called Sands place, 1859; named Ottawa place, 1873; name changed to Temple park, 1879; now called Mechanics' row.

***Ottawa street,** Rox.; from Sherman street to Laurel street; laid out, Sept. 7, 1871. L 687.

***Otter street,** B.; from Beacon street, northerly, to Charles river; same in 1847; laid out by Boston and Roxbury Mill Corporation, Feb. 26, 1849; accepted, July 1, 1857.

Overlook street, Rox., from Fisher avenue to Parker Hill avenue.

Overlook street, Breed's Island; from Gladstone to Farrington street; authority to open from Farrington street to Waldemar avenue, Aug. 26, 1896.

Owens street, Dor.; from Morton street.

Oxford place, B.; from Harrison avenue, easterly, then northerly and southerly, with opening from the south end easterly into Oxford street; from Harrison avenue, east, near Essex street, 1842.

***Oxford street**, B.; from Essex street to Beach street; same including Peck lane, 1842; accepted and named, Oct. 24, 1842.

***Oxford street**, Rox.; from Sudbury (now Weston) street to Tremont street; accepted conditionally, March 11, 1844; accepted finally, March 3, 1845; name changed to Newbern street, April 21, 1868.

Oxford terrace, B.; from Huntington avenue, near Dartmouth street, south-east, then north-east, 1884.

***P street**, So. B.; from Reserved Channel, north of East First street, to the Strandway; formerly to "Old Harbor," south of East Sixth street; from salt water on the south to the Harbor of Boston on the north, laid out and named, Feb. 27, 1805; laid out from low-water mark north of First street to Harbor line in Dorchester bay, Nov. 17, 1868.

***Pacific street**, So. B.: from East Fourth street to Thomas street (now Thomas park); laid out, Jan. 5, 1875. L 1003.

Packard's wharf, B.; from Atlantic avenue, south-easterly, nearly opposite Oliver street.

Paddy's alley, B.; from Ann (now North) street, north-westerly; prior to 1708 called Ball's alley, and also Perraway's alley; called Paddy's alley, 1708; from Ann street to Middle (now Hanover) street, 1732; a new street laid out in part over the old Paddy's alley, April 16, 1767, and relaid, June 17, 1773, being called Paddy-alley street; named North Centre street about 1773.

Paddock's mall, B., 1777; the west side of Common (now Tremont) street, opposite Rawson's lane (now Bromfield street).

Page avenue, Dor.; from McLellan street to Glenway street; Page avenue laid out under the name of Page street, Jan. 22, 1897. L 2825.

Page street, Dor., 1897; from McLellan street to Glenway street; Page avenue laid out with name of Page street, Jan. 22, 1897. L 2825.

Page terrace, Dor., 1895; from Page avenue, south-east.

Page's court, B., 1837; from North street, near Harris street; called Ann-street court from Ann (now North) street, west, near Bartlett (now Harris) street, 1830; named Page's court, 1837.

Page's court, B.; by plan of 1851, from Ann (now North) street, west, next north of Sun-court street; closed.

Page's court, So. B.; from West Broadway to Athens street, between D street and E street.

Page's yard, B.; from Ship (now Commercial) street, 1823; Richmond street extended through it in 1831.

Paine place, B., 1849; from Washington street, east, near and south of Bennet street; now built over.

***Paine street**, W. Rox., 1884; from Canterbury street to Walk Hill street; Sargent street laid out as Paine street, May 1, 1884. L 1768.

Pain's lane, W. Rox.; from end of Berry street; shown on plan 246, Vol. 3, Norfolk County Commissioners; included in Berry street; also called Paine's lane.

Paisley park, Dor., 1891; from Bournside street to Upland avenue; authority to open given by Street Commissioners, Oct. 1, 1891.

Palmer place, Rox.; from 65 Palmer street, south-westerly; named, March 14, 1871.

Palmer street, B., 1788; from Milk street, opposite Tanner's lane (now Bath street), southerly by the Rope-walks to Cow lane (now High street); called Hutchinson lane or street, 1732; called Palmer street, 1788; named Pearl street, 1800.

***Palmer street**, Rox.; from Washington street to Eustis street; name of Sumner street changed to Palmer street, April 21, 1868. L 1281.

Paris court, E. B.; from 79 Paris street between Decatur street and Wesley street; shown as extending to Chelsea street on atlas, 1884, and given as Parley court on atlas, 1874.

Paris place, E. B.; from easterly side of Paris street between Gove street and Porter street.

Paris place, B., 1848; name changed to Merrimac place, from Merrimac street, south, near Gouch (now Norman) street, 1857.

***Paris street**, E. B.; from Sumner street to Bennington street, near Putnam street; accepted to Maverick street, Aug. 27, 1849: the part laid out by East Boston Company laid out and named by City, July 28, 1851; accepted and laid out between Meridian street and Decatur street, July 12, 1852; accepted between Decatur street and Porter street, June 15, 1859; laid out from Porter street to Bennington street, Sept. 23, 1871., L 688, L 1653, L 2502, L 2718.

***Parish street**, Dor.; from Winter street, easterly; laid out, Aug. 27, 1884. L 1807, L 2310.

Park avenue, W. Rox.; from Centre street to Robin street; Park street so called on map, 1849.

Park lane, W. Rox., 1894; from Walnut avenue, near and north of Peter Parley street; formerly called Franklin Park terrace, and authority to open given under that name, by Street Commissioners, May 24, 1893; Park Lane laid out as Park Lane street, Nov. 23, 1895. L 2750.

Park place, B., 1836; from Hanover street, west, near Broad alley, probably changed to Parkman place.

Park place, B.; Park street so called in Directory, 1806.

Park place, Rox.; from 53 Yeoman street, south-westerly.

Park place, W. Rox.; from 6 Myrtle street, southerly.

Park place, W. Rox.; area at the junction of Forest Hills street and Morton street, so called on atlas of 1884.

***Park square**, B.; at the junction of Pleasant street, Boylston street and Columbus avenue; part of public highway at junction of Pleasant, Boylston, and Charles streets discontinued and enclosed as a public square and named Park square, Nov. 28, 1855. Vol. 31–72. L 613, L 878.

Park square, W. Rox.; north-easterly from and parallel with Park avenue or street; now a part of Irving street.

***Park street**, B., 1803; from Tremont street to Beacon street; prior to 1803 called Centry or Sentry street; named Park street, 1803; in 1806 Directory called Park place; confirmed as a public street, Sept. 15, 1834.

Park street, Rox.; name changed to Edgewood street, April 21, 1868; Edgewood street from Warren street to Blue Hill avenue was laid out, April 9, 1875.

Park street, Rox.; from Brookline avenue to Riverway; formerly from Binney street to Longwood street; part between Brookline avenue and Binney street laid out as Smyrna street, May 17, 1882. L 1610.

†**Park street**, Dor.; from Bernard street to Freeport street; from Commercial (now Freeport) street to Dorchester avenue located, Aug. 18, 1845; laid out from Dorchester avenue to Washington street, April 1, 1851; laid out from Washington street to the N. E. R.R., Sept. 8, 1886; part west of Washington street sometimes called West Park street. L 1182, L 1945.

†**Park street**, W. Rox.; from Montview street to Robin street; from Centre street to Robin street called Park avenue on map, 1849; laid out and accepted from Centre street to estate of Cox and others, March 29, 1872; laid out from a point between Pelton street and Anawan avenue (being about 2,000 feet from Centre street) to Martin street, Nov. 11, 1875. L 1090, L 1091.

***Park street**, Chsn.; from City square to Winthrop square; part of Warren street, commencing at City square with extension of same to Winthrop square, named Park street, Dec. 29, 1868. L 1549.

Parker avenue, Bri.; from North Harvard street, north-east, near Cambridge street.

Parker court, W. Rox.; from Paul Gore street, south-westerly, near Chestnut avenue.

Parker court, Bri.; from 48 Wexford street, south-west.

Parker place, Rox.; from Parker Hill avenue, at angle near Hillside street; westerly then south-westerly.

Parker place, Rox.; from Terrace street, opposite Alleghany street; formerly from Parker street, crossing Terrace street; part from Parker street to Terrace street laid out as Alleghany street, Oct. 2, 1877. L 1268.

Parker street, B., 1856; from Washington street to Harrison avenue; called Sprague street, 1855; named Parker street. Jan. 29, 1856; name changed to Rollins street. April 21, 1868. L 35.

***Parker street**, Rox.; from Boylston street to Centre street; laid out from Tremont street to Sewall, Day & Co.'s Works, Jan. 19, 1662, laid out from Heath street to Centre street, Jan. 19, 1662; named from Heath street by John Parker's to Worcester turnpike (now Tremont street) and across same to Mill-dam (now Beacon street), May 9, 1825; altered "from top of hill near Prospect street," Sept. 7, 1857; lines changed from Washington (now Tremont) street to Alleghany street, May 31, 1858; altered at junction with Heath street, Sept. 5, 1870; extended from Heath street to Centre street, Aug. 1, 1871; laid out between northerly line of Boylston street, extended and northerly end of part of Parker street south of Boylston street, now a public highway, Aug. 25, 1877; discontinued between Commonwealth avenue and Beacon street, Dec. 5, 1879; discontinued between West Chester park (now Massachusetts avenue) at Commonwealth avenue and Boylston street, Nov. 8, 1880. L 493, L 534, L 650, L 1260, L 1261, L 1262, L 1411, L 1504, L 1574, L 1845, L 1846, L 1847, L 1848, L 1849, L 2009, L 2588, L 2589.

***Parker street**, Chsn.; from Perkins street to Cambridge street; laid out and accepted, Sept. 18, 1865.

***Parker Hill avenue**, Rox.; from Huntington avenue to Parker street; name of Highland place changed to Parker Hill avenue, May 3, 1870; laid out from Tremont street (now Huntington avenue), and extended to Parker street, April 16, 1877. L 1234, L 1235, L 1236, L 1237.

Parker's alley, So. B.; from 222 West Fourth street to Silver street, now partly built over and remainder called Hayden place.

Parker's court, So. B.; from 228 West Fourth street to Silver street; shown on atlas, 1874; called Smith place on atlas, 1884, and not shown on later atlas.

Park lane street, W. Rox., 1895; from Walnut avenue north-westerly to near Olmstead street; laid out Nov. 23, 1895; formerly called Franklin Park terrace. L 2750.

Parkman place, B., 1825; from Hanover street, north-westerly, between Cross street and Parmenter street.

Parkman place, Dor.; from Parkman street, north, near Adams street.

***Parkman street,** B., 1868; from North Russell street, westerly, to North Grove street; called Vine street from North Russell street to Bridge (now North Anderson) street, 1806; extended to North Grove street, 1852; name changed to Parkman street, April 21, 1868. L 94, L 1754.

Parkman street, B., 1846; from Dover street, north; called Tuckerman street, 1831; named Parkman street, 1846; name changed to Albion street, 1849.

***Parkman street,** Dor.; from Dorchester avenue to Adams street; laid out and accepted, June 11, 1853. L 1210, L 1231, L 2093.

Parkman street, Bri., 1875; from Brooks street, north-west, near Faneuil station; part shown east from Brooks street on early atlas.

Parkman's corner, B., 1708-1732; corner of Ship (now Commercial) street and Battery alley (now street).

Parkway, E. B.; from Bennington street to Wood Island Park; includes what was formerly called Neptune street or avenue.

Parley avenue, W. Rox., 1880; from Centre street to Rockview street; same given Parley vale, Directory, 1884.

***Parmenter street,** B., 1870; from Hanover street to Salem street; called Bear, Beer or Bur lane, 1708; Bridge's lane, 1796; Richmond street, 1800; name changed to Parmenter street, December, 1870. L 319, L 331, L 443, L 2659.

***Parnell street,** B., 1880; from Lenox street to Sawyer street; called Plympton court, 1844; laid out and named Parnell street, Sept. 8, 1880. L 1489.

Parris place, B., 1845; from Poplar street, north, between Chambers street and Spring street; name changed to Melrose place, 1849.

Parrott's alley, B., 1800; from Water street to Milk street, nearly opposite Oliver street; probably the same as Board alley; now closed and occupied by the Mason building.

***Parsons street,** Bri., 1853; from Washington street to North Beacon street; laid out, June 3, 1842; accepted conditionally, July 18, 1842; laid out, June 24, 1853; accepted and named, Sept. 5, 1853; laid out from Beacon street to Faneuil street, May 19, 1856; accepted, March 9, 1857; relocated between Washington street, and Faneuil street, April 29, 1882. L 1608, L 1609.

Partridge street, W. Rox.; from La Grange street, opposite Adelaide terrace, to Cottage avenue.

***Passageway,** B.; from Faneuil Hall square to North street; very ancient, especially the northerly half next to North street; the City Solicitor decides that it is a public way, Sept. 23, 1879; named Bendall's lane, Feb. 27, 1882.

Passageway, B.; from Shawmut avenue to Tremont street between Upton street and Union park; laid out, 20 feet wide, Jan. 19, 1858, but City Solicitor rules (1879) that the action was illegal, there having been no order of notice; see Union Park passageway.

Passageway, Chsn., 1875; from Medford street to Prescott school; now partly built over by Medford-street Primary School-house.

Patten street, W. Rox., 1896; from Hyde Park avenue to Bourne street; authority to open given by Street Commissioners, Aug. 5, 1896.

Patterson street, Dor.; from Codman street, near Dorchester avenue to Brook street.

***Paul street,** B., 1868; from Tremont street to Emerald street; name, of Gardner (or Gardiner) street changed to Paul street, April 21, 1868; laid out, Dec. 31, 1870. L 546, L 566, L 837, L 838, L 1349.

***Paulding street,** Rox., 1884; from Dale street to Bainbridge street; laid out, Sept. 17, 1884. L 1821.

***Paul Gore street**, W. Rox.; from Centre street to Lamartine street; part from Centre street to Chestnut avenue laid out, Sept. 14, 1882; laid out from Chestnut avenue to Lamartine street, July 5, 1887. L 1638, L 2000, L 2781.

Paul Gore terrace, W. Rox.; from 82 Paul Gore street.

Payson avenue, Dor.; from Hancock street to Glendale street.

Payson court, So. B.; from 312 West Broadway to Athens street.

Payson place, Chsn., 1875; from 9 Elm street, near High street, south-easterly, then north-easterly, to Howard place.

***Peabody square**, Dor., 1893; the open space at the junction of Talbot avenue, Dorchester avenue and Ashmont street; named Nov. 20, 1893.

Peabody street, Rox.; from Brookline avenue to Binney street.

Peabody place, W. Rox.; from 219 Lamartine street, near Spring lane.

Peaceable street, Bri., 1875; from Rockland street to Winship street.

***Pearl place**, B. 1828; from Pearl street, east, between Milk street and High street; laid out and extended to Oliver street, July 23, 1869; name changed to Wendell street, being a continuation of that street, March 1, 1883. L 459, L 463.

Pearl place, E. B.; between and parallel with Webster street and Marginal street, near Cottage street.

***Pearl street**, B., 1800; from Milk street to Atlantic avenue; called Hutchinson lane, from Milk street to Cow lane (now High street), 1722; Hutchinson street, 1743; Palmer street, 1788: Green lane by plan of 1789; name of Hutchinson street changed to Pearl street, Jan. 22, 1800; extended to Purchase street, including Griffin's or Gridley's lane, 1821; extended from Purchase street to Broad street (now Atlantic avenue) July 10, 1837; extended from Milk street to Congress street at Water street, including portions of Bath street, April 18, 1873; last named portion called Post Office square, Dec. 28, 1874. Vol. 31, p. 6; Vol. 31, p. 27-65; Vol. 19, p. 69. L 2, L 82, L 656, L 846, L 853, L 915.

Pearl street, Rox.; name changed to King street, April 21, 1868; King street, from Roxbury street to Elmwood street, laid out, July 16, 1877.

***Pearl street**, Dor.; from Pleasant street to Dorchester avenue; Selectmen report in favor of acceptance, Sept. 12, 1855; laid out, July 13, 1859; laid out as a town way, March 5, 1860.

***Pearl street**, Chsn., 1845; from High street to Medford street; from Summer street to Bunker Hill street conveyed to Town by Oliver Holden, for a public highway, July 17, 1810, being called North Pleasant street; named Pearl street July 7, 1845; accepted conditionally, from Bunker Hill street to Medford street, May 4, 1856; same accepted Oct. 25, 1854; altered from Summer street to High street, Oct. 22, 1867.

Pearl street, Bri.; from Franklin street to Everett street; laid out by Selectmen, Dec. 16, 1873; laid out as Brentwood street, Aug. 13, 1889. L 2150.

Pearl-street place, Chsn.; from 90 Pearl street, north-westerly, near Medford street; same in 1875.

Pearl-street wharf, B.; from Atlantic avenue, south-easterly, at the foot of Pearl street.

Pearson's court, Rox.; from Kemble street.

Peck lane, B., 1796; from Essex street to Johonnot's wharf; same in 1817; included in Oxford street in 1842.

Peck's arch, B., 1800; entrance of Savage's or Williams court from Cornhill (now Washington street).

Peirse's alley, B., 1708; from King (now State) street to Corn Market (now Faneuil Hall square), 1708; called Change alley, 1788; Fitche's alley, 1796; Peirce's alley, 1800; Pierce alley, 1817; Flagg alley, 1828; Change avenue, 1841.

Pelham place, B.; from Pelham street, near Shawmut avenue, north-east.

***Pelham street,** B , 1868; from Washington street to Shawmut avenue; name of South Williams street changed to Pelham street, Jan. 4, 1868.

Pelton street, W. Rox.; from Park street, north-easterly, near Anawan avenue; same in 1874.

Pemberton corner, B.; corner Ann (now North) street and Swing Bridge lane (now Merchants' row), 1708.

Pemberton Hill, B.; that part of Common (now Tremont) street extending from its junction with Court street and Howard street; called Pemberton Hill, April 22, 1829; prior to 1835, south of Howard street and west of Tremont street between Somerset street and Tremont row.

Pemberton Hill street, B.; opposite Hanover street, 1839.

***Pemberton square,** B., 1838; from Tremont street, westerly, then northerly and southerly, then westerly to Somerset street; part running north and south formerly with park in centre; called Phillips place or square from Tremont street, west, opposite Court street, 1835; name changed to Pemberton square, 1838; laid out, Oct. 16, 1877. L 1279, L 1876, L 1912.

***Pemberton square,** B.; at the head of Cornhill contiguous to Court street and Tremont street; named Pemberton square, Feb. 19, 1838; same called Scollay square on account of naming Phillips square Pemberton square, June 25, 1838.

Pemberton's corner, B., 1708; corner Dock square and Wing's lane (now Elm street).

Pembroke court, B.; from Pembroke street, north-easterly, and then north-westerly and south-easterly; from Pembroke street, north, near Shawmut avenue, 1859.

***Pembroke street,** B., 1834; from Shawmut avenue to Warren avenue; laid out on the Neck, July 24, 1826; named from Tremont street to Suffolk street (now Shawmut avenue), Sept. 15, 1834; accepted Dec. 7, 1857; accepted west of Tremont street, Dec. 21, 1859; laid out as a public street from Tremont street to Warren avenue, May 21, 1867; laid out between Columbus avenue and B. & P.(now N. Y., N. H. & H.) R R., Dec. 7, 1869; part west of Columbus avenue named Berwick park, Dec. 21, 1869. L 115, L 354, L 502, L 516.

Pembroke street, Bri.; from Tremont street, near Newton line to said line; now wholly in Newton on account of change in boundary line.

***Penfield street,** W. Rox., 1892; from Brandon street to Birch street; Prospect street laid out as Penfield street, Sept. 23, 1892. L 2435.

Penneman's corner, B., 1708; corner of Marlboro' (now Washington) street and Summer street.

Penryth street, Rox.; from Pynchon street (now Columbus avenue) to Centre street.

People's Ferry avenue, B., 1854; from Commercial street, opposite Battery street, to the North Ferry; later called North Ferry avenue; Battery street extended to include same, Aug. 3, 1880. L 207, L 1474.

People's Ferry avenue, E. B.; from Sumner street, opposite Border street, to North Ferry; Border street extended to include same, Aug. 3, 1880. L 207.

Pepperell place, So. B.; from Dorchester avenue, westerly, between West Fourth street and Division street.

Pequot street, Rox.; from Wait street to Calumet street.

Perch street, Rox.; from Pike street, north-east.

Percival avenue, Dor.; from Bowdoin street to Fox avenue (now street); formerly from Church (now Bowdoin) street to Fox avenue; laid out as Percival street, March 21, 1888.

Percival court, } **Percival place**, } E. B.; from Orleans street, near Maverick street, north-westerly, then north-easterly.

Percival square, Dor., 1879; at junction of Bowdoin, Adams, and Church streets; laid out and named, April 7, 1879; named Eaton square, June 1, 1880.

***Percival street**, Dor., 1888; from Bowdoin street, forming the south side of Eaton square, to Fox avenue (now street); Percival avenue laid out as Percival street, March 21, 1888. L 2060.

Percy place, Rox.; from Roxbury street, northerly, nearly opposite Putnam street.

Percy street, W. Rox.; from Anson street to St. Mark street, near Forest Hills station.

Perham street, W. Rox., 1874; from Baker street, crossing Mt. Vernon street, West Roxbury Branch R.R.; authority to open from south-east of Lasell street to Baker street, given by Street Commissioners, March 5, 1895.

Perkins place, Rox.; from Roxbury street southerly, next west of Guild row; shown as Perkins street on atlases.

***Perkins street**, B., 1853; from Congress street to Pearl street; avenue for foot-passengers laid out from Atkinson (now Congress) street to Pearl street, nearly in line of continuation of Berry (now Channing) street, Jan. 30. 1826; passageway leading from between 67 and 69 Pearl street to Atkinson street named Perkins street, Sept. 12, 1853. Vol. 31, p. 88. L 911.

***Perkins street**, Rox. and W. Rox., 1825; from Centre street at junction with Day street, to Brookline line; Connecticut lane laid out, Jan. 19, 1662; same laid out, 1762; named Perkins street, from Centre street by Leonard Hyde's to Brookline line by the pond, May 9, 1825; lines established, Nov. 28, 1848; altered, etc., at junction with Prince street, Sept. 27, 1871.

Perkins street, W. Rox.; from Canterbury street to Grew avenue.

***Perkins street**, Chsn.; from Cambridge street to Somerville line, location of passageway reserved through Charlestown common altered and Perkins street laid out, running north-westerly from Cambridge road, May 6, 1822; laid out with present bounds, Oct. 25; 1852.

Perkins-street court, W. Rox.; from Perkins street, north, near and east of Prince street.

Perraway's alley, B.; a name of North Centre street prior to 1708; later called Paddy's alley.

***Perrin street**, Rox.; from Moreland street to Waverly street; accepted, July 27, 1863.

Perry court, Rox.; from Hampden street; name changed to Hampden place, May 9, 1876.

Perry place, Chsn.; from Pleasant street, easterly.

***Perry street**, B., 1853; from Washington street to Harrison avenue; laid out, Dec. 22, 1853; named, Dec. 29, 1853. Vol. 31, p. 98; Vol. 19, p. 126. L 4.

Perry street, Chsn.; from Decatur street; north-westerly; formerly from Chelsea street to and across Decatur street; part between

Chelsea street and Decatur street, laid out as Dupont street, Aug. 29, 1890. L 2258.

Perry's wharf, B.; from Lehigh street, south-easterly, adjoining Broadway.

Persia street, B., 1831; from Ann (now North) street to Fulton street; laid out and name changed to Ferry street, Aug. 1, 1842.

Perth street, Dor.; from Quincy street to Phipps avenue.

***Peterborough street,** Rox., 1896; from Audubon road to Audubon road; laid out, Nov. 16, 1896. L 2796, L 2606.

Peter Parley road, W. Rox.; from Forest Hills street to Walnut avenue; laid out as Peter Parley street, Aug. 28, 1891.

***Peter Parley street,** W. Rox., 1891; from Walnut avenue to Washington street; Peter Parley road, from Walnut avenue to Forest Hills street, laid out as Peter Parley street, Aug. 28, 1891; extension laid out from Forest Hills street to Washington street, Oct. 7, 1891. L 2332, L 2343.

Peters street, W. Rox.; from Neponset avenue, near Canterbury street.

***Peters street,** So. B., 1886; from East Seventh street to East Sixth street, near N street; laid out, July 31, 1886. L 1927.

Petrel street, W. Rox.; from Cottage avenue, opposite Shaw street, south-west.

Pevear court, Rox.; from Dudley street, south-westerly, opposite Winslow street; same called Pevear place and Pevear street.

Philip street, Dor.; from Taylor street, south-east to Milton Branch Railroad.

Phillips buildings, B., 1817; on Kilby and Water streets.

Phillips corner, B., 1732; corner of Cornhill (now Washington street) and Water street.

Phillips court, B., 1843; south-west from Leverett street, between Spring street and Ashland street, with two unnamed openings into Leverett street; one of the openings called Leverett avenue, 1859.

Phillips court, B., 1866; from Phillips street, southerly, between Grove street and West Cedar street; called Southac court, 1826; named Phillips court, 1866; on all recent atlases Southac court and Phillips court both appear.

Phillips place, B., 1829; from Tremont street, west, next north of Beacon street; called Tremont place, 1805; named Phillips place, 1829; now built over.

Phillips place or square, B., 1835; from Tremont street, west, opposite Court street; named Pemberton square, 1838.

Phillips place, So. B.; from West Fourth street, near and west of Dorchester avenue.

Phillips place, Dor.; from Dudley street, north-easterly, near and west of Belden street.

***Phillips square,** B.; junction of Harrison avenue, Essex street and Chauncey street; named, April 4, 1894.

***Phillips street,** B., 1866; from Irving street to West Cedar street; called Southac street, 1729; named Phillips street, Feb. 6, 1866. L 763.

***Phillips street,** Rox.; from Tremont street to Ward street; laid out from Tremont street to Smith street, July 24, 1879; laid out from Smith street to Ward street, July 3, 1883. L 1370, L 1687, L 1713, L 2038.

Phipps avenue, Rox. and Dor.; from Blue Hill avenue to Cedar (now Mascoma) street; also called Phipps street.

Phipps corner, B., 1708; corner of Salem street and Charles street.

Phipps lane, Chsn.; from Main street to Old Burying Ground; same as Phipps street.

Phipps place, B., 1835; from Charter street, south-westerly, towards Hull street, nearly opposite Foster street.

Phipps street, Rox. and Dor.; from Blue Hill avenue to Mascoma street; also called Phipps avenue.

***Phipps street,** Chsn.; from Main street, south-westerly, to Old Burying Ground; laid out, Oct. 17, 1839; accepted by Town, Nov. 11, 1839; called also Phipps lane.

Phoenix place, B., 1840; from Stillman street to Cooper street; closed.

Phoenix place, Rox.; from 75 Hampden street, westerly; now built over.

Pickering avenue, } Rox.; from Walnut avenue, southeasterly, between Rockland street and Dale street.
Pickering place, }

Pickering place, B.; from Rowe street, west, 1847–48; can not be now identified.

Pickering place, So. B.; from East Fifth street, southerly, between L street and M street.

***Piedmont street,** B., 1824; from Pleasant street to Ferdinand street; from Pleasant street to the water, 1824; extended to Ferdinand street, 1868; laid out, Sept. 25, 1868. L 393, L 394, L 396.

†**Pierce avenue,** Dor.; from Adams street, north-easterly, crossing Plain street towards Neponset avenue; laid out in part (probably between Newhall street and Plain street), March 1, 1869. L 711.

Pierce place, Dor.; from Hancock street, south-westerly, opposite Jerome street.

***Pierce square,** Dor., 1897; the open space at the junction of Adams street, Washington street and Dorchester avenue; named Jan. 18, 1897.

Pierce's or **Peirse's alley,** B.; now Change avenue; see Peirse's alley.

Pierpont street, Rox.; from Prentiss street to Station street, parallel with B. & P. (now N. Y., N. H. & H.) R.R.; laid out, Oct. 10, 1892; discontinued, Jan. 4, 1895. L 2440, L 2685, L 2686.

Pike alley, B., 1845; from Poplar street, south-westerly, north-westerly, then north-easterly, by two openings into Poplar street again; rear of the south side of Poplar street, near Chambers street; opening near Spring street now called Farwell avenue.

Pike street, Rox.; from Albany street to Fellows street.

Pilgrim place, Dor.; from Richfield street, north-easterly, between Columbia street and Norton street.

Pilgrim street, Rox.; from Punch Bowl road (now Brookline avenue) to Longwood creek and that portion of bridge over creek within Roxbury limits near Oakland place; money borrowed to build, Sept. 7, 1857; included in Longwood avenue as laid out by County Commissioners, June, 1857.

Pinckney lane, B., 1835; from Pinckney street to Mt. Vernon street; named Mt. Vernon avenue, 1846.

***Pinckney street,** B., 1803; from Joy street to Charles river; from Belknap (now Joy) street to Charles street, 1803; confirmed as a public street, Sept. 15, 1834; extended west of Charles street, Oct. 31, 1865. L 304, L 346.

Pine Grove terrace, Rox.; from 261 Heath street.

Pine Island, Rox.; north-east of Swett street at Roxbury Point.

Pine place, B., 1844; from Pine street to Oak place; closed.

***Pine street,** B., 1822; from Washington street to Harrison avenue; lines established, May 31, 1802; named Pine street, March 13, 1822; established as a public street of city, May 25, 1840. L 433.

Pine street, W. Rox.; from Albion (now Sycamore) street to Brown avenue, 1874; laid out, from Brown avenue to Sherwood street, with name of Ridge street, April 9, 1888, and from Sherwood street to Sycamore street, Oct. 3, 1891. L 2064.

Pine street, Chsn ; from Bunker Hill street to Bainbridge street; same in 1875. L 2738.

Pit's corner, B., 1732; corner Ann (now Commercial) street and Fish market (now North Market street).

Pitts alley, B.; from Pitts street, north-westerly; sometimes called Pitts place.

Pitts court, B., 1820; from Pitts street, north-westerly, near Green street.

Pitts lane, B., 1733; from Green street to the Mill-pond; named by Selectmen in 1788; named Pitts street, 1820.

Pitts place, } B., 1833; from Pitts street, north-westerly, near
Pitts-street place, } South Margin street.

***Pitts street**, B., 1820; from Green street to Merrimac street; Pitts lane, from Green street to the Mill-pond, 1733; filling begun, Sept. 30, 1807; named Pitts street, 1820. L 11.

***Plain street**, Dor.; from Chickatawbut street to Pierce avenue; laid out as Snow's court, June 5, 1867; located from Chickatawbut street to Pierce avenue, March 2, 1868. L 711.

Plainfield street, W. Rox.; from Williams street, south-westerly, to beyond Keyes street.

Plant avenue, Rox., 1896; from Parker street to Bickford street, near Centre street; authority to open given by Street Commissioners, Aug. 5, 1896.

Platt's corner, B., 1708; at the southerly end of Union street.

Pleasant place, B.; from Mahan place, southerly, and by two exits, westerly, into Pleasant street; see Pleasant-street place.

Pleasant place, Dor.; from Savin Hill avenue, north, near and west of Dorchester avenue.

Pleasant place, So. B.; from East Seventh street, south, between L street and M street; formerly called Mechanics place.

***Pleasant street**, B., 1743; from Washington street, opposite Broadway, to Park square; from Orange (now Washington) street, north-westerly, to the Common, 1743; laid out by George Tilley on his own land; accepted and recorded as a town street, May 5, 1773; from Orange street by the South Writing School, through what was called Tilley's land to the bottom of the Common and to Frog lane (now Boylston street), 1788; altered between Providence street and Boylston street, May 13, 1850. Vol. 31, p. 80, vol. 19, p. 96. L 47, L 387, L 391, L 392, L 393, L 394, L 475, L 548, L 549, L 565, L 590, L 613, L 724, L 726, L 878, L 1309, L 1448.

Pleasant street, Dor.; from South street to Union street, at Commercial Point.

***Pleasant street**, Dor., 1840; from Freeport street to East Cottage street at Town Meeting square; street from Stoughton Hall over the plain to Downer's, named Pleasant street, March 11, 1840. L 708, L 709, L 710, L 777, L 778, L 1502.

Pleasant street, W. Rox.; from Montgomery street to Webster street, near and parallel with Spring street; same in 1874.

Pleasant street, W. Rox.; from Mt. Vernon street to Dent street, near and parallel with West Roxbury Branch R.R.; same in 1874.

***Pleasant street**, Chsn.; from Main street to High street at Monument square; part of conveyed to Town, May 7, 1793; accepted from Back (now Warren) street to High street, June 6, 1823. L 1005.

Pleasant street, Chsn., 1819; from Summer street to Bunker Hill street; conveyed to Town by Oliver Holden, July 17, 1819, as Pleasant street; called North Pleasant street when name was changed to Pearl street, July 7, 1845.

Pleasant street, Bri.; from Franklin street to Everett street; laid out by Selectmen, Dec. 16, 1873; laid out as Holton street, Aug. 2, 1887. L 2007.

Pleasant-street court, B.; from Pleasant street, near Shawmut avenue, north-easterly.

Pleasant-street court, B., 1829; from Pleasant street to Church street; name changed to Berlin street, 1857; Tennyson street extended through Berlin street, 1869.

Pleasant-street court, Chsn.; from Pleasant street, north-easterly; same in 1875.

Pleasant-street place, B., 1846; from Pleasant street, east; northerly end called Pleasant place.

Plover street, W. Rox.; from Cottage avenue, near Sparrow street, south-west.

Plummer place, So. B.; from Middle street, south-easterly, towards Alger street.

Plymouth court, Rox.; from 979 Harrison avenue, north-westerly, near Hunneman street; same given as Hunneman court on atlas, 1884.

Plymouth place, B., 1825; from Front street (now Harrison avenue), west, to Newton place; laid out with Newton place as Knapp street, May 14, 1879. L 1351.

Plymouth street, B., 1800; from Summer street to Short lane or street (now Kingston street), 1800; laid out and made, from Summer street to Pond (now Bedford) street, and accepted by Town and named Plymouth street, May 13, 1800; called Kingston street at same date and since.

Plymouth street, B. and Rox., 1825; from Northampton street to Roxbury line, 1825; laid out from Eustis street to Boston line to meet Plymouth street, there, and accepted by Town, Dec. 16, 1833; part in Boston accepted and name changed to Harrison avenue, Aug. 9, 1859; no record of change of name of part in Roxbury.

Plymouth street, So. B.; name changed to Preble street, Aug. 7, 1855; (Preble street from Dorchester avenue to Liberty street and later extended to Vinton street).

***Plymouth street**, Rox.; from Longwood avenue to Bernier street; laid out, June 22, 1894. L 2600.

Plymouth street, Dor.; from Freeport (formerly Commercial) street to Neponset street; formerly from Commercial street to Pleasant street at Commercial Point.

Plympton court, B., 1844; from Lenox street, south, near Shawmut avenue; laid out from Lenox street to Sawyer street, with name of Parnell street, Sept. 8, 1880. L 1489.

***Plympton street**, B., 1849; from Harrison avenue to Albany street; named from Harrison avenue to a dock in South bay, May 14, 1849; accepted Oct. 30, 1860.

Point Shirley, B.; formerly a part of Boston and anciently called Pullen point; see Suffolk Deeds 48-136, Feb. 22, 1733.

***Polk street**, Chsn.; from Bunker Hill street to Medford street; laid out and accepted, July 2, 1867.

Pollard's corner, B., 1708; corner of Brattle street and Hillier's lane (now Brattle street).

†**Pomeroy street**, Bri., 1887; from Gordon street to west of Saunders

street; Orchard street, from Gordon street to Saunders street, laid out as Pomeroy street, June 9, 1887. L 1904.

Pomfret street, W. Rox.; from Corey street to Maple street.

Pond avenue, W. Rox.; from Chestnut street to Brookline line; laid out by County Commissioners, from Perkins street passing over a part of Chestnut street, through Brookline to Mill-dam or Punch Bowl road in Roxbury, November, 1867; part now called Chestnut street and part now in Riverway.

Pond place, B.; from Endicott street, easterly, north of Cooper street; from Pond (now Endicott) street, 1833; called Endicott-street place, 1837–42.

Pond street, B., 1708; from Newbury (now Washington) street to Blind (sometimes called Pond) lane, 1708; extended to Summer street, including Blind lane, 1803; name changed to Bedford street, Feb. 7, 1821.

Pond street, B., 1814; from junction Hanover street and Salem street to Charlestown bridge; called Mill lane, from Middle (now Hanover) street to the Mills, 1805; laid out May 26, 1806; laid out over the Mill-pond, Aug. 3, 1807; called Mill-pond street, from Mill lane to Prince street, 1807; lands exchanged for building (Pond street), 1808; from Hanover street to Charlestown bridge, 1814; altered in northerly part, 1828; name changed to Endicott street, June 13, 1836.

***Pond street**, Dor.; from Dorchesterway to East Cottage street; formerly from Boston street to Dorchester avenue; named from Five corners (now Edward Everett square) by the Great pond, to Mr. Moseley's, March 11, 1840; located, etc., Feb. 8, 1847; part between Pleasant street and Dorchester avenue changed to East Cottage street, March 1, 1893; part near Boston street taken into Dorchesterway. L 815, L 2533.

***Pond street**, W. Rox., 1825; from Centre street to Brookline line; named by Town, May 9, 1825; probably a public highway some time previous; County road from Roxbury to Brookline; altered, etc., April, 1838, and September, 1839. L 1062.

Pond-street place, B., 1833; from Endicott street, east, near and north of Cooper street; from Pond (now Endicott) street, 1833; called Endicott-street place, 1837–42; now Pond place or Pond-street place.

Ponemah street, Dor., 1895; from Blue Hill avenue, north-westerly; authority to open given by Street Commissioners, March 26, 1895.

Pontiac street, Rox.; from Alleghany street to Hillside street; authority to open given by Street Commissioners, April 12, 1894.

***Pontine street**, Dor.; from Norfolk avenue to Clifton street, laid out from Norfolk avenue to Batchelder street, Dec. 30, 1893; laid out from Batchelder street to Clifton street, Jan. 2, 1897. L 2582, L 2804.

Pope court, / **Pope-street court**, } E. B.; from Pope street to railroad, near and north-east of Curtis street.

†**Pope street**, E. B.; from junction Saratoga street and Swift street to Addison street; accepted at junction of Pope street and Saratoga street, Nov. 1, 1858; accepted between Saratoga street and Moore street, Dec. 10, 1861.

***Pope's Hill street**, Dor., 1882; from Neponset avenue to Commercial (now Freeport) street; Clay street laid out as Pope's Hill street, Dec. 8, 1882. L 1669.

Pope's wharf, B.; from Albany street, easterly, near and north of Dover street.

Poplar avenue, B., 1859; from Poplar street, northerly, between Auburn street and Charles street; called also Auburn avenue; included in Auburn street, Sept. 1, 1879.

Poplar avenue, B.; from Poplar street, northerly, between Auburn street and Charles street.

Poplar court, B.; from Poplar street, south-westerly, into Spring-street court; from Poplar street, southerly, near Kennard street, 1844.

Poplar place, B.; from Poplar street, north-easterly, near and east of Spring street; same in 1840.

***Poplar street**, B., 1800; from Chambers street to Charles street; new street west of Jeffrie and Russell's ropewalk, from Wiltshire (now Chambers) street to the water, named Poplar street, Feb. 12, 1800; to Brighton street, 1820; from Chambers street to North Charles street, 1859. L 2765.

***Poplar street**, W. Rox., 1825; from South street to Hyde Park line; named from South street, near Taft's across the turnpike, by Noah Davis' to Clapboard Hill, May 9, 1825 (from South street to Beech street); probably laid out as a highway some time previous; laid out by John Whittemore's land, near the Red Gate in line of old cart-path, to near Joseph Bailey's barn, Dorchester, at road from Lower Mills to Dedham, December, 1835; part between junction of Canterbury street and Beech street known as Sowden's Hill, 1859. L 2405, L 2570, L 2580.

Porcelain place, B.; from Poplar street, south-west, between Charles street and Brighton street; same in 1866.

Porter place, E. B.; from 134 Porter street, between Chelsea street and Bremen street.

***Porter street**, B., 1838; from Pleasant street, to Indiana place (now Corning street); from Pleasant street, west, 1838; to Indiana place, 1853; extended to Indiana place Dec. 1, 1857; accepted, Aug. 28, 1861. L 120, L 122½, L 548, L 724, L 838.

***Porter street**, E. B.; from Central square to Bremen street, with proposed extension to (proposed) Front street; accepted, from Central square to Chelsea street, June 3, 1856; accepted from Chelsea street to Bremen street, Sept. 17, 1857; extended through land of Boston & Worcester (now B. & A.) R.R. Co., Dec. 1, 1857.

***Porter street**, Rox., 1866; from Highland street to Lambert avenue; accepted and named, Oct. 29, 1866; name changed to Millmont street, April 21, 1868.

***Porter street**, W. Rox.; from Boylston avenue, southerly, to Bismarck street; laid out from Boylston avenue, Dec. 13, 1876; extension to Bismarck street laid out, June 16, 1892. L 1207, L 2403.

Portland place, B., 1820; from Portland street, north-easterly, between Hanover street and Sudbury street; now built over.

***Portland street**, B., 1807; from Hanover street to Causeway street; called Cold or Cole lane, from Hanover street to the Mill-pond, 1708; laid out and called Portland street, 1807; continued into the Mill-pond, Aug. 3, 1807; laid out across the Mill-pond to Causeway street, 1807. L 48, L 232, L 351, L 668, L 669, L 670, L 671, L 766, L 767, L 989, L 1602, L 1603, L 1604.

***Portland street**, B., 1842; from State street to Chatham street; Chatham row laid out near the head of Long wharf, May 9, 1827; called Portland street, 1842; renamed Chatham row, July 3, 1848.

***Portsmouth street**, Bri.; from Lincoln street to Waverley street; laid out, Nov. 2, 1893. L 2542.

†**Posen street**, Rox.; from Minden street, south-easterly, crossing Arklow street, also from Posen street, easterly, parallel with Minden street; part of Heath place laid out, from Minden street to Arklow street, with name of Posen street, Nov. 16, 1881. L 1568.

Post Office avenue, B., 1849; from Congress street, easterly, between State street and Exchange place; called Congress court, 1826; named Post Office avenue, 1849.

Post Office square, B., 1874; at junction of Congress, Pearl, Milk, Bath, and Water streets; parcel of land between proposed extension of Pearl street, Congress street and Milk street laid out as a public street, April 18, 1873; area included between Water, Milk, Congress, and Pearl streets named Post Office square, Dec. 28, 1874. L 87, L 846, L 1441.

Potomac street, W. Rox., 1896; from Mt. Vernon street to Yorktown street; authority to open given by Street Commissioners, Oct. 19, 1896.

***Powell street**, W. Rox.; from Summer street at Spring-street station, parallel with railroad, to Cass street; laid out, Dec. 10, 1883. L 1749.

†**Power street**, So. B.; from Boston street to Dorchester avenue; portion laid out eastwardly from Boston street, Dec. 24, 1875. L 1072.

Power's court, B.; from North street, westerly, between Salutation street and Hanover avenue; same in 1825; called also Ann-street court, 1830; called Powers (or Powar's) court again, 1840; now Powers court.

Powning's corner, B., 1708; corner Dock square and Crooked (afterwards Wilson's) lane (now Devonshire street), 1708.

Pratt court, Rox.; from Weston street, south-westerly, near and west of Cabot street; also called Pratt's court.

Pratt street, Dor.; from Ballou avenue to Lauriat avenue.

***Pratt street**, Bri.; from Linden street to Ashford street; given on chart 1875 as "street" from Linden street, easterly, towards B, & A. R.R., parallel with Ashford street; on chart of Boston, 1882, same called Pratt street; laid out from Linden street to Ashford street, May 9, 1887. L 1984.

***Preble street**, So. B.; from Dorchester avenue, easterly, then north-easterly, to Vinton street at O. C. (now N. Y., N. H. & H.) R.R.; name of Plymouth street changed to Preble street, Aug. 7, 1855; laid out from Dorchester avenue to Rogers street, Oct. 22, 1879; portion from Vinton street laid out, Feb. 7, 1881; laid out east of Rogers street to connect with last named part, Oct. 22, 1890. L 1209, L 1397, L 1415, L 1516, L 1761.

Prentice's corner, B., 1800; corner of Dock square and Hillier's lane (now Brattle street).

Prentice's wharf, B.; from Atlantic avenue, south-easterly, near and south of Congress street; now built over.

Prentiss place, Rox.; from Linden-Park street, northerly, between Cabot street and Lamont street; formerly called Linden place.

***Prentiss street**, Rox.; from Tremont street to Parker street; laid out, Dec. 30, 1869. L 507, L 508, L 2766.

Presby place, Rox.; from Winthrop street, north-easterly, near and west of Blue Hill avenue.

Prescott place, B., 1849; from Washington street, south-east, between East Lenox street and Thorndike street; named, May 14, 1849; Prescott place, from Washington street to Reed street, laid out and name changed to Newcomb street, Sept. 8, 1874. L 961.

Prescott place, Rox.; from Prescott street, north-westerly, between Eustis street and Hampden street.

Prescott place, Dor.; from Winter street to Church street.

Prescott place, Bri.; from Appianway, north-west.

***Prescott square**, E. B., 1875; between Eagle, Trenton, and Prescott streets; named Nov. 23, 1875.

†**Prescott street**, E. B.; from Eagle street to Boston, Revere Be[illegible] Lynn R.R.; accepted from Chelsea street to Bremen street, No[illegible] 1861; laid out from Trenton street to Eagle street, Sept. [illegible]g-authority to open part from near Orleans street to Boston, [illegible]eet, Beach & Lynn R.R. given by Street Commissioners, April [illegible] L 896, L 897.

***Prescott street**, Rox.; from Eustis street, north-easterly, then easterly to Hampden street; laid out, May 16, 1873. L 857.

***Prescott street**, Chsn., 1836; from junction of Devens street and Harvard street to Washington street; name of Middlegate street changed to Prescott street, Dec. 5, 1836.

Prescott-street avenue, Chsn.; from Bow (now Devens) street to Prescott street; same given, but unnamed in 1884.

Preston court, Dor.; from Gibson street, northerly, to Tenean creek, between Adams street and Brook street.

***Preston street**, Dor.; from Mills street to Freeport street; formerly from Mills street to Pleasant street; from Mill street to Commercial (now Freeport) street located, March 20, 1861; from Freeport street to Pleasant street now called South street. L 1857.

Price avenue, Dor.; (proposed) from Blue Hill avenue to Franklin Field.

Primus avenue, B., 1871; from Phillips street, southerly, near and east of West Cedar street; called Wilberforce place, 1843; named Primus avenue, 1871.

***Prince street**, B., 1708; from North square to Causeway street, opposite Charles River bridge; called Black Horse lane from Middle (now Hanover) street to Charlestown Ferry, 1698; highway laid out at lower end of Black Horse lane, Jan. 25, 1702; from Middle street to the salt water at the Ferry-way called Prince street, 1708; highway at lower end of Black Horse lane, now Prince street, widened and continued to low-water mark, March 2, 1721; commonly called Blackhorse lane in 1800; extended from Hanover street to North square, including parts of Bell alley and Garden-court street, July 11, 1833. L 151, L 2719, L 2764.

Prince street, B.; Lyman street, so called prior to 1812.

***Prince street**, W. Rox., 1855; from Pond street to Perkins street; laid out from road to Jamaica Plain Meeting-house to road from Roxbury through Brookline, September, 1828; called Cottage street on map, 1849; name of Cottage street changed to Prince street, April 2, 1855; altered, etc., at junction with Perkins street, near Jamaica pond, Sept. 27, 1871.

Prince-street avenue, B., 1833; from North Bennet street to Prince street; called School alley, 1732; Grammar alley, 1795; named Prince-street avenue, 1833; name changed to Bennet avenue, 1839.

Princeton place, E. B.; from Princeton street, south-easterly, between Prescott street and Putnam street.

***Princeton street**, E. B.; from Meridian street to Eagle square; accepted and laid out, Aug. 2, 1852, accepted and laid out, Dec. 18, 1855; accepted at junction Princeton street and Chelsea street, Nov. 1, 1858. L 93.

***Princeton street**, Chsn.; from Lexington street to Tufts street; part of Tufts street leading from and running at right angles with Lexington street called Princeton street, Oct. 6, 1851; laid out as a public way, July 13, 1863.

Princeton-street court, Chsn.; from Princeton street; extended to Medford street and laid out as Stone street, June 13, 1871.

Prior place, Dor.; from Richfield street north-west; now called Richfield park.

Prison lane, B., 1722; from Queen (now Court) street, south; probably the present east entrance of Court square.

Proctor court, Dor.; from Franklin court, northerly, between Massachusetts avenue and Norfolk avenue.

Proctor street, W. Rox.; from Fairview street to Walter street.

***Proctor street**, Rox.; from Adams street to East (now Hampden) street; accepted, March 7, 1853; name changed to Eustis street, April 21, 1868.

***Proctor street**, Rox., 1886; from Massachusetts avenue to Norfolk avenue; laid out from East Chester Park (now Massachusetts avenue) to Norfolk avenue, July 17, 1886. L 1922.

Proctor's lane, B., 1789; from Middle (now Hanover) street to Fish (now North) street; called Wood lane, 1708; named Proctor's lane, 1789; dock at bottom of Proctor's lane filled up, the Town to continue the passageway always open as any other public street, May 1, 1799; Richmond street extended through it, July 6, 1824.

Procyon place, Rox.; from Greenwich street, south-west.

Proprietor's way, Bri., 1814; from Washington street to South street; Seaver lane, 1842; later named Foster street.

***Prospect avenue**, W. Rox.; from Sycamore (formerly Albion) street to Brown avenue; laid out from Brown avenue to Sheldon street, Nov. 23, 1878; and from Sheldon street to Sycamore street, Oct. 13, 1891. L 1335, L 2347.

Prospect avenue, } Chsn., from Prospect street, easterly, near Chelsea
Prospect place, } street.

Prospect court, B.; from South Margin street, near Prospect street, 1849.

Prospect lane, B.; now Prospect street.

***Prospect street**, B.; from Merrimac street to Lyman street; from Leverett place (now Lyman street) to the Mill-pond, 1812; afterwards to Merrimac street; formerly called Prospect lane; accepted, conditionally, Sept. 10, 1827.

Prospect street, Rox.; from Parker street to High street (now Parker Hill avenue), 1849; name changed to Fisher avenue, April 21, 1868 (Fisher avenue from Parker street to Parker Hill avenue.)

Prospect street, Dor.; from Norfolk street to Milton avenue; laid out, as Edson street, Sept. 6, 1888. L 2091.

Prospect street, W. Rox.; from Charles street, north-easterly, to B. & P. (now N. Y., N. H. & H.) R.R., then north-westerly to Spring street.

Prospect street, W. Rox., 1878: from Brown avenue to Sheldon street; laid out as Prospect avenue, Nov. 23, 1878. L 1335.

Prospect street, W. Rox.; from Maple (now Birch) street to Brandon street; given on chart, 1884, as part of Birch street; laid out as Penfield street, Sept. 23, 1892.

***Prospect street**, Chsn.; from Chelsea street to Tremont street; laid out and accepted, Aug. 18, 1869; part of discontinued and new street laid out, April 12, 1870.

Prospect street, Bri.; Allston street laid out from North Beacon street (now Brighton avenue) to junction with a street formerly called Prospect street, near house of T. F. Frobisher, June, 1870.

***Providence street**, B., 1846; from Columbus avenue at Park square to Clarendon street; the flats deeded to City by Boston and Roxbury Mill Corporation, November, 1826; old way discontinued, April 27, 1846; new street east of the empty basin south of extension of Boylston street and north of depot of B. & P. (now N. Y., N. H. & H.) R.R., named Providence street, May 4, 1846; extended from the bend opposite Arlington street to Berkeley street, over land of Boston Water Power Co. and B. & P. R.R. Co., May 9, 1865; from Church street to Berkeley street discontinued, Dec. 10, 1866, and reconsidered, Dec. 13, 1866; part from Berkeley street to Clarendon street laid out, Oct. 22, 1885. L 287, L 328, L 746, L 1893, L 2456.

Province court or Province House court, B.; from Province street, easterly, towards Washington street, then southerly, crossing end of Ordway place; from Washington street through the archway in front of the so called Old Province House, to Province street, 1825.

Province House row, B. 1817; in Marlboro' (now Washington) street, in front of Old Province House; named and numbered, Oct. 8, 1817; so to avoid renumbering street.

***Province street,** B , 1833; from School street to Bromfield street; called Governor's alley, 1732; named Montgomery street, 1833; name of Governor's alley changed to Province street, June 10, 1833; same confirmed as a public way, Sept. 15, 1834. Vol. 31, p. 73. L-88, L 288, L 1601.

Public Garden, B.; between Charles, Boylston, Arlington and Beacon streets; the west side of Charles street, between Beacon street and Boylston street, 1837. L 171.

Pudding lane, B., 1708; from King (now State) street to Water street, "Pudden lane" after the fire enlarged into a street named Devonshire street, April 20, 1766.

Pulaski avenue, So. B.; from Athens street to West Third street, between F street and Dorchester street.

Pulling's corner, B., 1784; corner of Ann (now North) street and Cross street.

Pullen point, B.; old name for Point Shirley (see Suffolk Deeds, 48–136, Feb. 22, 1733).

Purchase place, B., 1827; from Purchase street, north, between Pearl street and Gibb's lane (now Oliver street); included in Hartford street, July 23, 1869. L 464.

***Purchase street,** B., 1747; from Broad street, at its junction with High street to Summer street, called Belcher's lane, 1708; from Summer street to Tilley's lane (now Gridley street), 1747; from Summer street to Batterymarch (now Broad) street, 1800; from Summer street to India wharf, 1817. Vol. 31, pp. 5, 67. vol. 19, p. 70, L 2, L 82, L. 327, L 464, L 466, L 468 L 469, L 470, L 471, L 821, L 922.

Puritan avenue, Dor.; from Richfield street, south-westerly.,

Putnam place, Rox.; from Roxbury street, south-westerly, then westerly, to Putnam street; name of Suffolk place changed to Putnam place, May 31, 1870 (same part given as Suffolk place on recent chart).

***Putnam square,** E. B., 1875; between White, Trenton and Putnam streets, Nov. 1, 1858; named, Nov. 23, 1875.

†**Putnam street,** E. B.; from Condor street to Bremen street, with proposed extension to (proposed) Front street; accepted from Condor street to Chelsea street, 1856; accepted from Chelsea street to Bremen street, 1861. L 676.

***Putnam street,** Rox.; from Roxbury street to Dudley street; accepted, Oct. 7, 1850, and March 3, 1851.

***Putnam street,** Chsn.; from Henley street to Common street; accepted, from turnpike (now Chelsea street) to houses of Robbins and Tapley, near Training Field, May 6, 1822.

Putnam street, Bri., 1875 (proposed); from Griggs street at Massachusetts (now Commonwealth) avenue, south-westerly, towards Warren street.

***Pynchon street,** Rox., 1868; from Tremont street to junction Heath street and Centre street; laid out as Lowell street from road near Guy Carleton's Factory in southerly direction to old Boston & Providence railroad near Hog bridge, September, 1833; name of Lowell street changed to Pynchon street, April 21, 1868; all of Pynchon street included in Columbus avenue, Jan. 4, 1895. L 768, L 1157.

***Q street,** So. B.; from harbor near East Second street to harbor south of East Sixth street, with proposed extension of to East First street; laid out and named from salt water on the south to Harbor of Boston on the north, Feb. 27, 1805; laid out from low-water mark north of First (now East First) street to harbor line in Dorchester Bay, Nov. 17, 1868; part south of East Sixth street now included in Marine Park. L 156, L 1446, L 1868, L 2057, L 2058, L 2135.

Quaker lane, B., 1708; from King (now State) street to Water street; called also Leveret's lane; with Dalton street named Congress street, Jan. 22, 1800.

Queen street, B., 1708; from Cornhill (now Washington street), opposite State street, to Hanover street; name changed to Court street, 1784.

Queen street, Dor.; from King street, south, between Neponset avenue and Train street.

Queensberry street, Rox., 1897; from Audubon road to Audubon road.

Quiet place, B., 1849; from Purchase street to Broad street (now Atlantic avenue), near Belmont (now Oliver) street; called Ingersoll place, 1847; built over prior to 1879.

Quincefield street, Dor., 1895; from Humphreys street, south-west, to Humphreys square; authority to open given by Street Commissioners, Nov. 14, 1895.

Quincy court, B.; from North street, south-easterly, near Richmond street; same in 1857; called on map, Quincy street.

Quincy lane, B., 1822; from Broad street to Hamilton street; called Hamilton avenue in 1823; closed in 1836.

Quincy place, B., 1812; from High street, north, near Washington (now Fort Hill) square; laid out and extended to Pearl place (now Wendell street), Dec. 15, 1873; name changed to Hartford street, being a continuation of the same, Feb. 28, 1882. L 836.

Quincy place, Rox.; from Quincy street, southerly, opposite Tupelo street.

Quincy place, Chsn.; from Quincy street, north-westerly, near Medford street.

Quincy row, B.; from Clinton street to South Market street; laid out, with name of Mercantile street, Dec. 19, 1879.

Quincy street, B.; from North street, south-easterly, near Richmond street; same called Quincy court in Directory and Records.

Quincy street, So. B.; name changed to Bowen street, April 21, 1868.

***Quincy street,** Rox. and Dor.; from Warren street to Bowdoin street; part in Roxbury, from Warren street to Grove Hall (now Blue Hill) avenue, laid out as South Dennis street, Jan. 19, 1662; confirmed, May 17, 1697; named Quincy street, Oct. 13, 1856; part in Dorchester closed by Selectmen, March 1, 1865; extended from Columbia street to Bellevue street, Nov. 15, 1870; laid out from Blue Hill avenue to Columbia street, Sept. 29, 1871; name of that part of Bellevue street, which was a continuation of Quincy street to Bowdoin street, changed to Quincy street, March 1, 1886. L 577, L 652, L 694, L 695, L 696, L 731, L 795, L 1558, L 1692.

Quincy street, Chsn.; from Bunker Hill street to Medford street; same in 1875; laid out under the name of St. Martin street, May 11, 1896. L 2762.

Quint avenue, Bri.; from Brighton avenue, south-west, near Allston street.

Radcliffe road, Dor.; from Randolph road, south-west, to Hyde Park line.

Railroad avenue, W. Rox.; from the end of Willow street, south-westerly, between Centre street and the railroad, near Highland station.

Railroad street, W. Rox.; from Willow street to Highland station; same as Railroad avenue.

Rainsford street, B.; Rainsford's lane so called in City Records, July 6, 1824, when made a part of Front street (now Harrison avenue).

Rainsford's corner, B.; corner of Charter street and North street, 1708; called Rainsford's corner, 1732.

***Raleigh street**, Rox.; from Beacon street to near Charles River; laid out, Nov. 11, 1890. L 2271.

Raleigh street, Dor.; from Glenway street to Greenwood street; authority to open given by Street Commissioners, March 28, 1893.

Ramsey street, Dor.; from Dudley street to Hamlet street, at Upham's corner.

Ramsey place, Dor.; from Ramsey street, north-west.

Rand place, Rox.; from Rand street, east, nearly opposite Fairbury street.

Rand square, Rox.; from Rand (the part now Julian) street, easterly; now a part of Julian street.

†**Rand street**, Rox.; from Julian street to Brookford street; formerly from Blue Hill avenue, nearly opposite Clifford street, easterly, southerly, south-westerly, to Brookford street; name of Bismarck street, from Blue Hill avenue, changed to Rand street, Dec. 30, 1871; laid out about 340 feet easterly from Blue Hill avenue, March 27, 1882; name changed to Julian street, March 1, 1892; part from Blue Hill avenue, opposite Woodbine street, easterly, laid out as part of Brookford street, July 6, 1883. L 1591, L 1715.

Rand street, W. Rox.; from Gardner street, south-west, to beyond Whiting street.

Randall street, Rox.: from Harrison avenue to Fellows street. L 1491.

Randlett place, Rox.; from Brookford (formerly Rand) street, southerly.

Randolph road, Dor.; from River street to Oakland street, nearly parallel with Hyde Park line; formerly Bird lane; authority to open given by Street Commissioners, April 16, 1896.

***Randolph street**, B.; from Harrison avenue to Albany street; same in 1870; laid out, Feb. 14, 1884. L 1756.

Randolph terrace, Dor.; from Beale street to Van Winkle street; near Shawmut Branch R.R.

Ransford's lane, B., 1708; from Essex street to Beach street, and so down to the sea, 1708; Rainsford's lane, from Essex street to Beach street, 1800; Rainsford street included in Front street (now Harrison avenue), July 6, 1824.

Ransom court, B.; from Cotting street, south-easterly; same in 1859; called Ransom street on plan.

Ransom road, Dor.; from Randolph road, south-west, to Hyde Park line.

Rasford's corner, B.; corner Essex street and Ransford's lane (now Harrison avenue), 1708.

Ravenswood park, W. Rox.; from Glen road, south-westerly, near Walnut avenue, 1853; now in Franklin Park.

Ravine lane, Bri.; from Englewood avenue to Roxbury avenue (now Sutherland road); afterward Elm street; now part of Strathmore road.

***Rawson street**, So. B.; from Boston street to Dorchester avenue; formerly Jackson street; laid out, Dec. 29, 1892. L 2484.

Rawson's lane, B.; from Marlborough (now Washington) street to the Common, 1708; from Marlborough street to Common (now Tremont) street, 1732; called Bromfield's lane, 1796; named Bromfield street, Nov. 10, 1828.

***Ray street**, Rox.; from Regent street, north-westerly, then north-easterly, crossing Hulbert street; laid out from Regent street to Hulbert street, Nov. 6, 1882; same called Roy street in 1884. L 1663.

Raymond street, Rox.; from Lamartine street to Gilbert street (now Chestnut avenue); now a part of Mozart street.

***Raymond street**, Bri.; from Franklin street to Everett street; formerly Vernon street; laid out, July 29, 1884. L 1796

Raymond street, W. Rox.; from south-east of Dunbar street to Joy street near Brookline line.

Raymond's corner, B.; corner Orange (now Washington) street and Frog lane (now Boylston street), 1800.

Read street, Dor.; from Glenway street to McLellan street; called Read avenue on plan, 1884.

***Reading street**, Rox.; from Kemble street to Swett street; name of Reed street changed to Reading street, July 28, 1874; called Reed street on plan, 1884; laid out from Kemble street to Swett street, June 23, 1891. L 2304.

Reed court, B.; from East Newton street to East Brookline street.

***Reed street**, B. and Rox.; from Northampton street to Hunneman street; from Northampton street to Roxbury line, 1855; laid out from Northampton street to south-westerly line of Thorndike street extended, Sept. 8, 1874; portion discontinued, Sept. 23, 1875; laid out from Thorndike street to Hunneman street May 29, 1896. L 959, L 960, L 1078, L 2769.

Reed street, Rox.; from Kemble street to Swett street; shown on map, 1849; from Island street to Swett street; name changed to Reading street, July 28, 1874; a portion of Kemble street from Reading street to Hampden street was once called Reed street.

Reed terrace, B.; from Reed street, nearly opposite Flagg street, south-east.

***Reed's court**, Rox.; from Yeoman street to Ambrose street; from Yeoman street, southwesterly, 1873; laid out and extended to Hartopp place (now Ambrose street), Feb. 25, 1875. L 1023.

***Reedsdale street**, Bri.; from Brighton avenue to Linden street, at Commonwealth avenue; laid out, Aug. 13, 1886. L 1928.

Regent court, Rox.; from Circuit street, north-westerly.

Regent place, Rox.; from Regent street, north-westerly.

Regent road, Dor.; from Oakland street to Randolph road; authority to open given by Street Commissioners, April 16, 1896.

Regent square, Rox.; from Regent street, south-easterly, between Circuit street and Rock street.

***Regent street**, Rox.; from Warren street to Dale street; part between St. James street and Alpine street accepted, conditionally, July 29, 1867; laid out from Warren street to Circuit street, Jan. 2, 1873; extended from Circuit street to Dale street, May 26, 1881. L 825, L 826, L 827, L 1528.

Reims place, Rox.; from Ward street, north-easterly, near N.Y., N. H & H. R.R.

***Remington street**, Dor.; from Centre street to Nixon street; laid out, June 23, 1885. L 1866.

Rena street, Bri.; from Western avenue, south-easterly, then south-westerly, to North Harvard street.

Renfrew court, Rox.; from Renfrew street, south-westerly.

Renfrew court, Rox.; from Harrison avenue, north-westerly and northerly. to the end of Renshaw court (plan, 1873); now part of Renfrew street.

Renfrew place, Rox.; from Renfrew street, south-westerly.

Renfrew road, Bri.; from Commonwealth avenue to Sidlaw road; authority to open given by Street Commissioners, Oct. 1, 1891.

***Renfrew street**, Rox.; from Eustis street to Winslow street; name of Brewster street changed to Renfrew street, April 20, 1869; laid out from Eustis street to Winslow street, Dec. 16, 1870; parts between Eustis street and Harrison avenue laid out on plan, 1873, as Renfrew court and Renshaw court. L 589, L 1075.

Renshaw court, Rox.; from Eustis street, south-westerly, to end of Renfrew court; now part of Renfrew street.

Reservoir lane, Bri.; from Beacon street, south-easterly, to Brookline line; same in 1875.

Revere avenue, B.; from Clinton street to Richmond street.

Revere place, B.; from Charter street, south-westerly, near Hanover street; same in 1843.

†**Revere street**, B., 1855; from Irving street to Charles River; called May street, 1733; named Revere street, Aug. 7, 1855, from South Russell street to Charles River; portion from South Russell street to Irving street discontinued, June 22, 1894. L 2615.

***Revere street**, W. Rox.; from Alveston street to junction Roanoke avenue and Elm street; from Alveston street to Union avenue (now Call street), 1874; Bishop street laid out over part from Roanoke avenue to Call street, April 16, 1877; Revere street laid out from Alveston street to Roanoke avenue, Nov. 9, 1878. L 1326.

Revere-street court, B.; from Revere street, north-westerly, near West Cedar street; called Sherman place, 1847; called May-street court, 1849; named Revere-street court, 1858; Hill's court, 1874; now Bellingham place.

Revere-street place, 1857; from Revere street, near Grove street; May-street place, 1844.

Rexham street, W. Rox.; from Brandon street, south, then south-east, to Colberg avenue.

Reynolds street, E. B.; from Addison street at junction with Bremen street to Trumbull street.

Rice street, E B.; from Coleridge street, north-westerly, to railroad crossing at Homer street.

***Rice street**, Dor., 1894; from Walnut street to Taylor street; formerly part of Wood street; laid out as Rice street, July 26, 1894. L 2608.

Rich street, Dor.; from Delhi street, south-east, towards West Selden street.

Richards avenue, W. Rox.; from Hyde Park avenue across Huntington avenue to Hyde Park line; called Richland street on plan, 1874; same called Richardson street, plan, 1884.

Richards corner, B.; corner of Ship (now North) street and White Bread alley (now Harris street), 1708.

Richards court, Dor.; from Olney (formerly Green) street; cannot be now identified.

Richards street, B.; from Harrison avenue to Reed street; same in 1874; now built over.

Richards street, Chsn.; from Medford street, north-easterly, nearly opposite Cook street.

***Richards street,** So. B., 1868; from Granite street crossing A street; name of Munroe street changed to Richards street, April 21, 1868; laid out, Nov. 17, 1868. L 255.

Richards street, Bri.; from Washington street, north-easterly, to Brighton Hill, then round the hill and crossing itself; same in 1875.

Richardson avenue, So. B. (proposed); from Hyde street, crossing Locust street.

Richardson park, Dor.; at junction of East Cottage street and Dorchester way.

Richardson place, B.; from Short (now Kingston) street, near Essex street, 1830–48.

Richardson place, B.; from Tremont street, easterly, opposite Van Rensselaer place, 1849; closed about 1865.

Richardson place, E. B.; from Saratoga street, near junction with Chelsea street, south-easterly, towards Bremen street.

Richardson street, Bri.; from Western avenue, south-east, then north-west to Mackin street. L 2782.

Richardson street, W. Rox; from Hyde Park avenue to Hyde Park line; same given as Richland street on plan, 1874, and Richards avenue in Directory, 1884.

Richardson's alley or lane, B.; Hawley street was so called at an early date.

***Richfield street,** Dor.; from Columbia street to Olney street; laid out, Sept. 28, 1886. L 1950.

Richfield park, Dor.; from Richfield street, south-west; formerly called Prior place.

Richland street, W. Rox.; from Hyde Park avenue to Hyde Park line; same called Richardson street on plan, 1884; Richards avenue, from Hyde Park avenue to Huntington avenue, 1880 and 1884.

Richmond avenue, B.; from Salem street, north-westerly, 1833; North Margin street extended through, 1841.

Richmond place, B.; from Richmond (now Parmenter) street, north, near Salem street, 1840; shown on plan, 1833, but not named.

Richmond road, Dor., 1896; from Oakland street to Randolph road; authority to open given by Street Commissioners, April 16, 1896.

***Richmond street,** B., 1800; from Atlantic avenue to Hanover street, opposite Parmenter street; from Middle (now Hanover) street to Back (now Salem) street called Bear, Beer, or Bur lane, 1708; Bridges lane, 1796; named Richmond street, Jan. 22, 1800; extended east to Fish (now North) street, 1820; extended through Proctor's lane to Fish street, July 6, 1824; extended to Commercial street, through Page's yard, 1831; extended westerly, across Salem street toward Haymarket square, through Bartlett place, Aug. 18, 1845; extended to Mercantile street, 1859; name of part between Salem street and Hanover street chonged to Parmenter street, Dec., 1870; extended from Commercial street to Atlantic avenue, Oct. 8, 1875. Vol. 31, p. 64. L 127, L 319, L 331, L 443, L 1042, L 1080.

***Richmond street,** Dor.; from Washington street to Adams street; straightened from Washington street to Dorchester avenue, Dec.

25, 1867; same part laid out as a highway, May, 1869; continuation to Adams street laid out, Aug. 12, 1869. L 1644, L 1645, L 2614.

*Richmond street, Chsn.; from Bow (now Devens) street to Canal street; from Bow street to Union street; accepted, Sept. 16, 1813; from Union street to Austin street accepted, April 5, 1824; laid out, extended and accepted from Austin street to Chapman street, Sept. 15, 1856; lines established between Bow street and Union street, Dec. 12, 1859; continued and laid out from Chapman street towards the river to a point that would intersect north-westerly line of Williams street extended south-westerly. June 29, 1863; extended and laid out from present terminus to Cambridge street, Sept. 30, 1867; name of Canal street extended to portion of Richmond street between Austin street and Canal street. June 16, 1874; Richmond street and Canal street called Rutherford avenue, May 28, 1878.

Richview street, Dor.; from Hillsdale street, south-west, to Dorchester Park.

Ricker street, W. Rox.; from Walker street, north-east, near Weld street.

†**Ridge street**, W. Rox.; from Brown avenue to Florence street; formerly called Pine street; laid out as Ridge street between Brown avenue and Sherwood street, April 19, 1888; from Sherwood street to Sycamore street, Oct. 3, 1891. L 2064, L 2341.

Ridge road, Bri.; from Dustin street to Etna street.

Ridge road, Dor.; from Oakland street to Randolph road, near Hyde Park line; authority to open given by Street Commissioners, April 16, 1896.

Ridgemont avenue, Bri.; from Allston Heights, south-west, crossing end of Eleanor street; authority to open given by Street Commissioners, Feb. 2, 1893; laid out as Ridgemont street, Dec. 14, 1894.

*Ridgemont street, Bri., 1894; from Allston Heights to west of Eleanor street; formerly Ridgemont avenue; laid out, Dec. 14, 1894. L 2669.

*Ridgeway lane, B., 1788; from Cambridge street to Derne street; same in 1788; taken as a town street, conditionally, Sept. 23, 1818.

*Rill street, Dor.; from Hancock street, south-westerly, crossing Ware street; laid out from Hancock street to Ware street, Sept. 30, 1881. L 1560.

*Ringgold street, B.; from Hanson street to Waltham street; same in 1846; laid out, May 5, 1868. L 379.

Riorden place, Chsn.; from Monument street, near Bunker Hill street, south-east; also called Monument place.

Ripley's wharf, B.: from Commercial street, opposite Commercial court, north-easterly.

Ritchie street, B.; from Salem street to Endicott street, 1840–1844; called Morton street before and since.

*Ritchie street, Rox.; from Centre street to Marcella street; a part of what formerly was Greenwood street; laid out, Dec. 31, 1888. L 2111.

River place, B., 1877; from River street, near Mt. Vernon street; called River-street place, 1861; River place, 1877.

*River street, B., 1843; from Beacon street to and across Mt. Vernon street; same called A street on plans of 1830; River street, from Beacon street to Mt. Vernon street, 1843; accepted, conditionally, Oct. 17, 1855; accepted between Mt. Vernon street and Chestnut street, Oct. 4, 1859; accepted, conditionally, from Chestnut street to Beacon street, Nov. 17, 1862; extended 134½ feet north of Mt. Vernon street, June 16, 1868; laid out from Beacon street to Chestnut street, Oct. 9, 1877. L 297, L 1274.

***River street**, Dor.; from Washington street (Lower Mills) to Hyde Park line; located, Dec. 1835; named, March 11, 1840; altered, etc., July 17. 1857; relocated, Nov. 27, 1858; altered, etc., April, 1859; relocated, Dec. 27, 1865; altered, etc., near Kenney's bridge, December, 1865. L 739, L 1223, L 1224, L 1225, L 1226, L 1227, L 1228, L 1501, L 1995, L 2065, L 2802.

River street, Bri., 1840; from Cambridgeport to Brighton, near Charles river; named River street, June 15, 1840; name changed to Western avenue, June 13, 1873.

River-street place, B.; from the end of River street, north of Mt. Vernon street, to Pinckney street; same in 1861.

Riverdale park, Rox.; Riverway sometimes so called.

***Riverdale street**, Bri.; from Western avenue to Raymond street; laid out, Dec. 19, 1889. L 2193.

Riverside avenue, E. B. (Breed's Island); from Saratoga street, opposite Bayswater street, nearly parallel with Belle Isle Inlet to Ashley avenue.

***Riverside street**, Rox.; from Tremont street to Columbus avenue; formerly from Tremont street to Cary street; named Dec. 27, 1871; laid out, Sept. 30, 1876; portion included in extension of Columbus avenue and portion west of Columbus avenue discontinued, Jan. 4, 1895. L 1181, L 2684.

Riverview avenue, Dor.; from Adams street, following irregularly the course of Neponset River two-thirds of its length, then curving north-easterly to end of Butler street; part from Adams street to railroad, laid out as Medway street, Oct. 21, 1889. L 2183.

Riverway, Rox.; the parkway leading from the Fens bridge to the junction of Tremont street and Heath street; sometimes called Riverdale park.

Roach street, Dor.; from Pleasant street to Dorchester avenue.

***Roanoke avenue**, W. Rox.; from Revere street at junction with Elm street, to Alveston street; in 1849, from Centre street to Green street, including what are now parts of Seaverns avenue, Roanoke avenue and Elm street; laid out from Revere street to Alveston street, May 1, 1876. L 1144.

Robbins court, B., 1822; from Middle (now Hanover) street, west; called Robinson's court, 1821; Robbin's court, 1822; North Hanover place or court, 1825; Hanover place, 1827; North Hanover court, 1840.

***Robert street**, W. Rox.; from Brookfield street to South Walter street; laid out, Dec. 27, 1893. L 2576.

Robert avenue, Dor.; from Magnolia street to Hartford street; shown on plan in 1889; now shown as Chamblet street.

***Robeson street**, W. Rox.; from Forest Hills street to Sigourney street; laid out, Sept. 17, 1884. L 1822.

Robin street, W. Rox.; from La Grange street to north-east of Park street.

Robin Hood street, Dor.; from Hartford street to Magnolia street; also called Robin Hood avenue; formerly called Homestead avenue.

Robinson avenue, Dor.; from Robinson street, north-westerly.

Robinson court, Dor.; from Savin Hill avenue, near railroad, north-easterly.

Robinson place, Dor.; from Brook avenue, south-easterly.

***Robinson street**, Dor.; from Adams street to Draper street; laid out, Nov. 10, 1871. L 714, L 2634.

Robinson's alley or **lane**, B.; from North street to Elits (now Unity) street, 1733; confirmed as a public way, Sept. 15, 1834; name changed to Webster avenue, March 28, 1855.

Robinson's court, B., 1821; from Middle (now Hanover) street, west, 1821; called Robbins court, 1822.

Robinwood avenue, W. Rox.; from Centre street to Enfield street; authority to open given by Street Commissioners, Dec. 28, 1892.

Rochdale street, Rox.; from Cobden street, north, to Fenner street; authority to open given by Street Commissioners, Feb. 6, 1893.

***Rochester street**, B.; from Harrison avenue to Albany street; from Harrison avenue, east, 1844; to Albany street, 1846; from Harrison avenue to Albany street, accepted and laid out as a public highway, Oct. 17, 1855.

Rock avenue, Dor.; from Norfolk street, north-west, nearly opposite Stanton street.

Rock road, Dor.; from Randolph road, south-west, to Hyde Park line.

***Rock street**, Rox.; from Rockland street to Regent street; laid out, March 21, 1884. L 1763.

Rockdale street, Dor.; from Oakland street, south-west; authority to open street given by Street Commissioners, Oct. 13, 1893.

Rockingham court, E. B.; from Orleans street, near Decatur street, north-westerly, to land E. (now B. & M.) R.R. Co.

Rockingham place, Rox.; from Cabot street, south-easterly, then south-westerly, to Roxbury street.

Rockingham road, Dor.; from Oakland street to Randolph road, near Hyde Park line; authority to open given by Street Commissioners, April 16, 1896.

***Rockland avenue**, Rox.; from Rockland street to Dale street, nearly opposite Laurel street; laid out Sept. 30, 1876. L 1180.

Rockland avenue, Dor.; from Woodward avenue to Grampian way.

Rockland place, E. B.; from Everett street to Maverick street; shown as Rockland court from Everett street, towards Maverick street in 1892.

Rockland place, Rox.; from Rockland street, north-easterly.

***Rockland street**, Rox.; from Warren street to Dale street; accepted conditionally, Oct. 30, 1865; laid out between Warren street and Walnut avenue, July 8, 1873; laid from Walnut avenue to Dale street, Dec. 6, 1875. L 877, L 1107, L 1108.

***Rockland street**, W. Rox.; from Washington street, south-east, to Dedham line; laid out April 5, 1872. L 974, L 975.

Rockland street, W. Rox.; from Washington street, near Parkway, south-east.

***Rockland street**, Bri.; from Washington street, east of Chestnut Hill avenue, south-westerly, crossing Chestnut Hill avenue; laid out southwardly from Chestnut Hill avenue, July 21, 1879. L 1368.

Rockland street, Bri.; named from "near Parish House," southerly, to South street, and continued to Brookline line, June 15, 1840, location altered, Sept. 9, 1856; accepted, June 1, 1857; accepted from South street to a point on Washington street opposite Market street, June 11, 1871; name changed to Chestnut Hill avenue, Dec. 27, 1872. L 1573.

Rockledge street, Rox., 1895; from Lambert avenue to Thornton street, opposite Juniper street; authority to open given by Street Commissioners, Sept. 13, 1895.

Rockview place, W. Rox.; from Rockview street, south-east, near Spring Park avenue.

***Rockview street,** W. Rox.; from Spring Park avenue to Green street; D street laid out from Spring Park avenue, and extended to Green street under name of Rockview street, May 26, 1880. L 1459, L 1460.

***Rockville park,** Rox.; from Warren street, easterly, 1885; formerly Allston place and Rockville place; name changed to Rockville park, March 1, 1885. L 403.

***Rockville place,** 1868, Rox.; from Warren street, easterly; name of Allston place changed to Rockville place, April 21, 1868; laid out, May 25, 1869; changed to Rockville park, March 1, 1885. L 403.

Rockville street, Dor.; from Blue Hill avenue to Oakland street; authority to owen given by Street Commissioners, May 2, 1892.

Rockway street, Dor.; from Rockville street to Chester street.

***Rockwell street,** Dor.; from Washington street to Milton avenue; formerly Homer street; no record of change of name, but Rockwell street laid out, Feb. 2, 1880. L 1434.

***Rockwood street,** W. Rox.; from Pond street to Brookline line; laid out, March 29, 1872; relocated, Sept. 30, 1880. L 1493.

Rocky Hill avenue, Dor.; from Davenport avenue, north-easterly, south-easterly, north-easterly, south-easterly, to Columbia street; portions called Arion street and Davenport square; the portion from Columbia street, north-west, called Rocky Hill in 1894.

Rocky Swamp lane, Rox.; an ancient road in Roxbury; part of rendered useless by Norfolk and Bristol turnpike (now Washington street); also called Jube's lane and the "road to Rocky swamp;" discontinued, September, 1806.

Rodman street, W. Rox., 1896; from Wachusett street to Patten street; authority to open given by Street Commissioners, Aug. 5, 1896.

Rodney street, Bri.; from Cambridge street, near Dustin street, north-east.

Roebuck passage, B., 1815; from the Town Dock to Ann (now North) street, 1815; called Fish lane, 1789; made a continuation of Merchants' row, Oct. 9, 1826.

Rogers avenue, Rox., 1872; from Ruggles street to Parker street; portion between Parker street and Huntington avenue laid out as Bryant street, May 21, 1884; portion from Ruggles street to near bend formerly called Ruggles place. L 418, L 1777.

Roger's corner, B., 1800; corner of Beacon street and Summer (now Mt. Vernon) street.

Rogers court, Rox.; from Rogers avenue, westerly, between Farnum place and Bay View place.

***Rogers street,** So. B.; from Dorchester street to Hyde street; name of Mechanics street, from Dorchester street to Preble street, changed to Rogers street Aug. 7, 1855; laid out, Nov. 13, 1875; laid out, from Preble street to Hyde street, Sept. 2, 1885. L 1093, L 1209, L 1879.

Roland road, Dor.; from Oakland street to Randolph road, near Hyde Park line; authority to open given by Street Commissioners, April 16, 1896.

Roland street, Chsn.; from B. & M. R.R. to Somerville line, near Crescent street.

Rollins court, Rox.; from Dennis street, south-east, nearly opposite Huckins street.

Rollins place, B.; from Revere street, northerly, to Garden-street court; same in 1843.

***Rollins street,** B., 1868; from Washington street to Harrison avenue; called Sprague street, 1855; named Parker street, 1856; name changed to Rollins street, April 21, 1868. L 35.

Romar terrace, Rox.; from Cedar street, south-west, between Cedar park and Centre street.

***Romsey street**, Dor.; from Dorchester avenue to Sydney street; laid out, from Dorchester avenue to Sagamore street, Aug. 23, 1888; laid out from Sagamore street to Sydney street, Jan. 4, 1896. L 2088, L 2754.

Ropemakers lane, Chsn., 1670; from Harvard street to Front street; mentioned to be widened, March 1, 1819; spoken of as "Arrow street formerly Ropemakers lane," April 12, 1819.

Rosamond place, W. Rox.; from Clarendon park near corner of Poplar street north-west.

Rosemary street, W. Rox.; from South street south-east between Hall street and Spalding street.

Rosalinda street, Dor., 1872; from Columbia street to Erie avenue, near present Walcott street; now abandoned.

Roseberry road, Dor.; from Randolph road, south-west, to Hyde Park line.

Roseclair street, Dor., 1894; from Dorchester avenue to Boston street; authority to open given by Street Commissioners, Oct. 3, 1894; authority to open from Boston street eastwardly, given by Street Commissioners, March 12, 1896.

Rosedale avenue, Dor.; from Washington street to Whitfield street; authority to open given by Street Commissioners, May 12, 1893; laid out as Rosedale street, March 16, 1895. L 2699.

***Rosedale street**, Dor., 1895; from Washington street to Whitfield street; formerly Rosedale avenue; laid out, March 16, 1895. L 2699.

Rosemont street, Dor.; from Samoset street to Adams street and from Adams street, south-easterly, to Gustin avenue.

Rosemont terrace, Dor.; from the portion of Rosemont street south-east of Adams street, southerly.

Rosewood street, Dor.; from Oakland street, south-west, near N. E. R.R.; authority to open given by Street Commissioners, Oct. 26, 1893.

Roslin avenue, W. Rox.; from Beech street to Norfolk street; from Washington street to Beech street, 1874; part from Washington street to Norfolk street laid out as Kittredge street, Dec. 22, 1882. L 1672, L 1673.

Roslin street, Rox.; from Warren street, easterly; laid out, with name of Carlisle street, Sept. 20, 1883. L 1732.

***Roslin street**, Dor.; from Washington street to Ocean street; laid out, July 31, 1873. L 885.

Roslindale avenue, W. Rox.; from Beech street to Dudley avenue; same in 1874.

Roslyn place, W. Rox.; from Chestnut avenue, north-west, near corner of Boylston street; called Roslin avenue in 1874.

Ross place, So. B.; from rear of O street between East Fifth street and East Sixth street.

Rosseter place, Dor.; from Rosseter street, south-west, opposite Olney street.

†**Rosseter street**, Dor.; from Bowdoin street to Eldon street; portion between Eldon street and Union avenue (now Olney street), formerly part of Bowdoin avenue, laid out as Rosseter street, Sept. 26, 1882; name of Union avenue from Olney street to Bullard street changed to Rosseter street, March 1, 1889. L 1643, L 1651.

Roswell street, Rox., 1896; from Langdon street to Shirley street; authority to open given by Street Commissioners, June 12, 1896.

Rougemont place, Rox.; from junction of Columbus avenue and West Walnut park, west.

***Round Hill street,** Rox.; from Day street, south-east, then north-east, then south-east, across Gay Head street, then south, then north-east to Walden street; laid out, Dec. 30, 1893. L 2566, L 2567.

Round lane, B., 1732; from Long lane (now Federal street) to Atkinson (now Congress) street, 1732; on Carleton's map, 1800, called Round street; name changed to Williams street, Jan. 10, 1821.

Rowe court, B., 1845; from Rowe (now Chauncey) street, west; Rowe place, 1820; Rowe court, 1840; Exeter place, 1845.

Rowe place, B.; from Rowe (now Chauncey) street, south-easterly; same in 1838.

Rowe place, B., 1820; from Rowe street, west, 1820; named Rowe court, 1840; Exeter place, 1845.

Rowe place, B., 1825; from Bedford street, south, 1825; named Rowe street, 1834; Chauncey street, 1856.

***Rowe street,** B., 1834; from Bedford street to Essex street; called Exeter street, 1805; Rowe place, from Bedford street, south, 1825; Rowe place, laid out from Bedford street to Essex street, and named Rowe street, Dec. 22, 1834; name of Rowe street changed to Chauncey street, April 15, 1856.

Rowe street, Dor.; from Houghton street, near Pope's Hill street, east.

Rowe street, W. Rox.; from Brown avenue to Sharon street; same in 1849. L 2308.

Rowe's lane, B., 1803; Pond street was so called, 1803.

Rowe's pasture or field, B., 1777; between Essex street and Pond (now Bedford) street.

Rowe's wharf, B.; from Atlantic avenue, north-easterly, opposite High street and Broad street.

***Rowena street,** Dor.; from Carruth street to Bushnell street; formerly part of Fuller street; laid out, Aug. 29, 1889. L 2158.

Roxbury avenue, Bri.; from Chestnut Hill avenue, north-easterly; crossing Englewood avenue; same in 1875; part from Chestnut Hill avenue to Englewood avenue laid out as Isleworth street, May 11, 1887; remainder laid out as a part of Sutherland road, Oct. 11. 1892. L 1985, L 2442.

***Roxbury street,** Rox.; from Washington street to Columbus avenue; laid out, Jan. 19, 1662, and named Washington street, May, 1825; name of Washington street between Guild row (now Washington street) and Pynchon street (now Columbus avenue) changed to Roxbury street, June 16, 1874. L 402, L 420, L 768.

Roxbury terrace, Rox.; from Roxbury street, north-west, formerly called Bates place; later Washington court.

Roxton street, Dor.; from Glenway street to Greenwood street.

Roy street, Rox.; from Regent street to and crossing Hulburt street; same as Ray street. L 1663.

Royal road, Bri.; from Cambridge street to Coolidge road; laid out as Royal street, Aug. 24, 1892. L 2428.

***Royal street,** Bri.; from Cambridge street to Coolidge street; formerly Royal road; laid out, Aug. 24, 1892. L 2428.

Royal Exchange lane, B.; Shrimpton's lane (now Exchange street) sometimes so called.

Royall's alley, B., 1732; from Ann (now North) street, east, to the Wharffe, 1732; same in 1800; where Blackstone street now is, or between Blackstone street and Barrett street.

***Roys street**, Rox.; from Lamartine street to Chestnut avenue; laid out, Oct. 6, 1880, from Lamartine street to Gilbert street (now Chestnut avenue). L 1497.

Rozella street, Dor., 1897; from Adams street, near King street, to Muzzy street; authority to open under the name of Adams terrace, given by Street Commissioners, Oct. 8, 1895.

Ruck's corner, B., 1732; corner of Charter street and Salem street, 1732.

Rugby street, W. Rox.; from Centre street, nearly opposite Ballard street, north-west to beyond Vane street.

Rugby street, Bri.; from Cambridge street, near Rodney street, north.

Ruggles court, Rox.; from Ruggles street, southerly, near corner Halleck street: also called Ruggles-street court.

Ruggles place, Rox., 1867; from Ruggles street at crossing of B. & P. (now N. Y., N. H. & H.) R.R. southerly to creek; part now called Rogers avenue and part abandoned. L 418.

Ruggles place, Dor.; from Washington street, south-easterly, then north-easterly, then northerly and parallel with Dorchester avenue, between Codman street and Richmond street.

***Ruggles street**, Rox., 1825; from Washington street to Back Bay Fens; portion from Cabot street to Gravelly Point laid out, Jan. 19, 1662; named from Worcester turnpike (now Roxbury street) to the cross-dam (now Parker street), May 9, 1825; line straightened Nov. 5, 1827; street from Tremont street near Boston line to Washington (now Roxbury) street by Linden park (now Linden Park street), part of which had been called Cabot street and part Ruggles street, named Cabot street throughout, Aug. 9, 1858; street from Parker street to Washington street, part of which had been known as Ruggles street and part as Water street, named Ruggles street throughout, Aug. 9, 1858; laid from Parker street to Back Bay Fens, June 10, 1896. L 385, L 659, L 884, L 895, L 1291, L 1310, L 1889, L 2773.

Rumney marsh; old name of Chelsea, which was a part of Boston until 1738.

Rupert street, Dor.; from Kilton street, south-east, near Washington street; authority to open under the name of Sidney street given by Street Commissioners, May 15, 1895.

***Ruskin street**, W. Rox.; from Weld street to Corey street; formerly Corey avenue; laid out, April 1, 1890. L 2216.

Russell court, B.; from North Russell street, westerly, near Parkman street; same in 1848.

Russell park, Dor., 1896; from Westville street, northwardly, nearly to Corona street; authority to open given by Street Commissioners, July 2, 1896.

Russell place, B.; from North Russell street, westerly, south of Russell court; same in 1847.

Russell place, B.; from Suffolk street (now Shawmut avenue) south-east, between Carney place (now Waterford street) and Garland street, 1859; closed about 1872.

Russell court, / **Russell place**, Rox.; from Ruggles street, north-westerly, to Madison court; laid out as Field street, Jan. 5, 1887. L 1971.

Russell place, Chsn.; from Russell street, north-east, near Harrison place.

Russell street, B., in 1795; from Cambridge street, northerly, 1800; named North Russell street, from Cambridge street to Eaton street, and South Russell street, from Cambridge street to May (now Revere) street, 1802; to Myrtle street, 1806.

***Russell street,** Chsn.; from Pearl street to Auburn street; Oliver Holden conveys land (now part of Russell street) running from Pleasant street nearly at right angles north-westerly to street laid out by Richard Sullivan (now Sullivan street), July 17, 1819; from Graves (now Sullivan) street to Eden street accepted, March 24, 1834; from Eden street to Oak street laid out, May 23, 1859; laid out from Oak street and extended to Auburn street, July 23, 1861.

Russell-street court, Chsn.; from Russell street, north-east, between Auburn street and Mead street.

Russell's wharf, B.; from Federal street, easterly; same from Purchase street, 1800.

Russell's wharf, B.; next northward from Old North Battery, easterly, to the water, 1800.

Russia wharf, B.; from Atlantic avenue, south-easterly, at corner of and parallel with Congress street.

***Ruth street,** E. B., 1892; from Webster street to Marginal street; formerly part of Terrace place; laid out from Webster street to Brigham street (formerly part of Terrace place), Nov. 26, 1892; extended to Marginal street, Oct. 12, 1893. L 2462, L 2463, L 2538.

***Rutherford avenue,** Chsn.; from Devens street to Cambridge street; Richmond street and Canal street named Rutherford avenue, May 28, 1878. L 1216, L 1217, L 1218, L 1219, L 1590, L 2021.

***Ruthven street,** Rox., 1884; from Walnut avenue to Elm Hill avenue; part from Walnut avenue to Humboldt avenue formerly called Oriole street; laid out as Ruthven street, Dec. 1, 1884; laid out from Humboldt avenue to Elm Hill avenue, Nov. 14, 1890. L 1837, L 2273.

Rutland place, B.; from Haven street, near corner Rutland street, south-easterly; same in 1866.

Rutland place, So. B.; from O street, near East Sixth street, westerly; also shown previously as Butland place; not shown in 1891.

***Rutland square,** B., 1866; from Tremont street to Columbus avenue; part of Rutland street, from Tremont street to Water Power Co.'s line, 125 feet easterly from Columbus avenue, accepted and named Rutland square, Oct. 9, 1866; laid out from B. W. P. Co.'s line to Columbus avenue, Dec. 24, 1867. L 340.

***Rutland street,** B., 1826; from Washington street to Tremont street; laid out from Washington street, west, July 24, 1826; from line of extension of Front street (now Harrison avenue) to Tremont street, 1836; accepted Dec. 7, 1857; part west of Tremont street, extended to line of B. W. P. Co., and accepted, Aug. 13, 1861; from Tremont street to Columbus avenue, 1861; from Tremont street to B. W. P. Co.'s line (a passageway 125 feet east from Columbus avenue) accepted and named Rutland square, Oct. 9, 1866; laid out from B. W. P. Co.'s line to Columbus avenue, Dec. 24, 1867; laid out from Columbus avenue to B. & P. (now N.Y., N.H. & H.) R.R., Dec. 7, 1869; part west of Columbus avenue named West Rutland square, July 25, 1871. L 502, L 516.

***Rutledge street,** W. Rox.; from Park street to Bellevue street; given as Farrington street on plan, 1874; laid out, June 15, 1877. L 1243.

Ruxton road, Dor.; from Ridge road to Regent road, near Hyde Park line.

***Sachem street,** Rox.; from Hillside street to Calumet street; laid out, Sept. 19, 1887. L 2023.

***Sackville street,** Chsn., 1887; from Bunker Hill street to Medford street; Webster street laid out, with name of Sackville street, Jan. 1, 1887. L 1968, L 1969.

Saco street, Dor. 1891; from Neponset avenue, near and south of Howe street; authority to open given by Street Commissioners, Oct. 1, 1891.

†**Sagamore street**, Dor.; from Savin Hill avenue to Soudan street; laid out from Savin Hill avenue to Romsey street, June 5, 1877. L 1242.

***Salcombe street**, Dor., 1892; from Stoughton street to Cushing avenue; authority to open given by Street Commissioners, Sept. 23, 1892; laid out June 5, 1895. L 2714.

Salem court, B.; from Salem street, south-east, near Tileston street; same in 1846.

Salem place, B.; from Salem street, north-westerly, between Cross street and Endicott street; same in 1839.

Salem place, B.; from Salem street to Cooper street, 1828; named Bartlett place, 1837.

***Salem street**, B.; from Hanover street to Charter street; from Prince street to Charter street, 1708; at one time called Green lane; from Hanover street to Charter street, 1824; the part from Hanover street to Prince street called Back street, 1708–1824. Vol. 31, p. 92. L 341, L 2188, L 2659.

Salem street, W. Rox.; from Corinth street, south-westerly; part from Corinth street to Albano street laid out, with name of Cohasset street, Oct. 30, 1889. L 2186.

***Salem street**, Chsn.; from Main street to High street; road leading from Main street, opposite Capt. Phipps to steps of Baptist Meeting-house accepted as a town road, March 12, 1804.

Salem-Hill court, Chsn.; from Pearl street, north-westerly, same in 1875.

***Salem-street avenue**, Chsn ; from Salem street to High street; from High street accepted as North street, Dec. 15, 1834; name of North street changed to Salem-street avenue, July 21, 1869.

Salem turnpike, Chsn.; from Charlestown (now City) square to Chelsea; from Charlestown square to the north-west corner of Navy Yard surrendered to Town by Salem turnpike and Chelsea Bridge Corporation and act of Legislature authorizing same passed, June 17, 1831; now Chelsea street.

Salt Alley, B.; from Salt lane, at Creek square, southerly.

***Salt lane**, B.; from Union street, easterly, to Creek square; from Union street to Creek lane, 1708; from Union street to Creek square, 1817.

Salter place, B.; from Prince street, south, near Salem street; same in 1834.

Salter's court, B.; a passageway to the Exchange Coffee House, between Congress street and Devonshire street, 1808; called Exchange square, 1818; named Congress square, 1821.

Salutation alley, B.; from North (now Hanover) street, down by the Salutation to Ship (now Commercial) street, 1708; called Salutation street, 1825; so called from a figure used as the sign of a tavern on that passageway which took off its hat to passengers; also because it led from Hanover street to the Salutation or Fort; the North Battery is called in old records the Salutation.

***Salutation street**, B.; from Hanover street to Commercial street; called Salutation alley, 1708; named Salutation street, 1825.

Salvisberg avenue, Rox.; from Hampshire street, near Vernon street, to Culvert place, now Downing street; same given Hunnewell court on chart, 1884; now called Whittier street.

Samoset street, Dor., 1892; from Centre street, near and east of O. C. (now N. Y., N. H. & H.) R.R; authority to open given by Street Commissioners, Aug. 3, 1892.

Samosett place, B.; from Prince street, north-easterly, near Hanover street; same in 1851; called Somerset place on chart.

Sanborn avenue, Dor.; from Harvard street to Bradshaw street.

Sands place, B.; from Washington street, east, near South May (now Savoy) street, 1859; named Ottawa place, 1873; Temple park, 1879; Mechanics row, 1894.

Sands place, B.; from Harrison avenue, westerly, near Savoy (formerly South May) street, leading into and sometimes called Ottawa place, Temple park, and Mechanics row.

Sanford place, B.; from East Lenox street, north-easterly, near Washington street; same in 1870.

***Sanford street**, Dor.; from Washington street to Cedar street (Lower Mills); named from Washington street, near the Mills, to Neponset (now Morton) street, March 11, 1840; accepted June 15, 1853.

Santuit street, Dor., 1896; from Welles avenue to Rosemont street.

Saratoga place, E. B.; from Saratoga street, near Meridian street, north-westerly.

***Saratoga street**, E. B.; from Central square to Winthrop line; laid out from Swift street, north-easterly, and extended north-easterly, towards Breed's Island or Belle Isle to centre of channel, Aug. 7, 1848; continued over Breed's Island to Chelsea-point bridge, Sept. 20, 1848; accepted and laid out from Meridian street to Marion street, Sept. 27, 1852; accepted from Central square to Swift street, Oct. 4, 1852; laid out and dedicated from Chelsea street to Swift street, July 28, 1858; accepted at junction with Pope street and junction with 40-foot strip of land adjoining land of E. (now B. & M.) R.R.; Nov. 1, 1858; accepted at junction with Chelsea street, Sept. 13, 1859; County road (now Saratoga street) over Breed's Island, straightened, Feb. 1, 1862. L 141, L 161, L 244, L 248, L 289, L 899, L 1457, L 1458, L 1487, L 1851, L 1930, L 2155, L 2617.

***Sargent street**, Dor.; from Howard avenue to Hartford street; laid out, Sept. 2, 1876. L 1165.

Sargent street, W. Rox.; from Canterbury street to Walk Hill street; laid out as Paine street, May 1, 1884. L 1768.

Sargent's wharf, B.; from Commercial street, south-easterly.

Sarsfield place, Bri.; from North Harvard street, north-west, near Western avenue.

***Sarsfield street**, Rox., 1887; from Tremont street to Grinnell street; Milford place laid out, with name of Sarsfield street, Dec. 10, 1887. L 2046.

***Saunders street**, Bri.; from Cambridge street to North Beacon street; laid out, Oct. 15, 1886. L 1953.

Savage court, E. B.; from Chelsea street, north-westerly, between Marion street and Porter street.

Savage's corner, B.; corner of Dock square and Shrimpton's lane (now Exchange street), 1708.

Savage's corner, B.; corner of Ann (now North) street and Scottow's (now Scott) alley, 1708.

Savage's court, B.; from Cornhill (now Washington street) through Webster's arch, westward, 1732; name changed to Williams court, 1789,

Saville street, W. Rox.; from Park street to Irving street.

***Savin street**, Rox.; from Warren street to Blue Hill avenue; laid out, April 9, 1875. L 1037, L 1038.

***Savin Hill avenue**, Dor.; from Pleasant street to Savin Hill station, O. C. (now N. Y., N. H. & H.) R.R.; thence around Savin Hill to same point; road to Savin Hill by Mr. Tuttle's named Savin Hill avenue, March 11, 1840; driveway around Savin Hill, before called in part Atlantic avenue and in part Indian way, laid out as a public highway with name of Savin Hill avenue, Aug. 12, 1869; laid out 50 feet wide from Pleasant street to O. C. (now N. Y., N. H. & H.) R.R., Aug. 6, 1875. L 761, L 1067, L 1068, L 1250, L 1760, L 2531.

***Savoy street**, B., 1892; from Washington street to Harrison avenue; South May street, laid out, with name of Savoy street, Nov. 29, 1892. L 2465.

***Sawyer avenue**, Dor.; from Pleasant street to Cushing avenue; from end of Savin Hill or Sawyer Hill avenue, southerly, then northwesterly, towards Hancock street; laid out from Pleasant street, including Savin Hill or Sawyer Hill avenue, July 16, 1877; extended to Cushing avenue, Oct. 28, 1881; street west from Pleasant street, given on chart 1874 as part of Savin Hill avenue, on chart 1884 as Sawyer Hill avenue. L 1250, L 1251, L 1561.

***Sawyer street**, B; from Shawmut avenue to Lenox street; same in 1845; laid out, Sept. 23, 1872. L 780.

Sawyer Hill avenue, Dor.; from Pleasant street, opposite Savin Hill avenue, to Sawyer avenue; given on chart 1874 as part of Savin Hill avenue, and by directories made a part of Sawyer avenue; laid out as Sawyer avenue, July 16, 1877.

Saxon court, E. B.; from Paris street, near Porter street, northwesterly.

Saxton street, Dor.; from Romsey street, south-westerly, crossing Belfort street; authority to open between Belfort street and Savin Hill avenue given by Street Commissioners, March 13, 1895.

Sayward place, So. B.; from Woodward street, near Dorchester avenue, north-easterly.

***Sayward street**, Dor.; from Columbia street to Bird street; laid out, July 26, 1883. L 1722.

Scarborough street, W. Rox.; from Walnut avenue to Morton street; from Walnut avenue to Forest Hills street, 1849; built from Forest Hills street to Canterbury street, paid for, Feb. 24, 1851; streets known as Forest Hills and Scarborough streets named Morton street, Dec. 5, 1859, remainder included in Franklin park.

Scarlet's wharf lane, B.; from Ann (now North) street, west, 1789; part of Fleet street, so called.

***Schiller street**, Rox.; from Heath street to Minden street; laid out, July 16, 1891. L 2316.

School alley, B.; from North Bennet street to Prince street, 1732; called Grammar alley on Carleton's map, 1795; opposite the North Grammar School into Prince street called School alley, 1800; named Bennet avenue, 1839.

School court, Rox.; from Tremont street to New Heath-place Schoolhouse; named, March 5, 1860; later called Cottage place.

***School street**, B.; from Washington street to Tremont street; from Cornhill (now Washington street,) west across Common (now Tremont) street to the head of the present Somerset street, 1708; called South Latin School street, 1789, from Cornhill to Common street the part west of Common street being called Beacon street, 1803; widened by laying out as a town way a strip of land before used as a common passageway, Oct. 9, 1843. L 88. L 2085.

***School street**, Rox. and W. Rox.; from Walnut avenue to Amory street; laid out, Jan. 19, 1662; named from Centre street to Back street (now Walnut avenue), May 9, 1825; name of part from Centre street to Boylston street changed to Amory street, April 21, 1868. L 1171, L 1586.

***School street**, Dor.; from Washington street to Harvard street; from Upper road to lane leading to John Pierce's house located, May 23,

1808; named from Upper road by No. 4 School to Mr. Carleton's, March 11, 1840.

***School street**, Chsn.; from Main street to Bunker Hill street; July 17, 1810, Oliver Holden conveys to Town for a public highway a parcel of land now used as road called Middle street, from Bartlett street, north-easterly, to Bunker Hill street, nearly parallel with Pleasant street; also road called Alfred street from Summer street, north-easterly, to Bartlett street. both now forming part of School street; part from High street to Main street formerly called School-House lane, accepted as School-House street, May 3, 1824. L 1490.

School street, Bri.; from Market street to Waverley street; same in 1875.

School-House court, Chsn.; from Charles street, south-easterly; same in 1875.

School-House lane, Chsn.; from Main street to High street; accepted as School-house street, May 3, 1824; now part of School street.

School-House street, Chsn.; from Main street to Bunker Hill street; name changed to Charles street, Sept. 30, 1850.

School-House street, Chsn.; from High street to Main street; formerly called School-House lane; accepted, May 3, 1824; now part of School street.

School-street place, W. Rox.; from School street, north-easterly.

School-street place, Chsn.; from School street, north-westerly.

Schrepel place, So. B.; from East Third street, north, near K street.

***Schuyler street**, Rox.; from Blue Hill avenue to Elm Hill avenue; Ashland street named Sea-view street April 21, 1868; Sea-view street, named Schuyler street, May 24, 1870; laid out from Maple street to Elm Hill avenue, Sept. 9, 1877. L 2016.

***Scollay square**, B.; at the junction of Tremont and Court streets, Cornhill and Tremont row; named Pemberton square, Feb. 19, 1838; name changed to Scollay square, June 25, 1838, in consequence of naming Phillips square Pemberton square; the site of Scollay's building which was taken by the city in 1870. L 580.

Scollay's building, B.; between Court and Tremont street, where Scollay square now is, 1809.

Sconce lane, B.; from Fort Hill to Battery March, 1708; called Sconce street, 1784; named Hamilton street, 1807.

Sconce street, B.; from Fort Hill to Batterymarch street; called Sconce lane, 1708; named Sconce street, 1784; name changed to Hamilton street, 1807.

***Scotia street**, Rox.; from Bothnia street to Dalton street; laid out, June 30, 1890. L 2236.

Scott alley, B.; from Ann (now North) street to Creek lane (now square); called Scottow's alley, 1708; named Scott alley, 1823.

Scott court, B.; from Suffolk street (now Shawmut avenue), south-east, near Roxbury line. 1835.

Scott court, B.; from Union street, west, toward Hanover street; called Minot's court, 1708; named Scott court, 1796; called Minot's court in Edes' list, 1800; a portion included in Friend street when extended from Hanover street to Union street, 1855; part between Friend street and Union street discontinued, March 23, 1857; what remained built over when Washington street was extended to Dock square in 1873. L 40, L 63.

Scott's court, Chsn.; from Chelsea street, north-westerly, near Medford street; same in 1875.

Scott place, So. B.; from East Fifth street, north, near N street.

Scottow's alley, B.; from Ann (now North) street to Creek lane (now square) 1708; named Scott alley, 1823.

Sea street, B., 1708; from Summer street to Windmill Point; from Summer street to South Boston Free Bridge, 1825; called Broad street, 1833; name changed to Sea street, 1842; changed to Federal street, 1856: East street, so called, on Hale's plan, 1819. Vol. 31, pp. 28, 54, 101. L 44, L 55.

Sea-street bridge, B.; from south end of Sea street to South Boston, 1828; now Federal-street bridge.

Seaborn street, Dor.; from Centre street to Kenwood street; authority to open, from Centre street to near Kenwood street, given by Street Commissioners, July 10, 1891.

Seabury place, B.; from Blossom street, opposite Fruit street, easterly, to Vine-street place, called Blossom-street place, 1843; named Seabury place, 1844.

Sears place, B.: from Anderson street, easterly; same in 1849 (from West Centre street, east, near May street).

***Seattle street**, Bri., 1891; from Cambridge street across Hopedale street; authority to open "near the corner of Cambridge street and North Harvard street" given by Street Commissioners, July 10, 1891; laid out from Cambridge street to a point near and north-west of Hopedale street, May 5, 1892. L 2398.

Seaver lane, Bri.; from Washington street to South street; laid out by Selectmen, Aug. 1, 1842; accepted, conditionally, Nov. 28, 1842; laid out, Jan. 15, 1843; accepted, April 10, 1843; name changed to Foster street, Nov. 20, 1848; called by both names by record up to 1855.

Seaver place, B.; from Tremont street, west, between Eliot street and Warrenton street; called Nassau court, 1825; named Seaver place, 1844. L 406.

***Seaver street**, E. B.; from Webster street to Sumner street; accepted and named, Oct. 7, 1853.

***Seaver street**, Rox. and Dor.; from Walnut avenue to Erie street; named from Back street (now Walnut avenue) to Brush Hill turnpike (now Blue Hill avenue), May 9, 1825; name of Egleston square, from Walnut avenue to Washington street, changed to Seaver street, March 1, 1882; extended from Blue Hill avenue to Columbia street at new Seaver street, Dec. 27, 1882; name of New Seaver street, from Columbia street to Erie street, changed to Seaver street, March 1, 1889; Columbus avenue extended over part from Washington street to Walnut avenue, Jan. 4, 1895. [Part from Blue Hill avenue to Walnut avenue included in Franklin Park by Park Commissioners, March 27, 1893, and same part relocated as a public street by Street Commissioners, Dec. 4, 1894.] L 597, L 602, L 930, L 1313, L 1676, L 2653, L 2654, L 2655.

***Seaverns avenue**, W. Rox.; from Centre street to Elm street; parts of shown as Roanoke avenue and Virginia avenue on map, 1849; extended through Starr lane and laid out as a public way, March 10, 1873. L 931, L 932, L 2503.

***Sea-view street**, Rox.; from Blue Hill avenue to Maple street; name of Ashland street changed to Sea-view street, April 20, 1869; name of Sea-view street changed to Schuyler street, May 24, 1870.

Sea-view street, B. I.; from Orient avenue to Tower street.

Second street, B., 1809; from Leverett street to Copper street; Second street leading southerly from Leverett street, accepted and recorded as a public street, May 12, 1828; confirmed as a public street, Sept. 15, 1834; name changed to Napier street, April 25 1855; named Barton street, 1868.

Second street, B.; Fulton street, so called on S. P. Fuller's plan of March 27, 1826; laid out from a street (now Clinton street) to be laid out north of the stores on North Market street to another street leading to Ann (now North) street to be laid out through land of Robert G. Shaw, Feb. 22, 1828.

***Second street,** So. B.; from Dorchester avenue to City Point; laid out parallel with Broadway and named, Feb. 27, 1805; made passable from Turnpike street to Dorchester street, Nov. 7, 1831; part southerly of the Brewery and the upland on margin of flats discontinued, Sept. 7, 1835; opened from P street to City fences, June 18, 1849; laid out from Federal street (now Dorchester avenue) to Dorchester street, and thence to low-water mark, Nov. 17, 1868; parts east and west of Dorchester street, named East and West Second street, Feb. 18, 1873. L 8, L 43, L 216, L 265, L 486, L 556.

Second street, Chsn.; from Lynde street to railroad; laid out from Lynde street to Front street by Charlestown Wharf Company; laid out again and accepted, Dec. 20, 1848; discontinued and acquired by the Eastern (now Boston & Maine) R.R., under authority of an act of the Legislature, but still open for a short distance from Lynde street.

Second-street court, B.; from Second street, south, 1835; called Second-street place and Napier-street place, 1855; Napier place, 1868.

Second-street place, B.; from Second street, south, 1855; called Second-street court, 1835; Second-street place and Napier-street place, 1855; Napier place, 1868.

†**Sedgwick street,** W. Rox.; from John A. Andrew street to South street; part of Walker street from John A. Andrew street, to Elm street, laid out as Sedgwick street, Dec. 5, 1881; another part of Walker street, from Elm street to South street, laid out as Sedgwick street, Dec. 7, 1887. L 1575, L 2045.

***Selden street,** Dor.; from Milton avenue to Forest Hills avenue (now Morton street); laid out, Dec. 4, 1893. L 2556, L 2557.

Selkirk road, Bri.; from Kilsyth road, crossing Sutherland and Chiswick roads, to Commonwealth avenue.

Selma street, E. B. (Breed's Island); from Gladstone street to Orient avenue; Bromley's atlas, 1892; now called Orienta place.

Selwyn street, W. Rox.; from Walter street, north-west, then south-west, to Farquhar street.

Seminary place, Chsn.; from Lawrence street to Austin street; same in 1875; laid out as Seminary street, Aug. 9, 1888. L 2087.

***Seminary street,** Chsn., 1888; from Lawrence street to Austin street; Seminary place laid out with name of Seminary street, Aug. 9, 1888. L 2087.

***Seneca street,** B.; from Harrison avenue to Albany street; called Erie street, 1844; named Seneca street, 1849; lower part of Seneca street, next to Albany street, accepted, Nov. 19, 1857. L 437, L 1535.

Seneca street, Rox.; from Dale street to Bower street; name changed to Laurel street, May 10, 1870.

Sentry Hill, B., 1708; afterwards Beacon Hill.

Sentry street, B.; from Beacon street, up Centrey Hill to the head of the present Temple street, 1708; called Century street, 1732; from Common (now Tremont) street to Beacon Hill, 1784; from the old Granary to the old Almshouse, 1800; the part north-west from Beacon street called Sumner (now Mt. Vernon) street, 1800; the part from Common street to Beacon street named Park street, 1803.

Sentry street, B.; a part of Sudbury street and a part of Queen (now Court) street were once so called.

Separate lane, B.; from Hanover street to the Mill-pond, 1722; name changed to Friend street, 1733.

Seven Star lane, B.; Summer street was sometimes so called, 1758–73.

***Seventh street**, So. B.; from Dorchester avenue to Dorchester street, and from G street to City Point; laid out parallel with Broadway, and named, Feb. 27, 1805; laid out from Federal street (now Dorchester avenue) to Dorchester street, and from G street to low-water mark, Nov. 17, 1868; called East and West Seventh streets, Feb. 18, 1873. L 199, L 226, L 227, L 655.

Seventh-street court, So. B.; from East Seventh street, northerly, near O street.

***Sever street**, Chsn.; from Haverhill street to Cambridge street; altered from Cambridge street to point opposite street (Gardner street) at westerly end of Sullivan square, Dec. 29, 1868; from Haverhill street to Kingston street accepted and named, June 28, 1870, L 1245.

Sewall place, B.; from Milk street, opposite Arch street; same, 1829 (from Milk street, north, opposite Morton place, now in Arch street).

Sewall place, Rox.; from Tremont street, southerly, near Parker street; laid out and extended to Delle avenue with name of Sewall street, March 3, 1891. L 2281.

Sewall street, B.; from Belknap (now Joy) street, west, 464 feet, parallel with Beacon street to Coventry street (now the easterly part of Walnut street), 1833; it ended at Coventry street, and Bishop-Stoke street ran from it to Beacon street; discontinued.

***Sewall street**, Rox., 1891; from Tremont street to Delle avenue; Sewall place laid out from Tremont street and extended to Delle avenue with name of Sewall street, March 3, 1891. L 2281.

Sewall street, Dor.; from Neponset avenue, easterly, between Boutwell street and Freeport street.

Sewall's court, Chsn.; from Arlington avenue, southerly, near Dorrance street.

Shailer avenue, Rox.; from Roxbury street, opposite Putnam street, to Linden park, now Linden-Park street.

***Shamrock street**, Dor.; from Dorchester avenue to Commercial (now Freeport) street; laid out, Aug. 2, 1883. L 1723.

***Shannon street**, Bri., 1892; from Washington street to Union street; Lexington avenue laid out with name of Shannon street, July 8, 1892. L 2412.

Sharkey place, Chsn.; from Beacham street, near corner of Arlington avenue, north-west.

Sharon court, E. B.; from Havre street, north-westerly, near Porter street.

***Sharon street**, B.; from Harrison avenue to Albany street; named from Harrison avenue, opposite centre of Franklin square, to Roxbury channel in South bay, May 14, 1849; accepted, Oct. 30, 1860. L 213.

Sharon street, W. Rox.; from Brown avenue to Canterbury street; same in 1849. L 2308.

Sharp court, Dor.; from Mather street, southerly, parallel with Allston street to unnamed place; called Sharp street in Bromley's atlas, 1894; given in directory as from Mather street to Allston street.

Sharp street, Dor.; from Mather street; same as Sharp court.

Shaving street, B.; from Federal street, easterly, then southerly, to Mt. Washington avenue; from Tirrell's wharf, east of Federal street, to Mt. Washington avenue, 1855.

Shaw street, W. Rox.; from La Grange street to Cottage avenue.

***Shawmut avenue,** B., Rox., and W. Rox.; from Tremont street to Roxbury street; part of Suffolk street, which in 1849 was also called South Suffolk street, from Dover street to Roxbury line, named Shawmut avenue, Oct. 20, 1851; name of Williams street changed to Shawmut avenue, April 2, 1855; extended from Arnold street to Roxbury line, Dec. 18, 1855; laid out and located by County Commissioners from end of Shawmut avenue at Boston line a new street over land of Davis to end of Williams street at Williams court, through Williams street to Washington (now Roxbury) street, through Roxbury street to Winslow street (now Guild row), through Winslow street to Dudley street, and over Norfolk and Bristol turnpike (now Washington street) to Dedham village, June, 1857; named Shawmut avenue, from Boston to West Roxbury line, Dec. 28, 1857; part in West Roxbury named Shawmut avenue, Feb. 3, 1858; part in Roxbury known as Dedham turnpike (now Washington street) reconstructed March, 1858; line changed near Edinboro' (now Thornton) street and Marcella street, April, 1858; relocated between Boston line and termination of Williams street, June, 1858; all that part which lies in the city of Roxbury accepted by County Commissioners, May 2, 1859; altered at junction of Bartlett street, Dec. 31, 1860; widened and extended from Dover street to Tremont street, including that part of Suffolk street between Dover street and Castle street, Oct. 10, 1870; from Washington (now Roxbury) street to Dudley street, in front of Universalist Church, named Guild row, June 16, 1874; name of Shawmut avenue from Dudley street to Dedham line changed to Washington street, June 16, 1874. Between Tremont street and Dover street. L 56, L 545, L 547, L 548, L 549, L 562, L 563, L 564, L 565, L 653, L 715, L 720, L 724, L 726, L 756, L 762, L 792, L 1349. Between Dover street and Roxbury line. Vol. 31, pp. 2, 8; L 22, L 30, L 121, L 615, L 640. In Roxbury District. L 384, L 402, L 615, L 659, L 945, L 946, L 993, L 994, L 995, L 996, L 997, L 998.

Shawmut park, Dor.; from King street, south, between Dorchester avenue and Adams street.

Shawmut place, B.; from Washington street, opposite Lenox street, named, May 14, 1849; included in extension of East Lenox street, 1851.

Shawmut place, Rox.; from Shawmut avenue, south-easterly, between Madison street and Williams street; included in the extension of Sterling street from Shawmut avenue to Washington street, Oct 4, 1884. L 1824.

Shawmut square, B.; between Washington, East Brookline, James, and East Newton streets; name changed to Franklin square, April 21, 1845.

***Shawmut street,** B.; from Pleasant street to Church street; from Pleasant street, west, 1825; to Church street, 1836; laid out, Sept. 25, 1868. L 387, L 397, L 475.

Shawmut street, W. Rox; from Florence street to railroad; map, 1849.

Shawmut terrace, B.; from Shawmut avenue, south-easterly, between Northampton street and Camden street.

***Sheafe street,** B., 1806; from Salem street to Snow-Hill street; from Salem street to Snow street, 1732; confirmed as a public street, Sept. 15, 1834.

Sheafe street, Chsn.; from Cook street, north-westerly, then north-easterly, to Cook-street court.

Sheafe's lane, B.; from Newbury (now Washington) street to the Common, 1732; named 1788; name changed to Avery street, Oct. 21, 1826; called also Coleburne's lane at an early date.

Shedd street, Bri.; from Champney street, north-westerly.

Sheep lane, B.; Sheafe's lane erroniously so called in directory, 1789.

Sheep Market, B.; the west side of Faneuil Hall square, so called, 1708.

Shelburne street, Dor.; from Buttonwood street, easterly; included in Dorchesterway.

***Shelby street**, E. B.; from Lexington street to Saratoga street; laid out, Oct. 9, 1877. L 1273.

***Sheldon street**, W. Rox.; from Prospect avenue to Ashland street; same in 1874; laid out, Nov. 23, 1878. L 1336.

***Shelton street**, Dor.; from Adams street to junction of Wrentham street and Bruce street; laid out, from Adams street, south-westerly, Sept. 19, 1882; extended to Wrentham street, Nov. 13, 1891. L 1639, L 2361.

***Shenandoah street**, Dor., 1892; from Carruth street to Wessex street; laid out, Nov. 3, 1892. L 2455.

***Shepard street**, Bri.; from Washington street to Union street.

Shepherd avenue, Rox.; from Huntington avenue, south-easterly, near Heath street.

Shepton street, Dor., 1896; from Shawmut park, westerly and easterly; authority to open given by Street Commissioners, June 23, 1896.

Shepton terrace, So. B.; from East Eighth street, between L street and M street, first south then east and west; called Shipton terrace in Bromley's atlas, 1891.

***Sherborn street**, Rox., 1894; from Commonwealth avenue to Charles river; laid out, Oct. 20, 1894. L 2633.

Sherbrook place, }
Sherbrooke place, } Rox.; from Tremont street, north-easterly, between Phillips street and Faxon street; formerly called Cherry place.

Sherburne's corner, B.; at the bend in Beacon street, then the east end of School street, at the present corner of Beacon street and Somerset street, about 1800; called also Sears' corner.

Sheridan avenue, Rox. and W. Rox.; from Centre street to Curtis street (now Chestnut avenue); street leading from Centre street, near Day street, to Boylston street named Sheridan avenue, July 7, 1868; Sheridan avenue, laid out from Centre street to Chestnut avenue and named Sheridan street, July 7, 1883. L 1716.

Sheridan court, Chsn.; from Tufts street, westerly.

Sheridan place, So. B.; from West Fifth street, near B street, south-westerly.

Sheridan street, Dor.; from Minot street, south-easterly, to brook; same called Sheridan place in directories.

***Sheridan street**, W. Rox., 1883; from Centre street to Chestnut avenue; Sheridan avenue laid out with name of Sheridan street, July 7, 1883. L 1716.

Sherlock street, Rox.; from Lambert avenue to Clarence street.

Sherman court, So. B.; from West Broadway to Athens street, between D street and E street.

Sherman place, B.; from May (now Revere) street, 1847; probably Hill's court, 1867.

Sherman place, B.; the west part of South May (now Savoy) street so called, 1850; so on map of 1855.

Sherman square, Chsn.; from Mystic avenue, easterly, between Sherman street and Dorrance street; same in 1875.

Sherman street, Chsn.; from Mystic avenue, next to B. & M. R.R., north, to Somerville line.

***Sherman street**, Rox.; from Bower street to Rockland street; laid out from Bower street to Dale street, Sept. 7, 1871; from Dale street, over Dale avenue, to Rockland street, Oct. 10, 1882. L 685, L 1646.

Sherman street, W. Rox.; from Poplar street opposite Augustus avenue, to Hawthorne street.

Sherwin street, B.; from Thorndike street near corner of Washington street, south-west.

Sherwood street, Rox.; from Bartlett street, crossing McGee street, to N.E. R.R.; shown on atlas, 1890.

***Sherwood street**, W. Rox., 1886; from Ashland street to Florence street; Hancock street laid out with name of Sherwood street, Oct. 25, 1886. L 1956, L 1957.

Ship street, B.; from Fleet street to the North Battery, 1708; straightened, etc., 1713; name of portion of Lynn street, from the North Battery to Winnisimmet Ferry, changed to Ship street, 1800; street running from Faneuil Hall Market, through Ann, Fish, and Ship streets to North street named Ann street throughout, July 6, 1824; from Fleet street to Commercial street called Ann street, 1824; from the foot of Ann street to the Ferry changed to Commercial street, and the remainder included in Ann (now North) street, 1833.

Shippie street, Chsn.; from Adams street to Chelsea street; name changed to Townsend street, March 14, 1831; made part of Chestnut street, June 20, 1846.

Shipton terrace, So. B.; from East Eighth street, between L street and M street, south, then east and west; called Shepton terrace in directory, 1894.

***Shirley street**, Rox.; from Dudley street to Norfolk avenue; laid out from Dudley street to George street, March 10, 1886; from George street to Norfolk avenue, Aug. 21, 1890. L 1791, L 1902, L 2257.

***Shoe and Leather street**, B.; from Fulton street to Ann (now North) street; having been made by John D. Williams at his own expense and given by him to City; laid out as a public street; at his request named Shoe and Leather street, Oct. 10, 1842; laid out as John street, Feb. 2, 1869.

Short lane, B.; from North Bennet street, 1796; to Tileston street, 1833; called Short street, 1849; named Wiggin street, 1878.

Short street, B.; on Price's map, 1733, from the angle in Southac street, north-west, to the water; since discontinued.

Short street, B.; from Pond street to Essex street, 1708; across Essex street to the water, 1769; from Pond street to Essex street, 1800; confirmed as a public street, Sept. 15, 1834; name of Short street discontinued and Kingston street, extended through it to Beach street, April 1, 1839.

Short street, B.; from North Bennet street to Tileston street; a part from North Bennet street called Short lane, 1796; extended to Tileston street, 1833, and named Short street, 1849; name changed to Wiggin street, April 24, 1878.

Short street, E. B.; from Everett street to Maverick street.

Short street, E B.; from Coleridge street to Cowper street.

Short street, So. B.; from Middle street to Tuckerman street.

Short street, Rox.; from Maple avenue (now Bellevue street) to Brookline avenue, formerly part of Appleton place.

Short street, Rox.; from Lawn street to Fisher avenue; laid out with name of Hayden street, June 28, 1886. L 1914.

Short street, Rox.; from Eustis street to Union street, 1849; extended to Dudley street, May, 1859; name changed to Winslow street, Dec. 17, 1860.

Short street, W. Rox.; from Mt. Vernon street to Walnut avenue (later Carl street, now Montview street); part of now known as Kirk street.

Short street, W. Rox.; from Washington street to Grove street; laid out with name of Stimson street, July 3, 1890. L 2238, L 2239.

Short street, W. Rox.; from Canterbury street to Dorchester line, 1849; now part of Berry street.

Short street, W. Rox.; from South street to Dedham turnpike (now Washington street); named, May 9, 1825; probably a public highway some time previous (now not shown).

***Short street,** Chsn.; from Bunker Hill street to Medford street; laid out and accepted, Aug. 21, 1860.

Short-street court, B.; rear of Short street, near Essex street, 1-27 name changed to Kington court or place, 1838.

Short-street court, Chsn.; from Short street, south-easterly.

Short-street place, Chsn.; from Short street, north-westerly.

Short Second street, B.; from Second street to Brighton street, 1849; called Napier street, 1855; called Little Napier street, 1855; named Barton court, 1868.

Shreve street, Dor.; from Norfolk street to Madison avenue; shown as Willowwood street on Bromley's atlas of Dorchester, 1894.

Shrimpton's corner, B.; corner of King (now State) street and Shrimpton's lane (now Exchange street), 1708.

Shrimpton's lane, B.; from Dock square to King (now State) street, 1708; called Exchange lane, 1789; sometimes called Royal Exchange lane; named Exchange street, 1816.

Shrimpton street, E. B., 1893; between Wood Island parkway and Prescott street; authority to open given by Street Commissioners, April 21, 1893.

Shurtleff court, Chsn.; from Rutherford avenue.

Shute street, B.; from Green street to Mr. Russell's ropewalk; Wiltshire street so called in Selectmen's list, 1788.

Sidlaw road, Bri., 1891; from Chestnut Hill avenue to Commonwealth avenue; authority to open given by Street Commissioners, Oct. 1, 1891.

Sidney street, Dor., 1895; from Kilton street, south-east, near Washington street; authority to open given by Street Commissioners, May 15, 1895; now called Rupert street.

Sigel place, Rox.; from Lamont street (formerly Linden avenue), west, near Vernon street; called Siegel court in directory, 1894.

Sigourney place, B.; from Hanover street, near Commercial street, westerly, then northerly; same in 1841.

***Sigourney street,** W. Rox.; from Walnut avenue to Glen road; laid out, May 19, 1884. L 1775, L 2134.

Silva place, Rox.; from Munroe street, southerly, near Hazelwood street.

***Silver street,** So. B.; from Dorchester avenue to G street, near West Broadway; accepted and laid out as public street, Nov. 29, 1852; opened and laid out from D street to E street, Sept. 18, 1861; extended Sept. 18, 1861; laid out from Dorchester avenue to A street, Sept. 1, 1871; laid out from A street to B street, Feb. 29, 1872; laid out from B street to C street, May 9, 1874; laid out from D street to E street, May 23, 1874; laid out from F street to Dorchester street, June 15, 1874; laid out from C street to D street, July 6, 1874; laid out from E street to F street, Sept. 29, 1874; laid out from Dorchester street to G street, June 5, 1876. L 166, L 645, L 646, L 742, L 925, L 933, L 938, L 968, L 1156, L 2746.

Silver-street place, So. B.; from Silver street, north-easterly, near Dorchester avenue.

***Simmons street**, Rox.; from Clay (now Linden-Park) street to Vernon street; laid out, Sept. 6, 1886. L 1943.

Simpkins' corner, B.; corner of Ann (now North) street and Royall's alley, 1732.

Simpson court, B.; from Van Rensselaer place, southerly; same in 1851.

Simpson's court, So. B.; from East Second street, northerly, between O street and P street; same given as Lauten place in directory, 1884.

Simpson's court, Chsn.; from Pearl street, south-east, near Medford street.

Sinclair place, Bri.; from North Beacon street, north-easterly, near Everett street.

Sinclair street, Rox.; from Elm Hill avenue to Landseer avenue; shown on plan dated June 1, 1881; abandoned.

Singleton street, B.; from Thorndike street, between Washington street and Reed street, south-west.

***Sister street**, B.; from Round lane (now Matthews street) north into Bury (now Channing) street, 1732; confirmed as a public street, Sept. 15, 1834; name changed to Leather square, Sept. 24, 1867. L 77, L 330.

***Sixth street**, So. B.; from Dorchester avenue to Dorchester street and from H street to City Point; laid out parallel with Broadway and named, Feb. 27, 1805; extended, March 27, 1867; portion adjacent to track of O. C. (now N. Y., N. H. & H.) R.R. Company discontinued, June 19, 1867; laid out from Foundry street (at Dorchester avenue) to Dorchester street and from H street to low-water mark, Nov. 17, 1868; called East and West Sixth streets, Feb. 18, 1873. Vol. 31, p. 48. L 7, L 336, L 355.

Sixth street, Chsn.; from Lynde street to Front street, 1875; to the railroad, 1884; laid out and accepted, July 31, 1855; discontinued and acquired by the Eastern (now Boston & Maine) R.R., under authority of an act of the Legislature, but still open for a short distance from Lynde street.

Sixth-street alley, So. B.; from West Sixth street to Bowen street, between D street and E street.

Skinner street, W. Rox.; from South street, north-easterly, then north-westerly, to Fairview street; laid out, with name of Conway street, July 21, 1885. L 1875.

Slate wharf, B.; from Commercial street, northerly, between land and wharves of the Boston Gaslight Company and Atkins wharf (now the City of Boston north paving yard).

Sleeper street, So. B.; north-east (to N. E. R.R. piers), and south-west across Congress street, near Fort Point Channel.

Sliding alley, B.; from Charter street to Lynn street, 1708; opened for use of town in 1719, having been fenced in; on Bonner's map, 1722; called Foster's lane, 1741; called Fuller street on Carleton's map, 1795; called Brewer's Hill in Edes' list, 1800; named Foster street, 1803.

Smith alley, B.; from North street to Commercial street, 1841; called Smith place on chart, 1883

Smith avenue, B.; from Kendall street to Hammond street.

Smith avenue, Dor.; a part of Union avenue so called on Mosoley's plan, 1869.

Smith court, B.; from Joy street, westerly; called May's court, 1812; named Smith court, 1848.

Smith court, Rox.; from Smith street, south-westerly, to Smith place (now Nichols or Nicholson court); called Smith-street court on chart, 1873; Smith-street place on chart, 1890.

Smith place, B.; from North street, south-easterly, to Commercial street; called Smith alley, 1841.

Smith place, B ; from Joy street, westerly; from Belknap (now Joy) street, west, south of Belknap place, 1842.

Smith place, So. B.; from West Fourth street to Silver street, between B street and C street.

Smith place, Rox.; from Phillips street, north-westerly, crossing the end of Smith court; same given Nichols court in 1884; given as Nicholson court in Directory of 1894 and in Bromley's atlas, 1890.

*__Smith street__, Rox.; from Parker street to Huntington avenue; laid out on chart, 1874, from Parker street to land of Redemptorist Fathers; extended to Bumstead lane, (now St. Alphonsus street,) Nov. 23, 1874; extended from Bumstead lane to Huntington avenue, April 27, 1891. L 986, L 2038, L 2289.

Smith street, Rox.; from Centre street down the hill to Worcester turnpike (now Roxbury street); named, May 9, 1825; name changed to Gardner street, Oct. 29, 1860.

Smith street, Bri.; from North Harvard street, near Western avenue, south-easterly, across Duck lane.

Smith-street court, Rox.; from Smith street, south-westerly, to Nichols (or Nicholson) court (formerly Smith court); same given Smith court on chart, 1873; Smith-street place, chart, 1890.

Smith-street place, Rox.; from Smith street, south-westerly, to Nicholson court (formerly Smith court); called also Smith-street court and Smith court.

Smith's corner, B.; corner of Fish (now North) street and Moon street, 1800.

*__Smyrna street__, Rox.; from Brookline avenue to Binney street; the part of private way called Park street, from Brookline avenue to Binney street, laid out and named Smyrna street, May 17, 1882. L 1610.

Snelling place, B.; from Hull street, north-easterly; same in 1844.

Snow Hill, B.; at the northern extremity of the town; later called Copp's Hill.

Snow street, B.; from Prince street to Hudson's Point, at foot of Charter street; Snow-Hill street so called on Bonner's map, 1722; also in list of 1732, and in Records, February, 1738.

Snow-Hill avenue, B.; from Snow-Hill street, west, opposite Sheafe street, 1830; exchanged for land to widen Prince street with Boston Gas Light Company, Dec. 8, 1866, and included in their land. L 151.

Snow-Hill court, B.; from Snow-Hill street, north-west, 1836; built over by Boston Gas Works.

Snow-Hill place, B.; from Snow-Hill street, south-easterly, next to Prince street; same in 1839.

*__Snow Hill street__, B.; from Prince street to Charter street; from Prince street to the end of Ferry-way by Hudson's Point, 1708; called Snow street in 1722, 1732, 1738; from Charlestown bridge up to the burying-ground on Copp's Hill, 1800; from Prince street across Copp's Hill to Charter street, 1817; laid out between Hull street and Charter street, April 10, 1837.

Snow's court, Dor.; from Chickatawbut street to Pierce avenue; laid out, June 5, 1867; located as Plain street, March 2, 1868.

***Soley street**, Chsn.; from Warren street to Monument square; new street laid out in place of Henley's lane and named Soley street, Dec. 24, 1850.

Soley's lane, Chsn.; mentioned, Nov. 14, 1782; no bounds given, no other mention.

Somerset court, B.; from Somerset street, west, 1809; name changed to Ashburton place, Nov. 13, 1845; extended to Bowdoin street in 1846.

Somerset place, B.; from Somerset street to Middlecot (now Bowdoin) street, 1807; from Somerset street to Bulfinch street, 1817; confirmed as a public way, Sept. 15, 1834; name changed to Allston street, Dec. 19, 1842.

Somerset place, B.; from Prince street, north-easterly, between Hanover street and Bennet avenue; given in directories, Samoset place.

***Somerset street**, B.; from Beacon street to Howard street; from Southac's court (now Howard street) to Beacon street, at Sherbourne's or Sears' corner, 1803; confirmed as a public street, Sept. 15, 1834. L 249, L 1876.

Sonoma street, Rox., 1892; from Maple street to Elm Hill avenue; authority to open given by Street Commissioners, June 16, 1892.

†**Sorrento street**, Bri., 1891; near the corner of Cambridge street and North Harvard street; authority to open given by Street Commissioners, July 10, 1891; laid out north-westerly from Cambridge street, May 6, 1892; from Cambridge street, north-westerly, across Hopedale street, 1894. L 2397.

Soudan street, Dor.; from Sydney street, west, crossing Sagamore street; Bromley's atlas, 1894; authority to open under name of Sudan street given by Street Commissioners, May 13, 1895.

South battery, B.; east of Fort Hill, near the junction of the present Purchase street and Broad street, 1722.

South bridge, B.; from Front street (now Harrison avenue) to South Boston, 1805; called Dover-street bridge, 1839.

South ferry, B.; from the end of Eastern avenue to East Boston.

South row, B.; on Marlboro' (now Washington) street, opposite School street, next north of the Old South Church, 1755–1824.

***South street**, B.; from Summer street to Lehigh street; from Summer street to the sea, 1708; Town slip carried out from the lower end of South street, April 14, 1712; extended to Beach street, Dec. 26, 1837; accepted from Beach street to Kneeland street, May 17, 1849; accepted from Kneeland street to Lehigh street, Nov. 15, 1852. Vol. 31, p. 90. L 948, L 1083, L 1449, L 1471, L 1596, L 1597.

South street, Dor.; from Commercial (now Freeport) street to Pleasant street (Commercial Point); from Commercial street to the water; given as a part of Preston street on Directory map and chart, 1884.

***South street**, W. Rox.; from Centre street, near Eliot street, to Centre street, near Church street; laid out from Centre street to Blue Marsh, Jan. 19, 1662; confirmed in 1685; extended in 1687; named from Center street, near Rev. Mr. Gray's Meeting-house, to Center street, near Rev. Mr. Flagg's Meeting-house, May 9, 1825; altered at Centre street, Sept. 27, 1871; relocated northerly from Washington street, Feb. 24, 1880. [A part near and north-east of Ashland street included in Dedham turnpike (now Washington street), 1808.] L 1436, L 2116, L 2277, L 2678, L 2736.

***South street**, Bri.; from Chestnut Hill avenue to Commonwealth avenue; named from Rockland street (now Chestnut Hill avenue) to Newton line, June 15, 1840; Commonwealth avenue extended over South street, from Chestnut Hill avenue to Newton line, Jan. 5, 1895. L 2651, L 2652.

South-street court, B.; from South street, east, opposite Essex street, 1818; included in extension of Essex street, from South street to Federal street, May 5, 1880. L 1450.

***South-street place**, B.; from South street, west, 1826; afterwards to Lincoln street; accepted and laid out as a public street, Oct. 22, 1855; name changed to Tufts street, Dec. 18, 1855.

Southac court, B.; from Southac (now Phillips) street, south, 1826; named Phillips court, 1866.

Southac place, B.; from Phillips (formerly Southac) street, southerly, near West Cedar street; same from Southac street, south, in 1841.

Southac street, B.; from Butolph (now Irving) street, nearly to the water, thence south to Beacon street, 1733; the portion of Southac street now called West Cedar street, south of the present Phillips street, was called George street in 1810; from Butolph street to George street, 1810; confirmed as a public street, Sept. 15, 1834; name changed to Phillips street, Feb. 6, 1866.

Southac's court, B.; from Tremont street, opposite Hanover street, west, in 17–2; named, 1732; from Court street, opposite the Orange Tree, westward, to Dr. Bulfinch's pasture, 1788; laid out, Oct. 2, 1816; from Court street to Bulfinch street, 1817; called Howard street from Tremont row to Bulfinch street, April 11, 1821.

South Allen court, B.; from South Allen street, south, 1822; name changed to McLean court, 1829.

South Allen street, B.; from Wiltshire (now Chambers) street, west, 1784; called Thirty-feet passage, west, to Mr. Dunn's, 1800; by directory plan, 1805, extends west to the water; from Wiltshire street, west, to Capt. Dunn's, 1807; accepted and name changed to McLean street, in honor of the benefactor of the General Hospital, to which it is a principal avenue, Dec. 22, 1828.

South Bennet place, B.; from South Bennet street, north, 1858 called Bennet place 1816 and 1880.

South Bennet street, B.; from Washington street to Harrison avenue; Bennet street was sometimes so called.

South Bridge street, B.; from Washington street to the South bridge (now Dover-street bridge), 1825; confirmed as a public street, Sept. 15, 1834; sometimes called Bridge street and East Dover street; name changed to Dover street, Nov. 10, 1834.

South Cedar place, B.; from Winchester street, southerly, between Church street and Pleasant street; see South Cedar-street place. L 392.

South Cedar street, B.; from Pleasant street, west, to Ferdinand street, 1825; accepted and laid out as a public street, Nov. 8, 1852; name changed to Winchester street, July 7, 1869. L 391, L 392, L 393, L 394, L 396, L 438.

South Cedar-street place, B.; from Winchester street, southerly, between Church street and Pleasant street; called Cedar-street place on chart, 1883; called Cedar-street court, 1831; Cedar-street place, 1840; South Cedar-street place, 1857. L 392.

South Dennis street, Rox.; from Warren street to Dorchester line, 1849; named Quincy street, June 2, 1851, but order not carried out; Dennis street from Grove Hall avenue, opposite Quincy street in Dorchester, to Warren street, named Quincy street, Oct. 13, 1856.

***South Eden street**, Chsn.; from Main street to Rutherford avenue; laid out and named, April 26, 1871.

Souther's corner, B.; corner of Milk street and Bishop's alley (now Hawley street), 1708.

Southern avenue, Dor.; from Washington street to Bernard street.

†**South Fairview street,** W. Rox.; from South street, south-west, then west, crossing Brookfield street and South Walter street; laid out from South street to South Walter street, March 30, 1895. L 2710.

South Foster place, B.; from Tremont street, west, between Boylston street and Eliot street, 1831; name changed to Van Rensselaer place, 1852.

South Hanover place, B.; from Hanover street, south-easterly, between Court street and Elm street, 1849; closed in 1853.

South Harvard street, Bri.; from Cambridge street, opposite Franklin street, to Brookline line; name of Cedar street changed to South Harvard street, Nov. 10, 1846; named Harvard avenue, Dec. 30, 1873.

South Huntington avenue, Rox., 1896; from Heath street to Castleton street; authority to open given by Street Commissioners, March 18, 1896.

South Latin School street, B.; School street so called in 1789.

South Lowell street, B ; from Shawmut avenue to Tremont street, 1848; name changed to Milford street, May 14, 1849.

***South Margin street,** B.; from Pitts street to Prospect street; laid out across the Mill-pond and named, Aug. 3, 1807. L 1221.

***South Market street,** B.; from Merchants' row to Atlantic avenue; laid out and named from Merchants' row by south side of Faneuil Hall Market to Commercial street, March 30, 1825; extended from Commercial street to Atlantic avenue, including street 40 feet wide known as City wharf, April 2, 1872. L 46, L 614, L 785.

South May street, B.; from Washington street to Harrison avenue; same in 1830; the west part called Sherman place on maps, 1850–1855; laid out with name of Savoy street, Nov. 29, 1892. L 2465.

South Quincy place, Chsn.; from Quincy street, north-west between Wellington place and North Quincy place.

***South Russell street,** B., 1795; from Cambridge street to Myrtle street; named from Cambridge street, south to May (now Revere) street, 1802; from Cambridge street to Myrtle street, 1806.

South Short street, Chsn.; from Short street, north-west between Bunker Hill street and Short-street place.

Southside park, Dor.; from Ashmont street, south, near Carruth street; appears on Bromley's atlas of 1894 as Arundel park.

South Suffolk street, B.; part of Suffolk street (now Shawmut avenue), from Dover street to Roxbury line, so called in 1849.

South Walter street, W. Rox.; from South street to South Fairview street. L 2709.

***South Williams street,** B.; from Washington street to Shawmut avenue, 1842; on petition for acceptance, Oct. 14, 1867, decided to be public, having been kept open for public use more than twenty years; name changed to Pelham street, Jan. 4, 1868.

***Southwood street,** Rox.; from Blue Hill avenue to Edgewood street; laid out, Aug. 17, 1891. L 2326.

South Worthington street, Rox.; from Tremont street, south-west, opposite Worthington street; also called Worthington place.

Sowden's Hill, W. Rox.; part of Poplar street, between its junction with Canterbury street and Beech street, so called in 1859.

Sowdon avenue, W. Rox., 1896; from Poplar street opposite Hillburn street, north-east.

Spalding street, W. Rox., 1894; from South street, near Morton street; authority to open given by Street Commissioners, Nov. 8, 1894.

Sparhawk avenue, Bri.; from Cambridge street to Sparhawk street; laid out, with name of Elko street, Aug. 10, 1893. L 2526.

Sparhawk street, Bri.; from Cambridge street to Market street; same in 1875; laid out, May 7, 1877. L 1240.

***Sparrow street**, W. Rox.; from Cottage avenue, across Partridge street.

Spear alley, B.; from Purchase street to Atlantic avenue; same in 1826.

†**Spear place**, B.; from Pleasant street, near Washington street, south-westerly, then north-westerly; same in 1838. L 549.

Spear's wharf, B.; from Atlantic avenue, south-easterly, near foot of Oliver street.

Speedwell street, Dor., 1893; near the south-east corner of Bowdoin street and Topliff street; authority to open given by Street Commissioners, Aug. 29, 1893; from Topliff street to Barrington street, south of Bowdoin street.

†**Spencer street**, Dor.; from Park street, south-easterly, crossing Wheatland avenue; laid out from Park street to Wheatland avenue, Dec. 28, 1893. L 2578.

Spice court, Chsn.; from Cambridge street, south-easterly, to near B. & M. R.R.; called Spice street on City map, 1891, and in Bromley's atlas of Charlestown of 1892.

Spinney street, W. Rox.; from Sparrow street to Cowing street.

Sprague street, B.; from Washington street to Harrison avenue; laid out, June 20, 1855; named changed to Parker street, Jan. 29, 1856; named Rollins street; 1868. L 35.

***Sprague street**, Chsn., 1892; from Bunker Hill street to Princeton street; Jerome place laid out from Bunker Hill street, and extended to Princeton street, with name of Sprague street, Aug. 11, 1892. L 2482.

Spring court, Rox.; from Fellows street, easterly, between Webber street and Hunneman street.

***Spring lane**, B.; from Washington street to Devonshire street; from Cornhill (now Washington street) to Joylieff's lane (now Devonshire street), 1708. L 423, L 2451.

Spring lane, W. Rox.; from Lamartine street to Chestnut avenue; same in 1874.

***Spring street**, B.; from Leverett street to Allen street; from Leverett street, west, to Wiltshire (now Chambers) street, 1733; from Leverett street to Poplar street, 1806; from the Almshouse to Poplar street, 1817; laid out and named, Oct. 24, 1825; accepted, and recorded as a public street, May 12, 1828; confirmed as a public street, Sept. 15, 1834.

Spring street, Dor ; from Savin Hill avenue to Bay street.

***Spring street**, W. Rox.; from Centre street to Dedham line; named from Center street to Baker street, May 9, 1825; probably a public highway some time previous; from Baker street to Dedham line by annexation from Dedham; Selectmen authorized to petition County Commissioners to lay out Spring street 50 feet wide from Centre street to Charles river or to Dedham line, Sept. 8, 1873. L 2488.

Spring street, Bri.; from Market street to Dustin street; same in 1875.

Spring-street court, B.; from Spring street, north-west, near corner of Allen street.

Spring terrace, Rox.; from Bower street, south-west, between Humboldt avenue and Sherman street.

Springdale street, Dor.; from Savin Hill avenue, next to N. Y., N. H. & H. R.R., south-west, then south-east, then curving southerly to Dorchester bay.

Springer court, So. B.; from East Eighth street to East Seventh street; laid out, with name of Springer street, June 10, 1885. L 1861.

***Springer street,** So. B., 1885; from East Seventh street to East Eighth street; Springer court laid out, with name of Springer street, June 10, 1885. L 1861.

***Springfield street,** B.; from Albany street to Columbus avenue; laid out on the Neck, from Washington street, west, July 24, 1826; the fifteenth of the new streets leading from Tremont street to Front street (now Harrison avenue) named Springfield street, Sept. 15, 1834; extended to Albany street, 1854; accepted, Dec. 7, 1857; accepted, Oct. 30, 1860; from Washington street to Albany street called East Springfield street; and from Washington street to Columbus avenue called West Springfield street, April 21, 1868. L 176, L 212, L 261, L 303.

***Spring Garden street,** Dor.; from Crescent avenue to Harbor View street; laid out, June 23, 1876. L 1159.

***Spring Park avenue,** W. Rox.; from Centre street to Chestnut avenue; laid out as a town way from Centre street to Chestnut street (now Chestnut avenue), Aug. 21, 1873; accepted by Town, Sept. 8, 1873.

Spring-street court, B.; from Spring street, north-westerly, to and across Poplar court; same in 1827 (from Spring street, west).

Spring-street place, B.; from Spring street, south, to Chambers street, 1828; included in Chambers street extended to Spring street, Jan. 6, 1872. L 732.

Springvale avenue, W. Rox.; from Spring street, northerly, then westerly, to Marshall street.

***Spruce street,** B.; from Beacon street, opposite the Common, to Chestnut street; same in 1822; confirmed as a public street, Sept. 15, 1834.

Spruce street, W. Rox.; from Florence street to Bourne street; same in 1874; laid out, with name of Catharine street, Dec. 28, 1893.

***Spurr street,** Bri., 1884; street connecting North Harvard street and Western avenue; named Spurr street, March 1, 1884.

St. Alphonsus avenue, Rox.; from Whitney street, south-east, to St. Alphonsus street.

***St. Alphonsus street,** Rox., 1893; from Huntington avenue to Calumet street; Bumstead lane laid out, with name of St. Alphonsus street, Dec. 20, 1893; extended over a private way and Delaware street to Calumet street, Sept. 23, 1895. L 2563, L 2564, L 2565, L 2734.

***St. Botolph street,** B. and Rox.; from Irvington street to Gainsborough street; given on chart, 1883, from B. & A. R.R., north-east of unnamed extension of Yarmouth (now Irvington) street, south-westerly to West Chester park (now Massachusetts avenue) and Camden (now Gainsborough) street; laid out from West Newton street to West Chester park, Jan. 19, 1880; extended from West Newton street to Harcourt street, Dec. 27, 1882; from Harcourt street to Irvington street, April 10, 1884; laid out from Massachusetts avenue to Gainsborough street, June 30, 1896. L 1428, L 1679, L 1766, L 2191, L 2774.

St. Catharine street, Rox.; from Parker street, east, between Centre street and Bromley park.

***St. Charles street,** B.; from Chandler street, northerly, to B. & A. R.R.; named, Dec. 5, 1871; laid out, Oct. 15, 1874. L 972.

St. Germain street, Rox., 1894; from Massachusetts avenue to Dalton street; Cromwell street laid out, with name of St. Germain street, Sept. 14, 1894. L 2618.

St. Gregory's court, Dor.; from Dorchester avenue, north-westerly, near Richmond street.

St. James avenue, B.; from Berkeley street to Huntington avenue; name of St. James street, from Berkeley street to Clarendon street, changed to St. James avenue, April 21, 1868; laid out, from Clarendon street to Huntington avenue, May 6, 1876; laid out, from Dartmouth street to Exeter street, Aug. 27, 1877; name of part between Huntington avenue and Exeter street changed to Blagden street, March 1, 1889. L 309, L 374, L 862, L 1147, L 1266, L 1699.

St. James Park, B.: from St. James avenue, southerly to the B. & P. (now N. Y., N. H. & H.) R.R.; now called Trinity place.

St. James place, Rox.; from St. James street, south-westerly, between Washington street and Alpine street.

***St. James street**, B., from Berkeley street on Back Bay land, 1860; laid out from Berkeley street to Clarendon street, April 7, 1868; name changed to St. James avenue, April 21, 1868.

***St. James street**, Rox.; from Warren street to Washington street; accepted, conditionally, Oct. 12, 1847; conditions complied with, July 31, 1848. L 863.

St. James terrace, Rox.; from St. James street, north-easterly, near Alpine street.

St. John avenue, E. B. (Breed's Island); from Walley street, west, then south, to Water avenue; shown in Bromley's atlas, 1892.

***St. John street**, W. Rox.; from Centre street to Rockview street; laid out, Oct. 25, 1886. L 1958.

***St. Joseph street**, W. Rox., 1892; from South street to Woodman street; St. Thomas street laid out, with name of St. Joseph street, Nov. 21, 1892. L 2458.

St. Mark street, W. Rox.; from South street, near Morton street, to Percy street.

St. Martin street, Chsn., 1896; from Bunker Hill street to Medford street; Quincy street, laid out, with name of St. Martin street, May 11, 1896. L 2762.

St. Mary's street, Rox.; from Brighton (now Commonwealth) avenue to Brookline Branch R.R.; included in Brookline when boundary line was changed in 1872.

***St. Paul street**, Rox.; from Falmouth street to Norway street; laid out from Falmouth street to Caledonia (now Norway) street, May 7, 1889. L 2128

St. Paul's row, B.; Common (now Tremont) street, near St. Paul's Church, 1826–30.

***St. Stephen street**, Rox., 1892; name of that part of Falmouth street, south-west of West Chester park (now Massachusetts avenue), changed to St. Stephen street, March 1, 1892. L 1296, L 1322, L 2129.

***Stacey street**, Chsn., 1889; from Main street to Dunstable street; Williams street laid out, with name of Stacey street, Oct. 7, 1889. L 2178.

***Stafford street**, Rox.; from Blue Hill avenue to Dennis street; laid out, Dec. 22, 1870. L 593.

Stanburyes corner, B.; "nigh the Mill Bridge, 1708."

Standard street, Dor., 1895; from River street, north-west, to beyond Manchester street.

Standish avenue, Dor.; from Park street to Harvard street; laid out, with name of Standish street, June 7, 1887. L 1993.

Standish court, B.; from Pitts street, west, near South Margin street; called Standish place, 1845; Standish court, 1874; Standish place on chart, 1883.

***Standish street**, Dor., 1887; from Harvard street to Park street; Standish avenue laid out, with name of Standish street, June 7, 1887. L 1993.

Stanhope place, B.; from Phillips street, southerly, between Garden street and Anderson s'reet; same in 1857 (from Southac street, south).

***Stanhope street**, B.: from Berkeley street, south-westerly, crossing Morgan street, then westerly; from Berkeley street, west, near Columbus avenue, 1866; laid out, Dec. 16, 1891. L 2375.

Staniford court, B.; from Staniford place, south, 1849.

Staniford place, B.; from Staniford street, south-easterly, between Cambridge street and Green street; same as in 1830.

***Staniford street**, B.; from Cambridge street to Causeway street; from Cambridge street to Green street, in 1722; named, 1732; from Cambridge street across Green lane (now Green street) to Leverett place, 1817; part from Green lane to Leverett place, afterwards Lyman street; no other mention of its being called Staniford street; extended from Green street, including parts of Lyman street and Chilson place, to Causeway street, May 11, 1886. L 1905.

Stanley avenue, E. B. (Breed's Island); from Ashley avenue to Belle Isle inlet; Bromley's atlas, 1892.

Stanley place, Chsn.; from Bow street, north-easterly, near Washington street.

†**Stanley street**, Dor., 1889; from Bellevue street to Sunset circle; Bellevue terrace laid out from Quincy street, south-west, crossing Kane street, with name of Stanley street, June 19, 1889; authority to open portion from Bellevue street, south-westerly, given by Street Commissioners, Oct. 14, 1896. L 2137.

Stanmore place, Rox.; from Warren street, opposite Dunreath place (now street), south-westerly, then north-westerly.

Stanton avenue, Dor.; from Norfolk street to Evans street; laid out with name of Stanton street, Feb. 8, 1889. L 2112.

Stanton place, Rox.; from Walnut avenue at its junction with Warren street, north-west.

***Stanton street**, Dor., 1889; from Norfolk street to Evans street; Stanton avenue, laid out, with name of Stanton street, Feb. 8, 1889. L 2112.

Stanwood avenue, Dor.; from Blue Hill avenue to Columbia street; laid out, with name of Stanwood street, July 11, 1885. L 1869, L 1870.

***Stanwood street**, Dor., 1885; from Columbia street to Blue Hill avenue; Stanwood avenue laid out as Stanwood street, July 11, 1885. L 1869, L 1870.

Stark street, Chsn.; from Cambridge street, opposite Parker street, to Roland street.

Starr lane, W. Rox.; from Centre street to Seaverns avenue; Virginia avenue, from Centre street to Roanoke avenue (now Elm street), 1849; Seaverns avenue extended through a part of Starr lane to junction of Elm street and Gordon street, March 10, 1873; from Gordon street to Starr (now Call) street, called Everett street, Dec. 4, 1877; same given as a part of Starr street on chart, 1874. L 2503.

Starr street, W. Rox.; from Gordon street to Keyes street; altered and constructed, March 10, 1873; part of, together with a part of Union avenue, named Call street, Dec. 4, 1877, and other part called Everett street, same date. L 1028, L 1029.

***State street**, B.; from Washington street to Long wharf; from Cornhill (now Washington street), both sides of the Town-House, east, to the sea, called King street, 1708; named State street, 1784; extended and named from Chatham row to Commercial street, April 13, 1858; extended along north side of State-street block and accepted, conditionally, April 13, 1858; extended to Atlantic avenue, March 27, 1876. L 134, L 262, L 1137, L 2113, L 2792.

State House avenue, B., 1827; from Beacon street, by the west side of the State House to Sumner (now Mt. Vernon) street, 1827; called also Hancock avenue.

Station square, W. Rox.; at the Mount Hope station, on the Providence division of the N.Y., N. H. & H. R.R.

***Station street,** Rox.; from Tremont street (now Columbus avenue) to Parker street; laid out, May 26, 1880. L 1463.

Stedman place, B.; from Washington street, east, next south of Kneeland street, 1859; closed in 1862.

Stedman street, W. Rox.; from Williams street, south-westerly, between Washington street and Forest Hills street, crossing Keyes street and Lotus place.

Steele's court, B.; from Chambers street, near Poplar street, to Leverett street, 1849; named Hammond avenue, 1850.

***Sterling street,** Rox.; from Washington street to Tremont street; laid out from Shawmut avenue to Warwick street, Sept. 1, 1871; extended to Cabot street, Oct. 9, 1883; name of Transit street, from Cabot street to Newbern street, changed to Sterling street, March 1, 1884; name of Newbern street, with a part of said Newbern street, to Tremont street, changed to Sterling street, March 1, 1884; extended from Shawmut avenue, over Shawmut place, to Washington street, Oct. 4, 1884. L 659, L 667, L 1559, L 1726, L 1824.

Stetson court, Chsn.; from Henley street, north-westerly, near Park street; same by chart, 1875.

Stetson place, B.; from West Cedar street, westerly, near Cambridge street; same in 1860.

***Stevens street,** B.; from Shawmut avenue to Lincoln place; same in 1864; laid out, Oct. 9, 1877. L 1276

Stevens's corner, B.; corner North (now Hanover) street and Love lane (now Tileston street), 1708; called Stephen's corner, 1732.

Stewart street, So. B. (proposed); from Dorchester avenue to Richardson avenue (proposed).

Still-House square, B; from the foot of Hawkins street by the Distill House to the Mill-pond, thence southerly to Sudbury street, 1743; named Adams street, 1846; now Bowker street; called also Distill-House square and Distillers square.

Stillman place, B.; from Stillman street to Cooper street; same in 1825.

***Stillman street,** B.; from Salem street to Charlestown street; laid out over the Mill-pond, 1807; from Back (now Salem) street to the Mill-pond, 1821; accepted, conditionally, Nov. 15, 1830; confirmed as a public street, Sept. 15, 1834; from Salem street to Charlestown street, 1835.

***Stimson street,** W. Rox., 1890; from Grove street to Centre street; laid out, including Short street (between Grove street and Washington street), July 3, 1890. L 2238, L 2239.

Stockmeath street, Dor.; from Eaton street to Bloomington street.

***Stockton street,** Dor., 1886; from Washington street to Milton avenue; Emery street laid out, with the name of Stockton street, Dec. 10, 1886. L 1965.

***Stoddard street,** B.; from Howard street to Court street; shown, 1722; called Stoddard's lane, from Cambridge (now Court) street to Southack's court (now Howard street), 1732; called Fitche's lane, 1788 to 1800; Stoddard's lane named Stoddard street, Oct. 19, 1829.

Stone place, Chsn.; from Edgeworth street, north-westerly, near Bunker Hill street.

***Stone street**, Chsn.; from Princeton street to Medford street; Princeton-street court extended from Princeton street to Medford street and laid out with name of Stone street, June 13, 1871.

Stonehurst street, Dor., 1893; near the south-east corner of Bowdoin street and Topliff street; authority to open given by Street Commissioners, Aug. 29, 1893; from Topliff street to Barrington street, south of Bowdoin street.

Stony Brook avenue, W. Rox.; from Brown avenue to Bourne street, 1849; later a part of Florence street.

Stony Brook place, Rox.; from Centre street, easterly, near Amory street.

Stony Brook street, W. Rox.; from Williams street, south-east of and near Washington street, parallel with Stony Brook, to Keyes street.

Stormont street, Rox.; from Elm Hill avenue to Landseer avenue, on plan dated June 1, 1881; now abandoned.

Story place, B.; from State street, west, between Devonshire street and Congress street, 1845; part of Half-square court; now Congress square.

Story place, W Rox ; from Greenough avenue, south-west, then west, near Centre street.

Story street, So. B.; from Dorchester avenue, crossing Washington avenue (proposed), to Richardson avenue (proposed).

***Story street**, So. B.; from G street, between East Fifth street and East Sixth street, with proposed extension to H street; called Bird lane, 1857; Story street, 1873; laid out, from G street to H street, June 30, 1890. L 2237.

***Stoughton street**, B.; from Harrison avenue to Albany street; between East Concord street and East Newton street; named from Harrison avenue, opposite Burying-ground, to Roxbury Channel in South bay, May 14, 1849; accepted, Oct. 30, 1860.

***Stoughton street**, Dor.; from Upham's corner to Pleasant street; altered near Deacon James Humphrey's house, April, 1800; street from Roxbury line through Burying-place lane called Stoughton street, March 11, 1840; altered near Brook street and Cottage (now East Cottage) street, June, 1856; widened to about 60 feet, October, 1871; name of part from Brook avenue to Upham's corner changed to Dudley street, June 30, 1874. L 702, L 703, L 704, L 705, L 706, L 707, L 757, L 758, L 782, L 783, L 784, L 880.

Stoughton-street place, Dor.; from Stoughton street, south, near Everett avenue.

Stratford avenue, Dor., 1893; between Anawan avenue and the N. Y., N. H. & H. R.R.; authority to open given by Street Commissioners, Nov. 17, 1893.

Stratford street, Dor., 1893; from Waldeck street, west, between Park street and Linsey street, near the Shawmut branch of the O. C. (now N. Y., N. H. & H.) R.R ; authority to open given by Street Commissioners, Jan. 18, 1893.

Strathmore road, Bri., 1891; between Chestnut Hill avenue and Brookline line; authority to open given by Street Commissioners, Oct. 1, 1891; formerly called Elm avenue; also Argyle road.

Stratton street, Bri.; from Bigelow street.

Strong place, B.; from Cambridge street, south, between Anderson street and Grove street.

Studley place, B.; from Eliot street, north, near Pleasant street; same in 1870.

***Sturbridge street**, Dor., 1890; from River street to Sanford street; laid out, Dec. 18, 1890. L 2275.

Sturgis place, B.; from Pearl street, east, near Milk street, 1833; included in Sturgis street, July 23, 1869; now Franklin street. L 459.

Sturgis street, B.; from Pearl street to Broad street, including Baker's alley, Sturgis place and Hamilton place; laid out, July 23, 1869; portions discontinued, April 15 and July 17, 1871; name of Sturgis street, from Oliver street to Broad street, changed to Franklin street, Sept 30, 1873. L 459, L 460, L 461, L 462, L 600.

Sudan street, Dor.; from Sydney street, north-west, between Harbor View street and Romsey street; authority to open given by Street Commissioners, Aug. 13, 1895.

Sudbury place, Rox.: from Weston street, south-west, between Tremont street and Windsor street; now Weston place.

***Sudbury square**, B.; from Sudbury street, west of 50 Portland street, same in 1709; the north part of Sudbury street and west of Cold lane (now Portland street).

***Sudbury street**, B.; from Haymarket square to Court street; from the head of School street to the Mill-pond and Cold lane (now Portland street) 1654; from the sign of the Orange Tree at the corner of Hanover street to the Mill-pond, and from thence to the lower end of Cold lane, 1708; the remainder of the street being called Sentry street; extended through Deacon street to Merrimac street, Sept. 2, 1839; from Court street to Portland street, 1850; Deacon street, from Portland street to Merrimac street, at Haymarket square, considered as continuation of and named Sudbury street, April 14, 1851; at one time the easterly end of Court street was called Sudbury street; the only street which, existing in Boston in 1645, retains at this day its original name. Vol. 31, p. 24. L 34, L 2167.

Sudbury street, Rox.; from Tremont street to Cabot street; accepted and named conditionally, March 11, 1844; accepted, finally, March 3, 1845; name changed to Weston street, April 21, 1868.

Suffolk avenue, B.; from Cornhill square, west, 1820; named Court avenue, 1837.

Suffolk Buildings, B.; corner of Congress street and State street, 1817.

Suffolk court, B.; from Washington street, east, 1806; called Suffolk place, 1809.

Suffolk Inns, B.; on the passageway from Cornhill (now Washington street) to the new Court-house, 1812.

Suffolk place, B.; from Bedford street, south-west; Suffolk court, from Washington street, east, called Suffolk place, 1809; to Bedford street, 1839; now built over.

Suffolk place, Rox.; from the end of Putnam place, east, then south; name changed to Putnam place, May 31, 1870, but still called Suffolk place on chart, 1884 and 1890.

Suffolk street, B.; from West Castle street to Dover street, 1829; laid out from South bridge in rear of Franklin School-house to westerly bounds of city lands, Dec. 13, 1830; street between Washington street and Tremont street, parallel with Washington street, to Roxbury line named Suffolk street, Sept. 15, 1834; part between Dover street and Castle street made in 1836–37; laid out and extended from Camden street to Lenox street, July 1, 1844; part south of Dover street called South Suffolk street, 1849–51; from Dover street to Roxbury line called Shawmut avenue, Oct. 20, 1851; from Dover street to Castle street named Shawmut avenue, 1870. Vol. 31, pp. 2, 8. L 56, L 545, L 547, L 562, L 563.

Suffolk street, Bri.; from Brighton (now Commonwealth) avenue, nearly opposite Malvern street, to Brookline line; abandoned.

Suffolk-street passageway, B.; passageway 20 feet wide laid out between land of George Archibald on south-easterly side of Suffolk street, July 25, 1831.

Sullivan place, B.; from Federal street, west, near Franklin street; same in 1824.

Sullivan square, Chsn ; between Main, Cambridge, Sever, and Gardner streets; square at the Neck in front of Hotel of Richard Sullivan named Sullivan square, Jan. 17, 1848; enlarged, Dec. 17, 1867.

Sullivan street, So. B.; from D street to Old Harbor street; the westerly portion accepted, July 5, 1860; about 40 feet east from D street laid out as a public street, Sept. 17, 1867; laid out from D street to Old Harbor street, Nov. 17, 1868; name changed to Ninth street, Nov. 17, 1868. L 96, L 191, L 192, L 194, L 273, L 309.

***Sullivan street,** Chsn.; from Main street to Bunker Hill street; from Main street to Bartlett street accepted as Graves street, Nov. 28, 1831; land given to town by Richard Sullivan as continuation of Graves street from Russell street to Bunker Hill street, Oct. 23, 1834; same accepted, Nov. 10, 1834; no record of change of name, but same soon after called Sullivan street. L 2005, L 2808.

Summer place, B.; from Arch street, west, near Franklin street; Bussey place so called for a short time previous to 1842.

***Summer street,** B.; from Washington street to Federal street; from Washington street to the sea, 1683; at some time previous to 1708 called the Mylne street; called also Seven Star Lane, 1758–73: owners have named a private way from Atlantic avenue, south-easterly, nearly opposite junction of Summer street and Federal street, Summer street. Vol. 31, pp. 20, 84; Vol. 19, p. 83. L 31, L 72, L 76, L 90, L 285, L 305, L 306, L 320, L 364, L 828, L 829, L 830, L 832.

†**Summer street,** W. Rox.; from Spring street to and across Ashland street; same in 1874; laid out from Spring street to Autumn street, April 29, 1878. L 1302.

***Summer street,** Chsn ; from Elm street to Pearl street; Oliver Holden conveyed to Town a parcel of land already used as a road called Summer street running from Elm street, north-west, July 17, 1819.

Summer street, Bri.; from Washington street to Warren street; near Brookline line ; called Corey road in 1896.

***Summit avenue,** Bri.; from Brookline line to Massachusetts (now Commonwealth) avenue; laid out from Allston street to Brookline line, by County Commissioners in 1867; laid out, Dec. 18, 1878, from Allston street to Massachusetts avenue, May 7, 1884; called Prospect street in 1861. Middlesex Lib. 854, fol. 413. L 1760.

Summit street, Rox.; from Circuit street to Regent street; laid out, with name of Herman street, Dec. 28, 1888. L 2109.

Summit street, W. Rox.; from Metropolitan avenue, south-westerly, across Hemman street; same in 1874.

Sumner court, Dor.; from Sumner street, south-easterly; formerly called Gulliver court and later Sumner-street place.

Sumner place, B.; from Friend street, north, between Hanover street and Sudbury street, 1850; closed.

Sumner place, E. B.; from Sumner street, near Seaver street, south-easterly.

Sumner place, Rox.; from Cabot street, south-easterly, near Vernon street.

***Sumner street**, B.; from Beacon street, north; called Sentry street, 1708–1800; from Beacon street, north, then west, around the new State House to Belknap (now Joy) street, 1800; extended west through Olive street to Charles street, 1824; Temple street extended over part running east of the State House to Beacon street, 1824; name changed to Mt. Vernon street, August, 1832.

Sumner street, E. B.; from New street to and crossing Jeffries street, with extension from New street to Week's wharf; laid out from Orleans street to London street, Aug. 7, 1848; accepted, Aug. 27, 1849; accepted from Cottage street to Orleans street, May 10, 1852; accepted from Cottage street to the water and from London street to New street, Oct. 25, 1852. L 1419, L 1506, L 2132, L 2172, L 2494.

***Sumner street**, Rox.; from Main (now Washington) street in Roxbury, continued until it meets another street opposite Capt. Aaron Davis' house; accepted, being commonly called Sumner street, April 1, 1816; from Washington street by Sumner School-house to Davis (now Albany) street, named May 9, 1825; extended to Mall street, April 2, 1855; lands exchanged to straighten line, February and July, 1860; name changed to Palmer street, April 21, 1868.

Sumner street, Dor.; from Stoughton street to Cottage (now East Cottage) street; named from Myrtle (now East Cottage) street by No. 1 School-house to Stoughton street, March 11, 1840; accepted, April 6, 1840. L 1714.

Sumner-street place, Dor.; from Sumner street, south-east, formerly called Gulliver court and now Sumner court.

Sun court, B.; the way leading south-easterly, from the North Meeting-house into Fish (now North) street. 1708; by plan of 1722 from Fleet street, south-westerly, by the North Meeting-house, then south-easterly, to Fish street and down to the sea; from Fish street, north-west, to Clarke's (now North) square, Moon street, being extended over the remainder to Fleet street, 1784; called Sun-court street, 1811.

***Sun-court street**, B.; from Moon street, at North square, to North street; from 1708 called Sun court; called Sun-court street in "Selectmen's Records," Nov. 27, 1811.

***Sunderland street**, Rox.; from Warren street, opposite Crawford street, to Blue Hill avenue, opposite Stanwood street; laid out, Oct. 6, 1880. L 1495.

Sunny court, Rox.; from Lamartine street, north-west, between Roys street and Hoffman street.

Sunnyside avenue, W. Rox.; from Arnold street to Agassiz avenue.

***Sunnyside street**, Rox., 1892; from Centre street, north, then west to Creighton street; a private way called Sunnyside terrace, laid out, with name of Sunnyside street, Dec. 28, 1892. L 2479, L 2480.

Sunnyside terrace, Rox.; from Centre street, north, then west to Creighton street; laid out, with name of Sunnyside street, Dec. 28, 1892. L 2479, L 2480.

Sunset circle, Dor., 1889; from Stanley street.

Sunset avenue, W. Rox.; from Wenham street.

***Sunset street**, Rox., 1891; from Parker Hill avenue to Hillside street; laid out, July 2, 1891. L 2306.

Surrey street, W. Rox.; from Canterbury street to the railroad, 1849; not in existence in 1874.

†**Surrey street**, Bri.; from Market street to Foster street; laid out, from Parsons street to Foster street, Sept. 4, 1884; at one time known as Kensington street. L 1817.

***Sussex street**, Rox., 1887; from Hammond street to Warwick street; laid out, Feb. 25, 1887. L 1978.

***Sutherland road**, Bri.; from Beacon street to Commonwealth avenue; name of Isleworth street, from Beacon street to Englewood avenue, changed to Sutherland road, March 1, 1892; laid out, from Englewood avenue to Commonwealth avenue, Oct. 11, 1892; formerly Roxbury avenue. L 1985, L 2442.

Sutton street, W. Rox.; from Berry street to Gilman street.

Sutton street, Dor.; from Morton street to Woolson street.

Swallow street, So. B.; from N street, easterly, between East Fifth street and East Sixth street.

Swallow street, W. Rox.; from La Grange street to Cottage avenue.

Swan avenue, E. B. (Breed's Island); from Ashley avenue to Belle Isle inlet; Bromley's atlas, 1892.

Swan court, Dor.; from Richmond street, between Butler street, and Adams street.

Swan place, So. B.; from Swan street, north-east, opposite Ontario street; discontinued and taken into estate of the O. C. (now N. Y., N. H. & H.) R.R. Co., under authority of chapter 127 of the Acts of the Legislature of 1893.

***Swan street**, So. B.; from Dorchester avenue, to Foundry street; accepted conditionally, Oct. 29, 1849; accepted, Dec. 18, 1854; laid out, Nov. 17, 1868; discontinued and taken into estate of the O. C. (now N. Y., N. H. & H.) R.R. Co., under authority of the Acts of the Legislature of 1893. L 223.

Swan street, W. Rox.; from Martin street, south-east, 1849; not in existence in 1874.

Swan's court, Dor.; from Olney street, south, near Blakeville street; given in directory only.

Sweetser's alley, B.; from Newbury (now Washington) street, east, nearly opposite Sheafe's lane (now Avery street), 1798; called Sweetser's court, 1809; Chickering place, 1855.

Sweetser's court, B.; see Sweetser's alley.

***Swett street**, Rox. and So. B.; from Albany street across South bay to Dorchester avenue; accepted from Northampton street at junction with Albany street to street leading to wharf of Thomas Simmons, March 7, 1859; width established from Davis (now Albany) street to Canal (now Hilton) street, June 25, 1866; laid out from Albany street to junction Boston street and Dorchester avenue, Jan. 2, 1875. L 377, L 1011, L 1012, L 1013, L 1014, L 1049, L 1150, L 1331, L 1352, L 1701.

†**Swift street**, E. B.; from Saratoga street to proposed part of Coleridge street; laid out from Bennington street to Saratoga street, Aug. 7, 1848.

Swift's corner, B.; corner Lynn (now Commercial) street and Henchman's lane (now Henchman street), 1800.

Swing bridge lane, B.; from Ann (now North) street to the Swing-ing-bridge, across the Town Dock, 1708; made part of Merchants' row, 1825.

†**Sycamore street**, W. Rox.; from Florence street to Kittredge street; laid out between Ashland street and Poplar street over private way called Albion street, July 6, 1880; from Ashland street to Florence street, Aug. 28, 1891; on chart, 1874, part from Roslin avenue (now Kittredge street) to Ashland street called Mt. Vernon street and part from Ashland street to Florence street called Albion street; no further record of changes of name. L 1468, L 2331.

Sydney place, Dor.; from Harvard street, westerly, then northerly, curving to meet end of Waterlow street; now Clinton street and a part of Waterlow street.

***Sydney street**, Dor.; from Savin Hill avenue to Crescent avenue; laid out from Savin Hill avenue to Harbor View street, Aug. 11, 1892; from Harbor View street to Crescent avenue, Oct. 16, 1894. L 2424, L 2425, L 2665.

***Sylvia street**, W. Rox., 1891; from Washington street to Forest Hills street; Bond avenue laid out, with name of Sylvia street, July 17, 1891. L 2317.

***Symmes street**, W. Rox., 1890; from Fairview street to Walter street; laid out, Feb. 11, 1890. L 2204.

T wharf, B.; from Atlantic avenue, opposite South Market street. Vol. 31, p. 47. L 1000, L 1001.

***Taber street**, Rox., 1868; from Warren street, south-east, crossing Harrison avenue and Winslow street; accepted as Union street, March 1, 1819; named Taber street, April 21, 1868. L 588, L 1746.

Taft court, W. Rox.; from Corinth street, nearly opposite Cohasset street, north-east, towards South street.

Taft's place, W. Rox.; from South street, north-east; near Washington street.

***Talbot avenue**, Dor.; from Blue Hill avenue to Dorchester avenue; first projected from junction Harvard street and Blue Hill avenue, easterly, to N. E. R.R ; Directory 1884 gives same from Washington street corner of Norfolk street to Blue Hill avenue corner of Harvard street; laid out from Blue Hill avenue to Washington street, March 29, 1888, and from Washington street to Dorchester avenue, including a part of Argyle street, Oct. 10, 1892. L 2062, L 2063, L 2437, L 2438, L 2758.

***Tamworth street**, B., 1880; from Boylston street to La Grange street; called Lowell court, from Boylston street, south, 1806; Lowell place, 1809; laid out as Tamworth street, April 28, 1880. L 1452.

Tanner's lane, B., 1708; from Milk street to Water street; called also Horn lane and Horse lane, 1795–1806; called Bath street, 1807; parts afterwards included in extension of Pearl street and Post Office square.

Tappan street, W. Rox.; from South street, north-east; laid out from South street, Nov. 11, 1896. L 2797.

Tattle street, B.; Hawkins street, from Cambridge street, north, then east, to Sudbury street, was sometimes so called, 1756–84, and according to Drake, commonly so called in 1800.

Taylor avenue, Dor.; from Stoughton (now Dudley) street, northerly, 1874; included in extension of Clifton street, June 15, 1883. L 1708.

***Taylor street**, B.; from Dwight street to Milford street; same in 1844 (from Groton, now Dwight street, to South Lowell, now Milford street); laid out, March 1, 1875. L 1026.

†**Taylor street**, Dor.; from Neponset avenue to Water street; part from Water street to O. C. (now N. Y., N. H. & H.) R.R.; laid out by Selectmen, March 21, 1866, and accepted by Town, April 2, 1866; laid out from Neponset avenue to Wood (now Rice) street, Jan. 31, 1876. L 1127.

Taylor street, Dor.; from Dudley street to Clifton street; laid out as Burgess street, July 12, 1888. L 2076.

Taylor street, Bri.; from Lake street, near Washington street, south-east.

Teevan place, Rox.; from 581 Shawmut avenue, near and north of Lenox street.

***Telegraph street**, So. B.; from Dorchester street to Old Harbor street, opposite Thomas park; laid out and extended 516 feet southerly from Dorchester street, to Dorchester street, Nov. 17, 1868. L 612.

Telegraph Hill, So. B.; formerly Dorchester Heights.

Telford street, Bri., 1897; from Western avenue, north-west, to Charles River Reservation, between Everett street and Antwerp street; authority to open given by Street Commissioners, Jan. 7, 1897.

Temple avenue, B., 1833; from Washington street, west, to Temple place; called Washington court, 1826; Temple avenue, 1833; included in Temple place, 1864.

Temple park, B., 1879; from Washington street, near South May (now Savoy) street; called Sands place, 1859; Ottawa place, 1873; Temple park, 1879; and is now called Mechanics row.

***Temple place**, B., 1830; from Tremont street to Washington street; called "Turnagaine alley from ye Comon, easterly," 1708; from Tremont street, east north of West street, 1830; extended to Washington street, 1864; named Autumn street, May 15, 1865; renamed Temple place, May 23, 1865; name of Avon street given to Temple place and Avon place, March 30, 1869; again changed to Temple place, June 9, 1869. L 274, L 290.

Temple place, Dor.; from Temple street, west, to unnamed street (now Sturbridge street); laid out as Monson street, March 21, 1890. L 2212.

***Temple street**, B., 1769; from Cambridge street to Derne street; from Cambridge street to the foot of Beacon Hill, 1769; extended to Sumner (now Mt. Vernon) street, 1820; the part of Sumner street which runs east of the State House to Beacon street named Temple street, July 6, 1824; same part named Mt. Vernon street, 1832; part of Temple street south of Derne street included in State House grounds by authority of an Act of the Legislature. L 1505, L 2105.

†**Temple street**, Dor.; from River street, north, crossing Sanford street; from River street to Sanford street laid out and widened, Feb. 20, 1852.

†**Temple street**, W. Rox.; from Baker street crossing Mt. Vernon street to West Roxbury Branch R.R.; laid out from Ivory street to Mt. Vernon street, July 16, 1877; laid out from Mt. Vernon street to Baker street, Sept. 14, 1894. L 1248, L 1249, L 2666.

Temple street, Chsn.; from Dorrance street to Sherman street.

Temple terrace, W. Rox., 1893; from Perham street to Temple street; authority to open given by Street Commissioners, March 5, 1895.

Templeton street, Dor.; from Adams street to Dorchester avenue; from Adams street, south-west, for a distance of about 800 feet, in 1884.

***Tenean street**, Dor.; from Freeport street to Fulton street, parallel with O. C. (now N. Y., N. H. & H.) R.R.; located from Water street to Commercial (now Freeport) street, March 26, 1860. L 1840.

Tennis court, B.; from Buckingham street, north, then east, near Dartmouth street.

***Tennyson street**, B.; from Columbus avenue to Pleasant street; from Church street, west, opposite Berlin street, 1856; name of Berlin street from Pleasant street to Church street, changed to Tennyson street, April 20, 1869. L 387, L 393, L 394, L 397.

Terrace avenue, W. Rox., 1874; from Sheridan avenue (now street), south-westerly, then south-easterly; part laid out as Cranston street, Nov. 11, 1890. L 2272.

Terrace avenue, E. B.; from Washburn avenue (now Walley street) to Chelsea avenue; part between Walley street and Breed street laid out, with the name of Gladstone street, Aug. 23, 1886. L 1933, L 1934, L 1935.

Terrace place, E. B.; from Webster street, near Seaver street, south-west, then south-east, parallel with Marginal street; part from

Webster street, south-west, then south-east, crossing Ida street, laid out with name of Brigham street, Nov. 26, 1892; part from Webster street opposite Lamson street, to Brigham street, laid out with name of Ruth street, Nov. 26, 1892; part between Ruth street and Brigham street, laid out as Ida street, Nov. 26, 1892.

*__Terrace street,__ Rox.; from Tremont street to New Heath street; from New Heath street to Alleghany street, 1873; Gore avenue laid out in part (about 200 feet south-west from Tremont street), April 17, 1875; name of last mentioned part changed to Terrace street, Sept. 23, 1875; laid out from New Heath street to Tremont street, including another part of Gore avenue, Oct. 9, 1875. L 1040, L 1087, L 1088.

*__Terry street,__ Rox., 1888; from Tremont street to Columbus avenue; Tremont place, from Tremont street to Cary street, laid out, Dec. 20, 1875, and named Terry street, March 1, 1888; part between Columbus avenue and Cary street discontinued, Jan. 4, 1895. L 1119, L 2684.

Tesla street, Dor., 1896; from River street to Edgewater drive; authority to open given by Street Commissioners, Feb. 24, 1896.

Texas avenue, Rox.; from Tremont street to Elmwood street; laid out as Texas street, Oct. 1, 1886. L 1952.

Texas court, Rox.; from Texas street, south-west.

*__Texas street,__ Rox.; from Tremont street to Elmwood street; Texas avenue laid out as Texas street, Oct. 1, 1886. L 1952.

Texas street, Bri., 1882; from Third street to Fifth street, near and parallel with B. & A. R.R.; now in Brighton cattle-yards.

Thacher avenue, B., 1835; from Thacher street to Cooper street; laid out as Lynn street, Sept. 10, 1884. L 1819.

Thacher avenue, Dor.; from Sawyer avenue, north-west; laid out as Cushing avenue and extended to Hancock street, in part over Upham avenue, Oct. 28, 1881. L 1562, L 1563, L 1564.

Thacher court or place, B.; from Thacher street, north, opposite Lynn street; called Thacher-street court, 1833; Thacher court, 1859; called both Thacher court and Thacher place, 1884; and Thacher court, 1890.

*__Thacher street,__ B., 1807; from Prince street to Charlestown street; laid out on the Mill-pond and named, 1807; from Prince street to Charlestown street, 1822; mistake in location rectified, 1827. L 366, L 1827, L 2262.

Thacher-street court, B., 1833; from Thacher street, north; called Thacher court or place, 1859, and Thacher court, 1890.

Thane street, Dor., 1895; from Harvard street at its junction with School street to Park street.

Thatcher road, Dor., 1896; from Dudley street to Cushing avenue; authority to open given by Street Commissioners, May 22, 1896.

Thaxter place, B., 1831; from Front street (now Harrison avenue), opposite Harvard street; probably included in Harvard street on its extension east in 1836.

Thayer street, B.; from Harrison avenue to Albany street, south of Bristol street.

Theatre alley, B., 1796; from Milk street to Franklin street; called Dinsdale's alley earlier; from Milk street to rear of theatre, 1817; south part called Odeon avenue, 1842–48; Devonshire street extended through it in 1859.

*__Thetford avenue,__ Dor.; from Norfolk street to Evans street; laid out, Sept. 27, 1875. L 1076.

*__Third street,__ So. B., 1805; laid out parallel with Broadway, and named, Feb. 27, 1805; portion between M street and N street discontinued, Dec. 31, 1857; laid out from Second (now West Second) street to Dorchester street, thence to M street and from N street to low-water mark, Nov. 17, 1868; called East and West Third streets, Feb. 18, 1873. L 8, L 123, L 143, L 155, L 157, L 160.

Third street, Chsn.; from Lynde street to the railroad; accepted from Lynde street to Front street by plan, October, 1860; discontinued and part taken by the Eastern (now B. & M.) R.R. by authority of an Act of the Legislature.

Third street, Bri., 1882; from North Beacon street to Texas street; now in Brighton cattle-yards.

Third-street court, So. B.; from 259 West Third street to Athens street, between E street and F street.

Third-street place, So. B.; from 239 West Third street, near E street, south-westerly; also called West Third-street place.

Thirteenth street, Rox.; from St. Botolph street to B. & P. (now N. Y., N. H. & H.) R.R.; abandoned.

Thirty-feet passage, B., 1784; from Wiltshire (now Chambers) street, west; called South Allen street, 1807; McLean street, 1829.

***Thomas park,** So. B.; around Telegraph Hill from G street, crossing Linden, Pacific, Atlantic, National and Old Harbor streets, to G street again; laid out as Thomas street, Nov. 17, 1868; named Thomas park, June 22, 1878. L 293, L 337, L 1890.

***Thomas street,** So. B.; around Telegraph Hill, 1855; laid out, Nov. 17, 1868; name changed to Thomas park, June 22, 1878, L 293, L 337.

***Thomas street,** W. Rox.; from Centre street to Brewer street; laid out, March 19, 1875. L 1031.

Thomas' corner, B., 1708; corner of Ann street and Paddy's alley (now North street and North Centre street) then so called.

Thompson court, S. B.; from Vinton street near Rogers street, north-east.

***Thompson square,** Chsn., 1875; junction of Main street and Warren street; name of La Fayette square changed to Thompson square, July 19, 1875. L 1086.

***Thompson street,** Chsn.; from Main street to Warren street; street to be laid out to cost $1,000, May 13, 1805; land conveyed by Oliver Holden and Timothy Thompson, 1805.

***Thompson's court,** B., 1856; from Revere street, north, near Grove street.

Thorn street, B.; from East Canton street to East Dedham street; named April 1, 1873; shown on atlas of 1890 as extending as far south as Stoughton street.

Thorndike place, B.; from Thorndike street near Reed street, north-east.

***Thorndike street,** B.; from Washington street to Harrison avenue; laid out, Sept. 25, 1874. L 956.

Thorndike street, Chsn.; from Main street to Rutherford avenue; same in 1875.

***Thornley street,** Dor.; from Dorchester avenue to Pleasant street; laid out, Sept. 10, 1874. L 963.

Thornton place, Rox.; from Thornton street, south-easterly, near and south of Valentine street.

***Thornton street,** Rox.; from Guild street to Marcella street; name of Edinboro' street (from Cedar street to Ellis street) changed to Thornton street, April 21, 1868; laid out from Ellis street to Shawmut avenue (now Washington street) and westerly over part of Vale street to Marcella street, Oct. 25, 1873; part from Washington street, westerly, to Thornton street "as recently laid out," named Valentine street, Oct. 19, 1875; extended from Cedar street over part of Cedar square to Guild street, Dec. 10, 1881. L 904, L 905, L 906, L 1580, L 1581, L 2309.

Thrush street, W. Rox.; from Heron street nearly opposite Grouse street, to Willet street.

Thurston street, B. I.; from Butler avenue to Bayswater street.

***Thwing street**, Rox., 1889; from Highland street, near Fulda street; Thwing terrace laid out as Thwing street, March 19, 1889. L 2115.

Thwing terrace, Rox.; from Highland street, north-west; laid out as Thwing street, March 19, 1889. L 2115.

***Tibbett's Town way**, Chsn.; from Mill street to Rutherford avenue; called Tibbett's Town way on chart, and shown on plans as extending nearly to Somerville line.

Tilden place, Rox.; from Auburn street, south-west, between Ruggles street and Vernon street; named, Sept. 1, 1868.

Tileston avenue, Dor.; from Blue Hill avenue, south of Walk Hill street, north-west, then north-east, crossing Walk Hill street to another part of Tileston avenue, leading from Blue Hill avenue, north of Walk Hill street; authority to open and extend the part north of Walk Hill street, given by Street Commissioners, Sept. 14, and Dec. 26, 1894, and March 26, 1895.

Tileston court, } B.; from Tileston street to Webster avenue; from
Tileston place, } Tileston street, near Hanover street, 1837.

Tileston place, Dor.; from 134 Neponset avenue, east, nearly opposite King street.

Tileston square, B.; from Atlantic avenue, south-east, between Congress street and Summer street.

***Tileston street**, B., 1821; from Hanover street to Salem street; called Love lane, 1708; also North Writing School street, 1789, named Tileston street, June 20, 1821.

Tileston street, B.; from Fellows street, north-westerly, near Northampton street.

Tileston street, Dor.; from Blue Hill avenue, near Walk Hill street, north-westerly; now called Tileston avenue.

Tileston wharf, B.; from Atlantic avenue, south-easterly, near N. E. R.R.; now built over.

Tilley's lane, B.; from Cow lane (now High street) to Belcher lane (now Purchase street); the third street from Summer street, shown in 1722; named, 1732; called Gridley's lane, 1795; Gridley street, from High street to Purchase street, 1825.

Tillson's lane, B.; Wilson's lane so called on plan, 1789.

Tirrell's wharf, B., from Shaving street, easterly.

Tilton street, Dor., 1895; from Washington street to Faxon street; authority to open given by Street Commissioners, May 15, 1895; now called Kilton street.

Tokio street, Dor., 1896; from River street to Edgewater drive; authority to open given by Street Commissioners, Feb. 24, 1896.

Tolman lane, Dor.; from angle in Ashmont street, south-westerly, nearly to Washington street; part of now included in Burt avenue.

Tolman place, Rox.; from Warren street, west, between St. James street, and Walnut avenue.

***Tolman street**, Dor.; from Neponset avenue to Norwood street; laid out, Dec. 8, 1893. L 2569.

Tonawanda street, Dor.; from Geneva avenue, south-west, to beyond Greenbrier street.

Tontine buildings, B.; in Franklin place, 1793.

***Topliff street**, Dor.; from Bowdoin street to Geneva avenue; laid out, Oct. 3, 1891. L 2342.

Torrey street, Dor.; from Washington street to Wentworth street.

Tower street, W. Rox., 1892; from Hyde Park avenue opposite Forest Hills station to Forest Hills cemetery; authority to open given by Street Commissioners, May 4, 1892; at one time called Foley street.

Tower street, B. I.; from Gladstone street to Farrington street.

Town dock, B.; originally an arm of the Town cove, sweeping inward from near the corner of the present Merchants' row and South Market street, on the south, and from Ann (now North) street on the opposite side, extending northwardly, almost to the foot of Brattle street; first called Bendall's dock, afterwards Town dock; connected by Mill-creek with Mill-pond; Swing bridge was built across nearly on line with present Merchants' row and a market place set up; all the north side of the Dock seems to have been known as the Fish market, 1708; Corn market and Corn court were on the south side of the dock, 1708.

Town dock, Chsn.; to be filled up and street laid out thereon, Feb. 4, 1839; report of Commissioners laying out Gray street over the Town dock from Chelsea street to Water street, March 28, 1842.

Town Hill court, Chsn.; from Harvard square to City square; part of now a covered passage.

Town Hill street, Chsn.; "doings of Selectmen in relation to fixing boundaries of Town Hill street," confirmed March 28, 1836; name changed to Harvard street, Nov. 7, 1836.

***Town Meeting square**, Dor.; junction Pond street, East Cottage street and Pleasant street; named, Jan. 24, 1894.

Town way, Bri.; private way from Market street, opposite house of Edward C. Sparhawk, to Parsons street, laid out as Town way, May 23, 1870; accepted as Arlington street, June 24, 1870.

Townsend place, B., 1841; from Commercial street, opposite Bartlett's wharf; sometimes called North Townsend place; part of included in Commercial street when widened in 1879; now included in park.

Townsend place, B., 1844; from Carver street, east, and then south, near Boylston street; sometimes called South Townsend place.

***Townsend street**, Rox., 1868; from Washington street to Warren street; name of Otis street changed to Townsend street, April 21, 1868; laid out, from Warren street to Walnut avenue, Jan. 6, 1872; laid out, from Walnut avenue to Washington street, July 26, 1875. L 733, L 734, L 1064, L 1065, L 2249.

Townsend street, Chsn., 1831; from Adams street to Chelsea street; name of Shippie street changed to Townsend street, March 14, 1831; name of Townsend street changed to Chestnut street, June 20, 1846.

Townsend's corner, B., 1708; corner of Tremont street and School street, the southerly termination of Tremont street, 1708.

***Train street**, Dor., 1852; from Ashmont street to Mill street; accepted and named, Dec. 22, 1852.

Trainer court, B., 1851; from Lenox street to Winfred court; from Lenox street, south, near Shawmut avenue, 1851; Trainer court and Winfred court included in the laying out of Dillon street, from Lenox street to Sawyer street, Oct. 24, 1887. L 2034.

Training-field, Chsn.; the square "anciently called Training-field," named Winthrop square, Jan. 17, 1848.

Training-field street, Chsn.; from the training field to Back (now Warren) street; laid out wider, May 12, 1804; accepted as so laid out, Jan. 7, 1805; laid out, May 21, 1827; name changed to Winthrop street, Dec. 5, 1836.

***Transit street**, Rox., 1881; from Cabot street to Newbern street; laid out, Sept. 23, 1881; name changed to Sterling street, March 1, 1884; also name of that part of Newbern street, from Tremont street to Transit street, changed to Sterling street, March 1, 1884. L 1559, L 1726.

Trant's alley, B., 1849; from Ann (now North) street, near North square; probably now North Brimmer place.

Trask place, Rox.; from Yeoman street to Orchard street; that part of Eaton street, between Yeoman street and Orchard street, so called previous to 1870; part from Yeoman street to Orchard park, laid out as Chadwick street, May 24, 1870, and extended to Hartopp place (now Ambrose street) Dec. 31, 1870; part from Orchard street to Hartopp place laid out as Orchard-Park street, Feb. 19, 1876. L 529.

Travers place, Rox.; from Adams street, north-west, between Eustis street and Orchard-Park street; directory gives this as Edward's place from 37 Adams street.

***Traverse street**, B , 1807; from Merrimac street to Charlestown street; laid out on the Mill-pond and named, August, 1807.

Travises corner, B., 1708; corner of Prince street and Snowhill street.

Tremlett park, Dor.; from Hooper street to Waldeck street, authority to open given by Street Commissioners, Oct. 1, 1891; laid out as Tremlett street, Aug. 10, 1893. L 2522.

***Tremlett street**, Dor., 1885; from Washington street to Waldeck street; laid out from Washington street to Hooper street, Sept. 16, 1885; authority to open Tremlett park from Hooper street to Waldeck street given by Street Commissioners, Oct. 1, 1891; Tremlett park laid out as Tremlett street, from Hooper street to Waldeck street, Aug. 10, 1893. L 1886, L 2522.

Tremont court, Rox.; from Terry street, north-east.

Tremont court, Chsn.; from 38 Tremont street, north-easterly.

Tremont place, B., 1829; from Beacon street, south, to the Granary Burying-ground.

Tremont place, B., 1805; from Tremont street, west, next north of Beacon street, opposite the Chapel, Tremont street, 1817; called Phillips place, 1829.

***Tremont place**, Rox.; from Tremont street to Cary street; laid out, Dec. 20, 1875; name changed to Terry street, March 1, 1888. L 1119.

Tremont place, Chsn.; from 22 Tremont street, north-easterly.

***Tremont row**, B., 1837; from Howard street to Pemberton square; called Sudbury street, 1654; called Pemberton Hill by Hale's plan, 1814; called Tremont row, from Beacon street to near the corner of Howard street, 1837; name changed to Tremont square and changed back to Tremont row, 1850; from Pemberton square to Howard street, part of Tremont street, 1852: Tremont row and Court street widened by removal of Scollay's building and steamer house No. 4, Nov. 4, 1870. L 580.

***Tremont street**, B. and Rox., 1708; from Court street at Scollay square to Huntington avenue at Francis street; called at different times Tra Mount, Tremount, Treamont, and Tremont; from School street to Court street called Sudbury street, 1654; from Hanover street to School street called Tra Mount street, 1708; in 1741 the part from Frog lane (now Boylston street) to Orange (now Washington) street, was called also Walker's lane or street; about 1777, from School street to Winter street was called Long Acre; between West street and Common street was called Colonnade row in 1810, and Fayette place, 1825–37; from Howard street over Pemberton Hill through Tremont, Common, and Nassau streets to Washington street named Common street, 1824; same named Tremont street,

1829; part from School street to Frog lane called Common street, 1722–1824, when it was included in Common street as above; from Frog lane to Hollis street, 1733, and from Frog lane to Dr. Byle's house, at corner of present Common street, 1744, called Clough street; same called Holyoke street, 1750; Nassau street, 1788; included in Common street, 1824; Tremont street, constructed from city lands, south, to Dedham street, June 9, 1831; continued to meet street then making in Roxbury, July 11, 1831; deed of F. C. Lowell of land formerly Cabot street, to be used as extension of Tremont street, June 18, 1832; from street next south of Dedham street to Roxbury line, opened for public travel, Sept. 17, 1832; from Pleasant street to city lands (except 106 feet) accepted Oct. 15, 1832; altered at junction of Pleasant street, July 29, 1833; street extending from Tremont street to Roxbury named Tremont street; from Byle's corner to Washington street, called Common street, Dec. 30, 1836; from Howard street to Tremont street, formerly called Common street or Pemberton Hill, named Tremont street, Nov. 4, 1844; part in Roxbury extended by County Commissioners of Norfolk for two miles and six rods from end of Tremont street at city line to Guy Carleton's morocco factory, intersecting the Worcester turnpike, October, 1831; the road leading from near Hog bridge in Roxbury to Boston line being circuitous, same altered and straightened by construction of new highway from near Hog bridge down the vale of Stony brook to near Guy Carleton's morocco factory, and thence to line of city of Boston, April, 1832; new road named Tremont street, May 25, 1832; accepted by county, Oct. 15, 1832; the south-westerly end where it intersects the old road from Roxbury to Brookline being unsafe because of close proximity of B. & P. (now N.Y., N.H. & H.) R.R. and sharp curve from Lowell street (later Pynchon street, now Columbus avenue), widened, June, 1825; name of Washington street from Tremont street to Brookline line, changed to Tremont street, April 21, 1868; Tremont street from Francis street to Brookline line included in the widening and extension of Huntington avenue, Jan. 5, 1895. Between Scollay square and Boylston street. L 282, L 310, L 753, L 1702, L 2824. Between Boylston street and Dover street. L 64, L 152, L 184, L 197, L 236, L 270, L 307, L 314, L 315, L 316, L 317, L 318, L 370, L 371, L 387, L 391, L 392, L 406, L 407, L 544, L 546, L 548, L 590, L 724, L 728, L 769, L 1764. Between Dover street and Roxbury line. Vol. 31. pp. 2, 7, 59. L 184, L 189, L 206. In Roxbury District. Vol. 31. pp. 7, 59. L 189, L 601, L 1045, L 1259, L 1262, L 1380, L 1480, L 1481, L 1482, L 1483, L 1484, L 1485, L 2024, L 2096, L 2142, L 2213, L 2445, L 2504, L 2768.

***Tremont street,** Chsn.; from Monument square to Chelsea street; name of part from Lexington street to Concord street changed to Monument square, Feb. 2, 1860; laid out as a public way from Lexington street to Edgeworth street, Sept. 7, 1863; name of Jay street (from Chelsea street to Edgeworth street) changed to Tremont street, making said street extend from Monument square to Chelsea street, Oct. 29, 1866.

***Tremont street,** Bri.; from Washington street at Oak square to Newton line; laid out by County Commissioners, July 25, 1861. L 2487.

***Trenton street,** E. B.; from Meridian street to East Eagle street; accepted and laid out, July 19, 1852; accepted at junction Trenton street and White street and at junction Trenton street and Eagle street, Nov. 1, 1858. L 106.

***Trenton street,** Chsn.; from Bartlett street to Bunker Hill street; laid out and accepted, Dec. 14, 1859.

Trescott place, Dor.; from 41 Harvard street, north-west, then north.

Trescott street, Dor.; from Pleasant street to F (now Bakersfield) street; authority to open, under name of A street given by Street Commissioners, May 4, 1892.

†**Trinity place**, B., 1876; from Huntington avenue to N. Y., N. H. & H. R.R.; from Huntington avenue to St. James avenue laid out, Nov. 24, 1876. L 1192.

Trinity triangle, B.; area bounded by Huntington avenue, Trinity place, and St. James avenue sometimes so called; included in Copley square, April 21, 1885.

Trowbridge court, Dor.; from Faulkner street to railroad near Field's Corner station.

***Troy street**, B., 1845; from Harrison avenue to Albany street; laid out and widened, June 20, 1871. L 625, L 697, L 2287.

***Trull street**, Dor.; from Hancock street to Bellevue street; laid out, Dec. 10, 1875. L 1114.

***Trumbull street**, B.; from Newland street to Ivanhoe street; laid out, Nov. 9, 1870. L 540, L 581.

Trumbull street, E. B.; from end of Reynolds street to end of Milton street.

***Truro street**, B.; from Yarmouth street to Harwich street; laid out, Oct. 21, 1882. L 1658.

Tucker place, B., 1859; from 52 Joy street, west.

Tucker street, B., 1803; from Leverett street, east, then south, to Green street, 1803; called also New Prince street previously to 1788; named Leverett place or alley, 1812; called Lyman place, 1834; Lyman street, 1856; part of Lyman street, near Green street, included in Staniford street, May 11, 1886.

Tucker street, Dor.; from Lauriat avenue to Chapman avenue.

Tuckerman street, B., 1831; from Dover street, north; named Parkman street, 1846; Albion street, 1849.

Tuckerman street, So. B.; from Dorchester street to Short street.

Tucker's corner, B., 1800; corner of Leverett street and Green lane.

†**Tudor street**, So. B.; from B street to Dorchester street; accepted and dedicated as a public highway between E street and F street, Sept. 8, 1864; laid out between C street and D street, Sept. 5, 1870; laid out between D street and E street, Nov. 15, 1873; laid out between F street and Dorchester street, Aug. 5, 1892. L 557, L 1488, L 2421.

Tudor's building, B., 1817; next the Court-house, Court street; now part of Young's Hotel.

Tufts court, Chsn.; from Tufts street to Corey street; named Tufts-street place, July 21, 1869; called also Tufts-street avenue on atlas, 1885 and 1892.

***Tufts street**, B., 1855; from South street to Kingston street; South-street place laid out, Oct. 23, 1855, and name changed to Tufts street, Dec. 18, 1855; laid out from Lincoln street to Kingston street, Sept. 28, 1889. L 1900, L 2170.

***Tufts street**, Chsn.; from Bunker Hill street to Medford street; accepted from Bunker Hill street to Benjamin Adams' line, March 24, 1834; continued to Lexington street, March 6, 1849; opened and graded from Tufts street to Lexington street (part last laid out), June 6, 1850; part leading from and at right angles with Lexington street named Princeton street, Oct. 6, 1851; laid out and accepted from Princeton street to Medford street, Sept. 15, 1856.

Tufts-street avenue, Chsn.; from Tufts street to Corey street; same named Tufts-street place, July 21, 1869; called also Tufts court, but Tufts-street avenue on atlas, 1885 and 1892.

Tufts-street court, Chsn.; south from Tufts-street avenue.

Tufts-street place, Chsn.; from Tufts street to Corey street; named, July 21, 1869; called Tufts court by directories and Tufts-street avenue by atlas, 1885 and 1892.

***Tupelo street,** Rox.; from Savin street to Quincy street; laid out, Nov. 23, 1881. L 1571.

Turnagaine alley, B., 1708; the alley leading from the Common, east, on the north side of Madam Usher's house; name changed to Temple place, 1830.

Turner street, B.; George street, now Hancock street, so called at one time.

***Turner street,** Rox.; from Haviland street to Astor street; laid out, including a part of Francis street, Nov. 16, 1894. L 2657, L 2658.

***Turnpike street,** So. B.; filled up and built from termination of South Boston turnpike (now Dorchester avenue) at Broadway to new bridge at First (now West First) street, Oct. 21, 1828: accepted between Dorchester line and Fourth (now West Fourth) street, Sept. 27, 1852; name changed to Dorchester avenue, March 27, 1854.

Turpin court, Dor.; from East Cottage (formerly Cottage) street; between Sumner street and Pleasant street, south-westerly; called Davis place on chart, 1884; now Cottage side, from East Cottage street to Willis street.

Tuttle avenue, Dor.; from Savin Hill avenue to Hartland street; laid out as Tuttle street, Nov. 16, 1891. L 2364.

***Tuttle street,** Dor., 1891; from Savin Hill avenue to Hartland street; Tuttle avenue laid out as Tuttle street, Nov. 16, 1891. L 2364.

Twelfth street, Rox.; from St. Botolph street to B. & P. (now N. Y., N. H. & H.) R.R.

Twombly place, Rox.; from 783 Parker street.

Tyler court, B., 1844; from Harrison avenue, opposite Pine street; closed.

Tyler place, B., 1842; from Tyler street, near Kneeland street, easterly.

***Tyler street,** B., 1841; from Beach street to Curve street; from Beach street, south, called Buffalo street, 1839; extended to Curve street and named Tyler street, 1841; accepted from Beach street to Kneeland street, Oct. 5, 1846, also, Oct. 18, 1847; accepted from Harvard street to Oak street, July 10, 1848; accepted from Harvard street to Kneeland street, and also from Oak street to Curve street, Jan. 5, 1856. L 1533.

Tyler's corner, B., 1732; corner of Ann street and Swing-bridge lane (now Hanover street and Merchants' row).

Tyng's alley, B., 1712; from Cornhill (now Washington street) into Brattle street; named, May 12, 1712.

Tyso park, Rox.; from Dennis street, south-east, nearly opposite Stafford street; shown in Bromley's atlas, 1890; now called Woodville park.

Tyson street, Dor ; (proposed) from Boston street, opposite Harvest street, north-westerly; shown on atlas, 1884.

***Ulmer street,** Rox.; from Minden street to Arklow street; a portion of Heath place from Minden street to Arklow street named Ulmer street, March 1, 1882. L 1117.

***Union avenue,** Dor., 1869; from Bowdoin street to Geneva avenue; laid out from Bowdoin street to Green street (now Geneva avenue), being called on Moseley's plan Smith avenue, Bowdoin avenue, and Love Lane avenue, but called Union avenue throughout, Dec. 28, 1869; accepted as Union street, April 5, 1852; part between Geneva avenue and Rosseter street named Olney street, March 1, 1888; part between Olney street and Bullard street named Rosseter street, March 1, 1889; part between Bowdoin avenue and Bowdoin street being a continuation of Bullard street, named Bullard street, March 1, 1889. L 1650, L 1651, L 1652, L 2020.

Union avenue, W. Rox.; from Walter street, near and north-east of South street; now included in Hewlett street.

Union aveuue, W. Rox; from Green street at Jamaica Plain station to Starr (now Everett) street, 1874; made part of Call street, Dec. 4, 1877.

†**Union avenue,** W. Rox.; from Washington street, north-west, then north-east, to Green street; same in 1874; part of from Green street parallel with Washington street laid out, Aug. 13, 1877. L 1257.

Union court, E. B.: from Everett street to Maverick street, near B., R. B. & L. R.R.

Union court, Chsn.; from Main street, westerly, near and south of Union street; same in 1875.

***Union park,** B. 1851; from Shawmut avenue to Montgomery street; from Shawmut avenue to Tremont street called Weston street or square, 1826; named Union park, May 19, 1851; new street from Washington street to Shawmut avenue in continuation of Union park opened, May 3, 1852, and named Union park, May 24, 1852; accepted and laid out as a public highway, Oct. 17, 1855; portion from Washington street to Shawmut avenue named Union-Park street, April 23, 1856; laid out by Water Power Company, west of Tremont street to street marked K (now Montgomery street); same part accepted, Sept. 2, 1861. Vol. 31, pp. 2, 7, 33. L 84.

Union Park passageway, B.; from Shawmut avenue to Tremont street, between Union Park and Upton street; laid out 20 feet wide and extended to Shawmut avenue and Tremont street, April 21, 1857; approved and dedicated as a public way, Jan. 19, 1858, but City Solicitor rules (1879) that the action was illegal, there having been no order of notice.

***Union-Park street,** B. 1856; from Shawmut avenue to Albany street; portion of Union park from Washington street to Shawmut avenue named Union-Park street, April 23, 1856; accepted Dec. 7, 1857; Blake's court, from Washington street to Harrison avenue, dedicated as a public highway and named Union-Park street, Oct. 16, 1860; extended with Waltham street from Harrison avenue to Albany street, Aug. 8, 1862. L 180, L 181, L 185, L 260, L 2520.

Union place, B.; from Wall street, west, between Causeway street and Cotting street; same in 1859.

Union place, E. B.; from Porter street, near Chelsea street, south-west, then north-west.

Union place, E. B.; from Princeton street, near Shelby street, southerly.

***Union square,** Bri.; junction of North Beacon street, Cambridge street, and Brighton avenue; same in 1875.

***Union street,** B., 1828; from Dock square to Haymarket square; the way leading from Platt's corner, north-west, crossing Hanover street to the Mill-pond, 1708; from the conduit at Dock head to the Mill-pond, 1732; previous to 1708 and until 1828, part from Hanover street to the Mill-pond called also Green Dragon lane; widened and named Union street, 1828; small portion discontinued between Hanover street and North Federal court, July 20, 1857; portion near estate of "Mary Homer's heirs" discontinued, Dec. 16, 1857. Vol. 31, p. 44. L 5, L 63, L 89.

Union street, Rox., 1825; from new lane (now Warren street) near Roxbury street as far as street is open, with passageway to Sumner (now Palmer) street accepted, March 1, 1819; named from Warren street to Sumner (now Palmer) street, May 9, 1825; name changed to Taber street, April 21, 1868.

Union street, Dor.; from Freeport street, north-east, to Pleasant street (Commercial Point).

***Union street**, Dor.; from Bowdoin street to Green (now Geneva avenue and Olney) street; Union avenue accepted as Union street, April 5, 1852.

†**Union street**, Chsn.; from Main street to railroad, south of Lynde street; from Main street to Washington street accepted, Sept. 16; 1813; laid out from Washington street to Lynde street, Sept. 17, 1896. L 2789.

***Union street**, Bri.; from Washington street to Chestnut Hill avenue; laid out from Rockland street (now Chestnut Hill avenue) to end of Shepard street, March 30, 1857; accepted, April 13, 1857; accepted from junction with Rockland street and Union street to Howard place, July 18, 1872.

Union terrace, W. Rox.; from Morton street to Forest Hills avenue near entrance to cemetery; same in 1874; part shown as Cary street on recent atlases.

Union wharf, B.; from Commercial street, east, between Battery street and Eastern avenue.

Unity court, B.; from Unity street, north-west, then north-east; same in 1830.

***Unity street**, B.; from Charter street to Tileston street; called Elias or Ellits street, 1733 to 1795; called also Clough street in 1756, Suffolk Deeds, Lib 89 fol. 148; called Unity street, from Charter street to Love lane (now Tileston street), 1795; confirmed as a public street, Sept. 15, 1834.

Upham avenue, Dor.; from Hancock street to beyond Cushing avenue; formerly from Hancock street easterly, then northerly, then north-westerly, to Hancock street again; called Upham street on recent atlases; Thacher avenue laid out as Cushing avenue, and extended in part over northerly part of Upham avenue to Hancock street, Oct. 28, 1881. L 1564.

Upham street, Dor.; see Upham avenue.

Upham street, So. B.; (proposed) from Dorchester avenue to Richardson avenue (proposed).

Upham's corner, Dor.; junction of Hancock, Stoughton, Boston and Dudley streets.

Upham's court, Dor.; from Boston street, east, opposite Hamlet street; same in 1874.

Upland avenue, Dor.; from Melville avenue to Park street; authority to open given by Street Commissioners, Oct. 1, 1891.

Upland place or **street**, Rox.; from Norfolk avenue, north-easterly, parallel with Magazine street; same in 1873.

Upper road, Dor.; from Roxbury to Milton; old name of Washington street.

Upton court or **street**, Bri.; from Western avenue, south-easterly, near Charles river; same in 1875; also called Upton's lane.

***Upton street**, B., 1857; from Shawmut avenue to Tremont street; called Chelsea street, 1826; named Upton street, April 21, 1857. Vol. 31, p. 7. L 294.

Usher's lane, B.; mentioned by Drake in 1677; probably Short street or Blind lane.

Utica place, B.; from Utica street, easterly, between Kneeland street and Beach street; same in 1842.

†**Utica street**, B., 1840; from Tufts street to south of Kneeland street; from Beach street near Lincoln street, 1840; extended to Harvard street (which part of Harvard street no longer exists), 1843; from Kneeland street to Harvard street accepted, Sept. 28, 1846; ex-

tended north to South-street place (now Tufts street), 1849; from Beach street to Kneeland street accepted, May 8, 1857; laid out from Beach street to Kneeland street, Sept. 29, 1884. L 1823.

Vale place, Rox.; part of Vale street from Marcella street to end of Thornton street; so called on chart, 1873; now part of Thornton street.

Vale street, W. Rox.; from La Grange street, south-west, between Pleasant street and Mt. Vernon street.

***Vale street,** So. B; from Dorchester street crossing Mercer street with proposed extension to "Old Harbor;" laid out from Dorchester street to Old Harbor street extended, Nov. 17, 1868. L 238.

***Vale street,** Rox.; from Thornton street to Marcella street; by chart, 1873, from Marcella street, generally south-easterly, then south-westerly, to Marcella street, the last part being called Vale place; Thornton street extended to Marcella street through part of Vale street, Oct. 25, 1873; Vale street laid out from Marcella street to Thornton street, Nov. 26, 1875. L 906, L 1098.

***Valentine street,** Rox.; from Washington street to Fulda street; part of Thornton street from Washington street, west, to Thornton street "as recently laid out" named Valentine street, Oct. 19, 1875; portion of discontinued, Aug. 9, 1876; laid out from Thornton street to Fulda street, June 23, 1890. L 905, L 2235.

Valley acre, B.; east, from Becon Hill, between the present Bowdoin street and Somerset street, 1777.

†**Vancouver street,** Rox.; from Ward street to Ruggles street; laid out from Huntington avenue to Ruggles street, May 20, 1896. L 2767.

Vandyke street, E. B.; from Addison street to Trumbull street.

Vane street, W. Rox.; from Holbrook street, south-west.

Van Ness terrace, Rox.; from No. 242 Warren street, at corner of Dunreath street.

Van Rensselaer place, B., 1852; from Tremont street, west, between Boylston street and Eliot street; called Foster court, 1826; Foster place or South Foster place, 1831; Van Rensselaer place, 1852.

Van Winkle street, Dor.; from Dorchester avenue to Shawmut Branch R.R., and from Shawmut Branch R.R. to Carruth street.

***Varney street,** W. Rox., 1894; from Wenham street to Wachusett street; Yale street laid out as Varney street, June 9, 1894. L 2599.

Vaughan avenue, Dor.; from Geneva avenue, easterly, between Columbia street and N. E. R.R.

Vaughan street, Dor.; from Blue Hill avenue to Harvard street.

Venice street, E. B.; (proposed) from Maverick street to proposed part of Putnam street.

Vera street, Dor., 1891; from Freeport street to Volga street.

Vermont avenue, W. Rox.; from Corey street, with proposed extension to Mt. Vernon street; laid out as Vermont street, Sept 30, 1895. L 2737.

Vermont street, W. Rox., 1895; from Corey street to Mt. Vernon street; Vermont avenue laid out with name of Vermont street and extended to Mt. Vernon street, Sept. 30, 1895. L 2737.

Vernon court, Rox.; from Vernon street, southerly, between Kent street and Vernon place.

Vernon place, B.; from Charter street, east, nearly opposite Unity street; same in 1825.

Vernon place, Rox.; from Vernon street, southerly, opposite Haskins street.

Vernon place, Bri.; from Vernon (now Raymond) street, north-easterly; part of Everett square, 1890; part included in laying out of Westford street, May 18, 1891.

Vernon street, B., 1828; from Leverett street, 1825; laid out and named, March 15, 1828; name changed to Willard street, April 21, 1868.

***Vernon street**, Rox.; from Washington street to Tremont street; from Washington street to the watering place laid out, Jan 19, 1662; Norfolk street accepted, extended to Washington street over a part of Williams street, and name changed to Vernon street, May 16, 1842; extended through Factory street and called Vernon street, May 16, 1842; from Washington street to Cabot street, 1849; extended from Cabot street through Foundry street to Tremont street, May 7, 1869. L 440, L 528, L 2175.

Vernon street, Bri.; from Franklin street to Everett street; laid out, Dec. 16, 1873; laid out as Raymond street, July 29, 1884. L 1796.

Vicksburg place, } So. B.; from East First street to East Second street,
Vicksburg street, } near I street.

***Victor street**, Dor., 1894; from Brook avenue to Dean street; Granville place laid out as Victor street, July 26, 1894. L 2672.

***Victoria street**, Dor.; from Dorchester avenue to Pleasant street; laid out from Dorchester avenue, north-westerly, towards Pleasant street, Jan. 14, 1884; extended to Pleasant street, May 21, 1886. L 1753, L 1906.

Vila street, Rox.; from Francis street to Longwood avenue.

Village place, B., 1833; from West Castle (now Castle) street to West Orange street, opposite Village street; now built over. L 546.

***Village street**, B.; from Dover street to Castle street; from Dover street, north, 1831; extended to Castle street and accepted, Nov. 20, 1855. L 54, L 544, L 546, L 724, L 838.

Vinal place, B.; from Harrison avenue near and south of Pine street, 1859; included in laying out of Broadway, July 3, 1880. L 1466.

Vincent court, B.; from Harvard street, south 1855; built over.

Vincent lane, B.; from Marlboro' (now Washington) street to Bishop's alley (now Hawley street), 1777; deeds of land to enlarge given Town provided street be called Franklin street, March 27, 1797; named Franklin street, 1798.

Vine avenue, Rox.; from Vine street, south-easterly, near Mt. Pleasant avenue.

***Vine street**, B.; from North Russell street to Bridge (now North Anderson) street, 1806; confirmed as a public street, Sept. 15, 1834. lower part from Bridge street to North Grove street accepted, May 10, 1852; name changed to Parkman street, April 21, 1868. L 94.

***Vine street**, Rox.; from Dudley street to Mt. Pleasant avenue; accepted conditionally, Nov. 17, 1851.

***Vine street**, Chsn.; from Chelsea street to Bunker Hill street; laid out according to its present bounds, Oct. 13, 1851; laid out and extended from Moulton street to Bunker Hill street, May 3, 1858. L 1986, L 2591, L 2738.

Vine-street place, B.; from Parkman street, northerly, to Seabury place; same in 1851; (from Vine, now Parkman, street, north).

Vinson street, Dor.; from Melville avenue to Geneva avenue; authority to open from Park street to Geneva avenue given by Street Commissioners, December 7 and December 30, 1891.

Vinton court, Chsn.; from Henley street, northerly; same in 1875.

***Vinton place**, So. B.; from Vinton street, north-east; so called in directory, but called Thomson court on atlases.

***Vinton street**, So. B.; from Dorchester street to O. C. (now N. Y., N. H. & H.) R.R.; laid out, Dec. 12, 1866; laid out from Dorchester street to the railroad, Nov. 17, 1868. L 345, L 1830.

Virginia avenue, Dor.; private way from Dudley street to Bird street; laid out and named Virginia street, March 21, 1881. L 1518.

Virginia avenue, W. Rox.; from Centre street to Roanoke avenue, 1849; now included in Starr lane and a part of Seaverns avenue.

***Virginia street**, Dor.; from Dudley street to Bird street; private way called Virginia avenue laid out as Virginia street, March 21, 1881, L 1518.

Volga street, Dor., 1891; from Neva street.

Von Hillern street, Dor.; (proposed) from Locust street to Mt. Vernon street, at Dorchesterway.

Vose street, Dor.; from Butler street, at junction with Riverview avenue to Crest avenue.

***Wabeno street**, Rox.; from Wyoming street to Waumbeck street; laid out, Oct. 27, 1887. L 2036.

***Wabon street**, Rox.; from Warren street to Wabeno street; laid out May 19, 1881. L 1523.

†**Wachusett street**, W. Rox., 1887; from Walk Hill street to south of Eldridge road; formerly Walk Hill avenue; laid out from Walk Hill street, north-easterly, Oct. 3, 1887; extended to what is now Weld Hill street, March 5, 1889; authority to open from Walk Hill street to south of Eldridge road given by Street Commissioners, Aug. 5, 1896. L 2028, L 2114.

Wadleigh place, So. B.; from Ellery street, south-westerly, to South bay.

Wadsworth corner, B., 1732; corner of Middle (now Hanover) street and Bell alley (now Prince street), then so called.

Wadsworth street, Bri.; from Pratt street, south-east, then south-west, to Ashford street.

***Wait street**, Rox., 1882; from Huntington avenue (formerly Tremont street) to Hillside street; shown as Garden street on plan dated 1845; private way called Hillside avenue, laid out and named Wait street, Oct. 24, 1882. L 1659.

Wakefield's alley, B., 1720; from Middle (now Hanover) street, east, north of Cross street; closed.

***Wakulla street**, Rox.; from Rockland street to Dale street; laid out, Dec. 6, 1875. L 1109.

Walcott street, So. B.; (proposed) from Richardson avenue (proposed) to and crossing Washington avenue (proposed).

Waldeck street, Dor.; from Melville avenue to Geneva avenue, parallel with Shawmut Branch R.R.; authority to open from Park street to point beyond Linsey street given by Street Commissioners, Jan. 18, 1893.

Waldemar avenue, Breed's Island; from Chelsea creek to Walley street; authority to open from Overlook street to Boston & Maine R.R. given by Street Commissioners, Aug. 26, 1896.

Walden park, Rox.; from Highland street, north-west; laid out as Morley street, Sept. 23, 1887. L 2027.

Walden place, Rox.; from Heath street, south-easterly; laid out, extended to Centre street, and named Walden street, Nov. 23, 1874. L 987.

***Walden street**, Rox., 1874; from Heath street to Centre street; Walden place laid out, extended to Centre street, and named Walden street, Nov. 23, 1874. L 987.

Walder street, B.; that part of Causeway street next Leverett street was so called at an early date.

Waldo street, B.; from St. Botolph street south-east between Gainsborough street and Whitman street.

Waldorf street, Dor.; from Ashmont street to Mellen street.

Wales corner, B., 1708; corner of Middle (now Hanover) street and Prince street then so called.

Wales lane, Dor., 1836; part of Columbia street, crossing Upper road (now Washington street) from Boston to Milton; Bowdoin avenue and Love lane so called on plan dated 1836.

Wales place, Dor.; from Columbia street to Olney-street place.

†**Wales street,** Dor.; from Blue Hill avenue to Nightingale street; laid out, Nov. 10, 1876; from Blue Hill avenue to Harvard street; from Harvard street to Nightingale street; authority to open given by Street Commissioners, Oct. 1, 1891. L 1190.

Wales wharf, B.; from Federal street, south-east, nearly opposite Beach street.

Walford street, Chsn.; from Bow street, south-west, to land of Fitchburg R.R.; shown as a passageway from Bow street to Front street in 1838; called Walford street, and shown as of same extent in 1874; portion closed by railroad taken by authority of Acts of Legislature of 1873.

***Walker avenue,** Chsn., 1847; from Walker street to Russell street; laid out, accepted and named, Aug. 28, 1847.

Walker avenue, Chsn., 1869; from Main street, south-west; West Walker street laid out 40 feet wide, Sept. 29, 1869; called also West Walker street and Walnut avenue; name changed to Lincoln street, Dec. 27, 1869.

Walker place, B., 1872; from Northampton street, south-west, between Washington street, and Shawmut avenue, nearly opposite Chester place.

Walker street, W. Rox.; from South street to John A. Andrew street; so shown, but not laid out, on plan dated 1871; part between John A. Andrew street and Elm street laid out as Sedgwick street, Dec. 5, 1881; Sedgwick street extended over Walker street to South street, Dec. 7, 1887. L 1575, L 2045.

***Walker street,** Chsn.; from Main street to Wall street; part from Main street to Russell street accepted, Nov. 28, 1831; remainder shown on plan dated 1848; extended from Russell street to Bunker Hill street, Nov. 25, 1867; discontinued between Wall street and Bunker Hill street, Oct. 4, 1869.

Walker street, W. Rox.; from Weld street to Joy street, near Brookline line.

Walker-street court, Chsn.; from Walker avenue, north-west.

Walker's lane, } B., 1741; from Orange (now Washington) street,
Walker street, } west, next south of Hollis street; Clough street, 1743; Nassau street, 1788; Common street, 1824; Tremont street, 1829; Common street again, 1836.

Walk Hill avenue, W. Rox.; from Walk Hill street, north-easterly, to unnamed street (now Weld Hill street) leading to cemetery; same given as Mountain street on map, 1849, but no record of change of name; laid out as Wachusett street Oct. 3, 1887, and March 5, 1889. L 2028.

Walk Hill road, Dor. and W. Rox.; an old name for Walk Hill street; part shown on plan dated 1833.

***Walk Hill street,** Dor. and W. Rox.; from South street at junction with Morton street to Norfolk street; laid out from road leading from Boies' Mill to Deacon James Baker's to Old road leading to

Meeting-house, Jamaica Plain, April, 1802; located by County Commissioners, April, 1804; named from Dedham turnpike (now Washington street) to Dorchester line, May, 1825; B & P. (now N.Y., N.H. & H.) R.R. having built 45½ rods of new road to avoid crossing said street near junction with Norfolk and Bristol turnpike (now Washington street) three times in about 50 rods, same accepted by County on plan of Old road, December, 1835; lines changed from railroad to Mountain street (now Wachusett street), Dec. 30, 1850; from Hyde Park avenue to Washington street laid out by County Commissioners, April 18, 1853; laid out at uniform width of 50 feet, July 3, 1871; altered from Hyde Park avenue to Stony brook, Sept. 27, 1871; name of Jamaica street, from Norfolk street to Walk Hill street, changed to Walk Hill street, being a continuation of the same, May 9, 1876; same part shown as Walk Hill street on plan dated 1838. L 942, L 943, L 944, L 1151, L 1344, L 2500, L 2785.

***Wall street**, B., 1839; from Minot street to Causeway street; from Minot street to the jail, 1839; extended to Causeway street, including Cotting court, Sept. 27, 1852.

Wall street, B., 1829; from Spruce street to Charles street; accepted and named Sept. 21, 1829; (no other record, the only street from Spruce street to Charles street of which there is record is Branch avenue (now street), which is nowhere given as Wall street).

Wall street, Rox., from Plymouth street south-east, on plan dated 1862; (the only street shown at present from Plymouth street is Woodstock street, which is very old).

***Wall street**, Chsn., 1860; from Sullivan street to Walker street; laid out and accepted from Sullivan street to Russell street, Nov. 30, 1860.

Wallace court, or place, Chsn., 1849; from Winthrop street, south-east; shown as an unnamed court from High (now Winthrop) street, south-east, on plan dated 1839; same named on plan dated 1849.

Wallace park, W. Rox.; from Bourne street, westerly, near Catherine street.

†**Walley street**, E. B. (Breed's Island); from Bennington street at junction with Ashley avenue to Revere line; part from Elm (now Leyden) street to Terrace avenue (now Gladstone street), formerly Washburn avenue laid out as Walley street, Aug. 23, 1886; extended from Leyden street over part of Ashley avenue to Bennington street, July 3, 1888. L 1932, L 2073.

Wallingford road, Bri., 1895; from Commonwealth avenue, north-westerly, to Chestnut Hill avenue; authority to open given by Street Commissioners, Jan. 1, 1895.

Wall's place, Chsn.; from Henley street, north, between Putnam street and Chelsea street.

Waln street, Rox., 1833; from Francis (now part of Turner) street, south-east, parallel with Baldwin street, to point about 220 feet north-west of Massachusetts avenue (formerly West Chester park); shown on plan dated 1833, from Francis street, south-east, to the channel in empty basin; part from point 220 feet north-west of Massachusetts avenue, south-east, abandoned.

***Walnut avenue**, Rox. and W. Rox., 1868; from Warren street to Forest Hills street (1884) (now to Sigourney street only); laid out as Back street, from Warren street to South street, Jan. 19, 1662; named Back street, May 9, 1825; name changed to Walnut street, Nov. 20, 1843; named Walnut avenue, April 21, 1868, but so given on plan dated 1862; laid out between Rockland street and Buena Vista avenue (now street), Dec. 15, 1868; part of nearly opposite Walnut park altered, Dec. 13, 1870; part of Walnut street from

Seaver street to Forest Hills street named Walnut avenue, March 1, 1884; part of south of Sigourney street now in Franklin park, L 419, L 578, L 824, L 1633, L 1816, L 2134 L 2377.

Walnut avenue, W. Rox.; from Corey street, south-west, towards Mt. Vernon street, 1853; later called Carl street; Carl street laid out as Montview street, from Corey street to Mt. Vernon street, Nov. 17, 1893.

Walnut avenue, Chsn., 1869; laid out from Main street, Sept. 29, 1869; called also Walker avenue and West Walker street; name changed to Lincoln street, Dec. 27, 1869.

Walnut court, Rox.; from Walnut avenue, south-east, between Pickering place and Dale street.

Walnut court, Chsn.; from Walnut street, north-west, near Medford street.

***Walnut park**, Rox.; from Washington street to Walnut avenue; accepted, July 27, 1863.

Walnut place, B., 1860; from Washington street to Reed street; laid out under the name of Flagg street, June 5, 1895. L 2703.

Walnut place, W. Rox.; from Green street, north-east, between Lamartine street and Chestnut avenue; laid out as Cheshire street, May 2, 1881. L 1521.

***Walnut street**, B., 1799; from Beacon street to Mt. Vernon street; the easterly half called Coventry street, 1733–91; from Beacon street to Olive (now Mt. Vernon) street called Walnut street, 1799; confirmed as a public street, Sept. 15, 1834; part of at one time called Bishop-Stoke street.

Walnut street, Rox.; from Cedar street, north-east, crossing Dorr street; formerly called Ascension street; now Lambert avenue.

***Walnut street**, Rox. and W. Rox., 1843; from Warren street to South street; laid out as Back street, Jan. 19, 1662; name changed to Walnut street, Nov. 20, 1843: boundary lines established from Dale street to Townsend street, Sept. 8, 1856; line changed, March 23, 1863; a part relocated and portion in West Roxbury accepted, March 21, 1864; named Walnut avenue, April 21, 1868; part from Seaver street to Forest Hills street named Walnut avenue, March 1, 1884; part now in Franklin park.

***Walnut street**, Dor.; from Neponset avenue to Ericsson street (Neponset); located as Pineneck lane, May 13, 1805; located as Walnut street from Neponset avenue to "Pineneck," April 3, 1854; street leading from house of William L. Clark to O. C. (now N. Y., N. H. & H.) R.R., accepted and named Walnut street, April 3, 1854; all parts of "Old road" leading from said house to Neponset turnpike (now avenue) not appearing on plan discontinued, April 3, 1854; part leading from O. C. R.R. to Neponset turnpike located, April 3, 1854; continued from Water street 1,072 feet, April 5, 1858. L 1063, L 2138.

Walnut street, W. Rox.; from Spring street to Belle avenue; shown in 1870.

***Walnut street**, Chsn.; from Bunker Hill street to Medford street; laid out and accepted, Aug. 6, 1866; laid out and accepted, Sept. 29, 1869; near location of former Mallet street. L 1185.

Walnut-street court, Dor.; from Walnut street, east, near Water street.

***Walpole street**, Rox., 1881; from Tremont street to Grinnell street; private way called Franklin place laid out from Tremont street and named Walpole street, Nov. 16, 1881; laid out from Berlin street to Grinnell street, April 2, 1890. L 1570, L 2217.

Walsh place, B., 1872; from Clark street, south-west, near Hanover street.

***Walter street,** W. Rox.; from Centre street to South street; part from Centre street, southward, past Weld street, shown but not named on plan dated 1815; named from Centre street to South street, May 9, 1825; probably a public highway some time previous. L 2736.

Walter's court, B., 1853; from Endicott street, east, near Cooper street; called Alton place, 1857; closed.

***Waltham street,** B., 1826; from Tremont street to Union-Park street; laid out on the Neck and named, July 24, 1826; from Tremont street to Suffolk street (now Shawmut avenue) named Waltham street, Sept. 15, 1834; extended from Suffolk street to Washington street, April 19, 1847; extended from Washington street to Harrison avenue, including part of Adams place, Sept. 18, 1848; lines established, Oct. 11, 1855; accepted, Dec. 7, 1857; extended with Union-Park street (they unite as Union-Park street a little south-east from Harrison avenue), from Harrison avenue to Albany street, Aug. 8, 1862. Vol. 31, p. 7. L 116, L 260, L 2520.

***Walton street,** Dor.; from Washington street to Harley street; laid out, July 31, 1873. L 887, L 2173.

***Wapping street,** Chsn., 1790; from Chelsea street to Water street; deed from Town to Mr. Jno. Harris of a piece of land at Wapping in lieu of land taken from him to accommodate the road, 1790; part of Wapping street discontinued on establishment of Navy Yard by a line across the same on easterly bounds of 21-foot passageway belonging to Town which leads to low-water mark, Jan. 14, 1801; widened in 1807 and 1830.

Wapping street, Chsn.; mentioned, Feb. 5, 1798, as a former name of Henley street (no other record).

Ward court, So. B.; from Ward street, north-easterly.

***Ward street,** So. B., 1855; from Dorchester street to Preble street; formerly called Centre street; named Ward street, Aug. 7, 1855; laid out, June 14, 1867. L 450, L 454, L 2392.

***Ward street,** Rox., 1853; from Huntington avenue to N. Y., N. H. & H. R.R.; from Bumstead lane (now St. Alphonsus street) crossing Phillips street, Parker street, and Halleck street to B. & P. (now N. Y., N. H. & H.) R.R., 1853; laid out 40 feet wide from Parker street, south-east, to Tremont street; seems to have been called at first Charles street, though shown as Ward street on plan dated 1853; name of Charles street changed to Ward street, April 21, 1868; laid out, June 14, 1869; laid out to B. & P. R.R., Nov. 15, 1877; laid out from Parker street to Huntington avenue, June 3, 1886. L 1290, L 1907, L 1908.

Ward's wharf, B.; from Federal street, east, near Federal-street bridge.

Ware place, B., 1853; from Richmond (now Parmenter) street, north, near Hanover street, 1853; not now named.

***Ware street,** Dor.; from Trull street to Rill street; laid out, March 26, 1880. L 1440.

***Wareham street,** B., 1849; from Harrison avenue at its junction with Malden street to Albany street; named from junction Harrison avenue and Malden street extended to a dock in South bay, May 14. 1849; accepted, Oct. 30, 1860.

Warland place, B.; from Hanover street, north-west, then north-east, near Commercial street; same in 1867.

Warner avenue, Dor.; from Harvard street to Park street; formerly from Glen road (now Glenway street) to Catholic cemetery; Glen avenue (now Glenway street) from Glen road (now Glenway street) to Harvard street, shown at one time as Warner avenue.

***Warren avenue,** B., 1867; from Berkeley street near Tremont street to Columbus square; called Avenue Three previous to 1855; laid out as a public street from West Canton street to Clarendon street, May 21, 1867; laid out from West Canton street to Columbus avenue, April 7, 1868; laid out from Clarendon street to Berkeley street, Nov. 17, 1868; portion bounded by Pembroke street, West Newton street and Columbus avenue named Columbus square, April 4, 1871. L 354.

***Warren avenue,** Chsn.; from City square to Warren bridge; laid out, accepted, and named Boston avenue, May 2, 1836; called Warren avenue in records of 1842, but no record of change of name. L 1709.

***Warren bridge,** B., 1828; from Causeway street, opposite the end of Beverly street, northerly, to Charlestown; from the foot of Haverhill street to Charlestown, 1828; since partly discontinued and now from the foot of Beverly street; discontinued in part again, Feb. 11, 1885, by which almost the entire bridge from line of solid filling at foot of Beverly street to solid filling on the north of the channel was moved easterly. L 1852.

Warren place, B., 1820; from Warren (now Warrenton) street to Pleasant street, 1820; name changed to Warrenton place, April 21, 1868.

***Warren place,** Rox.; from Warren street at junction with Harrison avenue to Pevear court; laid out from Warren street, June 20, 1874. L 717, L 940.

Warren place, Dor.; from Washington street, south-west, between Fuller street and Codman street; included in present Fairmount street.

***Warren square,** B., 1839; at the junction of Merrimac street, Market street, and Friend street; from Merrimac street to Friend street, 1839.

Warren square, W. Rox.; from Green street, by two branches north-east, to Centre place.

Warren street, B., 1788; from Hancock street, west, to Cambridge bay; named by Selectmen, July 4, 1788; from Hancock street to West Centre (now Anderson) street called Myrtle street, 1814; part near the river probably discontinued.

***Warren street,** B., 1795; from Orange (now Washington) street to Eliot street, 1795; confirmed as a public street, Sept. 15, 1834; name changed to Warrenton street, April 21, 1868.

***Warren street,** Rox., 1825; from Washington street to Blue Hill avenue; laid out, Jan. 19, 1662; named from Washington street through Upper road to Dorchester line, May 9, 1825; staked out, June 16, 1836; lines established near Dennis street, June 30, 1856; line established, Oct. 17, 1859. L 386, L 513, L 525, L 717, L 730, L 795, L 809, L 902, L 1264, L 1265, L 1369, L 1422, L 2004, L 2084.

***Warren street,** Chsn., 1786; from junction of Park street and Henley street to Main street at Thompson's square; street leading from Main street to Back street recorded by name of Warren street, Feb. 20, 1786; Back street from the square to Main street called Warren street, March 3, 1834; laid out near site of fire from the square to Joiner street, Dec. 7, 1835; land at junction Warren street and Joiner street given to Town by Henry Jacques, May 28, 1838; extended in a straight line from Joiner street to a point near junction with Winthrop square, Sept. 7, 1868; laid out from City square to Winthrop square, Nov. 30, 1868; name of Park street given to portion beginning at City square, with extension to Winthrop square, Dec. 29, 1868; Warren street and Main street merged together near Church court, May 19, 1869. L 1086.

***Warren street,** Bri., 1860; from Cambridge street to Brookline line; laid out by County Commissioners, Oct. 21, 1858; accepted by Commissioners, Jan. 2, 1860; named, March 5, 1860. L 2530.

Warrenton place, B., 1868; from Warrenton street to Pleasant street; called Warren place, 1820; named Warrenton place, April 21, 1868.

***Warrenton street**, B., 1868; from Washington street to Eliot street; called Warren street, 1795; confirmed as a public street, Sept. 15, 1834; named Warrenton street, April 21, 1868. L 1519.

***Warwick street**, Rox.; from Hammond street to Ruggles street; laid out, Sept. 1, 1871. L 663, L 664.

Washburn avenue, E. B. (Breed's Island); from Ashley avenue to beyond Bayswater street; formerly from Ashley avenue, parallel with B., R. B. & L. R R., to Revere line; changed to Walley street; laid out as Walley street from Elm (now Leyden) street to Terrace avenue (now Gladstone street), Aug. 23, 1886. L 1932.

Washburn place, B., 1846; from Charter street, south-westerly, to rear of burial ground; same in 1846; name changed to Hildreth place, 1874; Washburn place again, 1890.

***Washburn street**, So. B.; from Boston street to Dorchester avenue; laid out, easterly, from Boston street, Dec. 24, 1875; laid out from Dorchester avenue to Boston street, Dec. 17, 1889. L 1072, L 2190.

Washburn street, Bri.; from Harvard avenue, south-westerly, towards Warren street, crossing Gorham street and Griggs street; same in 1875; included in Massachusetts (now Commonwealth) avenue as laid out in 1883. L 1743.

Washington avenue, B., 1821; from Washington (now Fort Hill) square to Purchase street, 1821; accepted, April 8, 1829; street known as Washington square and Washington avenue called High street, Dec. 15, 1875. L 466, L 467.

Washington avenue, So. B.; (proposed) from Hyde street to Locust street.

Washington avenue, W. Rox.; from Spring street, south-easterly, near Dedham line; same in 1874.

Washington court, B., 1826; from Washington street, west, 1826; called Temple avenue, 1833; Temple place, 1864.

Washington court, B., 1845; from Washington street, west, near Medford court, 1845; to be accepted conditionally and when accepted to be called Marlboro' street, Oct. 28, 1856; called Marlboro' street, 1857; Marlboro' street accepted, Oct. 4, 1859; called Acton street, 1864.

Washington court, Rox.; from Roxbury street, opposite Highland street, northerly; formerly called Bates place; now called Roxbury terrace.

Washington court, Dor.; from Minot street, south-easterly; same given as Washington street, 1874, and Washington avenue, 1880 and 1884.

Washington Gardens, B., 1810; on Common (now Tremont) street, from West street to about the north line of the Masonic Temple and east, on West street, to about opposite Mason street, 1810.

Washington park, Rox., 1860; between Dale street, Bainbridge street, and Paulding street; named, Oct. 29, 1860.

Washington place, B., 1808; "all the buildings around the walk on Fort Hill," 1808; the square on summit of Fort Hill on outside of circular walk named Washington place, Sept. 19, 1810; called Washington square, 1837; named Washington square, April 7, 1845; named Fort Hill square, 1875.

Washington place, B.; from Webster avenue, north-east.

***Washington place**, B., 1837; from High street, south, to Belcher lane; same in 1837. L 218.

Washington place, So. B.; from Silver street, south-westerly, between A street and N. E. R.R.

Washington place, Rox.; from Roxbury street, north-east, near Allen place.

Washington place, Chsn.; from Washington street, north-easterly, between Devens street and Union street, near Washington square.

Washington Mechanic place, B., 1828–41; from Washington street, west, next south of Fayette court, 1828–41; closed.

Washington square, B , 1845; around the open space upon the top of Fort Hill; called Washington place, 1808; named Washington square, April 7, 1845; portions discontinued, July 8, 1871; park in centre of what was formerly called Washington square named Fort Hill square, Dec. 15, 1875; street formerly known as Washington square and Washington avenue named High street, Dec. 15, 1875. L 299, L 301, L 348, L 626, L 922.

Washington square, Chsn.; from Washington street, north-easterly, between Devens street and Union street; near Washington place.

***Washington street,** B , Rox., and W. Rox., 1788; from Haymarket square to Dedham line; from Dock square to School street called Cornhill, 1708; from School street to Summer street called Marlboro' street, 1708; from Summer street to Essex street called Newbury street, 1708; from Essex street to the fortification near the present line of Dover street called Orange street, 1708, from Beach street to Dover street having been so called from 1663; from Roxbury line to Orange street at fortification named Washington street, by the Selectmen, July 4, 1788: extended northerly through Orange street, Newbury street, Marlboro' street, and Cornhill to Dock square, July 6, 1824; extended from Cornhill to Haymarket square, Nov. 6, 1872; part in Roxbury laid out from Boston line to Roxbury street, Jan. 19, 1662; named from Boston line to Dedham and Worcester turnpikes, May 9, 1825; raised by B. & P. (now N.Y., N.H. & H.) R.R. over crossing near Wait's Mills, April, 1847; width adopted from Eliot square to Boston line, April 26, 1852; Norfolk and Bristol turnpike laid out as a public highway, part in Roxbury named Shawmut avenue and extended to Boston line to meet end of Shawmut avenue there, June, 1857; so much as lies in West Roxbury named Shawmut avenue, Feb. 3, 1858; prospective line established from Lowell (Pynchon) street (now Columbus avenue) to Parker street, July 2, 1860; name of Washington street from Tremont street at Pynchon street (now Columbus avenue) to Brookline line changed to Tremont street April 21, 1868; portion discontinued at junction of Gardner street, Dec. 15, 1868; name of Washington street from Guild row to Pynchon street changed to Roxbury street, June 16, 1874; name of Guild row (formerly Bartlett street) from Roxbury street to Dudley street and of Shawmut avenue from Dudley street to Dedham line changed to Washington street, June 16, 1874. Between Haymarket square and Boylston street. Vol. 19, pp. 84, 87, 88, 89; Vol. 31, pp. 4, 9, 17, 41, 50, 62, 63. L 65, L 67, L 102, L 124, L 147, L 206½, L 272, L 796, L 797, L 798, L 806, L 807, L 808, L 819, L 872, L 2451. Between Boylston street and Dover street. Vol. 19, p. 123; Vol. 31, p. 56. L 29, L 177, L 193, L 302, L 380, L 510, L 521, L 545, L 547, L 549, L 562, L 563, L 727, L 2002. Between Dover street and Roxbury line. L 26, L 372, L 1770, L 2385. Roxbury District. L 402, L 420, L 504, L 520, L 768, L 945, L 946, L 1429, L 1853, L 2004, L 2246, L 2247, L 2806. West Roxbury District. L 1453, L 1454, L 1486, L 1736, L 1737, L 1738, L 2069, L 2070, L 2071, L 2580.

***Washington street,** Rox. and Dor., 1840; from Grove Hall to Milton, in continuation of Warren street; road from Stephen Badlam's by Edmund Baker's house to Spurr's hill altered, September, 1797; road from William Walker's by Daniel Vose's house and over Neponset River to Milton located as a public highway, April, 1800; from S. Badlam's shop to lower bridge, Milton, altered and made a public highway, September, 1801; road at Spurr's hill altered, April, 1806; road east of Ebenr. Wale's house and to road leading to Four Corners (later Brush hill turnpike, now Blue Hill avenue) discontinued, April, 1806; road at Spurr's hill altered, April, 1807; road from Zebedee Cook, Jr.'s, garden, east side of Dorchester turnpike (now avenue) to new Town road, discontinued, July, 1824; Upper road from Roxbury to Lower Mills named Washington street, March 11, 1840; part from Warren street to Dorchester boundary line changed from Warren street to Washington street, March 1, 1886. L 570, L 739, L 776, L 1304, L 1897, L 1917, L 1918, L 1962, L 1987, L 2040, L 2173, L 2246, L 2247, L 2284, L 2386, L 2753, L 2794.

Washington street, Dor.; from Freeport street to Pleasant street (Commercial Point); formerly from Commercial (now Freeport) street to the water.

†**Washington street,** Chsn.; from Harvard street to the State Prison; from Bow street to David Goodwin's house accepted, Sept. 16, 1813; part of Arrow street from Harvard street to Bow street made a part of Washington street, Sept. 17, 1866.

Washington street, Chsn.; from Main street to Canal street (now Rutherford avenue); Winchester (now Dunstable) street erroneously so called in 1875.

***Washington street,** Bri., 1840; from Brookline line to Newton line (1884); named from Brookline through Brighton Centre to Angier's corner, June 15, 1840; accepted from junction Cambridge street and Washington street to Brookline line, Sept. 30, 1873; relocated between Cambridge street and Market street, Jan. 1, 1879. L 1423, L 1636, L 2559, L 2560, L 2561, L 2562, L 2721.

Washington terrace, Chsn.; from Washington street, south, nearly opposite Prescott street.

Wason place, Chsn.; from Everett street, south-easterly; same in 1875.

Water avenue, Breed's Island; from Belle Isle inlet to Walley street.

***Water street,** B., 1708; from Washington street, east, to Broad street; the street leading from Cox the butcher's shop in Cornhill, passing by Major Walley's as far as Mrs. Oliver's corner, named Water street, 1708; from Cornhill to Mackril lane (now Kilby street), 1732; from Cornhill to Oliver's dock, 1800; from Cornhill to Liberty square, 1817; extended east, through Liberty street to Broad street, March 20, 1826. L 91, L 99, L 164, L 401, L 810, L 853, L 856, L 982, L 2451.

Water street, Rox., 1845; new road from Ruggles (now Cabot) street to Williams street (now Shawmut avenue) across the marsh, named Water street, March 3, 1845; extended from Washington street to Parker street, April 2, 1855; extended to Washington street, Nov. 30, 1857; extended from Williams street to Washington street, Feb. 22, 1858; street from Parker street to Washington street, part of which has been called Ruggles street and part Water street named Ruggles street throughout, Aug. 9, 1858.

***Water street,** Dor.; from Taylor street to Fulton street (Neponset); laid out, April 5, 1858.

Water street, W. Rox.; from Williams street to Keyes street; same in 1874.

***Water street,** Chsn., 1780; from Warren avenue to the Navy Yard; New Fore street, "what is now called Water street," laid out 40 feet wide September, 1780; Thomas Edmands conveys to Town all the land laid out by the General Court for a public highway 40 feet wide and 80 feet long, from the west end of his house to Battery lane so called, March 2, 1802; altered, March 28, 1836; street laid out from Main street, near Water street, to Boston (now Warren) avenue, Jan. 15, 1846; same named Water street, being a continuation of that street, March 16, 1846. L 1974.

***Waterford street**, B., 1870; from Washington street to Shawmut avenue; called Carney place, 1831; named Waterford street, Nov. 8, 1871. L 545, L 562, L 728.

Waterlow street, Dor., 1874; from Harvard street, north-westerly, south-westerly, then southerly to Harvard street again; formerly from Harvard street, generally northerly, to end of Sydney place; named, Nov. 3, 1874; part changed to Elmont street; part of present Waterlow street from Clinton street, south-east, to Harvard street formerly a part of Sydney place.

Water's court, B.; from Endicott street, east, 1853; named Alton place, 1857.

Watson place, W. Rox.; from School street, north-easterly, near Weld avenue.

***Watson street**, B., 1886; from Northampton street to Camden street; formerly Baldwin street; laid out, May 10, 1886. L 1904.

Watti court, So. B.; from West Ninth street, near Dorchester street, south-west, to O. C. (now N. Y., N. H. & H.) R.R.; afterwards called Dana street; Dana street laid out as Mitchell street, Aug. 12, 1885.

***Waumbeck street**, Rox.; from Warren street at junction with Elm Hill avenue to Humboldt avenue; laid out from Elm Hill avenue to Wabeno street, Dec. 7, 1883; extended from Wabeno street to Humboldt avenue, July 27, 1886. L 1747.

Wauwatosa avenue, Breed's Island; from Chelsea creek to Saratoga street.

Waverly place, B., 1830; from South street, easterly; same in 1830. L 1471.

Waverly place, Bri.; from Waverly street, westerly.

Waverly street, B., 1859; from West Dedham street to Canton (now West Canton) street, 1859; name changed to Ivanhoe street, April 21, 1868, and name afterwards extended in both directions.

***Waverly street**, Rox.; from Warren street to Blue Hill avenue; laid out, July 27, 1863. L 903.

†**Waverly street**, Bri.; from Lincoln street to Western avenue; laid out from River street (now Western avenue) to Market street, June 3, 1842; accepted conditionally and then subject deferred, July 18, 1842; laid out, Aug. 24, 1853; accepted and named, Sept. 5, 1853; authority to open from angle in street to Lincoln street given by Street Commissioners, Oct. 14, 1892. L 2335.

Waverly terrace, B.; a block of brick buildings on the west side of Shawmut avenue, between Lenox street and Sawyer street, formerly so called; same in 1859.

Way place, Rox.; from Copeland street, south-easterly, nearly opposite Aspen st.

Way street, B.; from Dock square to Roebuck alley (now Merchants' row); dicontinued, April 16, 1838.

***Way street**, B., 1857–1864; from Harrison avenue to Albany street; from Washington street, east, called East Orange street, 1840; name of part from Harrison avenue to Lehigh street changed to Way street. Dec. 21, 1857, and back to East Orange street, Dec. 30, 1857; name changed again to Way street, March 22, 1864; portion between Albany street and Lehigh street discontinued when Broadway was extended. L 95, L 362, L 436, L 1529.

†**Wayland street**, Dor.; from Magnolia street to and beyond Balfour street; formerly Howard street, between Magnolia street and How-

ard avenue; name changed to Wayland street, March 1, 1888; authority to open from Howard avenue, north-west, given by Street Commissioners, May 25, 1893. L 550, L 2169.

***Wayne street**, Rox., 1868; from Blue Hill avenue to Maple street; accepted as Linden street, Oct. 24, 1864; named Wayne street, April 21, 1868; relocated, March 12, 1880. L 1438.

Webb park, So. B.; from East Sixth street, south, near I street.

***Webber street**, Rox., 1835; from Harrison avenue to Albany street; road leading from Davis (now Albany) street to Plymouth street (now Harrison avenue) accepted and named Webber street, Aug. 5, 1835. L 519.

Webb's corner, B., 1708; corner Union street and Marsh lane.

Weber street, W. Rox.; from Canterbury street, opposite Mt. Hope street, south-east, to Mt. Hope cemetery; same in 1874; Mt. Hope street extended over Weber street to Mt. Hope cemetery, July 22, 1892. L 2417.

***Webster avenue**, B., 1855; from Hanover street to Unity street; called Robinson's alley or lane, 1733; named Webster avenue, March 28, 1855. L 132.

Webster avenue, E. B.; from Webster street to Sumner street, near Cottage street.

Webster avenue, Chsn.; from Sackville street to Belmont street; Webster court so called on plan, 1885; called Webster-street court on plan, 1875.

Webster avenue, Bri.; from Brighton avenue, south, then west, to Webster street; formerly from Brighton avenue, south, then west, then north, to Cambridge street; portion from Cambridge street, south-east, now called Webster street.

Webster court, B.; from Webster avenue, north-east; same in 1857; same given on plan, 1883 and 1890, as Canny place.

Webster court, Chsn.; from Sackville street to Belmont street; called Webster-street court on plan, 1875, and Webster avenue on chart, 1885.

Webster place, B.; from Fleet street, north-easterly, near Hanover street; same in 1837.

Webster place, E. B.; from Webster street, between Sumner street and Lamson street, southerly.

Webster place, Bri.; from Webster street.

†**Webster street**, E. B.; from Mill street to Sumner street, near Jeffries street; accepted conditionally, Oct. 13, 1845; accepted and laid out as a public street from Lewis street to Cottage street, May 10, 1852; accepted from Cottage street to Sumner street, Oct. 11, 1852. Vol. 31, p. 42.

Webster street, So. B.; from West Fifth street, south-westerly, between B street and C street; abandoned; Directory shows Dunham park in same location.

Webster street, Rox.; name changed to Madison street, April 21, 1868; (Madison street, from Washington street to Shawmut avenue).

Webster street, W. Rox.; from Spring street to Linden street; same in 1874. L 2488.

Webster street, W. Rox.; from Whiting street, south-west; shown in 1890.

***Webster street**, Chsn.; from Bunker Hill street to Medford street; same in 1875; laid out as Sackville street, Jan. 1, 1887. L 1968, L 1969.

Webster street, Bri., 1873; from Everett (now Dunboy) street, west, crossing Bigelow street; laid out, Dec. 18, 1873.

Webster street, Bri.; from Cambridge street, south-east, formerly a part of Webster avenue.

Webster terrace, Bri.; from Webster street.

Webster-street court, Chsn.; from Sackville street to Belmont street; Webster court so called on plan, 1875; called Webster avenue on plan, 1885.

Webster's arch, B., 1732; the entrance from Cornhill (now Washington street) to Savage's court or Williams court, 1732.

Weeks place, Rox.; from Centre street, near Heath street, south-easterly.

Weitz street, Bri.; from Franklin street to Bayard street.

Welaka avenue, B. I., from Waldemar avenue to Overlook street.

***Weld avenue,** W. Rox.; from Columbus avenue to School street; accepted, Sept. 27, 1871; laid out, Jan. 5, 1875. L 1004.

***Weld Hill street,** W. Rox.; from Hyde Park avenue to Forest Hills cemetery; authority to open street given by Street Commissioners, May 4, 1892; laid out, Aug. 10, 1893. L 2525.

Weld park, W. Rox.; from Centre street, near May street, south-west.

***Weld street,** W. Rox., 1825; from Walter street to Baker street; named from Newton line by Weld place across Centre street to Walter street, May 9, 1825; from Willow street to Baker street by annexation from Newton. L 1792, L 2809, L 2810.

Weld street, W. Rox.; from Mt. Hope street south-west, now called Bradstreet avenue.

***Weldon street,** Rox.; from Holborn street to Quincy street; laid out Nov. 6, 1890. L 2269.

Weldon street, W. Rox.; from Walk Hill street to Hyde Park avenue; laid out from Walk Hill street to portion of running north-east to Hyde Park avenue as Wenham street, Nov. 30, 1891; part from Hyde Park avenue to Forest Hills cemetery laid out as Weld Hill street, Aug. 10, 1893. L 2368, L 2525.

***Well street,** B., 1808; from Custom-House street to Wharf street; same in 1808; confirmed as a public street, Sept. 15, 1834.

†**Welles avenue,** Dor.; from Washington street to Dorchester avenue; laid out from Washington street to Argyle street, Dec. 6, 1873. L 913, L 914, L 2173.

Wells place, B., 1848; from Washington street to Bradford street; laid out as Wilkes street, April 6, 1894. L 2586.

Welles place, B., 1857; from Joy street, west, near Cambridge street, 1857; closed.

Welles corner, B., 1732; corner Orange street and Frog lane (Washington street and Boylston street), 1732.

Welles corner, B., 1732; corner of Cambridge street and Green street, 1732.

Wellington place, Chsn.; from Quincy street, north-westerly.

***Wellington street,** B., 1870; from Columbus avenue, north-westerly; part of West Springfield street between Columbus avenue and B. & P. (now N. Y., N. H. & H.) R.R. named Wellington street, June 27, 1870. L 502, L 516.

Wellington street, E.B.; (proposed) from Maverick street to proposed part of Putnam street.

Wellingtons wharf, B.; from Federal street, easterly.

Wendell place, So. B.; from Preble street, southerly.

***Wendell street,** B., 1826; from Pearl street to Broad street; from Oliver street to Hamilton street named June 14, 1826; confirmed as a public street, Sept. 15, 1834; Humphrey place laid out and extended to Broad street, including part of Half Moon place, and its name changed to Wendell street, Dec. 30, 1870; laid out upon a new line near Broad street, on line of northerly side of Wharf street extended, April 2, 1872; name of Pearl place leading from Oliver street in continuation of Wendell street to Pearl street changed to Wendell street, March 1, 1883. L 460, L 463, L 682.

Wendell street, So. B.; from Preble street to Hyde street.

Wendell's lane, B., 1796; in Directory of 1796; probably Wendell street.

***Wenham street,** W. Rox., 1891; from Walk Hill street to Weld Hill street; formerly part of Weldon street; laid out, Nov. 30, 1891. L 2368.

***Wenonah street,** Rox.; from Elm Hill avenue, north-westerly, to Waumbeck street; laid out, Oct. 26, 1886. L 1959.

Wensley street, Rox., 1895; from Heath street to Bucknam street; authority to open given to Street Commissioners, Sept. 19, 1895.

Wensley's lane, B., 1744; from North Meeting-house down towards Charlestown river, Sept. 28, 1744, and same, May 4, 1758.

Wentworth place, B.; from Northampton street, south-west, near corner Shawmut avenue; same in 1867.

Wentworth street, Dor.; from Norfolk street, south-easterly, crossing Torrey street.

Wentworth's corner, B., 1800; corner Lynn street (now Commercial street) and Greenough's alley, 1800.

Wentworth's lane, B., 1732; from Allen's corner on Ann (now North) street, east. to the Wood wharffe, 1732; accepted conditionally, and named Barrett street, June 7, 1831; laid out from Ann street to Fulton street, and named Barrett street, Oct. 24, 1842.

Wesley avenue or street, Dor.; from Savin Hill avenue to the water.

Wesley place, B., 1836; from Hanover street, between Prince street and Parmenter street, north-westerly; same in 1836.

***Wesley place,** Chsn.; from Pearl street to Sullivan street; straightened, etc., and laid out, Dec. 31, 1867; discontinued, Sept. 14, 1868; laid out, etc., Sept. 22, 1868; called Wesley street, April 13, 1869.

Wesley street, E. B.; from Chelsea street to Paris street, near Meridian street.

Wesley street, So. B.; from Preble street to Hyde street.

***Wesley street,** Chsn.; from Pearl street to Sullivan street; name of Wesley place changed to Wesley street, April 13, 1869; see Wesley place.

Wessex street, Dor.; from Codman street to Weyanoke street.

***West street,** B.; from Washington street to Tremont street; from Newbury (now Washington) street, west, to the Common, 1708. L 24, L 196.

West street, E. B.; from Reynolds street to Homer street.

***West street,** Dor.; from John Whittemore's land, Roxbury, near the red gate, in line of old cart path to road from Lower Mills to Dedham; laid out, December, 1835; from Upper Mills to the Town House altered December, 1838; from River by Luke Trott's, to Roxbury line, named West street, March 11, 1840 (now Norfolk street).

West street, W. Rox.; from High street to Morrison street.

West street, W. Rox.; from Bellevue avenue to end of Orange street.

***West street,** Chsn.; from Alford street to Beacham street; laid out and accepted, June 24, 1872.

West Boston; the part of the Town west of Sudbury street from 1708 to 1800.

***West Boston bridge**; from the foot of Cambridge street to Cambridge, 1793.

Westbourne terrace, Bri.; from Corey road to Brookline line.

***West Broadway**, B. and So. B., 1873; from Albany street to South Boston; laid out as Broadway from Washington street, opposite Pleasant street, to South Boston and so called by records, charts, and directory; that part of Broadway from Dorchester avenue, opposite Broadway, to Dorchester street, opposite East Broadway, called West Broadway, Feb. 18, 1873. See Broadway. L 361, L 362, L 473, L 632, L 1532.

***West Brookline street**, B., 1868; from Washington street to Warren avenue; from Tremont street to Front street (now Harrison avenue) named Brookline street, Sept. 15, 1834; laid out from Tremont street to Water Power Company's line, Dec. 21, 1859; from Water Power Company's line to Warren avenue, May 21, 1867; from Washington street to Warren avenue called West Brookline street, April 21, 1868. L 138, L 354.

***West Canton street**, B., 1868; from Washington street to railroad at Carleton street; Canton street laid out on the Neck, July 24, 1826; named, from Tremont street to Front street (now Harrison avenue), Sept. 15, 1834; laid out from Tremont street to Boston Water Power Company's line, Dec. 21, 1859; West Canton street laid out between Tremont street and Warren avenue and accepted May 21, 1867; name of Canton street between Washington street and Warren avenue changed to West Canton street, April 21, 1868; laid out from Warren avenue to Appleton street at junction with Columbus avenue, Nov. 4, 1868; laid out from Columbus avenue to the B. & P. (now N. Y., N. H. & H.) R.R., Dec. 7, 1869. L 354, L 502, L 516, L 538.

***West Castle street**, B., 1732; from Orange (now Washington) street, west; name of West Castle street leading from Washington street to Tremont street changed to Castle street, June 23, 1874 (all intermediate record given under Castle street). L 563, L 566, L 837, L 838.

***West Cedar street**, B., 1826; from Chestnut street to Cambridge street; from Phillips street to the river called Southac street, 1733; from Chestnut street to Cambridge street called George street, 1810; from Chestnut street to Sumner (now Mt. Vernon) street named West Cedar street, 1826; from Sumner street to Pinckney street named West Cedar street, 1833; from Pinckney street to Cambridge street named West Cedar street, April 1, 1869. L 49.

West Centre street, B., 1733; from Cambridge street to May (now Myrtle street); extended to Pinckney street, 1833; name changed to Anderson street, May 21, 1861.

***West Chester avenue**, B., 1869; West Chester park and Chester square named West Chester avenue, July 13, 1869; part of West Chester avenue from Shawmut avenue to Tremont street called Chester square, Oct. 5, 1869; laid out from Boston Water Power Company's old line to Columbus avenue, Oct. 26, 1869; laid out from Columbus avenue to B. & P. (now N. Y., N. H. & H.) R.R., Dec. 7, 1869; street between Washington street and Tremont street part of which is called West Chester avenue and part Chester square, named Chester square throughout, April 5, 1870; between Tremont street and the B. & P. (now N. Y., N. H. & H.) R.R. called West Chester park, April 5, 1870; West Chester park, Chester square, Chester park, and East Chester park all changed to Massachusetts avenue, March 1, 1894. L 502, L 516.

***West Chester park**, B., 1859; from Tremont street, crossing Beacon street to Harvard bridge (Charles river); laid out and accepted from Tremont street to Boston Water Power Company's line, Dec. 21, 1859; West Chester park and Chester square named West Chester avenue, July 13, 1869; part of West Chester avenue, between Tremont street and B. & P. (now N. Y., N. H. & H.) R.R., called West Chester park, April 5, 1870; extended from B. & P. R.R. to Beacon street, July 5, 1873, and from Beacon street to the Charles river, May 21, 1889; name changed to Massachusetts avenue, March 1, 1894. L 452, L 502, L 516, L 805, L 805½, L 862, L 1140, L 1585, L 2133, L 2493.

***West Chester street**, B.; from Washington street across Tremont street to Back Bay land. 1854; from Washington street to Shawmut avenue, part of West Chester park, 1861, and named Chester square, 1864; West Chester park, Chester square, Chester park, and East Chester park all changed to Massachusetts avenue, March 1, 1894.

***West Concord street**, B., 1868; from Washington street to Tremont street; Concord street laid out on the Neck, July 24, 1826, and named from Tremont street to Front street (now Harrison avenue), Sept. 15, 1834; laid out from Tremont street to Water Power Company's line, Dec. 21, 1859; from Washington street to Tremont street named West Concord street, April 21, 1868; from Tremont street to Columbus avenue named Concord square, April 21, 1868; laid out from Columbus avenue to B. & P. (now N. Y., N. H. & H.) R.R., Dec. 7, 1869; same part named Greenwich park, March 29, 1870. Vol. 31, p. 1. L 502, L 516.

Westcott street, Dor.; from Park street to Talbot avenue, near and west of N. E. R.R.

***West Cottage street**, Rox. and Dor.; from Dudley street to Blue Hill avenue; laid out by Dorchester Selectmen from Stoughton (now Dudley) street to Brook avenue, Aug. 12, 1869; extended from Brook avenue to Blue Hill avenue, in part over part of Woodville square, Feb. 18, 1875. L 880, L 1027, L 1410.

***West Dedham street**, B., 1868; from Washington street to Tremont street; Dedham street laid out on the Neck, July 24, 1826; named from Tremont street to Front street (now Harrison avenue), Sept. 15, 1834; named West Dedham street, from Washington street to Tremont street, April 21, 1868. L 295, L 372.

***West Eagle street**, E. B.; from Border street to Brooks street, opposite Reservoir grounds; accepted as Eagle street, April 5, 1859.

***West Eighth street**, So. B.; from near O. C. (now N. Y., N. H. & H.) R.R. north-west from D street to Dorchester street; part of Eighth street called West Eighth street, Feb. 18, 1873; for record of laying out, see Eighth street. L 200, L 201, L 257, L 273, L 369.

***Westerly street**, Rox., 1893; from Centre street to Sunnyside street; Westerly terrace laid out as Westerly street, from Centre street to Sunnyside street, Nov. 1, 1893. L 2544.

Westerly terrace, Rox.; from Centre street to Sunnyside street; laid out as Westerly street, Nov. 1, 1893. L 2544.

***Western avenue**, B.; the Mill-dam from Charles street, west, 1821; part between Charles street and line near the toll-house presented by Boston & Roxbury Mill Corporation and accepted by City, Sept. 19, 1831; part between point accepted, Sept. 19, 1831, and street "leading to the water next westerly of dwelling-house of William W. Goddard" accepted and laid out as a public highway to be called Beacon street, April 21, 1857; from Otter street to "west end of new block of freestone-front houses" accepted and named Beacon street, May 27, 1858; from "Upham's house to a point distant 140 feet, westerly, from the south-easterly corner of Berkeley street," accepted and named Beacon street, Oct. 30, 1861; from Berkeley street to Clarendon street accepted and named Beacon street, May 26, 1863; from Clarendon street to Dedham (now Dartmouth) street accepted and named Beacon street, July 3, 1865; portions of Mill-dam road, known as Western avenue, lying in present limits of Boston, laid out, Dec. 7, 1868; part from Beacon street to Tremont street named Brookline avenue, 1868. L 416, L 417.

***Western avenue**, Bri.; from Cambridgeport bridge to Watertown bridge; name of River street changed to Western avenue, June 13, 1873; relocated by Street Commissioners, Oct. 3, 1877. L 1270, L 1271, L 1272, L 1967, L 2374, L 2423, L 2711.

Westfield street, B., 1875; from Tremont street, nearly opposite Northfield street, north-westerly; formerly from Tremont street to Columbus avenue.

***West Fifth street**, So. B., 1873; from Dorchester avenue to Dorchester street; part of Fifth street called West Fifth street, Feb. 18, 1873. Vol. 31, p. 38. L 183.

***West First street**, So. B., 1873; from Foundry street, easterly, to N. E. R.R. then south-easterly to Dorchester street; part of First street called West First street, Feb. 18, 1873. L 122, L 126, L 128.

***Westford street**, Bri., 1891; from Raymond street, near and east of Everett street to Raymond street; Everett square and Everett place laid out as Westford street, May 18, 1891. L 2293.

***West Fourth street**, So. B., 1873; from Dover-street bridge to Dorchester street; part of Fourth street called West Fourth street, Feb. 18, 1873. L 779, L 1319, L 1420, L 1421, L 2746.

West Haven street, B.; from Newland street, north-westerly, between Rutland street and West Newton street; same in 1867.

West Hill, B.; south of the foot of Cambridge street, by Charles river, 1722.

***Westland avenue**, Rox., 1878; from Massachusetts avenue to Parker street; laid out from West Chester park (now Massachusetts avenue) to Parker street; Dec. 27, 1878. L 1296 L 1345.

***Westminster avenue**, Rox.; from Washington street to Walnut avenue, April 25, 1864. L 741.

***Westminster street**, Rox.; from Hammond street to Ruggles street; laid out, Sept. 1, 1871. L 659, L 662.

Westminster terrace, Bri.; from 50 Chestnut Hill avenue.

Westmoreland street, Dor.; from Adams street, west, to Berkshire street.

West Newbury street, Rox.; from Jersey street (now Charlesgate-west) to Brookline avenue; laid out as Newbury street, March 30, 1894

***West Newton street**, B., 1868; from Washington street to and crossing Falmouth street; Newton street laid out on the Neck, July 24, 1826; named, from Tremont street to Front street (now Harrison avenue), Sept. 15, 1834; laid out from Tremont street to Boston Water Power Company's line, Aug. 13, 1861, and June 13, 1865; from Washington street to Columbus avenue named West Newton street, April 21, 1868; laid out from Water Power Company's line to Columbus avenue, July 14, 1868; laid out from Columbus avenue to B. & P. (now N. Y., N. H. & H.) R.R., Dec. 7, 1869; laid out from location of B. & P. R.R. to Huntington avenue, Dec. 27, 1878; laid out from Huntington avenue to land of B. & A. R.R., July 25, 1881. L 198, L 354, L 502, L 516, L 747, L 750, L 1542.

***West Ninth street**, So. B.; from D street to Dorchester street; part of Ninth street called West Ninth street, Feb. 18, 1873. L 96, L 194, L 273, L 369, L 1694.

Weston place, Rox.; from Weston street, south-east; formerly Sudbury place.

***Weston square**, B.; that part of public lands called Weston street and square named Union park, May 19, 1851.

***Weston street**, B.; laid out on the Neck, July 24, 1826; named from Tremont street to Suffolk street (now Shawmut avenue) Sept. 15, 1834; a mall or common laid out, Nov. 25, 1850; name changed to Union park, May 19, 1851. L 511, L 773, L 1377.

***Weston street**, Rox.; from Warwick street to Columbus avenue; name of Sudbury street (from Tremont street to Cabot street) changed to Weston street, April 21, 1868; laid out from Tremont street to Windsor street, Dec. 30, 1869; extended from Cabot street to Warwick street, Nov. 25, 1879. L 511, L 773, L 1377.

West Orange street, B., 1831; from Washington street, west, to Village place (from Castle street opposite Village street); called Orange place, 1825; named West Orange street, 1831; accepted, Dec. 18, 1854; portion between Washington street and Shawmut avenue discontinued as a public street, Feb. 3, 1872; named Orange street, 1874.

Westover street, W. Rox.; from Weld street to Joy street.

West Park street, Dor.; from Bernard street, near Harvard street station; Park street, west of Washington street, sometimes so called; part from Washington street to the N. E. R.R. laid out as Park street, Sept. 8, 1886.

West row, B.; on the part of Cambridge street, now Court street, near Bowdoin square, 1803–1830.

***West Rutland square**, B., 1871; from Columbus avenue, north-westerly, to Carleton street; part of Rutland street, west of Columbus avenue, named West Rutland square, July 25, 1871. L 502, L 516.

***West Second street**, So. B , 1873; from Dorchester avenue to Dorchester street; part of Second street called West Second street, Feb. 18, 1873. L 43, L 486, L 556.

West Selden street, Dor.; from Morton street to Crossman street.

***West Seventh street**, So. B., 1873; from Dorchester avenue to Dorchester street; part of Seventh street called West Seventh street, Feb. 18, 1873. L 199, L 226, L 227, L 655.

***West Sixth street**, So. B., 1873; from Dorchester avenue to Dorchester street; part of Sixth street called West Sixth street, Feb. 18, 1873. Vol. 31, p. 48.

West Sixth-street place, So. B.; from 62 West Sixth street, northeasterly.

***West Springfield street**, B., 1868; from Washington street to Columbus avenue; Springfield street laid out on the Neck, July 24, 1826; named from Tremont street to Front street (now Harrison avenue), Sept. 15, 1834; from Washington street to Columbus avenue called West Springfield street, April 21, 1868; laid out from Boston Water Power Company's old line to Columbus avenue, Oct. 26, 1869; laid out from Columbus avenue to B. & P. (now N. Y., N. H. & H.) R.R., Dec. 7, 1869; from Columbus avenue to B. & P. R.R. named Wellington street, June 27, 1870. L 452, L 502, L 516.

***West Third street**, So. B.; from West Second street to Dorchester street; part of Third street called West Third street, Feb. 18, 1873. L 160.

***Westville street**, Dor.; from Bowdoin street to Corwin street; formerly from Bowdoin street to Arcadia street; laid out from Bowdoin street to Draper street, including a part of Bowdoin square, Dec. 29, 1880; laid out from Draper street to Corwin (formerly Westville) street, Sept. 10, 1890; part of Westville street, 215 feet north from Arcadia street, laid out as Corwin street, Sept. 10, 1890. L 1513, L 1514, L 2260, L 2261.

***West Walker street**, Chsn.; laid out from Main street, Sept. 29, 1869; called also Walker avenue and Walnut avenue; name changed to Lincoln street, Dec. 27, 1869.

***West Walnut park,** Rox.; from Washington street, opposite Walnut park, north-westerly; laid out, Oct. 9, 1877. L 1275.

***West Windsor street,** Rox.; Windsor street, from Ruggles street to Weston street, sometimes so called.

West Wood Island, E. B.; south-easterly from proposed part of Cottage street, and south-westerly from Wood Island park.

***Wexford street,** Bri., 1886; from Market street to Hillside avenue; Winship avenue laid out as Wexford street, Dec. 10, 1896. L 1966.

Weyanoke park, Dor; between Shenandoah street and Weyanoke street.

Weyanoke street, Dor; from Carruth street to Wessex street.

***Wharf street,** B.; from Broad street to India street; same in 1808; confirmed as a public street, Sept. 15, 1834.

†**Wheatland avenue,** Dor.; from Washington street to N. E. R.R.; laid out from Washington street to Kilton street, June 24, 1879. L 1360, L 1361, L 1962.

Wheaton square, W. Rox.; from 208 Lamartine street.

***Wheeler street,** B., 1872; from Shawmut avenue to Indiana place (now Corning street); from Pleasant street, west, called Wheeler's court, 1829; laid out from Shawmut avenue and extended to Indiana place, Dec. 30, 1870; named Wheeler street, May 30, 1872. L 548, L 549, L 564, L 786.

Wheeler's corner, B., 1708; corner of Newbury (now Washington) street and Pond (now Bedford) street.

***Wheeler's court,** B., 1829; from Pleasant street, west, near Kirkland street; laid out, widened and extended from Shawmut avenue to Indiana place, (now Corning street), Dec. 30, 1870; named Wheeler street, May 30, 1872. L 548, L 549, L 564.

Wheeler's Point, B.; at the foot of Sea (now Federal) street, 1675; called Windmill Point, 1722.

Wheelock avenue, Dor.; from Hancock street, westerly, near Columbia street.

Whetcomb's or Whitcomb's corner, B., 1708; corner of School street and Tra Mount street.

Whipple avenue, W. Rox.; from Washington street, easterly to Stony brook.

Whipple street, Rox., 1892; from Haviland to south of Norway street.

Whitby street, B. I.; from Ashley avenue to Ford street.

White avenue, W. Rox.; from South street, westerly, then southerly, to Jamaica street; no record of change of name, but part northerly from Jamaica street laid out (from Jamaica street to White avenue, now Custer street) as Woodman street, Dec. 9, 1878; part from South street to Woodman street laid out as Custer street, May 19, 1881. L 1339, L 1522.

White Bread alley, B., 1708; the alley leading from North street down to Captain Richards' corner in Ship street; called Bartlett street, 1826; Harris street, 1868.

***White street,** E. B.; from Border street to Trenton street; accepted and laid out, Dec. 28, 1855; accepted at junction Eutaw street and White street, at junction Trenton street and White street, and at junction Monmouth street and White street, Nov. 1, 1858. Vol. 31, p. 23. L 21, L 78, L 606, L 1305.

White street, Dor.; from Glenway street to Bicknell street; laid out under the name of Bradshaw street, Jan. 3, 1896. L 2752.

White-street place, E. B.; from 38 White street, near Meridian street, northerly.

White's corner, B., 1800; corner Ann (now North) street and Centre (now North Centre) street.

White's (Major) corner, B., 1800; corner Essex street and Short (now Kingston) street.

†**Whitfield street**, Dor.; from Park street, south-easterly, crossing Wheatland avenue and Talbot avenue, to Norfolk street; laid out from Park street to Wheatland avenue, Oct. 14, 1890. L 2265.

***Whitford street**, W. Rox., 1888; from Kittredge street to Augustus avenue; part of Clarendon avenue laid out as Whitford street, Oct. 23, 1888. L 2099

***Whiting street**, Rox.; from Warren street to Winthrop street; Forest avenue laid out as Whiting street, March 19, 1884; extended through Homer place to Winthrop street, May 29, 1896. L 1762, L 2770.

Whiting street, W. Rox.; from Baker street to Rand street.

Whitman street, B ; from St. Botolph street south-east between Massachusetts avenue and Waldo street.

Whitman street, Dor.; from Norfolk street, south-east, near Edson street.

***Whitmore street**, B., 1886; from Kneeland street to Harvard street; Kneeland place included in laying out of Whitmore street, June 12, 1886. L 1910.

Whitney place, Rox.; from Tremont street, opposite Whitney street, southerly.

***Whitney street**, Rox.; from Tremont street to Conant street; laid out, July 15, 1876. L 1160, L 2339.

Whitney street, Bri., from Market street to Murdock street; same in 1875; authority to open given by Street Commissioners, Aug. 5, 1891; now called Mapleton street.

Whittier street, Rox.; from Hampshire street to Downing street; formerly Mahan avenue.

Whittler's alley, B.; from North street, near corner of Fleet street, south-east to Commercial street, opposite Eastern avenue.

Whitwell's corner, B., 1800; corner of Ann (now North) street and Dock square.

***Wicklow street**, Bri., from Market street to North Beacon street; private way known as Lyman avenue from Market street, and part of another private way known as Hillside avenue near North Beacon street, laid out as Wicklow street, Dec. 5, 1881. L 1577.

***Wiget street**, B., 1894; from Salem street to North Margin street; that part of North Margin street leading north-west from 90 Salem street called Wiget street, March 1, 1894.

***Wiggin street**, B., 1878; from North Bennet street to Tileston street; from North Bennet street called Short lane, 1796; extended to Tileston street, 1833; called Short street, 1849; name changed to Wiggin street, April 24, 1878.

Wiggin street, W. Rox.; from Beech street, south-west, between Washington street and Poplar street.

***Wigglesworth street**, Rox.; from Tremont street, crossing Huntington avenue, to Longwood avenue; laid out, Oct. 13, 1887. L 1831, L 2031, L 2032.

Wilberforce place, B., 1843; from Southac (now Phillips) street, south; name changed to Primus avenue, 1871.

Wilber court, E. B.; from 319 Sumner street, near Cottage street, south-westerly.

Wilbur street, Dor., 1896; from Cushing avenue to Upham avenue.

Wilder street, Dor.; from Washington street to Geneva avenue; new street opposite estate of Hon. Marshall P. Wilder named Wilder street, April 8, 1879; laid out, July 10, 1896. L 2780.

Wild's corner, B., 1800; corner School-street and Governor's alley (now Province street).

Wildwood street, Dor.; from Morton street to Woolson street.

***Wilkes street**, B., 1894; from Washington street to Bradford street; Wells place laid out as Wilkes street, April 6, 1894. L 2586.

Wilkes court, B.; at an early date, from Beer lane or Richmond (now Parmenter street).

Wilkins place, W. Rox.; from Sycamore street, north, between Poplar street and Hawthorne street.

Willard place, B.; from Washington street, westerly, between Lenox street and Camden street; same in 1846.

Willard place, Bri.; from North Harvard street, south-east, near the Charles river.

***Willard street**, B., 1868; from Leverett street to Lowell street; formerly from Leverett street, north-easterly, towards Lowell street; called Vernon street, 1825; named Willard street, April 21, 1868; April 19, 1881, the Supreme Court decided that Willard street had become public by dedication prior to statutes of 1846; extended to Lowell street, Sept. 17, 1888. L 2092.

Willet street, W. Rox.; from Washington street to Eagle street.

Williams avenue, Rox.; from Seaver street; laid out from Seaver street and extended to Munroe street and named Humboldt avenue, Dec. 30, 1882. L 1688, L 1689.

Williams court, B., 1788; from Washington street through arch at easterly end to Court square; formerly from Cornhill (now Washington street), west; called Savage's court, 1732; named Williams court, 1788 or 1789; accepted conditionally, June 21, 1862; acceptance rescinded, conditions not having been complied with, May 17, 1864. L 1350.

Williams court, Rox.; shown on plan, 1849, unnamed, from Washington street, north-westerly, crossing end of Williams street; after laying out of Shawmut avenue, through Williams street, Williams court widened at various times, being called both court and street until Oct. 25, 1872, when Williams street, was extended from Shawmut avenue to Westminster street.

Williams park, Dor.; from East street, south-east near Adams street.

Williams place, B.; from Charter street, south-west, nearly opposite Henchman street; now built over.

***Williams street**, B., 1821; from Federal street to Atkinson (now Congress) street; called Round lane, 1732; name changed to Williams street, Jan. 10, 1821; altered, 1867; name changed to Matthews street, April 21, 1868. L 350.

Williams street, Rox.; from Williams court to Washington (now Roxbury) street; named from Washington street by Sam Langley's to Worcester turnpike, May 9, 1825; continued and widened from S. Langley's house to Mr. William Bacon's fence, then turning and running toward Washington street, April 30, 1838; width and grade from Vernon street to Washington street established, Oct. 11, 1852; Shawmut avenue laid out over Williams street from end at Williams court to Washington (now Roxbury) street, June 3, 1857; laid out (conditionally) by County, Nov. 23, 1857.

***Williams street**, Rox.; from Washington street to Westminster street; laid out from "Mr. Bacon's fence toward Washington street," April 30, 1838; called Williams court where Shawmut avenue was built in 1857, and after that date both Williams court and street until Sept. 16, 1872, when Williams street was extended from Shawmut avenue to Westminster street. L 789.

***Williams street**, W. Rox.; from Forest Hills street to B. & P. (now N. Y., N. H. & H.) R.R.; formerly from Blue Hill avenue, crossing Washington street to B. & P. R.R.; once called Cook's lane; laid out from Blue Hill avenue to Walnut street (now avenue), Nov. 14, 1870; laid out from Walnut street across Forest Hills street and Stony brook to Shawmut avenue (now Washington street), Jan. 10, 1871, and March 5, 1872; laid out from Shawmut avenue to B. & P. R.R., opposite easterly end of Carolina avenue, Sept. 8, 1873; extension accepted as town way, Aug. 21, 1873; part between Blue Hill avenue and Forest Hills street included in Franklin park. L 970.

Williams street, W. Rox.; from South street to Bellevue avenue; laid out from Birch street at South street to Cottage (now Amherst) street, and named Brandon street, Sept. 14, 1881. L 1557.

Williams street, Chsn.; from Main street, westerly, between Dunstable street and Phipps street; same in 1875; Stacey street laid out from Main street to Dunstable street, including Williams street, Oct. 7, 1889. L 2178.

Williams terrace, Rox.; from Williams street near Westminster street, north-east, then south-east.

Williams corner, B., 1708; corner Fleet street and Middle (now Hanover) street.

Willicut place, Dor.; from Union avenue, now Rosseter street, south-westerly, south of Rosseter place.

Willis terrace, Rox.; from Roxbury street, south-west, opposite Washington place.

Willis street, Rox.; from Parker street, south-east, near Ruggles street.

***Willis street**, Dor.; from Pleasant street to Sumner street; laid out, Aug. 31, 1894. L 2527.

Willoughby place, Rox.; from Blanchard place (now Blanchard street), north-westerly.

†**Willow court**, Dor.; from Boston street, north-westerly, nearly to East Chester park (now Massachusetts avenue) at Oak street; from Captain Clapp's by Mrs. C. Howe's, named Willow court, March 11, 1840.

Willow park, Rox.; from Shawmut avenue, north-westerly, between Williams street and Ruggles street.

***Willow street**, B., 1823; from Chestnut street to Mt. Vernon street; called Maple street, 1822; name changed to Willow street, 1823.

†**Willow street**, W. Rox.; from Railroad street, crossing Centre street and Weld street, to Dunbar street; named from Centre street, near Clay brook to former Newton line, May 9, 1825; part between Centre street and Weld street probably a public highway some time previous.

Willowwood street, Dor., 1895; from Ballou avenue to Lauriat avenue; authority to open from Ballou avenue to Lauriat avenue, given by Street Commissioners, Jan. 30, 1896.

Wilmington avenue, Dor., 1895; from Codman street to Milton avenue; authority to open given by Street Commissioners, Dec. 4, 1895.

***Wilmont street**, Rox.; from Bainbridge street to Elmore street; laid out, July 20, 1880; name changed to Mayfair street, Feb. 16, 1882. L 1470.

Wilson street, W. Rox.; from Walnut street (now Walnut avenue), crossing Suffolk street, towards Blue Hill avenue; included in Franklin park, 1882.

***Wilson's lane,** B.; from King (now State) street to Dock square; called Crooked lane, 1708; name changed to Wilson's lane, May 12, 1712; Devonshire street extended through Wilson's lane to Dock square, June 6, 1872. L 767.

***Wilton street,** Bri.; from Cambridge street, north-westerly, to unnamed street near Harvard avenue; from Cambridge street to Braintree street laid out, Sept. 4, 1890. L 2259.

Wiltshire street, B.; from Green lane (now Green street), north, then west, then north-west, to the water, 1725; called Shute street in Selectmen's list, 1788; from Mr. Allen's house up by Phillips and Winthrop's new ropewalk, 1800; added to and called Chambers street, Sept. 18, 1811; accepted and recorded under name of Chambers street, May 26, 1868.

***Winchester street,** B.; from Pleasant street; to Ferdinand street; called South Cedar street, 1825; named Winchester street, July 7, 1869. L 387, L 391, L 392, L 393, L 394, L 396, L 438.

Winchester street, Chsn.; from Rutherford avenue; laid out from Rutherford avenue, name changed to Dunstable street and extended to Main street, Nov. 11, 1881; called Washington street on chart, 1875. L 1565.

Windham place, Bri.; from Warren street; (Directory, 1884).

Windmill Point, B.; from the foot of Sea (now Federal) street, west; called Wheeler's Point, 1675; named Windmill Point, 1722 (now Federal).

Windmill walk, B.; from Hanover street by the side of the Mill creek, 1796-1816.

***Windom street,** Bri.; near the corner of Cambridge street and North Harvard street; authority to open given by Street Commissioners, July 10, 1891; from Cambridge street to a point near and north-west of Home avenue (now Hopedale street); laid out, April 8, 1892. L 2391.

Windsor place, Rox.; from Windsor street, north-easterly, between Shawmut avenue and Westminster street.

Windsor road, Bri.; from Lanark road, to Kilsyth Road.

***Windsor street,** Rox.; from Ruggles street to Weston street; name of Clark street changed to Windsor street, April 21, 1868; laid out, Dec. 30, 1869; in Directory of 1894 this street is given as West Windsor street; all but a small portion included in the extension of Columbus avenue, Jan. 4, 1895; remaining portions discontinued, Feb. 5, 1896. L 512, L 2756.

***Windsor street,** Rox.; from Cabot street to Shawmut avenue; name of Clark street changed to Windsor street, April 21, 1868; laid out, Sept. 1, 1871; given as East Windsor street in Directory, 1894. L 659, L 655, L 666.

Winfred court, B.; from Sawyer street, east, to end of Trainer court; same in 1870; included in the laying out of Dillon street, from Lenox street to Sawyer street, Oct. 24, 1887. L 2034.

Wing's lane, B.; from Hanover street to Dock square; called Hudson's lane, 1658; named Wing's lane, 1708; name changed to Elm street, May 26, 1800.

Winnisimmet ferry, B.; from Commercial street, opposite the foot of Hanover street, north-easterly, to Chelsea; Hanover street, extended from Commercial street to Chelsea ferry, April 5, 1886.

Winship avenue, Bri.; from Market street to Hillside avenue; laid out as Wexford street, Dec. 10, 1886. L 1966.

Winship place, Bri.; from Washington street, near Chestnut Hill avenue, south-westerly, then south-easterly and north-westerly; same in 1875; laid out with name of Dighton place, Dec. 19, 1889. L 1850, L 2177, L 2195, L 2196.

Winship place, Bri.; from Winship street, south-east, nearly opposite Peaceable street.

***Winship street,** Bri.; from Washington street to Chestnut Hill avenue; laid out from Washington street to Union street, March 30, 1857; accepted April 13, 1857; accepted from Union street to Rockland street (now Chestnut Hill avenue), April 1, 1867; alterations by Selectmen accepted, May 18, 1871.

Winsley's corner, B.; corner of Bell alley (now Prince street) and Fleet street, 1708.

Winslow place, B.; from Chambers street, easterly, nearly opposite Allen street; same in 1844.

Winslow place, Rox.; from Washington street, north-westerly, between Ruggles street and William street.

***Winslow street,** Rox.; from Eustis street to Dudley street; Short street, from Eustis street to Union (now Taber) street, having been extended to Dudley street; named Winslow street, Dec. 17, 1860. L 1281.

Winslow street, W. Rox.; from Temple street to Dent street; same in 1874.

Winslow's corner, B.; corner Spring lane and Joyliff's lane (now Devonshire street), 1708.

Winsor wharf, B.; from Albany street, easterly.

Winter court, B.; from Winter street to Temple place, 1830; called Winter place, 1836.

Winter place, B.; from Winter street to Temple place; called Winter court, 1830; Winter place, 1836.

***Winter street,** B.; from Washington street to Tremont street; previous to 1708 called Bannister's lane and Blott's lane; named Winter street, from Newbury (now Washington) street, "nigh the upper end of Summer street, ward into the Common," 1708.

***Winter street,** Dor.; from junction of Adams street and East street to Hancock street; street from Meeting-House Hill by Mr. Swan's to East street named Winter street, March 11, 1840. L 787, L 2310.

Winthrop place, B.; from Summer street, north, to Otis place, 1821; portion discontinued, March 30, 1859; Devonshire street extended through Winthrop place to Summer street, April 23, 1861. L 133.

Winthrop place, Rox.; from Washington street to Shawmut avenue, between Ruggles street and Williams street.

***Winthrop square,** B.; at the junction of Devonshire street and Otis street; named, April 23, 1861. L 105, L 133, L 832.

Winthrop square, Chsn.; between Winthrop, Adams, and Common streets; anciently called the Training-field; named Winthrop square, Jan. 17, 1848; lines altered, May 30, 1871.

***Winthrop street,** E.B.; from Maverick square to Paris street; accepted, May 26, 1854.

†**Winthrop street,** Rox. and Dor.; from Warren street to and across Dennis street; part of Greenville street (from Grove Hall, now Blue Hill avenue, north-westerly) added to Winthrop street, making street extend from Warren street to Grove Hall avenue, April 2, 1855; from Warren street to Greenville street accepted, Oct. 20, 1856; extended from Blue Hill avenue to Dennis street, Sept. 2, 1884. L 1814.

***Winthrop street,** Chsn.; from Main street to Monument square; name of Training-field street changed to Winthrop street, Dec. 5, 1836; lines changed, Sept. 15, 1856; portion of High street between Monument court and junction of Adams and Winthrop streets named Winthrop street, Feb. 2, 1860.

***Wirt street**, Bri., 1891; from Washington street to Henshaw street; laid out, Nov. 13, 1891. L 2359, L 2721.

Wirth place, B.; from Camden street, south-westerly, between Washington street and Shawmut avenue; same in 1863; given on chart, 1890, Worth place.

Wise place, Rox.; from Centre street, southerly, parallel with Wyman place; laid out and extended to Roys street and called Wise street, March 5, 1883.

***Wise street**, Rox.; from Centre street to Roys street; Wise place laid out from Centre street, extended to Roys street, and called Wise street, March 5, 1883. L 1691.

Wistar place, Chsn.; from Elm street, north-westerly, near Bartlett street.

***Withington street**, Dor.; from Norfolk street to Torrey street; laid out, Oct. 7, 1889. L 2179.

***Wolcott street**, Dor., 1893; from Columbia street to Eric street; authority to open given by Street Commissioners, April 21, 1893; laid out July 10, 1896. L 2777.

Wolfert court, Rox.; from Fellows street, north-west, between Randall street and Fellows place.

Wood lane, B.; from Middle (now Hanover) street to Fish (now North) street, and so down to the sea, 1708; the Town slip at the lower end to be open forever, 1709; liberty given to build an open wharf at lower end to lie open for use of inhabitants, about 80 or 100 feet below highway, 1737; called Proctor's lane, 1796, but still called Wood lane on Carleton's map of 1800; made part of Richmond street, 1824.

Wood place, B.; from Eliot street, north, nearly opposite Warren (now Warrenton) street, 1856; closed.

†**Wood street**, Dor.; from Walnut street, north-westerly, near N. Y., N. H. & H. R.R.; part between Walnut street and Taylor street, laid out as Rice street, July 26, 1894. L 2608.

***Wood street**, Chsn.; from Main street to High street; accepted, Aug. 21, 1820.

Wood-street court, Dor.; from Walnut street to Wood street, now called Lorenzo street.

Wood-Island park, E. B.; from B., R. B. & L. R.R., south-easterly, to the water.

***Woodbine street**, Rox.; from Warren street to Blue Hill avenue; laid out, Dec. 16, 1870. L 592.

***Woodbury street**, B.; from Washington street to Shawmut avenue; Metropolitan place, from Washington street, west, laid out, extended to Shawmut avenue, including Amee place, and named Woodbury street, March 29, 1882. L 1594.

Woodcliff street, Dor.; from Howard avenue, south-east, opposite Dalmatia street.

Woodland avenue, Dor.; from Savin Hill avenue to Grampian way.

†**Woodland road**, W. Rox., 1892; from Pond street and May street; authority to open given by Street Commissioners, June 20, 1892; from Moss Hill road, westerly, to Moss Hill road again at its junction with Pond street; laid out for about 500 feet west from Moss Hill road, Oct. 12, 1894. L 2635.

Woodlawn avenue, Dor.; from West Selden street to Delhi street; (proposed).

Woodlawn street, W. Rox., 1892; between Hyde Park avenue and Forest Hills cemetery; authority to open given by Street Commissioners, May 4, 1892.

***Woodman street**, W. Rox.; from Custer street to Jamaica street; formerly a part of White avenue; laid out from Jamaica street to White avenue (now Custer street), Dec. 9, 1878. L 1339.

Woods place, Chsn.; from North Mead street, north-westerly, to Charlestown playground, then north-easterly.

***Woodside avenue**, W. Rox.; from Washington street to Forest Hills street; shown on map, 1849; laid out and accepted as Town way, Nov. 15, 1854.

***Woodstock avenue**, Bri.; from 44 Summit avenue.

Woodstock street, Rox.; from Maple avenue (now Bellevue street) to Plymouth street.

Woodville avenue, Rox.; from Blue Hill avenue, easterly, northerly, and westerly to Dennis street, 1873; same called later Woodville square; northerly and westerly parts later called Woodville street; now forming Woodville street, and a part of West Cottage street.

Woodville park, Rox.; from Dennis street, north-west, between Stafford street and Moreland street; called Tyso park in 1890.

Woodville square, Rox.; from West Cottage street, northerly, then westerly, to Dennis street; on chart, 1873, called Woodville avenue, from Blue Hill avenue, easterly, northerly, and westerly to Dennis street; later called Woodville square; West Cottage street extended to Blue Hill avenue in part over part of, Feb. 18, 1875; laid out from West Cottage street and Dennis street, March 26, 1877; name of, between West Cottage street and Dennis street, changed to Woodville street, March 1, 1890; name of Dennis street, from Woodville square to Blue Hill avenue, changed to Woodville street, March 1, 1890. L 1027.

***Woodville street**, Rox., 1890; from Blue Hill avenue to West Cottage street; name of Woodville square, from West Cottage street to Dennis street, changed to Woodville street, March 1, 1890; name of part of Dennis street, from Woodville square to Blue Hill avenue, changed to Woodville street, March 1, 1890. L 1085, L 1222.

***Woodward avenue**, Rox.; from Dudley street to George street; laid out, May 7, 1877. L 1232.

Woodward park, Dor.; from Dudley street, south-westerly, then north-westerly, to Howard avenue; part south-westerly from Dudley street laid out, with name of Folsom street, Aug. 5, 1884; remainder, between Folsom street and Howard avenue, called Woodward Park street in Directory and in Bromley's atlas, 1894. L 1798, L 2793.

Woodward place, So. B.; from Woodward street, southerly, near Dorchester avenue.

***Woodward street**, So. B.; from Dorchester street to Dorchester avenue; laid out and extended, Nov. 3, 1869. L 484.

***Woodward Park street**, Dor.; from Howard avenue to Folsom street; laid out, Oct. 29, 1896. L 2793.

Woolsey square, W. Rox.; open space around railway station at Green street station, between Green street and Gordon street; called also Depot square.

***Woolson street**, Dor.; from Blue Hill avenue to Norfolk street; laid out, Aug. 5, 1892. L 2420.

Worcester place, B.; from Washington street, north-westerly, between Lenox street and Clifton place; same in 1859.

***Worcester square**, B.; from Washington street to Harrison avenue; part of East Worcester street, 1834; called Worcester square, 1851;

accepted as laid out by the City of Boston in 1852, June 30, 1863. Vol. 31, p. 14. L 149.

*__Worcester street__, B.; from Washington street to Columbus avenue; laid out on the Neck, July 24, 1826; named from Tremont street to Front street (now Harrison avenue), Sept. 15, 1834; widened between Washington street and Harrison avenue and a common or mall laid out, to be completed by Jan. 1, 1852; Worcester street accepted, Dec. 7, 1857; extended west of Tremont street to Boston Water Power Co.'s line and accepted, Aug. 13, 1861; part between Washington street and Harrison avenue accepted and named Worcester square, June 30, 1863; laid out from Boston Water Power Co.'s old line to Columbus avenue, Oct. 26, 1869; laid out from Columbus avenue to B. & P. (now N.Y., N. H. & H.), R.R. Dec. 7, 1869; from Columbus avenue to B. & P. R.R. named Claremont park, Nov. 22, 1870. L 383, L 452, L 502, L 516.

Worcester street, Bri ; from Washington street to Mt. Vernon street, 1875; called Church street in 1885; no record; laid out, with name of Eastburn street, June 11, 1886. L 1911.

Worcester turnpike, Rox.; from Guild row to Brookline line; called Washington street, 1825; part between Guild row and Pynchon street (now Columbus avenue) named Roxbury street, June 16, 1874; part between Pynchon street and Brookline line named Tremont street, April 21, 1868; part between Francis street and Brookline line changed to Huntington avenue, Jan. 5, 1895.

†**Wordsworth street, E. B.**; from Pope street to Coleridge street; laid out, from Saratoga street to Milton street, Sept. 8, 1885. L 1885.

Worley street, W. Rox.; from Weld street, near Arnold street, south-easterly, to Dwinell street.

Wormwood street, So. B.; from A street south-east to N. E. R.R., between Congress street and Binford street.

Worthington place, Rox.; from Tremont street, southerly, opposite Worthington street; now South Worthington street.

*__Worthington street__, Rox.; from Tremont street to Longwood avenue laid out, Aug. 16, 1887. L 1831, L 2011, L 2012.

†**Wren street**, W. Rox.; from Rutledge street to Robin street; shown on map, but unnamed, 1849; laid out, from Rutledge street to Oriole street, Nov. 5, 1894. L 2668.

Wrentham park, Dor.; from Dorchester avenue, west, near Ashmont street.

*__Wrentham street__, Dor.; from Dorchester avenue to Bruce street, opposite Shelton street; formerly from Dorchester avenue to Ashmont street; laid out, from Ashmont street to Dell (now Dracut) street, March 27, 1890; name of part between Ashmont street and Dracut street changed to Bruce street, March 1, 1894; laid out, from Dorchester avenue to Shelton street, Oct. 4, 1894. L 2214, L 2667.

Wright's court, So. B.; from West Broadway to Athens street, between D street and E street.

Wright street, W. Rox.; from Sycamore street, south-east, then south-west to Hawthorne street.

Wybourne's lane, B.; Hawley street was so called at an early date.

Wyman place, B.; from Common street, north-easterly, near Washington street; same in 1868.

Wyman place, Rox.; from Centre street, southerly, opposite Parker street; Gilbert street (now Chestnut avenue) extended to Centre street over a part of Wyman place, Sept. 7, 1881. L 1499.

*__Wyman street__, Rox.; from Centre street to Lamartine street; accepted and named from Centre street to Curtis street (now Chestnut avenue), Nov. 26, 1866; extended to Lamartine street, June 5, 1877. L 1241, L 2119, L 2174.

Wyman street, W. Rox.; from Norfolk street, south-west.

†**Wyoming street,** Rox.; from Warren street to Humboldt avenue; laid out from Warren street to Wabeno street, Aug. 31, 1882; authority to open part from Wabeno street to Humboldt avenue given by Street Commissioners, June 9, 1891. L 1635.

Wyvern street, W. Rox., 1896; from Hyde Park avenue to Florence street; authority to open given by Street Commissioners, June 8, 1896.

***Yarmouth street,** B., 1869; from Columbus avenue to B. & P. (now N. Y., N. H. & H.) R.R. L 502, L 516.

Yendley place, Rox.; from Coventry street, north-east, north-west of Berlin street; included in the extension of Columbus avenue, Jan. 4, 1895. L 2682.

Yeoman court, Rox.; from Yeoman street, south-west, between Adams street and Chadwick street.

Yeoman place, Rox.; from Yeoman street, north-east, between Adams street and Chadwick street.

***Yeoman street,** Rox.; from Albany street to Hampden street.

York street, Dor.; from Glenway street to Greenwood street.

Yorktown street, W. Rox., 1896; from La Grange street to Potomac street; authority to open given by Street Commissioners, Oct. 19, 1896.

Young's court, B., 1860; from North street, west, between Cross street and Arch place; not in atlas or directories.

Zamora street, W. Rox., 1895; from Perkins street to Castleton street; authority to open given by Street Commissioners, Jan. 5, 1895.

Zeigler place, Rox.; from Zeigler street, south-west, between Winslow street and Dearborn street.

***Zeigler street,** Rox.; from Washington street to Dearborn street. L 504.

Zeller street, W. Rox.; from south-east of Selwyn street, north-west.

Zone street, B., 1840; from Grove street to the rear of West Cedar street; Myrtle street extended through it to May street, 1851.